Lars Powers and Mike Snell

Microsoft Visual Studio 2005

UNLEASHED

SAMS | 800 East 96th Street, Indianapolis, Indiana 46240 USA

Microsoft Visual Studio 2005 Unleashed

Copyright © 2007 by Sams Publishing

All rights reserved. No part of this book shall be reproduced, stored in a retrieval system, or transmitted by any means, electronic, mechanical, photocopying, recording, or otherwise, without written permission from the publisher. No patent liability is assumed with respect to the use of the information contained herein. Although every precaution has been taken in the preparation of this book, the publisher and author assume no responsibility for errors or omissions. Nor is any liability assumed for damages resulting from the use of the information contained herein.

International Standard Book Number: 0-672-32819-4

Printed in the United States of America

First Printing: 2006

09 08 07 06   4 3 2 1

Trademarks

All terms mentioned in this book that are known to be trademarks or service marks have been appropriately capitalized. Sams Publishing cannot attest to the accuracy of this information. Use of a term in this book should not be regarded as affecting the validity of any trademark or service mark.

Warning and Disclaimer

Every effort has been made to make this book as complete and as accurate as possible, but no warranty or fitness is implied. The information provided is on an "as is" basis. The authors and the publisher shall have neither liability nor responsibility to any person or entity with respect to any loss or damages arising from the information contained in this book.

Library of Congress Cataloging-in-Publication Data

Powers, Lars.
Snell, Mike.
  Microsoft Visual Studio 2005 Unleashed / Lars Powers and Mike Snell. – 1st ed.
    p. cm.
  Includes index.
  ISBN 0-672-32819-4 (alk. paper)
  1. Microsoft Visual Studio. 2. Microsoft .NET Framework. 3.
Application software–Development–Computer programs. I. Title.

TK5105.8885.M57W35 2006
006.7'882–dc22

                2006023540

Publisher
Paul Boger

Acquisitions Editor
Neil Rowe

Development Editor
Mark Renfrow

Managing Editor
Patrick Kanouse

Project Editors
Matthew Purcell
Seth Kerney

Copy Editor
Chuck Hutchinson

Indexer
Cheryl Lenser

Proofreader
Paula Lowell

Technical Editor
J. Boyd Nolan

Publishing Coordinator
Cindy Teeters

Interior Designer
Gary Adair

Cover Designer
Gary Adair

Safari
BOOKS ONLINE
ENABLED

The Safari® Enabled icon on the cover of your favorite technology book means the book is available through Safari Bookshelf. When you buy this book, you get free access to the online edition for 45 days. Safari Bookshelf is an electronic reference library that lets you easily search thousands of technical books, find code samples, download chapters, and access technical information whenever and wherever you need it.

To gain 45-day Safari Enabled access to this book:

▶ Go to http://www.samspublishing.com/safarienabled
▶ Complete the brief registration form
▶ Enter the coupon code 2TJP-2GIK-UJC4-4CKL-MAR7

If you have difficulty registering on Safari Bookshelf or accessing the online edition, please e-mail customer-service@safaribooksonline.com.

Contents at a Glance

Introduction 1

Part I   **An Introduction to Visual Studio 2005/.NET**

   1   A Quick Tour of Visual Studio 2005 7

   2   A Quick Tour of the IDE 37

   3   .NET Framework and Language Enhancements in 2005 63

Part II   **The Visual Studio 2005 Environment: In-depth**

   4   Solutions and Projects 89

   5   Browsers and Explorers 117

   6   Introducing the Editors and Designers 157

   7   Working with Visual Studio's Productivity Aids 201

   8   Refactoring Code 231

   9   Debugging with Visual Studio 2005 259

  10   The Visual Studio Automation Object Model 299

  11   Writing Macros, Add-ins, and Wizards 351

  12   The .NET Community: Consuming and Creating Shared Code 425

Part III   **Visual Studio 2005 at Work**

  13   Creating ASP.NET User Interfaces 465

  14   Building Windows Forms 517

  15   Working with Databases 553

  16   Web Services and Visual Studio 595

Part IV   **Visual Studio Team System**

  17   Team Collaboration and Visual Studio Team System 621

  18   Managing and Working with Team Projects 633

  19   Source Control 659

  20   Work Item Tracking 687

  21   Modeling 731

  22   Testing 769

  23   Team Foundation Build 811

       Index 833

Table of Contents

Introduction   **1**

Who Should Read This Book? 1

How Is This Book Organized? 2

    Part I: An Introduction to Visual Studio 2005 and .NET 2

    Part II: The Visual Studio 2005 Environment: In Depth 2

    Part III: Visual Studio 2005 at Work 2

    Part IV: Visual Studio Team System 2

Conventions Used in This Book 2

Part I   An Introduction to Visual Studio 2005/.NET

1   A Quick Tour of Visual Studio 2005   **7**

Some Welcome Enhancements 7

    Design, Write, and Discover Code 8

    Edit and Debug Code 16

    Share (and Consume) Code with a Community 20

    Target Different Customer Experiences 21

    Connect with Data 26

    Automate Application Testing 27

Sorting Through the SKUs 28

    Express Editions 29

    Standard Edition 30

    Visual Studio Professional Edition 30

    Visual Studio Team System 31

Summary 35

2   A Quick Tour of the IDE   **37**

Installation 37

    Choosing a Language 38

    Installing Source Control 38

    Configuring Your Development Environment 39

The Start Page 42

    Startup Options 43

Your First Project 43

The Menu Bar 44
The Many Toolbars 49
    The Standard Toolbar 50
The Toolbox 51
The Visual Designers 53
The Text Editors 53
    The Code Editors 54
    Editor Customizations 55
The Solution Explorer 57
The Properties Window 58
Managing the Many Windows of the IDE 59
    Pinning 59
    Docking 60
Summary 62

3   .NET Framework and Language Enhancements in 2005   63

Shared .NET Language Additions 63
    Generics 64
    Nullable Types 70
    Partial Types (Classes) 73
    Properties with Mixed Access Levels 73
    Ambiguous Namespaces 74
VB Language Enhancements 75
    The Continue Statement 76
    Unsigned Types 76
    IsNot Operator 76
    Using Block 77
    Form Access Similar to VB6 77
    Explicit Zero Lower Bound on an Array 77
    Operator Overloading 77
    Custom Events 78
C# Language Enhancements 78
    Anonymous Methods 79
    Static Classes 80
    Reference Two Versions of the Same Assembly 81
    Friend Assemblies 83
.NET Framework 2.0 Enhancements 83
    New Features of Core Technologies 84
Summary 84

Part II   The Visual Studio 2005 Environment In-depth

4   Solutions and Projects   89

Understanding Solutions 89
    Creating a Solution 90
    Working with Solutions 95
Getting Comfortable with Projects 100
    Creating a Project 101
    Working with Project Definition Files 103
    Working with Projects 110
Summary 115

5   Browsers and Explorers   117

Solution Explorer 117
    Visual Cues and Icons 118
    Managing Solutions 122
    Managing Projects 123
Class View 124
    Toolbar 124
    The Search Bar 125
    Objects Pane 125
    Members Pane 127
Server Explorer 129
    Data Connections 130
    Server Components 130
Object Browser 134
    Changing the Scope 134
    Browsing Objects 135
Performance Explorer 137
    Creating a Performance Session 137
    Configuring a Session 138
    Session Targets 142
    Reports 143
    Understanding Performance Reports 143
Macro Explorer 151
    The Macros Root Node 151
    Projects 151
    Modules 152
    Macro 152
Document Outline 152
    Editing Elements 154
Summary 154

6   Introducing the Editors and Designers   157

The Basics 157

    The Text Editor 158

    Visual Studio Designers 160

Coding with the Code Editor 161

    Opening an Editor 161

    Writing Code in the Code Editor 162

    Anatomy of the Code Editor Window 163

    Code Navigation Tools 166

    Searching Documents 168

    Debugging in the Text Editor 176

    Printing Code 179

    Using the Code Definition Window 180

Creating and Editing XML Documents and Schema 181

Developing Windows Forms Applications 184

    Customizing the Form's Appearance 185

    Adding Controls to a Form 186

    Writing Code 189

Developing Web Forms 192

    Designing a Web Form Application 192

Authoring Components and Controls 197

    Creating a New Component or Control 197

    Further Notes on Writing Component Code 199

Summary 200

7   Working with Visual Studio's Productivity Aids   201

Basic Aids in the Text Editor 203

    Change Tracking 203

    Coding Problem Indicators 204

    Active Hyperlinking 205

    Syntax Coloring 205

Outlining and Navigation 206

    Code Outlining 206

    HTML Navigation 208

Smart Tags and Smart Tasks 210

    HTML Designer 210

    Windows Forms Designer 211

    Code Editor 211

IntelliSense 212

    Complete Word 213

    Quick Info 214

    List Members 214

Parameter Info 215
Code Snippets and Template Code 216
Brace Matching 224
Customizing IntelliSense 225
The Task List 227
Comment Tasks 227
Shortcut Tasks 228
User Tasks 229
Summary 229

8   Refactoring Code   231

Visual Studio Refactoring Basics 232
Invoking the Refactoring Tools 233
Previewing Changes 236
Rename 237
Accessing the Rename Operation 238
Working with the Rename Dialog Box 239
Extract Method 241
Accessing the Extract Method Refactor 241
Extracting Methods 241
Generate Method Stub 247
Extract Interface 247
Accessing the Extract Interface Refactor 248
Extracting Interfaces 248
Refactor Parameters 250
Remove Parameters 250
Promote Local to Parameter 252
Reorder Parameters 254
Encapsulate Field 255
Accessing Encapsulate Field 255
The Encapsulate Field Dialog Box 255
Summary 256

9   Debugging with Visual Studio 2005   259

Debugging Basics 260
The Scenario 260
The Many Phases of Debugging 260
Debugging the Application (Self-Checking) 261
Debugging Basics Summary 269
The Visual Studio Debugger 270
The Debug Menu and Toolbar 270
Debug Options 275

Stepping In, Out, and Over Code 276
Indicating When to Break into Code 280
Working with Tracepoints (When Hit...) 288
Viewing Data in the Debugger 290
Using the Edit and Continue Feature 296
Remote Debugging 297
Summary 298

10   The Visual Studio Automation Object Model   299

An Overview of the Automation Object Model 300
Object Model Versions 300
Automation Categories 302
The DTE/DTE2 Root Object 302
Solution and Project Objects 304
Controlling Projects in a Solution 306
Accessing Code Within a Project 307
Windows 309
Referencing Windows 310
Interacting with Windows 311
Text Windows and Window Panes 314
The Tool Window Types 316
Linked Windows 325
Command Bars 327
Documents 331
Text Documents 332
Command Objects 344
Executing a Command 345
Mapping Key Bindings 346
Debugger Objects 347
Automation Events 348
Summary 349

11   Writing Macros, Add-ins, and Wizards   351

Writing Macros 352
Recording a Macro 352
Using the Macro Explorer 354
Using the Macro IDE 355
Handling Events 362
Invoking Macros 368
Writing Visual Studio Add-ins 372
Managing Add-ins 372
Running the Add-in Wizard 374

The Structure of an Add-in 383

A Sample Add-in: Color Palette 390

Creating a Visual Studio Wizard 414

Examining the Wizard Structure 415

Creating an Add New Item Wizard 418

Summary 423

12   The .NET Community: Consuming and Creating Shared Code   425

The Community Features of Visual Studio 425

The Visual Studio Start Page 426

The Community Menu 431

Discovering and Consuming Shared Content 442

Examining Shared Content Types 442

Finding the Right Content 443

Installing and Storing Shared Content 443

Giving Back to the Community 445

Creating Shared Items (Project and Item Templates) 445

Creating Project Templates 445

Creating Item Templates 451

Packaging Your Creation 452

Publishing Your Creation 461

Summary 461

Part III   Visual Studio 2005 at Work

13   Creating ASP.NET User Interfaces   465

The Basics of an ASP.NET Website 465

Creating a New Web Application Project 466

Controlling Project Properties and Options 476

Creating Web Pages 480

Designing Your User Interface 485

Determining Page Layout and Control Positioning 485

Creating a Common Look and Feel 487

Creating a User-Configurable UI 498

Working with the ASP.NET Controls 508

ASP.NET Control Enhancements 508

The New Controls Inside ASP.NET 508

Summary 515

14   Building Windows Forms   **517**

The Basics of Form Design 517
    Considering the End User 518
    Understanding the Role of UI Standards 519
    Planning the User Interface 520
Creating a Form 521
    The Windows Application Project Type 521
    Form Properties and Events 522
Adding Controls and Components 524
    Control Layout and Positioning 526
    Using Containers 530
    Control Appearance and Behavior 534
    Working with `ToolStrip` Controls 535
    Displaying Data 542
Creating Your Own Controls 546
    Subclassing an Existing Control 547
    Designing a User Control 548
    Creating a Custom Control 551
Summary 551

15   Working with Databases   **553**

Creating Tables and Relationships 553
    Creating a New SQL Server Database 554
    Defining Tables 556
    Using the Database Diagram Designer 557
Working with SQL Statements 562
    Writing a Query 562
    Creating Views 566
    Developing Stored Procedures 566
    Creating Triggers 570
    Creating User-Defined Functions 571
Using Database Projects 571
    Creating a Database Project 572
    Auto-Generating Scripts 573
    Executing a Script 574
Creating Database Objects in Managed Code 574
    Starting a SQL Server Project 575
    Creating a Stored Procedure in C# 576
Binding Controls to Data 579
    An Introduction to Data Binding 579
    Auto-Generating Bound Windows Forms Controls 580

Manually Binding Windows Forms Controls 586

Data Binding with Web Controls 589

Summary 594

16   Web Services and Visual Studio   595

Web Services Defined 596

Web Service Terms 596

The Components of a Web Service Project 597

.NET Web Services 598

ASP.NET Web Service Project 598

The Web Service Files 599

Developing a Web Service 600

Creating the Web Service 601

Accessing and Invoking the Web Service 604

Consuming a Web Service 611

Defining a Web Reference 611

Viewing the Web Reference 613

Calling the Web Service 614

Managing Web Service Exceptions 616

Creating a Web Service Exception 616

Handling a Web Service Exception 617

Summary 617

Part IV   Visual Studio 2005 Team System

17   Team Collaboration and Visual Studio Team System   621

A View of Software Development Projects 622

MSF Agile 622

MSF for CMMI 624

Introducing the Visual Studio Team System 625

Visual Studio Team Architect 626

Visual Studio Team Developer 627

Visual Studio Team Test 629

Team Foundation Server 630

Summary 632

18   Managing and Working with Team Projects   633

Anatomy of Team Foundation Server 633

The Application Tier 634

The Data Tier 636

Security 637

Managing a Team Project..639
    Creating a New Team Project...................................640
    Adding Users to a Project Team...............................643
    Controlling Project Structure and Iterations.................648
Contributing to a Project Team.......................................650
    Connecting to a Team Foundation Server.......................650
    Using Team Explorer..651
    Using the Project Portal.....................................651
    Using Microsoft Office.......................................652
    Using Project Alerts...654
    Working with Project Reports.................................655
Summary..657

19 Source Control   659

The Basics of Team Foundation Source Control.........................660
    Basic Architecture...660
    Security Rights and Permissions..............................661
Getting Started with Team Foundation Source Control..................662
    Configuring Visual Studio....................................662
    Using the Source Control Explorer Window.....................663
    Managing Workspaces..666
    Adding Files to Source Control...............................668
Editing Files Under Source Control...................................670
    Retrieving a File from the Source Repository.................671
    Checking in Your Changes.....................................671
    Understanding the Concept of Changesets......................677
    Shelving Your Code...678
    Merging Changes..680
Branching and Merging..682
    Branching..683
    Merging..684
Summary..685

20 Work Item Tracking   687

Understanding Work Items...688
    Understanding the Role of Work Items and the SDLC............688
    Picking the Work Item Set for Your Project...................688
    Identifying Work Item Commonalities..........................692
Using Team Explorer to Manage Work Items.............................701
Understanding Team Role Perspectives.................................707
    Project Vision...707
    Project Manager..708

Business Analyst 714
Developer 716
Tester 719
Customizing Work Items 722
Seeding the Process with Work Items 723
Customizing an Existing Work Item 727
Summary 730

21 Modeling   731

Team Architect Artifacts 732
Project Templates 732
Item Templates 733
Designing Your Application 734
Working with the Application Diagram 735
Defining a System 742
System Diagram 743
Defining Your Infrastructure 746
Logical Datacenter Diagram 746
Deploying Your Application 754
Deployment Diagram 755
Validate Deployment 756
Deployment Report 756
Implementing Your Application 758
Setting Implementation Properties 758
Generating Projects 759
Visually Developing Code 759
Class Diagram 760
Adding Items 760
Defining Relationships Between Classes 762
Defining Methods, Properties, Fields, and Events 765
Summary 767

22 Testing   769

Creating, Configuring, and Managing Tests 770
Test Projects 770
Test Items 772
Test Manager 773
Testing Configuration 775
Developer Testing 775
A Sample Unit Test 776
Writing Effective Unit Tests 777

Using Unit Test Classes and Methods 777
Creating Unit Tests 778
Running Unit Tests 780
Code Coverage Analysis 782
Web Testing 784
Recording a Web Test 785
Managing Web Test Requests 786
Running the Web Test and Viewing Results 787
Seeding a Web Test with Data 788
Extracting Values from Web Tests 793
Requesting Validation Rules 794
Load Testing 797
Creating a Load Test 797
Reviewing and Editing a Load Test 803
Running Load Tests and Reviewing Results 803
Manual Tests 805
Creating a Manual Test 805
Executing a Manual Test 805
Generic Tests 807
Ordered Tests 807
Creating an Ordered Test 808
Summary 808

23   Team Foundation Build   811

An Overview of Team Foundation Build 812
Team Foundation Build Architecture 812
Creating a New Build 815
Specifying New Build Information 815
Editing a Build Type 819
The Role of MSBuild 824
Starting a Build 825
Scheduling Builds 825
Invoking a Build 826
Monitoring and Analyzing Builds 828
Introducing the Team Build Browser 828
The Build Report 830
Summary 831

About the Authors

Lars Powers is an ISV Technical Advisor on the Microsoft Developer and Platform Evangelism team. He works with Microsoft's largest global ISV partners to help them craft solutions on top of Microsoft's next-generation technologies. Prior to joining Microsoft, Lars was an independent consultant providing training and mentoring on the .NET platform. Lars is also the co-author of *Visual Basic Programmer's Guide to the .NET Framework Class Library* (Sams Publishing, 2002).

Mike Snell has more than 14 years of experience as a software architect, consultant, and public speaker. He has led a number of enterprise-level projects and delivered training and mentoring to hundreds of developers. Mike has recently been working in Pittsburgh, Pennsylvania, to build the Microsoft Consulting Practice at CEI (www.ceiamerica.com). With his team of architects, he ensures the successful delivery of all Microsoft .NET projects for CEI's many clients.

Mike is also recognized as a Microsoft Regional Director (http://msdn.microsoft.com/isv/rd/default.aspx), Microsoft Certified Solution Developer (MCSD), and a Project Management Professional (PMP). He is also the co-author of *Visual Basic Programmer's Guide to the .NET Framework Class Library* (Sams Publishing, 2002).

Dedication

*With thanks and love to Mom and Dad, Kelsey, Carson, and
Cheryl. Ironically, it was your collective excitement over this book
that made it all worthwhile.*

—Lars Powers

*To Carrie, Allie, and Ben. Thanks for your patience and understand-
ing while I wrote this book (and your push to help me finish it).*

—Mike Snell

Acknowledgments

We would like to thank the great team at Sams Publishing for their many valuable contri-
butions and helping us get this book completed. This includes our development editor,
Mark Renfrow; our technical editor, J. Boyd Nolan; our copy editor, Chuck Hutchinson;
our two project editors, Seth Kerney and Matt Purcell; and finally, our acquisitions editor,
Neil Rowe.

Mike Snell: I would also like to thank the architects on my team for their insight and for
hearing me out on a number of topics that are included in this book. This team includes
Jason Agostoni, Geoff Tewksbury, Matt Trevors, and Stephen Johnston. I would also like
to thank another key member of the Microsoft Practice at CEI, Ryan Baker, for his encour-
agement and insight. Finally, I would like to thank my good friend and co-author, Lars
Powers. This was another great experience working together, thanks!

Lars Powers: I would like to thank the various members of the GISV technical team who,
at times, served as both endless wells of knowledge and strong supporters for this effort.
I'd also like to thank my co-author, Mike, for first convincing me to embark on this
project and then for being a solid peer and partner during the writing and editing process.
And finally, thanks to the various teams at Microsoft responsible for bringing Visual
Studio and the Visual Studio Team System concepts to life.

We Want to Hear from You!

As the reader of this book, *you* are our most important critic and commentator. We value your opinion and want to know what we're doing right, what we could do better, what areas you'd like to see us publish in, and any other words of wisdom you're willing to pass our way.

As an associate publisher for Sams Publishing, I welcome your comments. You can email or write me directly to let me know what you did or didn't like about this book—as well as what we can do to make our books better.

Please note that I cannot help you with technical problems related to the topic of this book. We do have a User Services group, however, where I will forward specific technical questions related to the book.

When you write, please be sure to include this book's title and author as well as your name, email address, and phone number. I will carefully review your comments and share them with the author and editors who worked on the book.

Email: feedback@samspublishing.com

Mail: Paul Boger
Associate Publisher
Sams Publishing
800 East 96th Street
Indianapolis, IN 46240 USA

For more information about this book or another Sams Publishing title, visit our website at www.samspublishing.com. Type the ISBN (excluding hyphens) or the title of a book in the Search field to find the page you're looking for.

Introduction

The release of Visual Studio 2005 and Visual Studio Team Systems marks a major revision to the .NET development experience. The languages have many improvements, the Framework has a number of additions, but most of all, the tools have been significantly enhanced. Visual Studio now contains code snippets, custom project templates, refactoring, data binding wizards, smart tags, modeling tools, automated testing tools, project and task management—just to name a few. These tools are meant to increase your productivity and success rate. This book is meant to help you unlock these tools so you realize these gains.

Who Should Read This Book?

Developers who rely on Visual Studio to get work done will want to read this book. It provides great detail on the many features inside the latest version of the IDE. The book covers all the following key topics:

- Understanding the basics of solutions, projects, editors, and designers
- Writing macros, add-ins, and wizards
- Debugging with the IDE
- Refactoring code
- Sharing code with team members and the larger community
- Writing ASP .NET applications
- Writing and consuming Web Services
- Coding with Windows forms
- Working with data and databases
- Using team collaboration and team systems
- Modeling with Team Architect
- Automating testing with Team Test
- Managing source code changes and builds

This book is not a language book. However, we do cover some of the new language features (such as generics) in both C# and Visual Basic. We also try to provide simple examples that can be read by developers of both languages. However, this book is purposefully focused on the tools that make up Visual Studio 2005.

How Is This Book Organized?

You can read this book cover to cover, or you can pick the chapters that apply most to your current need. We sometimes reference content between chapters, but for the most part, each chapter can stand by itself. This organization allows you to jump around and read as time (and interest) permits. There are four parts to the book; each part is described next.

Part I: An Introduction to Visual Studio 2005/.NET

The chapters in this part provide an overview of what to expect from Visual Studio 2005. Readers who are familiar only with prior versions of .NET will want to review these chapters. In addition, we cover the new language enhancement for the 2005 versions of VB and C#.

Part II: The Visual Studio 2005 Environment: In-depth

This part covers the core development experience relative to Visual Studio. It provides developers with a base understanding of the rich features of their primary tool. The chapters walk through the many menus and windows that define each tool. We cover projects, solutions, editors, designers, and other productivity tools and aids. We also dig into refactoring code, using the debugging toolset, working with the automation model inside Visual Studio, and preparing your code for sharing.

Part III: Visual Studio 2005 at Work

Part III focuses on how to work with the tools to write your applications. Each chapter provides an in-depth overview of how to use the IDE to help you get your application to production. We cover writing applications using ASP .NET, Web Services, Windows forms, and working with data and databases.

Part IV: Visual Studio 2005 Team System

Finally, Part IV covers how you can leverage Visual Studio Team System to enable better project visibility and team collaboration. These tools are totally new with Visual Studio 2005. We provide an in-depth exploration of team system projects, collaboration, and work item tracking. We also cover related features and tools that are brought to you by Team Systems, such as source code control, automated testing and test case management, visual modeling, and Team Foundation Build.

Conventions Used in This Book

The following typographic conventions are used in this book:

Code lines, commands, statements, variables, and any text you see onscreen appears in a monospace typeface. **`Bold monospace`** typeface is used to represent the user's input.

Placeholders in syntax descriptions appear in an *italic monospace* typeface. You replace the placeholder with the actual filename, parameter, or whatever element it represents.

Italics highlight technical terms when they're being defined.

A code continuation icon is used before a line of code that is really a continuation of the preceding line. Sometimes a line of code is too long to fit as a single line on the page. If you see ➡ before a line of code, remember that it's part of the line immediately above it.

The book also contains Notes, Tips, and Cautions to help you spot important or useful information more quickly.

PART I

An Introduction to Visual Studio 2005/.NET

IN THIS PART

CHAPTER 1   A Quick Tour of Visual Studio 2005   7

CHAPTER 2   A Quick Tour of the IDE   37

CHAPTER 3   .NET Framework and Language
             Enhancements in 2005   63

A Quick Tour of Visual Studio 2005

IN THIS CHAPTER

- Some Welcome Enhancements
- Sorting Through the SKUs

First encounters with a new programming tool can be tricky. You're often left feeling uneasy and alienated from your comfort zone. Let's face it; most of us are just starting to feel we've mastered the current tools and languages when along comes the next big wave. We're promised new levels of productivity; we're tempted by a sleek-looking Interactive Development Environment (IDE) and a set of cool new features. When the buzz finally becomes deafening, we pop in the freshly burned DVD only to quickly feel lost before even starting the exploration.

If you've been doing this very long, you've come to expect a new release the size of Visual Studio 2005 to come with new programming models, unfamiliar terms, fresh dialog boxes, and new ways to view code; it can be hard to find your footing on what seems to be unfamiliar ground. Sometimes, all you need is a map or a compass to point you in the right direction. We hope this chapter helps you get your bearings. We'll use this space to provide the highlights of the new tool and aid with sorting through the various new Visual Studio SKUs.

Some Welcome Enhancements

Visual Studio 2005 and the .NET Framework 2.0 introduce literally hundreds of new features to an already full-featured toolset. In fact, it's hard to believe Visual Studio 2003 needed so many improvements. In fact, the language enhancements are fairly minimal. This latest version is about increasing developer productivity, reducing mundane tasks, and involving the full project team in the software engineering process. The following sections highlight those enhancements that promise to make your work life easier.

Of course, we will go over each of these items in greater detail throughout the book; think of this section as your "executive overview" for the hurried developer.

> **NOTE**
>
> We are deliberately focusing here on Visual Studio enhancements. We will cover the .NET Framework and the .NET languages (including enhancements) in the chapters that follow.

Design, Write, and Discover Code

Every developer wants to write great code. Nobody deliberately sets out to write a bunch of spaghetti code that is impossible to decipher, maintain, or extend. So how does so much code end up that way? Developers often lack proper training (aren't allowed the time off for training) and are under tight time pressures to deliver to production (or get home to their lives). The complexity is not going away; if anything, it is mounting even higher. Deadlines, timelines, project schedules, and project managers will still be driving you to release your work as soon as you possibly can. So how does Visual Studio 2005 help? It can offer guidance and "training" right within the editor. It can do routine and mundane tasks for you, the right way. It can free you to focus on your business problems and produce a higher quality product in a shorter time frame. The following sections highlight some of the promising new features that do just that.

Architect and Design Your Code First

Most developers will agree that having a solid architecture and visualization of your code will lead to a better overall product and development experience. More often than not, however, architecture documents are created at the beginning of the project (if at all) in a tool like Visio only to become quickly outdated during the build phase. It seems there is never time enough to go back and update the diagrams. You are left to watch them rapidly deteriorate into "original design" or "system vision" documents—new labels put on what once represented the actual, physical structure of the application. Round-trip synchronization between the modeling tool and the development project was supposed to solve this problem. However, this solution was laden with its own issues: the principal among them is that developers want to see their code in their code window or IDE, not in yet another tool.

Visual Studio 2005 allows architects and developers to address this issue. Architects can work to create a full application design prior to cutting code. The modeling tools are built right into the IDE. Code and model are always in sync. The Class Designer, for instance, is simply a graphical view of your code. Edits within the designer are immediately reflected in the code and vice versa. The following sections describe the Visual Designers built into Visual Studio 2005.

Application Designer   The Application Designer allows architects to create a system definition model (SDM) that defines how different "applications" are combined for a given solution. An application in this sense refers to a website, web service, database, and so on. For example, a single solution might include a website that talks to a number of web services. These web services in turn might be communicating with a database or message queue. The Application Designer allows for this type of modeling. An architect can indicate which applications communicate with one another and can define the constraints between these relationships. Figure 1.1 provides a glimpse into the Application Designer.

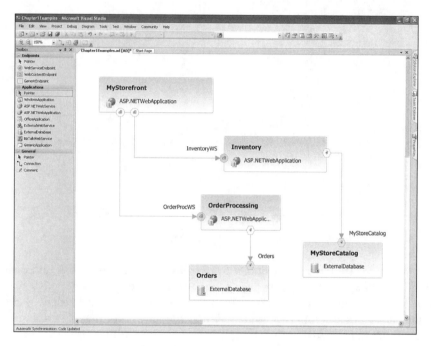

FIGURE 1.1   An e-commerce application seen through the Application Designer.

Class Designer   The Visual Studio 2005 Class Designer provides a graphical means for writing and modifying your objects. You can use it to define classes and their relationships, add properties and methods to those classes, and modify elements within a property or method; it even allows for the refactoring of code. A change to a given method name within the Class Designer, for instance, will change the method's name as well as update all of the method's callers to use the new name.

An added benefit of the designer is that it enables the rapid discovery of code. With the Class Designer, you can drop a few key classes on a model, let the tool determine the relationships that exist in the code, and quickly discover (with visual reference) how an application works. Figure 1.2 is a snapshot of the tool in action.

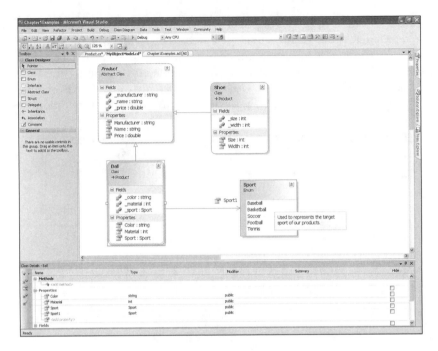

FIGURE 1.2   The Class Designer illustrating objects and their relationships.

Logical Datacenter Designer   The ability to model your datacenter is a dream come true for streamlining communications between the infrastructure and development teams. Visual Studio 2005 allows you to define the boundaries within your datacenter (zones), the traffic allowed between these boundaries, and the servers contained within each boundary. In addition, constraints can be applied to items within this logical model, including versions of software on machines, types of traffic allowed on the machine, application pools, global assembly cache information, session state management, and the like. Finally, these models can be signed and versioned (as they seldom change), and the application design can be vetted against this logical model. Figure 1.3 represents the logical deployment zones of an e-commerce application.

Deployment Designer   The application and Logical Datacenter Designers would be little more than pretty pictures if it were not for the Deployment Designer. This tool allows you to test your application's deployment against your logical datacenter. The tool verifies that you are allowed to make a deployment, allows you to drag and drop an application to a valid server, and verifies the deployment via a deployment compiler. For example, the tool does not allow you to place a web application on a database server that does not allow web traffic. In addition, during compilation, the deployment tool can determine whether the target server has the required software to run your application. Errors are output into a task list similar to coding errors. The intended effect is that deployment errors are found prior to moving code onto production servers, where errors can get very costly. Figure 1.4 shows the deployment diagram with the sample application deployed into the logical datacenter.

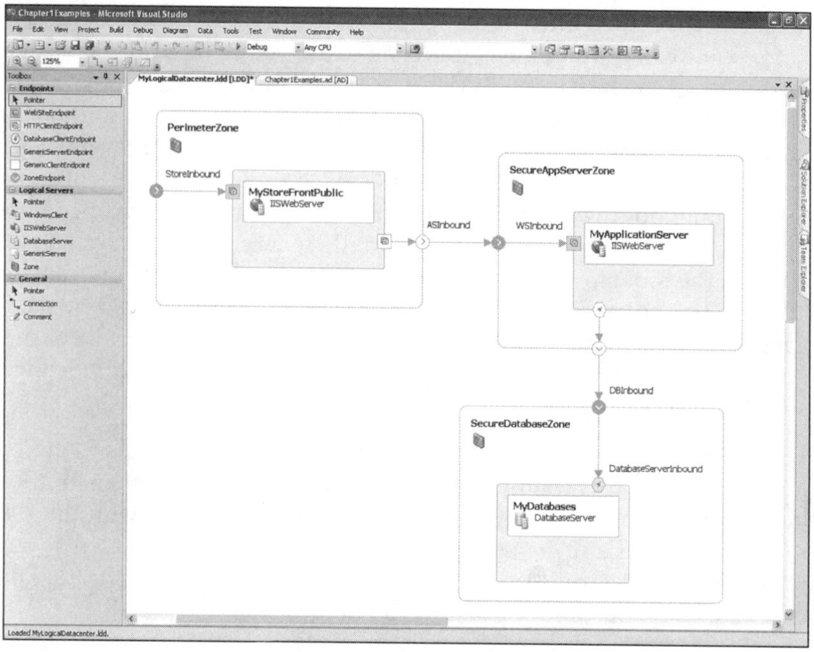

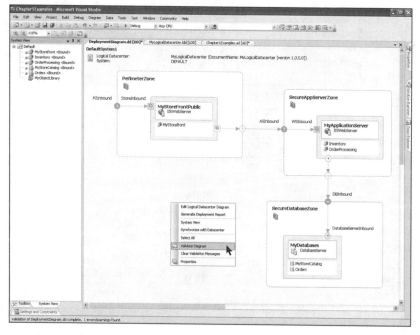

FIGURE 1.3   A logical representation of the servers within a sample datacenter.

FIGURE 1.4   A test deployment of an application into the logical datacenter.

Invoke Activities from the Editor

If you live in a code editor, you can get in a zone where you never want to touch a mouse again. The rhythm of the keys is soothing as you pound out line after line of code. Having to reach up for a menu item or dig for a feature that might provide you some automation is not acceptable. Microsoft has learned that a number of features within Visual Studio go unused because they cannot be found or take too much time to access; it's often easier to just keep the rhythm flowing and fix things with the keyboard rather than go hunting for a feature. Microsoft has worked to align itself with these folks; just look at the latest incarnation of Word. The tool provides help where it can by underlining spelling and grammar errors; autocorrecting commonly misspelled words; and using smart tags where it recognizes people, dates, and addresses. Microsoft has worked to bring even more of these paradigms into Visual Studio. The tool now brings the help to you rather than forcing you to grab for the mouse and go exploring, losing precious productivity in the process.

AutoCorrect (VB Only)   A smart enhancement to the IDE for Visual Basic developers is the AutoCorrect feature. This feature makes good on the premise, "If the IDE knows what's wrong with my code, why can't it fix it?" If you code an error with the 2005 editor, you're likely to get a smart-tag glyph that, when highlighted, presents you with options for correcting the given error. Figure 1.5 shows the AutoCorrect feature presenting two options for a read-only property that has a public "setter."

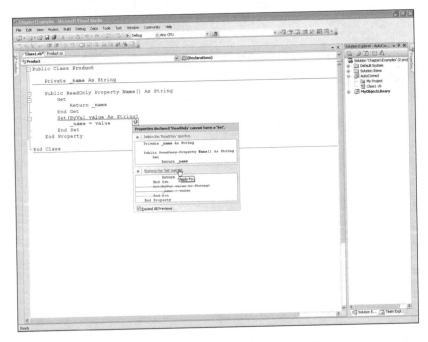

FIGURE 1.5   Invoking the AutoCorrect activity from the code editor.

Snippets   Snippet-like features have been available in code editors for a long time now: macros, cut-and-paste, code library products, and so on. If you've sat through a few demos (and what Microsoft developer hasn't?), I'm sure you've encountered a speaker relying on pasted code inside his or her toolbox to overcome typing deficiencies. This is a fine solution for very specific bits of code and one-developer scenarios. However, you have to remember both to create the code block and to use it. It's often easier to just start banging away at the keyboard using IntelliSense as your guide.

Think of the new snippet feature inside the Visual Studio code editor as an extension to IntelliSense that provides actual blocks of code to aid you with common programming tasks. A number of snippets ship with the product and, of course, you can easily create your own custom snippets (and share them with others). After using snippets for a short while, most developers will agree that having the snippet action part of the code window is an intuitive and welcome productivity enhancement. Figure 1.6 provides a glimpse of the snippet feature in action.

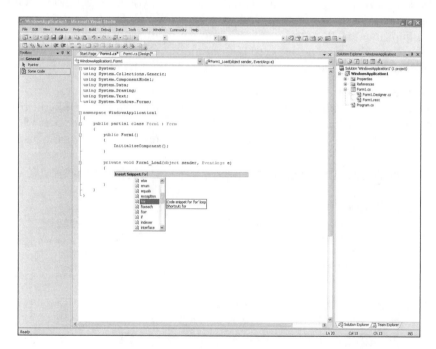

FIGURE 1.6   Code snippets automate common code blocks in an application.

My (VB Only)   The new My feature provides Visual Basic developers a speed-dial to a set of objects that provide common functionality to most applications. These objects, for the most part, wrap the .NET Framework and make it more accessible. Instead of navigating through the namespaces to determine how they might return the user's MyDocuments directory, for instance, VB developers can use the following:

```
My.Computer.FileSystem.GetDirectories( _
  My.Computer.FileSystem.SpecialDirectories.MyDocuments)
```

The functionality exposed by the My feature is sure to make some C# developers jealous. Some classes allow access to the assembly name, the path of the executing code, an audio file on the computer executing the code, the mouse and keyboard, the network and ports, resource files, the event log, user objects, and settings, for example. There is enough speed-dial access to provide a measurable boost in productivity of these basic Windows tasks.

Discover and Navigate Code

Most of us have at one time or another been presented with an unfamiliar code base and told to make enhancements and fixes to the same. It typically takes a ton of time stepping through all the code to decipher the various relationships and complexities that exist within. Tools like the aforementioned Class Designer can be a big help. In addition, the new features of Visual Studio 2005 described in the following sections will aid in the rapid navigation and "learning" of a code base.

Code Definition Window   When you're navigating code, you'll often run into a type that you need more information on. You might want to view the code behind the type to see how it is implemented. Previously, to jump between types, you either hunted for their underlying code files or used the Go to Definition from right-clicking on a given type. Visual Studio 2005 provides another tool: the code definition window.

Invoking this window splits the code editor between active code and a read-only view of referenced code. For example, if you are coding a class called Shoe that inherits from the abstract base class Product, you might want to be able to see the Product class without jumping from file to file. Figure 1.7 shows the code definition window doing just that.

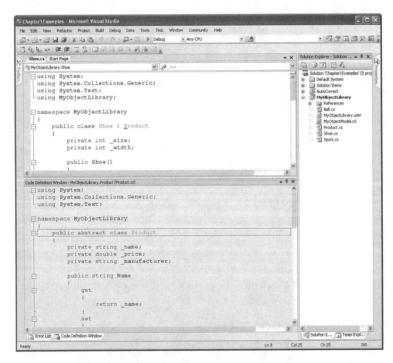

FIGURE 1.7   The code definition window allows a split-screen view of the active code editor and the code of its referenced types.

The code definition window is more than just a read-only view of referenced types. It allows you to clip text for pasting into your code; you can set breakpoints and bookmarks in this view as well. Of course, you can also easily jump to the actual code displayed in the code definition window by right-clicking and then choosing Edit Definition.

Class View Search   A new (and welcome) addition to the class viewer is search. It can be challenging to find the class you are looking for when working with thousands of lines of code across hundreds of classes—especially if your class files contain multiple classes within each file. In addition, you often need a quick search of the .NET Framework classes within the IDE. The class view search feature provides a means to quickly find all classes matching a given string. For example, Figure 1.8 shows a search for the string "Product".

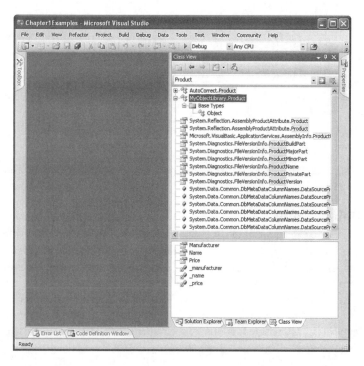

FIGURE 1.8   Class view search enables you to quickly find types within projects and/or the .NET Framework.

Find All References   Another great code navigation enhancement is Find All References. This option, available from a right-click on a given type, uses the compiler (not string checking) to find all the code files and locations that reference a given type. Figure 1.9 demonstrates this feature by searching for all references of a class called Product.

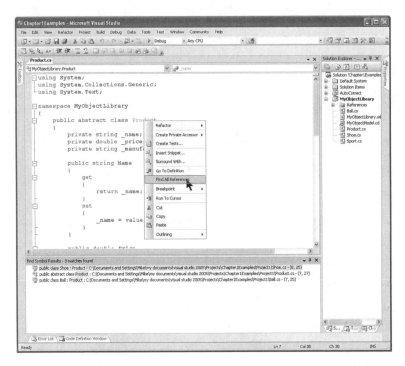

FIGURE 1.9   Find All References uses the compiler to find all uses of a given type.

Edit and Debug Code

When the code canvas is clean, there is nothing but opportunity staring us in the face. Some developers see this is a daunting task, whereas others (myself included) relish in creating something completely new. However, this is becoming more and more the exception to the average coding experience. Today's developers spend very little time doing fresh development. Instead, they tweak, modify, and enhance existing code. In doing so, they are often required to trace through the code and find glitches and the spot to apply the appropriate patch. Microsoft has put a lot of effort into improving this important part of everyday development. The following sections provide the highlights.

Refactoring (C# Only)

Developers often notice enhancements they would like to make to the readability of their code or to increase the probability of reuse or to eliminate duplication of similar code. This process is called *refactoring*. There's been a lot of talk around refactoring—especially as it relates to agile methods (write tests first, write code to satisfy tests, and then refactor to streamline the code base). The biggest issue with refactoring has been trying to make changes to a somewhat stable code base. Sweeping changes are okay in the initial development. However, the last thing anyone on the team wants as you move toward your production date is a change that might introduce more bugs into the code.

To aid in this dilemma, the Visual Studio C# editor provides a number of options for refactoring. It is possible with these tools to simply rename a method, for instance, and be assured that all code that calls that method will be changed. As another example, suppose you have a class that you would like to use as a model for a new class. You might want these classes to be based on a common interface. With the refactoring tools, you can simply extract the existing class as an interface and then implement that interface on the new class.

The refactoring engine uses the compiler to ensure proper and complete code coverage. It also searches comments and makes the proper changes there! In addition, it allows you to preview the changes as they are made (at least until you are comfortable with allowing the tool to modify your source). Refactoring features include all of the following:

- **Rename**—Allows the renaming of a fields, properties, methods, variables, and the like.

- **Extract Method**—Allows for the creation of a new method using existing (selected) lines of code within a given method.

- **Promote Local to Parameter**—Allows you to take a local member of a method and promote it to a parameter of the method. The tool will also work to update any callers of the method.

- **Reorder Parameters**—Allows for changing the order of parameters on a given method signature.

- **Remove Parameters**—Allows the removal of a given parameter from a method. This feature works to update the callers of the method to remove the value passed to the parameter.

- **Encapsulate Field**—Allows for quickly generating properties from a given field.

- **Extract Interface**—Takes an existing class or struct and generates a matching interface, allowing the type to now implement that interface.

The refactoring feature is invoked from either a right-click or a smart tag. The smart tag allows for automatic refactoring without searching for the feature. Figure 1.10 shows the refactoring tool moving through a series of changes in preview mode.

Refactoring for the VB Developer

Members of the Visual Basic development community were very outspoken when they heard they would not be getting the benefits of refactoring built into Visual Studio 2005. Fortunately, a third-party development house, DevExpress (www.devexpress.com), struck a deal with Microsoft to include a version of its product for all VB .NET developers.

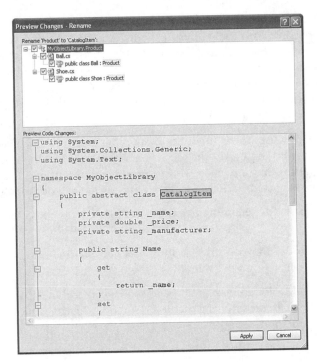

FIGURE 1.10   The refactoring tool allows for the preview of changes prior to execution.

Edit-and-Continue

Undoubtedly, the first thing you noticed when debugging your application, if you switched to .NET from a previous incarnation of Visual Basic, was the absence of *edit-and-continue*. You could no longer make a change in the debugger and continue to step through your code. Rather, you were forced to stop the application, make the change, recompile, and rebreak into your code. This was no small change for the VB folks out there, many of whom had incorporated edit-and-continue into their programming style. They might bang out the vast majority of their code and rely on a very long debug session to get the rest completed.

The good news is that edit-and-continue during debugging is back. There are some limitations (there were in prior VB versions as well), but for the most part you can make a change and keep on stepping. The better news is that this feature is not limited to VB: C# and C++ developers can also take advantage of this productivity enhancement.

Visualizers

Visualizers are another one of those features that will have you wondering how you lived without it. Imagine the last time you were trying to debug a problem with your data-driven application. Everything seemed right, so you figured the data must have been bad. Of course, it is almost impossible to see the data from the debug window. You either dig through a massive series of trivial properties, or you punt and jump out to a SQL window.

Now, with visualizers you can easily see the contents of a dataset represented as a table—right within the IDE in debug mode.

Visualizers allow for the meaningful, visual representation of a variable in debug mode. Visualizers can be invoked from DataTips, the Watch window, the Autos window, or the Locals window. Visualizers exist for data, XML, and HTML. There is also full support for writing custom visualizers and installing them in the IDE. Figure 1.11 shows the DataSet visualizer in action during a debugging session.

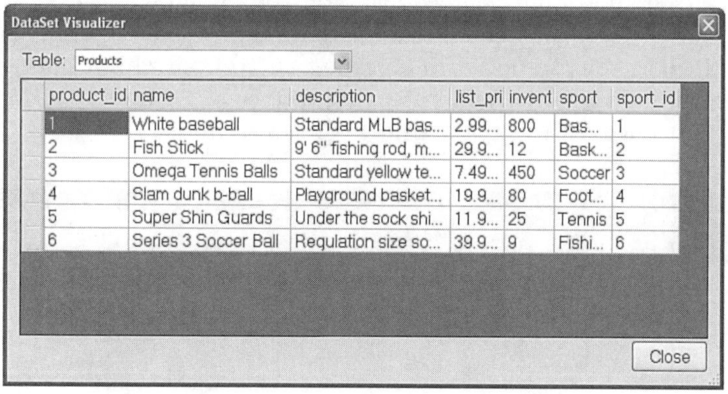

product_id	name	description	list_pri	invent	sport	sport_id
1	White baseball	Standard MLB bas...	2.99...	800	Bas...	1
2	Fish Stick	9' 6" fishing rod, m...	29.9...	12	Bask...	2
3	Omega Tennis Balls	Standard yellow te...	7.49...	450	Soccer	3
4	Slam dunk b-ball	Playground basket...	19.9...	80	Foot...	4
5	Super Shin Guards	Under the sock shi...	11.9...	25	Tennis	5
6	Series 3 Soccer Ball	Regulation size so...	39.9...	9	Fishi...	6

DataSet Visualizer
Table: Products
Close

FIGURE 1.11   A visual representation of a dataset in debug mode.

Additional Debugging Enhancements

The number of enhancements to the Visual Studio debugging experience is astonishing. We've already highlighted a few but would like to briefly bring a few more to your attention. The following sections describe some much-needed improvements to the .NET debugging experience.

IntelliSense in the Watch Window   You can now more easily add items to the Watch window simply by typing in the variable and navigating the underlying object model using IntelliSense right within the Watch window.

Improved Remote Debugging   Microsoft has greatly improved the setup of remote debugging. You now need to deploy only a single file to the remote machine to enable remote debugging. Microsoft has also worked to make sure it is a secure feature.

DataTips   You've had the ability to hover over a variable in the editor while in debug mode but were limited to a single string of text for display. DataTips provide the capability to present more data and allow you to drill into that data (similar to QuickWatch) right from a mouse-over.

Tracepoints   A new and improved breakpoint system in Visual Studio 2005 offers both better breakpoint management as well as the ability to create tracepoints. A *tracepoint* is a breakpoint that allows for a custom action to be executed when the code hits the tracepoint. Custom actions come in the form of printing a message to the output window or running a Visual Studio macro. It's nice to be able to write out trace messages during debugging without littering your code with trace statements.

FxCop Built-In Support   FxCop was an often underused code-analysis tool. I recall visiting one developer shop after another and finding out they had never heard of the tool or what it did. It checks a number of rules, including those surrounding naming conventions, performance enhancements, globalization violations, and design guidelines. You can turn rules on and off or even write your own rules.

The problem was FxCop required a download from Microsoft's GotDotNet site and installation on machines. The good news is that Microsoft has extended FxCop and built it directly into the IDE. You can now turn on code analysis from within a project's property page and start getting suggestions on improving your code. Figure 1.12 shows the rule settings of FxCop along with sample warnings generated from a compile.

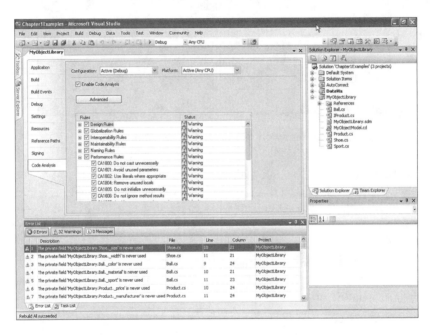

FIGURE 1.12   FxCop code analysis in action.

Share (and Consume) Code with a Community

Writing code is often a community thing. The developer community is broad and, for the most part, supportive of one another. Chances are, if you are having a problem, someone else has had the same issue. You can often reach out across the Internet and find solutions, components, sample code, articles, and the like that help to solve your issue. There is some kinship among developers that attracts them to posting sample code, newsgroup answers, and tips. Perhaps it is as simple as knowing that they may be the next in line to need an answer to a critical question, or maybe it's just the need to show off to one another. Either way, Microsoft has worked to extend the community atmosphere that pervades .NET.

New for 2005 is the ability to search communities (from within the IDE) for project templates, code snippets, samples, controls, starter kits, and add-ins. Microsoft has created a packaging and installation system surrounding .NET community content. You can now easily create new project templates, post them to community sites, find them within the IDE, and install them into your environment for use. See Chapter 12, "Writing Windows Forms Applications."

Target Different Customer Experiences

.NET has quickly become pervasive throughout the entire Microsoft product world (third-party vendors included). It took only a few short years, but it is now fair to say that .NET is everywhere; Windows programming and .NET programming are now synonymous.

As proof, we now have Windows Server 2003 with .NET built-in; we have a new version of SQL Server with support for hosting the .NET runtime and writing data access code as .NET code. The latest versions of Microsoft's server products like BizTalk and Commerce Server are built using .NET. The next version of its flagship operating system (codenamed Longhorn) has .NET embedded throughout—my cell phone is even running a version of the .NET Framework! Every application vendor on the Microsoft platform has a .NET version; we could go on and on. The point is that it is a great time to be writing .NET code. You can target so many solutions with a single framework!

The following sections highlight a number of the customer experiences you are able to target using Visual Studio 2005 and the latest version of the .NET Framework. In addition, Figure 1.13 shows the New Project dialog box in Visual Studio; it now represents the myriad of solutions that are possible with .NET.

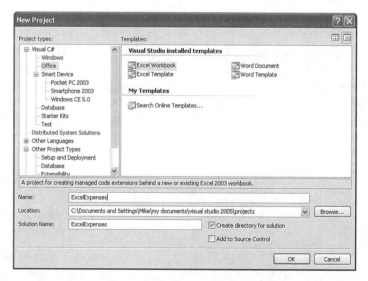

FIGURE 1.13   The many application faces of Visual Studio 2005.

Smart(er) Clients

Smart clients are rapidly becoming the user experience of choice for the business application. What *smart client* means, on the other hand, is still a topic of debate. The debate waivers between two principal ideals. The first represents a rich, windows-based UI application that is deployed and works across the Web, can work in a disconnected mode, understands how to update itself, and plays well in the security sandbox. The second is an application that uses MS Office as the user experience and combines some level of business functionality over the network.

Whatever your view of what makes a smart client (fundamentally, the two are not all that different), the good news is Visual Studio 2005 provides better support for both. The former representation (combination thick client and web application) is really an application design pattern. However, this pattern would not be as easy to create without things like click-once deployment, code-access security, support for disconnected data (and reconnecting that data), web services, and remoting infrastructure. The latter now has full support from within the IDE in the form of Visual Studio Tools for Office (VSTO for short).

Of course, we've been able to customize Office for a long time now; some of us still remember writing Excel macros on Windows 3.1 or automating Word with Word Basic. Visual Studio 2005 marks a new era for Office development with the complete support of building on the Office platform from within the Visual Studio 2005 IDE. With VSTO, you can now create Office-based projects and solutions inside the tool. This includes support for creating Word, Excel, and Outlook first-class projects. Figure 1.14 shows an Excel/C# solution within Visual Studio 2005.

> **NOTE**
>
> Building Office applications with Visual Studio 2005 requires the professional edition of Microsoft Office.

Smart Devices

Visual Studio 2005 extends your power to write applications that target mobile devices. You are free to target PDAs and mobile phones. The IDE provides UI, code, and debugging support for these applications. In addition, you can write both standard, forms-based mobile applications as well as ASP .NET mobile applications with the ASP .NET Mobile Designer. Figure 1.15 illustrates a standard SmartPhone application being developed leveraging Visual Studio.

Web Applications

There are major changes (and advancements) in store for web developers. Clearly, the vast majority of applications built these days involve some semblance of a web component—be it a full-blown browser-based, web application; a smart client that works across the Web; a web service; or otherwise. The point is that the majority of developers writing .NET code are targeting the Web at some level within their solution. It seems that Microsoft has remained heavily focused in this area for just these reasons. It is clear Microsoft has made another big investment in enhancing the web capabilities of .NET. We highlight some of these advancements in the following sections.

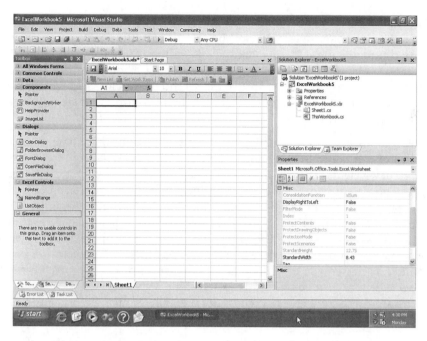

FIGURE 1.14   Visual Studio's support for Office applications.

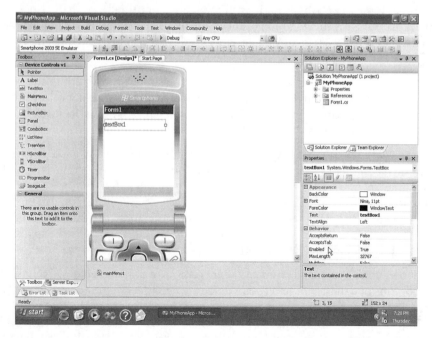

FIGURE 1.15   Visual Studio's support for targeting a SmartPhone.

A Full Toolbox   One of the first things you notice about ASP .NET is that there are many, many more controls than we web developers are used to (unless you've been purchasing third-party control libraries). The standard set of controls is still available for creating labels, text boxes, buttons, and the like. Of course, there are enhancements to these controls as well as some new standards like the Wizard control for creating web-based wizards or the MultiView for managing varied groups of controls that are influenced by user preference or identity.

Things get real interesting in the all new sets of controls. For instance, there is now a complete set of data controls including the GridView that takes the concept of the DataGrid to new heights. There is also the new ReportViewer control for displaying data as a report. There are new data source controls including an ObjectDataSource for binding directly to object data stored as a list or collection. Moving beyond data controls, there is a new SiteMapMath control that tracks a user's progress as he or she navigates through the various levels of your site and allows the user to jump back up the chain. There is an entirely new set of controls to manage user login to websites. Finally, if you've ever used SharePoint Portal Server, you have undoubtedly worked with zones and Web Parts. They allow users to define where functionality exists within a given page. Visual Studio 2005 ships with a similar set of Web Part controls for designing similar features into your application.

A Manageable User Experience   It seems the user experience (look and feel) of a website tends to evolve independently of the actual functionality of a site. Perhaps marketing is looking to keep the site fresh or inline with the latest campaign. As web developers, we have been planning for this for a long time with things like style sheets, include files, and user controls. ASP .NET 2.0 gives web developers additional tools for managing the user experience, namely themes, skins, and master pages.

A *theme* is a group of appearance properties that can be applied to an entire site, a given page, or a single control. You define themes based on common appearance properties that a page will contain (including images). For this reason, appearance properties are common across pages and controls in ASP .NET 2.0.

Creating a new theme is as simple as adding a new folder in your site's App_Themes directory. You then add theme-related files to the directory like a style sheet, images, and *skin* files. Skin files are new to ASP .NET 2.0. They enable you to define the look of a given control, such as a GridView, for your entire theme. With this feature, you can ensure all controls of a given type look identical across the site. You apply the theme to your entire website via a setting in the config file. Alternatively, you can apply a theme to a single page using the page directive's theme attribute.

Master pages evolve the include files and user controls of old to enable you to visually inherit portions of a master page. When you create a master page, you are defining the elements of the page that are common to all pages that derive from the master. Typically, this includes a header, some form of navigation, and a footer. In addition, the master page defines content areas to which subpages can add their functionality. Finally, this entire concept is supported visually through the Visual Studio designer. You can now see the layout of your pages during design! Figure 1.16 shows a subpage being created in the designer; the grayed-out areas are those common to the master page.

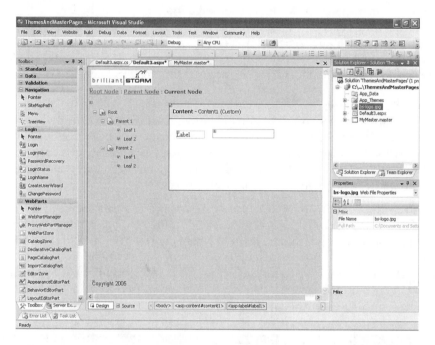

FIGURE 1.16   The designer view of a web page inheriting from a master page.

A Development Server   To test and debug applications effectively, most .NET web developers run a local copy of Internet Information Server (IIS) on their development machine (typically a Windows XP Professional box). The operations and infrastructure teams have typically turned a blind eye to this. However, as security becomes a bigger and bigger focus, a series of developer-hosted web servers on the network becomes difficult to manage at best and a security vulnerability at worst.

Solving this problem can be challenging; it often requires shared servers, remote debugging, or some level of virtual development. Each of these solutions has its own drawbacks. Chief among them is that the web developers can no longer cut the cord to the network and still be cutting code.

Visual Studio 2005 ships with a new tool to aid with this issue: ASP .NET Development Server (not a catchy name but effective nonetheless). This server has it roots in the server named Cassini that shipped with the free ASP .NET Web Matrix. With it, you are free to test your code locally, independent of IIS. Of course, the best feature is that it only serves pages to the local box; it is invisible on the network.

This server is not IIS. The biggest issue in this regard is that the ASP .NET Web Development Server runs with your local user credentials. Getting the security right will still require a walkthrough when you push things up to an IIS build or test server. Of course, you still can run a local copy of IIS on your machine if you prefer.

Connect with Data

Many of the advancements that .NET 2.0 makes relative to connecting with your data come in the form of easier-to-use, more connected tools and controls. There are a few advancements with respect to various data namespaces (System.Data, System.Data.SQLClient, and so on). However, the vast majority of improvements lie in the way Visual Studio and the new controls are working to bind to this data. The following sections describe some noticeable enhancements to the development experience.

Zero-Code Data Binding

Whether you are writing a new web form application that connects directly to your database or you have a three-tier application that delivers data to web controls via business objects or web services, Visual Studio makes great strides to automate this entire process. Visual Studio recognizes multiple data sources including business objects and lists, databases (SQL, Oracle, and others), XML, and web services.

Windows Forms   Windows form developers can simply add a data source to their application and make use of the tables and their relationships via drag-and-drop to a form. Visual Studio determines which data maps to which control (date data to calendar control, for instance) and how the data gets displayed in the form of parent-child relationships. Of course, you have complete control to override this information. Figure 1.17 shows a Windows form under development that connects users to orders and order details. The form is fully functional without writing a single line of code.

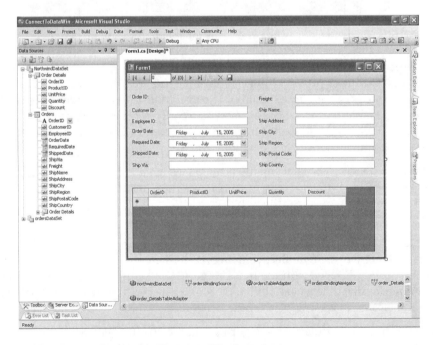

FIGURE 1.17   Zero-code data binding on a Windows form.

Web Forms   Developers of web forms have similar options for binding to data through the use of controls. A host of new data source controls allow for the configuration of a data connection (shared or otherwise) and the ability to work that data. Data source objects allow for defining selects, inserts, updates, and deletes across a variety of providers. Data source providers include the SqlDataSource object (used to connect to databases whether they are SQL Server or otherwise), AccessDataSource, ObjectDataSource, XmlDataSource, and SiteMapDataSource. Figure 1.18 shows the dialog box for defining an insert query to a SqlDataSource. Note that each parameter on the query can be linked to a control on the form (or the session, querystring, cookie, and the like).

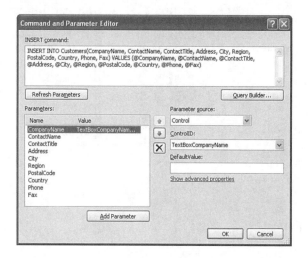

FIGURE 1.18   Data binding an insert query of a SqlDataSource control.

In addition to the data source objects, there are both new and improved controls that ease the burden of binding to and working with data. A new GridView control makes the process of working with lists of data much easier. The new FormView control allows you to build dynamic forms based on the rows in a database. Most ASP.NET controls now have a means to bind directly to a data source through the IDE. For instance, the DropDownList control allows you to pick a data source and to define a field that is displayed to the user and another whose value is posted to your code.

Automate Application Testing

Visual Studio 2005 empowers developers with testing tools to better ensure the quality of their code prior to deployment. These tools include automated unit testing, syntax checking, code coverage analysis, integrated FxCop features, object test bench, and more. As an example, developers can let Visual Studio generate unit tests based on their code base. This may fly in the face of test-driven development's mantra of test-first development, but it ensures a higher likelihood that tests will be developed for an application.

Developers may end up submitting a higher-quality product to the quality assurance team, but if you've spent time in this camp, you know what a manual, routine process this can be. Visual Studio now gives testers an arsenal of tools to call their own. You can write and track test cases, generate test coverage reports, track issues (and report on the same), execute load testing, and more. Figure 1.19 provides a glimpse into the features designed for testers. You can see the Test Manager screen in the background and the new test menu in the foreground.

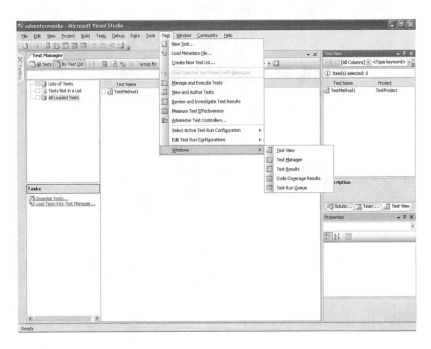

FIGURE 1.19   The Test Manager and the new test menu.

Finally, Visual Studio includes a new build engine that can be configured to execute tests when developers check in their code. If, for instance, you require the code not to break the build, you can configure an integration test to pass as part of the new build engine.

Sorting Through the SKUs

Visual Studio 2005 is not one, single product. It in fact comes in many flavors; each is baked for a different appetite. There is a recipe targeted at the hobbyist to the enterprise architect, the beta tester to the operations guy—and oh yeah, there are morsels for the developer, too! Microsoft is providing a smorgasbord of tools that invite the entire team to the software development project table.

New members of the team enjoying our favorite IDE means new features to serve their varied needs. For instance, the operations person is concerned about modeling the data-center, whereas a tester might be concerned about bug counts and expected load. A project manager tends to focus on tracking work items, whereas a developer wants to get some code written. This variety of needs results in multiple groups of features that pertain to a single role on the product life cycle—all stuffed into our favorite container: the Visual Studio IDE. Yes, it's getting crowded in here!

Microsoft has done a couple of things to both reduce complexity as well as to serve the new target users. Chief among them was to create multiple versions of the product, each targeted at an individual role on the team. Testers, for example, should not be forced to purchase a Class Designer. The same holds true for architects; they should not have to buy a test case management tool if they do not intend to use it.

Of course, some feature sets will overlap between roles. For example, both testers and developers write unit tests and are concerned with code coverage analysis of the various tests. Microsoft also understands there are those among our ranks who can't stand to not have it all. For them, Microsoft has created Team Suite—the full IDE experience that transcends all roles.

Sorting through all the new Visual Studio flavors can be confusing, for sure. You must understand that the new SKUs are an attempt to target individual roles as well as provide an integrated experience across the development life cycle. The new SKUs can also be seen as a direct response to Microsoft's new competition that sells all of these new features as separate products. We hope the following aids with your Visual Studio flavor selection.

Express Editions

The new Express Editions of the various Microsoft products are low-cost (between free and $50), low-barrier to entry versions targeted directly at the novice, hobbyist, student, or anyone else looking to write some code without breaking the bank. They can also be seen as Microsoft's answer to all the "freeware" tools available to today's developers. After all, if you are a college student looking to put up a buddy's website, you are more likely to look for the low-cost solution. Of course, five years down the road when you're making decisions for your company, Microsoft wants to be sure you've had a chance to work with its products.

The current Express Editions of Visual Studio include all the .NET languages: C#, Visual Basic, J#, and C++. However, each language is a separate downloadable product version. Microsoft has also created an Express version for the new SQL Server 2005 as well as an MSDN Express for providing help content. In addition, the Visual Studio Express Editions include built-in tutorial content/starter kits for developers who are new to the .NET Framework.

These editions purposely do not have all the power of their professional patriarch (such as a Class Designer, unit testing, enterprise templates, XSLT support, source code control, 64-bit support, and so on). In addition, they have a more streamlined user experience that does not expose the full complexity (or power) of the professional editions. However, developers will be able to create client/server form-based applications, websites, and even web services using the Visual Studio Express Editions.

NOTE

For more information regarding the Visual Studio Express Editions or to download one of these editions, you can visit Microsoft's site at the following URL: http://msdn.microsoft.com/howtobuy/vs2005/editions/stdexp/.

Standard Edition

The Standard version of Visual Studio is the base-level entry point for professional developers. This edition is similar in nature to the Express Editions. However, it contains all the .NET languages in a single package. In addition, it gives developers an expanded feature set over the Express versions. These additional capabilities include the following:

- Ability to target mobile devices

- Ability to work with database design beyond the local SQL Express Edition

- MSDN documentation

- Visual modeling via the visual Class Designer

- Support for XSLT

- Click Once deployment tool

- Consumption (not creation) of external add-ins

- Support for SQL Reporting Services

- Compatibility with Visual Source Safe (VSS)

Visual Studio Professional Edition

Most corporate developers and consultants will find a new home within one of the new Professional editions of Visual Studio. In fact, the product offerings are not that dissimilar to what you're used to with the current incarnations of Visual Studio. When you purchase Visual Studio Professional, you will still get all the language support (including VB, C#, C++, and J#) and, of course, the whole host of new enhancements.

The biggest difference (outside the new features) is how the product is packaged in an MSDN subscription. The first thing you'll notice is a subtle marketing change. Microsoft no longer sells an MSDN subscription that happens to include Visual Studio. Rather, it is now selling Visual Studio Professional with various MSDN flavors; gone are the universal, enterprise, and professional subscriptions. Keeping them around would lead folks to believe there was a one-to-one correlation. Therefore, Microsoft created the following flavors of Visual Studio combined with MSDN (listed from fewest features/applications to the most):

- **Visual Studio Professional only (without MSDN)**—Includes VB, C#, C++, and J#; allows for the creation of windows, web, and mobile applications; provides support for 64-bit development and enterprise templates; includes the Class Designer, the Server Explorer, and SQL developer edition.

- **Visual Studio Professional with MSDN Professional**—Includes all of the above plus the following: support for Excel, Word, and InfoPath projects; includes operating system licenses for development and testing; includes a copy of Virtual PC.

- **Visual Studio Professional with MSDN Premium**—Includes all of the above with the following extras: support for Access development extensions; adds support for modeling with Visio; includes Visual Source Safe; includes server licenses for development and testing; includes a copy of Microsoft Office, InfoPath, OneNote, Visio, Project, and MapPoint.

- **Visual Studio Tools for the Microsoft Office System**—Targeted at developers focused solely on Office automation. Comes in Visual Basic and C# flavors only. Does not include the capability to create mobile application or do 64-bit development.

NOTE

For more information regarding the Professional editions of Visual Studio, you can visit Microsoft's site at the following URL: http://msdn.microsoft.com/howtobuy/vs2005/editions/pro/.

Visual Studio Team System

Arguably the most exciting (and promising) innovation for Visual Studio 2005 lies within the new team system SKUs. These editions expand the product's focus beyond that of just software developers. Microsoft is now engaging directly with all members of the software life cycle—from project managers through operations.

Team System is an integrated, software development life cycle platform. The tools surrounding Team System are housed either within the IDE itself or within an Office application (like Project or Excel). Increased project communication and collaboration are at the heart of this platform. To enable a richer experience, Microsoft has created a central server application (backed by SQL Server 2005) that manages and tracks project work items across project roles.

This centralized system, called Team Foundation Server, allows for project-level synchronization among architects, developers, testers, project managers, and operations—all within the tool of their choice. For instance, developers can check out a work item (task) right from the IDE; they can also close that item right there. The same holds true for testers. They can identify an issue and create a new work item. Finally, project managers might choose to view, sort, and report on work items from Excel. They, too, can import, modify, and publish back to the central server from the tool of their choice. The following represents Microsoft's view of the project roles that Team System addresses:

- **Architect**—Software architects are responsible for an application's design. This certainly includes what we traditionally call *application design* such as classes, inheritance, function signatures, and the like. However, in today's service-oriented/distributed world, this often means the additional complexity of defining the interfaces and connections between discrete bits of application functionality. The modern business application is an amalgamation of other applications and data. For instance, a new application might be created to aggregate data from the order processing system and the customer relationship management system to provide a holistic view of corporate sales data.

  An architect's job doesn't end there. He or she must ensure the design will work within the confines of the datacenter. This includes verifying the application against current hardware, firewall rules, service packs, software versions, and so on. After all, who wants to spend four months creating an application only to be told by the infrastructure team that it does not fit within the deployment environment? Rather, the architect should be able to visually verify new distributed systems against a logical version of the datacenter.

- **Developer**—Developers make it all happen. They are responsible for building the application and writing the code that makes the magic happen. Microsoft understands and is trying to address our plight: We want to be free to write code that conforms to best practices. However, these practices are often a moving target—and there always seem to be more and more practices, patterns, and blocks. Team System is meant to help developers write secure and reliable code and ensure it all gets tested.

- **Tester**—Testers play a vital role in ensuring the overall quality of the project when it gets delivered to the end user. We all know that they typically get crunched when it comes to project time. Builds are not always ready. Features are still sneaking in. Team System wants to help make sure testers can get as much real testing done in the time they are given. The product understands that testers need to create test cases, write tests, execute tests, log and verify issues against code, and report code coverage and status information.

- **Project Manager**—Project managers (PMs) need to be able to orchestrate the entire team's effort. They are responsible for tracking actual progress against baseline plans. They often need to be able to collect work item status from multiple team members and allocate precious resources accordingly. Of course, most PMs don't use Visual Studio. Rather, their tool of choice is often Microsoft Project or Excel. The good news is that Team System ensures up-to-the-minute project task item tracking from the tool of choice.

- **Operations**—Operations want to make sure that what the folks in application development create can be deployed within the bounds of the organization. There is nothing worse than spending a few months on a hot new project only to find out during deployment that your architecture is not supported on the target servers. Perhaps you are using a newer version of the .NET Framework that has not been approved for production, or perhaps your application communicates directly to the database that is not allowed in the production setup.

Visual Studio Team Architect allows an architect to work with the operations person to define a logical representation of the datacenter environment. This includes typical server installs, communication between zones, and so on. This logical design can be controlled via versioning and digital signing. The architect can then work to verify the intended architecture against the logical datacenter. A compiler checks for inconsistencies and reports "errors" back to the architect—at design time, not during the final stage of production deployment.

The Server

Visual Studio Team Foundation Server is the core of Visual Studio Team System. This product is deployed onto a central server for the entire team to access. The result is a centralized, holistic management of the project—even across a distributed team.

> **NOTE**
>
> Microsoft's original announcement surrounding Team Foundation Server indicated that all development teams would have to come up with cash for this server SKU in addition to purchasing individual clients. Microsoft held down the entry cost for the product, but a lot of small development shops still balked at not being able to participate in this full life cycle tool.
>
> Microsoft heard and listened to a very important segment of its customer base. It decided to ship a five-user license for the server with each team client SKU. This will certainly help small development shops, spread some good PR, and help Microsoft ensure a widespread adoption of Visual Studio Team Foundation Server. Of course, despite pricing, Visual Studio Team Foundation Server was created for large, enterprise-scope development projects.

The functionality behind Team Foundation Server revolves around project management and source control. Project management and tracking are accomplished through work items. A *work item* can be a task on the project, an issue or bug, a software requirement, a feature, or a test scenario. In general a work item represents a generic unit of work on the project. Of course, work items are customizable and can have states, new fields, and business rules associated with them. Work items can also be driven by a methodology. Finally, work items play a central part in ensuring project team communication and reporting.

The source control features in Team Foundation Server complete the elevation of the entire Microsoft development product platform to a professional level. Development teams are no longer forced to live with the limitations of the previous incarnations of Visual Source Safe. You now are not required to go out and purchase a third-party source control system and live with its limited Visual Studio integration issues. Instead, Team Foundation Server brings you such enterprise class features as change sets, shelving, automatic build rules, the capability to associate work items to changed source, parallel development, a source control policy engine, branching, checkpoints, and more. And like the rest of Team Foundation Server, it is all extensible.

Surrounding these project management and source control features are a build management engine, a reporting infrastructure, and a project portal. The build tools allow for both automatic, scheduled builds as well as on-demand builds. Builds are reported against, documented, automatically tested, and analyzed for code coverage and churn, for example. The reporting engine and project portal combine to further enhance the view into the project by team members. Built on Windows SharePoint Services (WSS), it delivers the latest test and build reports, documentation, announcements, and quality analysis.

> **NOTE**
>
> Visual Studio Team Foundation Server ships with a new source control system based on SQL Server. For smaller development shops that need source control, a new version of Visual Source Safe fixes some of the issues that have plagued this product, including the lack of remote access capabilities. Thanks to new web service integration, remote access is now much more responsive.

The Client Tools

A number of new client versions of the Visual Studio toolset are used to access the foundation server. Each version includes a copy of Visual Studio 2005 Professional with the Class Designer and a license for Team Foundation Server. In addition, purchasing with MSDN premium will give you copies of the operating systems for development and testing, copies of Windows server for the same, Microsoft Office, Visio, Project, and MapPoint. What makes each of these SKUs unique and significant, however, is what additional goodies they do and do not contain. The intent is a targeted set of tools to a different role on the project. The following list outlines the features that drive these SKUs into their respective buckets:

- **Visual Studio Team Developer**—The SKU most likely to take hold with current VS developers, this product includes static code analysis, code profiling, dynamic code analysis, unit testing, and code coverage indicators.

- **Visual Studio Team Architect**—Designed for the software architect, this SKU improves design and design validation of distributed systems. Features include the first round of tools targeting the system definition model (SDM): SOA modeling tools, Distributed System Designer, Application Designer, and a Deployment Designer. Note: This version does not contain the team system features targeted at developers or testers.

- **Visual Studio Team Test**—Targeted at the software tester, this edition includes the ability to create unit tests, do code coverage analysis, manage and create test cases, and execute load tests. Purchasing MSDN Premium with the Team Test version gives testers a copy of Virtual Server to allow for deployment-testing scenarios.

- **Visual Studio Team Suite**—For those who must have it all (and have unlimited budgets), this SKU is the everything-but-the-kitchen-sink option. It includes all the features of Team Architect, Developer, and Test in a single package.

> **NOTE**
>
> To further compare the Visual Studio Team System SKUs and get up-to-date information on Microsoft's product bundling, you can visit Microsoft's site at http://msdn.microsoft.com/ howtobuy/vs2005/editions/team/compare/.

Summary

A new release of Visual Studio means a lot to all the various development camps out there. Visual Studio touches developers who write code in C++, C#, VB, J#, and many others. Literally millions of developers boot up and launch their favorite tool every day. They spend the vast majority of their working hours, days, weeks, and months architecting and building solutions with the tool. Added to this group are now the many testers, architects, and infrastructure people who will hopefully start to see what all the fuss is about.

CHAPTER 2

A Quick Tour of the IDE

IN THIS CHAPTER

- Installation
- The Start Page
- Your First Project
- The Menu Bar
- The Many Toolbars
- The Toolbox
- The Visual Designers
- The Text Editors
- The Solution Explorer
- The Properties Window
- Managing the Many Windows of the IDE

When you're traveling on unfamiliar ground, it's often wise to consult a tour guide. At minimum, a quick check of the map is in order before you set out for new adventures. The same holds true for approaching a new development tool the size and breadth of Visual Studio 2005. It is wise to familiarize yourself a bit with the tool before starting that first project off on the wrong foot.

This chapter is meant to be your quick, to-the-point guide. It serves to orient you before you set out. We'll cover the basics of installation; booting up the IDE; and getting to know the layout of the tool in terms of projects, editors, and designers. Let's get started.

Installation

The installation of Visual Studio 2005 remains similar to previous versions. The exception is the myriad of new SKUs and tools available for install. Depending on your purchase, a subset of these items will be available for your selection during install (see Chapter 1, "A Quick Tour of Visual Studio 2005"). If you are fortunate enough to own the Team Suite Edition, you'll be presented with the full set of options. Figure 2.1 shows the installation options selection dialog box for the Team Suite.

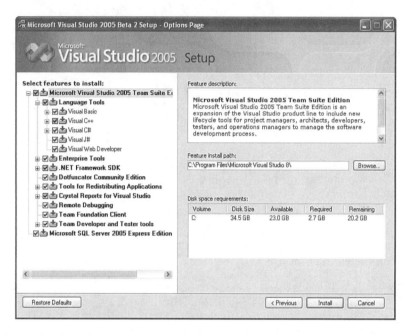

FIGURE 2.1   Visual Studio 2005 setup options page.

Choosing a Language

Setting up your development machine should be relatively straightforward. We suggest the average developer keep language installs to a primary language and perhaps one backup. You might use a secondary language for viewing sample code from MSDN or similar sites. Typically, this means if your primary language is Visual Basic, you install C# as a secondary language (and vice versa). This solves the problem of finding a great bit of code you want to embed in your project only to discover it's not available in your chosen language. Additionally, Visual Studio 2005 lets you configure your primary language (see the next section). We also believe that both C++ and J# are meant as primary languages. We cannot see a major benefit to choosing them as secondary languages to either VB or C# (unless, of course, you are constantly porting Java or something similar). Finally, choosing to install many languages, most of which you do not intend to use, not only takes up hard drive space, but it can also clutter your environment with too many choices. We do, however, recommend installing the full MSDN help system. There is always a possibility of finding a solution to a problem you are having inside an item targeted at a different language.

Installing Source Control

During install you'll need to consider your options surrounding source control and Team Foundation Server. If you are installing a development client SKU based on Team Systems, you will want to install the Team Foundation Client. This will allow you to connect to the new Team Systems Server and participate in item management, source control, report-ing, and so on.

If you are not working with Team Systems, we suggest you install the new version of Visual SourceSafe (VSS) 2005. This is a separate install from Visual Studio. If you are working on a team, the database will be installed on the server. The administration tools should be installed on either the administrator's box or the server. Each developer will simply install the client. If you are on your own, we still suggest that you use a local copy of VSS for managing your source code; you never know when a rollback will save the day. Figure 2.2 shows the new Visual SourceSafe tool in action.

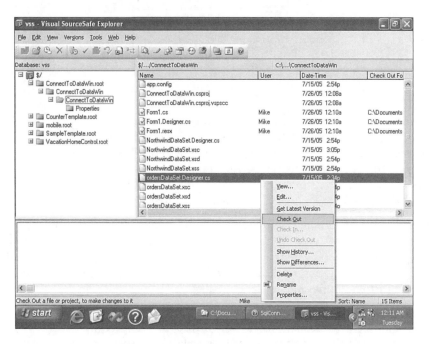

FIGURE 2.2   The New Visual SourceSafe 2005.

Configuring Your Development Environment

Booting the new IDE for the first time will result in a dialog box asking you to choose your environment settings. As Visual Studio becomes the central tool for so many devel-opers, testers, and project managers, it's harder and harder to satisfy them all with a single tool. To aid in this dilemma, Microsoft has created an entire set of environment settings that are configured for the average developer type. For instance, if you set your environment to C#, the new project dialog box will automatically highlight C# projects above other languages. Figure 2.3 shows the configuration options available to you.

FIGURE 2.3   The Environment Settings options dialog box.

Only your first use of Visual Studio will launch the default settings dialog box. On subsequent visits you'll go straight to the tool. However, you might consider switching your environment settings if you do a lot of switching from one language to another or if you switch roles. For example, C# developers might use the C# development settings the majority of the time. They might then toggle to the Tester or Project Management Settings if they intend to do a lot of testing for the project.

You manage your environment settings from the Tools menu's Import and Export Settings option. Figure 2.4 shows a screen from the resulting wizard. This screen allows you to choose settings to import. Note that there are several default setting groups, including those based on language and role (such as web developer, tester). In addition, you can browse to a custom settings file.

TIP

If you are like most developers, you are probably particular about your environment setup. There is nothing worse than having to work on a machine that has a different IDE configuration. You can be thankful that you can now use the Import and Export Settings Wizard to take your IDE settings with you.

Another key screen to this wizard is the settings selection screen. On this screen you decide which options are important for import. This allows you to pick and choose imported settings. For example, you may love the way a friend has configured her code editor in terms of font and contrasting colors, but you do not want all her other settings like keyboard configurations. Figure 2.5 provides a glimpse at the granular level to which you can manage your environment settings.

FIGURE 2.4   The Import and Export Settings Wizard.

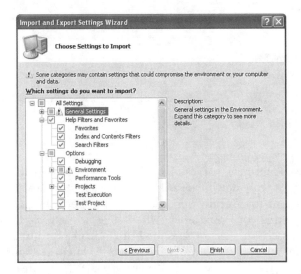

FIGURE 2.5   Choosing settings to import.

TIP

A great feature of the import and export settings tool is the ability to move help favorites. These favorites are finally abstracted from your default web browser favorites. In addition, they can now travel with you from machine to machine, so you do not have to spend another hour digging through the help file for a particularly important topic.

The Start Page

When you first get into the Visual Studio 2005 IDE, you are presented with the Start Page for the tool. This feature looked promising in previous versions but now seems to be actually useful in Visual Studio 2005. Figure 2.6 shows an example of the new Start Page.

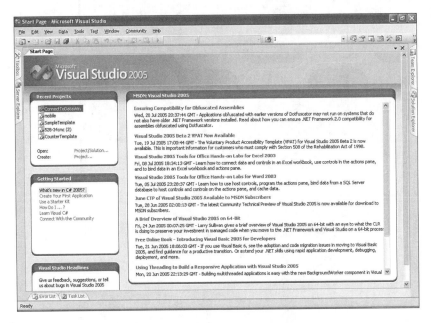

FIGURE 2.6   The Visual Studio 2005 Start Page.

The Start Page contains a number of web parts. Starting from the upper left, there is the Recent Projects area. From here, you can launch a project you were recently working on or create a new one. Moving down, you see the Getting Started area. This Web Part is useful if you are looking for learning opportunities with the tool. This can be a great place to set out exploring with a starter kit, what's new, or the new "How do I ...?" question-and-answer section. Below this is the headlines area for Visual Studio. Here, you are notified of recent releases or can provide feedback to Microsoft yourself. Finally, in the middle of the page are the headlines and offers from MSDN. This area can be useful to peruse at project startup—especially if you find yourself spending too much time on the project and feel yourself losing touch with the goings-on in the development world.

Startup Options

If you just don't like the Start Page or prefer to launch directly into the project you'll be spending the next few months of your life working on, you can customize what happens when the IDE boots. From the Options dialog box (Tools, Options), choose the Environment node and then the Startup leaf. Figure 2.7 shows some of the options available at startup.

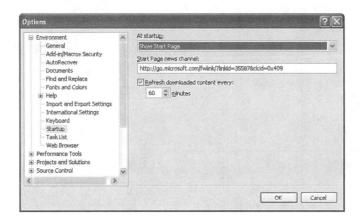

FIGURE 2.7   Startup options.

From here, you can configure where to get your start page news items. You can also tell the environment to load the last solution, show the new or open project dialog boxes, open your browser's home page, or do nothing (show an empty environment). You can also configure how often your content is automatically refreshed from the server.

Your First Project

The next, natural step is to create your first project. Doing so will quickly expose you to some of the basic project and file management features within the IDE. From the File menu, you're given the option to create a new project or website. The two are fundamentally not very different in terms of your first project. Projects are simply templates for windows, Office, mobile, and similar executable applications, whereas a website combines server-side code and markup language to send HTML to a browser.

Figure 2.8 shows a sample website inside the IDE. We chose C# as the target language of this website. Notice that the layout is relatively generic. You should expect a similar experience for your first few applications (until you've customized things). In the following sections, we will break down the many items on this screen; it might be useful to refer to this graphic to provide overall context as we discuss a given item.

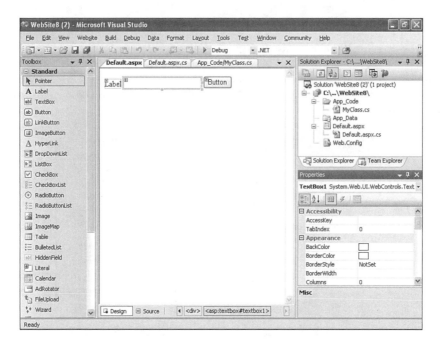

FIGURE 2.8   A sample web project inside the IDE.

The Menu Bar

If you've been working with previous versions, you should find the Visual Studio 2005 menu bar to be standard fare. It is very intuitive; options are where you'd expect them; and new menus appear depending on your place within the IDE, the tools you've chosen to install, and your default language. For example, a Refactor menu will appear when you are in the C# code editor; the Project menu shows up when you have a project open; and the File menu will configure itself differently depending on Visual Basic or C#. Table 2.1 lists (from left to right across the IDE) some of the more common menus, along with a description of each.

> **NOTE**
>
> Note that each menu screenshot in Table 2.1 was taken using the C# menu default settings. In each case, Visual Basic has an equivalent, albeit slightly different, menu. In addition, the keyboard shortcut callouts in the menu items are also those of C#. Visual Basic developers will recognize a lot of them as the same. All of them can be customized to an individual developer's preference.

TABLE 2.1   Visual Studio 2005 Menus

Menu	Figure	Description
File		The File menu is used to create new projects and add new items to the same. You can also save your work, work with projects under source control, and print your code.
Edit		The Edit menu is used for managing items on your Clipboard and fixing mistakes with Undo and Redo. In addition, the Edit menu provides access to important tools like Find and Replace and IntelliSense. The callout menu in the graphic at left shows some of the advanced options available from the Edit menu such as Format Document, which is useful to apply your formatting to code you are working with.

TABLE 2.1   Continued

Menu	Figure	Description
View	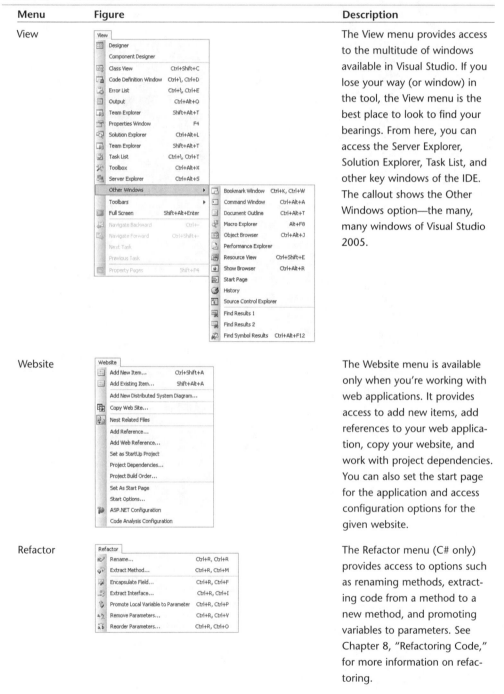	The View menu provides access to the multitude of windows available in Visual Studio. If you lose your way (or window) in the tool, the View menu is the best place to look to find your bearings. From here, you can access the Server Explorer, Solution Explorer, Task List, and other key windows of the IDE. The callout shows the Other Windows option—the many, many windows of Visual Studio 2005.
Website		The Website menu is available only when you're working with web applications. It provides access to add new items, add references to your web application, copy your website, and work with project dependencies. You can also set the start page for the application and access configuration options for the given website.
Refactor		The Refactor menu (C# only) provides access to options such as renaming methods, extracting code from a method to a new method, and promoting variables to parameters. See Chapter 8, "Refactoring Code," for more information on refactoring.

TABLE 2.1   Continued

Menu	Figure	Description
Project	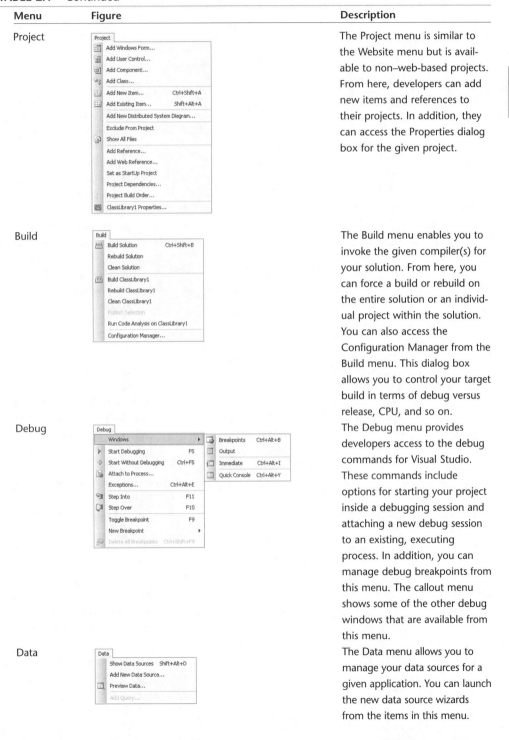	The Project menu is similar to the Website menu but is available to non–web-based projects. From here, developers can add new items and references to their projects. In addition, they can access the Properties dialog box for the given project.
Build		The Build menu enables you to invoke the given compiler(s) for your solution. From here, you can force a build or rebuild on the entire solution or an individual project within the solution. You can also access the Configuration Manager from the Build menu. This dialog box allows you to control your target build in terms of debug versus release, CPU, and so on.
Debug		The Debug menu provides developers access to the debug commands for Visual Studio. These commands include options for starting your project inside a debugging session and attaching a new debug session to an existing, executing process. In addition, you can manage debug breakpoints from this menu. The callout menu shows some of the other debug windows that are available from this menu.
Data		The Data menu allows you to manage your data sources for a given application. You can launch the new data source wizards from the items in this menu.

TABLE 2.1   Continued

Menu	Figure	Description
Format	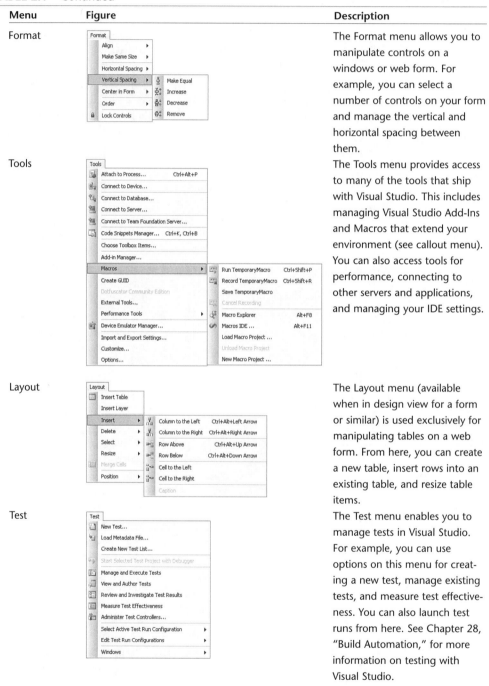	The Format menu allows you to manipulate controls on a windows or web form. For example, you can select a number of controls on your form and manage the vertical and horizontal spacing between them.
Tools		The Tools menu provides access to many of the tools that ship with Visual Studio. This includes managing Visual Studio Add-Ins and Macros that extend your environment (see callout menu). You can also access tools for performance, connecting to other servers and applications, and managing your IDE settings.
Layout		The Layout menu (available when in design view for a form or similar) is used exclusively for manipulating tables on a web form. From here, you can create a new table, insert rows into an existing table, and resize table items.
Test		The Test menu enables you to manage tests in Visual Studio. For example, you can use options on this menu for creating a new test, manage existing tests, and measure test effectiveness. You can also launch test runs from here. See Chapter 28, "Build Automation," for more information on testing with Visual Studio.

TABLE 2.1 Continued

Menu	Figure	Description
Window	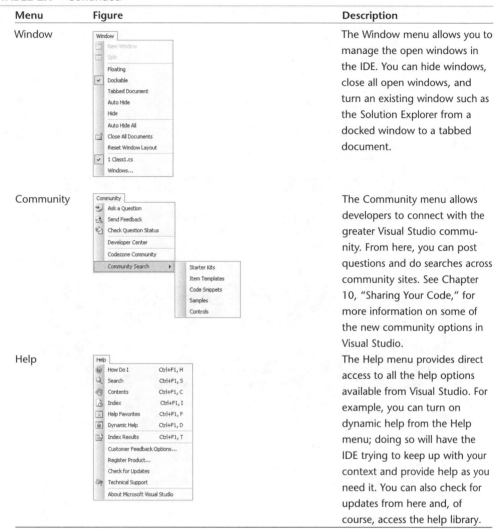	The Window menu allows you to manage the open windows in the IDE. You can hide windows, close all open windows, and turn an existing window such as the Solution Explorer from a docked window to a tabbed document.
Community		The Community menu allows developers to connect with the greater Visual Studio community. From here, you can post questions and do searches across community sites. See Chapter 10, "Sharing Your Code," for more information on some of the new community options in Visual Studio.
Help		The Help menu provides direct access to all the help options available from Visual Studio. For example, you can turn on dynamic help from the Help menu; doing so will have the IDE trying to keep up with your context and provide help as you need it. You can also check for updates from here and, of course, access the help library.

The Many Toolbars

Visual Studio includes more than 30 toolbars; there are three alone just for working with XML. If there is a set of commands that you use often, then there is a good chance there is a matching toolbar to group those commands. In the event that the standard toolbars that ship with Visual Studio don't meet your needs, you can create custom ones that do.

A large percentage of the toolbars are highly specialized. For example, if you are working with the Class Designer, you would, of course, use the Class Designer toolbar to manage class groups or change screen magnification. Or if you are building a SQL Query, you would use the Query Designer toolbar. We will not cover each of these toolbars for this reason. Instead, we will stick to our quick tour and cover the common ground here and save the sidetracks for future chapters.

The Standard Toolbar

The Standard toolbar will be present at all times during your IDE sessions (unless, of course, you customize things or turn it off). It provides quick access to all the commands you'll use over and over. The standard commands are on the top left: Create New Project, Add New Item, Open, and Save. These are followed by Cut, Copy, Paste, and Undo. Figure 2.9 shows the Standard toolbar undocked from the IDE.

TIP

We suggest you learn the keyboard equivalents for such standard commands as Cut, Copy, Past, Undo, and the like. You can then remove these toolbar icons from the toolbar to save precious screen real estate for commands that have you reaching for the mouse anyway (and have harder-to-remember shortcut keys).

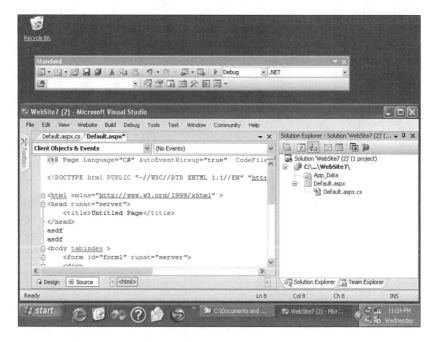

FIGURE 2.9   The Standard toolbar in Visual Studio 2005.

Additional items worth mentioning include the two navigation commands on the toolbar (document-like icons with a blue arrow pointing left on one and right on the other).

These buttons allow you to move backward and forward through your code and your solution. They keep track of special lines in your code or windows you have visited and provide one-click access up and down this line.

The button next to the navigation commands with the green arrow is often called the Run or Play button. This will initiate a build of your project and launch you into debug mode. Moving to the right (downward in the graphic), you see options for initiating a search within your code. This capability can be handy for quickly finding the place you left off or are looking for. To the right of this are icons for quick access to displaying one of the many windows of Visual Studio. Just like the View menu, these icons give you quick access to the Solution Explorer, Properties window, Object Browser, Toolbox, and so on. You even have an icon for Other Windows, which gives access to even more windows.

Finally, we recommend you do some of your own exploration into the many toolbars within Visual Studio. Often their usefulness presents itself only at the right moment. For instance, if you are editing a Windows form, having the Layout toolbar available to tweak the position of controls relative to one another can be a very valuable time-saver. Knowing these toolbars are available will increase the likelihood that you'll benefit from their value.

The Toolbox

The Visual Studio 2005 Toolbox has been significantly enhanced. It is now used to provide more than just access to the many controls when building forms. It now provides access to nearly anything that can be dragged onto one of the many designers used for creating forms, XML schemas, class diagrams, and the like. As an example, if you are building a web form, the Toolbox provides the many controls, grouped for easier access, which can be added to the form. Furthermore, if you are working on a class diagram, the Toolbox will give you access to classes, enums, and interfaces that can be added to the diagram.

Figure 2.10 shows the Toolbox in a standard configuration (undocked from the IDE) for building a web form. Note that the "Standard" group of controls is closed up to highlight some additional control groups. Note also some of the many new controls that have been added to ASP .NET (more on these in Chapter 11, "Writing ASP .NET Applications").

TIP

You can customize the Toolbox to your liking. For example, you can add your own groups (called *tabs*). You can also configure the Toolbox to show more icons on the screen at a time. As you familiarize yourself with the various standard controls, you can turn off their text descriptions and simply show them as icons. To do so, right-click the control group (tab) and turn off list view. Figure 2.11 illustrates the additional screen real estate you will gain in doing so.

FIGURE 2.10   The Visual Studio Toolbox configured for a web form.

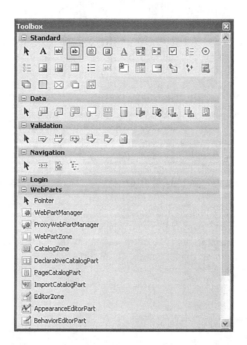

FIGURE 2.11   The Visual Studio Toolbox configured for more screen real estate.

The Visual Designers

Visual Designers are the canvases that you work on using the mouse to create items such as forms via drag, drop, move, resize, and the like. Visual Studio 2005 ships with many such Visual Designers. Together, they allow you to build the items that make up your application (and understanding of it). Items include Windows forms, web forms, class diagrams, logical datacenter diagrams, XML schemas, and more.

The Visual Designers all work mostly the same way. First, they take center stage within the IDE as tabbed windows surrounded by various menus, toolbars, and panes. Second, you use the Toolbox as your palette to place items on the designer. You then configure each item's many properties using the Properties window.

Figure 2.12 shows the Windows Forms Designer in action (the middle, highlighted tab). Note that the Toolbox is on the left and the Properties window is set on the bottom right. Additionally, many of the designers have their own toolbars. You can see from this graphic that the Layout toolbar is shown when working with forms. This allows you to easily position controls relative to one another. We will cover the majority of the visual designers in depth in the coming chapters.

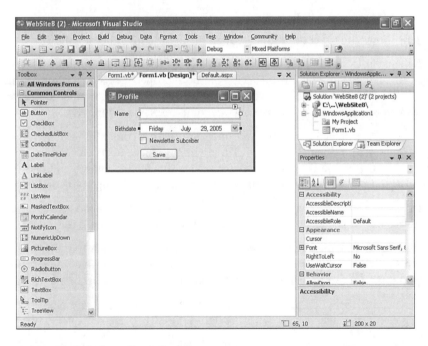

FIGURE 2.12   The Windows Form Designer.

The Text Editors

Visual Studio 2005 has several text editors or word (code) processors. Each text editor is based on a common core that provides the basic set of functionality for each editor such as the selection margin, the ability to collapse nested items, and colorization. Each editor derives from this core and is customized to give you the editors for code (C#, VB, and so on), the XML editor, the HTML (or aspx) editor, and style sheet editor.

The Code Editors

It is the code editor, for our money, where the magic happens. It is here that you get down to business leveraging your favorite language to define objects and their functionality. Of course, you can write code outside the Visual Studio editor, but why would you? You can also write a novel using Notepad or do your taxes by hand. A good code editor means higher productivity, plain and simple. and Visual Studio has some of the best code editors around.

The code editor is front and center when you're working on code. It handles indentation and whitespace to make your code clean and readable. It provides IntelliSense and statement completion to free you from having to look up (or memorize) every object library and keyword. It groups code into blocks; it provides color codes for keywords and comments; it highlights errors; it shows new code relative to previously compiled code. All in all, the Visual Studio code editor does quite a bit to keep you productive.

The C# Code Editor

Figure 2.13 shows the C# code editor. Some items to note include the following:

- The code is grouped into logical sections along the left side. You can use these minus signs to close up a whole class, method, property, or similar group. This capability allows you to hide code you are not working on at the moment. You can also create your own custom, named regions to do the same thing.

- New code is signaled inside the section groups with a colored line. Yellow is used for new code that has yet to be saved. The highlighted line turns green after a save and disappears after you close and reopen the file. This feature allows you (and the editor) to track where you have made changes to code during your current session.

- The name of the open code file is listed as the code window's tab across the top. The asterisk indicates the code has changed since the last time it was saved.

- IntelliSense is invoked as you type. You can use the arrow keys to quickly find the item in the list. Hovering over the item shows details for the given item (tip text to the right). You can press the Tab key to complete the item from IntelliSense.

- The code is highlighted in various colors. By default, keywords are blue, comments are green, text is black, your types are light blue, strings are red, and so on.

- The two drop-downs at the top of the code editor allow you to navigate between the classes in the file (left-side drop-down) and methods, fields, and properties within a given class (right-side drop-down).

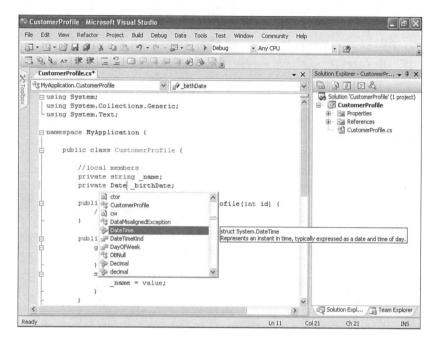

FIGURE 2.13   The C# code editor.

The Visual Basic Code Editor

The Visual Basic code editor works much the same way as the C# editor. Figure 2.14 shows the same code as in Figure 2.13 written inside the Visual Basic code editor. Some of the differences between the editors are as follows:

- Horizontal lines are used to separate methods and properties within the editor.

- The IntelliSense drop-down list is filtered into a common subset and all the possible values.

- The code navigation drop-downs at the top of the code editor allow you to navigate the entire, active object hierarchy (including events). The left-side drop-down shows namespaces, objects, and events. The right-side drop-down shows all methods for the given type, including those you have not overridden. Those items you have implemented are highlighted in bold.

Editor Customizations

Nearly every aspect of the text and code editors can be customized to your every whim. From our experience, it seems no two developers see their code the same way (except presenters and book writers, of course). From the Options dialog box, you can change the editor's background color or the color and font of various text within the editor; you can turn on line numbering, manage indenting and whitespace, and the list goes on.

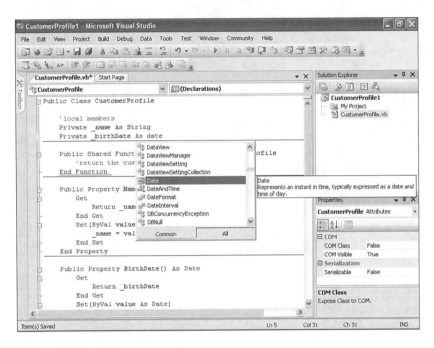

FIGURE 2.14   The Visual Basic code editor.

Figure 2.15 shows the Options dialog box set for Fonts and Colors. From here, you can tweak the many display items in the editor in terms of their color, font, and font size.

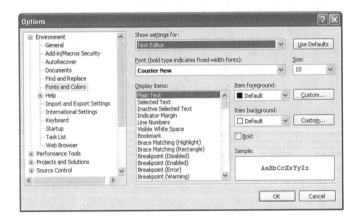

FIGURE 2.15   The Options dialog box set to Fonts and Colors.

If you dig a little deeper in the Options dialog box, you will come across the Text Editor node in the option tree. From here, you can manipulate even more settings for the text editor. For example, you can remove the horizontal procedure separators in the Visual Basic editor or turn off the automatic reformatting of code by the editor.

Even better, you can control how the editor automatically formats your code inside the C# editor. If you like to see all your curly braces on separate lines or prefer them to start on the line that starts the block, you can do so from here. Figure 2.16 shows some of the options available for formatting C# inside the editor.

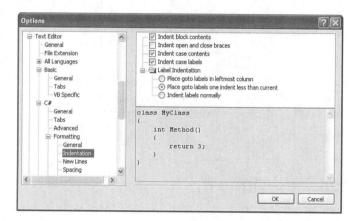

FIGURE 2.16   Controlling code formatting from the Options dialog box.

The Solution Explorer

The Solution Explorer allows you to group and manage the many files that make up your application. A solution simply contains multiple applications. An application can be a website, Windows application, class library, or console application. The files inside these containers represent your code in terms of forms and class files.

The Solution Explorer is the place where you typically start when adding a new item (class, image, form) to your application. It is also used to access these items. Double-clicking an item in the Solution Explorer opens the given designer or editor associated with the type of file you request. For example, opening a file with the extension .cs opens the C# code editor. Finally, you also use the Solution Explorer during source control scenarios to check items in and out of the source database.

Figure 2.17 shows the Solution Explorer undocked from the IDE. Note that a single solution is open (that is the limit), and the solution contains two applications (called *projects*). One is a website; the other is a Windows form application. The Solution Explorer is covered in depth in Chapter 5, "Browsers and Explorers."

FIGURE 2.17   The Visual Studio 2005 Solution Explorer.

The Properties Window

It seems with every new release and every new tool that programming becomes less and less about writing code and more and more about dragging, dropping, and configuring. The many tools, controls, and rich designers that free us from the repetitive code also now require our attention in the form of maintenance. This work is typically done through the manipulation of the literally hundreds of properties that work in concert to define our application. This is where the Properties window comes into play. It allows us to control the size, appearance, and behavior of our controls. Furthermore, the Properties window groups common properties into sets for easier access. Finally, the Properties window also gives us access to connecting the events for a given control to the code inside our application.

Figure 2.18 shows the Properties window (undocked from the IDE) for a button control. Note that the window groups similar properties into sections via the banded categories such as Appearance. You can turn off this capability and list properties in alphabetic order by clicking the AZ icon on the property toolbar. Another item worth noting is the lightning bolt icon also on the property toolbar. This gives you access to the events for the given control.

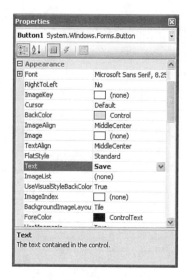

FIGURE 2.18   The Properties window in Visual Studio 2005.

Managing the Many Windows of the IDE

To round out our whirlwind tour, we thought it important to provide you guidance on customizing and managing the plethora of windows available within the IDE (lest they leave you with a postage-stamp size window in which to write your code). To manage these windows, you really need to know only two skills: pinning and docking.

Pinning

Pinning refers to the process of making a window stick in the open position. It is called pinning in reference to the visual cue you use to perform the act: a push-pin (refer to the Toolbox title bar inside Figure 2.19). Pinning is imperative because you sometimes want full-screen real estate for writing code or designing a form. In this case you should un-pin (hide) the various extraneous windows in your IDE. Note that when a window is un-pinned, a vertical tab represents the window (see the Solution Explorer tab inside Figure 2.19). Moving the mouse near this tab will result in the window unfolding for your use. After you use it, however, it will go back to its hiding spot.

Alternatively, you might be working to drop controls on that form. In doing so, you might want to pin (stick open) the Toolbox window (see Figure 2.19). This keeps open just the window you are working with and closes everything else.

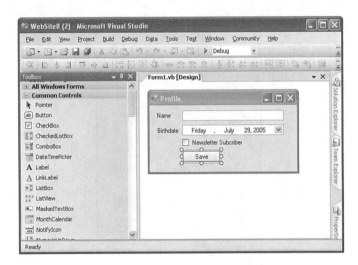

FIGURE 2.19   Pinned and un-pinned windows in the IDE.

Docking

Docking is the process of connecting windows to various sticky spots within the IDE. Typically, this means docking to the left, top, right, or bottom of the IDE. For example, the Toolbox is, by default, docked to the left side of the IDE. You may prefer to put it at the bottom of the screen, docked below the active designer (see Figure 2.20).

You can also dock windows to one another. For example, you may want to dock the Properties window below the Solution Explorer. Or you may want the Properties window to be a tab within the same window to which the Solution Explorer is docked (see Figure 2.20).

To help with docking, Visual Studio 2005 now provides a nice set of visual cues. First, you start with a pinned window (you cannot dock unpinned windows). You click and hold the title bar with the mouse. You then drag the window to where you want to dock it. Visual Studio will display some docking icons.

Four icons are at the edge of the IDE, one each at the left, top, right, and bottom. These icons are used for docking the window at the given edge of the IDE. Using these icons will result in the window's being docked across the full length (or width) of the IDE. Figure 2.21 shows the window housing the Solution Explorer and related tabs being docked to the full right of the IDE.

There is also an icon in the middle of the IDE. This icon is used for docking the selected window relative to the other windows in the IDE. For example, you might want to dock the Solution Explorer to the right side of the IDE but above the Toolbox. You would do so with the rightmost icon inside this center group. Finally, the centermost icon in the center group is used for docking a window to another window as a tabbed item (as in the Properties window in Figure 2.20).

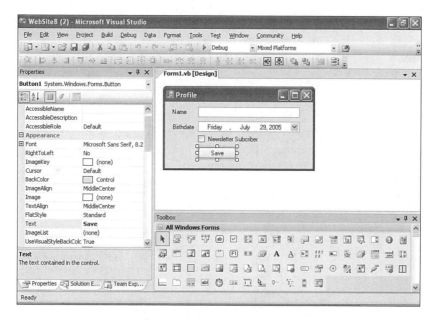

FIGURE 2.20   Some docking options in the IDE.

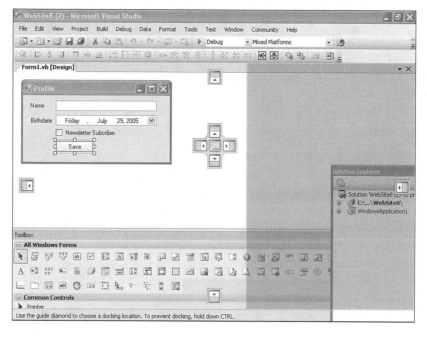

FIGURE 2.21   A window being docked.

Of course, you can also undock items. This is simply the process of floating windows off by themselves (outside, or on top of, the IDE). We have not seen much of this, but to do so, you simply grab (click with the mouse) a pinned window by the title bar and move it off to the side of the IDE or just don't choose a docking icon.

Summary

The whirlwind tour is over. We've covered the basics of installation, your first project, and the standard items you'll encounter when journeying out on your own. We hope you've found your bearings and can begin pushing onward.

CHAPTER 3

.NET Framework and Language Enhancements in 2005

IN THIS CHAPTER

- Shared .NET Language Additions
- VB Language Enhancements
- C# Language Enhancements
- .NET Framework 2.0 Enhancements

The majority of this book focuses on unlocking the productivity promises of the Visual Studio IDE. However, we thought it important to also cover some of the recent advances in the .NET languages and the Framework. These items (the IDE, the languages, and the Framework) all ship from Microsoft in concert. Therefore, any discussion of the new IDE would be incomplete without some mention of the elements that have been bound to it.

This chapter covers the enhancements relative to both Visual Basic .NET and C#. In addition, it highlights some of the key advances made in the Framework. Our assumption is that a majority of readers have some base-level understanding of either VB or a C-based language prior to the current version, along with a decent grasp of the .NET Framework. Therefore, our approach should give you insight into those enhancements that make .NET 2.0 a big leap forward over prior versions.

Shared .NET Language Additions

The .NET languages pick up a number of enhancements as a result of updates made to the common language runtime (CLR). Although there are specific enhancements for both Visual Basic and C#, respectively, the big advancements made in 2005 apply to both languages. Therefore, we will cover them as a group and provide examples in both languages. This group of .NET language enhancements includes the following key additions:

- Generics

- Nullable types

- Partial types

- Properties with mixed access levels

- Ambiguous namespaces

We will cover each of these items in detail in the coming sections. Again, we provide examples in both C# and VB because these enhancements apply to both languages. We will cover the VB and C# language-specific enhancements later in the chapter.

Generics

Generics are undoubtedly the biggest addition to .NET in version 2.0. As such, no book would be complete without covering their ins and outs. Generics may seem daunting at first—especially if you start looking through code that contains strange angle brackets in the case of C# or the Of keyword for Visual Basic. The following sections define generics, explain their importance, and show you how to use them in your code.

Generics Defined

The concept of *generics* is relatively straightforward. You need to develop an object (or define a parameter to a method), but you do not know the object's type when you write the code. Rather, you want to write the code *generically* and allow the caller to your code to determine the actual type of the object.

You could simply use the System.Object class to accomplish this. That is what we did prior to 2.0. However, imagine you also want to eliminate the need for boxing, runtime type checking, and explicit casting everywhere in your code. Now you can start to see the vision for generics.

The benefits of generics can best be seen through an example. The easiest example is that of creating a collection class that contains other objects. For our example, image you want to store a series of objects. You might do so by adding each object to an ArrayList. However, the compiler and runtime know only that you have some list of objects. The list could contain Order objects or Customer objects or both (or anything). The only way to know what is contained in the list is to write code to check for the type of the object in the list.

Of course, to get around this issue, you might write your own strongly typed lists. Although this approach is viable, it results in tedious code written over and over for each type you want to work with as a collection. The only real difference in the code is the type allowed in the list. In addition, you still have to do all the casting because the underlying list still simply contains types as System.Object.

Now imagine if you could write a single class that, when used, allows the user to define its type. You can then write one *generic* list class that, instead of containing types as System.Object, would contain objects as the type with which the class is defined. This allows a caller to the generic list to decide the list should be of type `Orders` or only contain `Customers`. This is precisely what generics afford us. Think of a generic class as a template for a class.

Generics come in two flavors: generic types and generic methods. *Generic types* are classes whose type is defined by the code that creates the class. A *generic method* is one that defines one or more generic type parameters. In this case, the generic parameter is used throughout the method but its type is defined only when the method is called. In addition, you can define constraints that control the creation of generics. In the coming sections, we'll look at all of these items.

The Benefits of Generics

Now you should plainly see some of the benefits that generics provide. Without them, any class that is written to manage different types must use `System.Object`. This presents a number of problems. First, there is no constraint or compiler checking on what goes into the object. The corollary is also true: You cannot know what you are getting out if you cannot constrain what goes in. Second, when you use the object, you must do type checking to verify its type and then do casting to cast it back to its original type. This, of course, comes with a performance penalty. Finally, if you use value types and store them in `System.Object`, then they get boxed. When you later retrieve this value type, it must be unboxed. Again, this adds unwanted code and unnecessary performance hits. Generics solve each of these issues. Let's look at how this is possible.

How .NET Manages Generics

When you compile a generic type, you generate Microsoft Intermediate Language (MSIL) code and metadata (just like all the rest of your .NET code). Of course, for the generic type or method, the compiler emits MSIL that defines your use of generic types.

With all MSIL code, when it is first accessed, the just-in-time (JIT) compiler compiles the MSIL into native code. When the JIT compiler encounters a generic, it knows the actual type that is being used in place of the generic. Therefore, it can substitute the real type for the generic type. This process is called *generic type instantiation*.

The newly compiled, native type is now used by subsequent, similar requests. In fact, all reference types are able to share a single generic type instantiation because, natively, references are simply pointers with the same representation. Of course, if a new value type is used in the generic type instantiation, the runtime will jit a new copy of the generic type.

This is how we get the benefits of generics both when we're writing our code and when it executes. Upon execution, all our code becomes native, strongly typed code. Now let's look at coding some generics.

Creating Generic Types

Generic types are classes that contain one or more elements whose type should be determined at instantiation (rather than during development). To define a generic type, you first declare a class and then define type parameters for the class. A *type parameter* is one that is passed to a class that defines the actual type for the generic. You can think of a type parameter as similar to method parameters. The big difference is that, instead of passing a value or a reference to an object, you are passing the type used by the generic.

NOTE

Most generic types are written to manage collections of objects or linked lists. Generics are not, however, limited to just managing collections. Any class you write can use generics.

As an example, suppose you are writing a class called Fields that works with name/value pairs similar to a Hashtable or Dictionary. You might declare the class as follows:

C#

```
public class Fields
```

VB

```
Public Class Fields
```

Let's also suppose that the class can work with a variety of types for its keys and a variety of types for its values. You want to write the class generically to support multiple types. However, after the class is instantiated, you want it to be constrained to the types used to create the class. To add the type parameters to the class declaration, you would then write the following:

C#

```
public class Fields<keyType, valueType>
```

VB

```
Public Class Fields(Of keyType, valueType)
```

In this case, keyType and valueType are type parameters that can be used in the rest of the class to reference the types that will be passed to the class. For example, you might then have an Add method in your class whose signature looks like the following:

C#

```
public void Add(keyType key, valueType value)
```

VB

```
Public Sub Add(key as keyType, value as valueType)
```

This indicates to the compiler that whatever types are used to create the class should also be used in this method. In fact, to consume the class, your code would first create an instance and pass type arguments to the instance. *Type arguments* are the types passed to type parameters. The following is an example:

C#
```
Fields<int, Field> myFields = new Fields<int, Field>();
```

VB
```
Dim myFields As New Fields(Of Integer, Field)
```

In this case a new instance of the generic `Fields` class is created that must contain `int` (`integer`) value for its keys and `Field` instances for its values. Calling the `Add` method of the newly created `Fields` object would then look like this:

C#
```
myFields.Add(1, new Field());
```

VB
```
myFields.Add(1, New Field())
```

If you try to pass another type to either parameter, you will get a compiler error because the object becomes strongly typed at this point.

> **TIP**
>
> When you see generics used, especially in C#, you will often see single letters used for defining type names. It is not uncommon to see <T> or <K>. You are not constrained to these short names. It is always better to provide somewhat more descriptive .names.

Creating Generic Methods

So far we've looked at generic type parameters. These type parameters end up defining variables with class-level scope. That is, the variable that defines the generic type is available throughout the entire class. As with any class you write, you may not need class-level scoping. Instead, it may be sufficient to define the elements passed to a given method. Generics are no different in this regard. You can define them at the class level (as we've shown) or at the method level (as we will see).

Generic methods work well for common, utility-like functions that execute a common operation on a variety of similar types. You define a generic method by indicating the existence of one or more generic types following the method name. You can then refer to these generic types inside the method's parameter list, its return type, and of course, the method body. The following shows the syntax for defining a generic method:

C#

```
public void Save<instanceType>(instanceType type)
```

VB

```
Public Sub Save(Of instanceType)(ByVal type As instanceType)
```

To call this generic method, you must define the type passed to the method as part of the call to the method. Suppose the Save method defined in the preceding example is contained in a class called Field. Now suppose you have created an instance of Field and have stored a reference to it in the variable named myField. The following code shows how you might call the Save method passing the type argument to the method:

C#

```
myField.Save<CustomerOrder>(new CustomerOrder());
```

VB

```
myField.Save(Of CustomerOrder)(New CustomerOrder())
```

We need to add a few notes on generic methods. First, you can often omit the type parameter when calling a generic method. The compiler can figure out the type based on the parameter passed to it. Therefore, the type parameter is optional when calling a generic method. However, it is generally preferable to pass the type because it makes your code more readable and saves the compiler from having to look it up. Second, generic methods can be declared as static (or shared). Finally, you can define constraints on generic methods (and classes), as we will see in the next section.

Getting Specific with Generics (Constraints)

When you first encounter generic methods, it can be easy to think of them as simple data storage devices. At first glance, they seem to have a huge flaw. This flaw can best be described with the question that might be gnawing at you, "Generics are great, but what if you want to call a method or property of a generic object whose type, by definition, you are unaware of?" This flaw seems to limit the use of generics. However, upon a closer look, you'll see that generic constraints allow you to overcome this perceived flaw.

Generic constraints are just what they sound like: They allow you to define restrictions on the types that a caller can use when creating an instance of your generic class or calling one of your generic methods. Generic constraints have the following three variations:

- **Derivation constraint**—Allows you to indicate that the generic type must implement one or more specific interfaces or derive from a base class.

- **Default constructor constraint**—Allows you to indicate that the generic type must expose a constructor without parameters.

- **Reference/value constraint**—Allows you to indicate that a generic type parameter must either be a reference or a value type.

Using a derivation constraint enables you to indicate one or more interfaces (or object types) that are allowed to be passed to the generic class. Doing so allows you to overcome the aforementioned flaw. For example, if in the `Fields` generic class defined previously you need to be able to call a method or property of the generic `valueType` (perhaps a property that aids in sorting the group of `Fields`), you can now do so, provided that method or property is defined on the interface or base class constraint. The following provides an example of defining a derivation constraint on a generic class:

C# Class Constraint

```
public class Fields<keyType, valueType> where keyType : ISort
```

VB Class Constraint

```
Public Class Fields(Of keyType, valueType As ISort)
```

In the preceding example, the class named `Fields`, which defines the two generic types `valueType` and `keyType`, contains a constraint on `keyType`. The constraint is that `keyType` must implement an interface called `ISort`. This now allows the generic class `Fields` to use methods of `ISort` without casting.

> **NOTE**
>
> You can define a derivation constraint for both generic classes and generic methods.

You can indicate any number of interfaces that the generic type must implement. However, you can indicate only a single base class from which the generic type can derive. You can, of course, pass to the generic type an object that itself inherits from this constraining base class.

> **NOTE**
>
> If you override a generic method in a base class, you *cannot* add (or remove) constraints to the generic method. Only the constraints defined in the base class will apply to the overridden method.

Generic Collections Namespace

Now that you've seen how to create your own generic classes, it is important to note that the .NET Framework provides a number of generic classes for you to use in your applications. The namespace `System.Collections.Generics` defines a number of generic collection classes designed to allow you to work with groups of objects in a strongly typed manner. A *generic collection* is a collection class that allows a developer to specify the type that is contained in the collection when declaring the collection.

NOTE

By default, Visual Studio adds a reference to the namespace `System.Collections.Generics` to all VB and C# code files.

The generic classes defined in this namespace are varied based on their usage. The classes include one called `List` designed for working with a simple list or array of objects. It also includes a `SortedList`, a `LinkedList`, a `Queue`, a `Stack`, and several `Dictionary` classes. These classes cover all the basics of working without strongly typed collection classes. In addition, the namespace also defines a number of interfaces that you can use when building your own generic collections.

Nullable Types

Most of us have written applications in which we were forced to declare a variable and choose a default value prior to knowing what value that variable should contain. For instance, imagine you have a class called `Person` with a Boolean property called `IsFemale`. If you do not implicitly know a person's sex at object instantiation, you are forced to pick a default, or you must implement the property as a tri-state enumeration (or similar) with values `Male`, `Female`, and `Unknown`.

The latter can be cumbersome, especially if the value is stored as a Boolean in the database. There are similar examples. Imagine if you are writing a `Test` class with an integer value called `Score`. If you are unsure of the `Score` value, you end up initializing this variable to zero (0). This value, of course, does not represent a real score. You then must program around this fact by either tracking zero as a magic number or carrying another property like `IsScoreSet`.

These examples are further amplified by the fact that the databases we work with all understand that a value can be null (or not set). We are often unable to use this feature unless we write code to do translation during our insert and select transactions.

Nullable types in .NET 2.0 are meant to free us from these issues. A *nullable type* is a special value type that can have a null assigned to it. This is unlike the value types we are accustomed to (`int`, `bool`, `double`, and so on); these are simply not initialized when declared. On the contrary, with nullable types, you can create integers, Booleans, doubles, and the like and assign them the value of null. You no longer have to guess (or code around) whether a variable has been set. This includes no longer having to provide a default value. Instead, you now can initialize or assign a variable to the value of null. You can now write code without default assumptions. In addition, nullable types also solve the issue of pushing and pulling nulls to and from the database. Let's look at how they work.

Declaring Nullable Types

Declaring a nullable type is very different between the C# and VB languages. However, both result in declaring the same nullable value type structure inside the .NET Framework (System.Nullable). This generic structure is defined by the type that is used in its declaration. For example, if you are defining a nullable integer, the generic structure returns an integer version. The following code snippets demonstrate how nullable types are declared in both C# and VBL:

A C# Nullable Type Example

```
bool? hasChildren = null;
```

A VB Nullable Type Example

```
Dim hasChildren As Nullable(Of Boolean) = Nothing
```

Notice that in the C# example, you can use the ? type modifier to indicate that a base type should be treated as a nullable type. This is simply a shortcut. It allows developers to use the standard syntax for creating types but simply add a question mark to turn that type to a nullable version. On the contrary, if you are coding in VB, you are required to be more explicit by defining the Nullable class as you would a similar generic. You can also use a similar syntax in C#, as in the following example:

```
System.Nullable<bool> hasChildren = null;
```

> **NOTE**
>
> Only value types can be nullable. Therefore, it is not valid to create a nullable string or a developer-defined class. However, you can create nullable instances of structures because they are value types.

Working with Nullable Types

The generic System.Nullable structure contains two read-only properties: HasValue and Value. These properties allow you to work with nullable types efficiently. The HasValue property is a Boolean value that indicates whether a given nullable type has a value assigned to it. You can use this property in If statements to determine whether a given variable has been assigned. In addition, you can simply check the variable for null (C# only). The following provides an example of each:

C# HasValue Example

```
If (hasChildren.HasValue) {…}
```

VB HasValue Example

```
If hasChildren.HasValue Then
```

C# Checking the Variable for Null

```
if (hasChildren != null) {…}
```

VB Checking the Variable Value for Null

```
If hasChildren.Value <> Nothing Then
```

The Value property simply returns the value contained by the Nullable structure. You can also access the value of the variable by calling the variable directly (without using the Value property). The distinction lies in that when HasValue is false, calls to the Value property will result in an exception being thrown. Whereas when you access the variable directly in this condition (HasValue = false), no exception is thrown. Therefore, it is important to know exactly the behavior you require and use these options correctly. The following provides an example of using the Value property:

C# Value Property Example

```
System.Nullable<bool> hasChildren = null;
Console.WriteLine(hasChildren);  //no exception is thrown
if (hasChildren != null) {
  Console.WriteLine(hasChildren.Value.ToString());
}
Console.WriteLine(hasChildren.Value); //throws InvalidOperationException
```

VB Value Property Example

```
Dim hasChildren As Nullable(Of Boolean) = Nothing
Console.WriteLine(hasChildren)  'no exception is thrown
If hasChildren.HasValue Then
  Console.WriteLine(hasChildren.Value.ToString())
End If
Console.WriteLine(hasChildren.Value)  'throws InvalidOperationException
```

In the preceding example, the call directly to hasChildren will not throw an exception. However, when you try to check the Value property when the variable is null, the Framework throws the InvalidOperationException.

Partial Types (Classes)

Partial types are simply a mechanism for defining a single class, struct, or interface across multiple code files. In fact, when your code is compiled, there is no such thing as a partial type. Rather, partial types exist only during development. The files that define a partial type are merged together into a singe class during compilation.

Partial types are meant to solve two problems. First, they allow developers to split large classes across multiple files. This potentially allows multiple team members to work on the same class without working on the same file (thus avoiding the related code-merge headaches). The other problem partial types solve is to further partition tool-generated code from that of the developer's. This keeps your code file clean (with only your work in it) and allows a tool to generate portions of the class behind the scenes. Visual Studio 2005 developers will immediately notice this when working with Windows forms, Web Service wrappers, ASP code-behind pages, and the like. If you've worked with these items in prior versions of .NET, you'll soon notice that when you're working in 2005, the generated code is now absent and the class that you write has been marked as partial.

Working with Partial Types

Partial types are declared as such using the keyword Partial. This keyword is actually the same in both C# and VB. You can apply this keyword to classes, structures, and interfaces. If you do so, the keyword must be the first word on the declaration (before Class, Structure, or Interface). Indicating a partial type tells the compiler to merge these items together upon compilation into a single .dll or .exe.

When defining partial types, you must follow a few simple guidelines. First, all types with the same name in the same namespace must use the Partial keyword. You cannot, for instance, declare a class as Partial Public Person in one file and then declare that same class as Public Person in another file under the same namespace. Of course, to do so, you would add the Partial keyword to the second declaration. Second, you must keep in mind that all modifiers of a partial type are merged together upon compilation. This includes class attributes, XML comments, and interface implementations. For example, if you use the attribute System.SerializableAttribute on a partial type, the attribute will be applied to all portions of the type when merged and compiled. Finally, it's important to note that all partial types must be compiled into the same assembly (.dll or .exe). You cannot compile a partial type across assemblies.

Properties with Mixed Access Levels

In prior versions of .NET, you were able to indicate the access level (public, private, protected, internal) only of an entire property. However, often you might need to make the property read (get) public but control the write (set) internally. The only real solution to this problem using prior .NET versions was not to implement the property set. You would then create another internal method for setting the value of the property. It would make your coding easier to write and understand if you had fine-grained control over access modifiers of your properties.

.NET 2.0 gives you control of the access modifiers at both the set and get methods of a property. Therefore, you are free to mark your property as public but make the set private or protected. The following code provides an example:

C# Mixed Property Access Levels

```csharp
private string _userId;
public string UserId {
  get { return _userId; }
  internal set { userId = value; }
}
```

VB Mixed Property Access Levels

```vb
Private _userId As String
Public Property UserId() As String
  Get
    Return _userId
  End Get
  Friend Set(ByVal value As String)
    _userId = value
  End Set
End Property
```

Ambiguous Namespaces

On large projects, it is possible to easily run into namespace conflicts with each other and with the .NET Framework (System namespace). Previously, these ambiguous references were not resolvable. Instead, you got an exception at compile time.

.NET 2.0 now allows developers to define a System namespace of their own without blocking access to the .NET version. For example, suppose you define a namespace called System and suddenly are unable to access the global version of System. In C# you would add the keyword global along with a namespace alias qualifier :: as in the following syntax:

```csharp
global::System.Double myDouble;
```

In VB the syntax is similar but uses the keyword Global:

```vb
Dim myDouble As Global.System.Double
```

To further manage namespace conflict, you can still define an alias when using (or importing) a namespace. This alias can then be used to reference types within the namespace. For example, suppose you had a conflict with the System.IO namespace. You could define an alias upon import as follows:

C#

```
using IoAlias = System.IO;
```

VB

```
Imports IoAlias = System.IO
```

You could then reference types by using the alias directly. Of course, Visual Studio still gives you complete IntelliSense on these items. The following provides an example of using the alias defined in the preceding example. Notice the new syntax that is possible in C# with the double colon operator:

C# new syntax

```
IoAlias::FileInfo file;
```

C# old syntax

```
IoAlias.FileInfo file;
```

VB

```
Dim file as IoAlias.FileInfo
```

VB Language Enhancements

Former VB developers will be pleased to find that the edit-and-continue feature is back in Visual Studio 2005! However, that's really an IDE feature. In fact, many new IDE features are considered language-specific. We intend to cover most (if not all) of them throughout the book. The IDE enhancements specific to VB include all of the following:

- Developing with My
- Edit-and-continue
- Code snippets
- IntelliSense enhancements
- Attribute editing in the Properties window
- Error correction and warning
- Exception Assistant

- XML documentation

- Document Outline window

- Project Designer

- Settings Designer

- Resource Designer

These enhancements (and more) help make VB great. However, in the following sections, we intend to focus on the language of VB. We want to point out the VB-specific additions that are so compelling in the 2005 release.

The `Continue` **Statement**

The new `Continue` statement in VB allows developers to skip to the next iteration in a loop. You use the `Continue` statement in combination with either `Do`, `For`, or `While` depending on the type of loop you're working with. If you want to short-circuit the loop and skip immediately to the next iteration, you simply use `Continue For¦Do¦While`, as in the following example:

```
Sub ProcessCustomers(ByVal customers() As Customer)
  Dim i As Integer
  For i = 0 To customers.GetUpperBound(0)
    If customers(i).HasTransactions = False Then Continue For
    ProcessCustomer(customers(i))
  Next
End Sub
```

Unsigned Types

Visual Basic developers can now use unsigned integer data types (`UShort`, `UInteger`, and `ULong`). In addition, the latest version of VB provides the signed type `SByte`. These new types allow VB developers to more easily call functions in the Windows API because these functions often take and return unsigned types. However, these unsigned types are not supported by the common language specification (CLS). Therefore, if you write code that uses these new types, CLS-compliant code may not be able to work with this code.

`IsNot` **Operator**

The new `IsNot` operator in VB allows developers to determine whether two objects are the same. Of course, VB developers could do this in prior versions by combining `Not` and `Is` as in `If Not myCustomer Is Nothing`. However, VB developers can now use the less awkward syntax of the `IsNot` operator, as in the following line of code. Note that this example is functionally equivalent to using the prior `Not … Is` syntax.

```
If cust IsNot Nothing Then
```

Using **Block**

VB developers who have spent some time with C# will undoubtedly love the capability to define an object's scope with a Using block. With this block, C# developers have been able to guarantee disposal of a resource when the application's execution left a given block for any reason. Good news: This feature has now been added to VB. Suppose, for example, that you want to open a connection to a database. You can now do so with the Using block. This way, when execution leaves this block for any reason, the object defined by the Using statement (SQL connection object) will be disposed of properly. The following code illustrates this new feature:

```
Using cnn As New System.Data.SqlClient.SqlConnection(cnnStr)
  'place code to use the sql connection here
End Using
```

Form Access Similar to VB6

Developers familiar with Visual Basic version 6 (prior to .NET) will recall having direct access to a form's properties and methods simply by using its name. In prior versions of .NET, developers were forced to create an instance of the form to access its properties. In VB8, developers can once again access a form's members by using its name directly.

Explicit Zero Lower Bound on an Array

In past incarnations of VB (prior to .NET) developers could indicate the upper and lower bounds of an array using the To keyword. Developers were able to define an array as starting at 1 and going "to" 10 for instance. This made code that used arrays very easy to read. However, with the advent of .NET and the common language specification (CLS), arrays were forced as zero (0) lower bounds. That is, every array in .NET starts with a zero element. This doesn't change with VB8. However, the ability to define your arrays as starting at 0 and going "to" an upper bound is back, simply for code readability. Therefore, you can define arrays as in the following line of code, but you must define the lower bound as zero (0):

```
Dim myIntArray(0 To 9) As Integer
```

Operator Overloading

If you have written class libraries long enough, you eventually need to define the behavior of your class when used with an operator such as addition (+), subtraction (-), multiplication (*), greater than (>), or similar. For example, if you need to calculate the result of how two versions of your class are added together with the + operator, you need to define the + operator behavior in your code. In prior versions of VB, you could not do this. VB8 allows for what is called *operator overloading*.

You define a new operator by using the keyword Operator (in place of Sub or Function), followed by the operator symbol you intend to overload (+, &, *, <>, and so on). You can then write this "function" as you would any other. It can take parameters and return a value. As an example, if you were going to define how two versions of your object are added together, you would define a + operator that took each version as a parameter and returned a third version as the result. The following code illustrates this structure:

```
Public Operator +(ByVal obj1 As MyObject, ByVal obj2 As MyObject) As MyObject
  'calculate objects and return a new version
End Operator
```

Custom Events

Visual Basic developers are now given control of what happens when delegates are registered with a given developer-defined event. VB has added the keyword Custom for use when declaring an event. When you use this keyword to declare an event, you are then required to define accessors for AddHandler, RemoveHandler, and RaiseEvent. These accessors override the default behavior of an event with your own custom code. This capability is useful in situations in which you want all your events to be fired asynchronously, or you need finite control over these operations.

C# Language Enhancements

The C# language takes another step forward in the 2005 release. We have already pointed out some of the common enhancements such as generics and nullable types. In addition, there are new IDE features for the C# developer. Some of these features include the following:

- Code snippets

- Refactoring

- IntelliSense updates

- Code wizards

- Project properties

We will cover those features throughout the book. However, here we intend to focus on C#-specific enhancements for 2005.

> **TIP**
>
> For more information on the C# language and the topics discussed here, Microsoft has created the "C# Language Specification 2.0." This Microsoft Word document is available for download at http://msdn.microsoft.com/library/default.asp?url=/library/en-us/dnvs05/html/cs3spec.asp. At this same URL, you can find the complete C# language reference and set of tutorials. In addition, the C# 3.0 specification is already out and ready for review and feedback.

Anonymous Methods

The term *anonymous method* sounds a bit daunting when you first come across it. However, an anonymous method is simply an unnamed block of code (not a method) that is passed directly to a delegate. First, this feature is available only to C# programmers. Second, it is useful only when you do not need the full power of a delegate—that is, when you do not require multiple listeners nor the ability to control (add and remove) who's listening.

The fastest way to understand anonymous methods is to compare the established, standard way of implementing a delegate to using an anonymous method. In prior versions of C#, to use a delegate, you had to write a method that was called by the delegate. This required you to both write a new method and connect that method to the delegate.

For an example, let's look at the way to connect code to a button's (System.Windows.Forms.Button) Click event. First, the Click event is a System.EventHandler (or delegate). You want to make sure that code you write in a method is connected to that delegate. Suppose the code is in a method that looks as follows:

```
private void button1_Click(object sender, EventArgs e) {
  label1.Text = "textBox.Text";
}
```

You then connect the method to the delegate. Of course, Visual Studio does the work for you behind the scenes. But you can also write this code manually. In addition, Visual Studio only takes care of connecting UI control delegates (events) to the methods. You are responsible for wiring up other delegates—whether they are custom or part of the framework. The following shows how Visual Studio connects the button1_Click method to the Button class's Click event:

```
this.button1.Click += new System.EventHandler(this.button1_Click);
```

As you can see, you have to both write a method for the code and connect that method to the delegate. Now let's look at what is possible with anonymous methods. As we've stated, you can simply pass code directly to the delegate. Therefore, you could add the following line of code to the form's constructor (after the call to InitializeComponents):

```
this.button1.Click += delegate {
  label1.Text = "Goodbye";
};
```

As you can see in the example, using an anonymous method involves using the keyword delegate. Of course, delegates can take parameters, so there is an optional parameter list after delegate (not shown in the example). Finally, there is the statement list (or block of code). This is the code passed anonymously (without a method name) to the delegate. This code is set off by curly braces.

NOTE

Anonymous methods have access to the variables that are in scope from the point where the anonymous method is created. These variables are called *outer variables* of the anonymous method (because the anonymous method itself can define its own *inner variables*). You need to know that by using these outer variables inside an anonymous method, they are considered *captured* by the anonymous method. This means that the lifetime of these captured variables is now dependent on the delegate being *garbage collected* (and not the method).

This section simply introduces anonymous methods. With them, you can write some reasonably sophisticated code (which can also be difficult to understand). As you might imagine, passing lines of code as parameters requires some careful thinking to stay out of trouble.

Static Classes

The new version of the .NET Framework provides language developers support for static classes. A *static class* is one whose every member is declared as a noninstance member (or static). That is, consumers of the class do not have to create an instance of the class to call its members. In fact, the Framework ensures that consumers cannot instantiate a static class. Static classes are common to the .NET Framework; however, the VB language does not currently allow for them. The C# language does. This is where we will focus our static class examples.

NOTE

You can approximate a static class in VB by creating a class with a private constructor. In addition, you would mark all the members on the class as Shared. The drawback is that you do not get compiler enforcement or the capability to use a static constructor.

Defining a Static Class

You create a static class by applying the Static keyword to the class declaration. The following line of code provides an example:

```
static class ProjectProperties { …
```

As indicated, declaring a class as static ensures that it cannot be instantiated. You still must explicitly declare all members of the class as static (they are not assumed as such). However, a static class will allow the compiler to verify that no instance members are added to the class by accident. You will receive a compiler error if you place a nonstatic member inside a static class; this includes both public and private members. Listing 3.1 provides a simple example of a static class and its members.

LISTING 3.1   A Static Class

```
namespace StaticClasses {
    static class ProjectProperties {
        static string _projectName;
        static ProjectProperties() {
            _projectName = "SomeNewProject";
        }
        public static string Name {
            get { return _projectName; }
        }
        public static DateTime GetDueDate() {
            //get the date the project is due
            DateTime dueDate = DateTime.Now.AddDays(10);
            return dueDate;
        }
    }
}
```

3

> **NOTE**
>
> Static classes are automatically sealed. That is, you cannot inherit or derive from a static class.

Constructors and Static Classes

You cannot create a constructor for a static class. However, if you need similar features of a constructor (like setting initial values), you can create what is called a *static constructor*. Listing 3.1 shows an example of the static constructor named ProjectProperties. Notice that this constructor initializes the value of the static member _projectName.

The .NET CLR loads the static class automatically when the containing namespace is loaded. In addition, when a static member is called, the static constructor is automatically called by the CLR. No instance of the class is necessary (or even possible) to call this special type of constructor.

Reference Two Versions of the Same Assembly

As a developer, you sometimes get stuck between needing the features of an older version of a component and wanting to upgrade to the latest version of that component. Often, this is the result of a third-party component that has evolved without concern for backward compatibility. In these cases, your options are limited to either a complete upgrade to the new component or sticking with the older version. C# 2.0 now provides an additional option: working with both versions through an external assembly alias.

The principal issue with working with multiple versions of the same assembly is resolving conflicts between the names of members that share the same namespace. Suppose, for instance, that you are working with an assembly that generates charts for your application. Suppose that the namespace is Charting and there is a class called Chart. When a new version of the assembly is released, you want to be able to keep all of your existing code as is but reference the new assembly for your new code. To do so in C# 2.0, you must follow a couple of steps.

First, you must define an alias for the newly referenced assembly. You do this through the Properties window for the selected reference. Figure 3.1 provides an example of setting this alias. Note that we are setting an alias for version 2 of the assembly (ChartV2). This ensures that calls to Charting.Chart will still point to version 1 of the assembly (ChartV1).

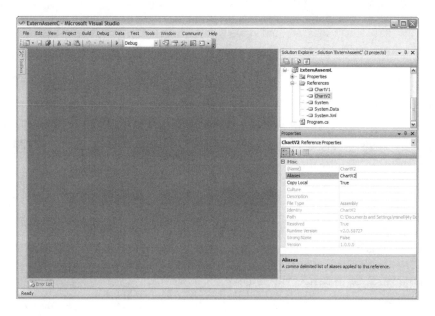

FIGURE 3.1   Defining a reference alias.

Next, in the code file where you plan to use the additional version of the assembly, you must define the external alias. You do so at the top of the file (before the Using statements) with the keyword extern. The following line shows an example of what would be placed at the top of the file to reference the second version of the Charting component:

```
extern alias ChartV2;
```

Finally, to use the members of the new version, you use the :: operator (as you would for another, similar C# alias). The following line of code provides an example:

```
ChartV2::Charting.Chart.GenerateChart();
```

Friend Assemblies

C# 2.0 allows you to combine assemblies in terms of what constitutes internal access. That is, you can define internal members but have them be accessible by external assemblies. This capability is useful if you intend to split an assembly across physical files but still want those assemblies to be accessible to one another as if they were internal.

> **NOTE**
>
> Friend assembles *do not* allow for access to private members.

You use the new attribute class `InternalsVisibleToAttribute` to mark an assembly as exposing its internal members as friends to another assembly. This attribute is applied at the assembly level. You pass the name and the public key token of the external assembly to the attribute. The compiler will then link these two assemblies as friends. The assembly containing the `InternalsVisibleToAttribute` will expose its internals to the other assembly (and not vice versa). You can also accomplish the same thing by using the command-line compiler switches.

Friend assemblies, like most things, come at a cost. If you define an assembly as a friend of another assembly, the two assemblies become coupled and need to coexist to be useful. That is, they are no longer a single unit of functionality. This can cause confusion and increase management of your assemblies. It is often easier to stay away from this feature unless you have a very specific need.

.NET Framework 2.0 Enhancements

Because there are so many new features in the .NET Framework, we could not begin to cover them in this limited space. Of course, we will do our best to point them out throughout the book. That said, we wanted to make sure to highlight some of those key enhancements that make this version of the .NET Framework such a great advancement. The following outlines a few of these items:

- **64-Bit support**—You can now compile your .NET application to target a 64-bit version of the operating system. This includes native support and WOW64 compatibility support (allows 32-bit applications to run on 64-bit systems).

- **ACL support**—.NET developers can now use access control list (ACL) features to manage permissions on resources from their code. New classes have been added to the IO namespace (and others) to help you grant users rights to files and the like.

- **Authenticated streams**—The new `NegotiateStream` class allows for secure (SSL encrypted) authentication between a client and a server (listener) when transmitting information across the wire. With it, you can securely pass the client's credentials through impersonation or delegation. In addition, the new `SslStream` class allows for the encryption of the data during the transfer.

- **Data Protection API (DPAPI)**—There is new support in .NET 2.0 for working with the DPAPI. Support includes the ability to encrypt passwords and connection strings on the server. Developers could tap into this in prior versions of .NET through a wrapper class available for download. In 2.0, this access is built into the Framework.

- **Network change discovery**—Your application can now be notified when it loses a connection to the network. With the `NetworkChange` class, developers can know when the computer hosting their application has lost its wireless connection or changed its IP address.

- **FTP support**—The `System.Net` namespace now provides classes for working with FTP. Developers can use the `WebRequest`, `WebResponse`, and `WebClient` classes to send and receive files over this protocol.

- **Globalization enhancements**—The new version of the Framework enables developers to define their own custom cultures. This gives you the ultimate flexibility when working with culture-related information in your application. In addition, .NET 2.0 provides updated Unicode support.

- **Greater caching control**—Developers can now use the `System.Net.Cache` namespace to programmatically control caching.

- **Serial I/O device support**—There is now a `SerialPort` class in the `System.IO` namespace. This class allows developers to work with devices that connect to a serial port on a computer.

- **Enhanced SMTP support**—The `System.Net.Mail` namespace enables developers to send email through an SMTP server.

- **Transactions**—.NET developers have a new `System.Transactions` namespace that allows .NET-developed classes to easily participate in a distributed transaction using the Microsoft Distributed Transaction Coordinator (MSDTC).

New Features of Core Technologies

ADO.NET, ASP.NET, and WinForms all have major advancements in the 2005 release. Each of these topics could be the subject of a separate book. ADO.NET, for instance, now has the support for user-defined type (UDT) and asynchronous database operations. Both ASP and WinForms have many new controls (and enhancements to the old controls). Both technologies, for example, bring back zero-code data binding. We suggest you explore each of these items in depth to see the many new advancements in these core areas.

Summary

This chapter presented those core enhancements to the .NET languages that are key to you, as a developer, in writing more and better code during your development day. Advancements such as generics will help you ensure type safety in collections and reduce error rates as a result. Similarly, nullable types will allow you to code without forcing values into unassigned variables and then coding around these "magic numbers." These and similar advancements made to both the C# and VB languages work to further evolve your toolset and increase your productivity.

Finally, this chapter briefly covered some of the new items inside the .NET Framework. Clearly, there is a lot that is new. The Framework is becoming so large that developers (and books) are often forced to specialize in a particular area. We suggest that you look at our list of enhancements and then jump off to your own specialty area for further exploration.

3

PART II

The Visual Studio 2005 Environment In-depth

IN THIS PART

CHAPTER 4	Solutions and Projects	89
CHAPTER 5	Browsers and Explorers	117
CHAPTER 6	Introducing the Editors and Designers	157
CHAPTER 7	Working with Visual Studio's Productivity Aids	201
CHAPTER 8	Refactoring Code	231
CHAPTER 9	Debugging with Visual Studio 2005	259
CHAPTER 10	The Visual Studio Automation Object Model	299
CHAPTER 11	Writing Macros, Add-ins, and Wizards	351
CHAPTER 12	The .NET Community: Consuming and Creating Shared Code	425

CHAPTER 4

Solutions and Projects

IN THIS CHAPTER

- Understanding Solutions

- Getting Comfortable with Projects

S*olutions* and *projects* are the containers Visual Studio uses to house and organize the code that you write within the IDE. Solutions are virtual containers; they group and apply properties across one or more projects. Projects are both virtual and physical in purpose. Besides functioning as organizational units for your code, they also map one to one with compiler targets. Put another way, Visual Studio turns projects into compiled code. Each project will result in the creation of a .NET component (such as a DLL or an EXE file).

> **NOTE**
>
> Web projects are compiled, but an assembly won't be generated until they are published. We cover more on the topic of web projects in Chapter 13, "Developing Smart Clients."

In this chapter, we will cover the roles of solutions and projects in the development process. We'll see how to create solutions and projects, examine their physical attributes, and discuss ways to best leverage their features.

Understanding Solutions

From a programming perspective, everything that you do within Visual Studio will take place within the context of a solution. As we mentioned in this chapter's introduction, solutions in and of themselves don't do anything other than serve as higher-level containers for other items. Projects are the most obvious items that can be placed inside solutions, but solutions can also contain miscellaneous files that may be germane to the solution itself, such as "read me" documents and design diagrams. Really, any file type can be added to a solution. Solutions can't, however, contain other solutions. In addition, Visual Studio will load only one solution at a time. If you need to work on more than one solution concurrently, you need to launch another instance of Visual Studio.

So what do solutions contribute to the development experience? Solutions are useful because they allow you to treat various different projects as one cohesive unit of work. By grouping multiple projects under a solution, you can work against those projects from within one instance of Visual Studio. In addition, a solution simplifies certain configuration tasks by allowing you to apply settings across all of the solution's child projects.

You can also "build" a solution. As mentioned previously, solutions themselves aren't compiled, per se, but their constituent projects can be built using a single build command issued against the solution. And, solutions are also a vehicle for physical file management: Because many items that show up in a solution are physical files located on disk, Visual Studio can manage those files in various ways (delete them, rename them, move them). So, it turns out that solutions are very useful constructs within Visual Studio.

The easiest way to explore solution capabilities and attributes is to create a solution in the IDE.

Creating a Solution

To create a solution, you first create a project. Because projects can't be loaded independent of a solution within Visual Studio, creating a project will cause a solution to be created at the same time.

> **NOTE**
>
> There actually is a way to create a blank, or empty, solution without also creating a project. If you expand the Other Project Types node that appears in the Project types list, you will see an option for Visual Studio Solutions. This contains a Blank Solution template. Blank solutions are useful when you are creating a new solution to house a series of already-existing projects; the blank solution obviates the need to worry about extra, unneeded projects being created on disk.

Launch the New Project dialog box by using the File menu and selecting the New, Project option (shown in Figure 4.1) or by using the Ctrl+Shift+N keyboard shortcut.

The New Project dialog box will be displayed with defaults for the project name, location, and solution name (see Figure 4.2). We'll take a detailed look at the various project types offered there when we discuss projects later in this chapter. Notice that at the bottom of the dialog box, a Solution Name field is displayed. This field allows you to customize the name of your solution prior to creating the solution. Just clicking OK at this point will do two things: A project of the indicated type and name will be created on disk (at the location specified), and a solution, with links to the project, will also be created on disk using the provided name.

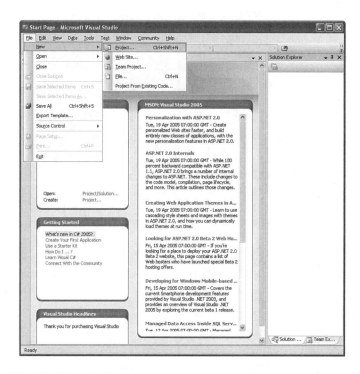

FIGURE 4.1   The File, New, Project menu.

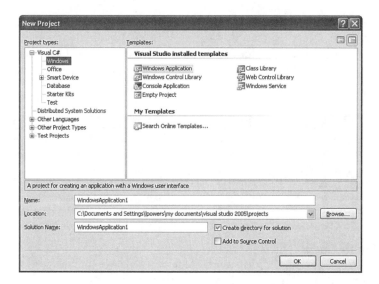

FIGURE 4.2   The New Project dialog box.

Assuming that you have selected something other than the Blank Solution project type, Visual Studio will now display the newly created solution and project in the Solution

Explorer window (we cover the Solution Explorer in depth in Chapter 5, "Browsers and Explorers"). In effect, Visual Studio has created the solution hierarchy shown in Figure 4.3.

FIGURE 4.3   A simple solution hierarchy.

Assuming that you have accepted the default locations and left the Create Directory for Solution box checked, the physical directory/file structure is created as shown in Figure 4.4.

FIGURE 4.4   The solution file hierarchy.

In this example, the first WindowsApplication1 folder holds the solution file and has a subfolder for each project. The second WindowsApplication1 folder contains the new Windows forms project. The source files are placed in the root of this folder, and any compiled output files sit underneath the bin directory and then under the specific build configuration (for example, Debug or Release).

CAUTION

By default, the solution is named after the project. There is potential for confusion here because you now have two folders/entities named WindowsApplication1. One refers to the solution; the other, the project. This is not an ideal way to physically organize your code on disk. It is recommended that you give the solution itself a unique name during the project creation process by simply overriding the default name given in the Solution Name field (refer to Figure 4.2).

The Solution Definition File

Visual Studio stores solution information inside two separate files: a solution definition file and a solution user options file. For the preceding example, Visual Studio created the solution definition file WindowsApplication1.sln and the solution user options file WindowsApplication1.suo in the indicated folder.

The solution definition file is responsible for actually describing any project relationships in the solution and for storing the various solution-level attributes that can be set. The solution user options file persists any customizations or changes that you, as a Visual Studio user, might have made to the way the solution is displayed within the IDE (such as whether the solution is expanded). In addition, certain source control settings and other IDE configuration data are stored here.

The solution user options file is, by default, marked as a hidden file, and its content is actually binary. Because its internal structure is not publicly documented, we won't attempt to dissect it here. The solution definition file, however, is simply a text file. Listing 4.1 shows the file content for a fairly complex sample solution.

LISTING 4.1   Sample Solution File

```
Microsoft Visual Studio Solution File, Format Version 9.00
# Visual Studio 2005
Project("{FAE04EC0-301F-11D3-BF4B-00C04F79EFBC}") = "Contoso.Fx.Integration",
➥ "ClassLibrary1\Contoso.Fx.Integration.csproj",
➥ "{DA0BA585-76C1-4F5E-B7EF-57254E185BE4}"
EndProject
Project("{FAE04EC0-301F-11D3-BF4B-00C04F79EFBC}") = "Contoso.Fx.Common",
➥ "Contoso.Fx.Common\Contoso.Fx.Common.csproj",
➥ "{A706BCAC-8FD7-4D8A-AC81-249ED61FDE72}"
EndProject
Project("{FAE04EC0-301F-11D3-BF4B-00C04F79EFBC}") = "Contoso.Fx.Analysis",
➥ "Contoso.Fx.Analysis\Contoso.Fx.Analysis.csproj",
➥ "{EB7D75D7-76FC-4EC0-A11E-2B54849CF6EB}"
EndProject
Project("{FAE04EC0-301F-11D3-BF4B-00C04F79EFBC}") = "Contoso.Fx.UI",
➥ "Contoso.Fx.UI\Contoso.Fx.UI.csproj",
➥ "{98317C19-F6E7-42AE-AC07-72425E851185}"
EndProject
Project("{2150E333-8FDC-42A3-9474-1A3956D46DE8}") = "Architecture Models",
➥ "Architecture Models", "{60777432-3B66-4E03-A337-0366F7E0C864}"
    ProjectSection(SolutionItems) = postProject
        ContosoSystemDiagram.sd = ContosoSystemDiagram.sd
    EndProjectSection
EndProject
Project("{FAE04EC0-301F-11D3-BF4B-00C04F79EFBC}") = "Contoso.UI.WindowsForms.
➥ OrderEntry", "Contoso.UI.WindowsForms.OrderEntry\Contoso.UI.WindowsForms.
➥ OrderEntry.csproj", "{49C79375-6238-40F1-94C8-4183B466FD79}"
EndProject
Project("{2150E333-8FDC-42A3-9474-1A3956D46DE8}") = "Class Libraries",
➥ "Class Libraries", "{E547969C-1B23-42DE-B2BB-A13B7E844A2B}"
EndProject
Project("{2150E333-8FDC-42A3-9474-1A3956D46DE8}") = "Controls", "Controls",
➥ "{ED2D843C-A708-41BE-BB52-35BFE4493035}"
EndProject
```

LISTING 4.1   Continued

```
Global
    GlobalSection(SolutionConfigurationPlatforms) = preSolution
        Debug¦Any CPU = Debug¦Any CPU
        Release¦Any CPU = Release¦Any CPU
    EndGlobalSection
    GlobalSection(ProjectConfigurationPlatforms) = postSolution
        {DA0BA585-76C1-4F5E-B7EF-57254E185BE4}.Debug¦Any CPU.ActiveCfg = Debug¦
➥ Any CPU
        {DA0BA585-76C1-4F5E-B7EF-57254E185BE4}.Debug¦Any CPU.Build.0 = Debug¦
➥ Any CPU
        {DA0BA585-76C1-4F5E-B7EF-57254E185BE4}.Release¦Any CPU.ActiveCfg = Release
➥ ¦Any CPU
        {DA0BA585-76C1-4F5E-B7EF-57254E185BE4}.Release¦Any CPU.Build.0 = Release¦
➥ Any CPU
        {A706BCAC-8FD7-4D8A-AC81-249ED61FDE72}.Debug¦Any CPU.ActiveCfg = Debug¦
➥ Any CPU
        {A706BCAC-8FD7-4D8A-AC81-249ED61FDE72}.Debug¦Any CPU.Build.0 = Debug¦
➥ Any CPU
        {A706BCAC-8FD7-4D8A-AC81-249ED61FDE72}.Release¦Any CPU.ActiveCfg = Release
➥ ¦Any CPU
        {A706BCAC-8FD7-4D8A-AC81-249ED61FDE72}.Release¦Any CPU.Build.0 = Release
➥ ¦Any CPU
        {EB7D75D7-76FC-4EC0-A11E-2B54849CF6EB}.Debug¦Any CPU.ActiveCfg = Debug¦
➥ Any CPU
        {EB7D75D7-76FC-4EC0-A11E-2B54849CF6EB}.Debug¦Any CPU.Build.0 = Debug¦
➥ Any CPU
        {EB7D75D7-76FC-4EC0-A11E-2B54849CF6EB}.Release¦Any CPU.ActiveCfg = Release
➥ ¦Any CPU
        {EB7D75D7-76FC-4EC0-A11E-2B54849CF6EB}.Release¦Any CPU.Build.0 = Release
➥ ¦Any CPU
        {98317C19-F6E7-42AE-AC07-72425E851185}.Debug¦Any CPU.ActiveCfg = Debug¦
➥ Any CPU
        {98317C19-F6E7-42AE-AC07-72425E851185}.Debug¦Any CPU.Build.0 = Debug¦
➥ Any CPU
        {98317C19-F6E7-42AE-AC07-72425E851185}.Release¦Any CPU.ActiveCfg = Release
➥ ¦Any CPU
        {98317C19-F6E7-42AE-AC07-72425E851185}.Release¦Any CPU.Build.0 = Release
➥ ¦Any CPU
        {49C79375-6238-40F1-94C8-4183B466FD79}.Debug¦Any CPU.ActiveCfg = Debug¦
➥ Any CPU
        {49C79375-6238-40F1-94C8-4183B466FD79}.Debug¦Any CPU.Build.0 = Debug¦
➥ Any CPU
        {49C79375-6238-40F1-94C8-4183B466FD79}.Release¦Any CPU.ActiveCfg = Release
➥ ¦Any CPU
```

LISTING 4.1   Continued

```
        {49C79375-6238-40F1-94C8-4183B466FD79}.Release¦Any CPU.Build.0 = Release
➥ ¦Any CPU
    EndGlobalSection
    GlobalSection(SolutionProperties) = preSolution
        HideSolutionNode = FALSE
    EndGlobalSection
    GlobalSection(NestedProjects) = preSolution
        {ED2D843C-A708-41BE-BB52-35BFE4493035} =
➥ {E547969C-1B23-42DE-B2BB-A13B7E844A2B}
        {EB7D75D7-76FC-4EC0-A11E-2B54849CF6EB} =
➥ {E547969C-1B23-42DE-B2BB-A13B7E844A2B}
        {A706BCAC-8FD7-4D8A-AC81-249ED61FDE72} =
➥ {E547969C-1B23-42DE-B2BB-A13B7E844A2B}
        {DA0BA585-76C1-4F5E-B7EF-57254E185BE4} =
➥ {E547969C-1B23-42DE-B2BB-A13B7E844A2B}
        {98317C19-F6E7-42AE-AC07-72425E851185} =
➥ {ED2D843C-A708-41BE-BB52-35BFE4493035}
    EndGlobalSection
EndGlobal
```

At the beginning of the file are references to the projects that belong to the solution. The references contain the project's name, its GUID, and a relative path to the project file itself (more on project files in a bit).

You can also see some of the various configuration attributes applied to the solution: The Debug and Release settings, for instance, show up here. Note that this project contains several solution folders: Architecture Models, Class Libraries, Controls, and Forms. They are represented in the solution file in much the same way as projects. In fact, the only difference is that they do not have a relative file path associated with them.

Working with Solutions

After you have created a solution, the primary vehicle is in place for interacting with your code base. In essence, this boils down to controlling the way that its constituent projects and files are built and deployed. Solutions also provide functionality outside the scope of projects. The primary tool for manipulating solutions and projects is the Solution Explorer. This tool is discussed in depth in Chapter 5. Here, we will look at the general procedures used to manage solutions by using the menu system in Visual Studio; keep in mind that most of the commands and actions discussed here can be initiated from the Solution Explorer.

Solution Items

In practice, the content you will add most often to a solution is project related. But items can be added directly to a solution as well. Collectively, the term *solution items* refers to any nonproject file that is attached to a solution. Because we know that solutions can't be compiled, it stands to reason that files added at the solution level serve no practical purpose from a compilation perspective. There are a variety of reasons, however, that you may want to add solution items to your solution. For instance, this is a convenient way to store documentation that applies to the solution as a whole. Because you can add any type of file to a solution, this could take the form of documents, notes to other developers, design specifications, or even source code files from other solutions that may have some impact or bearing on the work at hand.

By default, Visual Studio supports a few different types of solution items that can be created directly from within the IDE. They are grouped within four different categories. Within each category are various different file types that can be generated by Visual Studio. Table 4.1 shows the supported types.

TABLE 4.1   File Types Supported Within a Solution by Add New Item

Category	Item Type	File Extension
General	Text file	`.txt`
	Style sheet	`.css`
	XML schema	`.xsd`
	Bitmap file	`.bmp`
	Cursor file	`.cur`
	Visual C# class	`.cs`
	Visual Basic class	`.vb`
	HTML page	`.html`
	XML file	`.xml`
	XSLT file	`.xsl`
	Icon file	`.ico`
	Native resource template	`.rct`
	Visual J# class	`.jsl`
Performance	Blank performance session	`.psess`
	Performance wizard	`.psess`
Distributed System Diagrams	Application diagram	`.ad`
	System diagram	`.sd`
	Logical datacenter diagram	`.ldd`
Test Run Configuration	Test run configuration	`.testrunconfig`

NOTE

Keep in mind that you are in no way limited as to the type of file you can add to a solution. Even though Visual Studio supports only a limited number of file types that can be created within the IDE, you always have the option of creating a file *outside* the IDE and then adding it to a solution by using the Add Existing Item command.

Figure 4.5 shows the Add New Item – Solution Items dialog box that appears when you try to add a new item to a solution.

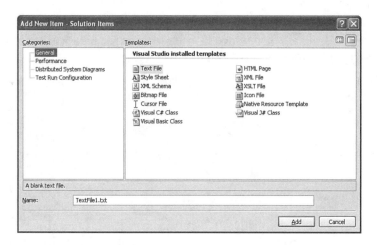

FIGURE 4.5   Adding a new solution item.

Solution Folders

To assist in organizing the various files in your solution, you can use *solution folders*. They are virtual folders implemented entirely within Visual Studio and do not cause physical file folders to be created on disk, and they exist solely to provide another grouping level within the solution. Solution folders can be nested and are especially useful in large solutions that contain many different projects and miscellaneous files. For example, you may want to group all of your web service projects under a single solution folder called Services, while grouping the Windows forms elements of your solution under a UI folder. Files added to a virtual folder are actually physically stored within the root of the solution directory structure.

Beyond providing a visual grouping element, solution folders also allow you to apply certain commands against all of the projects contained within an individual folder. For example, you can "unload" all of the projects within a virtual folder by issuing the unload command against the virtual folder.

Solution Properties

Several solution-level properties can be set from within the IDE. The Solution Property Pages dialog box gives you direct access to these properties and allows you to

- Set the startup project of the solution (this project will run when you start the debugger)

- Manage interproject dependencies

- Specify the location of source files to use when debugging

- Modify the solution build configurations

You launch this dialog box from the View menu or with the keyboard shortcut Shift+F4.

Specifying the Startup Project   Figure 4.6 shows the Startup Project property page. The property page categories are represented in a tree view to the left; expanding a tree node reveals the individual property pages available.

The Startup Project property page indicates whether the startup project should be the currently selected project, a single project, or multiple projects.

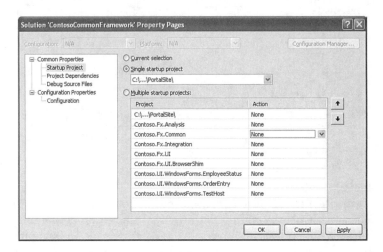

FIGURE 4.6   The Startup Project property page.

The default, and most typically used option, is to specify a single startup project. The project to run is specified in the drop-down box. If Current Selection is selected, the project that currently has focus in the Solution Explorer will be considered the startup project.

You also can launch multiple projects when the debugger is started. Each project currently loaded in the solution will appear in the list box with a default action of None. Projects set to None will not be executed by the debugger. You can also choose from the actions Start and Start Without Debugging. As their names suggest, the Start action will cause the indicated project to run within the debugger; Start Without Debugging will cause the project to run, but it will not be debugged.

Setting Project Dependencies   If a solution has projects that depend on one another—that is, one project relies on the types exposed by another project—Visual Studio will need to have a build order of precedence established among the projects. As an example, consider a Windows application project that consumes types that are exposed by a class library project. The build process will fail if the class library is not built first within the build sequence.

Most of the time, Visual Studio is able to determine the correct sequence. Sometimes, you may need to manually indicate that a project is dependent on other, specific projects. To supply this information, you use the Project Dependencies property page (see Figure 4.7). By selecting a project in the drop-down, you can indicate which other solutions it depends on by placing a check mark on any of the projects shown in the Depends On list.

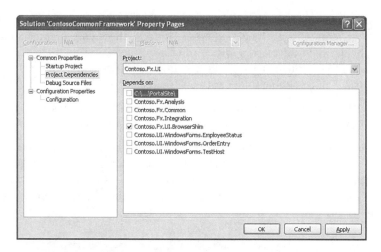

FIGURE 4.7   Project dependencies.

Source File Location for Debugging   In certain situations, you may need to explicitly point the Visual Studio debugger at source files to use when the debugger executes. One such scenario occurs when you are trying to debug a solution that references an object on a remote machine. If the source is not available locally for that remote object, you can explicitly point Visual Studio at the source files.

The Debug Source Files property page (see Figure 4.8) has two different list boxes. The top box contains a list of folders that hold source code specific to your debugging scenario. The bottom list box allows you to indicate specific files that the debugger should ignore (that is, should not load) when debugging.

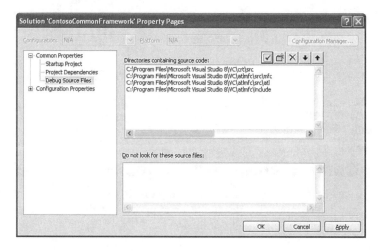

FIGURE 4.8   Source file locations.

To add an entry to either box, first place your cursor within the box and then click on the New Line button (top right of the dialog box). This will allow you to enter a fully qualified path to the desired folder. You remove an entry by selecting the item and then clicking on the Cut Line button. The Check Entries button allows you to double-check that all entries point to valid, reachable folder paths.

If the loaded solution has any Visual C++ projects, you will probably see several items already added into the Directories Containing Source Code list box.

Build Configuration Properties   Build configurations are covered in depth in Chapter 9, "Automation and Macros." On the Build Configuration property page (see Figure 4.9), you indicate how Visual Studio will build the projects contained within the solution. For each project, you can set a configuration and platform value. In addition, a check box allows you to indicate whether to build a particular project.

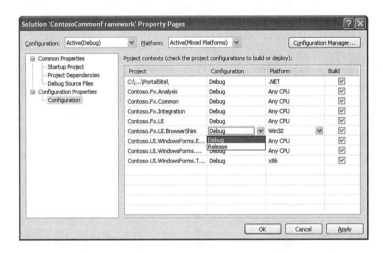

FIGURE 4.9   Build configuration properties.

See Chapter 9 for information on how to effectively use build configurations in your development.

Now that we have covered the concept of a solution in depth, let's examine how projects function within Visual Studio.

Getting Comfortable with Projects

Projects are where all of the real work is performed in Visual Studio. A project maps directly to a compiled component. Visual Studio supports a variety of different project types. Let's reexamine the project creation process.

Creating a Project

As we saw earlier when discussing solution creation, you create projects by selecting the New, Project option from the File menu. This launches the New Project dialog box (see Figure 4.10).

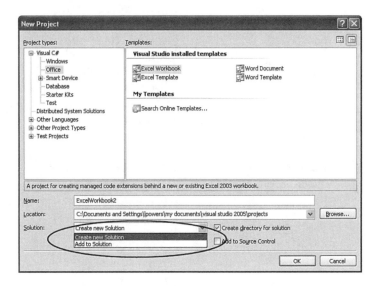

FIGURE 4.10   Adding a project to the current solution.

Table 4.2 shows the various project types supported in Visual Studio out of the box.

TABLE 4.2   Supported Project Types

Type	Language	Template
Database	Visual Basic, Visual C#	SQL Server project
Office	Visual Basic, Visual C#	Excel workbook
		Excel template
		Word document
		Word template
Smart Device	Visual Basic, Visual C#	Pocket PC 2003 – Device application
		Pocket PC 2003 – Control library
		Pocket PC 2003 – Empty project
		Pocket PC 2003 – Class library
		Pocket PC 2003 – Console application
		Smartphone 2003 – Device application
		Smartphone 2003 – Console application
		Smartphone 2003 – Class library
		Smartphone 2003 – Empty project
		Windows CE 5.0 – Device application

TABLE 4.2 Continued

Type	Language	Template
		Windows CE 5.0 – Control project
		Windows CE 5.0 – Empty project
		Windows CE 5.0 – Class library
		Windows CE 5.0 – Console application
	Visual C++	ATL Smart Device project
		MFC Smart Device project
		Win32 Smart Device project
		MFC Smart Device ActiveX control
		MFC Smart Device DLL
Starter Kits	Visual Basic, Visual C#	Screen Saver Starter Kit
		Movie Collection Starter Kit
	Visual J#	Calculator Starter Kit
Test	Visual Basic, Visual C#	Test project
Windows	Visual Basic, Visual C#, Visual J#	Windows application
		Windows control library
		Console application
		Empty project
		Class library
		Web control library
		Windows service
		Crystal Reports Application

> **NOTE**
>
> Visual Studio supports the ability to create new project types and templates. In fact, this is one easy way to enforce standards and propagate usage guidance within a development team. For more details, see Chapter 17, "Web Services and Visual Studio."

As outlined previously, creating a new project will also create a new containing solution. However, if you are creating a project and you already have a solution loaded in the IDE, the New Project dialog box will offer you the opportunity to add the new project to the existing solution. Compare Figure 4.10 with Figure 4.2; notice that there is a new option in the form of a drop-down box that allows you to indicate whether Visual Studio should create a new solution or add the project to the current solution.

Website Projects

Website projects are created in a slightly different way. Instead of selecting File, New, Project, you select File, New, Web Site. This launches the New Web Site dialog box (see Figure 4.11).

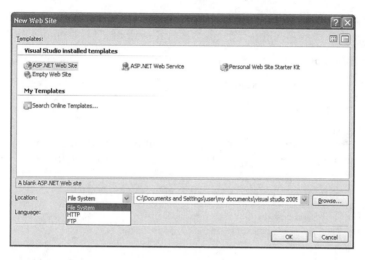

FIGURE 4.11   Creating a new website project.

As with other project types, you initiate website projects by selecting one of the predefined templates. In addition to the template, you also select a target source language and the location for the website. The location can be the file system, an HTTP site, or an FTP site. Unlike other project types, websites are not typically created within the physical folder tree that houses your solution. Even selecting the file system object will, by default, place the resulting source files in a Web Sites folder under the Visual Studio 2005 projects folder.

> **NOTE**
>
> The *target source language* for a website project simply represents the default language used for any code files. It does not constrain the languages you can use within the project. For instance, a website project created with C# as the target language can still contain Visual Basic code files.

After you have created the website, you manage and maintain it just like the other project types within the IDE.

Working with Project Definition Files

As with solutions, projects also maintain their structure information inside a file. These files have different extensions depending on their underlying language. Table 4.3 shows the various extensions that Visual Studio uses to identify project files.

TABLE 4.3   Project File Extensions

Project File Extension	Language
.vbproj	Visual Basic
.csproj	Visual C#
.vjsproj	Visual J#
.vcproj	Visual C++

Each project definition file contains all of the information necessary to describe the source files and the various project properties and options. This includes

- Build configurations

- Project references and dependencies

- Source code file locations/types

Visual Basic, Visual C#, and Visual J# project definition files are based on the same schema. Listing 4.2 contains a snippet from a Visual C# project definition file:

LISTING 4.2   Contents of a Visual C# Project Definition File

```
<Project DefaultTargets="Build"
➥xmlns="http://schemas.microsoft.com/developer/msbuild/2003">
  <PropertyGroup>
    <Configuration Condition=" '$(Configuration)' == '' ">Debug</Configuration>
    <Platform Condition=" '$(Platform)' == '' ">AnyCPU</Platform>
    <ProductVersion>8.0.50215</ProductVersion>
    <SchemaVersion>2.0</SchemaVersion>
    <ProjectGuid>{E22301F1-5AD6-4514-A05D-266158AB1CAB}</ProjectGuid>
    <OutputType>WinExe</OutputType>
    <AppDesignerFolder>Properties</AppDesignerFolder>
    <RootNamespace>WindowsApplication2</RootNamespace>
    <AssemblyName>WindowsApplication2</AssemblyName>
  </PropertyGroup>
  <PropertyGroup Condition=" '$(Configuration)¦$(Platform)' == 'Debug¦AnyCPU' ">
    <DebugSymbols>true</DebugSymbols>
    <DebugType>full</DebugType>
    <Optimize>false</Optimize>
    <OutputPath>bin\Debug\</OutputPath>
    <DefineConstants>DEBUG;TRACE</DefineConstants>
    <ErrorReport>prompt</ErrorReport>
    <WarningLevel>4</WarningLevel>
  </PropertyGroup>
  <PropertyGroup Condition=" '$(Configuration)¦$(Platform)' == 'Release¦AnyCPU' ">
    <DebugType>pdbonly</DebugType>
    <Optimize>true</Optimize>
    <OutputPath>bin\Release\</OutputPath>
    <DefineConstants>TRACE</DefineConstants>
    <ErrorReport>prompt</ErrorReport>
    <WarningLevel>4</WarningLevel>
  </PropertyGroup>
  <ItemGroup>
    <Reference Include="System" />
```

LISTING 4.2   Continued

```xml
    <Reference Include="System.Data" />
    <Reference Include="System.Deployment" />
    <Reference Include="System.Drawing" />
    <Reference Include="System.Windows.Forms" />
    <Reference Include="System.Xml" />
  </ItemGroup>
  <ItemGroup>
    <Compile Include="Form1.cs">
      <SubType>Form</SubType>
    </Compile>
    <Compile Include="Form1.Designer.cs">
      <DependentUpon>Form1.cs</DependentUpon>
    </Compile>
    <Compile Include="Program.cs" />
    <Compile Include="Properties\AssemblyInfo.cs" />
    <EmbeddedResource Include="Properties\Resources.resx">
      <Generator>ResXFileCodeGenerator</Generator>
      <LastGenOutput>Resources.Designer.cs</LastGenOutput>
      <SubType>Designer</SubType>
    </EmbeddedResource>
    <Compile Include="Properties\Resources.Designer.cs">
      <AutoGen>True</AutoGen>
      <DependentUpon>Resources.resx</DependentUpon>
    </Compile>
    <None Include="Properties\Settings.settings">
      <Generator>SettingsSingleFileGenerator</Generator>
      <LastGenOutput>Settings.Designer.cs</LastGenOutput>
    </None>
    <Compile Include="Properties\Settings.Designer.cs">
      <AutoGen>True</AutoGen>
      <DependentUpon>Settings.settings</DependentUpon>
      <DesignTimeSharedInput>True</DesignTimeSharedInput>
    </Compile>
  </ItemGroup>
  <Import Project="$(MSBuildBinPath)\Microsoft.CSharp.targets" />
</Project>
```

This project definition file would look relatively the same as a Visual Basic or Visual J# project. Visual C++ project files, however, use an entirely different schema. For completeness, and to contrast with the Visual Basic/Visual C#/Visual J# content, Listing 4.3 shows a sample Visual C++ project definition file in its entirety.

LISTING 4.3   Visual C++ Project Definition File

```xml
<?xml version="1.0" encoding="Windows-1252"?>
<VisualStudioProject
    ProjectType="Visual C++"
    Version="8.00"
    Name="Contoso.Fx.UI.BrowserShim"
    ProjectGUID="{BE574BF5-7FDA-46F2-A42E-4A35E5E338A0}"
    RootNamespace="ContosoFxUIBrowserShim"
    Keyword="MFCActiveXProj"
    SignManifests="true">
    <Platforms>
        <Platform Name="Win32" />
    </Platforms>
    <ToolFiles>
    </ToolFiles>
    <Configurations>
        <Configuration Name="Debug¦Win32" OutputDirectory="Debug"
            IntermediateDirectory="Debug" ConfigurationType="2"
            UseOfMFC="2" CharacterSet="1">
            <Tool Name="VCPreBuildEventTool" />
            <Tool Name="VCCustomBuildTool" />
            <Tool Name="VCXMLDataGeneratorTool" />
            <Tool Name="VCWebServiceProxyGeneratorTool" />
            <Tool
                Name="VCMIDLTool"
                PreprocessorDefinitions="_DEBUG"
                MkTypLibCompatible="false"
                TypeLibraryName="$(IntDir)/$(ProjectName).tlb"
                HeaderFileName="$(ProjectName)idl.h"
                ValidateParameters="false"
            />
            <Tool
                Name="VCCLCompilerTool"
                Optimization="0"
                PreprocessorDefinitions="WIN32;_WINDOWS;_DEBUG;_USRDLL"
                MinimalRebuild="true"
                BasicRuntimeChecks="3"
                RuntimeLibrary="3"
                TreatWChar_tAsBuiltInType="true"
                UsePrecompiledHeader="2"
                WarningLevel="3"
                Detect64BitPortabilityProblems="true"
                DebugInformationFormat="4"
            />
            <Tool Name="VCManagedResourceCompilerTool" />
```

LISTING 4.3   Continued

```
        <Tool
            Name="VCResourceCompilerTool"
            PreprocessorDefinitions="_DEBUG"
            Culture="1033"
            AdditionalIncludeDirectories="$(IntDir)"
        />
        <Tool Name="VCPreLinkEventTool" />
        <Tool
            Name="VCLinkerTool"
            RegisterOutput="true"
            OutputFile="$(OutDir)\$(ProjectName).ocx"
            LinkIncremental="2"
            ModuleDefinitionFile=".\Contoso.Fx.UI.BrowserShim.def"
            GenerateDebugInformation="true"
            SubSystem="2"
            TargetMachine="1"
        />
        <Tool Name="VCALinkTool" />
        <Tool Name="VCManifestTool" />
        <Tool Name="VCXDCMakeTool" />
        <Tool Name="VCBscMakeTool" />
        <Tool Name="VCFxCopTool" />
        <Tool Name="VCAppVerifierTool" />
        <Tool Name="VCWebDeploymentTool" />
        <Tool Name="VCPostBuildEventTool" />
    </Configuration>
    <Configuration
        Name="Release|Win32"
        OutputDirectory="Release"
        IntermediateDirectory="Release"
        ConfigurationType="2"
        UseOfMFC="2"
        CharacterSet="1"
        >
        <Tool Name="VCPreBuildEventTool" />
        <Tool Name="VCCustomBuildTool" />
        <Tool Name="VCXMLDataGeneratorTool" />
        <Tool Name="VCWebServiceProxyGeneratorTool" />
        <Tool
            Name="VCMIDLTool"
            PreprocessorDefinitions="NDEBUG"
            MkTypLibCompatible="false"
            TypeLibraryName="$(IntDir)/$(ProjectName).tlb"
            HeaderFileName="$(ProjectName)idl.h"
```

LISTING 4.3   Continued

```
                    ValidateParameters="false"
            />
            <Tool
                Name="VCCLCompilerTool"
                Optimization="2"
                PreprocessorDefinitions="WIN32;_WINDOWS;NDEBUG;_USRDLL"
                MinimalRebuild="false"
                RuntimeLibrary="2"
                TreatWChar_tAsBuiltInType="true"
                UsePrecompiledHeader="2"
                WarningLevel="3"
                Detect64BitPortabilityProblems="true"
                DebugInformationFormat="3"
            />
            <Tool Name="VCManagedResourceCompilerTool" />
            <Tool
                Name="VCResourceCompilerTool"
                PreprocessorDefinitions="NDEBUG"
                Culture="1033"
                AdditionalIncludeDirectories="$(IntDir)"
            />
            <Tool Name="VCPreLinkEventTool" />
            <Tool
                Name="VCLinkerTool"
                RegisterOutput="true"
                OutputFile="$(OutDir)\$(ProjectName).ocx"
                LinkIncremental="1"
                ModuleDefinitionFile=".\Contoso.Fx.UI.BrowserShim.def"
                GenerateDebugInformation="true"
                SubSystem="2"
                OptimizeReferences="2"
                EnableCOMDATFolding="2"
                TargetMachine="1"
            />
            <Tool Name="VCALinkTool" />
            <Tool Name="VCManifestTool" />
            <Tool Name="VCXDCMakeTool" />
            <Tool Name="VCBscMakeTool" />
            <Tool Name="VCFxCopTool" />
            <Tool Name="VCAppVerifierTool" />
            <Tool Name="VCWebDeploymentTool" />
            <Tool Name="VCPostBuildEventTool" />
        </Configuration>
    </Configurations>
```

LISTING 4.3   Continued

```
<References></References>
<Files>
    <Filter Name="Source Files"
        Filter="cpp;c;cc;cxx;def;odl;idl;hpj;bat;asm;asmx"
        UniqueIdentifier="{4FC737F1-C7A5-4376-A066-2A32D752A2FF}">
        <File RelativePath=".\Contoso.Fx.UI.BrowserShim.cpp"></File>
        <File RelativePath=".\Contoso.Fx.UI.BrowserShim.def"></File>
        <File RelativePath=".\Contoso.Fx.UI.BrowserShim.idl"></File>
        <File RelativePath=".\Contoso.Fx.UI.BrowserShimCtrl.cpp">
        </File>
        <File RelativePath=".\Contoso.Fx.UI.BrowserShimPropPage.cpp">
        </File>
        <File RelativePath=".\stdafx.cpp">
            <FileConfiguration Name="Debug¦Win32"     >
                <Tool Name="VCCLCompilerTool"
                    UsePrecompiledHeader="1" />
            </FileConfiguration>
            <FileConfiguration Name="Release¦Win32">
                <Tool Name="VCCLCompilerTool"
                    UsePrecompiledHeader="1" />
            </FileConfiguration>
        </File>
    </Filter>
    <Filter
        Name="Header Files"
        Filter="h;hpp;hxx;hm;inl;inc;xsd"
        UniqueIdentifier="{93995380-89BD-4b04-88EB-625FBE52EBFB}">
        <File RelativePath=".\Contoso.Fx.UI.BrowserShim.h"></File>
        <File RelativePath=".\Contoso.Fx.UI.BrowserShimCtrl.h"></File>
        <File RelativePath=".\Contoso.Fx.UI.BrowserShimPropPage.h">
        </File>
        <File RelativePath=".\Resource.h"></File>
        <File RelativePath=".\stdafx.h"></File>
    </Filter>
    <Filter Name="Resource Files"
 Filter="rc;ico;cur;bmp;dlg;rc2;rct;bin;rgs;gif;jpg;jpeg;jpe;resx;tiff;tif;
➥ png;wav"
        UniqueIdentifier="{67DA6AB6-F800-4c08-8B7A-83BB121AAD01}">
        <File RelativePath=".\Contoso.Fx.UI.BrowserShim.ico"></File>
        <File RelativePath=".\Contoso.Fx.UI.BrowserShim.rc"></File>
        <File RelativePath=".\Contoso.Fx.UI.BrowserShimCtrl.bmp"></File>
    </Filter>
```

LISTING 4.3   Continued

```
        <File RelativePath=".\ReadMe.txt"></File>
    </Files>
    <Globals></Globals>
</VisualStudioProject>
```

Working with Projects

As source code containers, projects principally act as a settings applicator. They are used to control and organize your source code files and the various properties associated with the whole build and compile process (we cover the build process in depth in Chapter 9). As with solutions, projects can contain various different items that are germane to their development. Projects are language specific. You cannot mix different languages within a specific project. There is no similar limitation with solutions: A solution can contain many projects, each one in a different language.

Project Items

After a project is created, it will, by default, already contain one or more project items. These default items will vary depending on the project template you selected and on the language of the project. For instance, creating a project using the C# windows application template would result in the formation of a Form1.cs file, a Form1.Designer.cs file, and a Program.cs file. Projects are also preconfigured with references and properties that make sense for the given project type: The windows application template contains a reference to the System.Windows.Forms assembly, whereas the class library template does not.

Projects, like solutions, can also have subfolders within them that you can employ to better manage and group project items. Unlike solutions, the folders that you create within a project are physical; they are created on disk within your project directory structure. These are examples of physical project items. Source code files are also physical in nature.

Projects can also contain virtual items—items that are merely pointers or links to items that don't actually manifest themselves physically within your project structure. They are, for example, references to other assemblies, database connections, and virtual folders (virtual folders are described in Chapter 5). Figure 4.12 illustrates a fully described solution and project.

FIGURE 4.12   Project structure.

Project Properties

Like solution properties, project properties are viewed and set using a series of property pages accessed through the Project, Properties menu. These property pages are hosted within a dialog box referred to as the *Project Designer*. Figure 4.13 shows the Project Designer that is displayed for a sample Visual Basic class library project. Different languages and different project types will actually surface different property pages within the Project Designer. For instance, the Application property page for a Visual Basic project looks different and contains slightly different information than an identical Visual C# project (although the basic intent of the page remains unchanged).

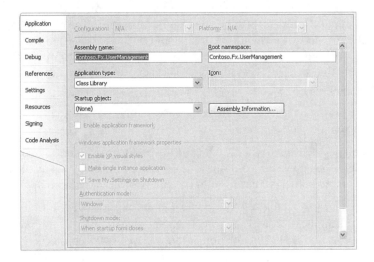

FIGURE 4.13   Setting properties using the Project Designer.

In general, you use project properties to control the following:

- General project attributes such as the assembly name and project type
- The way that the project will be built/compiled
- Debugger configuration for the project
- Resources used by the project
- Signing and security settings

Let's examine each of the available project property pages and discuss briefly the options that can be set on each.

Application   The Application property page allows you to set the assembly name, default/root namespace, application/output type, and the startup object. For Windows forms applications, authentication modes and visual styles are also controlled via this property page.

- **Assembly name**—This is the filename of the assembly that the project is compiled into. Typically, it defaults to the project name. The extension used is determined by the output type of the project.

- **Root/Default namespace**—This specifies a namespace to be used by any types declared within the project. This can also be declared manually in code.

- **Output type**—Displayed as the application type for Visual Basic projects, this value determines the fundamental project type (for example, class library, windows application, console application).

- **Startup object**—This object is used to set the entry point for the project. For windows applications, this will be the default form (or in the case of C#, the program entry point for the form) that should be launched when the application is executed. For console applications, this will be the main subroutine procedure that implements the console. Class library projects do not have an entry point and will be set to (Not set).

- **Icon**—This is the icon to associate with the assembly. It is not pertinent to class library or web projects.

- **Resource File**—This text box can be used to specify a path and filename for a resource file. Resource files contain nonexecutable content, such as strings, images, or even persisted objects, that need to be deployed along with an application.

- **Visual styles**—The Enable XP Visual Styles check box allows you to indicate whether the application will support XP themes when the user interface is rendered. This option is not applicable for non-Windows application projects.

- **Windows application properties**—Visual Basic provides a series of properties that apply specifically to Windows application projects. These properties allow you to set the splash screen associated with the project, the authentication mode supported by the project (Windows or application-defined), and the shutdown mode of the project. The shutdown mode specifies whether the application should shut down when the initial form is closed or when the last loaded form in the application is closed.

Build   The Build property page is used with Visual C# and Visual J# projects to tweak settings associated with build configurations. Using this dialog box, you can select whether the DEBUG and TRACE constants are turned on, and you can specify conditional compilation symbols. Settings that affect the warning and error levels and the build output are also housed here. For more exploration of the options available here, see Chapter 9.

Build Events   Visual Studio will trigger a pre- and post-build event for each project. On the Build Events page, you can specify commands that should be run during either of these events. This page also allows you to indicate when the post-build event runs: always, after a successful build, or when the build updates the project output. Build events are particularly useful for launching system tests and unit tests against a project that has just been recompiled. If you launch a suite of, say, unit tests from within the post-build event, the test cycle can be embedded within the build cycle.

NOTE

If you specify commands in the pre- or post-build events, Visual Studio will create a batch file for each event and place it into the `bin/debug` directory. These files, titled `PreBuildEvent.bat` and `PostBuildEvent.bat`, will house the commands you enter on the Build Events property page. In the event of an error running the build event commands, you can manually inspect and run these files to try to chase down the bug.

Code Analysis   Visual Studio offers the capability to run a series of rules and checks against your code base to enforce best practices, catch common errors, and apply intelligent coding guidance across a variety of topics such as performance, security, and globalization (to name just a few). The Code Analysis property page enables you to turn on code analysis for the current project, and it allows you to select which rules you want to run during the analysis process.

Compile (VB Only)   The Compile property page is used by Visual Basic projects to control which optimizations will be performed during compile and also to control general compilation options for the output path and warnings versus errors raised during the compilation process.

- **Compile options**—You use the Option strict and Option explicit drop-down to turn on or off these settings. You can also control whether the project will perform binary or text compares with the Option compare drop-down.

- **Compiler conditions**—Visual Basic allows you to customize the level of notification provided upon detecting any of a handful of conditions during the compilation process. For instance, one condition defined is Unused Local Variable. If this condition is detected in the source code during the compile, you can elect to have it treated as a warning or an error, or to have it ignored altogether.

- **Build events**—Visual Basic allows you to access the Build Events property page (see the previous section for an explanation) via a Build Events button located on this screen.

- **Misc compile options**—You can choose to disable all compiler warnings, treat all warnings as errors, and generate an XML documentation file during the compile process. This will result in an XML file with the same name as the project; it will contain all of the code comments parsed out of your source code in a predefined format.

Debug   The Debug property page allows you to affect the behavior of the Visual Studio debugger.

- **Start action**—You use this option to specify whether a custom program, a URL, or the current project itself should be started when the debugger is launched.

- **Start options**—You use this option to specify command-line arguments to pass to the running project, set the working directory for the project, and debug a process on a remote machine.

- **Enable debuggers**—You use the check boxes in this section to enable or disable such things as support for debugging unmanaged code, support for SQL stored procedure debugging, and use of Visual Studio as a host for the debugger process.

Publish   The Publish property page enables you to configure many ClickOnce-specific properties. You can specify the publish location for the application, the install location (if different from the publish location), and the various installation settings, including prerequisites and update options. You can also control the versioning scheme for the published assemblies.

References (Visual Basic)   The References property page is used within Visual Basic projects to select the assemblies referenced by the project and to import namespaces into the project. This screen also allows you to query the project in an attempt to determine whether some existing references are unused. You do this by using the Unused References button.

Reference Paths (Visual C#, Visual J#)   The Reference Paths property page allows you to provide path information meant to help Visual Studio find assemblies referenced by the project. Visual Studio will first attempt to resolve assembly references by looking in the current project directory. If the assembly is not found there, the paths provided on this property page will be used to search for the assemblies. Visual Studio will also probe the project's obj directory, but only after attempting to resolve first using the reference paths you have specified on this screen.

Resources   *Resources* are items such as strings, images, icons, audio, and files that are embedded in a project and used during design and runtime. The Resources property page allows you to add, edit, and delete resources associated with the project.

Security   For ClickOnce applications, the Security property page allows you to enforce code access security permissions for running the ClickOnce application. Various full trust and partial trust scenarios are supported.

Settings   *Application settings* are dynamically specified name/value pairs that can be used to store information specific to your project/application. The Settings property page allows you to add, edit, and delete these name/value pairs.

Each setting can be automatically scoped to the application or to the user, and can have a default value specified. Applications can then consume these settings at runtime.

Signing   The Signing property page allows you to have Visual Studio code sign the project assembly—and its ClickOnce manifests—by specifying a key file. You can also enable Delay signing from this screen.

Summary

Solutions and projects are the primary vehicles within Visual Studio for organizing and managing your code. They allow you to divide and conquer large solutions, and they provide a single point of access for various settings (at both the solution and project level). Solutions are the top-level container, and the first work item that Visual Studio creates when creating a new code project.

To summarize what we have learned about solutions:

- Solutions can be built (triggering a build of each of its projects) but cannot be compiled.

- Visual Studio can load only one solution at a time; to work on multiple solutions concurrently, you must have multiple copies of Visual Studio running.

- You can create folders within a solution to help group its content; these folders are virtual and do not represent physical file folders.

- Solutions are primarily used to group one or more projects together. Projects within a solution can be a mix of the various supported languages and project types.

- Solutions cannot contain other solutions.

- Besides projects, solutions can also contain miscellaneous files (called solution items) that typically represent information pertinent to the solution (readme files, system diagrams, and the like).

Although solutions are an important and necessary implement, it is the Visual Studio project that actually results in a compiled .NET component. Projects are created and based on templates available within the IDE that cover the various development scenarios, ranging from web application development to windows application development to smart device development.

To summarize what we have learned about projects:

- Projects exist to compile code into assemblies.

- Projects are based on a project template; project templates define the various artifacts, references, and so on that make sense for the project's context.

- Like solutions, projects also support subfolders to help you better organize your code. These folders are actual, physical folders that are created on disk.

- Projects contain project items. They can be source code files, references, and other items such as virtual folders and database connections.

We have seen how solutions and projects are physically manifested; in the next chapter we will cover the primary Visual Studio tools used to interact with solutions and projects.

CHAPTER 5

Browsers and Explorers

IN THIS CHAPTER

- Solution Explorer
- Class View
- Server Explorer
- Object Browser
- Performance Explorer
- Macro Explorer
- Document Outline

Visual Studio provides a cohesive and all-encompassing view of your solutions and projects by exposing them to you via *browsers* and *explorers*. These windows (which are confusingly also referred to as *view windows*) attempt to provide a visually structured representation of a large variety of elements—some code based, others not.

In general, you access and display these windows through the View menu. Some of these windows, such as the Solution Explorer and Class View, are staples of a developer's daily routine. Others touch on elements that are used during specific points within the development cycle or by more advanced Visual Studio IDE users.

In this chapter, we will examine each of the browser/ explorer windows in detail.

> **NOTE**
>
> As with many Visual Studio features, the actual browser and explorer tools available to you vary according to the Visual Studio version.

Solution Explorer

The Solution Explorer is the primary tool for viewing and manipulating solutions and projects. It provides a simple but powerful hierarchical view of all solution and project items, and it allows you to interact with each item directly via context menus and its toolbar.

Using Solution Explorer, you can launch an editor for any given file, add new items to a project or solution, and reorganize the structure of a project or solution. In addition, the Solution Explorer provides instant, at-a-glance information as to the currently selected project; the startup project for the solution; and the physical hierarchy of the solution, its projects, and their child items.

The Solution Explorer is simply another window hosted by Visual Studio. It can be docked, pinned, and placed anywhere within the Visual Studio environment. It is composed of a title bar, a toolbar, and a scrollable tree-view region (see Figure 5.1).

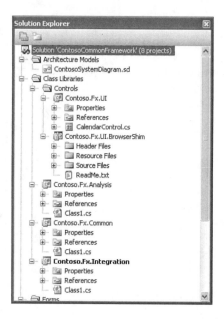

FIGURE 5.1   The Solution Explorer.

The tree view provides a graphics- and text-organizational view of the currently loaded solution. Figure 5.1 shows all of the various items and projects represented for an eight-project solution loaded in the IDE.

Visual Cues and Icons

Each item in the Solution Explorer is represented by a name and by an icon. Table 5.1 summarizes which icon is used to represent the supported item types.

> **NOTE**
>
> The icons shown in Table 5.1 are a representative list that correspond to specific project and solution items within the IDE. Other files added to a project or solution will be represented by the icon associated with their file type. For example, a Word document will be represented by the standard Word document icon in the Solution Explorer.

TABLE 5.1 Solution Explorer Item Types and Icons

Icon	Item	Notes
	About Box	Visual Basic only
	Application Diagram	
	ASP .NET Web Site	This represents the root node for an ASP .NET website project
	Bitmap File	
	Class Diagram	
	Component Class	
	Custom Control	
	DataSet	
	Dialog	Visual Basic only
	Folder	Solution folders or project folders
	Global Application Class	
	HTML Page	
	Icon File	
	Interface (Visual Basic)	
	Interface (Visual C#)	
	Logical Datacenter Diagram	
	Master Page	Web projects only
	Module	Visual Basic only
	My Project File	Visual Basic equivalent to the C# `Properties` Folder
	Partial Class	
	Project Reference	Visual C# only

TABLE 5.1　Continued

Icon	Item	Notes
	Properties Folder	Visual C# equivalent to the Visual Basic My Project File folder
	References Folder	Visual C# only
	Resources Folder	
	Settings Folder	
	Site Map	Web projects only
	Skin File	Web projects only
	Solution	The topmost root node visible within Solution Explorer
	Style Sheet	
	System Diagram	
	Text File	
	User Control	Any class that inherits directly from the UserControl class
	User Control (Web)	Class that inherits from System.Web.UI.UserControl
	VBScript/JScript File	
	Visual Basic Class File	
	Visual Basic Project	The root node for a Visual Basic project
	Visual C# Project	The root node for a Visual C# project
	Visual C# Class File	
	Web Configuration File	
	Web Form (.aspx)	
	Web Service	
	Windows Form	A file containing a class that implements the Form class

TABLE 5.1   Continued

Icon	Item	Notes
	Windows Form (Inherited)	
	Windows Form (MDI Parent)	Visual Basic only
	Web Project	
	XML File	
	XML Schema File	
	XSLT File	

Icon Overlays

To provide a visual cue about the status of a particular item, the Solution Explorer will overlay an additional graphical element over the item icon. These overlays are called *signal icons*. For example, when source code control is enabled, the Solution Explorer will visually indicate whether an item is checked out or not via a graphical overlay. Table 5.2 describes the signal icons used in the Solution Explorer.

TABLE 5.2   Solution Explorer Signal Icons

Icon	Description
	Item not found. The item was specified as part of the solution/project but can't be located.
	Checked in. The item is under source code control and is currently checked in.
	Checked out (exclusive). The item is under source code control and is currently checked out exclusively.
	Checked out (shared). The item is under source code control and is currently checked out in a shared mode.

The Solution Explorer supports different management actions depending on whether you are currently interacting with a solution or a project. In fact, supported commands may vary by project type as well. As an example, the Copy Web Project command button is available for web projects but not class library projects, whereas the Properties command button is available for all item types.

Table 5.3 shows the various toolbar command buttons supported by the Solution Explorer, along with their specific context.

TABLE 5.3   Solution Explorer Toolbar Buttons

Icon	Context	Description
	All	Properties button. Launches the Solution Properties dialog box.
	Solution, solution item, solution folder	Add New Solution Folder button. Creates a new solution folder in the currently loaded solution.
	Project, project item	Refresh. Refreshes the Solution Explorer's tree view of the project.
	Web project, web project item	Nest Related Files. Visual Studio can group certain project item constructs together. This is most commonly done with items such as code-behind files. This is a toggle button: Clicking it on will cause related files to be nested underneath the "parent" file. Clicking it off will cause all files to show up at the same level under the project.
	Project, project item	View Class Diagram. Creates a class diagram project item and launches the viewer for that item. All of the types contained within the project will be automatically added to the diagram.
	Web project, web project item	Copy Web Site. Copies the website to a specified location (available only for web projects).
	Web project, web project item	ASP .NET Configuration. Launches a browser to the ASP .NET Web Site Administration Tool. This feature is useful for setting up global security parameters and application-specific options.
	Solution, solution item, project, project item (only if items in the solution are currently hidden)	Unhide All. Unhides any hidden items in the solution.
	Project code files	View Code. Opens the current item in the code editor.
	Project code files with a UI (Windows form or web form)	View Designer. Opens the designer for the currently selected item.

Managing Solutions

Clicking on the solution in Solution Explorer will immediately expose all of the valid management commands for that solution. You access these commands either through the Solution Explorer toolbar or the context menu for the solution (accessed by right-clicking on the solution). Through the toolbar and the solution's context menu, the Solution Explorer allows you to

- View and set the properties for a solution
- Build/rebuild a solution
- Directly launch the configuration manager for a solution

- Set project dependencies and build order

- Add any of the various Visual Studio–supported solution and project items

- Add the solution to the source control

You can initiate some of these actions by using the Solution Explorer toolbar; you can access the balance in the context menu for a solution, as shown in Figure 5.2.

| Build Solution |
| Rebuild Solution |
| Clean Solution |
| Configuration Manager... |
| Project Dependencies... |
| Project Build Order... |
| Add ▶ |
| Set StartUp Projects... |
| Add Solution to Source Control... |
| Paste |
| Rename |
| Properties |

FIGURE 5.2   The solution context menu.

Managing Projects

Just as with solutions, Solution Explorer provides a variety of ways to manage projects within a solution. They include

- Opening a project item

- Building or rebuilding a project

- Adding items to a project

- Adding a reference to a project

- Cutting, pasting, renaming, or deleting a project within the solution tree

- Unloading a project

NOTE

The current startup project for a solution is indicated with a bold font (as is the Contoso.Fx.Integration project in Figure 5.1). If multiple projects are selected as startup projects, the solution name will instead be bolded.

The default action when you double-click an item is to open it within its default editor or designer. Multiple select and drag-and-drop operations are also supported. For instance, multiselecting several code files will allow you to open them simultaneously in their editor windows.

You can move and copy items within a solution, project, or between projects through the standard drag and drop using the left mouse button. You can also drag certain items from within a project and drop them onto a suitable designer surface. This is an easy way, for instance, to add classes to a class diagram: Simply highlight the code files that contain the types you want to add and drag them onto the class diagram designer window.

Class View

The Class View window is similar in design and function to the Solution Explorer window. It, too, provides a hierarchical view of project elements. However, the view here is not concerned with the physical files that constitute a solution or project; rather, this window provides a view of the various namespaces, types, interfaces, and enums within a project.

The Class View window is composed of four major visual components: a toolbar, a search bar, a tree view of types (called the *objects pane*), and a members pane.

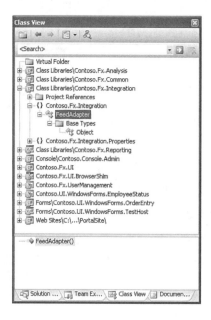

FIGURE 5.3   The Class View window.

Toolbar

The Class View window's toolbar provides easy access to command buttons for adding virtual folders, moving forward and back through the objects pane items, and controlling which objects are displayed.

Table 5.4 describes the various Class View toolbar buttons.

TABLE 5.4   Class View Toolbar Buttons

Icon	Description
	Class View new folder. Creates a virtual folder used to organize objects within the objects pane.
	Back. Causes the previously selected item to become the currently selected item.
	Forward. Causes the most recently selected item to become the currently selected item. This button is available only after using the Back button.
	Class view settings. Displays a drop-down list that allows you to select object types to display within the objects pane and the members pane. The available options include • Show Base Types • Show Derived Types • Show Project References • Show Hidden Types and References • Show Public Members • Show Protected Members • Show Private Members • Show Other Members • Show Inherited Members
	View Class Diagram. Creates a class diagram project item and launches the viewer for that item. All of the types contained within the project will be automatically added to the diagram.

The Search Bar

The search bar is a drop-down text box that provides a quick and easy way to filter the objects shown in the objects pane. When a search term (such as type name or namespace name) is entered, the Class View window will clear the objects pane and then repopulate it with only those objects that match the search term. Figure 5.4 shows the results of a search for FeedAdapter.

To restore the objects pane and remove the filter, click on the Clear Search button to the right of the Search button.

Recent search terms are saved for reuse in the drop-down list.

Objects Pane

The objects pane encloses a tree of objects grouped, at the highest level, by project. Each object is identified by an icon and by its name. Expanding a project node within the tree will reveal the various types contained within that project. Further parent-child relationships are also visible, such as the namespace-to-class relationship and the type-to-parent-type relationship.

Table 5.5 shows the icons used in the object pane.

5

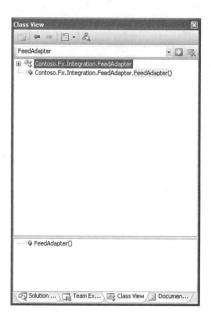

FIGURE 5.4   Filtering the objects pane.

TABLE 5.5   Objects Pane Icons

Icon	Description
	Class/Struct
	Delegate
	Enum
	Namespace
	Module
	Interface

Certain signal images are also overlaid on top of these icons to visually represent scope and access information for each object. These access type signal icons are shown in Table 5.6.

TABLE 5.6   Scope/Access Signal Icons

Icon	Description
	Private
	Internal/Friend
(n/a)	Public
	Protected

The depth of the various levels shown for each object will be dictated by the view settings in place at the time. For instance, turning on the Show Base Types option will append an additional base type level to the tree for each type. The object pane's principal duty is to allow quick and easy navigation back and forth through the object tree for each project. It exposes, in other words, an object-oriented view of each project.

Right-clicking within the objects pane will display the shortcut menu. The menu is essentially identical to the shortcut menu exposed by the Solution Explorer, with the exception of various Sort and Group by selections. The Sort options available here are

- **Sort Alphabetically**—The projects, namespaces, and types in the objects pane will be sorted in ascending, alphabetic order.

- **Sort by Object Type**—The types in the objects pane will be alphabetically sorted by their general classification (for example, in the following order: classes, enums, interfaces, structs).

- **Sort by Object Access**—The types will be sorted by their access modifier (public, private, protected, and so on).

- **Group by Object Type**—Another folder level will be added to the tree for each distinct object type present. For example, if a project contains both class and interface types, a class folder and an interface folder will be displayed in the objects pane tree, with their correlated types contained within.

Members Pane

The members pane reacts to the selection(s) made in the objects pane by displaying all of the members—properties, events, constants, variables, enums—defined on the selected type. Each member has a distinctive icon to immediately convey information such as scope and type; even member signatures show up here (note that the same signal icons used by the objects pane, and documented in Table 5.7, are used here as well).

The members pane is ideal for quickly visualizing type behavior and attributes: Just select the class/type in the objects pane and browse its members in the members pane.

TABLE 5.7   Members Pane Icons

Icon	Description
▤	Constant
▤◕	Method/Function
▤▦	Property
◕	Field

> **NOTE**
>
> Many developers will find that the bulk of their development tasks are more easily envisioned and acted on here within the Class View window as opposed to the Solution Explorer window. The available actions among the two are virtually identical, and the Class View window provides a much more code-focused perspective of your projects. Developers can spelunk through inheritance trees and see, at a glance, the various members implemented on each defined type within their project. The con to using the Class View is that source code control information is not visually surfaced here.

The members pane also exposes a context menu that has invaluable tools for browsing and editing code. For one, you can directly apply the Rename refactoring to a selected member. Other capabilities exposed here include the ability to immediately view the definition code for a member, to find every code location where the selected member is referenced, and to launch the Object Browser with the primary node for the member already selected for you.

The ability to alter the filter and display settings is also presented here. Figure 5.5 illustrates all of the available commands on this menu.

FIGURE 5.5   The members pane context menu.

Server Explorer

The Server Explorer window serves two purposes: It exposes various system services and resources that reside on your local machine and on remote machines, and it provides access to data connection objects. As with the other Visual Studio explorer windows, the systems, services, resources, and data connections are viewed in a graphical tree format. Systems appear under a top-level Servers node (your local machine will show up by default), and data connections appear under a top-level Data Connections node.

> **NOTE**
>
> The Server Explorer window content and configuration are not specific to a solution or project. Server Explorer settings are preserved as part of the IDE environment settings and are thus not subject to change on a per-solution (or project) basis.

A toolbar appears at the top of the Server Explorer window, providing one-click access to the Add Data Connection and Add Server functions (see Figure 5.6). You can also force a refresh of the window contents (a button is also provided to cancel the refresh because querying remote machines may be a lengthy process).

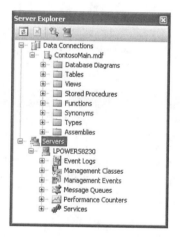

FIGURE 5.6   The Server Explorer window.

> **NOTE**
>
> The Express and Standard editions of Visual Studio do not have support for servers within the Server Explorer window; they are limited to data connections only. In fact, these versions of Visual Studio actually refer to this window as the Data Explorer window.

Data Connections

Data Connections represent a physical connection to a local or remote database. Through an established connection, you can gain access to and manipulate the various objects within a database. Each category of object will show up as a folder node under the Data Connections node. The tree items under each node allow you to directly interact with their physical database counterparts through a suite of designers and editors collectively referred to as *Visual Database Tools*. These tools are covered in depth in Chapter 15, "Working with Databases."

The following objects are exposed in the Server Explorer:

- Tables
- Views
- Stored procedures
- Functions
- Synonyms
- Types
- Assemblies

In general, you can create new database objects, edit or delete existing ones, and, where appropriate, query data from a database object (such as a table or view).

> **NOTE**
>
> The level of functionality and the number of object types you can access through the Server Explorer depend on both the version of Visual Studio you are using and the version of the database you are connecting to. In other words, not all functions are supported across all databases. The Visual Database Tools interact most effectively with Microsoft SQL Server, although most basic functions are supported against a variety of other relational database.

Server Components

The Servers node in Server Explorer exposes a variety of remote or local services and resources for direct management or use within a Visual Studio project. In essence, it is a management console for server-based components. By default, your local machine will be visible here as a server; to add other servers, right-click on the Servers node and select Add Server or simply click on the Connect to Server button in the Server Explorer toolbar. A dialog box will prompt you for a computer name or IP address for the server; this dialog box also supports the ability to connect via a different set of credentials.

Under the Servers node, the following component categories will appear as child nodes:

- Event Logs
- Management Classes

- Management Events
- Message Queues
- Performance Counters
- Services

Other component categories may also choose to register for display under the Servers node; the preceding list, however, represents the default, out-of-the-box functionality provided by Visual Studio 2005.

Event Logs

Under the Event Logs node, you can administer the separate application, security, and system event logs for the connected server. This includes clearing event log entries or drilling into and inspecting individual event log entries. Highlighting an event log or event log entry causes its properties to display in the Visual Studio property window, enabling you to view and edit their values. If you drag and drop one of the event logs into a project, a System.Diagnostics.EventLog or System.Diagnostic.EventLogEntry component instance will automatically be created.

Management Classes

The items under the Management Classes node represent various Windows Management Instrumentation (WMI) classes. Each of these classes maps to a logical or physical entity associated with a server. The available classes here are shown in Table 5.8.

TABLE 5.8   WMI Management Class Nodes

Title	WMI Class
Desktop Settings	Win32_Desktop
Disk Volumes	Win32_LogicalDisk
My Computer	Win32_ComputerSystem
Network Adapters	Win32_NetworkAdapter
Network Connections	Win32_NetworkConnection
NT Event Log Files	Win32_NTEventLogFile
Operating Systems	Win32_OperatingSystem
Printers	Win32_Printer
Processes	Win32_Process
Processors	Win32_Processor
Services	Win32_Service
Shares	Win32_Share
Software Products	Win32_Product
System Accounts	Win32_SystemAccount
Threads	Win32_Thread

A thorough discussion of WMI is beyond the scope of this chapter and this book; in summary, however, each of these nodes exposes various WMI class property groups (such

5

as precedents, antecedents, settings, dependents) and, in turn, each of these property groups will expose a span of commands, enabling you to directly affect a resource on the server. One simple example of how you might use this capability is to set access information for a share exposed on a remote server. When you expand nodes in the Server Explorer down to the share (via the Disk Volumes node), access to the share information is gained via the shortcut menu on the share. In this example, you would select the SetShareInfo action, which initiates a WMI dialog box allowing you to change various share attributes such as the description and maximum allowed users.

Management Events

The Management Events node contains a list of event queries; essentially, these are "listeners" that you establish to periodically poll the WMI eventing system on the server. These event queries are established through a dialog box (see Figure 5.7; you launch the dialog box by selecting Add Event Query on the shortcut menu). When an event is created, a child node to the Management Events node is created, and under this node, actual event instances will appear.

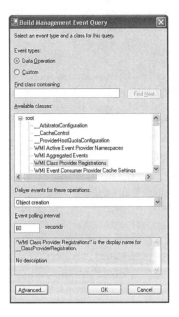

FIGURE 5.7   Creating a Management Event query.

Message Queues

If message queuing is installed on the target server, the Message Queues node displays all of the available message queues, along with any messages currently residing in each queue.

Performance Counters

Every performance counter installed on the target computer can be viewed in the Performance Counters node. Each performance counter is displayed within its category. Performance counter instances, if available, are also displayed.

Services

Each installed service is enumerated under the Services node. The shortcut menu off each service is used to control the service: Continue, start, stop, and pause actions are all supported (see Figure 5.8).

FIGURE 5.8   A service shortcut menu.

Programming with Server Explorer

Beyond allowing you to examine and manipulate data connections and server resources, the Server Explorer serves another task: By dragging and dropping items from the Server Explorer onto a Visual Studio design surface, you can quickly create components in code that directly reference the item in question. As an example, dragging the Application Log node (from Servers, Event Logs) onto an existing Windows form will create a System.Diagnostics.EventLog component instance that is preconfigured to point to the application log. You can then immediately write code to interact with the event log component. You could use the same process to quickly embed message queue access into your application or read from/write to a performance counter. Table 5.9 lists the various drag-and-drop operations that are possible, along with their results.

> **NOTE**
>
> Data connection items in the Server Explorer cannot be dragged onto a design surface. For more information regarding drag-and-drop development of database solutions, see Chapter 15.

TABLE 5.9   Server Explorer Drag and Drop

Under This Node	Dragging This	Does This
Event Logs	Event Log Category (for example, Application or System)	Creates a System.Diagnostics.EventLog component instance, configured for the appropriate event log
Management Classes	Management Class instance	Creates the appropriate WMI/CIMv2 component instance

TABLE 5.9   Continued

Under This Node	Dragging This	Does This
Management Events	Management Event Query	Creates a System.Management. ManagementEventWatcher component instance
Message Queues	Message Queue instance	Creates a System.Messaging.MessageQueue component instance for the selected queue
Performance Counters	Performance Counter or counter instance	Creates a System.Diagnostics. PerformanceCounter component instance, configured for the appropriate counter
Services	Service	Creates a System.ServiceProcess. ServiceController, provisioned for the indicated service

Object Browser

The Object Browser is similar in functionality and look and feel to the Class View window. It provides a hierarchical view of projects, assemblies, namespaces, types, enums, and interfaces. Unlike the Class View window, however, the Object Browser is capable of a much wider scope of objects. In addition to the currently loaded projects, the Object Browser is capable of displaying items from the entire .NET Framework, up to and including COM components and externally accessible objects. This is a great tool for finding and inspecting types, regardless of where they are physically located.

Changing the Scope

You can use the toolbar's Browse drop-down to filter or change the scope of the objects displayed within the Object Browser. The four different scoping options offered are shown in Table 5.10.

TABLE 5.10   Object Browser Scoping Options

Scope	Effect
All Components	This is a super-set of the other scopes offered. Selecting this option will show all types and members within the .NET Framework, the current solution, any libraries referenced by the current solution, and any individually selected components.
.NET Framework	Shows all objects within the .NET Framework.
My Solution	Shows all objects with the currently loaded solution, including any referenced components.
Custom Component Set	Shows any objects specifically added to the custom component set.

Editing the Custom Component Set

A *custom component set* is a list of components that you manually specify. Using a custom list might be useful in situations in which you want to browse a list of components from a variety of different "buckets." Instead of wading through each of the other scopes, you could include only those types that you care about in the component list.

You add to the custom component list by selecting the Edit Custom Component Set option in the Browse drop-down or by clicking on the ellipses to the right of the drop-down. This will launch an editor dialog box in which you can add or remove entries in this list (see Figure 5.9)

FIGURE 5.9   Editing the custom component set.

Adding a component to the set is as easy as selecting from one of the prepopulated object lists (available via the .NET, COM, or Projects tabs) or by browsing directly to the container assembly via the Browse tab. You can select an object or objects and then click the Add button. The current set members show up at the bottom of the dialog box. You can also select a current member and remove it from the list by clicking the Remove button.

Browsing Objects

The Object Browser consists of a toolbar and three different panes: an objects pane, a members pane, and a description pane. Again, the similarity here to the Class View window is obvious. The toolbar, objects pane, and members pane function identically to the Class View objects pane and members pane. You click down through the tree view to view each individual object's members; the toolbar aids in navigating deep trees by providing a forward and back button. Figure 5.10 shows the Object Browser in action.

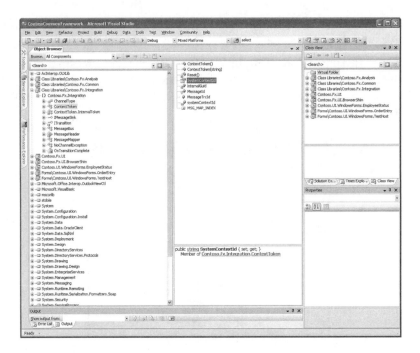

FIGURE 5.10   The Object Browser.

The hierarchical relationships, icons, and actions possible within the panes are the same (and therefore we won't rehash them here). The description pane, however, is a new concept.

Description Pane

When an item is selected in either the Object Browser's objects pane or members pane, the description pane will provide detailed information about the selected item. The data provided is quite extensive, and includes

- The name of the selected object

- The name of the parent of the selected object

- Code comments and in-line help associated with the selected object

Where possible, the description pane will embed hyperlinks within the data that it displays to allow you to easily navigate to related items. As an example, a declared property of type string might show the following description:

```
public string SystemContextId { set; get; }
    Member of Contoso.Fx.Integration.ContextToken
```

Note the use of hyperlinking: Clicking on the string identifier will navigate to the string data type within the Object Browser window. Similarly, clicking on the

Contoso.Fx.Integration.ContextToken hyperlink will navigate the browser to the class definition for the `ContextToken` class.

> **TIP**
>
> You can click on an assembly in the objects pane and quickly add it as a reference to the current project by clicking on the Add to References button, located on the Object Browser's toolbar.

Performance Explorer

The intent of the Performance Explorer window is to bring the world of performance profiling and reporting into the IDE. This is done through the concept of performance sessions; these are the primary vehicle, within Visual Studio, for evaluating and analyzing performance issues in code. The process of *profiling* involves the following actions:

1. Configuring an application for performance analysis

2. Collecting the performance data

3. Viewing/analyzing the collected data

The Performance Explorer provides a point-and-click interface for establishing performance sessions and analyzing the resulting datasets. It has a simple interface with a toolbar and a client area where data is displayed. The Performance Explorer is capable of displaying and managing multiple performance sessions at a time.

Creating a Performance Session

To create performance sessions, you use the Performance Wizard or the New Performance Session buttons (these buttons and others are described in Table 5.11). Clicking the New Performance Session button will create an empty performance session, whereas the Performance Wizard will guide you through setting the various properties of a performance session via a four-page wizard.

TABLE 5.11   Performance Explorer Toolbar Buttons

Icon	Action
	Performance Wizard. Launches the Performance Wizard to create a new performance session.
	New Performance Session. Creates a new, empty performance session.
	Launch. Runs a performance session against the specific target.
	Stop. Stops a currently running performance session.

TABLE 5.11   Performance Explorer Toolbar Buttons

Icon	Action
	Attach/Detach. Attaches or detaches a profiler to/from a currently running process. This action is valid and will appear only when the Sampling method is selected in the Method drop-down.
(n/a)	Method. This drop-down allows you to specify the profiling method (either Sampling or Instrumentation) for a performance session.

The Performance Wizard will collect information concerning

- The type of the assembly you are gathering data about

- The location of the assembly

- The method of performance profiling to implement

> **TIP**
>
> If a solution is currently loaded into Visual Studio, you can select one of its projects as the target of the performance session instead of browsing to an assembly on disk.

Performance profiling is conducted using either sampling or instrumentation. Sampling is used to profile an entire application; instrumentation is used to specifically target an individual module within an application.

After the basic session information has been collected, the wizard will close and the Performance Explorer will show a tree view of the session data. This tree view is organized into two major parent nodes: Targets (the assemblies or modules you identified in the wizard) and Reports (the actual performance data collected against the targets). Figure 5.11 shows a performance session as viewed within the Performance Explorer.

The Performance Explorer can display multiple sessions at one time. The shortcut menu for a session exposes several useful commands including the ability to launch the session, set the session as the current session, and edit the properties for the session.

Configuring a Session

To edit the individual properties of any given session, right-click on the session node (in the example shown in Figure 5.11, this is the node titled AdminConsole.psess), and select the Properties command. The Properties dialog box exposes a variety of basic and advanced properties for the selected session.

General Properties

The General Properties property page enables you to set general instrumentation properties. You can select the profiling method (sampling or instrumentation) and also enable/disable memory profiling during the session.

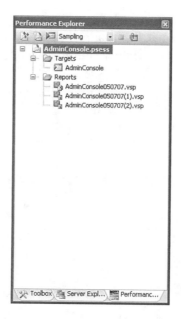

FIGURE 5.11   A performance session in the Performance Explorer.

Two check boxes control the collection of object allocation and lifetime statistics. If the Collect .NET Object Allocation Information box is not checked, the Allocation subreport will not be available for analysis. If the Also Collect .NET Object Lifetime Information box is not checked, the Objects Lifetime subreport will not be available.

You can also control how reports are named and stored:

- **Report Location**—The physical folder used to save the performance report.

- **Report Name**—The name of the report.

- **Automatically Add New Reports**—If checked, will cause new reports to automatically appear under the Reports node within the Performance Explorer.

- **Append Incrementing Number**—If checked, will cause an incrementing number to be appended to the report name and filename to prevent name collisions.

- **Use a Timestamp**—If checked, will use a time stamp basis for the report number.

Launch Properties
The Launch Properties page controls the binaries launched and their order. The available binaries appear in a list. Check those to launch in the performance session and use the up and down arrows to change the launch order.

Sampling Properties
Sampling events are the mechanism by which performance sessions collect data at specified intervals during a target run. Use the Sampling Properties page to change the

sampling event used by the profiler. You can also change the sampling interval (the time distance between sampling events). For example, you could decide to perform a performance sample after every five page faults. You would configure this by selecting Page Fault as the sample event and changing the sampling interval to 5.

If you select the Performance Counter sample event, you can then select from a list of all of the available performance counters. Figure 5.12 shows an example of sampling based on hardware interrupts. Note that the Summary section (toward the bottom of the dialog box) provides a plain-text description of the selected sampling event and interval.

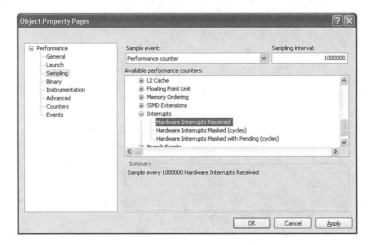

FIGURE 5.12   Configuring sample events for a performance session.

Binary Properties
As part of the instrumentation process, probes are automatically inserted into the session targets and assemblies. The Binary Properties property page will override this behavior and force the profiler to first make a copy of the binaries and place them in a specified directory before changing them.

- **Relocate Instrumented Binaries**—If checked, will cause the target binaries to be copied to a directory before instrumentation. The original binaries will not be touched.

- **Location to Place the Instrumented Binaries**—Specifies a physical location for the instrumented binaries.

Instrumentation Properties
You use the Instrumentation Properties property page to indicate executables or batch files that you want to run prior to or after a session's instrumentation. You could use this, for example, to make certain environment changes to a machine prior to profiling and then to return the machine to its prior state after profiling has completed.

- **Pre-Instrument Command Line**—Command to issue prior to instrumentation; this is typically used to specify a .cmd/.bat or executable to run prior to the session instrumentation.

- **Pre-Instrument Description**—A free-form description of the pre-instrument command.

- **Pre-Instrument Exclude**—Checking this box will cause the session to skip the pre-instrument command that you have specified (but will not remove it from the text box).

- **Post-Instrument Command Line**—Command to issue prior to instrumentation; this is typically used to specify a .cmd/.bat or executable to run prior to the session instrumentation.

- **Post-Instrument Description**—A description of the post-instrument command.

- **Post-Instrument Exclude**—Checking this box will cause the session to skip the pre-instrument command that you have specified (but will not remove it from the text box).

Advanced Properties

The VSInstr command-line tool is used to instrument and run profiling sessions within the IDE. This takes place behind the scenes when you use the Performance Explorer to create and run those sessions. Sometimes, though, you might need to pass command-line options to the VSInstr tool. The Advanced Properties page is used to do just that.

- **Additional instrumentation options**—This text box allows you to specify options for the VSInstr command-line tool.

Counters

CPUs generally implement their own performance counters. By checking the box on the Counters property page, you are asking the profiler to collect data directly from one or more of these counters. To select a counter, expand the available counters tree until the counter of interest is shown, highlight the counter, and then click on the arrow button to transfer it to the list of selected counters. Figure 5.13 shows how to select on-chip performance counters.

> **NOTE**
>
> The counters available are hardware dependent and will vary by chip type and manufacturer.

Events

.NET applications, and the runtime itself, are capable of registering and exposing a variety of event trace providers. The Performance Explorer can collect data from these providers during a performance session (see Figure 5.14).

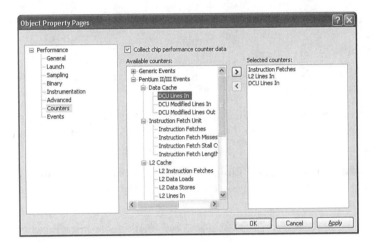

FIGURE 5.13   Selecting on-chip performance counters.

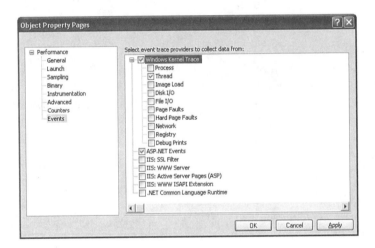

FIGURE 5.14   Collecting data from event trace providers.

Session Targets

Each session can have multiple targets; only one target, however, will be profiled when
the session is run. The "launch" target is denoted with a green "run" triangle. Right-clicking on a target will bring up the shortcut menu for targets. From this menu, you can
remove the target from the list, set the target as the launch target, or edit the properties
of the target. The properties selection will launch an Object Property dialog box in which
you can specify more advanced information that is not collected by the Performance
Wizard.

Launch Properties

Use the Launch property page to indicate executables or batch files that you want to run prior to or after a session's instrumentations.

- **Override Project Settings**—Checking this box enables you to manually specify the target executable and arguments.

- **Executable to Launch**—The executable assembly to launch as the target of the session.

- **Arguments**—Arguments to be passed to the target executable.

- **Working Directory**—The working directory for the target executable.

Instrumentation Properties

The Instrumentation Properties page is identical in form and function to the Instrumentation Properties page in the Session Properties dialog box (discussed previously).

Advanced Properties

This page is identical in form and function to the Advanced Properties page in the Session Properties dialog box (discussed previously).

Reports

The Reports node contains the analysis reports generated as the result of running a profile against a target. Clicking on a report will display its contents in a multitabbed window, similar to a Visual Studio editor window.

Report data can be exported into more consumable formats: Right-click on a report node and select Export Report from the shortcut menu. The Export Report dialog box, shown in Figure 5.15, will launch. When exporting a report, you can you select the desired subreports and the export format (CSV or XML).

Understanding Performance Reports

The reports generated from a performance session will vary in their form and content depending on whether the session was an instrumentation or sample session. As you can see in Figure 5.15, the profile data is organized across several subreports. With the exception of the Summary, each subreport is displayed in a tabular format with columns and rows; the columns represent the various data collection points (such as Number of Calls or Application Exclusive Time). The rows represent the entities specific to the subreport. For the Functions subreport, for example, these will be functions.

FIGURE 5.15   Exporting a report.

TIP

You can sort a specific subreport by clicking on a column heading. This will toggle between an ascending or descending sort on that column's data. This capability is obviously very useful on reports such as the Functions report: You can sort descending by the Number of Calls column to get a great sense of which routings are being used the most within a given application or module.

Table 5.12 provides an exhaustive list of all of the possible data points within each performance report.

TABLE 5.12   Performance Report Columns

Column	Subreport	Description
Application Exclusive Time	Functions, Caller/Callee	Execution time for a function that does not include the time for instrumentation, callees from the function, or transition events.
Application Inclusive Time	Functions, Caller/Callee	Same as the Application Exclusive Time sample, except callee times are included.
AVG Application Exclusive Time	Functions, Caller/Callee, Call Tree	The average Application Exclusive Time for all instances of a function within a given time range.
AVG Application Inclusive Time	Functions, Caller/Callee, Call Tree	The average Application Inclusive Time for all instances of a function within a given time range.

TABLE 5.12   Continued

Column	Subreport	Description
AVG Elapsed Exclusive Time	Functions, Caller/Callee, Call Tree	The average Elapsed Exclusive Time for all instances of a function within a given time range.
AVG Elapsed Inclusive Time	Functions, Caller/Callee, Call Tree	The average Elapsed Inclusive Time for all instances of a function within a given time range.
Class Name	Allocation	The name of the class.
Class Token	Allocation, Objects Lifetime	A metadata identifier for a class.
Elapsed Exclusive Time	Functions, Caller/Callee	Time for execution of a function; includes transition events but does not include time for any called functions.
Elapsed Inclusive Time	Functions, Caller/Callee	Time for execution of a function including transition events and execution time for all called functions.
Exclusive Allocations	Functions, Caller/Callee, Call Tree	Object allocations made in a function; excludes all called functions.
Exclusive Allocations %	Functions	Exclusive Allocations expressed as a percentage of all total allocations.
Exclusive Bytes Allocated	Functions, Caller/Callee, Call Tree	Bytes allocated in a function; excludes bytes allocated in any called function.
Exclusive Bytes %	Functions, Caller/Callee, Call Tree	Exclusive Bytes expressed as a percentage of all total bytes allocated.
Exclusive Samples	Functions, Caller/Callee	All samples made in a function; excludes samples in any called function.
Exclusive Transitions	Caller/Callee, Call Tree	Total number of transition events that occurred in a function, excluding any called functions.
Exclusive Transitions %	Functions, Caller/Callee, Call Tree	Inclusive Transitions expressed as a percentage of all total transition events.
Function Address	Functions, Caller/Callee, Call Tree, Allocation	The memory address of a function in hex.
Function Name	Functions, Caller/Callee, Call Tree, Allocation	The name of the function.
Gen 0 Bytes Collected	Objects Lifetime	Total number of bytes collected by the .NET Garbage Collector for a specific generation.
Gen 1 Bytes Collected	Objects Lifetime	Total number of bytes collected by the .NET Garbage Collector for a specific generation.

5

TABLE 5.12 Continued

Column	Subreport	Description
Gen 2 Bytes Collected	Objects Lifetime	Total number of bytes collected by the .NET Garbage Collector for a specific generation.
Gen 0 Instances Collected	Objects Lifetime	Total number of object instances collected by the .NET Garbage Collector for a specific generation.
Gen 1 Instances Collected	Objects Lifetime	Total number of object instances collected by the .NET Garbage Collector for a specific generation.
Gen 2 Instances Collected	Objects Lifetime	Total number of object instances collected by the .NET Garbage Collector for a specific generation.
Inclusive Allocations	Functions, Caller/Callee, Call Tree	Object allocations made in a function, including all called functions.
Inclusive Allocations %	Functions	Inclusive Allocations expressed as a percentage of all total allocations.
Inclusive Bytes Allocated	Functions, Caller/Callee, Call Tree	Bytes allocated in a function, including all bytes allocated in all called functions.
Inclusive Bytes %	Functions, Caller/Callee, Call Tree	Inclusive Bytes expressed as a percentage of all total bytes allocated.
Inclusive Samples	Functions, Caller/Callee	All samples made in a function, including all samples made in all called functions.
Inclusive Transitions	Caller/Callee, Call Tree	Count of transition events occurring in a function, including all transition events occurring in all called functions.
Inclusive Transitions %	Functions, Caller/Callee, Call Tree	Inclusive Transitions expressed as a percentage of all total transition events.
Instances	Allocation, Objects Lifetime	Total number of instances for a given object.
Instances Alive at End	Objects Lifetime	Total number of instances of a given object still alive (loaded in memory) at the time when the performance session ended.
Large Object Heap Bytes Collected	Objects Lifetime	Total number of large object instance bytes, placed on the heap, that were collected by the .NET Garbage Collector.

TABLE 5.12   Continued

Column	Subreport	Description
Large Object Heap Instances Collected	Objects Lifetime	Total number of large object instances, placed on the heap, that were collected by the .NET Garbage Collector.
Line Number	Functions, Caller/Callee, Call Tree, Allocation	The starting line number of a function (within the context of a source file).
MAX Application Exclusive Time	Functions, Caller/Callee, Call Tree	The largest Application Exclusive Time recorded during the performance session for all instances of a function.
MAX Application Inclusive Time	Functions, Caller/Callee, Call Tree	The largest Application Inclusive Time recorded during the performance session for all instances of a function.
MAX Elapsed Inclusive Time	Functions, Caller/Callee, Call Tree	The largest Elapsed Inclusive Time recorded during the performance session for all instances of a function.
MAX Elapsed Exclusive Time	Functions, Caller/Callee, Call Tree	The largest Elapsed Exclusive Time recorded during the performance session for all instances of a function.
MIN Application Exclusive Time	Functions, Caller/Callee, Call Tree	The smallest Application Exclusive Time recorded during the performance session for all instances of a function.
MIN Application Inclusive Time	Functions, Caller/Callee, Call Tree	The smallest Application Inclusive Time recorded during the performance session for all instances of a function.
MIN Elapsed Inclusive Time	Functions, Caller/Callee, Call Tree	The smallest Application Inclusive Time recorded during the performance session for all instances of a function.
MIN Elapsed Exclusive Time	Functions, Caller/Callee, Call Tree	The smallest Application Exclusive Time recorded during the performance session for all instances of a function.
Module Identifier	Functions, Caller/Callee, Call Tree	Within a process, a sequential number assigned to modules as they are loaded.
Module Name	Functions, Caller/Callee, Call Tree, Allocation	The name of the module.
Module Path	Functions, Caller/Callee, Call Tree, Allocation	Physical path to the module.
Number of Calls	Functions, Caller/Callee, Call Tree	Number of calls made to a function.

5

TABLE 5.12   Continued

Column	Subreport	Description
Parent Function Address	Call Tree	Address in memory of the caller function (in hex).
Percentage of Calls	Functions, Caller/Callee, Call Tree	Number of calls made to a function as a percentage of all calls made to all functions.
Process ID	Functions, Caller/Callee, Call Tree, Allocation, Objects Lifetime	Numeric ID for a given process.
Process Name	Functions, Caller/Callee, Call Tree, Allocation, Objects Lifetime	The name of the process.
Root Application Exclusive Time	Caller/Callee	The Application Exclusive Time for the root function of the selected function.
Root Application Inclusive Time	Caller/Callee	The Application Inclusive Time for the root function of the selected function.
Root Elapsed Exclusive Time	Caller/Callee	The Elapsed Exclusive Time for the root function of the selected function.
Root Elapsed Inclusive Time	Caller/Callee	The Elapsed Inclusive Time for the root function of the selected function.
Root Node Recursive	Functions, Caller/Callee, Call Tree	For a given function, indicates if it was called directly or indirectly in the recursive chain.
Source File Name	Functions, Caller/Callee, Call Tree, Allocation	Source file that contains the given function.
Time Exclusive CAP Overhead	Functions, Caller/Callee, Call Tree	The total time for all probes within the exclusive time of the function that were called by the parent function.
Time Inclusive CAP Overhead	Functions, Caller/Callee, Call Tree	The total time for all probes within the inclusive time of the function that were called by the parent function.
Total Bytes Allocated	Allocation, Objects Lifetime	For a given data type or class instance, total number of bytes allocated.
Type	Caller/Callee, Allocation	A number indicating caller/callee relationship: 0—Root function 1—Calling function 2—Called function
Unique ID	Functions, Caller/Callee, Call Tree	A number, in hex, used to identify a function.

TABLE 5.12   Continued

Column	Subreport	Description
Unique Process ID	Functions, Caller/Callee, Call Tree, Allocation, Objects Lifetime	A sequential number (unsigned integer) assigned to a process in order of its activation.
% Application Exclusive Time	Functions, Caller/Callee, Call Tree	Application Exclusive Time for a given function expressed as a percentage of the sum of all function application exclusive times.
% Application Inclusive Time	Functions, Caller/Callee, Call Tree	Application Inclusive Time for a given function expressed as a percentage of the sum of all function application inclusive times.
% Elapsed Exclusive Time	Functions, Caller/Callee, Call Tree	Elapsed Exclusive Time for a given function expressed as a percentage of the sum of all function elapsed exclusive times.
% Elapsed Inclusive Time	Functions, Caller/Callee, Call Tree	Elapsed Inclusive Time for a given function expressed as a percentage of the sum of all function elapsed inclusive times.
% of Total Bytes	Allocation, Objects Lifetime	A measure of the Total Bytes Allocated divided by the total bytes allocated for all data types or class instances during the performance session.
% Time Exclusive CAP Overhead	Functions, Caller/Callee, Call Tree	The Time Exclusive CAP Overhead expressed as a percentage of the sum of all exclusive CAP overhead timings.
% Time Inclusive CAP Overhead	Functions, Caller/Callee, Call Tree	The Time Inclusive CAP Overhead expressed as a percentage of the sum of all inclusive CAP overhead timings.

There are a total of six subreports (also referred to as views) within a performance report. Each subreport has a small set of data points displayed by default. You can add or remove data points (effectively, adding or removing columns in the subreport) by right-clicking in the report (or on any of the column headers) and selecting Add/Remove Columns. A list of all valid data points for the current subreport will display, enabling you to simply check the ones you want to view. Refer to Table 5.12.

Summary Subreport

The Summary subreport provides a summary of function statistics such as most-called functions, longest-running functions, and so on. Double-clicking on one of the listed functions will jump immediately to the function data in the Functions subreport (see the following section).

This tab is most useful in gaining an at-a-glance feel for performance hot spots within the profiled application or module.

Functions Subreport

The Functions subreport provides an exhaustive list of all functions that were called during the profile session. Each function is presented with timing data and, in the case of an instrumentation session, the number of calls made into that function.

Caller/Callee Subreport

The Caller/Callee tab presents caller/callee information in three separate panes. The middle pane will contain a selected, called function. Functions that appear in the top pane are functions that called the selected function (the caller function), and functions that appear in the bottom pane are functions that were called by the target function (the callee function).

This view is fully dynamic: Clicking on any of the functions that appear in any of the three panes will cause that function to be selected and thus placed in the middle pane, with the caller and callee panes changing to reflect the new selected function.

Call Tree Subreport

The Call Tree view shows you a trace of the call tree generated during the performance session. Each function call is represented within the call tree, and you can expand or collapse lists of called functions within a given root function.

You can reposition any calling function into the root node by using the right-click shortcut menu and selecting Set Root. You can redisplay the true root node by selecting Reset Root from the shortcut menu.

This view is particularly useful to gain insight into inclusive/exclusive function timings.

Allocation Subreport

The Allocation subreport is a list of the types/objects allocated during the performance session. Each type is displayed along with the function or functions responsible for its allocation.

The default columns within this view can be used to identify any types or function areas that are memory intensive.

Objects Lifetime Subreport

The Objects Lifetime view is similar to the Allocation view but instead focuses on the timed lifetime of all types/objects allocated during the session. Each class is represented as a row in the subreport.

> **NOTE**
>
> Although a large number of data points are useful when analyzing performance, two stand out as great trip-wires for finding code that isn't behaving as expected: Number of Calls and Elapsed Exclusive Time. If a function is looping more than expected or is taking longer to execute than expected, these two data points (both present by default on the Functions view) should immediately help you to identify those routines.

Macro Explorer

Macros are a series of consolidated commands that can be launched as one unit, typically through a key combination. As such, they are a huge productivity booster. You might use a macro, for instance, to automatically insert comments into your code, rearrange the windows within the IDE, or report on code statistics. Because macros can be wired into the extensibility object model, there are a host of functions accessible to you via macros.

The Macro Explorer, shown in Figure 5.16, is a tree-view window that exposes the list of macros within a solution.

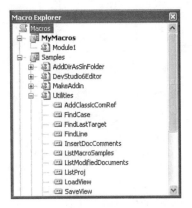

FIGURE 5.16   The Macro Explorer.

The Macros Root Node

The Macros root node has shortcut menu items for loading existing macro projects, creating a new macro project, or launching the Macros IDE. The Macros IDE is covered in depth in Chapter 11, "Writing Macros, Add-ins, and Wizards." Underneath the Macros root node, child nodes are organized hierarchically in the following fashion: projects → modules → macros.

Projects

A macro *project* is a logical and physical container for macros that can span a variety of different functions and intents. The projects themselves are physically stored as a

.vsmacros file. By default, macro projects reside within a separate VsMacros subdirectory within the Visual Studio projects directory.

At the projects level, you can

- Rename a project

- Create a new module within a project

- Unload a project (for example, unload it from the Macro Explorer window)

- Set the active "recording" project

If the Set as Recording Project option is selected, macros will be recorded into the selected project.

Modules

A *module* is a logical grouping of macros, typically used to store related macros. You might, for instance, create a module called FileUtilities to store macros designed to help with file management. With the module shortcut menu, you can

- Create a new macro

- Edit the module's macro code in the Macros IDE

- Rename the module

- Delete the module

Macro

The *macro* is analogous to a function. Right-clicking on the macro enables you to

- Run the macro

- Edit the macro within the Macros IDE

- Rename the macro

- Delete the macro

Document Outline

The Document Outline window exposes a hierarchical view of elements residing on a Windows form or web form. This window is a fantastic tool for "reparenting" form items or changing the z-order of a control within its parent. In addition, it assists with understanding the exact logical structure of a form that may have a lot happening on it from a visual perspective.

Figures 5.17 and 5.18 show the Document Outline windows for a simple web form and a slightly more complicated Windows form.

FIGURE 5.17   A web form.

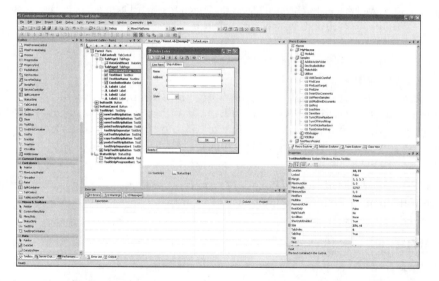

FIGURE 5.18   A Windows form.

The Document Outline toolbar allows you to control the display of the types within the tree view and also facilitates reordering and repositioning elements within the outline. Table 5.13 shows the toolbar commands available in the Document Outline window.

TABLE 5.13   Document Outline Toolbar Commands

Icon	Description
	Type Name Display Style. This drop-down button allows you to control how type names are displayed in the tree-view: <ul><li>None—No type names are displayed.</li><li>Short—The local, unqualified type name is displayed.</li><li>Long—The fully qualified type name is displayed.</li></ul>
	Expand All. Causes all of the parent nodes to expand.
	Collapse All. Causes all of the parent nodes to collapse.
	Move Down in Container. Moves the currently selected item down one place within its order in the current container.
	Move Up in Container. Moves the currently selected item up one place within its order in the current container.
	Move Out of Current Container. Moves the currently selected item out of its current container and places it in the next, higher container (or within the root level if no container exists).
	Move into Next Container. Moves the currently selected item out of its current container (or root level) and into the next container.

Editing Elements

The Document Outline makes it easy to instantly jump from the hierarchical element view directly to the underlying code for an item. If an item is currently being edited in the designer/code window, it will be highlighted within the outline tree. Conversely, selecting an item within the outline view will cause the item to be selected/highlighted within the designer/code window.

Besides the toolbar commands in Table 5.13, you can use drag-and-drop actions within the tree view to move elements around in the outline.

Summary

In this chapter, we have seen that browsers and explorers are Visual Studio windows that typically provide a hierarchical view of their content. They tend to share common interface elements (tree views, toolbars, and elements), and they are, in effect, the primary means to visualize and interact with project elements within the IDE.

Browsers and explorers provide simple point-and-click interfaces for

- Visualizing and organizing your solutions and projects on a file-by-file basis
- Visualizing and organizing your projects on a type-by-type, class-by-class basis
- Querying and interacting with server resources such as databases, performance counters, and message queues

- Browsing through type libraries

- Instrumenting assemblies and analyzing performance data

Although certain browsers/explorers touch underlying concepts that are fairly deep and complicated (performance profiling for instance), they are all geared toward a common goal: extending the reach of the IDE as a rapid application development tool for tasks beyond simple code file editing.

5

CHAPTER 6

Introducing the Editors and Designers

IN THIS CHAPTER

- The Basics
- Coding with the Code Editor
- Creating and Editing XML Documents and Schema
- Developing Windows Forms Applications
- Developing Web Forms
- Authoring Components and Controls

Although Visual Studio provides an impressive array of functionality for nearly all areas of the development process, its editors and designers are the real heart of the IDE. They are the bread-and-butter tools of the programmer: They enable you to write code, edit resources, design forms, and construct schemas. And, of course, each of these tools has key features designed to boost your productivity and the quality of your output.

This chapter is squarely focused on using these editors and designers to create solutions within the IDE.

The Basics

Broadly speaking, a Visual Studio editor is a text editor (think word processor) that allows you to write specific output efficiently. A designer is a visual editor, allowing you to work with visual concepts directly instead of text. Many document types are supported by both designers and editors: You can build a form, for instance, by using the drag-and-drop convenience of the Windows Forms designer or by hand-crafting the code within a text editor; or you can build an XML file using the same mechanisms.

The Visual Studio text editor provides the core text-editing functionality for all of the editors. This functionality is then inherited and added upon to create editors specific for a given document type. Thus, you have a code editor for source code files, XML editor for markup, a CSS editor for style sheets, and so on.

Likewise, designers will manifest themselves in ways specific to their role. The HTML designer is part text editor and part graphical tool, and the Windows and web forms designers are superb WYSIWYG form builders.

The Text Editor

There are a few text-editing features that we all take for granted: selecting parts of an existing body of text, inserting text into a document, copying and pasting text, and so on. As you would expect, the text editor window supports all of these features in a way that will be familiar to anyone who has used a Windows-based word processor.

You select text, for instance, by using the following familiar actions:

1. Place the cursor at the start of the text you want to select.

2. While holding down the left mouse button, sweep the mouse to the end of the text you want selected.

3. Release the left mouse button.

In addition to this "standard" selection method, the Visual Studio text editor also supports "column mode" selection. Instead of your selecting text in a linear fashion from left to right, line-by-line, column mode instead allows you to drag a selection rectangle across a text field. Any text character caught within the selection rectangle will be part of the selected text. This is called *column mode* because it allows you to create a selection area that captures columns of text characters instead of just lines. The procedure is largely the same:

1. Place the cursor at the start of the text you want to select.

2. While holding down the Alt key *and* the left mouse button, expand the bounds of the selection rectangle until it includes the desired text.

3. Release the left mouse button and Alt key.

After you've selected text, you can copy, cut, or drag it to a new location within the text editor. As with text selection, the commands for cutting, copying, and pasting text remain unchanged from their basic, standard implementation in other Windows applications: You first select text and then cut or copy it using the Edit menu, toolbar, or the text editor's shortcut menu.

By dragging a text selection, you can reposition it within the current text editor; place it in another, previously opened text editor window; or even drag the selection into the command or watch windows.

Line Wrapping and Virtual Space

The default behavior of the text editor is not to automatically wrap any text for you. In other words, as you type, your text or code will simply keep trailing on to the right of the editor. If you exceed the bounds of the currently viewable area, the editor window will simply scroll to the right to allow you to continue typing. However, the text editor window can behave more like a word processor where the document content is typically constrained horizontally to its virtual sheet of paper.

TIP

With word wrapping turned on, Visual Studio will automatically wrap your text onto the next line. You can also have the IDE place a visual glyph, which indicates that a wrap has taken place. Both of these options are controlled on the Options dialog box, under the TextEditor, All Languages, General page (shown in Figure 6.1).

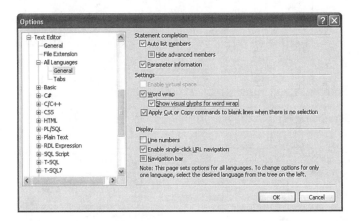

FIGURE 6.1   Editor Options dialog box.

If you override the default behavior, turn wrapping on, and then type a line of code that exceeds the editor's width, you can see that the editor window (see Figure 6.2) automatically wraps the source to fit within the boundaries of the window and provides an icon to the far right of the editor to indicate that a wrap has taken place. Word wrapping is useful for keeping all of your code in plain sight (without the need for scrolling horizontally).

The other option on the Text Editor Options dialog box, Enable Virtual Space, is a mutually exclusive feature to word wrapping. That is, you can enable virtual space or word wrapping, but not both. Virtual Space refers to the capability to type text anywhere within the editor window without entering a bunch of spaces or tabs in the text area. This feature is useful in situations in which you want to place, for example, a code comment to the right of a few lines of code. Instead of tabbing each code comment over (or padding spaces before them) to get them to indent and line up nicely, you can simply place the cursor at the exact column within the text editor where you want your comments to appear. See Figure 6.3 for an example; the code comments in the screenshot were not preceded by any spaces or tabs. They were simply typed directly into their current positions.

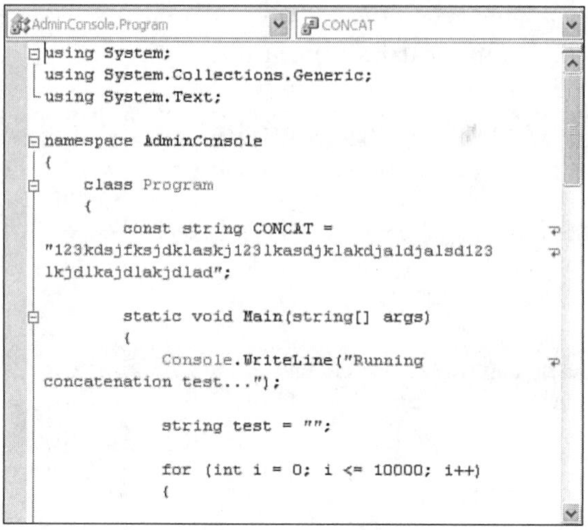

FIGURE 6.2   Word wrapping in the editor.

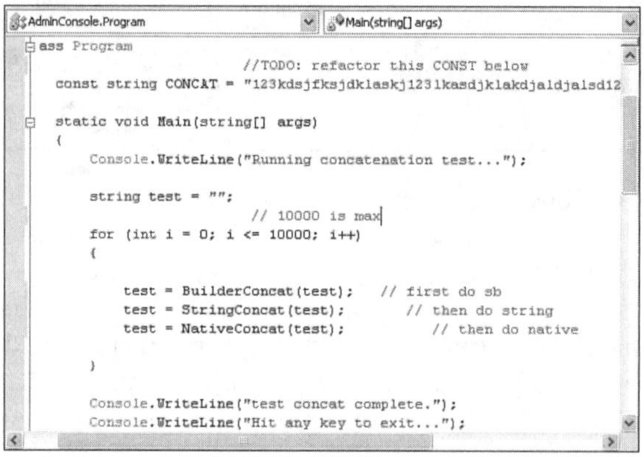

FIGURE 6.3   Virtual spacing in the editor window.

Visual Studio Designers

Designers are much more visual in nature than the text editors within Visual Studio; they provide a graphical perspective of a particular solution artifact. Thus, a form will appear within a designer just as it would to the end user: as visual constructs made up of buttons, borders, menus, and frames. The code to implement the items shown in a designer is actually written by Visual Studio itself.

Like the various editors, the designers are all similar in form and function. They occupy space within the tabbed documents area of the IDE (just as the editors do). They may take on different behaviors depending on their target use. The Windows Forms designer and the component designer both appear nearly the same, but there are subtle differences in their usage.

Coding with the Code Editor

Writing code and creating other syntax-based files are really all about typing text. The text editor window is the Visual Studio tool directly mapped to the task of creating source code text files. It is the keystone of development inside the IDE. It supports text entry and basic text operations such as selecting text regions, dragging and dropping text fragments, and setting tab stops. With basic text features alone, the editor would be sufficient to code with. However, the features layered on top for debugging, code formatting, code guidance, and customization really make this tool shine.

As we mentioned previously, the text editor actually has a few different personalities within the IDE. The code editor is designed to support creating and editing source code files, the XML editor is targeted at XML files, and the CSS editor is targeted at CSS files. Although there may be subtle differences with the way that code or markup is displayed in these windows, they all share the user interface and the same set of editing functionality.

> **TIP**
>
> Each editor type is fully customizable. Just fire up the Options dialog box (by choosing Tools, Options) and locate the Text Editor node. Under this node are separate pages that allow customization of each editor type.

Opening an Editor

There are two ways to launch a text editor (or any other editor in the IDE for that matter). The first way involves using the Solution Explorer: Select an existing code file, text file, or other type file and double-click on the file. If it is a code file, you can also right-click on it and select View Code. The file content will be loaded into a new editor window.

The second way to launch an editor window is to choose File, New, File. This will launch the New File dialog box. Selecting a code template from this dialog box will launch a code editor prefilled with the initial code stubs relevant to the template selected.

> **TIP**
>
> The text editor windows live as tabbed windows front-and-center within the IDE. If multiple code editors are open, they will each be accessible by their tab. If a lot of editors are open at one time, finding the exact window you are looking for by cycling through the tabs may be cumbersome. There are two fast ways for quickly locating and selecting a code editor window. First, you can use Solution Explorer. Double-clicking on the code file again within the Solution Explorer will select and display the associated code editor window. Second, you can use the Window menu. Each open code editor window will be shown by name in the windows list under the Window menu.

Writing Code in the Code Editor

Because the code editor's primary purpose is "word processing" for source code, let's first look at writing the simplest of routines—a "Hello, World" function—from the ground up using the code editor.

Figure 6.4 shows a code editor with an initial stubbed-out console file. This was produced by creating a new Visual C# Console project using the Solution Explorer. Double-clicking on the Program.cs file within that new project displays the source code for this console application.

FIGURE 6.4   Initial template console code.

As you can see, Visual Studio, as a result of the template used for creating the project, has already filled in some code:

```
using System;
using System.Collections.Generic;
using System.Text;

namespace HelloWorld
{
    class Program
    {
        static void Main(string[] args)
        {
        }
    }
}
```

To demonstrate the code editor in action, we'll examine a "Hello, World!" application. In this case, you will create a console application that outputs the "Hello, World!" string to the console window.

Within the Main routine, add the following:

```
Console.WriteLine("Hello, World!");
```

To begin writing the code, you simply place your cursor in the window by clicking within the Main routine's braces, press Enter to get some space for the new line of code, and type the Console.WriteLine syntax.

These and other productivity enhancers are discussed at great length in the next chapter. Here, we will focus on the basics of editing and writing code in the editor window.

Now that you have seen the code editor in action (albeit for a very simple example), you're ready to dig more into the constituent components of the editor window.

Anatomy of the Code Editor Window

Editor windows, as you have seen, live as tabbed windows within the IDE and are typically front-and-center visually in terms of windows layout. As you can see with the code editor window in Figure 6.5, each text editor window consists of three primary regions: a code pane, a selection margin, and an indicator margin. There are also both horizontal and vertical scrollbars for navigating around the displayed file.

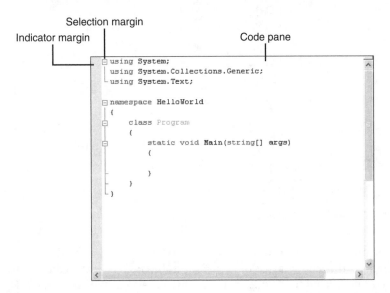

FIGURE 6.5   The components of the code editor window.

These regions, and their functionality, remain the same for all editor types within the IDE.

The code editor adds an additional set of UI elements that are not present with the other editors: Two drop-down boxes at the top of the code editor window enable you to quickly navigate through source code by selecting a type in the left drop-down and then selecting a specific type member (property, field, function, and so on) in the right drop-down (these drop-downs are called *class* and *method name*, respectively, in Visual Basic). This will jog the current cursor location directly to the indicated type.

NOTE

The type drop-down displays only those types that are declared in the file currently displayed in the editor; it won't display a list that is global to the entire solution, project, or even namespace. Likewise, the type member drop-down displays only members for the selected type.

The Code Pane

The code pane is the place where the document (source code, XML, and so on) is displayed and edited. This region provides basic text-editing functionality, in addition to the more advanced productivity features of the editor, such as IntelliSense.

Right-clicking within the code pane provides a shortcut menu (see Figure 6.6) that includes standard cut, copy, and paste verbs, along with an assortment of other handy editing actions.

FIGURE 6.6   Code editor shortcut menu.

The Indicator Margin

The indicator margin is the slim, gray-colored margin to the far left of the editor. This margin area is used to mark a line of code that contains a breakpoint or bookmark. Figure 6.7 shows the "Hello, World" example with a bookmark placed on the Main routine and a breakpoint placed on the Console.WriteLine command.

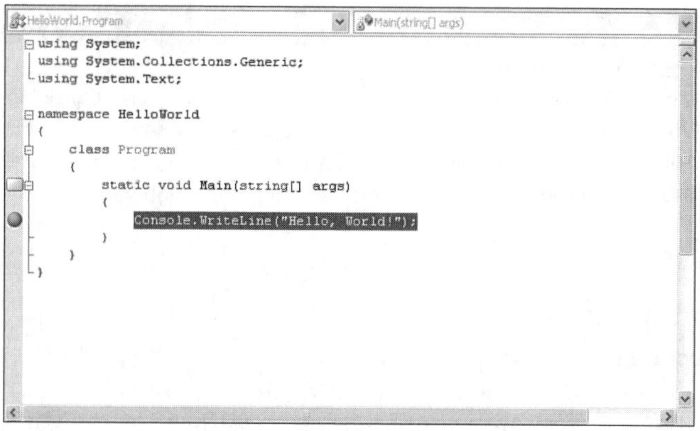

FIGURE 6.7 Bookmarks and breakpoints.

Clicking within the indicator margin will toggle a breakpoint on or off for the line of code you have selected (we cover more on the topic of breakpoints later in this chapter and in Chapter 9, "Debugging with Visual Studio 2005").

The Selection Margin

The selection margin is a narrow region between the indicator margin and the editing area of the code pane. It provides

- The ability to select an entire line of text by clicking within the selection margin.

- A visual indication—via colored indicator bars—of those lines of code that have changed during the current editing session.

- Line numbers if this option has been turned on. See the following section where we discuss customizing the text editor's behavior.

You can clearly see the "changed text" indicator and line numbers in action in Figure 6.8.

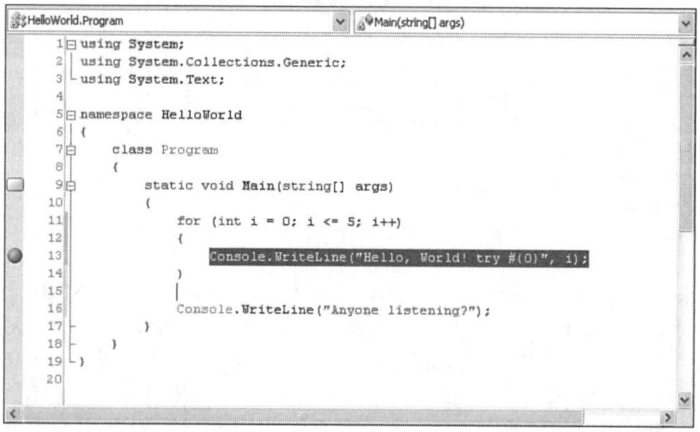

FIGURE 6.8 Changed text indicators.

TIP

Visual Studio provides a dedicated toolbar for the text editor. You can view this toolbar by selecting View, Toolbars, Text Editor. It exposes buttons for the Member List, Quick Info, Parameter
List, and Word Completion IntelliSense features, in addition to indenting, commenting, and
bookmark navigation buttons. The navigation buttons are arguably the most useful here because
they provide easily accessible forward and back navigation through your code.

Code Navigation Tools

As the lines of code in any given project increase, the concept of effectively navigating
through the code base—that is, quickly and easily finding lines of interest among the
potentially thousands or even millions of lines of code—becomes an issue.

The text editor comes equipped with several tools to help you mark lines of code, search
and replace text across source files, and, in general, maintain your situational awareness
from within a long code listing.

Line Numbering

As we mentioned in the discussion of the text editor's selection margin, line numbering
can be enabled for any given document loaded into an editor. This option is controlled in
the Options dialog box within the Text Editor, All Languages, General page, or selectively
under the individual languages and their General page.

By themselves, line numbers would be fairly useless. The capability to immediately jump
to a line of code completes the equation and provides some real benefit from a navigation
perspective. While within a text editor, press the Ctrl+G key combination to jump to a
line of code. This triggers the Go To Line dialog box (see Figure 6.9), which provides a
text box for specifying the line number to jump to and even indicates the valid "scope"
for the jump by providing a line number range for the current document. Entering a valid
line number here will move the current cursor position to the start of that line.

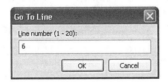

FIGURE 6.9   Jumping to a line.

Bookmarks

Bookmarks tackle the problem of navigating through large code files. By placing a bookmark on a line of code, you can instantly navigate back to that line of code at any time.
When dealing with a series of bookmarks, you can jump back and forth through the
bookmarked lines of code. This turns out to be a surprisingly useful feature. If you are a
developer who is dealing with a large base of source code, there will inevitably be points

of interest within the source code that you want to view in the editor. Recall that the text editor window does provide a means of navigating via type and member drop-downs; these are not, however, the best tools for the job when your "line of interest" may be an arbitrary statement buried deep within a million lines of code.

Bookmarks are visually rendered in the indicator margin of the text editor (refer to Figure 6.8; a bookmark appears on line 9).

To add a bookmark or navigate through your bookmarks, you use either the text editor toolbar or the Bookmarks window.

You can view the Bookmarks window, shown in Figure 6.10, by choosing View, Other Windows, Bookmarks Window. You will notice that this window provides a toolbar for bookmark actions and provides a list of all available bookmarks, along with their actual physical location (filename and line number within that file).

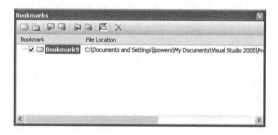

FIGURE 6.10   The Bookmarks window.

To toggle a bookmark for a given line of code, you first place your cursor on the desired line within the text editor and then click on the Toggle bookmark button. The same process is used to toggle the bookmark off. Using the forward and back buttons within the bookmarks window will jump the text editor's cursor location back and forth through all available bookmarks.

TIP

Use the Bookmarks window to navigate through code across projects. You are not limited to bookmarks placed within a single code file; they can, in fact, be in *any* loaded code file. The list of bookmarks in this window is also a useful mechanism for quickly toggling a bookmark on or off (via the check box next to the bookmark) and for assigning a meaningful name to a bookmark. Right-clicking on a bookmark will allow you to rename it something more meaningful than "Bookmark7."

Bookmark Folders   One interesting feature with the Bookmarks window is the capability to create a bookmark folder. This is a logical organizational bucket for related bookmarks. For instance, you may want to place bookmarks for a specific math algorithm under a folder called MathFuncs. To do this, you would first create a folder by using the New Folder button the toolbar. You can rename the folder to whatever makes sense for your particular scenario. Then you can create a bookmark and drag and drop it into the folder.

See Figure 6.11 for a look at a populated Bookmarks window. Note that two folders are in use, in addition to bookmarks being shown for a variety of different source code files.

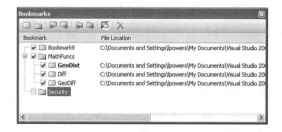

FIGURE 6.11   The Bookmarks window with folders.

Searching Documents

The text editor window provides an extensive search-and-replace capability. Three primary methods of searching are supported: Quick Find (ideal for finding text fragments within the current document or set of open documents), Search In Files (ideal for finding text in a file residing anywhere with a folder structure), and Find Symbol (ideal for searching on objects or members by name). All of these search mechanisms are triggered through the Find and Replace window; a drop-down button on the Find and Replace window will control the mode of the window, which directly maps to the three search methods just itemized.

This same window is used to perform text substitution. This Replace functionality has two different modes that equate to the first two search modes. Thus, you have Quick Replace, which functions in a similar fashion to Quick Find, and Replace In Files, which functions in a similar fashion to Search In Files.

Let's take a closer look at each of these search-and-replace modes individually.

Quick Find/Quick Replace

Figure 6.12 illustrates the Find and Replace window in Quick Find mode. You have three pieces of information to fill in here: You need to indicate what you are searching for, what you want to search in, and you can also select from different options to fine-tune your search parameters.

The Find What drop-down, obviously, specifies the string to search for. This drop-down will hold the last 20 strings used in a Find operation, making it easy to reuse a previous search: Just select it from the list.

The Look In drop-down sets the scope of the search. For Quick Find searches, you have a few different options to choose from:

- **Current Document**—This option indicates the currently active document within the text editor.

- **Selection**—If a portion of a document is selected within a text editor, this option will limit the search to only the selected text.

- **All Open Documents**—The search will be performed across any open documents.

- **Current Type**—If the cursor is currently positioned within an object or namespace code block, the "current type" option will allow you to search within that code block. Note that this option will use the name of the code block itself and won't display as "current type." Consider this example: A code editor window is open, and the cursor is placed within the definition for a class called `MessageBus`, within the `Contoso.Fx.Integration` namespace. The Look In drop-down will display an option called `Contoso.Fx.Integration.MessageBus` to limit the scope of the search to just this class. If the cursor is not positioned within a code block, this option will simply not display.

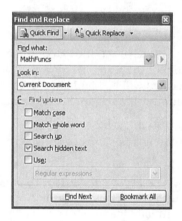

FIGURE 6.12   Quick Find mode.

Fine-Tuning Your Search   Below the Look In control is a series of check boxes for fine-tuning the search. The effects these options have on your search are self-explanatory:

- Match Case will cause the search to be executed against the exact case you used in the Find What drop-down.

- Match Whole Word will force the search to match only on the entire string as entered in the Find What drop-down.

- Search Up causes the search to move from bottom to top in a document (as opposed to the default top-to-bottom search).

- Search Hidden Text (selected by default) will search code regions that are currently not visible (in other words, collapsed code regions, a hidden outline region, design time metadata, and so on).

- Use Wildcards/Use Regular Expressions will change how the search engine performs matching on the Find What string. A standard search does a character match for the target string. You can also, however, use wildcard conventions (such as `Message*` to find any string starting with the text `Message`) or a full-blown regular expression to perform even more intricate searches. You would enter a regular expression as the Find What string.

TIP

If you elect to use wildcards or regular expressions for your search, there is a tool that can help you to write the correct syntax for the search phrase. If the Use check box is selected, a small button located directly to the right of the Find What drop-down will become enabled. This button will display the expression builder: a fly-out menu of expression syntax choices along with their descriptions. The context of this menu will change depending on whether you have indicated wildcard or regular expressions.

Finding Search Results   After you have specified all of the criteria for your search, the Find Next button at the bottom of the search window will launch the search. Any matches within the scope specified will be highlighted for you within the document. Clicking on the Find Next button will move to the next match until there are no more matches found.

You also have the option of placing a bookmark against any matches. Just click the Bookmark All button.

Replacing Text   You set the Quick Replace mode (see Figure 6.13) by clicking on the rightmost of the two mode buttons (in the same fashion that you set Quick Find mode). The Quick Replace process is virtually identical to Quick Find; a single additional field, used to specify the replacement text, is added to the dialog box. The Find What, Look In, and Find Options fields all remain the same in form and function.

Two buttons are added to the dialog box to initiate the string replacement: Replace, which will replace the first instance found with the Replace With text, and Replace All, which will replace all instances found with the Replace With text. Note that any replacements made can always be undone via the Undo command under the Edit menu. These two buttons take the place of the Bookmark All button, which is not available in this mode.

NOTE

Although a complete discussion of regular expressions is outside the scope of this book, you should note that the Replace With box is capable of supporting tagged expressions. For more information on how you might use this to your advantage during replace operations, consult a regular expression reference manual and look at the MSDN Regular Expressions help topic for Visual Studio.

FIGURE 6.13   Quick Replace mode.

Find In Files/Replace In Files

Figure 6.14 depicts the Find and Replace dialog box in Find In Files mode. The operation of this mode is similar to Quick Find, with a few minor differences. You still have to specify the "what" and the "where" components of the search. And you still can fine-tune your search, although you lose the Search Up and Search Hidden options because they don't make sense for a file-based search. The major differences with this mode are (1) the available search scopes you can specify in the Look In drop-down and (2) the way search results are displayed. Let's look at these two differences in turn.

The search scope is notable in that it allows you to select the entire solution as your search target (in addition to the scopes supported for Quick Find). In addition, notice that you now have a Choose Search Folders button located just to the right of the Look In drop-down.

Building Search Folder Sets   Clicking the Search Folders button will launch a dialog box; this dialog box allows you to build up a set of directories as the scope of the search. You can name this folder set and even set the search order for the directories. Figure 6.15 captures this dialog box as a search set called ClassLibCode is built. You can see that two directories have been added to the set and that you can add more by simply browsing to the folder with the Available Folders control and adding them to the Selected Folders list.

The Find Results Window   With Quick Find, the search results are simply highlighted (or bookmarked) right within the text editor window. The Find In Files mode will display its search results in a separate, dedicated Find Results window (see Figure 6.16). You can redirect the output to one of two results windows by selecting either the Find Results 1 Window or Find Results 2 Window option at the bottom of the search dialog box. These windows are identical; two options provided here allow you to keep different search results separate and avoid the confusion that the co-mingling of matches would cause if you were constrained to just one output window.

FIGURE 6.14   Find In Files mode.

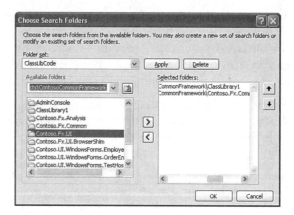

FIGURE 6.15   Building a Search Folder set.

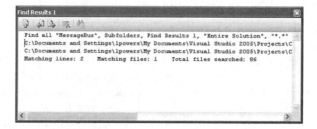

FIGURE 6.16   The Find Results window.

In Figure 6.16 you see the results of a simple search conducted across all of the files in a solution. The interior of the Find Results window provides the following information:

- A description of the search performed (for example, `Find all "MessageBus"`, `Subfolders, Find Results 1, "Entire Solution"`).

- The matches returned from the search. Match information includes the file path and name, the line number within the file, and a verbatim repeat of the exact line of code containing the match.

- A summary of the find results including the number of matching lines of code, the number of files containing matches, and the total number of files searched.

Double-clicking on one of the results lines in the window will jog the cursor location directly to the matching line within the editor. Note that this window has a toolbar. From left to right, the buttons on this toolbar allow you to

- Jump to the matched line of code within the text editor. (First, place your cursor on the match inside the Find Results window and then click on the Go to the Location of the Current Line button.)

- Move back and forth through the list of matches. Each matched item will be high-lighted in the Find Results window and in the Text Editor window.

- Clear the Find Results window.

- Cancel any ongoing searches.

Replacing In Files   The Replace In Files mode builds from the Find in Files mode by providing all of the same functionality and adding back the ability to cycle through matching results in the Text Editor window. Replace, Replace All, and Skip File buttons also make an appearance in this mode (see Figure 6.17).

We've already covered the Replace and Replace All functions. Each file that matches the search phrase will be opened in a separate text editor window, and the replacements will be made directly in that window. If performing a Replace All, the replacements will be made and then saved directly into the containing file. You also have the option, via the Keep Modified Files Open after Replace All check box, to have Visual Studio keep any files touched open inside their respective text editors. This allows you to selectively save or discard the replacements as you see fit.

You can elect to skip files during the search-and-replace process by using the Skip File button. This button is available only if more than one file has been selected as part of the search scope. Clicking this button tells the search engine to skip the current file being processed and continue with the next in-scope file.

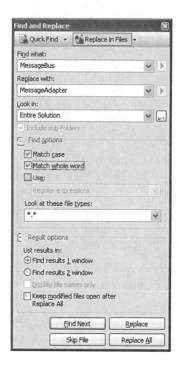

FIGURE 6.17   Replace In Files mode.

Find Symbol

The last search mode supported by the Find and Replace dialog box is called Find Symbol. It is used to search out lines of code in which a symbol is defined, referenced, or used. This tighter search scope makes this the preferred mechanism for, say, finding all places where a class called CustomAnalyzer is referenced. You could use the other Find modes to locate this text, but the Find Symbol algorithm's tighter scope is much more relevant to this kind of search because it will not rove over any non-symbol text in the document. In addition, the Find Symbol function uses reflection and the compiler to find symbol references; this is not a simple text search with a different scope.

The Find Symbol search also has two other distinguishing characteristics over the normal Find/Replace. It is able to search external components even in the absence of source code. As an example, you can opt to select .NET Framework in the Look In drop-down. Figure 6.18 shows the results of searching for the String symbol in the framework itself.

The second difference with Find Symbol is the capability to immediately jump to a referenced object's definition or browse its definition using the object browser. You can access both of these functions, Go To Definition and Browse Definition, by right-clicking on any of the matches displayed in the results window.

FIGURE 6.18   Find Symbol Results window.

> **NOTE**
>
> If you are searching for a symbol within a library where you do not have access to the source code, the option to view the symbol's definition in source (for example, Go To Definition) will obviously not be available. However, you can still leverage the Browse Definition function to instantly pull the definition open in the object browser. It turns out that this is a great way to understand and explore libraries not of your own creation.

Incremental Search

Incremental Search functions without the aid of a dialog box. With a text editor open, select Edit, Advanced, Incremental Search (or press Ctrl+I). While Incremental Search is active, you will see a visual pointer cue composed of binoculars and a down arrow. If you start typing a search string, character-by-character, the first match found will be highlighted within the text editor window itself. With each successive character, the search string is altered and the search itself is re-executed. The current search string is displayed on the Visual Studio status bar. Figure 6.19 illustrates an Incremental Search in progress; the characters *M E S S A* have been entered, and you can see the first match flagged within the text editor.

By default, the search function works from the top of the document to the bottom, and from left to right. You can reverse the direction of the search by using the Ctrl+Shift+I key combination.

To jump to the next match within the document, use the Ctrl+I key combination.

Clicking anywhere within the document or pressing the Esc key will cancel the incremental search.

> **NOTE**
>
> Incremental searches are always performed in a manner that is not case sensitive and will always match on substrings.

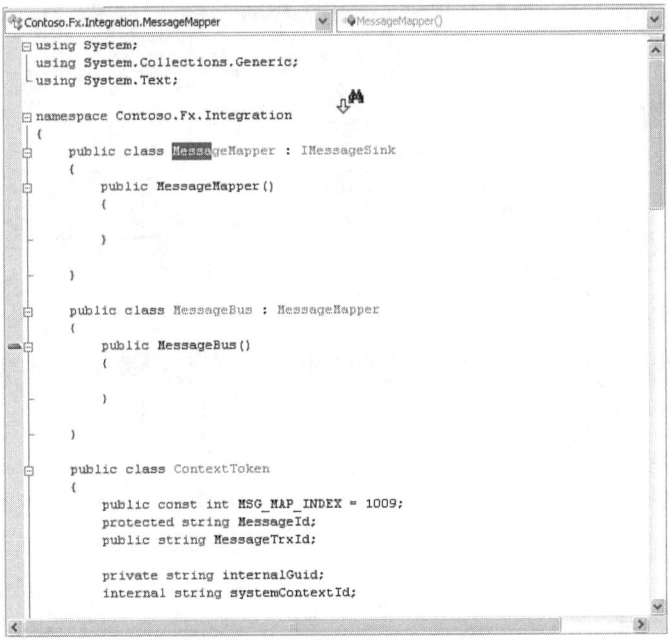

FIGURE 6.19   Incremental search.

Debugging in the Text Editor

The text editor—more specifically, the code editor—has several interactive features that facilitate with the code debugging process. Debugging activities within the text editor primarily center on breakpoints and runtime code control. We will cover general Visual Studio debugging in greater detail in Chapter 9.

A breakpoint is simply a location (for example, line of code) that is flagged for the debugger; when the debugger encounters a breakpoint, the currently executing program is paused immediately prior to executing that line of code. While the program is in this paused state, you can inspect the state of variables or even affect variable state by assigning new values. You can also interactively control the code flow at this point by skipping over the next line of code or directly to another line of code and continuing from there—all of this without actually leaving the IDE.

Setting a Breakpoint

To set a breakpoint using the code editor, first locate the line of code you want to pause on and then click on that line of code within the indicator margin. This will set the breakpoint, which can now be visually identified by a red ball in the indicator margin. Hovering over the breakpoint indicator margin will show a ToolTip indicating some basic information about that breakpoint: the code filename, the line number within that code file, the type you are in (if any), and line number within that type.

In Figure 6.20, a breakpoint has been set within a class called `MessageMapper`. The ToolTip information shows that you are on line 3 in the `MessageMapper` type, but within the overall code file (`Integration.cs`), you are on line number 9.

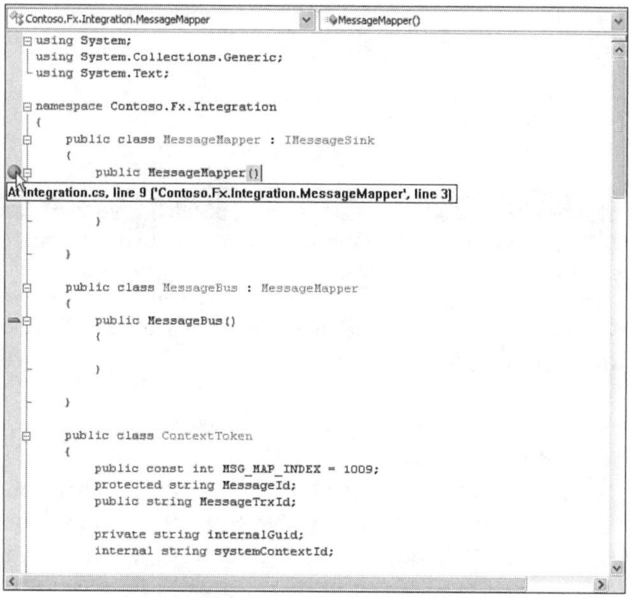

FIGURE 6.20   Setting a breakpoint.

Clicking on the breakpoint again will remove it.

The breakpoint we have set is a simple one in that it will suspend the program on that line of code without regard for any other variable or factor. Simple breakpoints are, however, only the tip of the iceberg. Breakpoints support an extensive set of conditions used to fine-tune and control what will actually trigger the breakpoints. For instance, you can set a breakpoint to activate the state of a variable or the number of times program execution will "hit" the breakpoint. You also can configure conditional breakpoints by simply pointing and clicking within the code editor window.

Configuring a Breakpoint

Right-clicking on the breakpoint indicator will reveal the context menu (see Figure 6.21) for configuring the breakpoint.

It is from here that you can indicate special conditions for triggering the breakpoint and even disable or enable the breakpoint. Disabling the breakpoint, rather than deleting it, keeps its location intact if you ever need to re-enable it.

FIGURE 6.21   Configuring a breakpoint.

TIP

Visual Basic actually provides a command word that allows you to programmatically trigger a breakpoint within your code. The Stop statement, like a breakpoint, will suspend execution of the executing code. This capability is useful when you're running the application outside the IDE. Any time a Stop statement is encountered during runtime, the Visual Studio debugger will launch and attach to the program.

Controlling the Flow of Running Code

When a program is run within the IDE, it will continue along its path of execution through the code base until it hits a breakpoint or Stop statement, is paused manually, or terminates either by reaching the end of its code path or by a manual stop.

TIP

The VCR-like controls and their shortcut keys (available under the Debug menu or on the Debug toolbar) are, by far, the easiest way to start, pause, or stop code within the IDE.

When a breakpoint is hit, the code editor will visually indicate the line of code where execution has paused. Figure 6.22 shows a slightly modified version of the "Hello, World" program, suspended at a breakpoint. A yellow arrow in the indicator margin flags the next statement that will execute when you resume running the program. In this case, because the breakpoint is also here, the next statement indicator appears in the margin embedded within the breakpoint glyph.

When execution is paused, you may change the next line of code to be executed. By default, of course, this will be the line of code where operations were paused (recall that execution stops just prior to running the line of code matched with the breakpoint). But you can manually specify the next line of code to run by right-clicking on the target line and then selecting Set Next Statement.

In Figure 6.23, this feature has been used to jump out of the WriteLine loop. Normal flow through the code has been circumvented, and instead of continuing to spin through the for loop, the program will immediately execute the line of code just after the loop. You can see the arrow and highlighting, which show that the next line of code and the breakpoint are no longer at the same location within the code file.

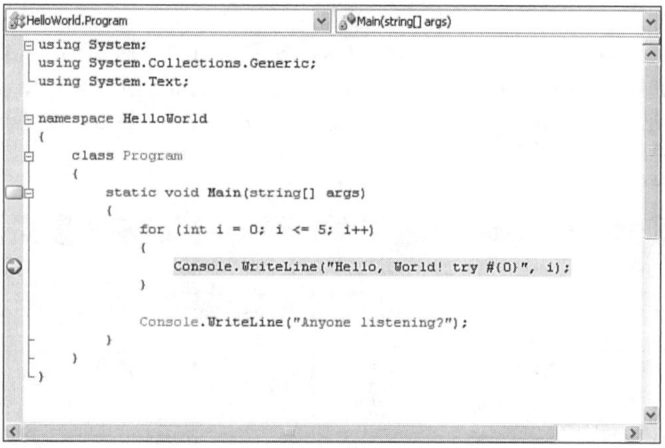

FIGURE 6.22   Stopping at a breakpoint.

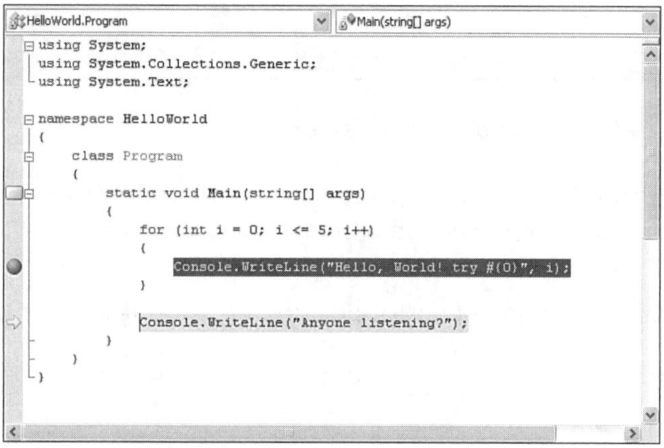

FIGURE 6.23   Setting the Next Run Statement.

You can also create a sort of virtual breakpoint by selecting Run To Cursor from the editor's context menu. This will cause the program to run until it hits the line of code that you have selected, at which point it will pause much as if you had set a breakpoint there.

Printing Code

To print the current text editor's contents, select Print from the File menu. The Print dialog box is fairly standard, allowing you to select your printer and set basic print properties. Two Visual Studio–specific options bear mentioning here. The Print What section in this dialog box controls whether line numbers will be produced in the printout and whether collapsed regions will be included in the printed content.

Colors and Fonts

By default, the font colors and markup that you see in the text editor window will be sent to the printer as is (assuming that you are printing to a color printer). If you so desire, you can tweak all these settings from the Fonts and Colors page in the Options dialog box (see Figure 6.24).

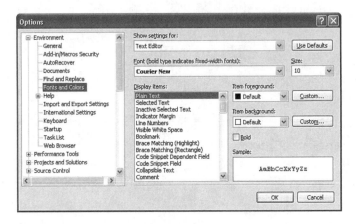

FIGURE 6.24   The Fonts and Colors Options dialog box.

This is the same dialog box used to control font and color settings for many of the IDE's constituent parts. You access the printer settings by selecting Printer in the Show Settings For drop-down at the top of the dialog box.

Figure 6.25 provides a snapshot of output produced by printing a code file.

```
C:\Documents and Settings\lpowers\My ...\HelloWorld\Program.cs                          1

1  using System;
2  using System.Collections.Generic;
3  using System.Text;
4
5  namespace HelloWorld
6  {
7      class Program
8      {
9          static void Main(string[] args)
10         {
11             for (int i = 0; i <= 5; i++)
12             {
13                 Console.WriteLine("Hello, World! try #{0}", i);
14             }
15             Console.WriteLine("Anyone listening?");
16         }
17     }
18 }
19
```

FIGURE 6.25   Code printout.

Using the Code Definition Window

The code definition window is a "helper" window that works in close conjunction with the code editor window by displaying definitions for symbols selected within the code editor. It is actually a near clone of the code editor window, with one big exception: It is read-only and does not permit edits to its content.

The code definition window content is refreshed any time the cursor position is moved within the code editor window. If the cursor or caret is placed in a symbol/type, the code definition window will show you how that symbol is defined.

Figure 6.26 shows an open code editor and a code definition window; the cursor in the editor is positioned on an internal field, _state, defined within the class InternalToken.

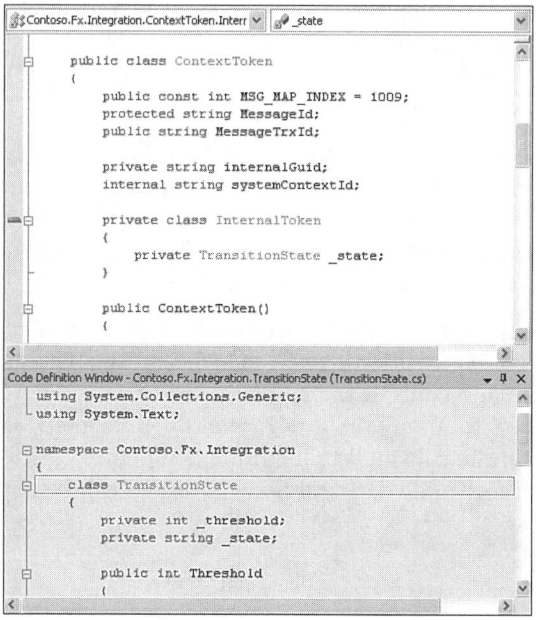

FIGURE 6.26   The code definition window.

The code definition window has reacted to the cursor position by showing the source code that actually defines the type of the _state field. You can see from the figure that the code definition window is a fairly featured adaptation of a text editor window: It supports bookmarks, breakpoints, and various navigation aids. Although you cannot edit code using this window, you are not prevented from copying code out of the window.

Creating and Editing XML Documents and Schema

The text editor is equally adept, and just as productive, at editing documents with XML and HTML content. There is also a specific CSS editor for writing and editing cascading style sheets.

Both HTML and XML documents contain structured content involving concepts of nodes and tags, attributes, and node containership. CSS documents fall into this camp, too. The XML, HTML, and CSS editors are aware of the syntactical requirements for their respective defining structures and provide appropriate IntelliSense and formatting help where possible. For a proper treatment of the various editing, validation, and productivity aids available with these editors, see Chapter 7, "Working with Visual Studio's Productivity Aids."

In the following section, we will look at the core editing features supported for the XML, HTML, and CSS document types.

Working with XML Data

XML documents are edited using either a document view or data view. The document view provides standard text editing of the document content; this is the default view you see when loading XML into the XML editor by, for instance, double-clicking an XML file in the Solution Explorer.

The data view presents the XML as a data grid, allowing you to easily add and edit the core XML data contained within the document. You access the data view by first opening the XML document and then selecting the Data Grid command under the View menu. (You can also get access to this command from the shortcut menu. Right-click anywhere within the open XML editor and select View Data Grid.)

The standard document view is typically used to edit the structure of the XML document, while the data grid view excels at letting you quickly edit the data within the XML structures. You can compare and contrast the two views using a simple product catalog sample XML document. Figure 6.27 shows the text view of the document, and Figure 6.28 shows the data view. Notice in the data view that editing is supported across multiple tables and datasets and that both core node data and node attributes can be populated and edited in the grid.

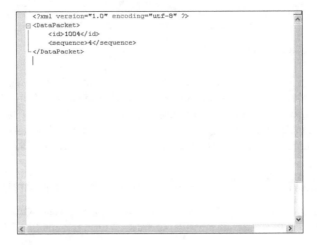

FIGURE 6.27   XML document: text view.

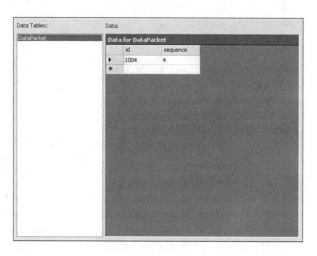

FIGURE 6.28   XML document: data view.

Inferring Schema   The XML Editor can automatically generate an XML schema document (XSD) based on a valid XML document. While the XML document is open, select Create Schema from the XML main menu. This will create an XSD document and open it in the XML editor (as a separate document). From there, you can make any needed changes to the XSD document and save it to disk. You can also include it in your project at this point.

NOTE

If you run the Create Schema command against an XML document that already contains a Document Type Definition (DTD) or XML-Data Reduced (XDR) schema, the XML inference algorithm will use these schemas as the basis for the conversion as opposed to the actual data within the XML document.

Running XSLT Against XML   The XML menu also houses an option to run an XSLT style sheet against an XML document and view the output within a new editor window. You must first attach the XSLT sheet to the XML document; the Properties window for the XML document will include a `Stylesheet` property. Entering the full path and filename of the XSLT in this property will attach the stylesheet. Alternatively, you can manually code the stylesheet into the XML document's prolog section by typing an `xml-stylesheet` Processing Instruction prolog into the document, like this:

```
<?xml-stylesheet type='text/xsl' href='myxsl.xsl'?>
```

When a stylesheet is associated, selecting the Show XSLT Output option from the XML menu will run the transforms against the XML document and show you the results in a separate editor window.

Working with Cascading Style Sheets

The CSS Editor allows you to build and edit cascading style sheet documents. Because CSS documents are, at their core, text documents, the editor doesn't need to provide much more than standard text-editing features to be effective. There are, however, a few built-in tools available from the editor that allow you to add style rules and build styles using dialog boxes as opposed to free-form text entry.

Adding Style Rules   Right-click within the CSS editor to access the shortcut menu. From there, select the Add Style Rule option. The Add Style Rule dialog box allows you to input an element, class name, or class ID and even define a hierarchy between the rules. Committing the change from this dialog box will inject the necessary content into the CSS editor to create the rule.

Defining Style Sheet Attributes   After you've added a style to the CSS document by either writing the style syntax manually or by using the aforementioned Add Style Rule dialog box, you can edit the attributes of that style using the Style Builder dialog box. You launch this dialog box by right-clicking anywhere within the previously entered style section and then selecting the Build Style option. When you use this dialog box, it is possible to fully describe the style across several different categories from font to layout to list formatting.

Developing Windows Forms Applications

The Visual Studio .NET Windows Forms designer enables drag-and-drop development of Windows forms applications. Also known as WinForms, these applications manifest all or part of their user interface as windows on the desktop.

The process of building a Windows Forms application starts the same as all other project types within Visual Studio: You select the Windows Application project template from the New Project dialog box and set up the location for the applications source. From there, Visual Studio will stub out an initial project, and the Windows Forms designer will load, as shown in Figure 6.29.

As you can see from the figure, a design-time "mock up" of the actual form is visible within the designer. This is the canvas for your user interface. Using this canvas, you can add controls and visual elements to the form, tweak the look and feel of the form itself, and launch directly to the code that is wired to the form. Changes made in the designer are actually implemented as changes made to the form's resource file (`.resx`). In other words, the designer is really an XML editor with a graphical presentation; behind the scenes, it is manipulating the form's underlying XML description in order to visually realize the form that you see within the designer.

To investigate how the designer works, start with a simple design premise: Say you want to take the blank form that Visual Studio generated for you and create a login dialog box that allows users to input a name and password and confirm their entries by clicking an OK button. A Cancel button should also be available to allow users to dismiss the form.

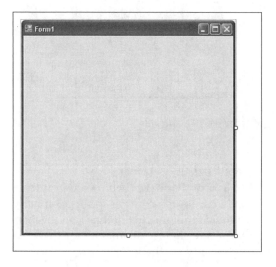

FIGURE 6.29   Initial form in the Windows Forms designer.

NOTE

Don't get confused about the various representations that a form can have, such as message box or dialog box. From a development perspective, they are all windows and are therefore all forms.

The designer in this exercise allows you, the developer, to craft the form and its actions while writing as little code as possible. Using drag-and-drop operations and Property dialog boxes, you should be able to customize the look and feel of the application without ever dealing with the code editor.

Customizing the Form's Appearance

There are a few obvious visual elements in the designer. For one, the form itself is shown complete with borders, title bar, client area, and Min/Max/Close buttons. In addition, you can see grab handles at the corners of the form and at the 12, 3, 6, and 9 o'clock positions. The grab handles are used to resize the form. To change other attributes of the form, you use the property grid for the form. The property grid will allow you to set the background color, border appearance and behavior, title text, and so on.

In Figure 6.30, the title of the form has been changed to Login, and the border behavior has been changed to match a dialog box as opposed to a normal, resizable window.

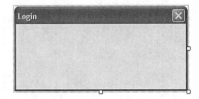

FIGURE 6.30   Editing the form's size and title.

Adding Controls to a Form

Controls are adornments to a form that have their own user interface. (There is such a thing as UI-less controls; we'll cover such controls in this chapter when we discuss component design.) They provide the principal interaction mechanism method with a form. Put another way, a form is really just a container for the various controls that will implement the desired functionality for the form.

You can add controls to a form quite easily by dragging and dropping them from the Toolbox. Continuing the metaphor of the designer as a canvas, the Toolbox is the palette.

The Toolbox

The Toolbox is a dockable window within the IDE; it is viewable only when you are editing a project element that supports Toolbox functionality. To make sure the Toolbox is visible, select it from the View menu (or use the Ctrl+W, X shortcut).

The Toolbox groups the controls in a tabbed tree. Simply expand the tab grouping (such as Common Controls or Menus & Toolbars), and you will see a list of the available controls. In this case, you want two text box controls to hold the login ID and password text, a few label controls to describe the text box controls, and the OK and Cancel buttons to commit or cancel the entries. All of these controls can be located under the Common Controls tab (see Figure 6.31)

FIGURE 6.31   The Toolbox.

To place a control on the form, drag its representation from the Toolbox onto the form. Some controls, referred to as *components*, don't actually have a visual user interface. The timer is one example of a component. When you drag a component to a form, it is placed in a separate area of the designer called the *component tray*. The component tray allows you to select one of the added components and access its properties via the Properties window.

Arranging Controls

When you are designing a form, control layout becomes an important issue. You are typically concerned about ensuring that controls are aligned either horizontally or vertically, that controls and control groups are positioned with equal and common margins between their edges, that margins are enforced along the form borders, and so on.

The designer provides three distinct sets of tools and aids that assist with form layout. First, you have the options available to you under the Format menu. With a form loaded in the designer, you can select different groups of controls and use the commands under the Format menu to align these controls vertically or horizontally with one another, standardize and increase or decrease the spacing between controls, center the controls within the form, and even alter the controls' appearance attributes so that they are of equal size in either dimension.

The other layout tools within the designer are interactive in nature and are surfaced through two different modes: snap line and grid positioning. You can toggle between these two modes via the Windows Forms Designer Options dialog box (choose Tool, Options and then the Windows Forms Designer tab). The property called `LayoutMode` can be set to either `SnapToGrid` or `SnapLines`.

Using the Layout Grid   The layout grid is, as its name implies, a grid that is laid on top of the form. The grid itself is visually represented within the designer by dots representing the intersection of the grid squares. As you drag and move controls over the surface of the grid, the designer will automatically snap the control's leading edges to one of the grid's square edges.

> **TIP**
>
> Even with the grid layout turned on, you can circumvent the snapping behavior by selecting a control, holding down the Ctrl key, and using the arrow keys to move the control up, down, right, or left one pixel at a time.

The size of the grid squares (and thus the spacing of these guide dots) is controlled by the `GridSize` property (also located in the Options dialog box). A smaller grid size equates to a tighter spacing of guide dots, which in turns equates to more finely grained control over control placement.

Figure 6.32 shows the login form with the layout grid in evidence. Note that the grid was used to make sure that

- The text boxes are aligned with one another (and are the same length).

- The labels are aligned vertically with the text boxes and horizontally with each other.

- The buttons are aligned vertically and have an appropriate buffer area between their control edges and the form's border.

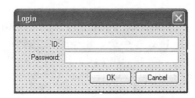

FIGURE 6.32   The layout grid.

Using Snap Lines   Snap lines are a slightly more intelligent mechanism for positioning controls. With snap lines, there is no grid visible on the form's surface. Instead, the designer draws visual hints while a control is in motion on the form.

Figure 6.33 illustrates snap lines in action; this figure shows the process of positioning the OK button.

FIGURE 6.33   Using snap lines.

Note that the control has "snapped" into a position that is located a set distance away from the form border (indicated by the thin blue line extending down from the button to the form edge). The button snap position also sufficiently spaces the control from its neighboring Cancel button, as indicated by the thin blue line extending from the right edge of the button to the left edge of the Cancel button. The snap line algorithm has also determined that you are trying to create a row of buttons and thus need to vertically align the current control to its neighbor. This is actually done using the interior text of the buttons; the thin pink line running under the text of both buttons clearly shows that they are perfectly aligned.

The snap line algorithms automatically take into account the recommended margins and spacing distances as discussed in the Windows User Interface Guidelines adopted by Microsoft. This feature takes the guesswork out of many layout decisions and helps to ensure some commonality and standards adherence within the Windows Forms applications.

> **NOTE**
>
> Changes made to the layout modes of the designer typically do not take effect immediately. You may need to close the designer and reopen it after making a change (such as switching between SnapLine mode and SnapToGrid mode).

Resizing Controls and Editing Attributes

When a control is in place on its parent form, you can interact with the control in various ways. You can set control properties using the Properties window. You also can alter the sizing and shape of the control by dragging the grab handles on the sides of the control.

Writing Code

Although the designer excels at enabling developers to visually construct a user interface, its ability to actually implement behavior is limited. You can use the designer to place a button, but responding to a click on the button and reacting in some way are still the domain of code.

At the code level, a form is simply a class that encapsulates all of the form's behavior. For simplicity and ease of development, Visual Studio pushes all of the code that it writes via the designer into clearly marked regions and, in the case of Windows forms, a separate code file. The file is named after the primary form code file like this: `<FormName>.Designer.<language extension>`. As an example, the login form is accompanied by a `Login.Designer.cs` file that implements the designer-written code.

Listing 6.1 shows what Visual Studio has generated in the way of code to implement the changes made through the designer.

LISTING 6.1   Windows Forms Designer–Generated Code

```
namespace Contoso.UI.WindowsForms.OrderEntry
{
    partial class Login
    {
        /// <summary>
        /// Required designer variable.
        /// </summary>
        private System.ComponentModel.IContainer components = null;

        /// <summary>
        /// Clean up any resources being used.
        /// </summary>
        /// <param name="disposing">true if managed resources should be disposed;
        /// otherwise, false.</param>
        protected override void Dispose(bool disposing)
        {
```

LISTING 6.1   Continued

```
        if (disposing && (components != null))
        {
            components.Dispose();
        }
        base.Dispose(disposing);
    }

    #region Windows Form Designer generated code

    /// <summary>
    /// Required method for Designer support - do not modify
    /// the contents of this method with the code editor.
    /// </summary>
    private void InitializeComponent()
    {
        this.label1 = new System.Windows.Forms.Label();
        this.label2 = new System.Windows.Forms.Label();
        this.textBoxID = new System.Windows.Forms.TextBox();
        this.textBoxPassword = new System.Windows.Forms.TextBox();
        this.buttonCancel = new System.Windows.Forms.Button();
        this.buttonOk = new System.Windows.Forms.Button();
        this.SuspendLayout();
        //
        // label1
        //
        this.label1.AutoSize = true;
        this.label1.Location = new System.Drawing.Point(61, 23);
        this.label1.Name = "label1";
        this.label1.Size = new System.Drawing.Size(17, 13);
        this.label1.TabIndex = 0;
        this.label1.Text = "ID:";
        //
        // label2
        //
        this.label2.AutoSize = true;
        this.label2.Location = new System.Drawing.Point(26, 46);
        this.label2.Name = "label2";
        this.label2.Size = new System.Drawing.Size(52, 13);
        this.label2.TabIndex = 1;
        this.label2.Text = "Password:";
        //
        // textBoxID
        //
        this.textBoxID.Location = new System.Drawing.Point(85, 20);
```

LISTING 6.1   Continued

```
this.textBoxID.Name = "textBoxID";
this.textBoxID.Size = new System.Drawing.Size(195, 20);
this.textBoxID.TabIndex = 2;
//
// textBoxPassword
//
this.textBoxPassword.Location = new System.Drawing.Point(85, 46);
this.textBoxPassword.Name = "textBoxPassword";
this.textBoxPassword.Size = new System.Drawing.Size(195, 20);
this.textBoxPassword.TabIndex = 3;
//
// buttonCancel
//
this.buttonCancel.DialogResult =
   System.Windows.Forms.DialogResult.Cancel;
this.buttonCancel.Location = new System.Drawing.Point(205, 72);
this.buttonCancel.Name = "buttonCancel";
this.buttonCancel.Size = new System.Drawing.Size(75, 23);
this.buttonCancel.TabIndex = 4;
this.buttonCancel.Text = "Cancel";
//
// buttonOk
//
this.buttonOk.Location = new System.Drawing.Point(124, 72);
this.buttonOk.Name = "buttonOk";
this.buttonOk.Size = new System.Drawing.Size(75, 23);
this.buttonOk.TabIndex = 5;
this.buttonOk.Text = "OK";
//
// Login
//
this.AcceptButton = this.buttonOk;
this.AutoScaleDimensions = new System.Drawing.SizeF(6F, 13F);
this.AutoScaleMode = System.Windows.Forms.AutoScaleMode.Font;
this.CancelButton = this.buttonCancel;
this.ClientSize = new System.Drawing.Size(292, 109);
this.Controls.Add(this.buttonOk);
this.Controls.Add(this.buttonCancel);
this.Controls.Add(this.textBoxPassword);
this.Controls.Add(this.textBoxID);
this.Controls.Add(this.label2);
this.Controls.Add(this.label1);
this.FormBorderStyle =
   System.Windows.Forms.FormBorderStyle.FixedDialog;
```

6

LISTING 6.1 Continued

```
            this.MaximizeBox = false;
            this.MinimizeBox = false;
            this.Name = "Login";
            this.ShowInTaskbar = false;
            this.SizeGripStyle = System.Windows.Forms.SizeGripStyle.Hide;
            this.Text = "Login";
            this.ResumeLayout(false);
            this.PerformLayout();

        }

        #endregion

        private System.Windows.Forms.Label label1;
        private System.Windows.Forms.Label label2;
        private System.Windows.Forms.TextBox textBoxID;
        private System.Windows.Forms.TextBox textBoxPassword;
        private System.Windows.Forms.Button buttonCancel;
        private System.Windows.Forms.Button buttonOk;
    }
}
```

Developing Web Forms

Web forms represent the user interface element to a web application. Traditionally with .NET, the term *web form* is used to refer specifically to pages processed dynamically on the server (using ASP .NET). We use a broader definition here and use the term to refer to any web page, static or dynamic, that can be developed and designed within the Visual Studio IDE.

The HTML designer (also referred to as the Web designer) is the sister application to the Windows Forms designer; it allows you to visually design and edit the markup for a web page. As with the Windows Forms designer, it works in conjunction with the HTML designer and source view to cover all of the bases needed for web page design. We will cover the entire web application development process in depth in Chapter 13, "Writing ASP.NET Applications"; in the following sections, we will simply cover the basics of the web designers and editors.

Designing a Web Form Application

Web page design starts first with a web project. Select File, New Web Site, and from the dialog box, select the ASP .NET Web Site option. After you set the source code directory and source language, click OK to have Visual Studio create the project and its initial web page.

The web designer looks similar to the Windows Forms designer; it has a document window that acts as a canvas, allowing objects from the Toolbox to be placed and positioned on its surface. View tabs are oriented at the bottom of the designer. These tabs, not present in the other designers, allow you to quickly switch between design view and source view. In this case, source view is the actual HTML markup for the page you are designing.

Now examine what happens when you try to mimic the login form that was previously built using Windows forms. (There is actually a prebuilt login form component that you could use here; for the sake of demonstrating the development process, however, we will go ahead and cobble together our own simplistic one for comparison's sake.)

Adding and Arranging Controls

The process of adding and arranging controls doesn't change from the Windows Forms designer process. Simply drag the controls from the Toolbox onto the designer's surface. In this case, you want two labels, two text boxes, and an OK button (because this isn't a dialog box, you can dispense with the Cancel button). Changing control properties is also handled the same way via the Properties window. You can select the labels and command buttons and set their text this way.

> **NOTE**
>
> As you add controls to a web page, you should note that the default layout mode is relative. That is, controls are not placed at absolute coordinates on the screen but instead are placed relative to one another. Absolute positioning is accommodated via style sheets. For instance, you can select a label control, edit its style properties, and select Absolutely Position as the position mode. This will now allow you to range freely over the form with the control.

A formatting toolbar is provided by default; it supplies buttons for common text formatting actions such as changing font styles, colors, paragraph indenting, and bulleting.

To line up control edges the way you want, you can press Shift+Enter to insert spacing between the controls as necessary (this will generate a break tag, <br>, in the HTML). In this case, a break was added between the first text box and the second label, and between the second text box and the first button. Figure 6.34 shows the design in progress. The text boxes don't line up and you will probably want to apply a style for the label fonts and buttons, but the general layout and intent are evident.

Editing Markup

As controls and other elements are added and manipulated on the designer's surface, HTML is created to implement the design and layout. As a designer or developer, you are free to work at either the visual level with the designer or the text/source level with the HTML Source Editor. Like the other editors within Visual Studio 2005, the HTML Source Editor supports IntelliSense and other interactive features for navigating and validating markup.

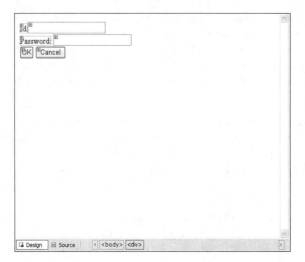

FIGURE 6.34   Creating a web form.

To toggle between the designer and the HTML editor, use the Design and Source tabs at the bottom of the document tab. Figure 6.35 provides a peek at the HTML generated by the designer when you added the controls for the login page. Toward the bottom of the document tab, you will see the Design and Source tabs, with the Source tab selected.

```
Client Objects & Events                        (No Events)
    <%@ Page Language="C#" AutoEventWireup="true" CodeFile="Defaul

    <!DOCTYPE html PUBLIC "-//W3C//DTD XHTML 1.1//EN" "http://www.
    <html xmlns="http://www.w3.org/1999/xhtml">
    <head runat="server">
        <title>Login Page</title>
    </head>
    <body>
        <form id="form1" runat="server">
            <div>
                <asp:Label ID="Label1" runat="server" Text="Id:"><
                    runat="server"></asp:TextBox><br />
                <asp:Label ID="Label2" runat="server" Text="Passwo
                <asp:TextBox ID="TextBox2" runat="server"></asp:Te
                <asp:Button ID="Button1" runat="server" Text="OK"
                <asp:Button ID="Button2" runat="server" Text="Canc
            </form>
    </body>
    </html>
```

FIGURE 6.35   Web form: source view.

Using the HTML editor, you can write your own HTML and then toggle back to the designer view to see how your changes will look within the browser. As with the design surface, a toolbar is provided here. The HTML source editing toolbar provides quick access to code "forward and back" navigation, commenting, and schema validation options (we'll discuss this specific part in a bit).

One key feature realized with the HTML editor is the concept of source format preservation: The HTML source editor works very hard to respect the way that you, the developer, want your markup formatted. This includes the placement of carriage returns and whitespace, the use of indentation, and even how you want to handle word and line wrapping. In short, Visual Studio will never reformat HTML code that you have written!

Working with Tables   HTML tables provide a quick and easy way to align controls on a web page. With Visual Studio 2005, there is a dedicated Insert Table dialog box that provides extensive control over table layout and appearance. To place a table onto the design surface, select Insert Table from the Layout menu. The Insert Table dialog box supports custom table layouts where you specify the row and column attributes and the general style attributes such as borders and padding. Through this dialog box, you can also select from a list of preformatted table templates.

After you've added a table to the designer, it is fully interactive for drag-and-drop resizing of its columns and rows.

Formatting Options   In addition to preserving the format of HTML that you write, Visual Studio 2005 also provides fine-grained control over how the designer generates and formats the HTML that it produces. You use the HTML page and its subpages in the Options dialog box (Tools, Options, Text Editor, HTML) to configure indentation style, quotation use, word wrapping, and tag casing (see Figure 6.36).

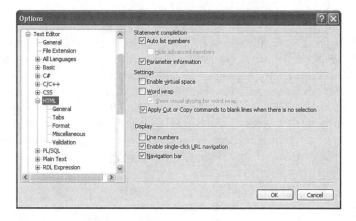

FIGURE 6.36   HTML formatting options.

Settings can be applied globally for all markup, or you can set options on a per-tag basis by clicking the Tag Specific Options button (Text Editor, HTML, Format). As an example, this level of control is useful if your particular coding style uses line breaks within your table column tabs (<td>), but not with your table row tags (<tr>). In Figure 6.37, the tr tag is being set to support line breaks before and after the tag, but not within the tag.

FIGURE 6.37   Setting HTML formatting at the tag level.

Browser Output and Validation

The result of all of the design effort put into an HTML document is its final rendering within a browser. With various flavors of browsers in use supporting various levels of HTML specifications (including XHTML), it is difficult to ensure that the page's design intent actually matches reality. Visual Studio's browser target settings help with this problem by enabling you to easily target a specific HTML standard or *browser*. As you type HTML into the source editor, Visual Studio will validate the syntax on-the-fly against your selected browser target. If a piece of markup violates the rules of your particular validation target, it will be flagged by the familiar red squiggly line (complete with a ToolTip explaining the exact violation), and the error will be listed within the Task List window.

The target can be selected on the HTML designer or source editor toolbar: Just pick the target from the drop-down.

> **NOTE**
>
> The validation rules for a given browser or standard can actually be customized to support targets that may not ship out of the box with Visual Studio.

Standards Compliance   The HTML code generated by the HTML designer is, by default, XHTML compliant; tags, for instance, are well formed with regards to XHTML requirements. Using the various XHTML validation targets will help you to ensure that the code you write is compliant as well.

Visual Studio also focuses on providing compliance with accessibility standards: those standards that govern the display of web pages for persons with disabilities. You launch the Accessibility Checker by using the Check Page for Accessibility button on the HTML Source Editing or Formatting toolbars.

Figure 6.38 shows the Accessibility Validation dialog box. You can select the specific standards you want to have your HTML validated against. You can also select the level of feedback that you receive (errors, warnings, or a text checklist). Each item flagged by the checker will appear in the Task List window for resolution. For more details on the two standards supported here (WCAG and Access Board Section 508), see their respective websites: http://www.w3.org/TR/WCAG10/ and http://www.access-board.gov/508.htm.

FIGURE 6.38   Setting accessibility validation options.

Authoring Components and Controls

Referring to our earlier discussion of Windows forms, components are nonvisual controls or classes. This is a good generic definition, but a more specific one is this: A component is any class that inherits from `System.ComponentModel.IComponent`. This particular interface provides support for designability and resource handling. If you need a designable control that does not have a user interface of its own, you will work with a component. And in Visual Studio, the component designer is the tool used to develop components.

Controls are similar in function but not form: A control is a reusable chunk of code that *does* have a visual element to it.

Creating a New Component or Control

You kick off the process of authoring a component by using the Add New Item dialog box (from the Project menu). Selecting Component Class in this dialog box will add the stub code file to your current project and will launch the component designer. To start control development, you use the Add New User Control dialog box.

NOTE

Essentially two different "types" of controls can be authored within Visual Studio: custom controls and user controls. Custom controls inherit directly from the System.Windows.Forms. Control class; they are typically code intensive because you, the developer, are responsible for writing all of the code necessary to render the control's visual portion. User controls (sometimes called composite controls) inherit from the System.Windows.forms.UserControl class. User controls are advantageous because they can be built quickly by compositing other controls together that are already available in the Toolbox. These controls already have their user interface portion coded for you.

Both the control and the component designer work on the same principles as the Windows Forms designer: the designers allow you to drag an object from the Toolbox onto the design surface.

Assume that you need a component that will send a signal across a serial port every *x* minutes. Because Visual Studio already provides a timer and a serial port component, which are accessible from the Toolbox, you can use the component designer to add these objects to your own custom component and then leverage and access their intrinsic properties and methods (essentially, using them as building blocks to get your desired functionality).

Figure 6.39 shows the component designer for this fictional custom component; two objects have been added: a timer and a process component.

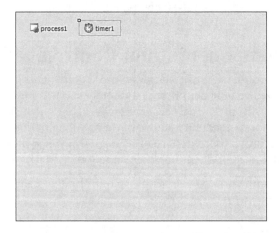

FIGURE 6.39   The component designer.

A similar scenario can be envisioned with a user control. You can take the example of a login "form," consisting of two text boxes, two labels, and two buttons, and actually make that a control—one that can be easily included in the Toolbox and dropped onto a Windows form or web form.

Further Notes on Writing Component Code

Because the component has no visual aspect to it, you don't have the layout and formatting features that you see with the Windows Forms designer. However, the concept of drag-and-drop programming is alive and well. Visual Studio, behind the scenes, injects the code to programmatically add the given class to the component's container. From there, you can edit the various objects' properties, double-click an object to get to its code, and so on.

When you simply drag the timer and process objects over from the Toolbox, Visual Studio aggregates these objects into the component by automatically writing the code shown in Listing 6.2.

LISTING 6.2   Component Designer–Generated Code

```
namespace Contoso.UI.WindowsForms.OrderEntry
{
    partial class MyComponent
    {
        /// <summary>
        /// Required designer variable.
        /// </summary>
        private System.ComponentModel.IContainer components = null;

        /// <summary>
        /// Clean up any resources being used.
        /// </summary>
        /// <param name="disposing">true if managed resources should be
        /// disposed; otherwise, false.</param>
        protected override void Dispose(bool disposing)
        {
            if (disposing && (components != null))
            {
                components.Dispose();
            }
            base.Dispose(disposing);
        }

        #region Component Designer generated code

        /// <summary>
        /// Required method for Designer support - do not modify
        /// the contents of this method with the code editor.
        /// </summary>
        private void InitializeComponent()
        {
            this.components = new System.ComponentModel.Container();
```

LISTING 6.2   Continued

```
        this.timer1 = new System.Windows.Forms.Timer(this.components);
        this.serialPort1 = new System.IO.Ports.SerialPort(this.components);


    }

    #endregion

    private System.Windows.Forms.Timer timer1;
    private System.IO.Ports.SerialPort serialPort1;



    }
}
```

Writing code "behind" one of the objects placed on the component designer canvas is easy: Double-click the object's icon, and the code editor will be launched. For instance, double-clicking on the timer icon on the designer surface will cause the `timer1_Tick` routine to be created and then launched in the code editor.

Summary

Visual Studio provides a full array of editors and designers. They cover the gamut of solution development activities from WYSIWYG positioning of graphical controls to finely tuned text editing for a certain language, syntax, or markup.

This chapter described how to leverage the basics within these editors and designers. It also described how the editor and designer relationship provides two complementary views of the same solution artifact, in effect working together to provide you, the developer, with the right tool for the right task at hand.

In subsequent chapters, we'll look at the more advanced options and productivity features available within these tools and even look at end-to-end development efforts involved in building a web application or Windows forms application.

CHAPTER 7

Working with Visual Studio's Productivity Aids

IN THIS CHAPTER

- Basic Aids in the Text Editor
- Outlining and Navigation
- Smart Tags and Smart Tasks
- IntelliSense
- The Task List

In the preceding chapter, we discussed the basic capabilities of the designers and editors in Visual Studio 2005. In this chapter, we will travel a bit deeper into their capabilities and those of other Visual Studio tools by examining the many productivity aids provided by the IDE. Many of these productivity enhancers are embedded within the text editors. Others are more generic in nature. But they all have one common goal: helping you, the developer, write code quickly and correctly.

If you recall from Chapter 6, "Introducing the Editors and Designers," in our coverage of the editors we used a very basic code scenario: a console application that printed "Hello, World!" to the console. In Figure 7.1, you see what the final code looks like in the code editor window.

If you have followed along by re-creating this project and typing the "Hello, World!" code in Visual Studio, you will notice that the productivity features of the code editor have already kicked into gear. For one, as you start to type code into the template file, the code editor has tabbed the cursor in for you, placing it at a new location for writing nicely indented code.

Second, as you type your first line of code, Visual Studio reacts to your every keystroke by interpreting what you are trying to write and extending help in various forms (see Figure 7.2). You are given hints in terms of completing your in-progress source, provided information on the members you are in the process of selecting, and given information on the parameters required to complete a particular method. These features are collectively referred to as *IntelliSense*, and we will explore its forms and functions in depth in this chapter.

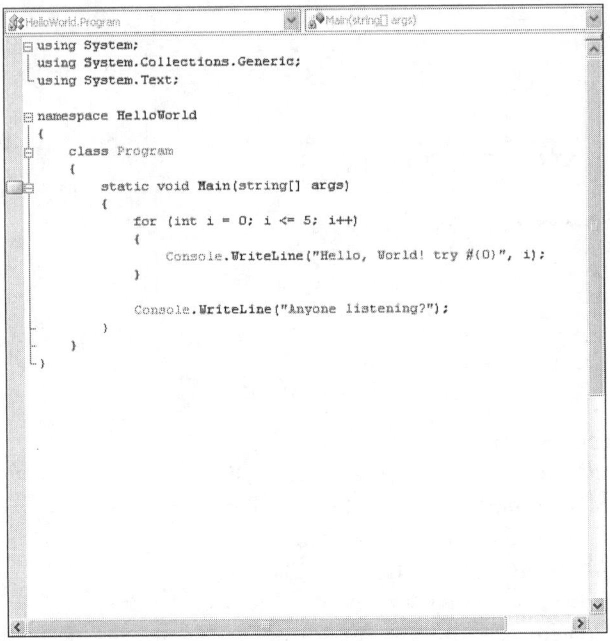

HelloWorld.Program
Main(string[] args)
using System;
using System.Collections.Generic;
using System.Text;
namespace HelloWorld
{
class Program
{
static void Main(string[] args)
{
for (int i = 0; i <= 5; i++)
{
Console.WriteLine("Hello, World! try #{0}", i);
}
Console.WriteLine("Anyone listening?");
}
}
}

FIGURE 7.1 "Hello, World" in the code editor.

HelloWorld.Program
Main(string[] args)
using System;
using System.Collections.Generic;
using System.Text;
namespace HelloWorld
{
class Program
{
static void Main(string[] args)
{
for (int
}
}
}
in
indexer
IndexOutOfRangeException
InsufficientMemoryException
int
Int16
Int32
Int64
interface
IntPtr
struct System.Int32
Represents a 32-bit signed integer.

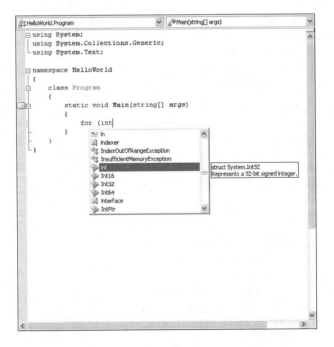

FIGURE 7.2 IntelliSense in action.

As you type, the IDE is also constantly checking what you have written with the compiler. If compile errors exist, they are dynamically displayed for you in the output window.

So, for this one simple line of code, Visual Studio has been hard at work improving your coding productivity by doing the following:

- Intelligently indenting the code

- Suggesting code syntax

- Displaying member descriptions to help you select the correct code syntax

- Visually matching up delimiting parentheses

- Flagging code errors by constantly background compiling the current version of the source code

These features subtly help and coach you through the code-writing process by accelerating the act of coding itself.

Basic Aids in the Text Editor

The text editor user interface itself exposes visual constructs that help you with common problem areas encountered during the code-writing process. These basic aids provide support for determining what has changed within a code document and what compile problems exist in a document. Additionally, the discrete syntax elements for each individual language are visually delineated for you using colored text.

Change Tracking

When you are in the midst of editing a source code file, it is tremendously useful to understand which lines of code have been committed (that is, saved to disk) and which have not. Change tracking provides this functionality: A yellow vertical bar in the text editor's selection margin will span any lines in the editor that have been changed but not saved. If content has been changed and subsequently saved, it will be marked with a green vertical bar in the selection margin.

By looking at the yellow and green tracking bars, you can quickly differentiate between

- Code that hasn't been touched since the file was loaded (no bar)

- Code that has been touched and saved since the file was loaded (green bar)

- Code that has been touched but not saved since the file was loaded (yellow bar)

Change tracking is valid only for as long as the editor window is open. In other words, change tracking is significant only for the current document "session"; if you close and re-open the window, the track bars will be gone because you have established a new working session with that specific document.

Figure 7.3 shows a section of a code file displaying the different flavors of change tracking bars.

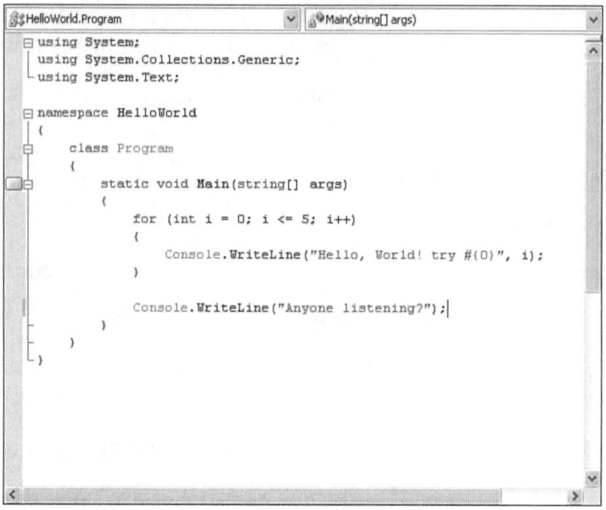

```csharp
using System;
using System.Collections.Generic;
using System.Text;

namespace HelloWorld
{
    class Program
    {
        static void Main(string[] args)
        {
            for (int i = 0; i <= 5; i++)
            {
                Console.WriteLine("Hello, World! try #(0)", i);
            }

            Console.WriteLine("Anyone listening?");
        }
    }
}
```

FIGURE 7.3   Change tracking.

Coding Problem Indicators

The Visual Studio compiler works in conjunction with the code editor window to flag any problems found within a source code document. The compiler can even work in the background, enabling the editor window to flag problems as you type (as opposed to waiting for the project to be compiled).

Coding problems are flagged using "squiggles": wavy, color-coded lines placed under the offending piece of code. These squiggles are the same mechanism Microsoft Word uses to flag spelling and grammar problems. The squiggle colors indicate a specific class of problem. Table 7.1 shows how these colors map to an underlying problem.

TABLE 7.1   Coding Problem Indicator Colors

Color	Problem
Red	Syntax error; the code will not compile because of the syntax requirements and rules of the language.
Blue	Semantic error; this is the result of the compiler not being able to resolve the type or code construct within the current context. For instance, a type name that doesn't exist within the compiled context of the current project will be flagged with a blue squiggle. Typically, these are good indicators for typos (e.g., misspelling a class name).
Purple	Warning; the purple squiggle denotes code that has triggered a compiler warning.

Hovering the mouse pointer over the problem indicator will reveal the actual compiler error or warning message, as demonstrated in Figure 7.4.

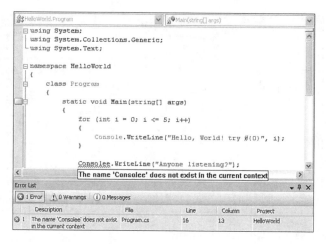

FIGURE 7.4   Coding problem indicators.

Active Hyperlinking

Text editors support clickable hyperlinks within documents; clicking on a link will launch a browser redirected at the URL. One great use of this feature is to embed URLs to supporting documentation or other helpful reference information within code comments.

Syntax Coloring

The text editor can parse and distinctly color different code constructs to make them that much easier to identify on sight. As an example, the code editor window will, by default, color any code comments green. Code identifiers are black, keywords are blue, strings are colored red, and so on.

In fact, the number of unique elements that the text editor is capable of parsing and coloring is immense: The text editor window recognizes more than 100 different elements. And, you can customize and color each one of them to your heart's content through the Environments node in the Options dialog box. Do you like working with larger fonts? Would a higher contrast benefit your programming activities? How about squeezing more code into your viewable screen real estate? These are just a few reasons you might stray from the defaults with this dialog box.

Figure 7.5 shows the fonts and colors dialog box that allows you to specify foreground and background colors for code, HTML, CSS, or other elements. Select the element in the display item list and change its syntax coloring via the foreground and background color drop-downs.

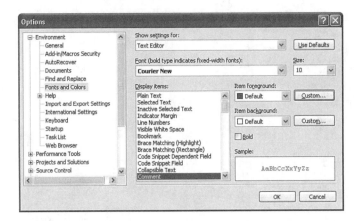

FIGURE 7.5   Setting font and color options.

NOTE

The dialog box shown in Figure 7.5 actually enables you to control much more than the syntax coloring for the text editor; you can change the coloring schemes used in all of the different windows within Visual Studio. The item you select in the Show Settings For drop-down will determine the portion of the IDE you are customizing and will alter the list of items in the Display Items list.

You can always use the Use Defaults button at the top right of the dialog box to restore the default coloring schemes.

Outlining and Navigation

Certain documents, such as source code files and markup files, have a natural parent-child aspect to their organization and syntax. XML nodes, for instance, can contain other nodes. Likewise, functions and other programming language constructs such as loops and try/catch blocks act as a container for other lines of code. Outlining is the concept of visually representing this parent-child relationship.

Code Outlining

Code outlining is used within the code editor; it allows you to collapse or expand regions of code along these container boundaries. A series of grouping lines and expand/collapse boxes are drawn in the selection margin. These expand/collapse boxes are clickable, enabling you to hide or display lines of code based on the logical groupings.

TIP

Both Visual Basic and C# provide a way to manually create named regions of code via a special region keyword. Use #region/#endregion (#Region and #End Region for Visual Basic) to create your own artificial code container that will be appropriately parsed by the code outliner. Because each region is named, this is a handy approach for organizing and segregating the logical sections of your code. In fact, to use one example, the code generated for you by the Windows Forms Designer is automatically tucked within a "Windows Forms Designer generated code" region.

Code outlining is best understood using a simple example. First, refer to Figure 7.1. This is the initial console application code. It contains a routine called Main, a class declaration, a namespace declaration, and several using statements. The code outline groupings that you see in the selection margin visually indicate code regions that can be collapsed or hidden from view.

Because the class declaration is a logical container, the selection margin for that line of code contains a collapse box (a box with a minus sign). A line is drawn from the collapse box to the end of the container (in this case, because you are dealing with C#, the class declaration is delimited by a curly brace). If you click on the collapse box for the class declaration, Visual Studio will hide all of the code contained within that declaration.

Figure 7.6 shows how the editor window looks with this code hidden from view. Note that the collapse box has changed to a plus sign, indicating that you can click on the box to reshow the now-hidden code, and that the first line of code for the class declaration has been altered to include a trailing box with ellipses.

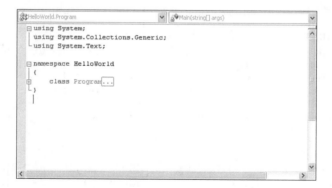

FIGURE 7.6   Collapsed outline region.

The HTML Editor also supports outlining in this fashion. HTML elements can be expanded or collapsed to show or hide their containing elements.

Using the Outlining Menu

Several code outlining commands are available under the Edit, Outlining menu (see Figure 7.7).

- **Toggle Outlining Expansion**—Based on the current cursor position in the editor window, hides or unhides the outline region.

- **Toggle All Outlining**—Hides or unhides all outline regions in the editor.

FIGURE 7.7   The Edit, Outlining menu.

- **Stop Outlining**—Turns off automatic code outlining (any hidden regions will be expanded). This command is available only if automatic outlining is turned on.

- **Stop Hiding Current**—Removes the outline for the currently selected region. This command is available only if automatic outlining has been turned off.

- **Collapse to Definitions**—Hides all procedure regions. This command is useful for distilling a type down to single lines of code for all of its members.

- **Start Automatic Outlining**—Enables the code outlining feature. This command is available only if outlining is currently turned off.

Code outlining is a convenience mechanism: By hiding currently irrelevant sections of code, you decrease the visible surface of the code file and increase code readability. You can pick and choose the specific regions to view based on the task at hand.

TIP

If you place the mouse pointer over the ellipses box of a hidden code region, the contents of that hidden region will be displayed to you in a ToolTip-style box; this is done without your having to actually expand/reshow the code region.

HTML Navigation

One problem with large or complex web pages is that navigation through the HTML can be problematic with multiple levels and layers of tag nesting. Envision a page containing a table within a table within a table. When you are editing the HTML (through either the designer or the editor), how can you tell exactly where you are? Put another way, how can you tell where the current focus is within the markup hierarchy?

Using the Tag Navigator

The tag navigator is Visual Studio's answer to this question. The navigator appears as a series of buttons at the bottom of the web page editor, just to the right of the designer/editor tabs. A breadcrumb of tags is shown (as buttons) that leads from the tag which currently has focus all the way to the outermost tag. If this path is too long to actually display within the confines of the editor window, it will be truncated at the parent tag side; a button will allow you to display more tags toward the parent.

Figure 7.8 picks up a scenario we dealt with in Chapter 6: an HTML login page. While you're editing the OK button in the sample login page, the tag navigator shows the path all the way back to the parent-enclosing <html> tag.

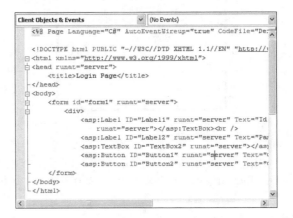

FIGURE 7.8   The tag navigator.

Each tag button displayed by the navigator can be used to directly select the inclusive or exclusive contents of that tag. A drop-down triggered by the tag button will contain options for selecting the tag or selecting the tag content. The former will cause the tag itself, in addition to all of its enclosed content, to be selected. The latter will exclude the tag begin and end, but will still select all of its enclosed content.

The navigator is a great mechanism for quickly moving up and down within a large HTML documents tag tree.

Using the Document Outline Window

The Document Outline window displays a tree-view representation of the HTML elements on a page. This hierarchical display is also a great navigation tool because it allows you to take in the entire structure of your web page in one glance and immediately jump to any of the elements within the page.

To use the Document Outline window, choose Document Outline from the View menu. Figure 7.9 shows a sample outline window. The exact elements displayed within this window will vary slightly depending on the current view you are in. In the design view, the document outline will include only those HTML elements that are within the body element. In source view, elements within the head and page elements are also displayed. The outline will also show script and code elements in the source view.

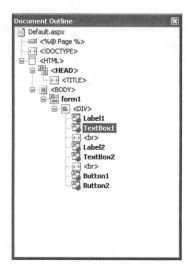

FIGURE 7.9   The Document Outline window.

Clicking on an element will navigate to that element (and select it) within the designer window, and, of course, you can expand or collapse the tree nodes as needed.

Smart Tags and Smart Tasks

Smart tags and *smart tasks* (the terms can essentially be used interchangeably) are menu- or IntelliSense-driven features for automating common control configuration and coding tasks within the IDE. Designers and editors both implement smart tags in a variety of different scenarios. In the following sections, we will examine a few of the ways that smart tags make your life easier, starting first with the HTML Designer.

HTML Designer

As controls are placed onto the HTML designer, a pop-up list of common tasks appears. These tasks, collectively referred to as *smart tasks*, allow you to "set the dials" for a given control to quickly configure it for the task at hand.

When you drag new controls onto the designer surface, a pop-up list of common tasks automatically appears. You can use the common tasks list to quickly configure a control's properties, as well as walk through common operations you might perform with it. For example, when you add a `GridView` control to a web page, a common task list appears that allows you to quickly enable sorting, paging, or editing for the `GridView`. When you add a TextBox control to a web page, a common task list appears that enables you to quickly associate a validation control with the control.

The Windows Forms designer also plays host to smart tags.

Windows Forms Designer

With the Windows Forms designer, the functionality of smart tags remains consistent; they do, however, take a slightly different form. A form control that supports this functionality will show a smart tag glyph somewhere within its bounds (typically to the top right of the control). This glyph, when clicked, will open a small drop-down of tasks. Figure 7.10 contains a snapshot of the smart tag in action for a tab control.

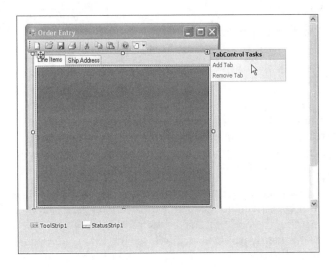

FIGURE 7.10   TabControl smart tag.

Code Editor

Smart tags can also appear within code. One example can be found on interfaces. Normally, implementing an interface is a fairly code-intensive task. You have to individually create a member to map to each member defined on the interface. The smart tag in this case allows you to automatically create those members using two different naming modes:

- **Explicit naming**—Members have the name of the derived interface.

- **Implicit naming**—Member names do not reference the name of the derived interface.

See Figure 7.11 to view this smart tag in action.

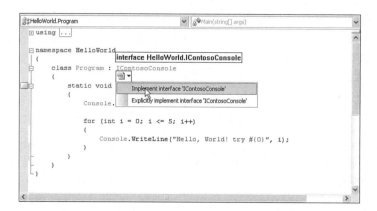

FIGURE 7.11   "Implement Interface" smart tag.

IntelliSense

IntelliSense is the name applied to a collection of different coding aids surfaced within the text editor window. Its sole purpose in life is to help you, the developer, write a syntactically correct line of code *quickly*. In addition, it tries to provide enough guidance to help you write lines of code that are correct *in context*—that is, code that makes sense given the surrounding lines of code.

As you type within the text editor, IntelliSense is the behind-the-scenes agent responsible for providing a list of code fragments that match the characters you have already entered, highlighting/preselecting the one that makes the most sense given the surrounding context, and, if so commanded, automatically inserting that code fragment in-line. This saves you the time of looking up types and members in the reference documentation and saves time again by inserting code without it being necessary for you to actually type the characters for that code.

We'll spend a lot of time in this section discussing IntelliSense in the context of editing code, but you should know that IntelliSense also works with other document types such as XML documents, HTML documents, and XSLT files.

> **TIP**
>
> Attaching a schema to an XML document is beneficial from an IntelliSense perspective. The schema is used to further enhance the capabilities of the List Members function (see its section later in this chapter).

There are many discrete pieces to IntelliSense that seamlessly work in conjunction with one another *as you are writing code*. Let's look at them one by one.

Complete Word

Complete Word is the basic time-saving kernel of IntelliSense. After you have typed enough characters for IntelliSense to recognize what you are trying to write, a guess is made as to the complete word you are in the process of typing. This guess is then presented to you within a list of possible alternatives (referred to as the *completion list*) and can be inserted into the code editor with one keystroke. This is in contrast to your completing the word manually by typing all of its characters.

Figure 7.12 illustrates the process: Based on the context of the code and based on the characters typed into the editor, a list of possible words is displayed. One of these selections will be selected as the most viable candidate; you may select any entry in the list (via the arrow keys or the mouse). Pressing the Tab key will automatically inject the word into the editor for you.

> **NOTE**
>
> Complete Word takes the actual code context into account for a variety of different situations. For instance, if you are in the midst of keying in the exception type in a `try/catch` block, IntelliSense will display only exception types in the completion list. Likewise, typing an attribute will trigger a completion list filtered only for attributes; when you're implementing an interface, only interface types will be displayed, and so on. This IntelliSense feature is enabled for all sorts of content: Beyond C# and Visual Basic code, IntelliSense completion works for other files as well, such as HTML tags, CSS style attributes, `.config` files, and HTML script blocks, just to name a few.

You can manually invoke Complete Word at any time by using the Ctrl+Spacebar or Alt+Right-arrow key combinations.

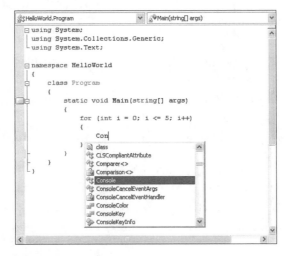

FIGURE 7.12   IntelliSense: Complete Word.

Quick Info

Quick Info displays the complete code declaration and help information for any code construct. It is invoked by hovering the mouse pointer over an identifier; a pop-up box will display the information available for that identifier.

Figure 7.13 shows Quick Info being displayed for the `Console.ReadLine` function. You are provided with the declaration syntax for the member, a brief description of the member, and a list of its exception classes.

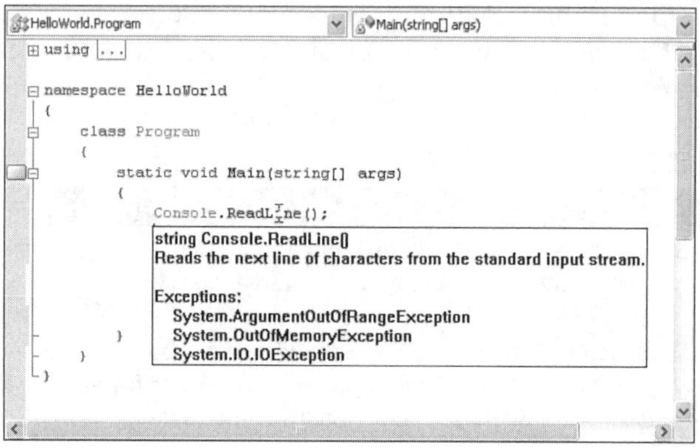

FIGURE 7.13   IntelliSense: Quick Info.

List Members

For any given type or namespace, the IntelliSense List Members feature will display a scrollable list of all valid member variables and functions specific to that type. To see the List Members function in action, perform the following steps in an open code editor window:

1. Type the name of a class (Ctrl+Space will give you the IntelliSense window with possible class names).

2. Type a period; this indicates to IntelliSense that you have finished with the type name and are now "scoped in" to that type's members.

3. The list of valid members will now be displayed. You can manually scroll through the list and select the desired member at this point, or, if you are well aware of the member you are trying to code, you can simply continue typing until IntelliSense has captured enough characters to select the member you are looking for.

4. Leverage Complete Word by pressing the Tab key to automatically insert the member into your line of code (thus saving you the typing effort).

This feature also operates in conjunction with Quick Info: As you select different members in the members list, a quick info pop-up will be displayed for that member.

> **NOTE**
>
> IntelliSense maintains a record of the most frequently used/selected members from the List Members and Complete Word functions. This record is used to help avoid displaying or selecting members that you have rarely, if ever, used for a given type.

Parameter Info

Parameter Info, as its name implies, is designed to provide interactive guidance for the parameters needed for any given function call. This feature is especially useful for making function calls that have a long list of parameters and/or a long overload list.

Parameter Info is initiated whenever you type an opening parenthesis after a function name. To see how this works, perform these steps:

1. Type the name of a function.

2. Type an open parenthesis.

3. A pop-up box will show the function signature. If there are multiple valid signatures (for example, multiple overloaded versions of this function), you can scroll through the different signatures by using the small up/down arrow cues.

4. After selecting the desired signature, you can start typing the actual parameters you want to pass in to the function.

5. As you type, the parameter info pop-up will continue coaching you through the parameter list by bolding the current parameter you are working on. As each successive parameter is highlighted, the definition for that parameter will appear.

In Figure 7.14, the second parameter for the `Console` object's `SetWindowPosition` function is currently being entered.

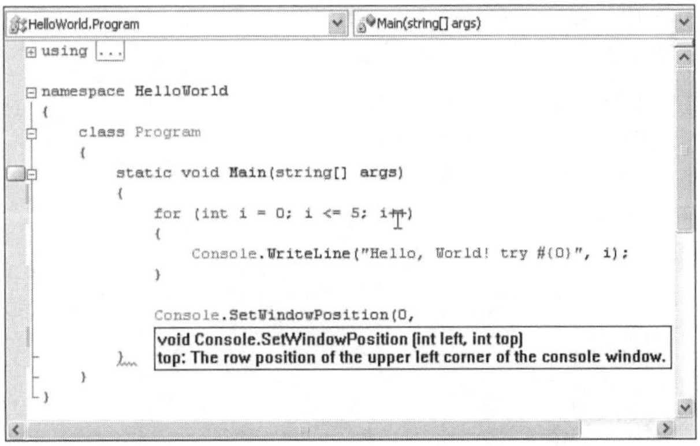

FIGURE 7.14   IntelliSense: Parameter Info.

Code Snippets and Template Code

Code snippets are prestocked lines of code available for selection and insertion into the text editor. Each code snippet is referenced by a name referred to as its *alias*. Code snippets are used to automate what would normally be non–value-added, repetitive typing. You can create your own code snippets or use the default library of common code elements provided by Visual Studio.

Using the Code Snippet Inserter

You insert snippets by right-clicking at the intended insertion point within an open text editor window and then selecting Insert Snippet from the shortcut menu. This will launch the Code Snippet Inserter, which is a drop-down (or series of drop-downs) that works much like the IntelliSense Complete Word feature. Each item in the inserter represents a snippet, represented by its alias. Selecting an alias will expand the snippet into the active document.

With C#, the Code Snippet Inserter is a single drop-down with all available aliases listed. Visual Basic provides an added feature here: Its inserter is actually categorized. To contrast the way the inserter works across these languages, let's look at some snapshots from the IDE.

In C#   First, let's look at how the inserter works with C#. Starting from a bare-bones class file, Figure 7.15 shows the results of expanding the `ctor` snippet into the window. The constructor code is left in place. It is syntactically correct and even has the correct constructor name (referring back to the class name). You can see that snippets can't do everything for you—you still have to write meaningful code inside the constructor—but snippets can eliminate tedious code that really doesn't require much intellectual horsepower to generate.

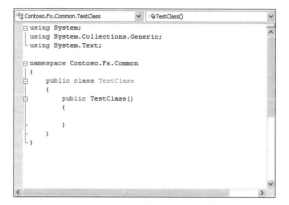

FIGURE 7.15   The `ctor` code snippet.

In Visual Basic   Now for Visual Basic: In Figure 7.16, a snippet designed to help manipulate the opacity of the Windows forms object is being selected. Note that these are folders displayed within the inserter's drop-down. They help to categorize and place an organizational hierarchy over the snippet library. The opacity snippet is located within the Windows Forms Applications folder. Selecting this folder will cause a placeholder to be displayed within the text editor window, and the inserter will now refresh to show only those snippets that have been placed in the Windows Forms Applications category.

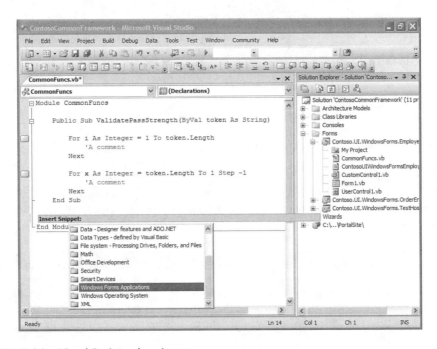

FIGURE 7.16   Visual Basic code snippets.

> **TIP**
>
> A quick, alternate way to display the Code Snippet Inserter is to type a question mark and then press the Tab key. This works only with Visual Basic code documents.

The example here presents yet another level of category folders from which you can select the Forms folder (pressing the Backspace key will back up one category level). You have finally drilled down to the actual list of snippets.

Double-clicking the Create Transparent Windows Forms snippet will get you the code snippet you have been hunting for, but you still aren't done yet. In Figure 7.17, the snippet is selected, and the inserter has injected the template code into the Visual Basic code for you, but the inserter (at least in this case) wasn't intelligent enough to know the name of the form you are trying to make transparent.

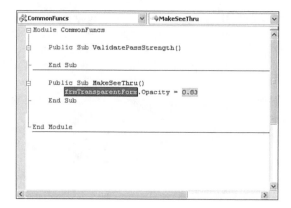

FIGURE 7.17   Form transparency snippet.

The snippet code has the form name filled in with a default, dummy name that is already highlighted. You merely have to start typing the form name you need, and it will replace the dummy name. The opacity value is also a dummy value that you can quickly correct at this time.

> **TIP**
>
> Snippets may have one or more placeholder values: fragments of code that you will want and probably need to change. You can cycle through each of the placeholder values by pressing the Tab key. When a placeholder is highlighted (in blue), you can start typing to replace the syntax with something that makes sense for your specific code context.

Surrounding Code with Snippets

C# and XML documents have one additional style of code snippets that bears mentioning: Surround With snippets. Surround With snippets are still snippets at their core (they are simply prestocked lines of code), but they differ in how they are able to insert themselves into your code.

Using a Surround With snippet, you can stack enclosing text around a selection with the text editor. As an example, perhaps you have a few different class declarations that you would like to nest within a namespace. When you use the Surround With snippet, this is a simple two-step process: Highlight the class definitions and fire up the Code Snippet Inserter. This time, instead of selecting Insert Snippet from the shortcut menu, you select Surround With. The insert works the same way, but this time has applied the snippet (in this case, a namespace snippet) in a different fashion. Compare the before and after text shown in Figures 7.18 and 7.19.

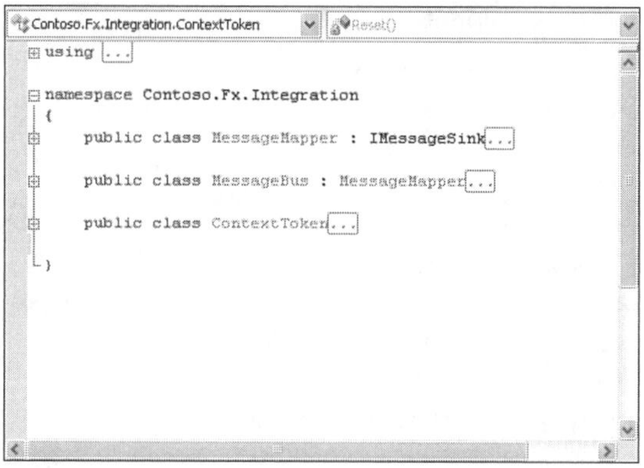

FIGURE 7.18   Before inserting a Surrounds With snippet.

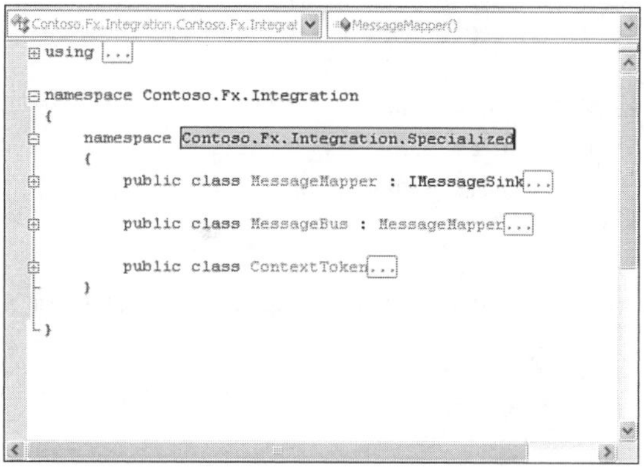

FIGURE 7.19   After inserting a Surrounds With snippet.

Creating Your Own Code Snippets

Because code snippets are stored in XML files, you can create your own snippets quite easily. The key is to understand the XML schema that defines a snippet, and the best way to do that is to look at the XML source data for some of the snippets included with the IDE.

Snippets are stored on a per-language basis under the install directory for Visual Studio. For example, the Visual Basic snippets can be found, by default, in the folders under the C:\Program Files\Microsoft Visual Studio 8\Vb\Snippets directory. Although snippet files are XML, they carry a .Snippet extension.

The XML Snippet Format   Listing 7.1 provides the XML for the C# constructor snippet:

LISTING 7.1   C# Constructor Snippet

```xml
<?xml version="1.0" encoding="utf-8" ?>
<CodeSnippets xmlns="http://schemas.microsoft.com/VisualStudio/2005/CodeSnippet">
    <CodeSnippet Format="1.0.0">
        <Header>
            <Title>ctor</Title>
            <Shortcut>ctor</Shortcut>
            <Description>Code snippet for constructor</Description>
            <Author>Microsoft Corporation</Author>
            <SnippetTypes>
                <SnippetType>Expansion</SnippetType>
            </SnippetTypes>
        </Header>
        <Snippet>
            <Declarations>
                <Literal Editable="false">
                    <ID>classname</ID>
                    <ToolTip>Class name</ToolTip>
                    <Function>ClassName()</Function>
                    <Default>ClassNamePlaceholder</Default>
                </Literal>
            </Declarations>
            <Code Language="csharp"><![CDATA[public $classname$ ()
{
    $end$
}]]>
            </Code>
        </Snippet>
    </CodeSnippet>
</CodeSnippets>
```

The basic structure of this particular snippet declaration is described in Table 7.2. A more complete schema reference is available as a part of the Visual Studio MSDN help collection; it is located under Integrated Development Environment for Visual Studio, Reference, XML Schema References, Code Snippets Schema Reference.

TABLE 7.2   XML Snippet File Node Descriptions

XML Node	Description
`<CodeSnippets>`	The parent element for all code snippet information. It references the specific XML namespace used to define snippets within Visual Studio 2005.
`<CodeSnippet>`	The root element for a single code snippet. This tag sets the format version information for the snippet (for the initial release of VS 2005, this should be set to 1.0.0.0). Although multiple `CodeSnippet` elements are possible within the parent `<CodeSnippets>` element, the convention is to place one snippet per file.

TABLE 7.2   Continued

XML Node	Description
`<Header>`	A metadata container element for data that describes the snippet.
`<Title>`	The title of the code snippet.
`<Shortcut>`	Typically, the same as the title, this is the text that will appear in the code snippet insertion drop-downs.
`<Description>`	A description of the snippet.
`<Author>`	The author of the snippet.
`<SnippetTypes>`	The parent element for holding elements describing the snippet's type.
`<SnippetType>`	The type of the snippet: Expansion, Refactoring, or Surrounds With. You cannot create custom refactoring snippets. This property is really used to tell Visual Studio where the snippet can be inserted within the editor window: Expansion snippets insert at the current cursor position, while Surrounds With snippets get inserted before and after the code body identified by the current cursor position or selection.
`<Snippet>`	The root element for the snippet code.
`<Declarations>`	The root element for the literals and objects used by the snippet.
`<Literal>`	A string whose value can be interactively set as part of the snippet expansion process. The `Editable` attribute on this tag indicates whether the literal is static or editable. The `ctor` snippet is an example of one without an editable literal; contrast this with the form transparency snippet that you saw—an example of a snippet with an editable literal that allows you to set the form name as part of the snippet insertion.
`<ID>`	A unique ID for the literal.
`<ToolTip>`	A ToolTip to display when the cursor is placed over the literal.
`<Function>`	The name of a function (see Table 7.3) to call when the literal receives focus. Functions are available only in C# snippets.
`<Default>`	The default string literal to insert into the editor.
`<Code>`	An element that contains the actual code to insert.

The trick to writing a snippet is to understand how literals and variable replacement works. Say that you wanted to create a C# snippet that writes out a simple code comment indicating that a class has been reviewed and approved as part of a code review process. In other words, you want something like this:

```
// Code review of ContextToken.
//    Reviewer: Lars Powers
//    Date: 1/1/2006
//    Approval: Approved
```

In this snippet, you need to treat four literals as variable; they can change each time the snippet is used: the class name, the reviewer's name, the date, and the approval. You can set them up within the declarations section like this:

```
<Declarations>
    <Literal Editable="False">
        <ID>classname</ID>
        <ToolTip>Class name/type being reviewed</ToolTip>
        <Function>ClassName()</Function>
        <Default>ClassNameGoesHere</Default>
    </Literal>
    <Literal Editable="True">
        <ID>reviewer</ID>
        <ToolTip>Replace with the reviewer's name</ToolTip>
        <Default>ReviewerName</Default>
    </Literal>
    <Literal Editable="True">
        <ID>currdate</ID>
        <ToolTip>Replace with the review date</ToolTip>
        <Default>ReviewDate</Default>
    </Literal>
    <Literal Editable="True">
        <ID>approval</ID>
        <ToolTip>Replace with Approved or Rejected</ToolTip>
        <Default>Approved</Default>
    </Literal>
</Declarations>
```

Notice that you are actually calling a function to prepopulate the class name within the snippet. Functions are available only with C# (with a subset also available in J#) and are documented in Table 7.3. The rest of the literals rely on the developer to type over the placeholder value with the correct value.

TABLE 7.3   Code Snippet Functions

Function	Description
GenerateSwitchCases(*enumliteral*)	Creates the syntax for a switch statement that includes a case statement for each value defined by the enumeration represented by *enumliteral* (C#/J#).
ClassName()	Inserts the name of the class containing the code snippet (C#/J#).
SimpleTypeName(*typename*)	Takes the type name referenced by *typename* and returns the shortest name possible given the using statements in effect for the current code block.
	Example: SimpleTypeName(System.Exception) would return Exception if a using System statement is present (C#).
CallBase(*parameter*)	Is useful when stubbing out members that implement or return the base type: when you specify get, set, or method as the parameter, a call will be created against the base class for that specific property accessor or method (C#).

You should also provide some basic header information for the snippet:

```
<Header>
    <Title>review</Title>
    <Shortcut>review</Shortcut>
    <Description>Code review comment</Description>
    <Author>L. Powers</Author>
    <SnippetTypes>
        <SnippetType>Expansion</SnippetType>
    </SnippetTypes>
</Header>
<Snippet>
```

At this point, the snippet is syntactically complete. Although this snippet is writing comments into the editor, the same exact process and structure would apply for emitting code into the editor. If you wanted to write a Surrounds With snippet, you would change the <SnippetType> to Surrounds With.

Now, you need to make Visual Studio aware of the snippet.

Adding a Snippet to Visual Studio   You can use Visual Studio's own XML editor to create the XML document and save it to a directory (a big bonus for doing so is that you can leverage IntelliSense triggered by the XML snippet schema to help you with your element names and relationships). The Visual Studio installer creates a default directory to place your custom snippets located in your My Documents folder: `\My Documents\Visual Studio 2005\Code Snippets\VC#\My Code Snippets`. If you place your XML template here, Visual Studio will automatically include your snippet for use.

The Code Snippets Manager is the central control dialog box for browsing the available snippets, adding new ones, or removing a snippet (see Figure 7.20). As you can see, the review snippet shows up under the My Code Snippets folder.

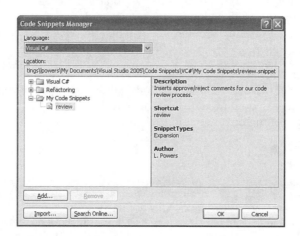

FIGURE 7.20   The Code Snippets Manager.

You can also opt to include other folders besides the standard ones. To do so, click on the Add button to enter additional folders for Visual Studio to use when displaying the list of snippets.

Figure 7.21 shows the results of the custom snippet.

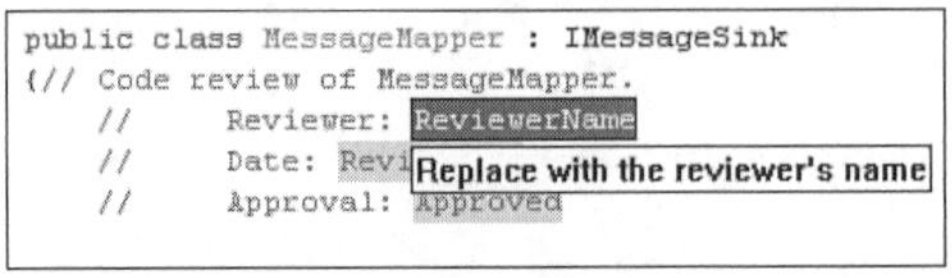

```
public class MessageMapper : IMessageSink
{// Code review of MessageMapper.
    //     Reviewer: ReviewerName
    //     Date: Revi Replace with the reviewer's name
    //     Approval: Approved
```

FIGURE 7.21   Results of a custom code snippet.

> **TIP**
>
> Snippets can also be browsed and shared online (see Chapter 12, "The .NET Community Consuming and Creating Shared Code," for a discussion of online communities). A great way to further your understanding of code snippet structure and functions is to browse your way through the snippet files included in Visual Studio, as well as those created by the developer community as a whole.

Snippets in the Toolbox

Although this capability is technically not part of the official code snippet technology within Visual Studio, you can also store snippets of code in the Toolbox. First, select the text in the editor and then drag and drop it onto the Toolbox. You can then reuse this snippet at any time by dragging it back from the Toolbox into an open editor window.

Brace Matching

Programming languages make use of parentheses, braces, brackets, and other delimiters to delimit function arguments, mathematical functions/order of operation, and bodies of code. It can be difficult to visually determine whether you have missed a matching delimiter—that is, if you have more opening delimiters than you have closing delimiters—especially with highly nested lines of code.

Brace matching refers to visual cues that the code editor uses to make you aware of your matching delimiters. As you type code into the editor, any time you enter a closing delimiter, the matching opening delimiter and the closing delimiter will briefly be highlighted. In Figure 7.22, brace matching helps to indicate the matching delimiters for the interior for loop.

> **TIP**
>
> You also can trigger brace matching simply by placing the cursor directly to the left of an opening delimiter or the right of a closing delimiter. If you are browsing through a routine congested with parentheses and braces, you can quickly sort out the matching pairs by moving your cursor around to the various delimiters.

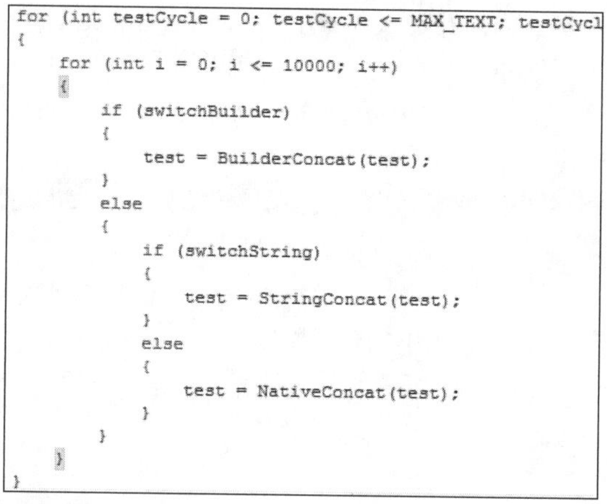

```
for (int testCycle = 0; testCycle <= MAX_TEXT; testCycl
{
    for (int i = 0; i <= 10000; i++)
    {
        if (switchBuilder)
        {
            test = BuilderConcat(test);
        }
        else
        {
            if (switchString)
            {
                test = StringConcat(test);
            }
            else
            {
                test = NativeConcat(test);
            }
        }
    }
}
```

FIGURE 7.22   Brace matching.

Although this feature is referred to as brace matching, it actually functions with the following delimiters:

- Parentheses ( )
- Brackets [ ], <>
- Quotation marks " "
- Braces { }

In the case of C#, brace matching also works with the following keyword pairs (which essentially function as delimiters using keywords):

- # region, #endregion
- #if, #else, #endif
- case, break
- default, break
- for, break, continue
- if, else
- while, break, continue

Customizing IntelliSense

Certain IntelliSense features can be customized, on a per-language basis, within the Visual Studio Options dialog box. If you launch the Options dialog box (located under the Tools menu) and then navigate to the Text Editor node, you will find IntelliSense options confusingly scattered under both the General and IntelliSense pages.

Figure 7.23 shows the IntelliSense editor Options dialog box for Visual C#.

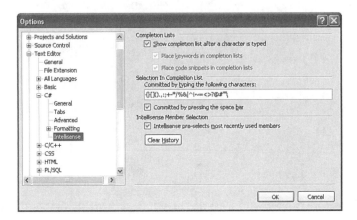

FIGURE 7.23   IntelliSense options.

Completion Lists in this dialog box refer to any of the IntelliSense features that facilitate autocompletion of code such as List Members and Complete Word. Table 7.4 itemizes the options available in this dialog box.

TABLE 7.4   IntelliSense Options

Option	Effect
Show Completion List After a Character Is Typed	Checking this box causes the Complete Word feature to automatically run after a single character is typed in the editor window.
Place Keywords in Completion Lists	If this box is checked, language keywords will be displayed within the completion list. As an example, for C#, this would cause keywords such as class or string to be included in the completion list.
Place Code Snippets in Completion Lists	Checking this box will place code snippet alias names into any displayed completion lists.
Committed by Typing the Following Characters	This check box contains any of the characters that will cause IntelliSense to execute a completion action. In other words, typing any of the characters in this text box while a completion list is displayed will cause IntelliSense to insert the current selection into the editor window.
Committed by Pressing the Space Bar	Checking this box adds the space character to the list of characters that will fire a completion commit.
IntelliSense Pre-selects Most Recently Used Members	If this box is checked, IntelliSense will maintain and use a historical list of the most frequently used members for a given type. This MFU list is then used to preselect members in a completion list.

The Task List

The Task List is essentially an integrated "to do" list; it captures all of the items that, for one reason or another, need attention and tracking. The Task List window then surfaces this list and allows you to interact with it. To show the window, select the View menu and choose the Task List entry. Figure 7.24 illustrates the Task List window displaying a series of user tasks. Tasks belong to one of three categories—comment tasks, shortcut tasks, and user tasks—and only one category can be displayed at a time.

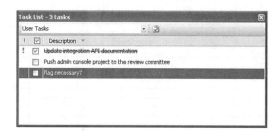

FIGURE 7.24   The Task List window.

The drop-down at the top of the Task List window enables you to select the current category. Each category will have slightly different columns that it shows for each task category type, but they will all have a Priority and a Description column. For instance, user tasks and shortcut tasks provide a check box that is used to track task completion; shortcut and comment tasks display a filename and line number, and so on.

You can sort the tasks by any of the columns shown in the list. Right-clicking on the column headers will provide a shortcut menu that allows you to control the sort behavior, as well as which columns (from a list of all supported columns) should be displayed.

Comment Tasks

Comment tasks are created within your code. Placing a code comment with a special string literal/token will cause Visual Studio to add that comment to the comment task list. Three of these tokens are defined by Visual Studio: HACK, TODO, and UNDONE.

As an example, the following C# code would result in four different comment tasks in the task list:

```
namespace Contoso.Fx.Integration.Specialized
{
    //TODO: Implement second constructor
    public class MessageMapper : IMessageSink
    {
        public MessageMapper()
        {
        }
    }
```

```
//TODO: Check on IMap interface implementation
public class MessageBus : MessageMapper
{
    public MessageBus()
    {
        //UNDONE: MessageBus ctor
    }
}

//HACK: re-write of TokenStruct
public class ContextToken
{
    public ContextToken()
    {
    }
    public ContextToken(string guid)
    {
    }
}
}
```

Double-clicking on the comment task will take you directly to the referenced comment line within the editor window.

Custom Comment Tokens

If needed, you can add your own set of tokens that will be recognized as comment tasks. From the Tools, Options dialog box, select the Task List page under the Environment section; this dialog box provides options for adding, editing, or deleting the list of comment tokens recognized by the task list.

In Figure 7.25 a REVIEW token has been added to the standard list. Note that you can also set a priority against each of the tokens and fine-tune some of the display behavior by using the Task List Options check boxes, which control whether task deletions are confirmed, and by setting whether filenames or complete file paths are displayed within the task list.

Shortcut Tasks

Shortcut tasks are actually links to a line of code. You add them using the Bookmarks menu by placing the cursor on a line within the editor and then selecting Edit, Bookmarks, Add Task List Shortcut. The actual content of that line of code will show up as the task description.

Double-clicking on the task will take you directly to the bookmarked line within the editor window.

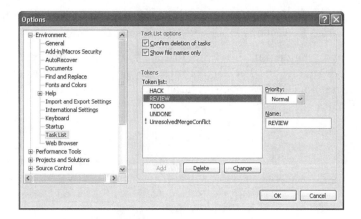

FIGURE 7.25   Adding a custom comment task token.

User Tasks

User tasks are entered directly into the task window. A Create User Task button will show next to the category drop-down on the Task List window (refer to Figure 7.24); this button will add a new entry within the list. You can type directly into the description column to add the task's title.

Unlike shortcut and comment tasks, user tasks aren't linked to a specific line of code.

> **NOTE**
>
> Visual Studio's automation model provides complete control over task lists. Using the exposed automation objects such as TaskList and TaskListEvents, you can, for example, programmatically add or remove tasks from the list; respond to a task being added, edited, or even selected; and control the linking between a task and an editor.

Summary

Visual Studio 2005 carries a staggering number of features designed to boost your productivity. This chapter described the many facets of the IntelliSense technology, ranging from statement completion to the new code snippet technology, and you learned how to work with the various IntelliSense features both to write code faster and improve the quality of your code.

We covered how to navigate and browse through sometimes complicated and congested code files.

We also introduced code snippets and discussed the different types of code snippets and their usefulness.

Last, we covered how to use the Task List window to its fullest potential, to help organize and track the various to-do items inherent with any programming project.

From a productivity standpoint, Visual Studio 2005 truly is more than the sum of its parts: In synergy with one another, each of these features knocks down substantial hurdles and pain points for developers, regardless of their background, skill level, or language preference.

CHAPTER **8**

Refactoring Code

Whether or not you realize it, if you are like most developers, you are always refactoring code. Every time you change your code to reduce duplication or rename items for the sake of clarity, you are refactoring. Refactoring is simply putting a name to a common development task. The strict definition of the term is, "A change made to the internal structure of software to make it easier to understand and cheaper to modify without changing its observable behavior." That is, refactoring does not add features to the application. Instead, it improves the general maintenance of the code base.

The term *refactoring* has received a large amount of attention as of late. A number of good books have been written touting the many benefits of refactoring code as you are building your application. This is when you are closest to the code and thus able to quickly make these maintenance-type changes. Many of these books are on the subject of extreme programming. Refactoring has become one of the key tenets of the extreme programmer. In extreme programming your code base builds feature by feature to satisfy a series of tests. This can result in code that works wonderfully but does not look like it was designed as a cohesive unit. To combat this, you would be wise to go over the code base at frequent intervals and thus improve the general quality of the code (remove duplication, create common interfaces, rename items, put things into logical groups, and so on).

Perhaps because of all this attention, a new set of features has arisen inside code editors to aid with refactoring. These features have their basis in a real need. No developer wants to introduce errors into a relatively stable code base simply for the sake of improving maintenance—especially when running a tight schedule. Imagine explaining to your

IN THIS CHAPTER

- Visual Studio Refactoring Basics
- Rename
- Extract Method
- Extract Interface
- Refactor Parameters
- Encapsulate Field

manager or client that the large spike in bugs is a result of sweeping changes you made to the code to improve future maintenance and readability. We can be thankful that the C# editor inside Visual Studio 2005 provides a reliable set of refactoring tools. These tools let you make changes to the code base without the concern of creating more issues than you are solving.

Refactoring for the VB Developer

We are focusing this chapter on the refactoring tools built into Visual Studio 2005. These tools are strictly for the C# code editor. Fortunately, Visual Basic developers do have an option for refactoring. A third-party development house, DevExpress (www.devexpress.com), struck a deal with Microsoft to include a version of its product for all Visual Studio 2005 VB .NET developers. We cannot cover this tool in this book, but users should find many similarities between the two products.

Visual Studio Refactoring Basics

The Visual Studio refactoring tools work to ensure you see the promises of refactoring: increased reuse of your code, fewer rewrites, reduced duplication, and better readability. These tools work to instill confidence in the edits they make to your code. They do so by using a common refactoring engine based on the C# compiler rather than string matching and search-and-replace. The engine and compiler work together to cover the entire code base (and its references) to find all possible changes that need to be made as part of a given refactor operation. The engine even searches out code comments and tries to update them to reflect new type names. In addition, you can preview changes to your code before they happen. This adds further to your comfort level with the modifications these tools are making to your code.

Table 8.1 presents a high-level overview of the many refactoring operations that are possible with the C# editor. We will cover each of them in great detail in the coming sections. Prior to this, however, we will cover some of the common elements of the refactoring process. These elements include both invoking a refactoring tool inside Visual Studio and previewing the refactoring changes as they happen.

TABLE 8.1   Refactoring Tools Inside the Visual Studio 2005 C# Editor

Tool	Description
Rename	Renames fields, properties, methods, and variables.
Extract Method	Creates a new method using existing code within a different method or routine.
Promote Local to Parameter	Moves a local member of a method to a parameter of the method.
Reorder Parameters	Changes the order of parameters for a given method.
Remove Parameters	Removes a parameter from a method.
Encapsulate Field	Quickly creates a property from an existing field.
Extract Interface	Creates an interface from an existing class or structure.

Invoking the Refactoring Tools

The refactoring tools are available from wherever you work on your C# code inside Visual Studio. You can invoke them in a number of ways. For example, if you are working inside the code editor, you can invoke the Rename tool using a smart tag. You can also select and right-click code to reveal the refactoring options; these same options are available on the menu bar through the Refactor menu. Finally, you can refactor directly from the Class Designer as you edit and change various items within a given class.

Using the Refactor Menu (and Right-Click)

The most common place to invoke the refactoring commands is from the actual refactoring menu. This menu item is added to the IDE when you have a C# code window open and active. Figure 8.1 shows the menu being invoked. Note that the portion of code you are trying to refactor is highlighted in the IDE. In this case, we want to rename the class Product because we have determined that all our products are books. Therefore, we will rename the class Product to Book.

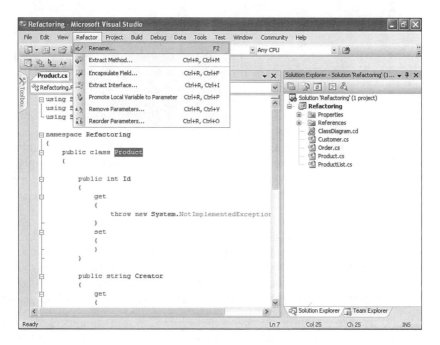

FIGURE 8.1   The Refactor menu in action.

This same menu is available via a right-click within the editor. Again, you either high-light a word or section of code (or simply position the cursor accordingly) and then right-click. The top item in this menu is Refactor. This menu folds out to reveal the full Refactor menu (as shown in Figure 8.2).

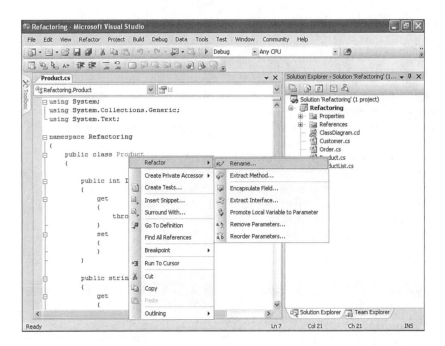

FIGURE 8.2   The Refactor menu invoked via a right-click with the mouse.

Refactoring in the Code Window via Smart Tags

The smart tag was introduced in Microsoft Office. Its goal was simple: Try to understand what the user was typing and offer additional, "smart" functionality. For example, as you type in the Word editor, it tries to understand when you've typed a name or address. In these cases, the editor provides you with additional functionally such as Create contact or Schedule appointment.

The C# code editor provides a similar, smart-tag–like feature. The editor detects your typing and understands when you have made a change to your code that is the equivalent of a refactor. In these cases the editor creates a smart tag that can be used to invoke the refactoring tool. This allows you to stay in the code editor but still take advantage of the increased productivity and reduced error rate that the refactoring tool can provide.

As an example, suppose you have a property named ID. You want to rename this item to Identifier. You open the class file and position your cursor near the property name. You then type the new property name. The C# code editor detects your change and underlines the final character of the changed name. Figure 8.3 shows an example of this. Notice the small rectangle beneath the *r* in *identifier*.

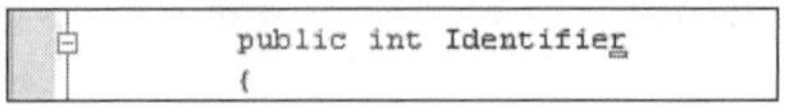

```
        public int Identifier
        {
```

FIGURE 8.3   Renaming a property invokes a smart tag for refactoring.

This small rectangle hovering underneath the change is your visual cue that the C# code editor thinks it can help you. You can position your mouse cursor next to the rectangle to reveal an in-line menu that indicates how the editor might help. Figure 8.4 shows the smart tag as it is invoked relative to the previous example.

TIP

You can also invoke smart tags without grabbing for the mouse. To do so, press the key combination Shift+Alt+F10.

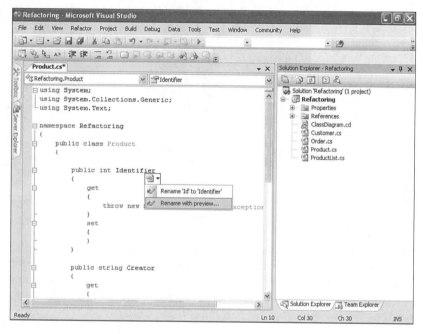

FIGURE 8.4   Invoking a refactor via a smart tag.

Using the Class Designer to Refactor

Visual Studio 2005 provides a Visual Designer for working with classes. This Class Designer allows you to view the contents of your classes and their relationships. It can also be used as a productivity tool; you can create new classes and modify existing classes directly within the designer (see Chapter 21, "Modeling," for additional details.)

The Visual Studio Class Designer exposes the refactoring tool when you're working with C# classes. This ensures that code modifications made using this Visual Designer take full advantage of refactoring. For instance, suppose you want to rename a property from within the Class Designer but also want to make sure that the references to that property are automatically updated. You can do so by right-clicking the property within the Class Designer and choosing the Refactor menu's Rename option. Figure 8.5 shows refactoring from directly within the Class Designer.

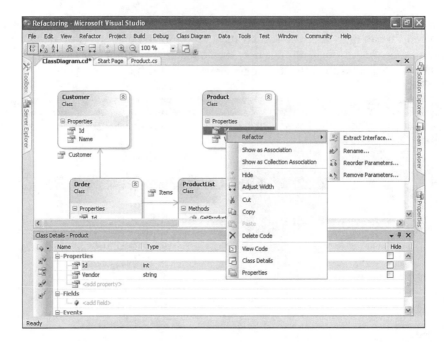

FIGURE 8.5   Invoking refactoring from within the Visual Studio Class Designer.

Previewing Changes

As you become comfortable with the refactoring tools, you may decide to simply let them do their thing without much oversight on your part. However, if you are like most developers, then no one (or no tool) touches your code without your consent. Fortunately for us, the refactoring tools provide a preview option. This option lets you follow the tool through its changes and, in turn, accept or reject a given change.

The Preview Changes dialog box is invoked as an option (check box) on a given refactoring operation (or in the case of a smart tag, from a second menu item on the smart tag menu). Figure 8.6 provides an example of selecting the Preview Reference Changes option from the Rename refactor operation.

After the refactoring operation is invoked with Preview Changes, Visual Studio presents you with the Preview Changes dialog box. The top portion of this dialog box lists all of the changes the given refactor operation intends to make. This list is presented as a tree, with the outer branch representing where you intend to originate the change. The leafs under this branch are all files where changes will happen. Nested beneath the filenames are the actual places within the code that a change will be made. You use this list to select each item you would like to preview. Figure 8.7 shows an example of the many changes required when changing a class name from Order to CustomerOrder.

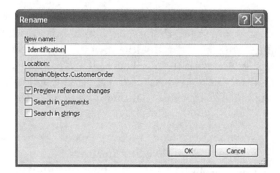

FIGURE 8.6   Invoking a refactor operation with Preview Reference Changes.

FIGURE 8.7   Previewing changes of a Rename operation.

As each item in the Preview Changes tree is clicked, the corresponding code is displayed below the tree in the Preview Code Changes section of the dialog box. This allows developers to quickly review where changes will be made. To prevent a given change, you can simply uncheck the item in the tree view. Of course, you can prevent entire file changes by unchecking further up in the hierarchy at the file level. When you are finished with your preview and satisfied with the proposed changes, you simply click the Apply button to commit the changes to your code.

Rename

Renaming code elements is the most common refactoring operation. In a typical refactoring session, renaming often makes up the bulk of the work. However, most renaming happens outside the normal refactoring window. Developers do not typically wait until the code base is operational and say to themselves, "Okay, now I will go back and rename these 10 items for clarity." Although this does happen, the more likely scenario is that as you build your application, you consistently rename items to correct mistakes or make things clearer and more readable. Of course, as the code base builds, renaming classes, methods, fields, and the like becomes more and more difficult without introducing new bugs into your code.

Therefore, the ability to rename items with the confidence that you will not introduce bugs into your code is paramount. The C# editor in Visual Studio 2005 provides just this feature. With it, you can rename all relevant code items including namespaces, classes, fields, properties, methods, and variables. In fact, the Rename operation can even search through your code comments and update them accordingly.

Accessing the Rename Operation

You can rename from many places within the IDE. In the previous "Invoking the Refactoring Tools" section, we looked at accessing Rename from the Refactor menu, a right-click, a smart tag, and the Class Designer. You can also access Rename from the Object Browser and the Solution Explorer. In addition, if you use the Properties dialog box to change the name of a control you've placed on a form, the Rename operation is invoked behind the scenes and the control gets renamed appropriately.

From the Object Browser, you can access the Rename operation only from the Refactor menu. Of course, you need to be browsing your own types in your solution. You simply select the item you want to rename and then click the Refactor menu. Figure 8.8 shows an example of the Object Browser and Rename operation working together.

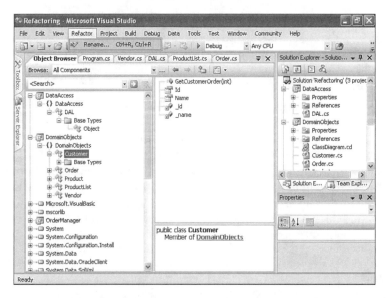

FIGURE 8.8   Accessing the Rename operation from the Object Browser.

You can rename within the Solution Explorer for filenames that equate to class names. For instance, if you select a file named Customer, right-click, and choose Rename, Visual Studio will rename the file. In addition, it will search the code within the file for any class that had the same name as the file. So if you had a Customer class and a Customer.cs file, a Rename operation will rename the file as well as the class (and all references to the class). Note that while an undo on the Rename operation will roll back a change, in the case of a filename change, Undo reverts the code but does not change the filename back to its original name.

> **TIP**
>
> You can access the Rename operation from a set of command keys. Past versions of Visual Studio introduced the concept of *chords*. They are like traditional keyboard commands, but you press (or *play*) them in sequence. For instance, to invoke the Rename operation without touching your mouse, position your cursor over what you want to rename. Then press the sequence Ctrl+R, Ctrl+R. Pressing this combination in sequence will bring up the Refactoring, Rename dialog box relative to the code element behind your cursor.

Working with the Rename Dialog Box

The Rename dialog box allows you to specify a few options when invoking a given Rename refactor operation. Figure 8.9 presents an example of the dialog box. The two text boxes on the form allow you to define the rename itself. In the New Name section, you indicate the new name of the element to be renamed. The Location text box indicates the namespace of the element to be renamed. Of course, all referenced locations will also be searched.

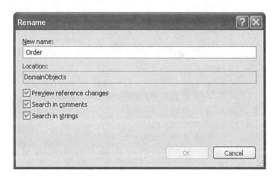

FIGURE 8.9   The Rename dialog box.

The Rename dialog box also presents developers with a few options (all off by default) when doing a rename. The three check boxes below the Location text box allow you to set the options as described in Table 8.2.

TABLE 8.2   The Rename Dialog Box Options

Option	Description
Preview Reference Changes	This option allows you to indicate whether you want to preview the changes before they are applied to your code. This capability can be especially useful if you are renaming for the first time or you intend to rename items inside strings or comments. Renaming strings and comments does not use the compiler. Instead it uses string matching. Therefore, it may not always be accurate or the intended result. Figure 8.10 shows the Preview Changes – Rename dialog box with a string rename (specifically the text on a button).
Search in Comments	This option allows you to indicate whether the Rename operation should search your comments for possible textual references that should be renamed. Comments often refer to types and hence need to be synced with changes. The alternative is a set of very confusing comments. Figure 8.10 shows the Preview Changes – Rename dialog box with a Comments folder and a sample comment that needs to be renamed.
Search in Strings	This preference allows you to indicate whether the Rename operation should search inside your literal strings for references to a given item name. String literals include constants, control names, form names, and so on. This capability is most useful if there is a tight coupling between your code and the elements within your user interface.

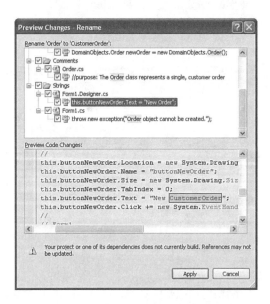

FIGURE 8.10   The Preview Changes – Rename dialog box.

Extract Method

When developers go back and take a look at their code, perhaps during a periodic code review or after a particularly long session of heads-down development, they often find methods that are too long or course-grained, contain duplicate code, or are just poorly organized. A common thing to do is pass over the code and create fine-grained, discrete methods to reduce these issues and make for a more readable, reusable, and maintainable code base.

The problem, of course, is that doing this is time consuming and often introduces bugs into the code. The C# code editor in Visual Studio 2005 provides an Extract Method refactoring tool to ensure a quick, bug-free experience when you're working to better organize your code. With this tool, you can create a new method using existing code.

Accessing the Extract Method Refactor

To access the Extract Method refactor operation, you first must select a portion of code to refactor. You then can use the Refactor menu and select the Extract Method menu item. You can also invoke the Extract Method from the context menu via a right-click.

> **TIP**
>
> To invoke the Extract Method operation from the keyboard, first select the section of code you want to extract. Next, play the chord Ctrl+R, Ctrl+M.

Extracting Methods

With the Extract Method operation, you can create (or extract) a new method from multiple lines of code, a single line, or an expression within a given line of code. In each case, the method is created immediately following the method from which the code was extracted. The extracted code is replaced by a call to the new method.

Listing 8.1 provides an example of a typical, overlong method. We've added line numbers for reference purposes. When you're reviewing code, methods such as these are common and exactly what you should be looking for. The method is designed as a static call that returns a given customer's Order object based on the customer's ID number and the order ID number. However, the order, the order line items, and the customer details are all retrieved from discreet database calls and stored in domain-specific objects. These objects are then stored on the order as properties.

LISTING 8.1   A Long Static Method

```
01   public static Order GetCustomerOrder(int customerId, int orderId) {
02
03      DataAccess.DAL dal = new DataAccess.DAL();
04      Order order = new Order();
05
06      //get order details
```

LISTING 8.1   Continued

```
07    System.Data.DataTable dtOrder = dal.GetData("customerOrder", orderId);
08
09    //validate order against customer
10    if (customerId != (int)dtOrder.Rows[0]["customer_id"]) {
11      throw new ApplicationException("Invalid order for the given customer.");
12    }
13    order.Id = (string)dtOrder.Rows[0]["id"];
14
15    //get order items
16    List<OrderItem> items = new List<OrderItem>();
17    System.Data.DataTable dtItems = dal.GetData("orderItems", orderId);
18    foreach (System.Data.DataRow r in dtItems.Rows) {
19      OrderItem item = new OrderItem((int)r["product_id"], orderId);
20      item.Name = (string)r["name"];
21      item.Description = (string)r["description"];
22      item.Quantity = (int)r["quantity"];
23      item.UnitPrice = (double)r["unit_price"];
24      items.Add(item);
25    }
26    order.Items = items;
27
28    //get customer details
29    System.Data.DataTable dtCustomer = dal.GetData("customer", customerId);
30    Customer cust = new Customer(customerId);
31    cust.Name = (string)dtCustomer.Rows[0]["name"];
32    order.Customer = cust;
33
34    return order;
35  }
```

Opportunities for method extraction inside this one method are numerous. You might consider extracting the call to initialize the Order object, the call to get order items, and the call to get customer details. Doing so will result in better organized code (thus, more readable), more opportunities for reuse, and an easier-to-maintain code base. Let's look at doing these extractions.

First, you'll extract the call that sets up the order. Knowing what to select for extraction requires a bit of experience with the tool. In this case, extract lines 3–13. This takes the code from the DataAccess setup through the order initialization. However, doing so confuses the Extract Method operation somewhat because you are setting up both a DataAccess object and an Order object in the first two operations. The Extract Method understands you need these two objects further in your method. Therefore, it will create both objects as *out* parameters of the method. What you want is the method to return an instance of the Order object and set up its own DataAccess object. You can accomplish this with the following steps:

1. Select lines 4–13 (order creation through initialization).

2. Select the Extract Method refactor operation (menu, right-click, or keyboard chord).

3. Visual Studio will then present the Extract Method dialog box, as shown in Figure 8.11. This dialog box presents the new method name (NewMethod by default) and the method signature. If the method signature does not look right, you can cancel the operation and refine your code selection. In this case, the method is static; returns an Order object; and takes customerId, orderId, and DataAccess objects. We do not want the latter in our function signature but will deal with this momentarily.

4. Rename the method to something meaningful. In this case, rename it to InitCustomerOrder.

5. Click the OK button to allow the method to be extracted.

6. The new method is created, and the old method is replaced by the following call:

```
Order order = InitCustomerOrder(customerId, orderId, dal);
```

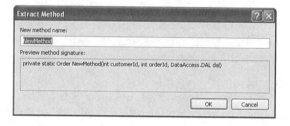

FIGURE 8.11   Extracting code to a method to initialize the order.

NOTE

Extracted methods are created as private by default.

You still have one issue with the extracted method: It takes an instance of DataAccess when you would prefer that it created its own instance. Fortunately, you can use another refactoring operation to deal with this issue. In this case, use the Remove Parameters refactor. This refactoring operation is covered later in this chapter. It is important to point out that removing the parameter results in removing it from both the method signature and the call to the method. It does not, however, put the call to create that DataAccess object inside the new method (nor does it remove it from the old method). You must take these two steps manually.

Next, let's extract the call to get order items. Begin by selecting lines 16–25 (see Listing 8.1). Note that we do not want to select the call to set the order's property (line 26); we simply want to return an object that represents all line items for a given order. Figure 8.12 shows the selection and method extraction. In this case, name the new method GetOrderItems. After the method is extracted, it is replaced by the following call to the new method:

```
List<OrderItem> items = GetOrderItems(orderId, dal);
```

Again you have the issue with the DataAccess object being passed into the new method. You solve this issue in the same manner as you did previously.

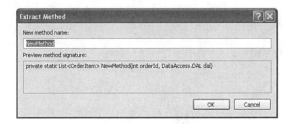

FIGURE 8.12   Extracting code to a method to return order items.

Finally, let's look at extracting the portion of the method that gets the customer details. By now, this procedure should be reasonably straightforward. You select the code (lines 29–31) and choose the Extract Method operation. You name the new method GetCustomer and deal with the extracted DataAccess parameter.

The newly organized (and much shorter) method looks like Listing 8.2. In addition, you now have three new tight, discrete methods that you may be able to reuse in the future (and perhaps make public). These new methods can be found in Listing 8.3.

LISTING 8.2   The Static Method After the Extractions

```
public static Order GetCustomerOrder(int customerId, int orderId) {

  Order order = InitCustomerOrder(customerId, orderId);

  //get order items
  List<OrderItem> items = GetOrderItems(orderId);
  order.Items = items;

  //get customer details
  Customer cust = GetCustomer(customerId);
  order.Customer = cust;

  return order;
}
```

LISTING 8.3   The Extractions

```
private static Customer NewMethod(int customerId) {
  DataAccess.DAL dal = new DataAccess.DAL();
  System.Data.DataTable dtCustomer = dal.GetData("customer", customerId);
  Customer cust = new Customer(customerId);
  cust.Name = (string)dtCustomer.Rows[0]["name"];
  return cust;
}

private static List<OrderItem> GetOrderItems(int orderId) {
  List<OrderItem> items = new List<OrderItem>();
  DataAccess.DAL dal = new DataAccess.DAL();
  System.Data.DataTable dtItems = dal.GetData("orderItems", orderId);
  foreach (System.Data.DataRow r in dtItems.Rows) {
    OrderItem item = new OrderItem((int)r["product_id"], orderId);
    item.Name = (string)r["name"];
    item.Description = (string)r["description"];
    item.Quantity = (int)r["quantity"];
    item.UnitPrice = (double)r["unit_price"];
    items.Add(item);
  }
  return items;
}

private static Order InitCustomerOrder(int customerId, int orderId) {

  Order order = new Order();

  //get order details
  DataAccess.DAL dal = new DataAccess.DAL();
  System.Data.DataTable dtOrder = dal.GetData("customerOrder", orderId);

  //validate order against customer
  if (customerId != (int)dtOrder.Rows[0]["customer_id"]) {
    throw new ApplicationException("Invalid order for the given customer.");
  }
  order.Id = (string)dtOrder.Rows[0]["id"];
  return order;
}
```

8

> **NOTE**
>
> Extract Method does not allow you to choose where to put the extracted method. Many times you might find a bit of code that really needs to be extracted into a method of another, different class. For this, you have to extract the method and then move things around manually.

Extracting a Single Line of Code

Sometimes, you might want to extract a single line of code or a portion of a line of code as its own method. For example, you may have a calculation that is done as part of a line of code but is common enough to warrant its own method. Alternatively, you might need to extract an object assignment to add additional logic to it. In either case, the C# code editor supports this type of extraction.

Let's look at an example. Suppose you have the following line of code that calculates an order's total inside a loop through the order items list:

```
total = total + item.Quantity * item.UnitPrice;
```

You may want to extract the portion of the assignment that calculates a line item's total (quantity * unit price). To do so, you simply select the portion of code and invoke the Extract Method refactor. Figure 8.13 shows this operation in action.

FIGURE 8.13   Extracting a portion of a line of code.

Notice that, by default, the new method would like an instance of OrderItem. You may prefer to pass both quantity and unit price instead. You would have to make this change manually. You could do so by creating the variables in the new method and doing a Promote Local to Parameter refactor (covered later in this chapter). Alternatively, if quantity and unit price were assigned to variables prior to doing the extraction, you would get a new method that accepted these parameters (instead of an OrderItem instance). Figure 8.14 demonstrates this fact.

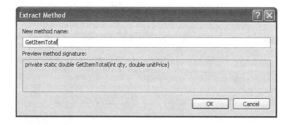

FIGURE 8.14   An alternative extraction of a portion of a line of code.

The resulting refactor replaces a portion of the line of code with the following:

```
total = total + GetItemTotal(qty, unitPrice);
```

It also adds the new method as follows:

```
private static double GetItemTotal(int qty, double unitPrice) {
  return qty * unitPrice;
}
```

Generate Method Stub

You can get Visual Studio to automatically generate a method stub for you. This is not strictly a refactoring operation but can provide some similar increases in productivity. The scenario where this is applicable is as follows. Suppose you are writing code that calls a method off one of your objects. However, that method does not exist. You can still write code to make the call to the nonexistent method. Visual Studio will then recognize that this method does not exist and provide you with a smart tag (see Figure 8.15) to create the method.

System.Data.DataSet ds = dal.GetData(orderId);
Generate method stub for 'GetData' in 'DataAccess.DAL'

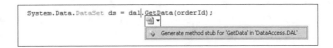

FIGURE 8.15 Generate a method stub for a nonexistent method.

Clicking on the smart tag will result in Visual Studio extracting the method call to a newly generated method in the target assembly and class. Figure 8.16 shows the new method. Note that Visual Studio even provided a readable name for the method's parameter. This name was based on the variable inside the calling method.

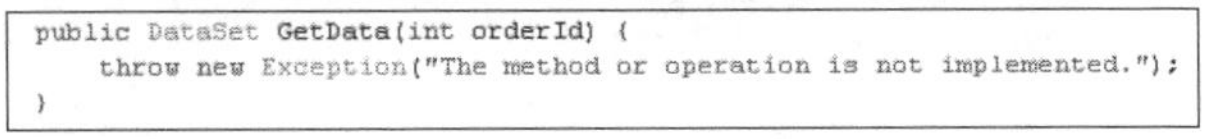

public DataSet GetData(int orderId) {
throw new Exception("The method or operation is not implemented.");
}

FIGURE 8.16 The generated method stub.

Extract Interface

When classes contain the same subset of members, it can be useful to define a common contract that each class shares. This, of course, is done via an interface. Some basic advantages to defining interfaces is that your code becomes more readable, is easier to maintain, and operates the same for like members. However, developers often don't realize the commonality between their classes until after those classes are coded. This makes creating interfaces sometimes a bit too painful of an operation.

The C# editor in Visual Studio 2005 provides the Extract Interface refactoring operation to make this process easier. It allows you to take an existing class or struct and automatically generate a matching interface that the existing class will then implement.

Accessing the Extract Interface Refactor

To access the Extract Interface refactor operation, you first must position your cursor in a class, struct, or another interface that contains the members you want to extract. You then can use the Refactor menu and select the Extract Interface menu item. You can also invoke Extract Interface from the context menu via a right-click.

TIP

To invoke the Extract Interface operation from the keyboard, first position your cursor in the class, struct, or interface that contains the members you want to extract. Next, play the chord Ctrl+R, Ctrl+I.

Extracting Interfaces

To better understand the Extract Interface operation, let's look at an example. Suppose you review your code and notice that a number of your domain objects share similar properties and methods. Let's say the objects Customer, Vendor, Manufacturer, SalesAgent, and Product all contain properties for Id and Name and methods for Get, Save, and Delete. In this case, you should consider extracting this commonality into an interface that each object would implement. Let's look at how the Extract Interface refactoring operation aids in this regard.

First, you position your cursor on the target class whose members you want to extract. In the example, choose the Customer class. Invoking the Extract Interface operation presents a dialog box named the same. Figure 8.17 shows this dialog box relative to the example.

FIGURE 8.17   Extracting an interface.

Notice that you first define a name for the interface. By default, the tool names the interface with the name of the class preceded by the letter *I* for interface—in this case,

`ICustomer`. Of course, we are going to use our interface across our domain, so we will change this to `IDomainObject`.

The Extract Interface dialog box also shows the generated name and the new filename for the interface. The generated name is simply the fully qualified name of the interface. This will be used by the class for implementation of the interface. The New File Name text box shows the C# filename for the interface. All extracted interfaces result in the creation of a new file. The tool tries to keep the filename in sync with the interface name.

The last thing to do is select which members of the object you want to publish as an interface. Of course, only public members are displayed in this list. For this example, select all of the public members: `Id`, `Name`, `Get`, `Save`, and `Delete`.

Clicking the OK button generates the interface. The only change that is made to the `Customer` class is that it now implements the new interface, as in the following line of code:

```
public class Customer : DomainObjects.IDomainObject
```

The interface is then extracted to a new file. Listing 8.4 shows the newly extracted interface.

LISTING 8.4   The Extracted Interface

```
using System;
namespace DomainObjects {
  interface IDomainObject {
    void Delete();
    void Get(int id);
    int Id { get; }
    string Name { get; set; }
    void Save();
  }
}
```

The next step in the example is to go out to each additional domain object and implement the new interface. This has to be done without the benefit of refactoring. However, Visual Studio does provide a smart tag for implementing an interface. Figure 8.18 shows the smart tag that results from typing : `IDomainObject` after the `Vendor` class declaration.

In this case you have two options: Implement the interface or explicitly implement the interface. The former checks the current class to see whether there are implementations that apply. The latter generates code that explicitly calls the interface items. It puts all this code inside a region for the given interface. This capability can be very useful if you're stubbing out a new class based on the interface. The following lines of code provide an example of an explicit interface member declaration:

```
void IDomainObject.Get(int id) {
  throw new Exception("The method or operation is not implemented.");
}
```

8

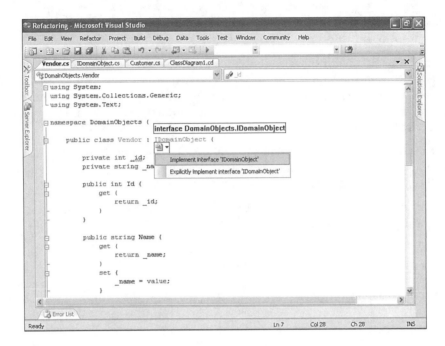

FIGURE 8.18   Implementing an interface.

Refactor Parameters

You sometimes need to change your method signatures by removing an item, adding a local variable as a parameter, or by reordering the existing parameters. These changes require that all calls to the method also be changed. Doing this manually can introduce new bugs into the code. For example, suppose you want to swap the order of two parameters with the same type (int, for example). If you forget to change a call to the method, it may still work; it just won't work right. These bugs can be challenging to find. Therefore, Visual Studio provides refactoring operations for removing, promoting, and reordering parameters.

Remove Parameters

The Remove Parameters refactor operation allows you to select one or more parameters from a given method, constructor, or delegate and have it removed from the method. It also works to update any callers to the method and remove the value passed to the parameter.

You invoke the Remove Parameters operation by positioning your cursor inside the method signature and then selecting the Remove Parameters menu item from the Refactor menu. You can also get to this operation through the context menu (right-click). In addition, this operation is available from the Class Designer from inside both the class view and the class details view.

TIP

To invoke the Remove Parameters operation from the keyboard, first position your cursor in the method that contains the parameters you want to remove. Next, play the keyboard chord Ctrl+R, Ctrl+V.

Let's look at an example. Suppose you have a method with the following signature:

```
public static Order GetCustomerOrder(int customerId, int orderId)
```

This method returns an Order object based on both a customer and an order identification number. Suppose you determine that the order ID is sufficient for returning an order. In this case, you invoke the Remove Parameters refactor and are then presented with the Remove Parameters dialog box (see Figure 8.19). Method parameters are listed at the top. To remove one, you select it and click the Remove button. The item to be removed is then updated with a strikethrough. If you change your mind, you can use the Restore button to cancel individual parameter removals.

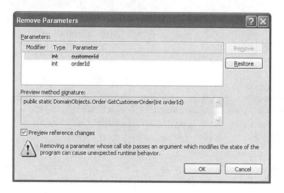

FIGURE 8.19   The Remove Parameters dialog box.

When you are ready to make the removal, you can choose to preview the changes or simply apply them all at once. The preview option works the same as other previews. It simply shows you each change in a tree view and allows you to see the details behind the change. You can, of course, also uncheck specific changes. When finished, you apply the final set of removals to your code.

CAUTION

It is common to declare a local variable inside a method and pass that local variable as a call to another method. If you use the refactoring operation to remove the parameter on the method you are calling, the local variable still exists in your calling method. Be careful to make sure that this is what you intended; if not, you will have to remove the local variable manually.

Promote Local to Parameter

One common developer activity is to take a variable from within a method and make it a parameter of the method. As an example, you might look up a value inside a method and assign that value to a local variable. Instead of doing the lookup inside the method, you might want to have the value passed to the method (perhaps you would use the Extract Method refactor to push the value assignment to a new method).

This change of taking a local variable and creating a parameter can be done automatically via the Promote Local Variable to Parameter refactoring operation. It allows you to select a local member of a given method and promote it to a parameter of the method. The tool also works to update any callers of the method.

You invoke the Promote Local Variable to Parameter operation by positioning your cursor on a line of code that declares a variable. You then select the Promote Local Variable to Parameter menu item from the Refactor menu. You can also get to this operation through the context menu (right-click).

> **TIP**
>
> To invoke the Promote Local Variable to Parameter operation from the keyboard, first position your cursor on the line of code that contains the variable declaration. Next, play the keyboard chord Ctrl+R, Ctrl+P.

> **NOTE**
>
> You can promote locals only where they have been initialized. Otherwise, the operation gives an error because it does not know how to update callers to the method. In fact, if the declaration and initialization are on separate lines of code, you cannot use the refactor. This refactoring method works best when both declaration and initialization (assignment) are done on the same line.

Let's walk through an example. Suppose you have a method that takes an order ID and returns an `Order` object, as in the following method signature:

```
public static Order GetCustomerOrder(int orderId)
```

When looking through this method, you notice that there is a variable assignment that retrieves a customer ID as follows:

```
int customerId = GetCustomerId(orderId);
```

Suppose you determine that looking up a customer ID from an order ID is very inefficient for a couple of reasons. First, you already should know the customer ID before calling the method. Second, you plan to look up the order inside this method. By looking up the customer ID from the order, you look up the order twice. Therefore, you identify this variable assignment as a good candidate for promoting to the method signature. To do so, you first must right-click the line of code that does the assignment and then choose Promote Local Variable to Parameter from the Refactor context menu.

In this case, there is no preview of the change. Instead, Visual Studio does the refactor. The assignment is removed from the method. The method signature is changed to read as follows:

```
public static Order GetCustomerOrder(int orderId, int customerId)
```

In addition, clients who called into this method also get updated. In this case, a call to GetCustomerOrder would now include the code that previously did the variable assignment, GetCustomerId(orderId). The following is an example:

```
Order newOrder = Customer.GetCustomerOrder(odrId, GetCustomerId(orderId));
```

One negative here is that the code that called to the Customer object defined the order ID variable with the name odrId. Refactoring used the variable assignment code which defined order ID as orderId. This will result in a compile error that you will have to fix manually. Of course, this would not be the case with constants or in situations in which you use consistent variable names to mean the same thing.

Some Promoting Tips

Constants work as the best type of local variable for promoting to parameters. The reason is that there is no issue with updating calling clients. If you have a local variable with a constant value assigned, you can update callers with that set value.

When you promote a variable that includes an object call in the assignment, however, you will get the warning dialog box shown in Figure 8.20. Promoting a variable whose assignment is the result of a call to another method requires that callers that require an update as a result of the promotion should also be able to call the object that does the assignment.

FIGURE 8.20   Promoting warning.

As an example, suppose you have the variable declaration and assignment as follows:

```
int CustomerId = GetCustomerFromOrder(orderId)
```

If you promote CustomerId to a parameter, callers to the method will have to have a reference to the object that contains GetCustomerFromOrder. If they do not, you will end up with a compiler error (and hence the warning). Whether this is an issue depends on how you've organized your code and reference.

When you promote a local variable as a parameter, the parameter is attached to the end of the function signature. This may be your intention. However, you might want to order things differently for better code readability and maintenance. To do so, you would then combine the Reorder Parameters refactor with the promotion. We will look at this operation next.

Reorder Parameters

You move parameters around in a method typically just for readability and maintenance. You might want the more important parameters to appear first on the method signature, or you might try to keep the order similar across like methods or overloads. The Reorder Parameters refactor operation allows you to change the order in which parameters exist on a given method, constructor, or delegate. It also works to update any callers to the method and rearrange the parameters passed on the call.

You invoke the Reorder Parameters operation by positioning your cursor inside the method signature that contains the parameters you want to reorder and then selecting the Reorder Parameters menu item from the Refactor menu. You can also get to this operation through the context menu (right-click). In addition, this operation is available from the Class Designer.

> **TIP**
>
> To invoke the Reorder Parameters operation from the keyboard, first position your cursor in the method that contains the parameters you want to rearrange. Next, play the keyboard chord Ctrl+R, Ctrl+O.

Let's look at an example. Suppose you just ran the Promote Local Variable example that promoted a customer ID local to a parameter of the method. The following is the method signature for reference:

```
private static Order InitCustomerOrder(int orderId, int customerId)
```

This method is called `InitCustomerOrder`. Suppose that because `customer` comes first in the method name, you want to make that the first parameter of the method. To do so, you position the cursor on the method and invoke the Reorder Parameters refactor. This presents the Reorder Parameters dialog box.

This dialog box allows you to modify the order of the parameters on the given method. At the top, it lists all the parameters of the method. To the right of this list, there are two buttons. The up-arrow button moves the selected parameter in the list up. The down arrow does the opposite. You use these buttons to get the order of the parameters the way you want them. Figure 8.21 shows this example loaded into the Reorder Parameters dialog box.

Notice that as you change parameter order, the resulting method signature is displayed below the parameter list. You also have the option to preview any changes that will be made to callers of the method. Clicking the OK button will apply the changes to both the method and its callers.

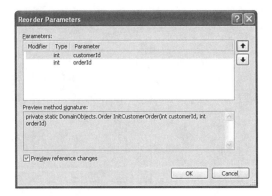

FIGURE 8.21   The Reorder Parameters dialog box.

Encapsulate Field

It's common to have a private field in your object from which you need to create a property. These fields might have been built as private because they were only used internally to the object. Alternatively, a developer may have simply defined a public field instead of encapsulating it as a property. In either case, if you need to make an actual property out of a field, you can do so with the Encapsulate Field refactor operation.

Accessing Encapsulate Field

The Encapsulate Field operation allows you to quickly generate properties from a given field. Properties, of course, allow you to protect the field from direct access and to know when the given field is being modified or accessed. To encapsulate a field, you simply position your cursor over the field and select the Encapsulate Field option from the Refactor menu. You can also do so from the context menu (right-click) or the Class Designer.

> **TIP**
>
> To invoke the Encapsulate Field operation from the keyboard, first position your cursor on the field that you want to encapsulate. Next, play the keyboard chord Ctrl+R, Ctrl+F.

The Encapsulate Field Dialog Box

The Encapsulate Field dialog box, shown in Figure 8.22, allows you to set a few options for this refactor. First, it presents the field you are refactoring in a read-only text box. Next, it allows you to define a name for the new property. The good news is that the tool will try to name your property correctly. For example, if you have a private field named _score, the tool will choose Score for the property name by default.

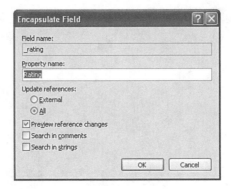

FIGURE 8.22   The Encapsulate Field dialog box.

An additional option on this dialog box is the choice of which references you would like to have updated. This refers to existing references to the field. Suppose you have a public field. This field may be called both from within the object that defines the field as well as by other, external objects. You may want to force external callers to use the new property. For this, you would use the External setting. In this case, the object that contains the field would still reference the local, private field (and not the property). Setting the Update Reference option to All results in both the external and internal callers using the property.

When you apply the encapsulation, the tool changes your internal field to private (if it was not already private) and then generates a property. The property includes both get and set accessors for the field. If the field was declared as read-only, the encapsulation generates only a get accessor.

Let's look at the code. Suppose you have the following field declaration:

```
private int _rating;
```

You want to encapsulate this private into a public property. Figure 8.22 shows the selected options for the encapsulation. The code that is generated is as follows:

```
private int _rating;
public int Rating {
    get { return _rating; }
    set { _rating = value; }
}
```

In addition, internal callers to the field (the field was private) are now updated to use the property internally (due to the All selection for the Update References option).

Summary

This chapter showed how the refactoring tools built into the C# editor for Visual Studio 2005 can greatly increase productivity and decrease unwanted side effects (bugs) when you're making sweeping changes to your code to improve maintenance, reuse, and readability. The refactoring tools use the compiler and not text searching. This improves confidence in and reliability of the tools.

These tools can be accessed using the keyboard, the Refactor menu, a context menu, or the Class Designer. Actual refactoring operation access, of course, depends on code selection context.

The refactoring tools allow you to change your code in many ways. You can easily rename items in your code. You can take existing lines of code and extract them to new methods. Your objects can be used as the basis to define new interfaces. Method signatures can be modified using the Remove, Promote Local Variable, and Reorder refactoring operations. Finally, you can take existing fields and quickly encapsulate them into properties.

CHAPTER 9

Debugging with Visual Studio 2005

IN THIS CHAPTER

- Debugging Basics
- The Visual Studio Debugger

Today's developers may spend as much time debugging their code as they do writing it. This is due in some part to the nature of today's highly dependent and distributed applications. These applications are built to leverage existing functionality, frameworks, building blocks, libraries, and so on. In addition, they often communicate with other applications, services, components, databases, and even data exchanges. In addition, developers also demand more assistance from their debugger to help increase their productivity. Visual Studio 2005 tries to address these needs by offering a number of advancements in the debugging process. Some highlights include

- Edit and Continue for both VB and C# developers

- Easier setup for secure remote debugging

- Visualizers and debugger DataTips

- Just-my-code debugging

- Better breakpoints and the addition of tracepoints

- The Exception Assistant window

- Debugging support at design time

We will cover all of these features and more in this chapter. Of course, if you are just getting started with .NET, more than just this list is new to you. The Visual Studio debugger has been evolving since the first release of .NET, which provided a unified debugger with the capability to debug across languages. In this chapter, we will start by covering the basics of debugging an application. We will then discuss the Visual Studio 2005 debugger in depth.

Debugging Basics

A typical scenario for a developer writing an application today is to start building a screen or form and build up the code that surrounds it. In addition, the developer may rely on a framework or a few building blocks that provide added functionality. The application may also communicate with a services layer and most definitely a database. Even the most typical applications have a lot of moving parts. These moving parts make the task of finding and eliminating errors in the code all the more complex. The tools that help you track down and purge errors from your code not only have to keep up with this complexity, but also must ease the effort involved with the debugging process. In the following sections, we will cover how a developer would use the tools built into Visual Studio 2005 to debug a typical development scenario.

The Scenario

We want to define an application scenario that we can use to both introduce the basics of debugging as well as function as a base for us to build on throughout the chapter when demonstrating the many features of the debugging tools. In this scenario, imagine you are writing a web page that allows customers to view and edit their profiles. This screen offers new functionality to a larger, existing application. The following are some of the conditions that surround this application scenario:

- The customers' profiles are stored in a SQL 2005 database.

- A data access library abstracts access to the database.

- A web service provides the customers' profile information.

Your task is to write this page using the web service to return customers' profiles and write users' changes to their profiles back to the database using the data access library. The application you will be debugging in this scenario is written in C#. However, the debugging tools in Visual Studio are equally applicable to both C# and Visual Basic. That is, everything we discuss here applies to both languages unless specified as otherwise.

The Many Phases of Debugging

Nearly every time developers open the IDE, they are in some way debugging their code. The line between debugging and writing code, in fact, is becoming more and more blurred. For example, the code editor helps eliminate errors in your code as you write it. It highlights items where errors are present and allows you to fix them. You are then both writing and debugging simultaneously.

In addition, the compiler acts as another debugging tool. The first time you click the Run button, the compiler checks your code and reports a list of errors for you to fix prior to continuing. This is debugging. The steps or phases of the debugging process can be broken into the following:

- **Coding**—The editor helps you by pointing out issues and possible resolutions.

- **Compiling**—The compiler checks your code and reports errors prior to continuing.

- **Self-checking**—You run the application in debug mode and step through screens and code to verify functionality.

- **Unit testing**—You write and run unit tests to check your application.

- **Responding to issues**—When an issue has been logged against the code, you must re-create and debug a specific scenario.

In this chapter, we will concentrate on two of these phases: self-checking and responding to issues. These are the two phases in which developers will get the most use of the debugging tools built into Visual Studio. We will therefore assume that the code is written and compiles. Let's start by looking at how to self-check the code.

Debugging the Application (Self-Checking)

In this scenario, you have just started writing a web page to edit a customer's profile. Assume that you've laid out the page, connected to the profile web service, and have written the code to save a user's profile to the database. You now need to start self-checking your work to make sure everything operates as you expect.

The first step is to start your application in debug mode. This will allow you to break into your code if an error occurs. In development, this is typically your default setting. You invoke debug mode by clicking the Run button (the green arrow on the Debug toolbar), making sure your configuration is also set to Debug (the default). Figure 9.1 shows the sample application about to be run in debug mode for the first time.

FIGURE 9.1   Starting the debugger.

Enabling Debugging on a Website

This example is a web application. As such, it requires you to set up debugging on server-side code whose errors and information are output to a remote client. Of course, you are developing on a single development machine. However, sometimes you may have to debug a process on a test server.

In either case, you have to enable debugging through the configuration file (`web.config`) for your application. Visual Studio will actually initially prompt you to add a config file and enable debugging. Figure 9.2 shows this prompt. Clicking the OK button adds the configuration file to the application and starts the debugging session.

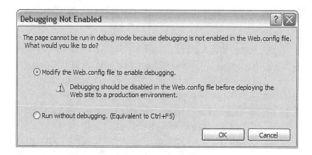

FIGURE 9.2   Allowing Visual Studio to enable debugging.

> **NOTE**
>
> It is important that you turn off debugging prior to deploying to production. Having debugging enabled in a production environment is a security risk. With debugging enabled, ASP.NET writes the details of your errors to a web page. These details provide valuable clues to would-be hackers about how your application is put together. In some instances, the error could include user credentials that are being used to access secured resources.

To turn off debug mode, you must edit the web configuration file. Specifically, you edit the `Compilation` element under the `system.web` node. You set debug equal to `false` (as in off). The following is an example of the XML:

```
<system.web>
  <compilation debug="true"/>
    ...
</system.web>
```

Starting in Debug Mode

The most typical scenario for starting a debug session is just clicking the Run button on the toolbar. This will compile the application and bring up the initial form or page. You also have the option to start without debugging. This capability is useful if you intend to attach to a running process or simply want to run through the application as a user might see it (without breaking into the IDE).

You can also start by stepping into code, line-by-line. This approach is useful if you want to see all of your code as it executes (rather than just errors). You might desire this if you are getting some unexpected behavior. Stepping line-by-line gives you an exact understanding of what is going on with your code (rather than just your assumed understanding).

Stepping into code on a web form is typically done by first opening the main source. You then right-click and select the Run To Cursor option from the shortcut menu. Figure 9.3 shows an example. This command tells Visual Studio to run the application until it gets to this point. At that time, the IDE will open into debug mode, where you can step through each line of code (or continue and so on).

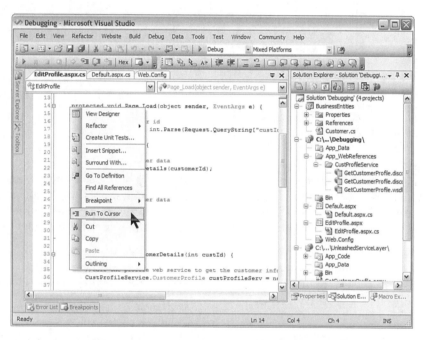

FIGURE 9.3   After selecting Run to Cursor, you can start debugging.

Breaking on an Error

Not everything you find in debug mode is an error that results in a break in the code. Often, issues arise just because you're looking at the behavior of the application. For example, a control could be out of place, the tab order could be wrong, and so on. For these items, you still have to rely on your eyes. The debugging tools in Visual Studio help you respond to hard errors in your code.

By default, when unhandled exceptions occur in your code, the debugger will break execution and bring up the IDE with the offending code highlighted. The key in that sentence is "unhandled exceptions." They represent places in your code where you do not have try-catch blocks to manage an exception. This is typically a good default setting. However, you often need to see handled exceptions as well.

Fortunately, the errors that result in a break in the IDE are a configurable set. For example, you may handle a specific exception in your code and not want to be dumped to the IDE every time it occurs. Rather, you want to be notified only of those especially exceptional conditions. The Exceptions dialog box allows you to manage the set of exceptions you're concerned with. You access this dialog box by choosing Debug, Exceptions (or pressing Ctrl+D, E). Figure 9.4 shows the dialog box.

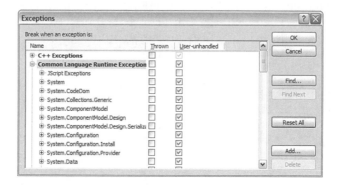

FIGURE 9.4   Determining where Visual Studio breaks.

In the Exceptions dialog box, the various exceptions are categorized for easy access (there is also a Find feature). The two columns of check boxes are of primary interest: one for Thrown and one for User-unhandled. Notice that, by default, the setting for all exceptions in the .NET Framework is User-unhandled. This indicates that the debugger should break execution only when a given exception is thrown and it is not handled by your code.

Adding Thrown to the mix will tell the debugger to break execution even if you have code to handle the exception. The debugger will react by breaking on the line of the exception, before your handler is called.

For the most part, you would simply toggle Thrown at the CLR level. You probably do not need to get more granular, but you can if you need to. However, doing so often results in confusion.

Debugging an Error

The first step in debugging your application is to click that Run button. You are then in debug mode. As it happens, the sample application throws an exception upon the initial run. The debugger responds by breaking into the code and showing the offending line. Figure 9.5 shows a typical view of the editor when it breaks on an error.

There are a few items to point out about the standard debug session shown in Figure 9.5. First, Visual Studio has highlighted the line on which the error was thrown. You can see this clearly by the arrow and the highlighted text.

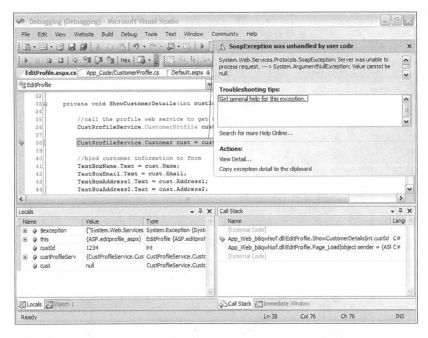

FIGURE 9.5   The debugger breaking execution.

Next, notice the window in the upper right of the image. This is the Exception Assistant, which is new to Visual Studio 2005. It provides details on the exception and offers tips for troubleshooting and fixing the given issue. From this window, you can access a few actions, including searching online help for more information on the exception.

At the bottom of the screen are a few additional helpful windows. The Locals window on the left automatically shows the value assigned to all local variables in the code where the exception was thrown. This gives you easy access to key information that might be contributing to the issue. Notice that to the right of this window is a tab called Watch 1. This is a watch window; it keeps track of any custom watch scenarios you set up (more on this later).

The window on the bottom right of the screen is the Call Stack. It shows the order in which various components of your application were called. You can look at the Call Stack to find out how you got to where you are. You can also use it to navigate to any code referenced in the stack. Finally, the tab next to this gives you access to the Immediate window. It allows you to type in code commands and get the results in the editor (more on this to come).

Attaching to the Web Service   After you examine your error, you can see it is being thrown inside the web service process. Unfortunately, the code called by the web service is being run in a separate process than the one you are debugging. When you debug an application, you debug (or shadow) a running process such as an executable (`.exe`).

To debug code in the web service process, you must both have the source code and attach to the executing process. In this case, all the code for the running application is in the solution. Therefore, you need to attach to the process.

Attaching to the process will enable you to debug code in libraries called by the web service. However, it will not, by default, enable you to debug the web service itself. The reason is that you have not enabled debugging for the web service. Recall Figure 9.2. Here, you turned on debugging for the web application. You need to do the same thing for the web service if you intend to step through code in the web service. You would do so by adding a `web.config` file to the site and setting the debug attribute to `true`.

In this case, however, do not end the debug session. You can see that the error is in code contained in a library that is called by the web service, and not the web service itself. Therefore, you simply attach to the web service process and debug code in the `DataAccessLib` project. To attach to the web service process, you choose the Attach to Process option from the Debug menu. This brings up the dialog box shown in Figure 9.6.

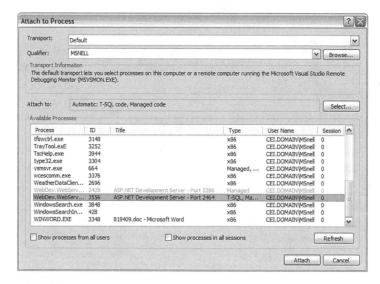

FIGURE 9.6   Attaching to a process.

In Figure 9.6 notice that the currently attached process is grayed out. This is a visual indicator that you are already attached to the web server running the UI. Beneath this, you see the web service process. To attach the debug session to this process, you simply highlight it and click the Attach button. You are now debugging both processes and can therefore set a breakpoint where the error might be occurring.

NOTE

If debugging is enabled on both the website and web service applications, Visual Studio still attaches only to the startup project's process. Therefore, if you want to debug code in the web service, you still need to attach to that process (in addition to enabling debugging).

TIP

If you have set a web reference to a web service in your solution and then you enable debugging in that web service, you may get errors from Visual Studio. These errors indicate that the remote server is now rejecting your connection. Unfortunately, the only way around this problem seems to be to delete the web reference and re-add it. If debugging was enabled in your web service prior to setting the web reference, you should be okay.

Setting the Breakpoint   To get the debugger to break into your code when it reaches a specific line, you set a breakpoint on that line. You do so by clicking on the indicator bar for the given line. Alternatively, you can right-click on the line and choose Insert Breakpoint from the Breakpoint context menu. In the example, the error may be coming from the code that gets the customer data from the database. Therefore, you need to navigate to the `DataAccessLib` project, open the `Customer.cs` file, and set a breakpoint, as shown in Figure 9.7.

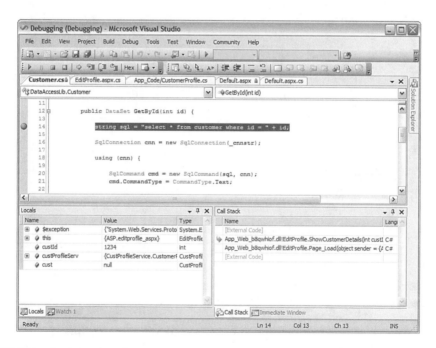

FIGURE 9.7   Setting a breakpoint.

Continuing the Debugging   After you've navigated off the executing code during a debug session, it can often be hard to find your way back. The line that was executing could be buried in any one of the open code windows. Thankfully, you can use the Show Next Statement button (yellow arrow icon) on the Debug toolbar to take you back. This will return you to the line that was executing when the debugger broke.

In the example, rerun the call to the web service so you can now hit your breakpoint and step through the code. To do so, you must move the current execution point in the code. This can be accomplished by right-clicking the line where you want execution to start (or rerun) and selecting Set Next Statement from the context menu. Figure 9.8 shows this menu option.

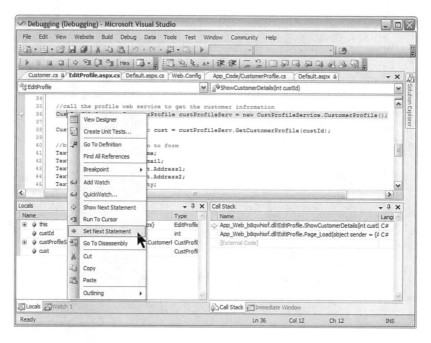

FIGURE 9.8   The Set Next Statement option.

Now that you have backed up the execution point, you are ready to continue the debugging. You can do this by clicking the Run button again. This is essentially indicating you are done with the break and want to continue execution.

Stepping to Find the Error   In the example, the debugger will break execution as soon as it hits the breakpoint in the web service. This will allow you to step through the code. To step line-by-line through the code, you can click the Step Into button on the Debug toolbar or press the F11 function key. This will execute the code one line at a time, allowing you to view both execution flow as well as the state of the application as code executes. Doing so with the example allows you to see the error. It seems that an instance of the DataSet object was not set prior to your trying to fill it.

In most scenarios, you can make this fix during the debug session and continue stepping through or running the code. Unfortunately, in this example you cannot make the change while debugging. You cannot invoke Edit and Continue with an attached process. Figure 9.9 shows the message you get when you try.

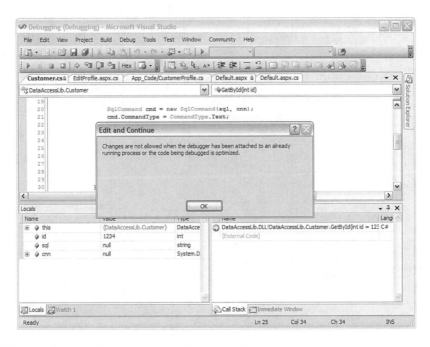

FIGURE 9.9   Edit and Continue error with an attached process.

So instead of using Edit and Continue, you can bookmark the line where you want to make the change using the Text Editor toolbar. You then click the Stop button on the Debug toolbar to stop the debug session. You can now make your change.

To continue through self-checking, you would next restart the debugging process. However, prior to this, you may want to clear the breakpoint you had set. To do so, select the Breakpoints toolbar item. This brings up the Breakpoints window, as shown in Figure 9.10. From this window you can view all breakpoints in the application. Here, you select and clear the breakpoint by clicking the Delete button from the Breakpoint toolbar. Finally, you click the Run button to continue the debug, self-check session.

Debugging Basics Summary

You have now set up your scenario and debugged your first error. This example was meant to introduce you to the basics of doing debugging in Visual Studio 2005. If you are familiar with prior IDE versions, you probably noticed a lot of similarities. Walking through the scenario showed the many tools inside the debugging environment, including the Debug toolbar and menu, the Breakpoints window, the watch window, and so on. Now that you have a grasp of the basics, in the next section we intend to explore these debug elements in greater detail.

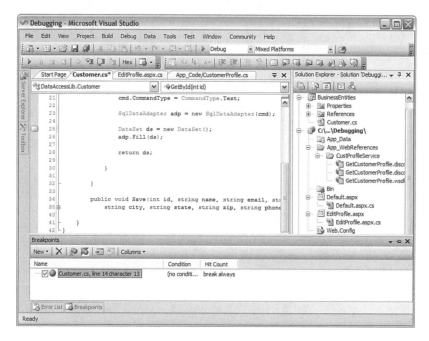

FIGURE 9.10   Breakpoints window.

The Visual Studio Debugger

The debugger built into Visual Studio 2005 is one of the largest and most complex tools in the IDE. With such a large feature-set area, we cannot cover every scenario you will encounter. However, we hope to expose the most commonly applicable features in this section. We will continue to work with the customer profile scenario for our examples.

The Debug Menu and Toolbar

The Debug menu and related toolbar provide your first-level access to starting debug sessions, stepping into code, managing breakpoints, and accessing the many features of debugging with Visual Studio. There are two states to the debug window: at rest and debug mode. In the at-rest state, the Debug menu allows you to start a debug session, attach code to a running process, or access some of the many debug windows. Figure 9.11 shows the menu in this state.

When the debugger is engaged and you are working through a debug session, the state of the Debug menu changes. It now provides a number of additional options to those provided by the at-rest state. These options include those designed to move through the code, restart the session, and access even more debug-related windows. Figure 9.12 shows the Debug menu during a debug session.

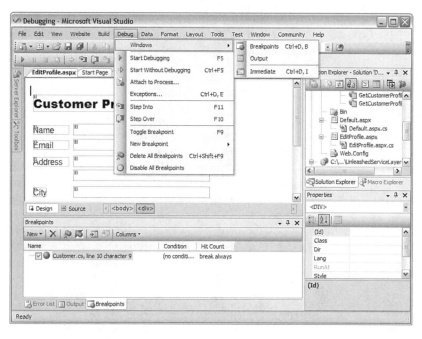

FIGURE 9.11   The Debug menu at rest.

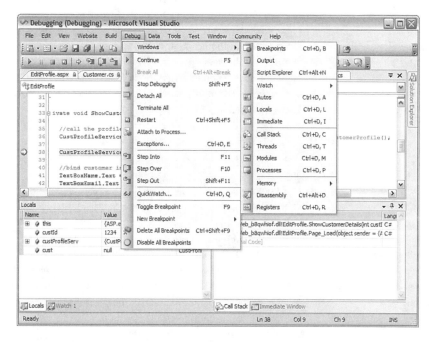

FIGURE 9.12   The Debug menu during a debug session.

Let's look at the many options provided by the Debug menu. Table 9.1 presents all the items available from the toolbar, whether an at-rest option or one that is available only during a debug session. When reading through the table, refer to the preceding figures to get context on any given item.

TABLE 9.1   The Debug Menu Items

Menu Item	Description
Windows, Breakpoints	Opens the Breakpoints window in the IDE. This window provides access to all the breakpoints in the option solution.
Windows, Output	Shows the Output window in the IDE. The Output window is a running log of the many messages that are emitted by the IDE, the compiler, and the debugger. This information can be useful during a debug session.
Windows, Immediate	Opens the Immediate window in the IDE. This window allows you to execute commands. For example, during design, you can call your methods directly from the Immediate window and have them enter breakpoints and so on.
Start Debugging, Continue	Either starts your application in debug mode or continues running the application if already in debug mode.
Start Without Debugging	Starts your application. However, it does not connect the debugger to the process. Therefore, this more closely represents what users would see when they run your application.
Attach to Process	Allows you to attach the debugger (and your code) to a running process (executable).
Exceptions	Opens the Exceptions option dialog box. This dialog box allows you to choose how the debugger breaks on any given exception.
Step Into	Starts the application in debug mode when your application is in design mode. For most projects, clicking the Step Into command invokes the debugger on the first executing line of the application. In this way, you can step into the application from the first line. If you are in a debug session, Step Into advances the debugger a line. If you choose to "step into" a function, the debugger will do so line-by-line.
Step Over	Functions the same as Step Into with one major difference: If you choose to "step over" a function, the line calling the function will be executed (along with the function), and the debugger will set the next line (after the function call) as the next line to be debugged.
Toggle Breakpoint	Toggles the breakpoint on the current line of code. If the breakpoint is set, toggling it will remove it. If it is not set, toggling will set it.
New Breakpoint, Break at Function	Brings up the New Breakpoint dialog box. This dialog box allows you to indicate where in a given function the code should break.
Delete All Breakpoints	Removes all breakpoints from your solution.

TABLE 9.1   Continued

Menu Item	Description
Disable All Breakpoints	Disables breakpoints in the solution without deleting them. You can also disable individual breakpoints. This capability is very useful if you want to keep the breakpoints around for later but simply don't want to hit that one at the moment.
Enable All Breakpoints	Enables all breakpoints that have been disabled due to a call to Disable All Breakpoints.
Break All	Allows you to break the application into the debugger manually (without having to hit a breakpoint) during a debug session. This capability is useful to gain access to the debug information such as watch windows.
Stop Debugging	Terminates the debugging session. It also terminates the process you are debugging, provided that process was started by Visual Studio.
Detach All	Detaches the debugger from executing process. This allows your application to continue running after the debugger is through with it.
Terminate All	Stops debugging and terminates all processes to which you are attached.
Restart	Stops the debugging session and restarts it. Similar to clicking both Stop Debugging and Start Debugging in sequence.
Step Out	Tells the debugger to execute the current function and then break back into debugging after the function has finished. This capability is useful if you step into a function but then want to have that function just execute and yet return you to debug mode when it is complete.
QuickWatch	Brings up the QuickWatch window when the debugger is in break mode. The QuickWatch window shows one variable or expression you are watching and its value. QuickWatch's usefulness has been replaced by the new DataTips (more on this to come).
Windows, Script Editor	Opens the script editor. This feature is useful for debugging client- and server-side script.
Windows, Watch	Opens one of many possible watch windows in the IDE. Watch windows represent items and expressions you are keeping a close eye on through the debug session.
Windows, Autos	Opens the Autos window. This window shows variables (and their value) in the current line of code and the prior line of code.
Windows, Locals	Opens the Locals window in the IDE. This window shows variables in the local scope (function).
Windows, Call Stack	Shows the list of functions that are on the stack. Also indicates the current stack frame (function). This selected item is what defines the content from the Locals, watch, and Autos windows.
Windows, Threads	Shows the Threads window in the IDE. From here, you can view and control the threads in the application you are debugging.
Windows, Modules	Shows the Modules window in the IDE. This window lists the DLLs and EXEs used by your application.

TABLE 9.1   Continued

Menu Item	Description
Windows, Processes	Shows the Processes window in the IDE. This window lists the processes to which the debug session is attached.
Windows, Memory	Opens the Memory window for a view at the memory used by your application. This is valid only when address-level debugging is enabled from the Options dialog box.
Windows, Disassembly	Opens the Disassembly window. This window shows the assembly code corresponding to the compiler instructions. This is valid only when address-level debugging is enabled from the Options dialog box.
Windows, Registers	Opens the Registers window so that you can view register values change as you step through code. This is valid only when address-level debugging is enabled from the Options dialog box.

The Debug Toolbar

The Debug toolbar provides quick access to some of the key items available on the Debug menu. From here, you can manage your debug session. For example, you can start or continue a debug session, stop an executing session, step through lines of code, and so on.

Figure 9.13 presents the Debug toolbar during an active debug session. In design mode, the Continue button would read Start Debugging, and a number of these items would be disabled. We have added callouts for each item on the toolbar. You can cross-reference these callouts back to Table 9.1 for further information.

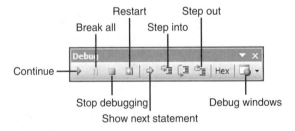

FIGURE 9.13   The Debug toolbar during break mode.

> **NOTE**
>
> In Figure 9.13 the Breakpoints window icon on the right of the figure with the callout "Debug windows" actually is a drop-down menu. This menu provides access to the many debug windows that are available to developers.

Debug Options

You can control the many debugging options in Visual Studio through the Options dialog box. The Debugging node on the options tree provides access to these debugging switches. Figure 9.14 shows the general debugging settings.

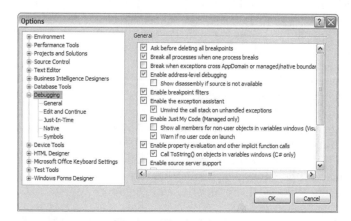

FIGURE 9.14   The Debug Options dialog box.

The general settings list provides access to turn on and off many debugging options. These options include all of the following:

- Turn on and off breakpoint filters

- Enable or disable the warning dialog box associated with clearing all breakpoints

- Turn on or off the Exception Assistant

- Enable or disable just-my-code debugging

- Require source code to exactly match that being debugged (or not)

- And many more

There are additional debug option dialog boxes, which provide access to more debug settings. For instance, you can control how Edit and Continue works (you can also turn off this feature). There are settings for which type of code (Managed, Native, Script) is enabled for just-in-time debugging. You also have the option for using additional debug symbol files (.pdb and .dbg). These files can be helpful if you do not have the source code associated with a particular library you need to debug, such as Windows source or a third-party component.

These many options help you customize your debug experience. However, for this chapter, we are going to accept the default options and debug accordingly.

Stepping In, Out, and Over Code

Probably the most common debug operation for developers is stepping through their code line-by-line and examining the data emitted by the application and the debugger. Code stepping is just that, examining a line, executing the line, and examining the results (and then repeating the process over and over). Because this is such a dominant activity, becoming efficient with the step operations in Visual Studio is important for maximizing the use of your time during a debug session. Here, we will cover each of the stepping options and provide examples accordingly.

Beginning a Debug Session (Stepping into Code)

The Step Into command is available from both the Debug menu and toolbar (you can also press F11 as a shortcut). There are two behaviors commonly associated with this one command. The first is related to when you invoke the command for an application that is not currently running in debug mode. In this case, the application will be compiled, started, and the first line presented to you in the debug window for stepping purposes. This is, in essence, stepping into your application. Figure 9.15 shows a Windows form application in debug mode as the result of a call to Step Into.

NOTE

For web applications, using Step Into or Step Over does not work the same. Instead, your application simply runs in debug mode in the case of websites. The debugger does not break on the first line of your application. To do this, you must set a breakpoint or choose the Run To Cursor option (see the following section).

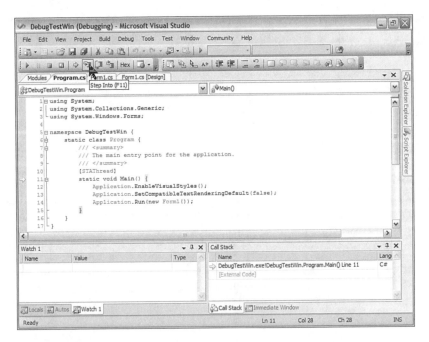

FIGURE 9.15 Using Step Into to start an application.

A call to the Step Over command (Debug menu, toolbar, or F10) while your application is at rest will result in the same behavior as Step Into. That is, your application (provided it is not a website) will be compiled and started in a debug session on the first line of code.

Run To Cursor   One of the more handy (and overlooked) features of the debug toolset is Run To Cursor. This feature works the way it sounds. You set your cursor position on some code and invoke the command. The application is compiled and run until it hits the line of code where your cursor is placed. At this point, the debugger breaks the application and presents the line of code for you to step through. This capability is especially handy because this is how many developers work. They are looking at a specific line (or lines) of code and want to debug this line. They do not need to start from the first line and often do not want to be bothered with breakpoints. The Run To Cursor feature is therefore an efficient means to get the debugger on the same page as you. Figure 9.16 shows this feature being invoked from the context menu.

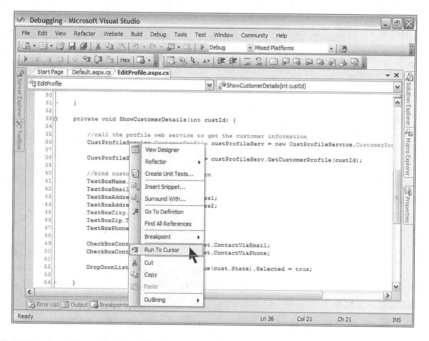

FIGURE 9.16   Invoking the Run To Cursor command.

Run To Cursor works even if the user is required to activate some portion of the code prior to the code's reaching the cursor position. In this way, it really is an invisible, temporary breakpoint. For instance, in the example, users are presented with a default page. From here, they can select to edit their profiles as an option. If you set the Run To Cursor command on a line inside the edit profile screen, the debugger will still execute the application and wait until the users (testers or developers) invoke the given line of code.

Start Debugging   You can also start your debug session by selecting the Start Debugging option (green "play" arrow) from the Debug menu or toolbar (or F5). This starts a debug session but does not break into code unless an exception occurs or a breakpoint is encountered. This is a common operation for developers testing their code without wanting to walk through it or those who use a lot of breakpoints.

Break All   Finally, if your application is running and you want to enter break mode, you can do so at any time by invoking the Break All command from the Debug menu or toolbar (or Ctrl+Alt+Break). The Break All feature is represented by the pause icon. This stops your application wherever it is in execution and allows you to interrogate the debugger for information. The Break All command is especially useful if you need to break into a long-running process or loop.

Walking Through Your Code

During a debug session, you have basically three options for moving through your code. You can step into a line or function, step over a given function, and step out of a function. Let's look at each option.

Step Into

The Step Into command (F11) allows you to progress through your code one line at a time. Invoking this command will execute the current line of code and position your cursor on the next line to be executed. The important distinction between stepping into and other similar commands is how Step Into handles lines of code that contain function calls. If you are positioned on such a line, calling Step Into will take you to the first line inside the function (provided you have the appropriate debug symbols loaded).

As an example, look at Figure 9.17. It shows the sample web service making a call to the data access library's method named `Customer.GetById`. In this case, both projects are loaded in the solution; thus, you have access to their debug symbols. Therefore, a call to Step Into will result in your stepping into the first line of `GetById`.

Figure 9.18 shows stepping into this function. Notice that you are now positioned to step line-by-line through this function. Of course, when you reach the end of this function, the debugger will return you to the next line in the calling function (line 23 in the web service depicted in Figure 9.17).

Step Over   The Step Over command (F10) allows you to maintain focus on the current procedure without stepping into any methods called by it. That is, calling Step Over will execute line-by-line but will not take you into any function calls, constructors, or property calls.

As an example, consider Figure 9.17. Here, the debugger is positioned on the call to `Customer.GetById`. If you called the Step Over command, the `GetById` function would execute without your stepping through it. Instead, the next line to execute in step mode would be the line following the call to `GetById`. Of course, any exception thrown by the function you step over will result in the debugger breaking into your code as normal.

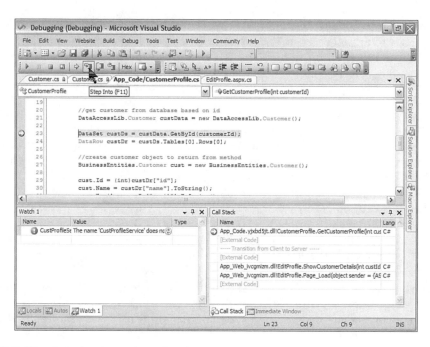

FIGURE 9.17   Stepping into a line of code.

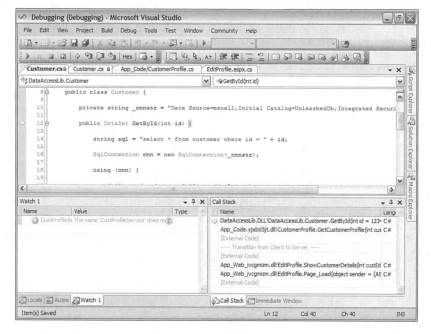

FIGURE 9.18   The results of stepping into a function.

Step Out   The Step Out command (Shift+F11) is another useful tool. It allows you to tell the debugger to finish executing the current method you are debugging but return to break mode as soon as it is finished. This is a great tool when you get stuck in a long method you wished you had stepped over. In addition, you may step into a given function only to debug a portion of it and then want to step out.

As an example, refer again to Figure 9.18. Recall that you stepped into this method from the code in Figure 9.17. Suppose you start stepping through a couple of lines of code. After you take a look and verify that a connection is made to the database, you simply want to have the function complete and return to debugging back in the calling function (line 23 of Figure 9.17). To do so, you simply invoke Step Out.

Continuing Execution

When you are in a debug session, the Start Debugging (or Run) command changes to Continue. The Continue command is available when you are paused on a given line of code in the debugger. It enables you to let the application continue to run on its own without stepping through each line. For example, suppose you walked through the lines of code you wanted to see, and now you want to continue checking your application from a user's perspective. Using Continue, you tell the application and debugger to keep running until either an exception occurs or a breakpoint is hit.

Ending a Debug Session

You can end your debug session in few ways. One common method is to kill the currently executing application. This might be done by closing the browser window for a web application or clicking the Close (or X) button of a Windows application. Calls in your code that terminate your application will also end a debug session.

There are also a couple of options available to you from the Debug window. The Terminate All command kills all processes that the debugger is attached to and ends the debug session. There is also the Detach All option. Figure 9.19 shows both options in the toolbar. Detach All simply detaches the debugger from all running processes without terminating them. This capability can be useful if you've temporarily attached to a running process, debugged it, and want to leave it running.

Indicating When to Break into Code

You control the debugger through breakpoints and tracepoints. With these, you can tell the debugger when you are interested in breaking into code or receiving information about your application. Breakpoints allow you to indicate when the debugger should stop on a specific line in your code. Tracepoints are new to Visual Studio 2005. They are a type of breakpoint that allows you to perform an action when a given line of your code is reached. This typically involves emitting data about your application to the output window. Mastering the use of breakpoints will reduce the time it takes to zero in on and fix issues with your code.

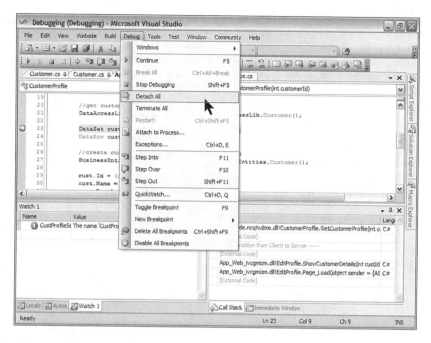

FIGURE 9.19   Detaching from a process.

Setting a Breakpoint

The most common method of setting a breakpoint is to first find the line of code on which you want the debugger to stop. You then click in the code editor's indicator margin for the given line of code. Doing so will place a red circle in the indicator margin and highlight the line of code as red. Of course, these are the default colors; you can change the look of breakpoints in the Tools, Options dialog box under the Environment node, Fonts and Colors.

There are a few additional ways to set breakpoints. For instance, you can right-click a given line of code and choose Insert Breakpoint from the Breakpoint context menu. You can also choose New Breakpoint from the Debug menu (or press Ctrl+D, N). This option brings up the New Breakpoint dialog box in which you can set a function breakpoint.

Setting a Function Breakpoint   A function breakpoint is just a breakpoint that is set through the New Breakpoint dialog box. It is called a *function breakpoint* because it is typically set at the beginning of the function (but does not need to be). From the New Breakpoint dialog box, you can manually set the function on which you want to break, the line of code in the function, and even the character on the line.

If your cursor is on a function or on a call to a function when you invoke this dialog box, the name of the function will automatically be placed in the dialog box. You can also type a function name in the dialog box. Figure 9.20 shows the New Breakpoint dialog box in action. Notice that you can manually set the line and even the character on the line where the breakpoint should be placed.

> **NOTE**
>
> If you specify an overloaded function in the New Breakpoint dialog box, you must specify the actual function on which you want to break. You do so by indicating the correct parameter types for the given overload. For example, the current `ShowCustomerDetails` takes a customer ID as an `int`. If you had an overload that also looked up a customer by name (as a string), you would indicate this overload in the Function field as `ShowCustomerDetails(string)`.

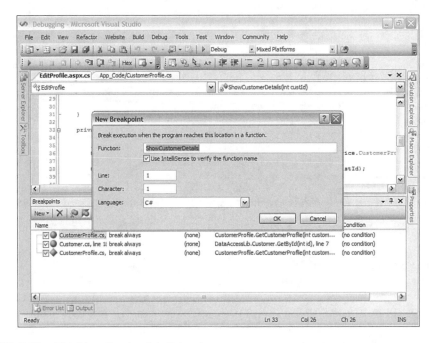

FIGURE 9.20   The New Breakpoint dialog box.

Recognizing the Many Breakpoints of Visual Studio

Visual Studio 2005 has a number of breakpoint icons. These icons allow you to easily recognize the type of breakpoint associated with a given line of code. For instance, a round, filled circle is a common breakpoint, whereas a round, hollow circle represents a common breakpoint that has been disabled. We've provided Table 9.2 for reference purposes. It shows some of the more common icons associated with breakpoints and presents a description of each.

TABLE 9.2   The Breakpoint Icons

Icon	Description
●	This icon indicates a standard, enabled breakpoint. When the debugger encounters this line of code, it will stop the application and break into debug mode.
◆	This icon indicates a standard tracepoint. When the debugger hits this line of code, it will perform the action associated with the tracepoint.

TABLE 9.2   The Breakpoint Icons

Icon	Description
⊕	The plus icon inside the breakpoint indicates an advanced breakpoint that contains a condition, hit count, or filter.
◈	The plus icon inside the tracepoint indicates an advanced tracepoint that contains a condition, hit count, or filter.
○	An empty or hollow breakpoint indicates a disabled breakpoint. The breakpoint is still associated with the line of code. However, the debugger will not recognize the disabled breakpoint until it has been re-enabled. Hollow icons are associated with types of breakpoint icons such as tracepoints, advanced items, and even breakpoint errors and warnings. In all conditions, the hollow icon indicates the item is disabled.
◌	Represents a breakpoint warning indicating that a breakpoint cannot be set due to a temporary condition. This can be the result of debugging not being enabled for a website or debug symbols not being loaded. These icons are set by Visual Studio.
◇	Represents a tracepoint warning (see preceding description).

Working with the Breakpoints Window

The Breakpoints window in Visual Studio provides a convenient way to organize and manage the many conditions on which you intend to break into the debugger. You access this window from the Debug menu or toolbar (or by pressing Ctrl+D, B). Figure 9.21 shows the Breakpoints menu inside Visual Studio.

The Breakpoints Window Toolbar   The Breakpoints window has its own toolbar that allows you to manage the breakpoints in the window. The commands available from the toolbar are described in detail in Table 9.3.

TABLE 9.3   The Breakpoints Window Toolbar

Item	Description
New ▾	Brings up the new Breakpoints window, allowing you to set a breakpoint at a function.
✕	Allows you to delete the selected breakpoint in the list.
🗙	Deletes all breakpoints in the window.
🏷	Toggles all breakpoints as either on or off. If all breakpoints are enabled, clicking this icon allows you to keep the breakpoints but turn them all off as a group. If all breakpoints are disabled, this command will enable them as a group.
⬲	Allows you to go to the source code associated with the selected breakpoint.

TABLE 9.3   Continued

Item	Description
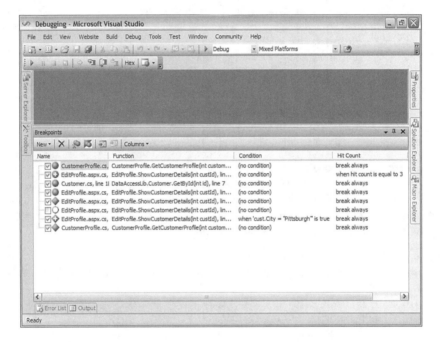	Allows you to go to the disassembly information associated with the selected breakpoint.
	Allows you to choose which columns you want to view in the Breakpoints window. Each column provides information about a given breakpoint. For example, you can see information on the condition associated with each breakpoint, the filename, the function, the filter, the process, and so on.

FIGURE 9.21   The Breakpoints window.

Managing Each Individual Breakpoint   The Breakpoints window also gives you access to each individual breakpoint. It serves as a launching point for setting the many options associated with a breakpoint. For example, you can disable a single breakpoint by toggling the check box associated with the breakpoint in the list. In addition, you can set the many properties and conditions associated with a breakpoint. Figure 9.22 shows both a disabled tracepoint and the context menu associated with an individual breakpoint.

Notice that from this context menu, you can delete the breakpoint and navigate to its related source code. More important, however, is the access to setting the conditions and filters associated with the breakpoint. We will cover using each of these in the next section.

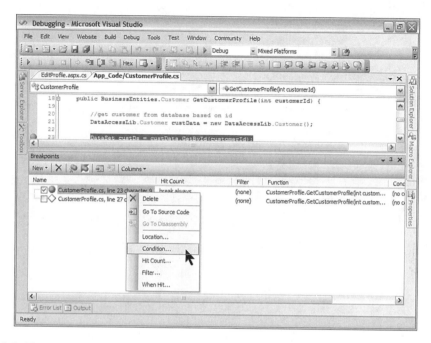

FIGURE 9.22   Managing an individual breakpoint.

Breaking Based on Conditions

Often, setting a simple breakpoint is not sufficient (or efficient). For instance, if you are looking for a particular condition to be true in your code—a condition that seems to be causing an exception—then you would prefer to break based on that condition. This saves the time of constantly breaking into a function only to examine a few data points and determine that you have not hit your condition. The following sections highlight the conditional options available for breakpoints.

Setting a Breakpoint Condition   A breakpoint condition allows you to break into the debugger or perform an action (tracepoint) when a specific condition is either evaluated as true or has changed. Often, you know that the bug you are working on occurs only based on a very specific condition. Breakpoint conditions are the perfect answer for finding that intermittent bug.

To set a condition, you select the breakpoint on which you want to apply a condition. You then choose the Condition option from the right-click context menu. This will bring up the Breakpoint Condition dialog box, as shown in Figure 9.23. Notice that when setting the condition, you have access to IntelliSense (you can invoke IntelliSense either when you click a dot or press Ctrl+Space).

When you set a condition, you have two options: Is True and Has Changed. The Is True option allows you to set a Boolean condition that, when evaluated to true, results in the debugger's breaking into the given line of code.

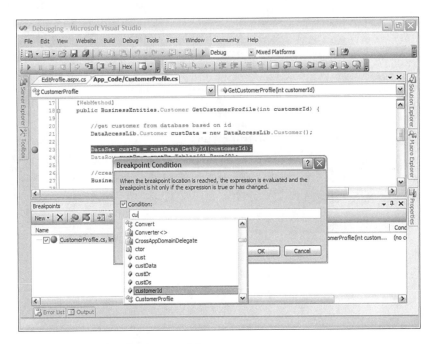

FIGURE 9.23   Setting a breakpoint condition.

For an example, refer to the sample application. Suppose that you are notified of an error that happens only for a specific customer. You might go to the Customer class and set a breakpoint inside the GetCustomerProfile function. You might then add the Is True condition, customerId=1234, to the breakpoint (where customerId is the parameter to the function). This will tell the debugger not to stop on this line of code unless this condition is met. Figure 9.24 shows this condition in the dialog box. It also presents the two options available for conditions.

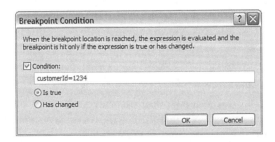

FIGURE 9.24   The Breakpoint Condition dialog box.

The Has Changed option tells the debugger to break when the value of an expression changes. The first pass through your code sets the value for the first evaluation. If the value changes after that, the debugger will break on a given line. This capability can be useful when you have fields or properties with initial values and you want to track when

those values are being changed. In addition, Has Changed can be useful in looping and
if...then scenarios where you are interested in only whether the results of your code
changed a particular value.

TIP

Your breakpoint information is persisted between debug sessions. That is, when you close Visual
Studio for the day, your breakpoints are still there when you return. This validates the time you
might spend setting some sophisticated debugging options. They can remain in your application
and turned on and off as required.

Setting a Breakpoint Filter   Breakpoint filters allow you to specify a specific machine,
process, or thread on which you want to break. For instance, if your error condition
seems to happen only on a certain machine or within a certain process, then you can
debug this condition specifically with a filter. Filters are most useful in complex debugging scenarios where your application is highly distributed.

To use this feature, you can specify the machine by name, the process by name or ID, or
the thread by name or ID. You can also use specify combinations with & (and), ¦¦ (or),
and ! (not). This allows you to get to a specific thread on a specific process on a certain
machine. Figure 9.25 shows the dialog box in which you set breakpoint filters.

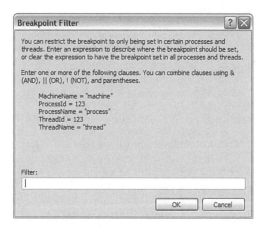

FIGURE 9.25   The Breakpoint Filter dialog box.

Using a Hit Count with a Breakpoint   Using the Hit Count command, you can tell the
debugger that you want to break when a given line of code is reached a number of times.
This feature is useful only if you cannot set a better condition and know that when you
pass over your code a certain number of times something bad happens. However, the Hit
Count option might be more useful in tracepoint scenarios where you are emitting data
about what is happening in your code.

Figure 9.26 shows the Breakpoint Hit Count dialog box. Notice that this screenshot was
taken during an active debug session. You can add any of these conditions to breakpoints

during an active debug session. In addition, notice that the current hit count is set to one (1). You have the option to click the Reset button and turn the hit count back to zero and continue debugging from that point.

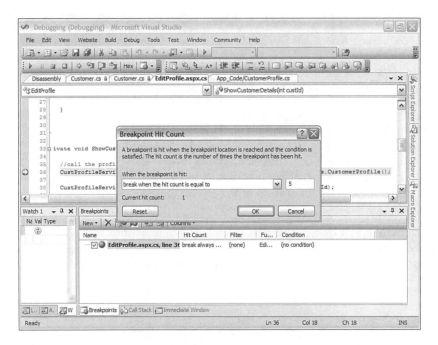

FIGURE 9.26   Setting a breakpoint hit count.

This dialog box also provides a few options for setting the actual hit count. In the dropdown list under When the Breakpoint Is Hit, the following options are available:

- Break Always (the default and does not invoke the hit count option)

- Break When the Hit Count Is Equal To

- Break When the Hit Count Is a Multiple Of

- Break When the Hit Count Is Greater Than or Equal To

TIP

You can combine all the breakpoint conditions we've discussed to create even more specific conditions for your breakpoints.

Working with Tracepoints (When Hit...)

Tracepoints allow you to emit data to the Output window or run a Visual Studio macro when a specific breakpoint is hit. This capability can be very useful if you want to keep a running log of what is happening as your application runs in debug mode. You can then review this log to get valuable information about specific conditions and order of execution when an exception is thrown.

You can set tracepoints explicitly by right-clicking a line of code and choosing Insert Tracepoint from the Breakpoint menu. In addition, selecting the When Hit command from the context menu for a breakpoint (in the Breakpoints window) will bring up a tracepoint dialog box, which is titled When Breakpoint Is Hit, as shown in Figure 9.27.

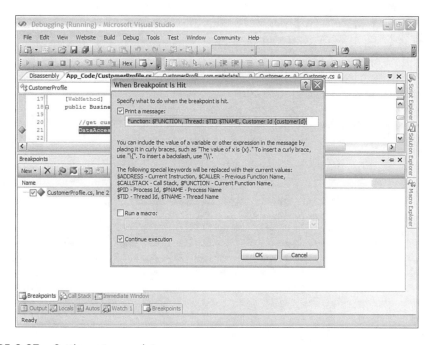

FIGURE 9.27   Setting a tracepoint.

The options available for the When Breakpoint Is Hit dialog box include printing a message to the output window, running a macro, and continuing execution. You can choose any combination of these options. The first, printing a message, allows you to output data about your function. There are a number of keywords you can use to output data, such as $FUNCTION for the function name and $CALLER for the name of the calling function. A full list is printed in the dialog box in Figure 9.27. You can also output your specific variable values. You do so by enclosing the variable names in curly braces.

The Continue Execution option allows you to indicate whether this is a true tracepoint or a breakpoint that contains a tracing action. If you choose to continue, you only get the trace action (message and/or macro). If you indicate not to continue, you get the trace action; plus, the debugger stops on this line of code, just like a simple breakpoint. This is essentially applying a When Hit action to a standard breakpoint.

Finally, when you select the Run a Macro option, the dialog box gives you a list of all the macros loaded in your environment for selection.

You can also combine tracepoint actions with conditions. When you do so, the action fires only when the breakpoint condition is met.

As an example, we have set a tracepoint inside the web service `GetCustomerProfile` (see Figure 9.27). This tracepoint prints a message to the output window when the line of code is hit and simply continues the application executing. The message we intend to print is as follows:

```
Function: $FUNCTION, Thread: $TID $TNAME, Customer Id {customerId}
```

This message will print the function name, thread ID and name (if any), and the value of the variable, `customerId`. Figure 9.28 shows two passes through the tracepoint output in the Output window.

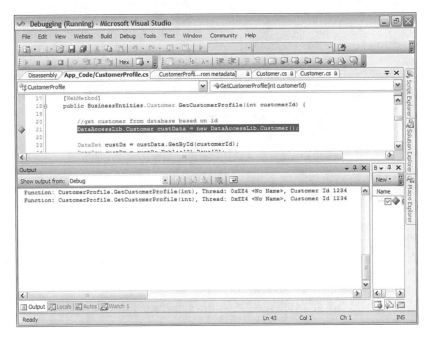

FIGURE 9.28   The results of a tracepoint.

Viewing Data in the Debugger

After the debugger has thrown you into break mode, the next challenge is to filter all the data your application is emitting. Getting to the right data will help you find problems faster and fix them faster. Visual Studio tries to make the data available where you want it. For example, DataTips show you variable values right in the code editor. There are many similar improvements in the way Visual Studio shows debugging data in the 2005 edition. We will cover these and more throughout the following sections.

Watching Variables

A common activity in a debug session is to view the values associated with the many types in your application. There are a number of windows available to help you here. The two most obvious are the Locals and Autos windows.

Locals Window   The Locals window shows all the variables and their values for the current debug scope. This gives you a view of everything available in the current, executing method. The variables in this window are set automatically by the debugger. They are organized alphabetically in a list by name. In addition, hierarchy is also shown. For example, if a given variable relates to object type, that object's members are listed inside the variable (as a tree).

Figure 9.29 shows an example of the Locals window. In it, you can see the sample application paused inside the GetCustomerProfile method. Notice that the cust variable is expanded to show the various properties and fields associated with this object. As values are set, the results are shown in the Value column.

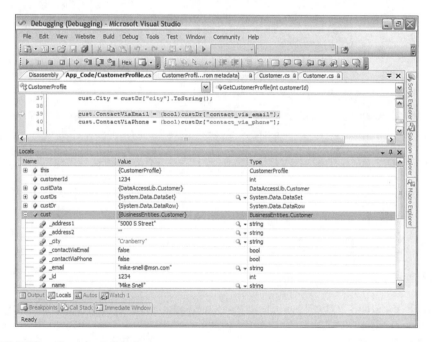

FIGURE 9.29   The Locals window.

TIP

You can edit a value in the Locals or Autos window. To do so, right-click the variable and choose Edit Value from the context menu. You can then change the value of the variable similar to using the Immediate window.

The Autos Window   Often, viewing all the locals provides too many options to sort through. This can be true when there is just too much in scope in the given process or function. To hone in on the value of the code you are looking at, you can use the Autos window. This window shows the value of variables and expressions that are in the current executing line of code or in the prior line of code. This allows you to really focus on just the values you are currently debugging.

Figure 9.30 shows the Autos window for the same line of code as was shown in Figure 9.29. Notice the difference in what is shown. Also, notice that Visual Studio has even added specific expressions that differ from the code to the watch list. For example, the call to custDr["city"] is shown as a watch item.

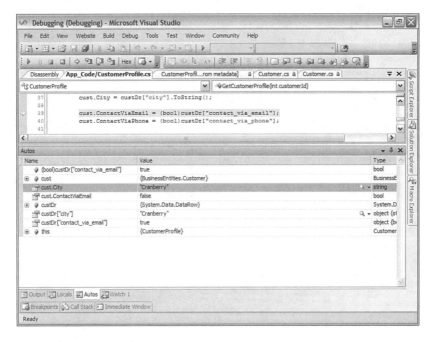

FIGURE 9.30   The Autos window.

The Watch Windows   The Visual Studio watch windows allow you to set a custom list of variables and expressions that you want to keep an eye on. In this way, you decide the items in which you are interested. The watch windows look and behave just like the Locals and Autos windows. In addition, the items you place in watch windows persist from one debug session to another.

You access each watch window from the Debug menu or toolbar. The four watch windows are named Watch 1 through Watch 4. Having four watch windows allows you to set up four custom lists. This capability can be especially helpful if each custom list applies to a separate scope in your application.

You add a variable or expression to the watch window from either the code editor or the QuickWatch window. If you are in the code editor, you select a variable or highlight an expression, right-click, and choose the Add Watch menu item. This will take the highlighted variable or expression and place it in the watch window. You can also drag and drop the highlighted item into a watch window.

QuickWatch   The QuickWatch window is very similar to the other watch windows. However, it allows you to focus on a single variable or expression. The QuickWatch window is used less often now that DataTips exist. From the QuickWatch window, you can write expressions and add them to the watch window. When writing your expression, you have access to IntelliSense. Figure 9.31 shows the QuickWatch window.

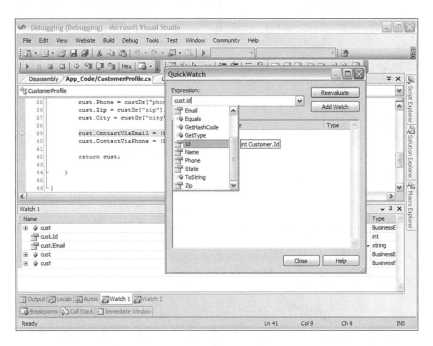

FIGURE 9.31   The QuickWatch window.

The item you add to QuickWatch will be evaluated when you click the Reevaluate button. Clicking the Add Watch button will send the variable to the watch window.

Getting Data Tips

In prior versions of Visual Studio, you could highlight a section of code and view a ToolTip that indicated the value of the variable or expression. In 2005, this concept is expanded considerably with DataTips. DataTips allow you to highlight a variable or expression in the code editor and get watch information right there in the editor. This feature is more how developers work. For example, if you are looking at a line of code, you might highlight something in that line to evaluate it. Previously, this meant doing a QuickWatch. Now it simply unfolds in a DataTip.

Figure 9.32 provides an example. Here, the cursor is positioned over the cust variable that is of type Customer. Clicking on the plus sign to expand this variable unfolds the many members of the object. You can scroll through this list using the arrow at the bottom of the window. You can also right-click any member in the list and edit its value, copy it, or add it to the watch window. The magnifying glass icon next to the items in the list allows you to select a specific visualizer for a given item (more on these shortly).

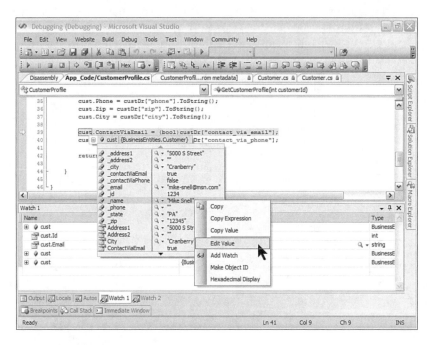

FIGURE 9.32   The DataTips window.

You can still select an expression and have it evaluated as a DataTip. For example, if you select the portion of line 39 in Figure 9.32 that reads (bool)custDr["contact_via_ email"], a DataTip will show this variable and its value of true.

> **TIP**
>
> The DataTips window can often get in the way of viewing code. Sometimes, you need to see the DataTips and the code underneath. In this case, holding the Control (Ctrl) key will make the DataTips window transparent for as long as you press it.

Visualizing Data

When you are looking at variable values, what you really want to get to is the data behind the object. Sometimes this data is obscured by the object model itself. For example, suppose you are looking for the data that is contained in a DataSet object. To find it, you have to dig many layers deep in a watch window or a DataTip. You have to traverse the inner workings of the object model just to get at something as basic as the data contained by the object. If you've spent much time doing this in prior versions of Visual Studio, you know how frustrating it can be.

Visual Studio 2005 tries to take away this frustration and provide quick, easy access to the data contained in an object. It does so through a new tool called *visualizers*. Visualizers are meant to present the object's data in a meaningful way.

A few visualizers ship with Visual Studio by default. They include the following:

- **HTML**—Shows a browser-like dialog box with the HTML interpreted as a user might see it

- **XML**—Shows the XML in a structured format

- **Text**—Shows a string value in an easy-to-read format

- **DataSet**—Shows the contents of the `DataSet`, `DataView`, and `DataTable` objects

There is also a framework for writing and installing visualizers in Visual Studio. You can write your own and plug them into the debugger. You can also download additional visualizers and install them. The possibilities of visualizers are many: as many ways as there are to structure and view data. A few ideas might be a tree-view visualizer that displays hierarchical data or an image visualizer that shows image data structures.

You invoke a visualizer from one of the many places you view data values. This includes watch windows and DataTips. Visualizers are represented by a magnifying glass icon. Figure 9.33 shows launching a visualizer using this icon.

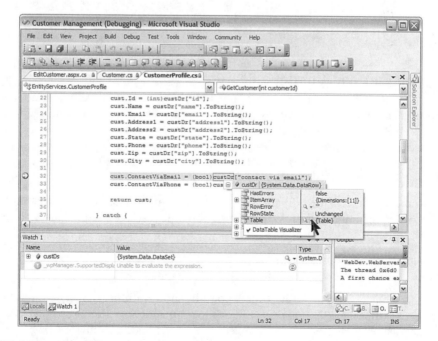

FIGURE 9.33   Launching a visualizer from the DataTip.

For a visualizer example, refer to the `DataSet` problem. Rather than digging through the object hierarchy to get at the data, you can now invoke the `DataSet` visualizer right from a DataTip. Figure 9.34 shows the visualizer in action for the customer `DataSet` object in the sample application.

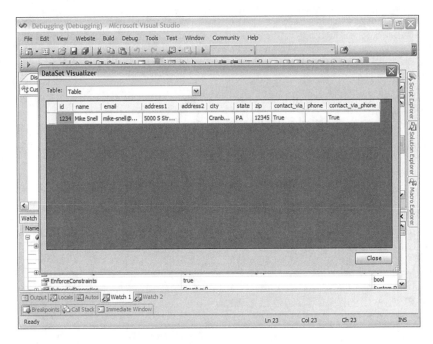

FIGURE 9.34   The DataSet Visualizer.

Using the Edit and Continue Feature

Edit and Continue allows you to change code as you debug without killing your debug session. You can make a modification to a line of code or even fix a bug and keep working in break mode. Visual Basic developers who worked in versions prior to .NET should recall this powerful tool. Its absence in .NET made it one of the most requested features. The good news is that Edit and Continue was added in 2005 to both Visual Basic and C#.

There is no trick to invoking Edit and Continue. You simply make your code change during a debug session and then keep running through your code with a Step command or Continue.

The feature is turned on by default. If it is turned off, you can re-enable it using the Options dialog box available from the Tools menu.

Not all code changes you make are eligible for Edit and Continue. In fact, it should be used only in minor fixes. Any major additions to your code should not be done in debug mode just as a best practice. If your change is within the body of a method, it has a higher likelihood of passing the Edit and Continue test. Most code changes outside the method body require the debugger to restart. Some common changes that are not eligible for Edit and Continue include

- Changing code on the current, active statement

- Changing code on any calls on the stack that lead to the current, active statement

- Adding new types, methods, fields, events, or properties

- Changing a method signature

For a more exhaustive list, search MSDN for "Edit and Continue." There are similar lists for both Visual Basic and C#.

Remote Debugging

Remote debugging allows you to connect to a running application on another machine or domain and debug that application in its environment. This is often the only way to experience errors that are occurring on specific hardware. We've all heard the developer's cry, "Works on my machine." Remote debugging helps those developers figure out why their application doesn't work in other environments.

In a number of scenarios, remote debugging makes a lot of sense. They include debugging SQL server–stored procedures, web services, web applications, remote services or processes, and so on.

The hardest part about doing remote debugging is getting it set up properly. The actual debugging is no different from the debugging we've discussed thus far. However, the setup requires you to jump through a lot of hoops in terms of installation and security. These hoops are necessary because you do not, by default, want developers to easily connect debug sessions to applications on your servers.

There is some good news. Visual Studio 2005 tries to minimize and simplify the setup and configuration of remote debugging. Microsoft has introduced the Remote Debugging Monitor (`msvsmon.exe`) for this purpose. However, developers will still find the setup tasks somewhat arduous (but rewarding when finished). We will not cover the setup in great detail here. We suggest querying MSDN for "Remote Debugging" to get the full walk-through.

We do offer the following, however, as a set of high-level tasks that you will need to complete to get remote debugging working:

1. Install the remote debugging monitor (`msvsmon.exe`) on the remote machine being debugged. You install it using the setup application, `rdbsetup.exe`. You can also run it from a file share.

2. Configure remote debugging permissions. Typically, this means giving your user account administrative access to the machine being debugged.

3. Run the remote debugging monitor on the remote machine. This is a Windows application (with a GUI). You can also set the monitor to run as a Windows service. This capability can be useful for specific server scenarios and ASP .NET remote debugging.

4. If your debug machine is running XP with SP2, you will have to configure the firewall for remote debugging (see MSDN documentation for details).

5. Run Visual Studio on your debug machine as you would to debug any process. Open the project that contains the source for the process you want to debug.

6. Attach to the running process on the remote machine using Attach to Process. You will have to browse to the machine you want to debug and find the process running on that machine.

As you can see, getting remote debugging set up can be a challenge. However, if you have a test environment that you typically debug, the setup should be a one-time operation. From there, you should be able to debug in a more realistic environment as well as walk through SQL stored procedures.

Summary

This chapter presented the Visual Studio 2005 debugger. We covered setting breakpoints in code as well as setting conditions for when those breakpoints are hit. We discussed stepping through code after hitting that breakpoint. In addition, we presented tracepoints, which perform an action (such as printing a message to the output window) when a line of code is hit in the debugger. The chapter also examined the many ways you can see the data presented by the debugger, including the watch windows, visualizers, and DataTips.

The many enhancements in the Visual Studio 2005 debugger are sure to speed your overall development effort. This is a key skill to have. Just like the better you become at coding to anticipate errors and prevent them, honing your skills with the debugging tools is yet another way to unlock additional productivity.

CHAPTER 10

The Visual Studio Automation Object Model

IN THIS CHAPTER

- An Overview of the Automation Object Model

- Solution and Project Objects

- Windows

- Command Bars

- Documents

- Command Objects

- Debugger Objects

- Automation Events

Visual Studio is built to be "extensible." It ships with its own API to enable you, the developer, to control many of the pieces of the IDE.

The API is called the *Visual Studio automation object model*, and understanding its capabilities is the key to unlocking your ability to program and control the IDE itself by writing code in the form of macros and add-ins (discussed in Chapter 11, "Writing Macros, Add-Ins, and Wizards").

In this chapter, we discuss the layout and structure of the automation object model. We map the various objects in the object model to their IDE counterparts, delve into the various ways to interact with these objects through managed code, and, we hope, start to see a glimpse of the possibilities in terms of Visual Studio customization.

To drive home the object model concepts and place them in context, we have provided various code snippets and listings, nearly 100% of which are written in Visual Basic. The reason is that Visual Basic is the language of macros (other languages are not supported), and macros are by far the easiest and quickest way to reach out and touch elements of the IDE. As such, macros are a perfect vehicle for exploring and understanding the object model. In Chapter 11, we'll move beyond the object model and work to understand how to use, write, and run macros and add-ins (add-ins don't suffer from the Visual Basic limitation, so we'll switch gears and provide a majority of our add-in code using C#).

Don't worry too much about the mechanics of writing an add-in or macro at this point; concentrate instead on understanding the automation objects and how they are referenced and used. For the ambitious, know that the code listings here can be pasted directly into the Macros IDE Editor and run as is.

An Overview of the Automation Object Model

The automation object model is a structured class library with a top-level root object called DTE (or DTE2; more on this in a bit), which stands for Development Tools Environment. By referencing the assembly that implements the DTE/DTE2 object, you can instance this root object and use its members and child classes to access the IDE components.

Object Model Versions

The automation object model is actually implemented across two different, complementary primary interoperable assemblies: EnvDTE and EnvDTE80. EnvDTE is the original automation assembly distributed with previous versions of Visual Studio .NET. EnvDTE80 is a new library distributed with Visual Studio 2005. Visual Studio 2005 provides enhanced automation functionality. Because of this, Microsoft was faced with a common design decision: Replace or upgrade the current EnvDTE and risk introducing incompatibilities with current macros and add-ins, or ship a new assembly that could be leveraged in cases in which the new functionality was desired (existing code would still target the previous, unchanged library).

The latter path was chosen, and thus EnvDTE80 (80 represents version 8.0) represents the latest automation functions, while EnvDTE provides the base level of functionality and backward compatibility.

Within the EnvDTE80 assembly, you will find types that supersede their predecessors from the EnvDTE assembly. In these cases, the type name has been appended with a 2 to indicate the revised version. Thus, we have DTE and DTE2, Solution and Solution2, and so on.

Table 10.1 provides a side-by-side listing of some of the most important types implemented in EnvDTE and EnvDTE80. This type list is incomplete; it should be considered for reference only. This table is useful, however, for identifying some of the newly minted types in the new automation assembly; in the next section, we'll see how these types can be organized into broad Visual Studio automation categories and how they map onto physical IDE constructs.

TABLE 10.1   EnvDTE and EnvDTE80 Types

EnvDTE **Type**	EnvDTE80 **Type**	Description
AddIn		Represents a VS add-in.
Breakpoint	Breakpoint2	Returns the debugger object.
BuildDependencies		For the selected project, represents a collection of BuildDependency objects.
BuildDependency		For the selected project, represents the projects that it depends on for a successful build.

TABLE 10.1   Continued

EnvDTE Type	EnvDTE80 Type	Description
BuildEvents		Exposes a list of events relevant to a solution build.
Command		Represents a command action in the IDE.
Commands	Commands2	Returns a collection of all commands supported in the IDE.
CommandWindow		Represents the command window.
Configuration		Represents a project's configuration properties.
Debugger	Debugger2	Represents the Visual Studio debugger.
DebuggerEvents		Exposes events from the debugger.
Document		Represents an open document in the IDE.
Documents		Returns a collection of all open documents in the IDE.
DTE	DTE2	Represents the IDE; this is the top-level root object for the automation object model.
EditPoint	EditPoint2	Represents a text operation point within a document.
Events	Events2	Exposes all automation events.
Find	Find2	Represents the Find capability for text searches in the IDE.
HTMLWindow		Represents an HTML window.
OutputWindow		Represents the output window.
Program	(Process2)	Represents a program running within the IDE; useful for examining processes and threads within the program. EnvDTE80 functionality is provided by the Process2 object.
Project		Represents a project loaded in the IDE.
ProjectItem		Represents an item contained within a given project.
ProjectItems		Returns a collection of all items contained within a project.
Property		Represents a generic property for an object (this can be used across a variety of objects in the automation library).
SelectedItem		Represents projects or project items that are currently selected in the IDE.
Solution	Solution2	Represents the solution currently loaded in Visual Studio.
SourceControl	SourceControl2	Represents the source control system of record within Visual Studio.
TaskItem		Represents an item in the task list window.
TaskItems	TaskItems2	Returns a collection of all items in the task list window.
TaskList		Represents the task list window.
TextDocument		Represents a text file open in the IDE.

10

TABLE 10.1   Continued

EnvDTE **Type**	EnvDTE80 **Type**	**Description**
TextPane	TextPane2	Represents a pane within an open text editor window.
TextWindow		Represents a text window.
ToolBox		Represents the Toolbox window.
ToolBoxItem	ToolBoxItem2	Represents an item within the Toolbox window.
ToolBoxTab	ToolBoxTab2	Represents a tab of items on the Toolbox window.
Window	Window2	Represents, generically, any window within the IDE.
Windows	Windows2	Returns a collection of all windows within the IDE.

Automation Categories

Because any automation effort with Visual Studio starts with the object model, you should understand first how it maps onto the IDE constructs and determine the exact capabilities that it exposes.

In general, you can think of the object model classes as being organized into categories that directly speak to these IDE concepts:

- Solutions and projects
- Windows and command bars (toolbars and menu bars)
- Documents
- Commands
- Debugger
- Events

Each of the objects in these categories touches a different piece of the IDE, and access to each object is always through the root-level DTE2 object.

The DTE/DTE2 Root Object

The DTE/DTE2 object represents the tip of the API tree. You can think of it as representing Visual Studio itself, with the objects under it mapping to the various constituent parts of the IDE.

As mentioned previously, DTE2 is the object used with Visual Studio 2005, with DTE providing compatibility with previous versions. In this chapter, unless we specifically need to differentiate between their capabilities, we will generically refer to the DTE and DTE2 objects as simply DTE.

The DTE properties are used to gain a reference to a specific IDE object (or collection of objects). Methods on the object are used to execute commands in the IDE, launch wizards, or close the IDE.

Table 10.2 shows the major properties and methods defined on the DTE2 object; they have been organized within the six object categories itemized in the preceding section.

TABLE 10.2   DTE2 Properties and Methods for IDE Access

Category	Property	Description
Commands	Commands	Returns a collection of Command objects; in general, a command is an action that can be carried out within the IDE such as opening or saving a file.
Debugger	Debugger	Returns the debugger object.
Documents	ActiveDocument	Returns a Document object representing the currently active document.
Documents	Documents	Returns a collection of Document objects representing all open documents.
Event Notification	Events	Returns the Events object for handling event notifications.
Solutions and Projects	ActiveSolutionProjects	Returns a collection of the Project objects representing the projects that are currently selected within the Solution Explorer.
Solutions and Projects	Solution	Returns the Solution object for the currently loaded solution.
Windows and Command Bars	ActiveWindow	Returns a Window object representing the window within the IDE that currently has focus.
Windows and Command Bars	CommandBars	Returns a collection of CommandBar objects representing all the toolbars and menu bars.
Windows and Command Bars	MainWindow	Returns a Window object representing the IDE window itself.
Windows and Command Bars	StatusBar	Returns a StatusBar object representing Visual Studio's status bar.
Windows and Command Bars	ToolWindows	Returns a ToolWindows instance, which in turns provides access to a few of the most prominent tool windows: the command window, error list, output window, Solution Explorer, task list, and Toolbox.
Windows and Command Bars	WindowConfigurations	Returns a collection of WindowConfiguration objects; these objects represent the various window layouts in use by Visual Studio.

10

TABLE 10.2 Continued

Category	Method	Description
Commands	ExecuteCommand	Executes an environment command.
--	LaunchWizard	Starts the identified wizard with the given parameters.
--	Quit	Closes Visual Studio.

> **NOTE**
>
> The mechanics of referencing and instancing a DTE object change slightly depending on whether you are writing an add-in or a macro, so we'll cover the specifics in the macro and add-in sections in Chapter 11.

In summary, the DTE object is a tool for directly interacting with certain IDE components and providing access to the deeper layers of the API with its property collections. If you move one level down in the API, you find the major objects that form the keystone for automation.

Solution **and** Project **Objects**

The Solution object represents the currently loaded solution. The individual projects within the solution are available via Project objects returned within the Solution.Projects collection. Items within a project are accessed in a similar fashion through the Project.ProjectItems collection.

As you can see from Figure 10.1, this hierarchy exactly mirrors the solution/project hierarchy that we first discussed in Chapter 4, "Solutions and Projects."

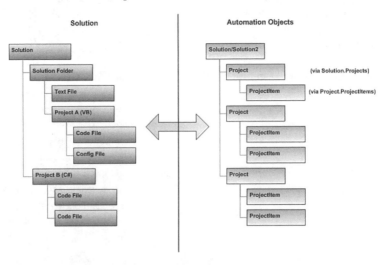

FIGURE 10.1 Mapping the solution/project hierarchy.

There are some mismatches here—solution folders, for instance, are treated as projects—but for the most part, the object model tree closely resembles the solution project tree that you are used to.

The Solution object and Solution2 object members allow you to interact with the current solution to perform common tasks such as

- Determining the number of projects in the solution (Count property)
- Adding a project to the solution based on a project file (AddFromFile method)
- Creating a new solution or closing the current one (Create and Close methods)
- Saving the solution (SaveAs method)
- Removing a project from the solution (Remove method)

You can also directly retrieve a reference to any of the projects within the currently loaded solution by iterating over the Solution.Projects collection. As an example of interacting with the Solution and Project objects, this Visual Basic code snippet removes the first project from the current solution:

```
Dim sol As Solution = DTE.Solution
Dim proj As Project = sol.Projects.Item(1)

If proj.Saved Then
            sol.Remove(proj)
Else
     ...
End If
```

Table 10.3 provides the combined list of the most commonly used properties and methods implemented by Solution2.

TABLE 10.3   Primary Solution/Solution2 Object Members

Property	Description
AddIns	Returns a collection of AddIn objects associated with the current solution.
Count	Returns a count of the projects within the solution.
DTE	Provides a reference back to the parent DTE object.
FullName	Provides the full path and name of the solution file.
IsOpen	Indicates whether a solution is open.
Projects	Returns a collection of Project objects representing all the projects within the solution.
Properties	Returns a collection of Property objects that expose all the solution's properties.
Saved	Indicates whether the solution has been saved since the last modification.
SolutionBuild	Returns a reference to a SolutionBuild object. This is the entry point to the build automation objects applicable for the current solution.

10

TABLE 10.3 Continued

Method	Description
AddFromFile	Adds a project to the solution using an existing project file.
AddFromTemplate	Takes an existing project, clones it, and adds it to the solution.
AddSolutionFolder	Creates a new solution folder in the solution.
Close	Closes the solution.
Create	Creates an empty solution.
FindProjectItem	Initiates a search for a given item in one of the solution's projects.
Item	Returns a `Project` instance.
Open	Opens a solution (using a specific view).
Remove	Removes a project from the solution.
SaveAs	Saves the solution.

Controlling Projects in a Solution

One of the things that the `Solution` object is good for is retrieving references to the various projects that belong to the solution. Each `Project` object has its own set of useful members for interacting with the projects and their items. By using these members, you can interact with the projects in various, expected ways, such as renaming a project, deleting a project, and saving a project.

See Table 10.4 for a summary of the most common `Project` members.

TABLE 10.4 Primary `Project` Object Members

Property	Description
AddIns	Returns a collection of `AddIn` objects associated with the current solution.
Count	Returns a count of the project within the solution.
DTE	Provides a reference back to the parent `DTE` object.
FullName	Provides the full path and name of the solution file.
IsOpen	Indicates whether a solution is open.
Projects	Returns a collection of `Project` objects representing all the projects within the solution.
Properties	Returns a collection of `Property` objects that expose all the solution's properties.
Saved	Indicates whether the solution has been saved since the last modification.
SolutionBuild	Returns a reference to a `SolutionBuild` object. This is the entry point to the build automation objects applicable for the current solution.
Method	**Description**
AddFromFile	Adds a project to the solution using an existing project file.
AddFromTemplate	Takes an existing project, clones it, and adds it to the solution.
AddSolutionFolder	Creates a new solution folder in the solution.
Close	Closes the solution.
Create	Creates an empty solution.
FindProjectItem	Initiates a search for a given item in one of the solution's projects.
Item	Returns a `Project` instance.

TABLE 10.4   Continued

Property	Description
Open	Opens a solution (using a specific view).
Remove	Removes a project from the solution.
SaveAs	Saves the solution.

Accessing Code Within a Project

Beyond the basic project attributes and items, one of the cooler things that can be accessed via a `Project` instance is the actual code within the project's source files. Through the `CodeModel` property, you can access an entire line of proxy objects representing the code constructs within a project. For instance, the `CodeClass` interface allows you to examine *and edit* the code for a given class in a given project.

> **NOTE**
>
> Support for the different CodeModel entities varies from language to language. The MSDN documentation for each CodeModel type clearly indicates the source language support for that element.

After grabbing a `CodeModel` reference from a `Project` instance, you can access its `CodeElements` collection (which is, not surprisingly, a collection of `CodeElement` objects). A `CodeElement` is nothing more than a generic representation of a certain code structure within a project. The `CodeElement` object is generic, but it provides a property, `Kind`. This property is used to determine the exact native type of the code object contained within the `CodeElement`.

The `CodeElement.Kind` property is an enumeration (of type `vsCMElement`) that identifies the specific type of code construct lurking within the `CodeElement` object. Using the `Kind` property, you can first determine the true nature of the code element and then cast the `CodeElement` object to its strong type. Here is a snippet of C# code that does just that:

```
if (element.Kind == vsCMElement.vsCMElementClass)
        CodeClass myClass = (CodeClass)element;
```

For a better grasp of the code model hierarchy, consider the C# code presented in Listing 10.1; this is a "shell" solution that merely implements a namespace, a class within that namespace, and a function within the class.

LISTING 10.1   A Simple Namespace and Class Implementation

```
using System;
using System.Collections.Generic;
using System.Text;

namespace MyNamespace
{
```

LISTING 10.1   Continued

```
class MyClass
{
    public string SumInt(int x, int y)
    {
        return x + y;
    }
}
}
```

If you map the code in Listing 10.1 to the code object model, you would end up with the structure you see in Figure 10.2.

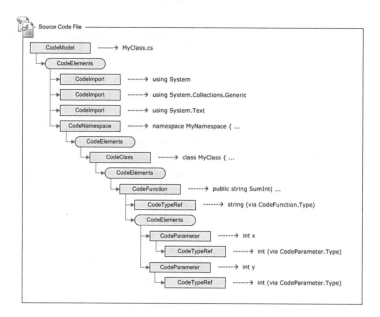

FIGURE 10.2   Simple code model object hierarchy.

To get an idea of the complete depth of the code model tree that can be accessed through the CodeElements collection, consult Table 10.5; this table shows all the possible vsCMElement values, the type they are used to represent, and a brief description of the type.

TABLE 10.5   Mapping the vsCMElement Enumeration Values

Enumeration Value	Type	Description
vsCMElementAssignmentStmt		An assignment statement
vsCMElementAttribute		An attribute
vsCMElementClass	CodeClass	A class

TABLE 10.5 Continued

Enumeration Value	Type	Description
vsCMElementDeclareDecl		A declaration
vsCMElementDefineStmt		A define statement
vsCMElementDelegate	CodeDelegate	A delegate
vsCMElementEnum	CodeEnum	An enumeration
vsCMElementEvent	CodeEvent	An event
vsCMElementEventsDeclaration		An event declaration
vsCMElementFunction	CodeFunction	A function
vsCMElementFunctionInvokeStmt		A statement invoking a function
vsCMElementIDLCoClass		An IDL co-class
vsCMElementIDLImport		An IDL import statement
vsCMElementIDLImportLib		An IDL import library
vsCMElementIDLLibrary		An IDL library
vsCMElementImplementsStmt		An implements statement
vsCMElementImportStmt	CodeImport	An import statement
vsCMElementIncludeStmt		An include statement
vsCMElementInheritsStmt		An inherits statement
vsCMElementInterface	CodeInterface	An interface
vsCMElementLocalDeclStmt		A local declaration statement
vsCMElementMacro		A macro
vsCMElementMap		A map
vsCMElementMapEntry		A map entry
vsCMElementModule		A module
vsCMElementNamespace	CodeNamespace	A namespace
vsCMElementOptionStmt		An option statement
vsCMElementOther	CodeElement	A code element not otherwise identified in this enum
vsCMElementParameter	CodeParameter	A parameter
vsCMElementProperty	CodeProperty	A property
vsCMElementPropertySetStmt		A property set statement
vsCMElementStruct	CodeStruct	A structure
vsCMElementTypeDef		A type definition
vsCMElementUDTDecl		A user-defined type
vsCMElementUnion		A union
vsCMElementUsingStmt	CodeImport	A using statement
vsCMElementVariable		A variable
vsCMElementVBAttributeGroup		A Visual Basic attribute group
vsCMElementVBAttributeStmt		A Visual Basic attribute statement
vsCMElementVCBase		A Visual C++ base

Windows

The visible, content portion of Visual Studio is represented by Window objects. Window objects are instances of open windows within the IDE such as the Solution Explorer, the task list window, an open code editor window, and so on. Even the IDE itself is represented by a `Window` object.

Any given window is either a document window or a tool window. Document windows host documents that are editable by the Text Editor. Tool windows contain controls that display information relevant to the current context of the IDE; the Solution Explorer and task list windows are examples of tool windows, and a VB source code file open in an editor is an example of a document window.

Referencing Windows

If you need to retrieve an instance of a specific window, you have a few different options, each optimal for a given situation. For starters, the main IDE window is always available directly from the `DTE` object:

```
Dim IDE As Window
IDE = DTE.MainWindow
```

Obviously, if you need to perform a specific action against the IDE window, this is your quickest route.

The `DTE.ActiveWindow` property also provides direct and quick access to a `Window` object, in this case the currently active window:

```
Dim CurrentWindow As Window
CurrentWindow = DTE.ActiveWindow
```

The tool windows within the IDE—that is, the command window, the error list window, the output window, the Solution Explorer, the task list window, and the Toolbox—also have a direct way to retrieve their object model instances: You use the `DTE.ToolWindows` property. This property returns a `ToolWindows` object that exposes a separate property for each of the tool windows.

This Visual Basic code grabs a reference to the task list window and closes it:

```
Dim taskwin As Window

taskwin = DTE.ToolWindows.TaskList
taskwin.Close()
```

And finally, the fourth way to access an IDE window is through the `DTE.Windows` collection; this collection holds an entry for each IDE window. You can access a window from the collection by using either an integer representing the window's position within the collection, or by providing an object or string that represents the window you are trying to retrieve.

The following code grabs a handle to the Solution Explorer window:

```
Dim windows As Windows2 = DTE.Windows
Dim window As Window = windows.Item(Constants.vsWindowKindSolutionExplorer)
```

Interacting with Windows

Table 10.6 itemizes the properties and methods available on each `Window` object.

TABLE 10.6   Window Object Members

Property	Description
AutoHides	A Boolean flag indicating whether the window can be hidden (applies only to tool windows).
Caption	The title/caption of the window.
Collection	The Windows collection that the current Window object belongs to.
CommandBars	A CommandBars collection of the command bars implemented by the window.
ContextAttributes	A collection of ContextAttribute objects; they are used to associate the current context of the window with the Dynamic Help window.
Document	If the Window object is hosting a document, this returns a reference to the document.
DTE	A reference to the root DTE object.
Height	The height of the window in pixels.
IsFloating	A Boolean flag indicating whether the window is floating or docked.
Left	The distance, in pixels, between the window's left edge and its container's left edge.
Linkable	A Boolean flag indicating whether the window can be docked with other windows.
LinkedWindowFrame	Returns a reference to the Window object that is acting as the frame for a docked window.
LinkedWindows	A collection of Window objects representing the windows that are linked together within the same frame.
Object	Returns an object proxy that represents the window and can be referenced by name.
ObjectKind	A GUID indicating the type of the object returned from Window.Object.
Project	A Project instance representing the project containing the Window object.
ProjectItem	A ProjectItem instance representing the project item containing the Window object.
Selection	Returns an object representing the currently selected item in the window (for document windows, this might be text; for tool windows, this might be an item in a list, and so on).
Top	The distance, in pixels, between the window's top edge and its parent's top edge.
Visible	A Boolean flag indicating whether the window is visible or hidden.

10

TABLE 10.6   Continued

Property	Description
Width	The width of the window in pixels.
WindowState	Gets or sets the current state of the window (via a vsWindowState enum value: vsWindowStateMaximize, vsWindowStateMinimize, vsWindowStateNormal).

Method	Description
Activate	Gives the window focus.
Close	Closes the window; you can indicate, with a vsSaveChanges enum value, whether the window's hosted document should be saved or not saved, or whether the IDE should prompt the user to make that decision.
SetSelectionContainer	Passes an array of objects to the Properties window when the Window object has focus. This property is mainly used for custom tool windows where you need to control what is displayed in the Properties window.
SetTabPicture	Specifies an object to use as a tab image; this image is displayed whenever the window is part of a tab group within the IDE.

Beyond the basics (such as using the Height and Width properties to query or affect a window's dimensions, or setting focus to the window with the SetFocus method), a few properties deserve special mention:

- The Document property gives you a way to programmatically interact with the document that the window is hosting (if any).

- The Project and ProjectItem properties serve to bridge the Window portion of the API with the Project/Solution portion; in a similar vein as the Document property, you can use these properties to interact with the project that is related to the window, or the project item (such as the VB code file, text file, resource file, and so on).

- If you are dealing with a tool window, the SetTabPicture method provides a way to set the tab icon that is displayed when the tool window is part of a group of tabbed windows (for instance, the Toolbox window displays a wrench and hammer picture on its tab when part of a tabbed group).

- Again, specifically for tool windows only, the SetSelectionContainer can be used to supply one or more objects for display within the Properties window. This capability is useful if you have a custom window where you need to control what is displayed in the Properties window when the window has focus (all the standard VS windows already do this for you).

Listing 10.2 contains a simple macro illustrating the use of the Window object; in this example, each window is queried to determine its type, and then a summary of each window is output in a simple message box.

LISTING 10.2   VB Macro for Querying the Windows Collection

```vb
Imports EnvDTE
Imports EnvDTE80
Imports System.Diagnostics
Imports System.Windows.Forms


Public Module MacroExamples

    Public Sub InventoryWindows()
        ' Get collection of all open windows
        Dim windows As Windows2 = DTE.Windows

        ' Count the nbr of open windows
        Dim windowCount As Integer = windows.Count

        ' Local vars for looping and holding window and string
        ' results
        Dim idx As Integer
        Dim results As String
        Dim window As Window2

        results = windowCount.ToString + " windows open..." + vbCrLf

        ' Iterate the collection of windows
        For idx = 1 To windowCount

            window = windows.Item(idx)
            Dim title As String = window.Caption

            ' If the window is hosting a document, a valid Document
            ' object will be returned through Window.Document
            If Not (window.Document Is Nothing) Then
                ' Write this out as a document window
                Dim docName As String = window.Document.Name
                results = results + "Window '" + title + "' is a document window"
                    + vbCrLf
            Else
                ' If no document was present, this is a tool window
                ' (tool windows don't host documents)
                results = results + "Window '" + title + "' is a tool window"
                    + vbCrLf
            End If
```

10

LISTING 10.2   Continued

```
        Next

        ' Show the results
        MessageBox.Show(results, "Window Documents", MessageBoxButtons.OK, _
            MessageBoxIcon.Information)

    End Sub

End Module
```

> **NOTE**
>
> If you want to embed your own custom control inside a tool window, you have to write an add-in and use the `Windows.CreateToolWindow` method. We cover this scenario in Chapter 11.

Text Windows and Window Panes

Text windows have their own specific object abstraction in addition to the generic `Window` object: The `TextWindow` object is used to represent text editor windows. To obtain a reference to a window's `TextWindow` object, you retrieve the `Window` object's value and assign it into a `TextWindow` type:

```
Dim textWindow As TextWindow
textWindow = DTE.ActiveWindow.Object
```

The `TextWindow` object doesn't provide much functionality over and above the functionality found in the `Window` type; its real value is the access it provides to window panes.

Text editor windows in Visual Studio can be split into two panes; with a text editor open, simply select Split from the Window menu to create a new pane within the window. The `TextWindow.ActivePane` property returns a `TextPane` object representing the currently active pane in the window, and the `TextWindow.Panes` property provides access to all the panes within a text window:

```
' Get pane instance from collection
Dim newPane As TextPane2
newPane = textWindow.Panes.Item(1)

' Get currently active pane
Dim currPane As TextPane2
currPane = textWindow.ActivePane
```

One of the more useful things you can do with the TextPane object is to scroll the client area of the pane (for example, the visible portion of the document within the pane) so that a specific range of text is visible. This is done via the TextPane.TryToShow method.

Here is the definition for the method:

```
Function TryToShow( Point As TextPoint, Optional How As vsPaneShowHow, _
    PointOrCount As Object)
```

The TextPoint parameter represents the specific location within the text document that you want visible in the text pane (we discuss TextPoint objects in depth in a later section of this chapter; see "Editing Text Documents"). The vsPaneShowHow value specifies how the pane should behave when scrolling to the indicated location:

- vsPaneShowHow.vsPaneShowCentered will cause the pane to center the text/text selection in the middle of the pane (horizontally and vertically).

- vsPaneShowHow.vsPaneShowTop will place the text point at the top of the viewable region in the pane.

- vsPaneShowHow.vsPaneShowAsIs will show the text point as is with no changes in horizontal or vertical orientation within the viewable region in the pane.

The last parameter, the PointOrCount object, is used to specify the end of the text area that you want displayed. If you provide an integer here, this represents a count of characters past the original text point; if you provide another text point, then the selection is considered to be that text that resides between the two text points.

The TextPane object is also used to access the Incremental Search feature for a specific window pane. Listing 10.3 shows an example of this feature in action.

LISTING 10.3   Controlling Incremental Search

```
Imports EnvDTE
Imports EnvDTE80
Imports Microsoft.VisualStudio.CommandBars
Imports System.Diagnostics
Imports System.Windows.Forms


Public Module MacroExamples

    Public Sub IncrementalSearch()
        ' Grab references to the active window;
        ' we assume, for this example, that the window
        ' is a text window.
        Dim window As Window2 = DTE.ActiveWindow
```

LISTING 10.3   Continued

```
        ' Grab a TextWindow instance that maps to our
        ' active window
        Dim txtWindow As TextWindow = window.Object


        ' Get the active pane from the text window
        Dim pane As TextPane2 = txtWindow.ActivePane


        'Using the active pane, get an IncrementalSearch object
        ' for the pane
        Dim search As IncrementalSearch = pane.IncrementalSearch


        ' Try to find our IMessageMapper interface by looking
        ' for the string "IM"
        ' Configure the search:
        '    search forward in the document
        '    append the chars that we are searching for
        '    quit the search
        search.StartForward()
        search.AppendCharAndSearch(AscW("I"))
        search.AppendCharAndSearch(AscW("M"))


        ' To remove us from incremental search mode,
        ' we can call IncrementalSearch.Exit()...
        'search.Exit()


    End Sub
End Module
```

The Tool Window Types

In addition to having a `Window` object abstraction, each default tool window in the IDE—the command window, output window, Toolbox window, and task list window—is also represented by a discrete type that exposes methods and properties unique to that tool window. Table 10.7 lists the default tool windows and their underlying type in the automation object model.

TABLE 10.7   Tool Windows and Their Types

Tool Window	Type
Command Window	`CommandWindow`
Output Window	`OutputWindow`
Task List Window	`TaskList`
Toolbox Window	`ToolBox`

To reference one of these objects, you first start with its `Window` representation and then cast its `Window.Object` value to the matching type. For instance, this VB snippet starts with a `Window` reference to the task list window and then uses that `Window` object to obtain a reference to the `TaskList` object:

```
Dim windows As Windows = DTE.Windows
Dim twindow As Window = _
    DTE.Windows.Item(EnvDTE.Constants.vsWindowKindTaskList)
```

Tasks and the Task List Window

The `TaskList` object enables you to access the items currently displayed in the task list window; each item in the window is represented by its own `TaskItem` object. The `TaskItem` object exposes methods and properties that allow you to manipulate the task items. For instance, you can mark an item as complete, get or set the line number associated with the task, and change the priority of the task.

You remove tasks from the list by using the `TaskItem.Delete` method and add them by using the `TaskItems.Add` method. The `Add` method allows you to specify the task category, subcategory, description, priority, icon, and so on:

```
Dim tlist As TaskList = CType(twindow.Object, TaskList)

tlist.TaskItems.Add("Best Practices", "Coding Style", _
    "Use of brace indenting is inconsistent", _
    vsTaskPriority.vsTaskPriorityMedium, _
    vsTaskIcon.vsTaskIconUser, True, _
    "S:\ContosoCommonFramework\Contoso.Fx.Common\Class1.cs", _
    7, True, True)
```

Table 10.8 provides an inventory of the `TaskItem` members.

TABLE 10.8   `TaskItem` Members

Property	Description
Category	The category of the task.
Checked	A Boolean flag indicating whether the task is marked as completed (a check mark appears in the check box next to the task).
Collection	The `TaskList` collection that the current `TaskItem` object belongs to.
Description	The description of the task.
Displayed	A Boolean flag indicating whether the task is currently visible in the task list window.
DTE	A reference to the root `DTE` object.
FileName	The name of the file associated with the task (if any).
IsSettable	By passing in a `vsTaskListColumn` enum value to this property, you can determine whether that column is editable or not.
Line	The line number associated with the task.

10

TABLE 10.8   Continued

Property	Description
Priority	A `vsTaskPriority` value indicating the task's priority level. Possible values include `vsTaskPriorityHigh`, `vsTaskPriorityMedium`, and `vsTaskPriorityLow`.
SubCategory	The subcategory of the task.
LinkedWindows	A collection of `Window` objects representing the windows that are linked together within the same frame.
Object	Returns an object proxy that represents the `Window` and can be referenced by name.
ObjectKind	A GUID indicating the type of the object returned from `Window.Object`.
Project	A `Project` instance representing the project containing the `Window` object.
ProjectItem	A `ProjectItem` instance representing the project item containing the `Window` object.
Selection	Returns an object representing the currently selected item in the `Window` (for document windows, this might be text; for tool windows, this might be an item in a list, and so on).
Top	The distance, in pixels, between the window's top edge and its parent's top edge.
Visible	A Boolean flag indicating whether the window is visible or hidden.
Width	The width of the window in pixels.
WindowState	Gets or sets the current state of the window (via a `vsWindowState` enum value: `vsWindowStateMaximize`, `vsWindowStateMinimize`, `vsWindowStateNormal`).
Method	**Description**
Delete	Removes the task from the task list window.
Navigate	Causes the IDE to navigate to the location (for example, file and line) associated to the task.
Select	Selects or moves the focus to the task within the task list window.

Listing 10.4 contains a short VB macro demonstrating the use of the `TaskList`, `TaskItems`, and `TaskItem` objects to iterate the tasks and toggle their completed status.

LISTING 10.4   Toggling Task Item Completion

```
Imports EnvDTE
Imports EnvDTE80
Imports Microsoft.VisualStudio.CommandBars
Imports System.Diagnostics
Imports System.Windows.Forms


Public Module MacroExamples

    Public Sub ToggleAllTasks()
```

LISTING 10.4   Continued

```
        ' Reference the windows collection
        Dim windows As Windows = DTE.Windows

        ' Pluck the task list window from the collection
        Dim twindow As Window = _
            DTE.Windows.Item(EnvDTE.Constants.vsWindowKindTaskList)

        ' Convert the window object to a TaskList instance by
        ' casting its Object property
        Dim tlist As TaskList = CType(twindow.Object, TaskList)

        ' Iterate all of the task items in the task list
        For Each task As TaskItem In tlist.TaskItems
            ' Toggle the "completed" check mark on each item
            task.Checked = Not task.Checked
        Next


    End Sub
End Module
```

The ToolBox

Four objects are used to programmatically interface with the Toolbox:

- `ToolBox`—An object representing the Toolbox itself

- `ToolBoxTabs`—A collection representing the tab panes on the Toolbox

- `ToolBoxItems`—A collection representing the items within a tab on the Toolbox

- `ToolBoxItem`—A discrete item displayed within a Toolbox tab

Figure 10.3 illustrates the Toolbox object hierarchy.

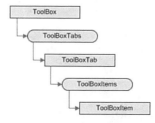

FIGURE 10.3   ToolBox object hierarchy.

10

These objects are used primarily to add, remove, or alter the items hosted by the Toolbox. For instance, you can easily add a custom tab to the Toolbox by using the `ToolBoxTabs` collection:

```
Dim tBox As ToolBox
Dim myTab As ToolBoxTab
tBox = DTE.Windows.Item(Constants.vsWindowKindToolbox).Object
myTab = tBox.ToolBoxTabs.Add("My TBox Tab")
```

You can also add items to any tab with the `ToolBoxItems.Add` method, which accepts a name for the item to add, a "data" object representing the item, and a `vsToolBoxItem-Format` enum, which specifies the format of the item. The `Add` method uses the `vsToolBoxItemFormat` to determine how to interpret the "data" object value. For instance, if you wanted to add a .NET control to the tab created in the previous code snippet, you could accomplish that with just one line of code:

```
tlBoxTab.ToolBoxItems.Add("ContosoControl", _
        "C:\Contoso\Controls\CalendarControl.dll", _
        vsToolBoxItemFormat.vsToolBoxItemFormatDotNETComponent)
```

Notice that the item, in this case, is represented by a path to the assembly that implements the control and that it has an item format of `vsToolBoxItemFormatDotNET-Component`.

Listing 10.5 contains a VB function that adds a tab to the Toolbox, adds a control and a text fragment to the tab, and then removes the tab.

LISTING 10.5   Adding and Removing Items in the Toolbox Window

```
Imports EnvDTE
Imports EnvDTE80
Imports Microsoft.VisualStudio.CommandBars
Imports System.Diagnostics
Imports System.Windows.Forms


    Public Sub AddAToolBoxTab()
        Dim toolBox As ToolBox
        Dim tabs As ToolBoxTabs
        Dim tab As ToolBoxTab
        Dim tabItems As ToolBoxItems
        Dim win As Window

        Try
            ' Get a reference to the toolbox
            win = DTE.Windows.Item(Constants.vsWindowKindToolbox)
            toolBox = win.Object
```

LISTING 10.5   Continued

```
' Get a reference to the toolbox tabs collection
tabs = toolBox.ToolBoxTabs

' Add a new tab to the ToolBox
tab = tabs.Add("New ToolBox Tab")

' Make the added tab the active tab
tab.Activate()

tabItems = tab.ToolBoxItems

With tabItems
    ' Add a piece of text to the toolbox.
    ' Clicking on the text will add it to
    ' the active document...
    .Add("Code Comment", _
        "This is some text to add to the toolbox", _
        vsToolBoxItemFormat.vsToolBoxItemFormatText)

    'Now add a control to the toolbox.
    'When adding a control, you need to specify
    'the path to the assembly; you can add all
    'classes from the assembly (shown below)
    'or just one of the classes (see MSDN
    'docs for that syntax)
    .Add("My Login Control", _
        "C:\MyComponents\Contoso\LoginControl.dll", _
        vsToolBoxItemFormat.vsToolBoxItemFormatDotNETComponent)

    'For demonstration purposes, let's remove
    'the items that we had just added, and then
    'remove the newly created tab...

    'Put up a messagebox to confirm the deletes
    MessageBox.Show("Click OK to delete the tab and added items.", _
        "Delete Toolbox Tab Items", MessageBoxButtons.OK, _
        MessageBoxIcon.Information)

    'Delete the tab
    tab.Delete()

End With
```

10

LISTING 10.5   Continued

```
    Catch ex As Exception
        MsgBox("Error: " & ex.ToString())
    End Try


End Sub
```

Executing Commands in the Command Window

The command window is a tool window used to execute IDE commands or aliases. IDE commands are essentially ways to tell the IDE to perform some action. Some commands map directly to menu items (such as File Open), whereas others don't have menu equivalents.

The CommandWindow object permits you to programmatically pipe commands into the command window and execute them. You can also output a text string (for informational purposes) to the window and clear its current content:

```
' Get a reference to the command window
Dim cmdWindow As CommandWindow = _
    DTE.Windows.Item(Constants.vsWindowKindCommandWindow).Object


' Display some text in the command window
cmdWindow.OutputString("Hello, World!")


' Clear the command window
cmdWindow.Clear()
```

Listing 10.6 shows how to programmatically execute commands in the CommandWindow object.

LISTING 10.6   Executing Commands in the Command Window

```
Imports EnvDTE
Imports EnvDTE80
Imports Microsoft.VisualStudio.CommandBars
Imports System.Diagnostics
Imports System.Windows.Forms


Public Module MacroExamples

    Public Sub ExecCommandWindow()
        Dim cmdWindow As CommandWindow = _
            DTE.Windows.Item(Constants.vsWindowKindCommandWindow).Object
```

LISTING 10.6   Continued

```
          ' Display some text in the command window
          cmdWindow.OutputString("Executing command from the automation OM...")

          ' Send some command strings to the command window and execute
          ' them...

          ' This command will start logging all input/output in the
          ' command window to the specified file
          cmdWindow.SendInput("Tools.LogCommandWindowOutput cmdwindow.log", True)

          ' Open a file in a code editor:
          '    1. We use an alias, 'of', for the File.OpenFile command
          '    2. This command takes quote-delimited parameters (in this case,
          '       the name of the editor to load the file in)
          Dim cmd As String = "of "
          cmd = cmd & """C:\Contoso\ContosoCommonFramework\Integration\
➥Integration.cs"""
          cmd = cmd & "/e:""CSharp Editor"""

          cmdWindow.SendInput(cmd, True)

          cmdWindow.SendInput("Edit.Find MessageTrxId", True)

          ' Turn off logging
          cmdWindow.SendInput("Tools.LogCommandWindowOutput /off", True)

      End Sub
End Module
```

Output Window

The output window displays messages generated from a variety of different sources in the IDE. A prime example is the messages generated by the compiler when a project is being built. For a deeper look at the functionality provided by the output window, see Chapter 9, "Debugging with Visual Studio 2005."

The output window is controlled through three objects:

- `OutputWindow` is the root object representing the output window.

- `OutputWindowPanes` is a collection of `OutputWindowPane` objects.

- `OutputWindowPane` represents one of the current panes within the output window.

Using these objects, you can add or remove panes from the output window, output text to any one of the panes, and respond to events transpiring in the window.

The following VB code fragment retrieves a reference to the output window and writes a test string in the Build pane:

```
Dim outWindow As OutputWindow = _
DTE.Windows.Item(Constants.vsWindowKindOutput).Object

Dim pane As OutputWindowPane = _
    outWindow.OutputWindowPanes.Item("Build")

pane.OutputString("test")
```

Using the OutputWindowPane object, you can also add items simultaneously to a specific output pane and the task list window. The OutputWindowPane.OutputTaskItemString method writes text into the output window and simultaneously adds that text as a task to the task list window:

```
Dim output As String = "Exception handler not found"
Dim task As String = "Add exception handler"
pane.OutputTaskItemString(output, _
  vsTaskPriority.vsTaskPriorityMedium,  "", vsTaskIcon.vsTaskIconNone, _
  "", 0, task, True)
```

Because most of the output window actions are conducted against a specific pane, most of the useful methods are concentrated in the OutputWindowPane object. For your reference, the OutputWindowPane members are itemized in Table 10.9.

TABLE 10.9   OutputWindowPane Members

Property	Description
Collection	The OutputWindowPanes collection that the current OutputWindowPane object belongs to
DTE	A reference to the root DTE object
Guid	The GUID for the output window pane
Name	The name of the output window pane
TextDocument	A TextDocument object representing the window pane's content
Method	**Description**
Activate	Moves the focus to the output window
Clear	Clears the contents of the window pane
ForceItemsToTaskList	Writes all task items not yet written to the task list window
OutputString	Writes a string to the output window pane
OutputTaskItemString	Writes a string to the output window pane and simultaneously adds a task to the task list window

Listing 10.7 demonstrates controlling the output window by adding a new pane to the window, writing text into that pane, and then clearing its content.

LISTING 10.7   Writing to the Output Window

```
Imports EnvDTE
Imports EnvDTE80
Imports Microsoft.VisualStudio.CommandBars
Imports System.Diagnostics
Imports System.Windows.Forms


Public Module MacroExamples

    Public Sub WriteToOutputWindow()

        ' Grab a reference to the output window
        Dim outWindow As OutputWindow = _
            DTE.Windows.Item(Constants.vsWindowKindOutput).Object

        ' Create a new pane in the output window
        Dim pane As OutputWindowPane = _
            outWindow.OutputWindowPanes.Add("New Pane")

        pane.OutputString("Text in the 'New Pane'")

        pane.Clear()

    End Sub
End Module
```

Linked Windows

Tool windows can be positioned in a variety of ways within the IDE: You can float tool windows around within the overall IDE container; you can dock a tool window to one of the sides of the IDE; you can join windows together, pin and unpin them; and so on (see the section "Managing the Many Windows of the IDE" in Chapter 2, "A Quick Tour of the IDE," for an introduction to window layout).

A *linked window* refers to two or more tool windows that have been aggregated together. Figure 10.4 shows one common example of this: The Toolbox and Solution Explorer and the Data Sources window have all been joined together in a common frame. Each window that is part of the frame can be viewed by clicking on its tab.

By joining together two or more tool windows, you actually create an additional window object—called a *linked window* or *window frame*—that functions as the container for its hosted tool windows and is available as a part of the DTE.Windows collection.

10

FIGURE 10.4   Linked windows.

By using the `Window.LinkedWindows` and `Window.WindowFrame` properties and the `Windows2.CreateLinkedWindowFrame` method, you can programmatically link and unlink any available tool windows. The Visual Basic code in Listing 10.8 demonstrates this process by doing the following:

1. You grab the window objects for the Toolbox window and the Solution Explorer window.

2. You programmatically join these two windows together, effectively creating the linked window that you see in Figure 10.4.

3. After joining the windows together, you get a reference to the newly created linked window and use its `LinkedWindows` property to unlink the windows that were previously just linked together.

LISTING 10.8   Linking and Unlinking Tool Windows

```
Imports EnvDTE
Imports EnvDTE80
Imports System.Diagnostics
Imports System.Windows.Forms

Public Module MacroExamples

    Public Sub LinkUnLink()
        Dim windows As Windows2 = DTE.Windows

        ' Grab references to the solution explorer and the toolbox
        Dim solExplorer As Window2 = _
```

LISTING 10.8   Continued

```vb
        windows.Item(Constants.vsWindowKindSolutionExplorer)
    Dim toolbox As Window2 = windows.Item(Constants.vsWindowKindToolbox)

    ' Use the Windows2 collection to create a linked window/window
    ' frame to hold the toolbox and solution explorer windows
    Dim windowFrame As Window2
    windowFrame = windows.CreateLinkedWindowFrame(solExplorer, _
        toolbox, vsLinkedWindowType.vsLinkedWindowTypeTabbed)

    ' At this point, we have created a linked window with two tabbed
    ' "interior" windows: the solution explorer, and the toolbox...

    MessageBox.Show("Press OK to Unlink the windows", "LinkUnLink", _
        MessageBoxButtons.OK, MessageBoxIcon.None)

    ' To unlink the windows:
    '    -- Use the window frame's LinkedWindows collection
    '    -- Remove the window objects from this collection

    windowFrame.LinkedWindows.Remove(toolbox)
    windowFrame.LinkedWindows.Remove(solExplorer)

    End Sub
End Module
```

Command Bars

A command bar is a menu bar or toolbar; from an object model perspective, these are represented by `CommandBar` objects. Because menu bars and toolbars are hosted within a window, you reference specific `CommandBar` objects via the `Window` object, through the `Window.CommandBars` property. In turn, every `CommandBar` plays host to controls such as buttons, drop-downs, and so on. Figure 10.5 shows the Solution Explorer tool window with its command bar highlighted.

Note that there are six buttons hosted on the command bar.

> **NOTE**
>
> Unlike the `Windows` collection, which holds only an instance of each open window, the `CommandBars` collection holds instances for every single registered command bar, regardless of whether the command bar is currently being shown in the window.

The VB code in Listing 10.9 queries the `CommandBar` object for the Solution Explorer window and prints out the `CommandBar` objects that it finds.

Solution Explorer Command Bar

FIGURE 10.5   The Solution Explorer tool window and its command bar.

LISTING 10.9   Querying the CommandBar Object

```
Imports EnvDTE
Imports EnvDTE80
Imports Microsoft.VisualStudio.CommandBars
Imports System.Diagnostics
Imports System.Windows.Forms


Public Module MacroExamples

    Public Sub QueryCommandBar()
        Dim windows As Windows2 = DTE.Windows

        ' Grab reference to the solution explorer
        Dim solExplorer As Window2 = _
            windows.Item(Constants.vsWindowKindSolutionExplorer)

        ' Retrieve the solution explorer's command bar object
        Dim cmdBar As CommandBar = CType(solExplorer.CommandBars(1), CommandBar)

        ' Start building our output string
        Dim output As String = "Command bar contains: " + vbCrLf
```

LISTING 10.9   Continued

```
    ' Get a reference to the controls hosted in the
    ' command bar
    Dim controls As CommandBarControls = cmdBar.Controls

    ' Count integer
    Dim i As Integer = 1

    ' Iterate the controls in the command bar
    For Each control As CommandBarControl In controls

        If control.Enabled Then

            output = output + i.ToString() + " " + _
                control.Type.ToString() + _
                ": " + control.Caption + vbCrLf

            i = i + 1

        End If

    Next

    MessageBox.Show(output, "Solution Explorer Command Bar", _
        MessageBoxButtons.OK)

    End Sub
End Module
```

Correlate the results in Figure 10.6 with Figure 10.4: Six buttons are visible on the tool window, and the code has found six items in the CommandBarControls collection (which is returned through the CommandBar.Controls property). Removing the following check against the Enabled property would result in many more controls produced in the message box:

```
If control.Enabled Then
```

FIGURE 10.6   Controls found in the command bar.

Notice in Listing 10.9 that you have to explicitly cast the object returned from the `Window.CommandBars` property: this is, interestingly, not a strongly typed property, and it returns an `Object` instead of an actual `CommandBars` instance.

TIP

Use the `CommandBar.Type` property to determine whether a command bar is a toolbar or a menu bar. A value of `MsoBarType.msoBarTypeNormal` indicates that the command bar is a toolbar, whereas a value of `MsoBarType.msoBarTypeMenu` indicates that the command bar is a menu bar.

The `CommandBar` object properties and methods are documented in Table 10.10.

TABLE 10.10 CommandBar Members

Property	Description
AdaptiveMenu	For menu bars, this Boolean flag indicates whether the command bar has *adaptive menus* enabled. (Adaptive menus, sometimes referred to as *personalized menus*, are menus that alter their drop-down content based on projected or actual usage by the user; the intent is to display only those commands that are useful on the menu and hide the other nonessential commands.)
Application	An object representing the parent application to the command bar.
BuiltIn	Boolean flag used to distinguish between built-in and custom command bars.
Context	A string indicating where the `CommandBar` is saved (the format and expected content of this string are dictated by the hosting application).
Controls	A `CommandBarControls` collection containing `CommandBarControl` objects; each of these objects represents a control displayed by the command bar.
Creator	An integer value that identifies the application hosting the `CommandBar`.
Enabled	A Boolean flag indicating whether the command bar is enabled.
Height	The height of the command bar in pixels.
Index	The index of the command bar in the command bar collection.
Left	The distance, in pixels, between the left side of the command bar and the left edge of its parent container.
Name	The name of the command bar.
NameLocal	The localized name of the command bar.
Parent	An object that is the parent of the command bar.
Position	An `MsoBarPosition` enum value used to get or set the position of the command bar (for example, `MsoBarPosition.msoBarTop`).
Protection	An `MsoBarProtection` enum value that identifies the protection employed against used modification (for example, `MsoBarProtection.msoBarNoMove`).
RowIndex	An integer representing the docking row of the command bar.
Top	The distance, in pixels, between the top of the command bar and the top edge of its parent container.
Type	The type of the command bar (as an `MsobarType` enum value; for example, `MsoBarType.msoBarTypeNormal`).

TABLE 10.10 Continued

Property	Description
Visible	A Boolean flag indicating whether the command bar is currently visible.
Width	The width of the command bar in pixels.
Method	**Description**
Delete	Removes the command bar from its parent collection.
FindControl	Enables you to retrieve a reference to a control hosted by the command bar that fits various parameters such as its type, ID, tag, and visibility.
Reset	Resets one of the built-in command bars to its default configuration.
ShowPopup	Displays a pop-up representing a command bar.

> **NOTE**
>
> Previous versions of Visual Studio actually relied on a Microsoft Office assembly for the CommandBar object definition (Microsoft.Office.Core). Visual Studio 2005 provides its own implementation of the CommandBar object that is defined in the Microsoft.VisualStudio.CommandBars namespace, although you will find some types that carry their nomenclature over from the MS Office assembly, such as the various MsoXXX enums.

Documents

Document objects are used to represent an open document in the IDE. To contrast this abstraction with that provided by the Window object: A Window object is used to represent the physical UI aspects of a document window, whereas a Document object is used to represent the physical document that is being displayed within that document window.

A document could be a designer, such as the Windows Forms designer, or it could be a text-based document such as a readme file or a C# code file open in an editor.

Just as you get a list of all open windows using the DTE.Windows collection, you can use the DTE.Documents collection to retrieve a list of all open documents:

```
Dim documents As Documents = DTE.Documents
```

The Documents collection is indexed by the document's Name property, which is, in effect, the document's filename without the path information. This makes it easy to quickly retrieve a Document instance:

```
Dim documents As Documents = DTE.Documents
Dim readme As Document = documents.Item("ReadMe.txt")
```

Using the Document object, you can

- Close the document (and optionally save changes)

- Retrieve the filename and path of the document

- Determine whether the document has been modified since the last time it was saved

- Determine what, if anything, is currently selected within the document

- Obtain a `ProjectItem` instance representing the project item that is associated with the document

- Read and edit the contents of text documents

Table 10.11 contains the member descriptions for the `Document` object.

TABLE 10.11   Document Members

Property	Description
ActiveWindow	The currently active window associated with the document (null or `Nothing` value indicates that there is no active window).
Collection	The collection of `Document` objects to which this instance belongs.
DTE	The root-level `DTE` object.
Extender	Returns a `Document` extender object.
ExtenderCATID	The extender category ID for the object.
ExtenderNames	A list of extenders available for the current `Document` object.
FullName	The full path and filename of the document.
Kind	A GUID representing the kind of document.
Name	The name (essentially, the filename without path information) for the document.
Path	The path of the document's file excluding the filename.
ProjectItem	The `ProjectItem` instance associated with the document.
Saved	Indicates whether the solution has been saved since the last modification.
Selection	An object representing the current selection in the document (if any).
Windows	The `Windows` collection containing the window displaying the document.
Method	**Description**
Activate	Moves the focus to the document.
Close	Closes the document. You can indicate, with a `vsSaveChanges` enum value, whether the window's hosted document should be saved or not saved, or whether the IDE should prompt the user to make that decision.
NewWindow	Opens the document in a new window and returns the new window's `Window` object.
Object	Returns an object proxy that represents the window and can be referenced by name.
Redo	Re-executes the last user action in the document.
Save	Saves the document.
Undo	Reverses the last used action in the document.

Text Documents

As we mentioned, documents can have textual or nontextual content. For those documents with textual content, a separate object—`TextDocument`—exists. The `TextDocument` object provides access to control functions specifically related to text content.

If you have a valid `Document` object to start with, and if that document object refers to a text document, then a `TextDocument` instance can be referenced from the `Document.Object` property like this:

```
Dim doc As TextDocument
doc = myDocument.Object
```

Table 10.12 contains the `TextDocument` members.

TABLE 10.12   TextDocument Members

Property	Description
DTE	The root-level DTE object
EndPoint	A TextPoint object positioned at the end of the document
Parent	Gets the parent object of the text document
Selection	Returns a TextSelection object representing the currently selected text in the document
StartPoint	A TextPoint object positioned at the start of the document
Method	**Description**
ClearBookmarks	Removes any unnamed bookmarks present in the document
CreateEditPoint	Returns an edit point at the specific location (if no location is specified, the beginning of the document is assumed)
MarkText	Bookmarks lines in the document that match the specified string pattern
ReplacePattern	Replaces any text in the document that matches the pattern

> **TIP**
>
> A text document will be represented by both a `Document` instance and a `TextDocument` instance. Nontext documents, such as a Windows form open in a Windows Forms designer window, will have a `Document` representation but no corresponding `TextDocument` representation. Unfortunately, there isn't a great way to distinguish whether a document is text based or not during runtime. One approach is to attempt a cast or assignment to a `TextDocument` object and catch any exceptions that might occur during the assignment.

Two `TextDocument` methods are useful for manipulating bookmarks within the document: `ClearBookmarks` will remove any unnamed bookmarks from the document, and `MarkText` will perform a string pattern search and place bookmarks against the resulting document lines. A simple macro to bookmark `For` loops in a VB document is presented in Listing 10.10.

LISTING 10.10   Bookmarking For Loops in a VB Document

```
Imports EnvDTE
Imports EnvDTE80
Imports Microsoft.VisualStudio.CommandBars
```

10

LISTING 10.10 Continued

```vb
Imports System.Diagnostics
Imports System.Windows.Forms


Public Module MacroExamples

    ' Bookmark all 'For' tokens in the current
    ' document
    Public Sub BookmarkFor()
        Dim doc As Document
        Dim txtDoc As TextDocument

        ' Reference the current document
        doc = DTE.ActiveDocument

        ' Retrieve a TextDocument instance from
        ' the document
        txtDoc = doc.Object

        ' Call the MarkText method with the 'For' string
        Dim found As Boolean = _
            txtDoc.MarkText("For", vsFindOptions.vsFindOptionsFromStart)

        ' MarkText returns a boolean flag indicating whether or not
        ' the search pattern was found in the textdocument
        If found Then
            MessageBox.Show("All instances of 'For' have been bookmarked.")
        Else
            MessageBox.Show("No instances of 'For' were found.")
        End If
    End Sub
End Module
```

The other key functionality exposed by the `TextDocument` object is the capability to read and edit the text within the document.

Editing Text Documents

From a Visual Studio perspective, text in a text document actually has two distinct "representations": a virtual one and a physical one. The physical representation is the straight, unadulterated code file that sits on disk. The virtual representation is what Visual Studio presents on the screen: It is an *interpreted* view of the text in the code file that takes into account various editor document features such as code outlining/regions, virtual spacing, word wrapping, and so on.

Figure 10.7 shows this relationship. When displaying a text document, Visual Studio reads the source file into a text buffer, and then the text editor presents one view of that text file to you (based on options you have configured for the editor).

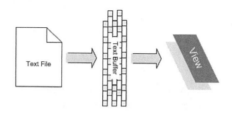

Text File

Text Buffer

View

FIGURE 10.7   Presentation of text documents within the IDE.

Text in a document is manipulated or read either on the buffered text or on the "view" text that you see in the editor. There are four different automation objects that allow you to affect text; two work on the text buffer and two work on the editor view.

For the text buffer:

- TextPoint objects are used to locate specific points within a text document. By querying the TextPoint properties, you can determine the line number of the text point, the number of characters it is offset from the start of a line, the number of characters it is offset from the start of the document, and its display column within the text editor window. You can also retrieve a reference to a CodeModel object representing the code at the text point's current location.

- The EditPoint object inherits from the TextPoint object; this is the primary object used for manipulating text in the text buffer. You can add, delete, or move text using edit points, and they can be moved around within the text buffer.

And, for the editor view:

- The VirtualPoint object is equivalent to the TextPoint object except that it can be used to query text locations that reside in the "virtual" space of the text view (virtual space is the whitespace that exists after the last character in a document line). VirtualPoint instances are returned through the TextSelection object.

- The TextSelection object operates on text within the text editor view as opposed to the text buffer and is equivalent to the EditPoint interface. When you use the TextSelection object, you are actively affecting the text that is being displayed within the text editor. The methods and properties of this object, therefore, end up being programmatic approximations of the various ways that you would manually affect text: You can page up or page down within the view; cut, copy, and paste text; select a range of text; or even outline and expand or collapse regions of text.

Because the VirtualPoint object is nearly identical to the TextPoint object, and the TextSelection object is nearly identical to the EditPoint object, we won't bother to cover each of these four objects in detail. Instead, we will focus on text buffer operations using EditPoint and TextPoint. You should be able to easily apply the concepts here to the text view.

Because EditPoint objects expose the most functionality and play the central role with text editing, we have provided a list of their type members in Table 10.13.

TABLE 10.13   EditPoint2 Members

Property	Description
AbsoluteCharOffset	The number of characters from the start of the document to the current location of the edit point
AtEndOfDocument	Boolean flag indicating whether the point is at the end of the document
AtEndOfLine	Boolean flag indicating whether the point is at the end of a line in the document
AtStartOfDocument	Boolean flag indicating whether the point is at the beginning of the document
AtStartOfLine	Boolean flag indicating whether the point is at the start of a line in the document
CodeElement	Returns the code element that maps to the edit point's current location
DisplayColumn	The column number of the edit point
DTE	Returns the root automation DTE object
Line	The line number where the point is positioned
LineCharOffset	The character offset, within a line, of the edit point
LineLength	The length of the line where the edit point is positioned
Parent	Returns the parent object of the EditPoint2 object
Method	**Description**
ChangeCase	Changes the case of a range of text
CharLeft	Moves the edit point to the left the specified number of characters
CharRight	Moves the edit point to the right the specified number of characters
ClearBookmark	Clears any unnamed bookmarks that exist on the point's current line location
Copy	Copies a range of text to the Clipboard
CreateEditPoint	Creates a new EditPoint2 object at the same location as the current EditPoint2 object
Cut	Cuts a range of text and places it on the Clipboard
Delete	Deletes a range of text from the document
DeleteWhitespace	Deletes any whitespace found around the edit point
EndOfDocument	Moves the edit point to the end of the document
EndOfLine	Moves the edit point to the end of the current line
EqualTo	A Boolean value indicating whether the edit point's AbsoluteCharOffset value is equal to another edit point's offset
FindPattern	Finds any matching string patterns in the document
GetLines	A string representing the text between two lines in the document
GetText	A string representing the text between the edit point and another location in the document

TABLE 10.13   Continued

Method	Description
GreaterThan	A Boolean value indicating whether the edit point's AbsoluteCharOffset value is greater than another edit point's offset
Indent	Indents the selected lines by the given number of levels
Insert	Inserts a string into the document, starting at the edit point's current location
InsertFromFile	Inserts the entire contents of a text file into the document starting at the edit point's current location
LessThan	Returns a Boolean value indicating whether the edit point's AbsoluteCharOffset value is less than another edit point's offset
LineDown	Moves the point down one or more lines
LineUp	Moves the point up one or more lines
MoveToAbsoluteOffset	Moves the edit point to the given character offset
MoveToLineAndOffset	Moves the edit point to the given line and to the character offset within that line
MoveToPoint	Moves the edit point to the location of another EditPoint or TextPoint object
NextBookmark	Moves the edit point to the next available bookmark in the document
OutlineSection	Creates an outline section between the point's current location and another location in the document
PadToColumn	Pads spaces in the current line up to the indicated column number
Paste	Pastes the contents of the Clipboard to the edit point's current location
PreviousBookmark	Moves the edit point to the previous bookmark
ReadOnly	Returns a Boolean flag indicating whether a text range in the document is read only
ReplacePattern	Replaces any text that matches the provided pattern
ReplaceText	Replaces a range of text with the provided string
SetBookmark	Creates an unnamed bookmark on the edit point's current line in the document
StartOfDocument	Moves the edit point to the start of the document
StartOfLine	Moves the edit point to the beginning of the line where it is positioned
TryToShow	Attempts to display the point's current location within the text editor window
Unindent	Removes the given number of indentation levels from a range of lines in the document
WordLeft	Moves the edit point to the left the given number of words
WordRight	Moves the edit point to the right the given number of words

10

Now let's look at various text manipulation scenarios.

Adding Text   EditPoint objects are the key to adding text, and you create them either by using a TextDocument object or by using a TextPoint object.

A TextPoint instance can create an EditPoint instance in its same exact location by calling TextPoint.CreateInstance. With the TextDocument type, you can call the CreateEditPoint method and pass in a valid TextPoint.

Because TextPoint objects are used to locate specific points in a document, a TextPoint object is leveraged as an input parameter to CreateEditPoint. In essence, the TextPoint object tells the method where to create the edit point. If you do not provide a TextPoint object, the edit point will be created at the start of the document.

This code snippet shows an edit point being created at the end of a document:

```
Dim doc As Document = DTE.ActiveDocument
Dim txtDoc As TextDocument = doc.Object

Dim tp As TextPoint = txtDoc.EndPoint
Dim ep As EditPoint2 = txtDoc.CreateEditPoint(tp)
' This line of code would have the same effect
ep = tp.CreateEditPoint
```

After creating an edit point, you can use it to add text into the document (remember, you are editing the buffered text whenever you use an EditPoint object). To inject a string into the document, you use the Insert method:

```
' Insert a C# comment line
ep.Insert("// some comment")
```

You can even grab the contents of a file and throw that into the document with the EditPoint.InsertFromFile method:

```
' Insert comments from a comments file
ep.InsertFromFile("C:\Contoso\std comments.txt")
```

Editing Text   The EditPoint object supports deleting, replacing, cutting, copying, and pasting text in a document.

Some of these operations require more than a single point to operate. For instance, if you wanted to cut a word or an entire line of code from a document, you would need to specify a start point and end point that define that range of text (see Figure 10.8).

FIGURE 10.8   Using points within a document to select text.

This snippet uses two end points, one at the start of a document and one at the end, to delete the entire contents of the document:

```
Dim doc As Document = DTE.ActiveDocument
Dim txtDoc As TextDocument = doc.Object

Dim tpStart As TextPoint = txtDoc.StartPoint
Dim tpEnd As TextPoint = txtDoc.EndPoint

Dim epStart As EditPoint2 = txtDoc.CreateEditPoint(tpStart)
Dim epEnd As EditPoint2 = txtDoc.CreateEditPoint(tpEnd)
epStart.Delete(epEnd)
```

Besides accepting a second EditPoint, the methods that operate on a range of text will also accept an integer identifying a count of characters. This also has the effect of defining a select. For example, this snippet cuts the first 10 characters from a document:

```
epStart.Cut(10)
```

Repositioning an EditPoint   After establishing an EditPoint, you can move it to any given location in the document by using various methods. The CharLeft and CharRight methods will move the point any number of characters to the left or right, while the WordLeft and WordRight methods perform the same operation with words:

```
' Move the edit point 4 words to the right
epStart.WordRight(4)
```

The LineUp and LineDown methods will jog the point up or down the specified number of lines. You can also move EditPoints to any given line within a document by using MoveToLineAndOffset. This method will also position the point any number of characters into the line:

```
' Move the edit point to line 100, and then
' in 5 characters to the right
epStart.MoveToLineAndOffset(100, 5)
```

The macro code in Listing 10.11 pulls together some of the areas that we have covered with editing text documents. This macro and its supporting functions illustrate the use of EditPoints to write text into a document. In this case, the macro automatically inserts a comment "flowerbox" immediately preceding a routine. To accomplish this, the macro goes through the following process:

1. A reference is obtained for the current document in the IDE.

2. The active cursor location in that document is obtained via the TextDocument.Selection.ActivePoint property.

3. An EditPoint is created using the VirtualPoint returned from the ActivePoint.

4. A second EditPoint is then created; these two points are used to obtain the entire content of the routine definition line.

5. The routine definition is then parsed to try to ferret out items such as its name, return value, and parameter list.

6. A string is built using the routine information and is inserted into the text document using an EditPoint.

LISTING 10.11   Inserting Comments into a Text Window

```
Imports EnvDTE
Imports EnvDTE80
Imports Microsoft.VisualStudio.CommandBars
Imports System
Imports System.Collections
Imports System.Diagnostics
Imports System.Text
Imports System.Windows.Forms


Public Module MacroExamples

    ' This routine demonstrates various text editing scenarios
    ' using the EditPoint and TextPoint types. If you place your
    ' cursor on a subroutine or function, it will build a default
    ' "flower box" comment area, insert it immediately above the
    ' sub/function, and outline it.
    '
    ' To use:
    '    1) put cursor anywhere on the Sub/Function line
    '    2) run macro
    '    The macro will fail silently (e.g., will not insert any
    '    comments) if it is unable to determine the start
    '    of the Sub/Function
    '
    Public Sub InsertTemplateFlowerbox()

        ' Get reference to the active document
        Dim doc As Document = DTE.ActiveDocument
        Dim txtDoc As TextDocument = doc.Object
        Dim isFunc As Boolean

        Try
            Dim ep As EditPoint2 = txtDoc.Selection.ActivePoint.CreateEditPoint()
```

LISTING 10.11   Continued

```
        ep.StartOfLine()
        Dim ep2 As EditPoint2 = ep.CreateEditPoint()
        ep2.EndOfLine()

        Dim lineText As String = ep.GetText(ep2).Trim()

        If InStr(lineText, " Function ") > 0 Then
            isFunc = True
        ElseIf InStr(lineText, " Sub ") > 0 Then
            isFunc = False
        Else
            Exit Sub
        End If

        ' Parse out info that we can derive from the routine
        ' definition: the return value type (if this is a function),
        ' the names of the parameters, and the name of the routine.
        Dim returnType As String = ""
        If isFunc Then
            returnType = ParseRetValueType(lineText)
        End If

        Dim parameters As String() = ParseParameters(lineText)
        Dim name As String = ParseRoutineName(lineText)
        Dim commentBlock As String = BuildCommentBlock(isFunc, name, _
returnType, parameters)

        ' Move the edit point up one line (to position
        ' immediately preceding the routine)
        ep.LineUp(1)

        ' Give us some room by inserting a new blank line
        ep.InsertNewLine()

        ' Insert our comment block
        ep.Insert(commentBlock.ToString())

    Catch ex As Exception

    End Try

End Sub
Private Function BuildCommentBlock(ByVal isFunc As Boolean, _
```

10

LISTING 10.11   Continued

```vb
        ByVal name As String, _
        ByVal returnType As String, ByVal parameters As String())

        Try
            Dim comment As StringBuilder = New StringBuilder()

            ' Build up a sample comment block using the passed in info
            comment.Append("'''''''''''''''''''''''''''''''''''''''''''''''''''''''")
            comment.Append(vbCrLf)
            comment.Append("' Routine: " + name)
            comment.Append(vbCrLf)
            comment.Append("' Description: [insert routine desc here]")
            comment.Append(vbCrLf)
            comment.Append("'")
            comment.Append(vbCrLf)
            If isFunc Then
                comment.Append("' Returns: A " & returnType & _
" [insert return value description here]")
            End If
            comment.Append(vbCrLf)
            comment.Append("'")
            comment.Append(vbCrLf)
            comment.Append("' Parameters:")
            comment.Append(vbCrLf)
            For i As Integer = 0 To parameters.GetUpperBound(0)
                comment.Append("'        ")
                comment.Append(parameters(i))
                comment.Append(": [insert parameter description here]")
                comment.Append(vbCrLf)
            Next
            comment.Append("'''''''''''''''''''''''''''''''''''''''''''''''''''''''")

            Return comment.ToString()

        Catch ex As Exception
            Return ""
        End Try

    End Function
    Private Function ParseRetValueType(ByVal code As String) As String
        Try
            ' Parse out the return value of a function (VB)
            ' Search for 'As', starting from the end of the string
```

LISTING 10.11   Continued

```
            Dim length As Integer = code.Length
            Dim index As Integer = code.LastIndexOf(" As ")

            Dim retVal As String = code.Substring(index + 3, length - (index + 3))

            Return retVal.Trim()

        Catch ex As Exception

            Return ""
        End Try
    End Function
    Private Function ParseParameters(ByVal code As String) As String()
        Try
            ' Parse out the parameters specified (if any) for
            ' a VB sub/func definition
            Dim length As Integer = code.Length
            Dim indexStart As Integer = code.IndexOf("(")
            Dim indexEnd As Integer = code.LastIndexOf(")")

            Dim params As String = code.Substring(indexStart + 1, _
indexEnd - (indexStart + 1))

            Return params.Split(",")

        Catch ex As Exception
            Return Nothing
        End Try
    End Function
    Private Function ParseRoutineName(ByVal code As String) As String
        Try
            Dim name As String
            Dim length As Integer = code.Length
            Dim indexStart As Integer = code.IndexOf(" Sub ")
            Dim indexEnd As Integer = code.IndexOf("(")

            If indexStart = -1 Then
                indexStart = code.IndexOf(" Function ")
                If indexStart <> -1 Then
                    indexStart = indexStart + 9
                End If
            Else
```

10

LISTING 10.11   Continued

```
                indexStart = indexStart + 5
          End If

          name = code.Substring(indexStart, indexEnd - indexStart)

          Return name.Trim()

      Catch ex As Exception
          Return ""
      End Try
    End Function
End Module
```

Command Objects

Every action that is possible to execute through the menus and toolbars in Visual Studio is generically referred to as a *command*. For example, pasting text into a window is a command, as is building a project, toggling a breakpoint, and closing a window.

For each command supported in the IDE, there is a corresponding Command object; the DTE.Commands collection holds all the valid Command object instances. Each command is keyed by a name that categorizes, describes, and uniquely identifies the command. The "paste" command, for instance, is available via the string key "Edit.Paste". If you wanted to retrieve the Command object mapping to the paste command, you would pull from the Commands collection using that string key:

```
Dim commands As Commands2 = DTE.Commands
Dim cmd As Command = commands.Item("Edit.Paste")
```

You can query a command's name via its Name property:

```
' name would = "Edit.Paste"
Dim name As String = cmd.Name
```

Table 10.14 contains the members declared on the Command interface.

TABLE 10.14   Command Members

Property	Description
Bindings	The keystrokes that can be used to invoke the command
Collection	The Commands collection that the Command object belongs to
DTE	A reference to the root-level DTE object
GUID	A GUID that identifies the command's group
ID	An integer that identifies the command within its group
IsAvailable	A Boolean flag that indicates whether the command is currently enabled

TABLE 10.14   Continued

Property	Description
`LocalizedName`	The localized name of the command
`Name`	The name of the command
Method	**Description**
`AddControl`	Creates a control for the command that can be hosted in a command bar
`Delete`	Removes a named command that was previously added with the `Commands.AddNamedCommand` method

The list of all available commands is extremely long (nearly 3,000 total), and it is therefore impossible to cover every one of them here, or even a large portion of them. To get an idea, however, of the specific commands available, you can visit the dialog box used to customize the Visual Studio toolbars. If you select the Customize option from the View, Toolbars menu, and then click on the Commands tab, you can investigate all the various commands by category (see Figure 10.9). Another alternative would be to programmatically iterate the `DTE.Commands` collection and view them that way. In fact, in the following chapter, we use this as one scenario for showcasing add-in development.

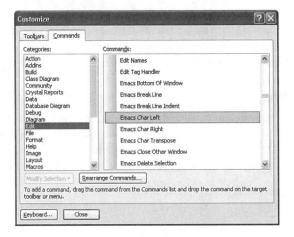

FIGURE 10.9   Using the Customize dialog box to view commands.

So, although we can't cover all the commands, you can learn how to perform common tasks with the Command objects such as executing a command, checking on a command's current status, and even adding your own commands to the command library.

Executing a Command

Commands can be executed in two different ways. The DTE object has an `ExecuteCommand` method that you can use to trigger a command based on its name:

```
DTE.ExecuteCommand("Window.CloseDocumentWindow")
```

The `Commands` collection is also a vehicle for launching commands through its `Raise` method. Instead of using the command's name, the `Raise` method uses its GUID and ID to identify the command:

```
Dim commands As Commands2 = DTE.Commands
Dim cmd As Command = commands.Item("Window.CloseDocumentWindow")
Dim customIn, customOut As Object

commands.Raise(cmd.Guid, cmd.ID, customin, customout)
```

Some commands accept arguments. The `Shell` command is one example. It is used to launch an external application into the shell environment and thus takes the application filename as one of its parameters. You can launch this command by using the `ExecuteCommand` method like this:

```
Dim commands As Commands2 = DTE.Commands
Dim cmd As Command = commands.Item("Tools.Shell")
Dim arg1 = "MyApp.exe "

DTE.ExecuteCommand(cmd.Name, arg1)
```

The `Raise` method also works with arguments: The last two parameters provided to the `Raise` method are used to specify an array of arguments to be used by the command and an array of output values returned from the command.

Mapping Key Bindings

Most commands can be invoked by a keyboard shortcut in addition to a menu entry or button on a command bar. You can set these keyboard shortcuts on a per-command basis by using the `Command.Bindings` property. This property returns or accepts a `SafeArray` (essentially an array of objects) that contains each shortcut as an element of the array.

Key bindings are represented as strings with the following format:

```
"[scopename]::[modifier+][key]".
```

Scopename is used to refer to the scope where the shortcut is valid, such as Text Editor or Global. The *modifier* token is used to specify the key modifier such as `"ctrl+"`, `"alt+"`, or `"shift+"` (modifiers are not required). And the *key* is the keyboard key that will be pressed (in conjunction with the modifier if present) to invoke the command.

To add a binding to an existing command, you first need to retrieve the current array of binding values, add your binding string to the array, and then assign the whole array back into the `Bindings` property like this:

```
Dim commands As Commands2 = DTE.Commands
Dim cmd As Command = _
    commands.Item("File.SaveSelectedItems")
```

```
Dim bindings() As Object

bindings = cmd.Bindings

' Increase the array size by 1 to hold the new binding
ReDim Preserve bindings(bindings.GetUpperBound(0) + 1)

' Assign the new binding into the array
bindings(bindings.GetUpperBound(0)) = "Global::Shift+F2"

' Assign the array back to the command object
cmd.Bindings = bindings
```

> **NOTE**
>
> You can create your own named commands that can be launched from a command bar in the IDE (or from the command window for that matter). The `Command` object itself is added to the `Commands` collection by calling `Commands.AddNamedCommand`. The code that will run when the command is executed will have to be implemented by an add-in. We'll cover this scenario in Chapter 11.

Debugger Objects

The automation object model provides a `Debugger` object that allows you to control the Visual Studio debugger. A `Debugger` instance can be obtained through the `DTE.Debugger` property:

```
Dim debugger As Debugger
debugger = DTE.Debugger
```

With a valid `Debugger` object, you can

- Set breakpoints
- Start and stop the debugger for a given process
- Control the various execution stepping actions supported by the debugger such as Step Into, Step Over, and Step Out
- Issue the Run to Cursor command to the debugger
- Query the debugger for its current mode (for example, break mode, design mode, or run mode)

The following code starts the debugger if it isn't already started:

```
Dim debugger As Debugger2
debugger = DTE.Debugger
```

10

```
If debugger.CurrentMode <> dbgDebugMode.dbgRunMode Then
    debugger.Go()
End If
```

Automation Events

If your macro or add-in needs to be notified when a certain event occurs, various event objects are supported in all the automation object categories previously discussed. There are events for windows, events for editors, events for projects, and so on. For every event supported by the IDE, a corresponding class in the automation model allows you to hook the event and take action if the event is raised. The event objects tree is rooted in the DTE.Events property, as depicted in Figure 10.10.

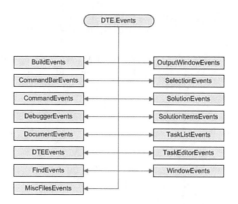

FIGURE 10.10   Event types.

Because events are handled differently depending on whether you are working with code in an add-in or code in a macro, we will wait until the next chapter to cover the details of handling events. The basic premise, however, is fairly simple: You obtain a reference to the event object that you are interested in and then write an event handler that responds to one of that object's published events.

This code, for instance, is how you might handle the "build complete" event from inside a Visual Basic add-in:

```
Dim WithEvents bldevents As BuildEvents
bldevents = DTE.Events.BuildEvents
```

After instantiating a BuildEvents object, you now have to write the actual event handler:

```
Private Sub bldevents_OnBuildDone(ByVal Scope As EnvDTE.vsBuildScope, _
    ByVal Action As EnvDTE.vsBuildAction) Handles bldevents.OnBuildDone
        ' Code to handle the event goes here
    End Sub
```

Summary

The Visual Studio automation object model is a deep and wide API that exposes many of the IDE components to managed code running as a macro or an add-in. In this chapter, we documented how this API is organized and described its capabilities in terms of controlling the Visual Studio debugger, editors, windows, tool windows, solutions, and projects.

We also discussed the eventing model exposed by the API and looked at the API's capabilities with regards to accessing the underlying code structure for a project, issuing commands inside the IDE, and editing text documents programmatically.

Using the methods and properties expressed on the automation objects, you can automate common tasks in the IDE and extend Visual Studio in ways that address your specific development tool needs.

In the next chapter, we will directly build on the concepts discussed here and specifically walk you through the process of building add-ins and writing macros that talk to the automation objects.

10

CHAPTER 11

Writing Macros, Add-ins, and Wizards

In the preceding chapter, we examined the API available for developers to customize, tweak, and control various portions of the Visual Studio IDE. This chapter will take that knowledge and show you how to write macros and add-ins that leverage the automation object model.

A macro's purpose is to provide you with an approach for writing your own task automation applets. In previous chapters, you saw many IDE features that automate repetitive tasks. The built-in refactoring support, IntelliSense word completion, code snippets, and others certainly fall into that category. And as you develop solutions with Visual Studio, you will find yourself performing additional repetitive tasks that beg for a solution. Macros are the means to that end.

Macros can be hand-crafted or generated for you by recording certain actions within the IDE. In fact, Visual Studio even has a separate macro development environment—the Macros IDE—designed to help you quickly develop macro solutions.

If macros represent the quick and easy approach to automation, then add-ins are their more complex, and more powerful, counterparts. Add-ins are compiled projects written in Visual Basic, Visual C#, Visual J#, or even Visual C++. Add-ins are useful for covering more advanced extensibility scenarios up to and including surfacing your own custom forms, tool windows, and designers in the IDE.

Another topic we'll tackle in this chapter is that of creating and customizing Visual Studio wizards. Wizards are launched any time you create a new project or add an item to a project. These wizards typically present one or more dialog boxes to capture preferences from the user and then use those preferences to create a project structure, generate default code, or perform even more complicated tasks. Wizards work in conjunction with template files to drive the initial structure for a code file or entire project. The entire framework for wizards and templates is available to customize to fit your particular needs.

Writing Macros

As we have already established, macros are Visual Basic routines that interact with the automation object model to control various aspects of the IDE. Although macros can certainly be complex pieces of logic, their real value lies in the fact that it is relatively simple to write short, quick routines that take some of the manual pain away from the development process. Macros aren't used so much to add new functionality to the IDE as they are to batch together actions in the IDE and enable a single invocation point for those actions.

If you think about the common tasks that you perform while developing a Visual Studio solution, the macro's value lies in its capability to help you automate those tasks where it makes sense. Chapter 10, "The Visual Studio Automation Object Model," included a macro sample that inserts a comment flowerbox at the start of a function or subroutine. The goal with that macro was to reduce the time required to fully comment routines. That particular macro wasn't complicated, nor did it solve a particularly egregious software engineering problem. Its intent, rather, was to take a small edge off a very manual component to the code-writing process: commenting your code. So the macro development process really starts with first identifying an opportunity for automation. The next step is to understand the IDE objects you will have to touch to effect a solution. The final step is tying those objects together with Visual Basic code in the form of a macro.

We have already covered two of the three pieces of knowledge that enable you to become proficient with macros: We discussed the automation object model in-depth in the preceding chapter, and we summarized the scenarios where macros shine. The third and final piece is understanding the mechanics of writing a macro from start to finish and then executing the macro in the IDE.

Recording a Macro

The simplest way to create a macro is to record one: Just turn on Visual Studio's macro recorder and perform a series of actions in the IDE. The macro recorder will turn your IDE interactions into macro code.

To start recording a macro, select Tools, Macros, Record TemporaryMacro (or press Shift+Ctrl+R). This will immediately start the recorder; a small toolbar, as shown in Figure 11.1, will appear at this point to allow you to control the recording.

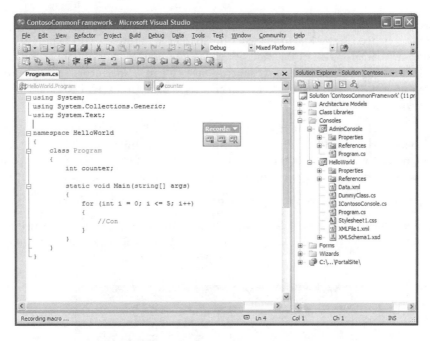

FIGURE 11.1   The Macro Recorder toolbar.

The three buttons on the toolbar allow you to pause and resume the recording, stop the recording, or cancel the recording. Pausing the recording will do just that: The recorder will stop recording your actions in the IDE, although it will still remain active. Clicking the button a second time will resume recording. If you stop the recording, this will cause the macro code to be generated and saved for later execution. Canceling the recording will stop the recorder but will not save the macro.

With the recorder running, perform a series of actions in the IDE. Suppose that you wanted to have an easy way to expand all of the project nodes (and their subnodes) in the Solution Explorer window. To record this action, you would simply click on each of the project items in the Solution Explorer to expand them in their tree view. When you are finished going through every project and project item, click on the Stop Recording button. The macro will be stored at this point as a "temporary" macro. It will not be saved to disk at this stage, but you can immediately run it by selecting Run Temporary Macro from the Tools, Macros menu.

> **NOTE**
>
> Only one temporary macro is stored at a time in Visual Studio. This means that if you record another temporary macro, it simply replaces the current temporary macro. If you want to have the macro around for a while, you can store it on disk by selecting Tools, Macros, Save TemporaryMacro. If it is not already displayed, this selection will show the Macro Explorer.

Using the Macro Explorer

We briefly touched on the Macro Explorer in Chapter 5, "Browsers and Explorers"; it is a tool window that shows all of the macros available to you. Macros are organized in projects and modules. The temporary macro that you just created will show up under the MyMacros project, under a module called RecordingModule, and it will be called TemporaryMacro.

If you have selected to save the temporary macro, Visual Studio will automatically place that TemporaryMacro node in edit mode with the name highlighted. This is your cue to type in a name for the macro. Pressing Enter will commit the name change and cause the macro to be saved to disk. If you don't change the name, it will not be saved.

Using the Macro Explorer, you can rename or delete macros and run macros.

To execute a macro, just double-click on its node in the Macro Explorer. This will immediately run the macro's code. While a macro is running, you will see an animated icon and a status message on Visual Studio's status bar (see Figure 11.2).

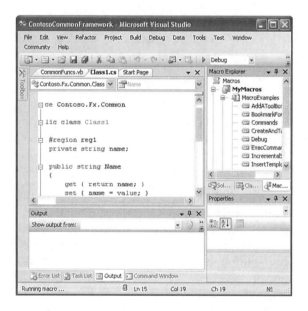

FIGURE 11.2   A running macro.

TIP

Macros don't have any default or prebuilt notification mechanism that tells you when the macro has completed or if the macro has encountered an error. If you want to track a macro's progress, you will need to edit the macro accordingly so that it outputs messages to the output window, through message boxes, or other means.

To see the Visual Basic code responsible for implementing the macro, you right-click on the macro in the Macro Explorer and select Edit. This will launch the Macro IDE. The IDE can also be launched by selecting Tools, Macros, Macros IDE (or pressing Ctrl+F11).

Using the Macro IDE

The Macros IDE, shown in Figure 11.3, is essentially a specialized version of Visual Studio, trimmed down and streamlined to support the macro development process.

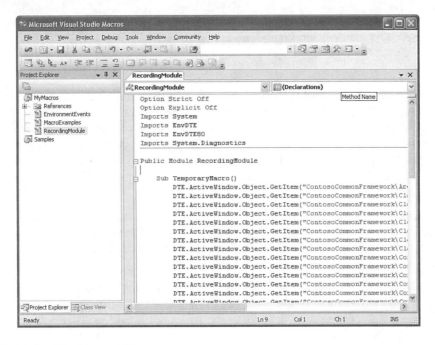

FIGURE 11.3   The Macros IDE.

Immediately, you can see that this is, in fact, the Visual Studio user interface that you are, by now, used to working with. Everything behaves the same: Tool windows can be docked, float, pinned, and so on. The code editor window that you use to edit your macro code works the same with IntelliSense, outlining, and all of the other productivity aids that you have come to expect. Although the Macros IDE behaves identically to the full-blown Visual Studio IDE, there are some differences. For instance, it has only a subset of the tool windows and document windows supported in the full IDE. Language support in the code editor is limited strictly to Visual Basic (because that is the only macro language supported), and you can't design forms or any similar artifact here.

Working with Macro Projects

The Project Explorer tool window works on the same principles as the Solution Explorer; it presents a tree view of your work items. In the case of macros, the tree nodes are organized like this: project -> module. Individual macros are displayed in the code editor window (note that this is essentially the same as the Macro Explorer view, with the exception that the Macro Explorer's tree shows each individual macro by name).

In our case, we recorded a temporary macro, and it shows up under the `MyMacros` project, in the module named `RecordingModule`. If you look back at Figure 11.3, you will see a portion of the code that was created when the macro was recorded; it is all contained in a Visual Basic sub called `TemporaryMacro()`.

> **TIP**
>
> When you use the macro recorder, the code that it emits is automatically stored in the `MyMacros` project. To change this, just right-click any other macro project in the Macro Explorer and select Set as Recording Project.

Macro projects map one-to-one with a folder on disk; they are not the same as Visual Studio projects. By default, you have a `MyMacros` project (which maps to the folder `MyMacros` under `My Documents\Visual Studio 2005\Projects\VSMacros80`) and a `Samples` project (which maps to a `Samples` folder under the same directory tree). Within each macro project directory, there will be a .vsmacros file whose name is the same as the project directory's name. Thus, there is a `Samples.vsmacros` file in the `Samples` folder and a `MyMacros.vsmacros` file in the `MyMacros` folder.

The .vsmacro file contains all of the code for the individual macros (and modules) within the project that it maps to. This is a huge difference from the way that Visual Studio works with project files: A macro does not map to its own file like a project item does in, say, a Visual Basic class library project.

Sharing Macros   You might be surprised to learn that the native storage format for macros is binary. Technically, the .vsmacros file is a COM-structured storage file; within this file resides all of the source code for every macro in the project. There is a way, however, to export a macro, module, or macro project to a Visual Basic (.vb) file. To do so, perform the following steps:

1. Right-click the macro module in the Macros IDE Project Explorer.

2. Select Export <*ModuleName*>. The Export File dialog box will launch (see Figure 11.4).

3. Select a location and filename, and the macro code will be written into the file in plain text.

After a macro module has been exported, you can then physically share it with other developers by simply passing the file around. Importing a previously exported macro file is easy: From the Macros IDE, you select Project, Add Existing Item and select the macro .vb file to import; this will place it into the macro project currently selected in the Project Explorer.

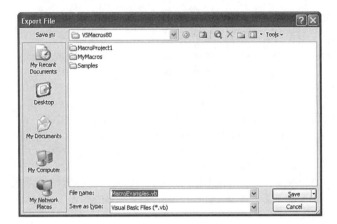

FIGURE 11.4   Exporting a macro module.

Adding a Project   Confusingly, the capability to add a macro project is not present in the Macros IDE. It is, however, an option in the Visual Studio IDE: Select Tools, Macros, Load Macro Project. From there, you simply browse for the .vsmacros file that contains the project you want to load. If you want to create a new, empty macro project, you select Tools, Macros, New Macro Project.

After a macro project has been added, it is immediately accessible in the Macros IDE.

Writing a Macro

If you revisit the code that was generated for you when you recorded your Solution Explorer node expansions, you can see that the macro recorder has generated the code in Listing 11.1.

LISTING 11.1   Recorder-Generated Macro Code

```
Option Strict Off
Option Explicit Off
Imports System
Imports EnvDTE
Imports EnvDTE80
Imports System.Diagnostics


Public Module RecordingModule

    Sub TemporaryMacro()
DTE.ActiveWindow.Object.GetItem("ContosoCommonFramework\Architecture Models").
➥UIHierarchyItems.Expanded = True
DTE.ActiveWindow.Object.GetItem("ContosoCommonFramework\Class Libraries").
➥UIHierarchyItems.Expanded = True
DTE.ActiveWindow.Object.GetItem("ContosoCommonFramework\Class
➥Libraries\Contoso.Fx.Analysis\Properties").UIHierarchyItems.Expanded = True
```

LISTING 11.1   Continued

```
DTE.ActiveWindow.Object.GetItem("ContosoCommonFramework\Class
➥Libraries\Contoso.Fx.Analysis\References").UIHierarchyItems.Expanded = True
DTE.ActiveWindow.Object.GetItem("ContosoCommonFramework\Class
➥Libraries\Contoso.Fx.Common\Properties").UIHierarchyItems.Expanded = True
DTE.ActiveWindow.Object.GetItem("ContosoCommonFramework\Class
➥Libraries\Contoso.Fx.Common\References").UIHierarchyItems.Expanded = True
DTE.ActiveWindow.Object.GetItem("ContosoCommonFramework\Class
➥Libraries\Contoso.Fx.Integration\Properties").UIHierarchyItems.Expanded = True
DTE.ActiveWindow.Object.GetItem("ContosoCommonFramework\Class
➥Libraries\Contoso.Fx.Integration\References").UIHierarchyItems.Expanded = True
DTE.ActiveWindow.Object.GetItem("ContosoCommonFramework\Consoles\AdminConsole").
➥UIHierarchyItems.Expanded = True
DTE.ActiveWindow.Object.GetItem("ContosoCommonFramework\Consoles\HelloWorld").
➥UIHierarchyItems.Expanded = True
DTE.ActiveWindow.Object.GetItem("ContosoCommonFramework\Consoles").
➥UIHierarchyItems.Expanded = True
DTE.ActiveWindow.Object.GetItem("ContosoCommonFramework\Consoles\AdminConsole
➥\Properties").UIHierarchyItems.Expanded = True
DTE.ActiveWindow.Object.GetItem("ContosoCommonFramework\Consoles\AdminConsole
➥\References").UIHierarchyItems.Expanded = True
DTE.ActiveWindow.Object.GetItem("ContosoCommonFramework\Consoles\HelloWorld
➥\Properties").UIHierarchyItems.Expanded = True
DTE.ActiveWindow.Object.GetItem("ContosoCommonFramework\Consoles\HelloWorld
➥\References").UIHierarchyItems.Expanded = True
DTE.ActiveWindow.Object.GetItem("ContosoCommonFramework\Consoles\HelloWorld
➥\XMLSchema1.xsd").UIHierarchyItems.Expanded = True
DTE.ActiveWindow.Object.GetItem("ContosoCommonFramework\Forms").UIHierarchyItems.
➥Expanded = True
DTE.ActiveWindow.Object.GetItem("ContosoCommonFramework\Forms\Contoso.UI.
➥WindowsForms.TestHost\Properties").UIHierarchyItems.Expanded = True
DTE.ActiveWindow.Object.GetItem("ContosoCommonFramework\Forms\Contoso.UI.
➥WindowsForms.TestHost\References").UIHierarchyItems.Expanded = True
DTE.ActiveWindow.Object.GetItem("ContosoCommonFramework\Forms\Contoso.UI.
➥WindowsForms.TestHost\Form1.jsl").UIHierarchyItems.Expanded = True
DTE.ActiveWindow.Object.GetItem("ContosoCommonFramework\C:\...\PortalSite\").
➥UIHierarchyItems.Expanded = True
    End Sub
End Module
```

In the case of the recorded macro, the generated code is straightforward, and it represents
a verbatim replay of what you manually accomplished in the Solution Explorer window.
The macro references each individual item in the explorer window by using the
`ActiveWindow.Object.GetItem` method, passing in the object's name to get a

`UIHierarchyItem` reference. From there, it is a simple property set to expand all of the items below (by setting `UIHierarchyItems.Expand = True`).

The code is complete and works, but it's probably not exactly what you were looking for. For instance, it references the projects and project items that you expanded by their path and name. This means that the macro is certainly not generic (it would work only with the Contoso sample solution), and even then the code is fairly brittle: If you add or remove a project or project item, the macro won't know and will still try to set the prior item's `Expanded` property. To really make the macro useful, you will want to rework the code here. The advantage of using the recorder is that it produces, if nothing else, a valid starting point for macro development. In fact, it has highlighted the use of an object, `UIHierarchyItem`, which we did not discuss in the preceding chapter. An eye for general program structure would tell you that there should be a way to refactor these lines of code into a loop, recursively expanding nodes out in the tree until all have been expanded. Perhaps instead of just expanding or collapsing nodes, you could also try toggling this property.

You edit macro code using the code editor just as you would to edit any other document with Visual Studio. To rework this macro, you can start by establishing a *recursive* helper routine that takes in a `UIHierarchyItem` object, toggles its `Expanded` property to `True`, and calls itself for each sub item found in the `UIHierarchyItems` collection:

```
For Each subNode As UIHierarchyItem In node.UIHierarchyItems
    ExpandNodes(subNode)
Next
node.UIHierarchyItems.Expanded = True
```

> **NOTE**
>
> Unlike the editors in the main Visual Studio IDE, the text editor in the Macros IDE will automatically save the file that you are editing when you close it. This will be done without any prompting whatsoever. Unless you undo changes that you have made while editing, they will be committed after you close the editor, regardless of whether you have explicitly saved them.

Then, to kick things off, you need a parent, controlling routine that instantiates a window object (representing the Solution Explorer) and grabs the root-level `UIHierarchy` object from the window. From there, you loop the first level of nodes in the tree and call down into the recursive routine:

```
Dim tree As UIHierarchy
Dim explorer As Window2

explorer = DTE.Windows.Item(Constants.vsWindowKindSolutionExplorer)

tree = explorer.Object
```

```
For Each node As UIHierarchyItem In tree.UIHierarchyItems
    ExpandNodes(node)
Next
```

To go one step further, if you modify the recursive routine to take in a Boolean value, you now have a general-purpose routine that can either expand or collapse a series of nodes. Putting it all together, you end up with two macros: One will expand all nodes in the Solution Explorer tree, and one will collapse all nodes in the Solution Explorer tree. In Listing 11.2, you see these two macros as public subroutines called ExpandAll and CollapseAll. The private routine ExpandCollapseNodes is called by both of the macros.

LISTING 11.2   Macro: Expand/Collapse All Solution Explorer Nodes

```
Imports EnvDTE
Imports EnvDTE80
Imports Microsoft.VisualStudio.CommandBars
Imports System
Imports System.Collections
Imports System.Diagnostics
Imports System.Text
Imports System.Windows.Forms


Public Module MacroExamples

    ' Expands all nodes in the Solution Explorer
    Public Sub ExpandAll()
        Dim tree As UIHierarchy
        Dim explorer As Window2

        ' Reference to the solution explorer window
        explorer = DTE.Windows.Item(Constants.vsWindowKindSolutionExplorer)

        ' Reference to the UIHierarchy object obtained from the
        ' solution explorer window
        tree = explorer.Object

        ' Iterate the top level nodes, call recursive routine to
        ' expand each node
        For Each node As UIHierarchyItem In tree.UIHierarchyItems
            ExpandCollapseNodes(node, True)
        Next


    End Sub
```

LISTING 11.2   Continued

```
' Collapses all nodes in the Solution Explorer
Public Sub CollapseAll()
    Dim tree As UIHierarchy
    Dim explorer As Window2

    ' Reference to the solution explorer window
    explorer = DTE.Windows.Item(Constants.vsWindowKindSolutionExplorer)

    ' Reference to the UIHierarchy object obtained from the
    ' solution explorer window
    tree = explorer.Object

    ' Iterate the top level nodes, call recursive routine to
    ' expand each node
    For Each node As UIHierarchyItem In tree.UIHierarchyItems
        ExpandCollapseNodes(node, True)
    Next

End Sub

' Recursive routine for expanding or collapsing all of the sub nodes
' of a given UIHierarchyItem
Private Sub ExpandCollapseNodes(ByRef node As UIHierarchyItem,
    ByVal expanded _As Boolean)
' For Each subNode As UIHierarchyItem In node.UIHierarchyItems
        ' Re-call this routine with the new subnode as the parent node
        ExpandCollapseNodes(subNode, expanded)
    Next

    ' Perform the collapse/expansion
    node.UIHierarchyItems.Expanded = True

End Sub
End Module
```

Compared with the code that the macro recorder emitted for you, there isn't a whole lot of similarity; but again, the recorded code *was* useful from an education perspective, alerting you to the approach and concept of using the UIHierarchy/UIHierarchyItem/ UIHierarchyItems objects to handle the node expansion.

Debugging
The debug experience with macros is similar to that of debugging other Visual Studio projects. The runtime debugger in the Macros IDE supports all of the familiar concepts of breakpoints and the *Step Into* and *Step Over* commands.

If you were unsure of your recursive code, you might choose to place a breakpoint in the recursive routine and monitor the progress of the macro. The Macros IDE also supports the error list window, which will flag any syntax errors for you. See Figure 11.5 for a glimpse of a breakpoint and the error list window in the Macros IDE.

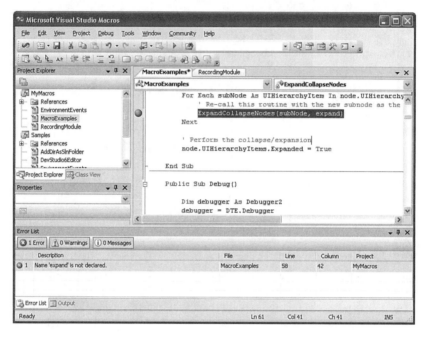

FIGURE 11.5   Debugging a macro.

NOTE

If debugging is taking place in the Macros IDE, the main IDE will be inaccessible. You won't be able to perform tasks in the main IDE.

Handling Events

We covered the individual event classes in Chapter 10; every event exposed in the IDE is available via these automation classes. To handle an event in a macro, you need to have two things: an event definition and an event handler.

Every macro project has, by default, an `EnvironmentEvents` module. This module is automatically created for you every time you create a new macro project, and it implements event definitions for many of the automation events. If you need to handle any of the following event categories, the event definition is already taken care of for you:

- Core DTE events
- Document events

- Window events

- Task List events

- Search events

- Output window events

- Selection events

- Build events

- Solution events

- Solution item events

- File events

- Debugger events

- Project events

- Key press events

- Code model events

Listing 11.3 shows the EnvironmentEvents source code (generated by Visual Studio) that is responsible for implementing these event definitions.

LISTING 11.3   EnvironmentEvents Module

```
Option Strict Off
Option Explicit Off
Imports EnvDTE
Imports EnvDTE80
Imports System.Diagnostics


Public Module EnvironmentEvents

#Region "Automatically generated code, do not modify"
'Automatically generated code, do not modify
'Event Sources Begin
    <System.ContextStaticAttribute()> _
    Public WithEvents DTEEvents As EnvDTE.DTEEvents

    <System.ContextStaticAttribute()> _
    Public WithEvents DocumentEvents As EnvDTE.DocumentEvents

    <System.ContextStaticAttribute()> _
    Public WithEvents WindowEvents As EnvDTE.WindowEvents
```

LISTING 11.3   Continued

```
    <System.ContextStaticAttribute()> _
    Public WithEvents TaskListEvents As EnvDTE.TaskListEvents

    <System.ContextStaticAttribute()> _
    Public WithEvents FindEvents As EnvDTE.FindEvents

    <System.ContextStaticAttribute()> _
    Public WithEvents OutputWindowEvents As EnvDTE.OutputWindowEvents

    <System.ContextStaticAttribute()> _
    Public WithEvents SelectionEvents As EnvDTE.SelectionEvents

    <System.ContextStaticAttribute()> _
    Public WithEvents BuildEvents As EnvDTE.BuildEvents

    <System.ContextStaticAttribute()> _
    Public WithEvents SolutionEvents As EnvDTE.SolutionEvents

    <System.ContextStaticAttribute()> _
    Public WithEvents SolutionItemsEvents As EnvDTE.ProjectItemsEvents

    <System.ContextStaticAttribute()> _
    Public WithEvents MiscFilesEvents As EnvDTE.ProjectItemsEvents

    <System.ContextStaticAttribute()> _
    Public WithEvents DebuggerEvents As EnvDTE.DebuggerEvents

    <System.ContextStaticAttribute()> _
    Public WithEvents ProjectsEvents As EnvDTE.ProjectsEvents

    <System.ContextStaticAttribute()> _
    Public WithEvents TextDocumentKeyPressEvents As
        EnvDTE80.TextDocumentKeyPressEvents

    <System.ContextStaticAttribute()> _
    Public WithEvents CodeModelEvents As EnvDTE80.CodeModelEvents

    <System.ContextStaticAttribute()> _
    Public WithEvents DebuggerProcessEvents As EnvDTE80.DebuggerProcessEvents

    <System.ContextStaticAttribute()> _
    Public WithEvents DebuggerExpressionEvaluationEvents As
        EnvDTE80.DebuggerExpressionEvaluationEvents
'Event Sources End
```

LISTING 11.3   Continued

```
'End of automatically generated code
#End Region

End Module
```

Writing the Event Handler

In addition to defining the various event objects for you, the IDE can also be leveraged to insert the actual event handler skeleton code for you. First, open the `EnvironmentEvents` module in the code editor. Then use the type drop-down (the leftmost drop-down at the top of the code editor) to select the event class that you want. Figure 11.6 shows the process of selecting the `SolutionEvents` type.

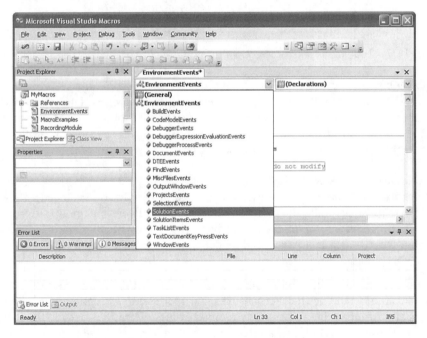

FIGURE 11.6   Selecting a macro event type.

When you have the type selected, the declarations drop-down (the drop-down at the far-right, top of the code editor) will hold a list of the events defined for that event object. If you were interested in receiving notification, for example, every time a solution was opened, you would select the `Opened` event. Immediately after you select this event, the event handler code will be injected into the code editor. In this case, the following code results from the selection:

```
Private Sub SolutionEvents_Opened() Handles SolutionEvents.Opened

End Sub
```

You can leave this code as is in the `EnvironmentEvents` module (a reasonable practice), or you can cut and paste it into any other module in the project. With the event handler in place, you just need to worry about writing the code that deals with the event.

You should know that every time you load a macro project with events (in other words, every time you add a macro project with events to your list of macros), a security dialog box will be displayed (shown in Figure 11.7).

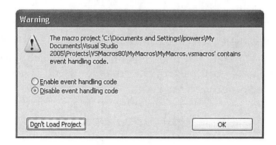

FIGURE 11.7   Loading a macro project with events.

This dialog box merely alerts you to the fact that the macro contains event interception code and enables you to disable the event objects in the macro; the latter is probably a good idea when you're opening a macro from an untrusted source. You also have the option to simply abort the project load process by clicking on the Don't Load Project button to the bottom left of the security dialog box.

Adding a New Event Declaration

If you need access to an event that isn't predeclared for you in the `EnvironmentEvents` module, it is possible to add the event declaration manually. As a demonstration, let's add a new event handler for the `WindowHiding` event exposed by the `WindowVisibilityEvents` class. This event, which is not included by default, will tell you whenever a tool window in the IDE is hidden.

First, you need to add the event declaration somewhere within the macro project. The obvious location would be the `EvironmentEvents` module; this keeps all of the event code in one spot. Just remember to place any manual event declarations outside the region marked as `"Automatically generated code, do not modify"`. Here is the event declaration for the `WindowVisibilityEvents` class:

```
<System.ContextStaticAttribute()> _
Public WithEvents WindowVisibilityEvents As EnvDTE80.WindowVisibilityEvents
```

Now for the event handler: Just as you did in the previous example, select the type `WindowVisibilityEvents` in the type drop-down and the event `WindowHiding` in the members drop-down. This will create a skeleton event handler routine (to which you have the display of a message box):

```
Private Sub WindowVisibilityEvents_WindowHiding(ByVal Window As _
        EnvDTE.Window) Handles WindowVisibilityEvents.WindowHiding

    MessageBox.Show("WindowHiding fired for " & Window.Caption)

End Sub
```

Initializing the Event Object

Although you have declared the event object and have written the event handler, you still aren't finished: You also need to initialize the event object. The macro runtime itself has two events that you need to hook to ensure that the event object is initialized correctly every time the macro runtime starts or resets itself. Without this step, the event object is syntactically complete but won't receive any events from the main IDE.

There are two events that you need to concern yourself with, both exposed by the DTEEvents class. The first is DTEEvents.OnMacrosRuntimeReset; this event is fired whenever the runtime is reset for any reason. Because a runtime-reset causes all global state to be cleared, including event connections, this would essentially prevent any event interception from happening if you didn't initialize the event object as a step in the reset process.

Handling this event is the same as handling any other: You use the type and member drop-downs to generate the skeleton code for you, and then you insert the code that you need to initialize the event object:

```
Private Sub DTEEvents_OnMacrosRuntimeReset() Handles
    DTEEvents.OnMacrosRuntimeReset
     WindowVisibilityEvents = CType(DTE.Events, Events2).WindowVisibilityEvents
End Sub
```

The second event that you need to hook is the DTEEvents.OnStartupComplete event. This event is fired when the runtime and macro environment has completed its startup process:

```
Private Sub DTEEvents_OnStartupComplete() Handles DTEEvents.OnStartupComplete
    WindowVisibilityEvents = CType(DTE.Events, Events2).WindowVisibilityEvents
End Sub
```

By initializing the event object every time the runtime starts or resets itself, you ensure that you maintain a viable, active link to the eventing engine in the IDE.

To test the event handler, you simply switch to the main IDE and close or hide any of the tool windows by clicking on their Close button. If you have done everything correctly, you will see the message box shown in Figure 11.8.

FIGURE 11.8   Catching the `WindowHiding` event.

NOTE

If you have added a new event declaration to your macro project and are unable to get its event handler to fire, a few things may have gone wrong. First, make sure that you have correctly added the event class initialization code to both the `OnStartupComplete` and `OnMacrosRuntimeReset` events. Second, you may need to unload and reload your macro project to establish the "wiring" for your event. To unload the macro project, shut down the Macros IDE (if it is open), and from the Main IDE's Macro Explorer window, right-click on the macro project that you have added the event(s) to and select Unload Macro Project. Then add the macro project back in by right-clicking the root Macros node in the Macro Explorer and selecting Load Project. Make sure you have selected Enable Event Handling Code in the security dialog box that will trigger when you try to load the project.

Invoking Macros

From the discussion of the Macro Explorer, you know that one way to run a macro is to simply double-click on the specific macro in the explorer window. One of the more common things you will want to do with certain macros is provide an alternative (and potentially easier) way to trigger a macro from the main IDE through toolbar buttons, menu items, and keyboard shortcuts.

Triggering Macros from Toolbars and Menus

If you wanted to provide quick access to the node expansion and node collapse macros, you could assign them as toolbar buttons or menu items in the main IDE. You do this through the Customize dialog box as follows:

1. Display the dialog box by selecting Tools, Customize.

2. Select the Commands tab.

3. Select the Macros category in the categories list. Each individual macro in all of the currently loaded macro projects will be displayed in the commands list box (they will follow the format *[Macro Project Name]*.*[Macro Module Name]*.*[Macro Subroutine Name]*).

4. With the macro selected, drag it onto any of the visible toolbars or menus (see Figure 11.9).

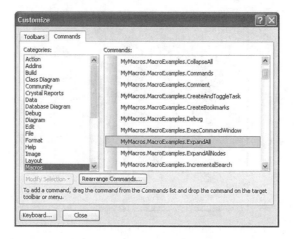

FIGURE 11.9   Drag the macro from the list to the toolbar or menu.

After you add the button or menu item, the item will remain highlighted/selected; if you now click on the Modify Selection button in the Customize dialog box, a drop-down menu (displayed in Figure 11.10) will appear that allows you to change the appearance of the button or menu item.

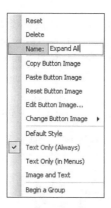

FIGURE 11.10   The Modify Selection drop-down.

Using this interactive drop-down, you can change the text that appears for the item, assign a picture to the item, or even "paint" your own picture using the Button Editor (see Figure 11.11). You launch this dialog box by selecting the Edit Button Image option from this drop-down.

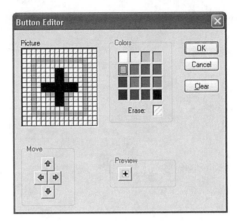

FIGURE 11.11   Assigning a button image.

Assigning Keyboard Shortcuts to Macros

To launch a macro via a keyboard shortcut, you need to assign the key sequence to the macro using the Options dialog box as follows:

1. Open the Options dialog box by selecting Tools, Options.

2. Under the Environment node, select the Keyboard page.

3. In the Keyboard settings page, select the macro in the list of commands (you can filter this list by typing the name of the macro or by just typing **macros** in the text box labeled Show Commands Containing). Each macro is listed by its macro project, module name, and then macro name.

4. Put the cursor in the Press Shortcut Keys text box and then hold down the key or keys you want to use to trigger the macro (see Figure 11.12).

5. Click on the Assign button; your macro can now be launched through the key combination that you entered.

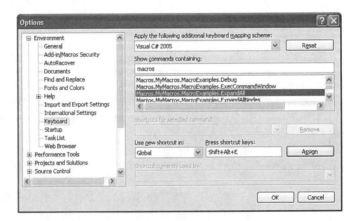

FIGURE 11.12   Assigning a keyboard shortcut to a macro.

11

> **NOTE**
>
> Visual Studio already has many different key combinations assigned to its various actions and commands. If you happen to press a key combination that is already in use, the command that currently uses that key combination will be displayed in the drop-down at the bottom of the Options dialog box (see Figure 11.12). At this point, you can either choose a different set of keys to use, or you can overwrite the key assignments. Overwriting is probably not a good idea if you are replacing one of the more common commands such as cut, open file, and so on.

Running Macros from the Command Window

As you have seen from the steps to trigger a macro via toolbar/menu and keyboard shortcut, each macro is exposed in the IDE via a command (see the section "Command Objects" in Chapter 10). The command window is purpose-built to execute commands, so macros can be run from the command window prompt as well.

With your cursor at the prompt in the command window, just type the letter m to trigger the window's IntelliSense and thus display a list of all macros. Scroll down and select the macro you want to run; then press Enter. The macro will execute.

Macros with Parameters   Although, in general, it makes sense for macros to execute without any required user interaction, it may sometimes be beneficial to write macros that accept parameters as part of their function/sub definition.

Consider the `ResizeIDE` macro in Listing 11.4. It takes in width and height values as parameters and then resizes the main IDE window according to those values.

LISTING 11.4   Resizing the IDE

```
Option Strict Off
Option Explicit Off
Imports EnvDTE
Imports EnvDTE80


Public Module MacroExamples

    Public Sub ResizeIDE(Optional ByVal width As Integer = 800, _
      Optional ByVal height As Integer = 600)
        Dim ide As Window2 = DTE.MainWindow

        ide.Width = width
        ide.Height = height


    End Sub
End Module
```

If you were to call this macro from the command window, you would have to pass these parameters in like this:

```
Macros.MyMacros.MacroExamples.ResizeIDE 800 600
```

> **NOTE**
>
> If you write a macro that accepts parameters, those parameters must be declared as optional, and you must provide default values for the parameters. Although you won't receive any errors, if you write a macro with nonoptional parameters, the macro won't be registered. You won't see it in the Macro Explorer, and you won't be able to run the macro.

Writing Visual Studio Add-ins

Up to this point, we have confined our Visual Studio automation discussions to macros. As you have seen, macros are an ideal way to control a variety of items in the IDE. Within a macro, you have access to the entire automation object model, macros are easy to write, and they come complete with their own development environment. Even with all of these positives, however, there are limitations to what a macro can do:

- A macro can't be used to create and display custom tool windows.
- A macro is incapable of exposing any sort of user interface beyond simple dialog boxes and message boxes.
- A macro can't implement a property page hosted in the Options dialog box.
- A macro can't dynamically enable or disable menu and toolbar items in the IDE.
- A macro can't be compiled and distributed as a binary.

Visual Studio add-ins can do all of the preceding and more. Put simply, add-ins present deeper IDE integration options to developers. So, what exactly is an add-in? An add-in is a compiled DLL containing a COM object that implements a specific interface, `IDTExtensibility2`, which provides the add-in with a direct connection to the IDE. As we have mentioned previously, you can write add-ins in your managed language of choice. Because we have spent so much time working with Visual Basic syntax in the macro world in this chapter, all of the add-in examples will be done in C#.

Probably the simplest way to get started with add-ins is to run the Add-in Wizard. As with the macro recorder, the wizard will give you a starting point for implementing your own add-ins, and by examining the code that the Add-in Wizard creates, you can learn a great deal about the makeup of an add-in.

Managing Add-ins

Visual Studio add-ins are controlled with the Visual Studio Add-in Manager. It allows you to do two things: load and unload any registered add-in and specify how an add-in can be loaded. To access the Add-in Manager, select Tools, Add-in Manager (see Figure 11.13).

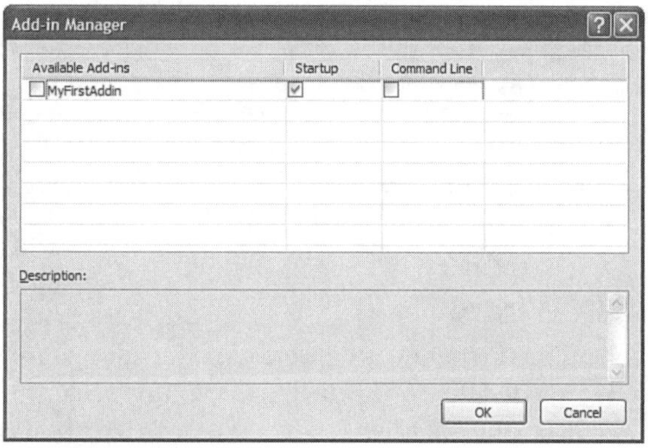

FIGURE 11.13   Managing add-ins.

This dialog box will always display a list of any available add-ins on the local machine. Checking or unchecking the box next to an add-in's name will cause the add-in to immediately load or unload. The Startup check box determines whether the add-in will load automatically when Visual Studio is started. The Command Line check box performs the same action if Visual Studio is started via the command line (such as when you are launching Visual Studio as part of an automated build scenario).

Add-in Automation Objects

To programmatically manage add-ins, you use the DTE.AddIns collection, which contains an AddIn instance for every currently registered add-in (whether or not it is loaded).

You can directly reference add-ins from the DTE.AddIns collection by using their name like this:

```
AddIn addIn = this.DTE.AddIns.Item("MyFirstAddIn")
```

With a valid add-in object, you can use its properties to determine whether it is loaded, query its name, or retrieve the add-in's ProgID:

```
bool isLoaded = addIn.Connected;
string name = addIn.Name;
string id = addIn.ProgId;
```

> **NOTE**
>
> We use the term *registered* to denote an add-in that has been installed on the local machine and registered with Visual Studio. In versions prior to Visual Studio 2005, this meant that a Registry entry was created for the add-in. This concept has now been replaced with XML files: Visual Studio looks for XML files with an .addin extension to determine the list of add-ins available to be loaded (an add-in is "loaded" when it has been connected to, and loaded within, an application's host process). These .addin files are created for you automatically by the Add-in Wizard, but they can be easily created or edited by hand as well. To get a feeling for the information and

structure of these files, look in the `Visual Studio 2005\Addins` folder under your local `My Documents` directory. Each registered add-in will appear here; you can poke through an add-in file by loading it into Visual Studio, Notepad, or any other text editor.

So, how do you go about creating your own add-in? The easiest way is to start with the Add-in Wizard.

Running the Add-in Wizard

The Add-in Wizard is launched whenever you try to create a new project of the type Visual Studio Add-in. From the File, New Project dialog box, select the Extensibility node in the project types tree (Visual C#, Other Project Types, Extensibility). From here, you can see two project templates: Visual Studio Add-in and Shared Add-in (see Figure 11.14).

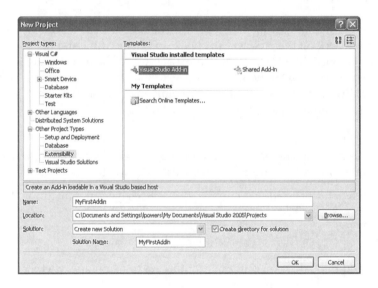

FIGURE 11.14 Selecting the Visual Studio add-in project type.

We'll touch on the differences between these two project types in a bit; for now, we are interested in the Visual Studio Add-in template.

Clicking OK will start the Add-in Wizard.

Selecting a Language
After an initial welcome page, you can select the language you want to use for the add-in (see Figure 11.15).

The list of languages available will depend on two things:

- The languages installed as part of your Visual Studio package
- The type of add-in (shared or Visual Studio)

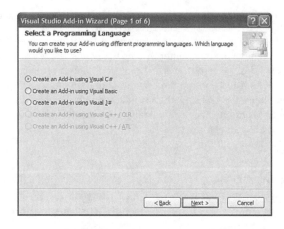

FIGURE 11.15   Picking your add-in language.

Visual Studio add-ins support Visual C#, Visual Basic, Visual J#, and both managed and unmanaged Visual C++.

Picking an Application Host
After selecting a language, you are presented with a question about "application hosts." This screen, shown in Figure 11.15, is really just asking where you want the add-in to run.

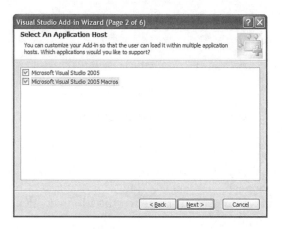

FIGURE 11.16   Selecting the application host.

Because you have indicated that this is a Visual Studio Add-in and not a shared add-in, your host options essentially are the Visual Studio IDE or the Macros IDE.

NOTE

This is a good time to discuss the differences between a Visual Studio add-in and a shared add-in. A *shared add-in* is the moniker given for add-ins hosted inside a Microsoft Office application, such as Microsoft Word or Microsoft Excel. A *Visual Studio add-in* can only be hosted within the Visual Studio or Macros IDE. If you run through the Add-in Wizard for a shared add-in, you will find that the page which asks you to select an application host (or hosts) will be populated with a list of the installed Microsoft Office applications; you won't be able to select Visual Studio as an application host for a shared add-in.

Describing the Add-in

The name and description you enter on page 3 of the wizard (see Figure 11.17) are visible in the Add-in Manager when the add-in is selected. This information is intended to give users an idea as to the add-in's functionality and purpose.

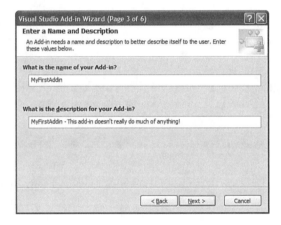

FIGURE 11.17   Giving the add-in a name and description.

Setting Add-in Options

The next wizard page, shown in Figure 11.18, allows you to specify various add-in options. You can indicate whether you want the add-in to appear in the Tools menu, when you want the add-in to load, and whether the add-in could potentially display a modal dialog box during its operation.

Setting About Box Information

The second-to-last wizard page captures the text that Visual Studio will display in its About Box dialog box (see Figure 11.19).

This is the place to include such details as where users can contact the author of the add-in, support and licensing information, copyright and version information, and so on.

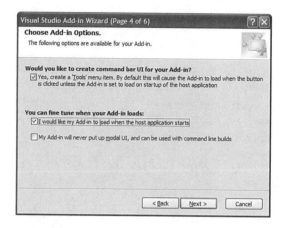

FIGURE 11.18   Setting add-in options.

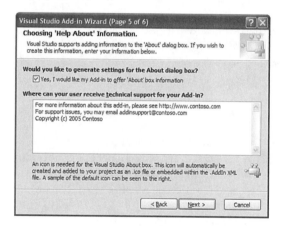

FIGURE 11.19   Entering text for the Visual Studio About Box dialog box.

Finishing the Wizard

The last page of the wizard contains a summary of the options that you have selected. After you click the Finish button, the wizard will start creating the code for your add-in based on all the selections you have made in the wizard.

Because add-ins are DLLs, the Add-in Wizard will create the add-in source as part of a class library project in the IDE. The primary code file that is created implements a class called Connect. This class inherits from all of the necessary COM interfaces to make the add-in work in the context of the IDE.

Listing 11.5 shows the Connect class as it was generated by the Add-in Wizard.

LISTING 11.5   Code Generated by the Add-in Wizard

```csharp
using System;
using Extensibility;
using EnvDTE;
using EnvDTE80;
using Microsoft.VisualStudio.CommandBars;
using System.Resources;
using System.Reflection;
using System.Globalization;

namespace MyFirstAddin
{
    /// <summary>The object for implementing an Add-in.</summary>
    /// <seealso class='IDTExtensibility2' />
    public class Connect : IDTExtensibility2, IDTCommandTarget
    {
        /// <summary>Implements the constructor for the Add-in object.
        ///     Place your initialization code within
        ///     this method.</summary>
        public Connect()
        {
        }

        /// <summary>Implements the OnConnection method of
        ///     the IDTExtensibility2 interface. Receives notification
        ///     that the Add-in is being loaded.</summary>
        /// <param term='application'>Root object of the host
        ///     application.</param>
        /// <param term='connectMode'>Describes how the Add-in
        ///     is being loaded.</param>
        /// <param term='addInInst'>Object representing this
        ///     Add-in.</param>
        /// <seealso class='IDTExtensibility2' />
        public void OnConnection(object application,
                ext_ConnectMode connectMode, object addInInst,
                ref Array custom)
        {
            _applicationObject = (DTE2)application;
            _addInInstance = (AddIn)addInInst;
            if(connectMode == ext_ConnectMode.ext_cm_UISetup)
            {
                object []contextGUIDS = new object[] { };
                Commands2 commands =
                            (Commands2)_applicationObject.Commands;
                string toolsMenuName;
```

LISTING 11.5   Continued

```
try
{
    //If you would like to move the
                    //command to a different menu,
                    //change the word "Tools" to the
    //  English version of the menu.
                    //This code will take the culture,
                    //append on the name of the menu
    //  then add the command to that menu.
                    //You can find a list of all the top-level
                    // menus in the file CommandBar.resx.
    ResourceManager resourceManager =
      new ResourceManager("MyFirstAddin.CommandBar",
      Assembly.GetExecutingAssembly());
    CultureInfo cultureInfo = new
        System.Globalization.CultureInfo
        (_applicationObject.LocaleID);
    string resourceName =
      String.Concat(cultureInfo.TwoLetterISOLanguageName,
      "Tools");
    toolsMenuName = resourceManager.GetString(resourceName);
}
catch
{
    //We tried to find a localized version of
                    // the word Tools, but one was not found.
    //  Default to the en-US word, which may
                    //work for the current culture.
    toolsMenuName = "Tools";
}

//Place the command on the tools menu.
//Find the MenuBar command bar, which is the
            //top-level command bar holding all the main
            //menu items:
Microsoft.VisualStudio.CommandBars.CommandBar menuBarCommandBar =
  ((Microsoft.VisualStudio.CommandBars.CommandBars)
  _applicationObject.CommandBars)["MenuBar"];

//Find the Tools command bar on the MenuBar command bar:
CommandBarControl toolsControl =
  menuBarCommandBar.Controls[toolsMenuName];
CommandBarPopup toolsPopup = (CommandBarPopup)toolsControl;
```

LISTING 11.5   Continued

```csharp
                //This try/catch block can be duplicated if you wish to
                //add multiple commands to be handled by your Add-in,
                //just make sure you also update the QueryStatus/Exec
                //method to include the new command names.
                try
                {
                    //Add a command to the Commands collection:
                    Command command = commands.AddNamedCommand2(_addInInstance,
                      "MyFirstAddin", "MyFirstAddin",
                      "Executes the command for MyFirstAddin", true, 59,
                      ref contextGUIDS,
                      (int)vsCommandStatus.vsCommandStatusSupported
                        +(int)vsCommandStatus.vsCommandStatusEnabled,
                      (int)vsCommandStyle.vsCommandStylePictAndText,
                      vsCommandControlType.vsCommandControlTypeButton);

                    //Add a control for the command to the tools menu:
                    if((command != null) && (toolsPopup != null))
                    {
                        command.AddControl(toolsPopup.CommandBar, 1);
                    }
                }
                catch(System.ArgumentException)
                {
                    //If we are here, then the exception is probably because a
                    //command with that name already exists. If so there is no
                    //If so there is no need to recreate the command
                    // and we can safely ignore the exception.
                }
            }
        }


        /// <summary>Implements the OnDisconnection method of the
        /// IDTExtensibility2 interface. Receives notification that the Add-in
        /// is being unloaded.</summary>
        /// <param term='disconnectMode'>Describes how the Add-in is being
        /// unloaded.</param>
        /// <param term='custom'>Array of parameters that are host application
        /// specific.</param>
        /// <seealso class='IDTExtensibility2' />
        public void OnDisconnection(ext_DisconnectMode disconnectMode,
➥ref Array custom)
        {
        }
```

LISTING 11.5   Continued

```
/// <summary>Implements the OnAddInsUpdate method of the IDTExtensibility2
/// interface. Receives notification when the collection of Add-ins has
///changed.</summary>
/// <param term='custom'>Array of parameters that are host application
/// specific.</param>
/// <seealso class='IDTExtensibility2' />
public void OnAddInsUpdate(ref Array custom)
{
}


/// <summary>Implements the OnStartupComplete method of the
/// IDTExtensibility2 interface. Receives notification that the host
/// application has completed loading.</summary>
/// <param term='custom'>Array of parameters that are host application
/// specific.</param>
/// <seealso class='IDTExtensibility2' />
public void OnStartupComplete(ref Array custom)
{
}


/// <summary>Implements the OnBeginShutdown method of the IDTExtensibility2
/// interface. Receives notification that the host application is being
/// unloaded.</summary>
/// <param term='custom'>Array of parameters that are host application
///specific.</param>
/// <seealso class='IDTExtensibility2' />
public void OnBeginShutdown(ref Array custom)
{
}


/// <summary>Implements the QueryStatus method of the IDTCommandTarget
/// interface. This is called when the command's availability is
/// updated</summary>
/// <param term='commandName'>The name of the command to determine state
/// for.</param>
/// <param term='neededText'>Text that is needed for the command.</param>
/// <param term='status'>The state of the command in the user
/// interface.</param>
/// <param term='commandText'>Text requested by the neededText
/// parameter.</param>
/// <seealso class='Exec' />
public void QueryStatus(string commandName, vsCommandStatusTextWanted
    neededText, ref vsCommandStatus status, ref object commandText)
{
```

LISTING 11.5   Continued

```
            if(neededText ==
             vsCommandStatusTextWanted.vsCommandStatusTextWantedNone)
            {
                if(commandName == "MyFirstAddin.Connect.MyFirstAddin")
                {
                    status = (vsCommandStatus)vsCommandStatus.
➥vsCommandStatusSupported¦vsCommandStatus.vsCommandStatusEnabled;
                    return;
                }
            }
        }


        /// <summary>Implements the Exec method of the IDTCommandTarget
        /// interface. This is called when the command is invoked.</summary>
        /// <param term='commandName'>The name of the command to execute.</param>
        /// <param term='executeOption'>Describes how the command should be
        /// run.</param>
        /// <param term='varIn'>Parameters passed from the caller to the command
        /// handler.</param>
        /// <param term='varOut'>Parameters passed from the command handler to
        /// the caller.</param>
        /// <param term='handled'>Informs the caller if the command was handled
        /// or not.</param>
        /// <seealso class='Exec' />
        public void Exec(string commandName, vsCommandExecOption executeOption,
            ref object varIn, ref object varOut, ref bool handled)
        {
            handled = false;
            if(executeOption == vsCommandExecOption.vsCommandExecOptionDoDefault)
            {
                if(commandName == "MyFirstAddin.Connect.MyFirstAddin")
                {
                    handled = true;
                    return;
                }
            }
        }
        private DTE2 _applicationObject;
        private AddIn _addInInstance;
    }
}
```

At this stage, the add-in doesn't actually *do* anything. You still have to implement the custom logic for the add-in. What the wizard has done, however, is implement much (if not all) of the tedious plumbing required to wire the add-in into the IDE, expose it on the Tools menu, and intercept the appropriate extensibility events to make the add-in work.

Now that you have a baseline of code to work with, you're ready to examine the source to understand the overall structure and layout of an add-in.

The Structure of an Add-in

The first thing to notice is that the Connect class inherits from two different interfaces: IDTCommandTarget and IDTExtensibility2.

```
public class Connect : IDTExtensibility2, IDTCommandTarget
```

The IDTCommandTarget interface provides the functionality necessary to expose the add-in via a command bar. The code to inherit from this interface was added by the wizard because the Yes, Create a Tools Menu Item box was checked on page 4.

The IDTExtensibility2 interface provides the eventing glue for add-ins. It is responsible for all of the events that constitute the life span of an add-in.

The Life Cycle of an Add-in

Add-ins progress through a sequence of events every time they are loaded or unloaded in their application host. Each of these events is represented by a method defined on the IDTExtensibility2 interface. These methods are documented in Table 11.1.

TABLE 11.1   IDTExtensibility2 Methods

Method	Description
OnAddInsUpdate	Called whenever an add-in is either loaded or unloaded
OnBeginShutdown	Called if Visual Studio is shut down while an add-in is loaded
OnConnection	Called when an add-in is loaded
OnDisconnection	Called when an add-in is unloaded
OnStartupComplete	Called when the add-in loads if this add-in is set to load when Visual Studio starts

The diagrams in Figure 11.20 and Figure 11.21 show how these methods (which really represent events) fall onto the normal load and unload path for an add-in.

If you look back at the template code for the add-in, you can see that each one of these IDTExtensibility2 methods has been implemented. The OnDisconnection, OnAddInsUpdate, OnStartupComplete, and OnBeginShutdown methods are empty; the wizard has merely implemented the method signature. The OnConnection method, however, already has a fair bit of code to it before you even lift a hand to modify or add to the wizard-generated code.

Now you're ready to investigate what happens in each of the IDTExtensibility2 methods.

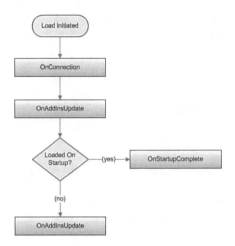

FIGURE 11.20   Load sequence of events.

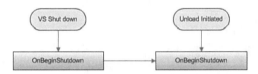

FIGURE 11.21   Unload sequence of events.

OnAddInsUpdate   The OnAddInsUpdate method is called when any add-in is loaded or unloaded from Visual Studio; because of this, the OnAddInsUpdate method is primarily useful for enforcing or dealing with dependencies between add-ins. If your add-in depends on or otherwise uses the functionality contained in another add-in, this is the ideal injection point for containing the logic that deals with that relationship.

Here is the OnAddInsUpdate method as implemented by the Add-in Wizard:

```
/// <summary>Implements the OnAddInsUpdate method of the IDTExtensibility2
/// interface. Receives notification when the collection of Add-ins has
/// changed.</summary>
/// <param term='custom'>Array of parameters that are host application
/// specific.</param>
/// <seealso class='IDTExtensibility2' />
public void OnAddInsUpdate(ref Array custom)
{
}
```

> **TIP**
>
> Because you don't know which add-in has triggered the OnAddInsUpdate method, you would need to iterate through the DTE.AddIns collection and query each add-in's Connected property to determine its current state.

OnBeginShutdown   OnBeginShutdown is called for every running add-in when Visual Studio begins its shutdown sequence. If an IDE requires any clean-up code (including perhaps resetting IDE settings that have been changed during the add-in's life), you would place that code within this method.

A user may elect to cancel Visual Studio's shutdown process. OnBeginShutdown will fire regardless of whether the Visual Studio shutdown process was successful. This forces you, as an add-in author, to always assume that Visual Studio has, in fact, terminated and therefore act accordingly in your code.

Here is the OnBeginShutdown method:

```
/// <summary>Implements the OnBeginShutdown method of the
IDTExtensibility2 interface. Receives notification that the host
application is being unloaded.</summary>
/// <param term='custom'>Array of parameters that are host
application specific.</param>
/// <seealso class='IDTExtensibility2' />
public void OnBeginShutdown(ref Array custom)
{
}
```

OnConnection   OnConnection indicates that an add-in has been loaded. It accepts four parameters:

```
public void OnConnection(object application, ext_ConnectMode connectMode,
    object addInInst, ref Array custom)
```

The first parameter, application, is the most important; it provides a reference to the DTE object representing the IDE. You know from the preceding chapter that the DTE object is the key to accessing the entire automation object model. With macros, the DTE object is held as a global variable. For add-ins, the OnConnection method is the sole provider of this object, thus providing the crucial link between the add-in and its host IDE.

The second parameter, connectMode, is an ext_ConnectMode enumeration. It indicates exactly how the add-in was loaded (see Table 11.2 for a list of the possible ext_ConnectMode values).

TABLE 11.2   ext_ConnectMode Members

Member	Description
ext_cm_AfterStartup	The add-in was loaded after Visual Studio was started.
ext_cm_CommandLine	The add-in was loaded from the command line.
ext_cm_External	n/a (Visual Studio 2005 does not use this value.)
ext_cm_Solution	The add-in was loaded with a Visual Studio solution.
ext_cm_Startup	The add-in was loaded when Visual Studio started.
ext_cm_UISetup	The add-in was loaded for UI setup (this represents the initial load of an add-in).

The addInInst parameter is actually a reference to the add-in itself. And last, the custom parameter is an empty Array object. This array is passed by reference and can be used to pass parameters into and out of the add-in.

The Add-in Wizard has taken the first two parameters, explicitly cast them to their underlying types, and assigned them into two class fields for later reference:

```
_applicationObject = (DTE2)application;
_addInInstance = (AddIn)addInInst;
```

The next block of code examines the ext_ConnectMode value. If this is the first time that the add-in was loaded (for example, ext_ConnectMode is equal to ext_cm_UISetup), then the code does two things: It creates a Tools menu entry for the add-in, and it creates a custom, named command to launch the add-in (this named command is called when you select the add-in from the Tools menu).

```
if(connectMode == ext_ConnectMode.ext_cm_UISetup)
{
        object []contextGUIDS = new object[] { };
        Commands2 commands = (Commands2)_applicationObject.Commands;
    string toolsMenuName;

    try
    {
        //If you would like to move the command to a different menu, change the
        // word "Tools" to the English version of the menu.
        //   This code will take the culture, append on the name of the menu
        //   then add the command to that menu. You can find a list of all
        //   the top-level menus in the file
        //   CommandBar.resx.
        ResourceManager resourceManager = new _
                    ResourceManager("MyFirstAddin.CommandBar", _
                    Assembly.GetExecutingAssembly());
        CultureInfo cultureInfo = new _
                    System.Globalization.CultureInfo(_applicationObject.LocaleID);
        string resourceName = String.Concat(cultureInfo.TwoLetterISOLanguageName,
"Tools");
        toolsMenuName = resourceManager.GetString(resourceName);
    }
    catch
    {
        //We tried to find a localized version of the word Tools, but one
        //was not found.
        //   Default to the en-US word, which may work for the current culture.
        toolsMenuName = "Tools";
    }
    //Place the command on the tools menu.
```

```
//Find the MenuBar command bar, which is the top-level command bar holding
//all the main menu items:
Microsoft.VisualStudio.CommandBars.CommandBar menuBarCommandBar = _
    ((Microsoft.VisualStudio.CommandBars.CommandBars)__
    applicationObject.CommandBars)["MenuBar"];

//Find the Tools command bar on the MenuBar command bar:
CommandBarControl toolsControl = menuBarCommandBar.Controls[toolsMenuName];
CommandBarPopup toolsPopup = (CommandBarPopup)toolsControl;

//This try/catch block can be duplicated if you wish to add multiple commands
//to be handled by your Add-in,
// just make sure you also update the QueryStatus/Exec method to include
// the new command names.
try
{
    //Add a command to the Commands collection:
    Command command = commands.AddNamedCommand2(_addInInstance, _
                "MyFirstAddin", "MyFirstAddin", _
                "Executes the command for MyFirstAddin", true, 59, _
                ref contextGUIDS,
                (int)vsCommandStatus.vsCommandStatusSupported
                 +(int)vsCommandStatus.vsCommandStatusEnabled,
                (int)vsCommandStyle.vsCommandStylePictAndText,
                 vsCommandControlType.vsCommandControlTypeButton);

    //Add a control for the command to the tools menu:
    if((command != null) && (toolsPopup != null))
    {
        command.AddControl(toolsPopup.CommandBar, 1);
    }
}
catch(System.ArgumentException)
{
    //If we are here, then the exception is probably because a command with
    //that name already exists. If so there is no need to recreate the
    //command and we can
    // safely ignore the exception.
}
```

TIP

You can see that the Add-in Wizard is quite liberal with its code comments; when you set out to write your own add-in, it is often useful to read the auto-generated comments and use copy/paste methods to duplicate functionality that the wizard has generated for you.

OnDisconnection   OnDisconnection fires when the add-in is unloaded from Visual Studio. This is the opposite action from that signaled by the OnConnection method. As with OnConnection, an enumeration—ext_DisconnectMode—is provided to this method that indicates the circumstances surrounding the unload action. For a list of the possible ext_DisconnectMode values, see Table 11.3.

TABLE 11.3   ext_DisconnectMode Members

Member	Description
ext_dm_HostShutdown	The add-in was unloaded because Visual Studio was shut down.
ext_dm_SolutionClosed	The add-in was unloaded because the solution was closed.
ext_dm_UISetupComplete	The add-in was unloaded after UI setup was complete.
ext_dm_UserClosed	The add-in was manually or programmatically unloaded. (This is used only if Visual Studio is still running; otherwise, ext_dm_HostShutdown will be used.)

Here is the OnDisconnection method:

```
/// <summary>Implements the OnDisconnection method of the IDTExtensibility2 inter-
face. Receives notification that the Add-in is being unloaded.</summary>
/// <param term='disconnectMode'>Describes how the Add-in is being
/// unloaded.</param>
/// <param term='custom'>Array of parameters that are host application
/// specific.</param>
/// <seealso class='IDTExtensibility2' />
public void OnDisconnection(ext_DisconnectMode disconnectMode, ref Array custom)
{
}
```

OnStartupComplete   If an add-in is set to load automatically during Visual Studio startup, the OnStartupComplete method will fire after that add-in has been loaded.

Here is the OnStartupComplete method:

```
/// <summary>Implements the OnStartupComplete method of the IDTExtensibility2
/// interface. Receives notification that the host application has completed
/// loading.</summary>
/// <param term='custom'>Array of parameters that are host application
/// specific.</param>
/// <seealso class='IDTExtensibility2' />
public void OnStartupComplete(ref Array custom)
{
}
```

Reacting to Commands

Add-ins can react to commands issued within the IDE. If you recall from the discussion on commands in the preceding chapter, and in the previous section on macros, this is done through the concept of "named commands." A named command is really nothing more than an action that has a name attached to it. You already know that Visual Studio comes with its own extensive set of commands that cover a wide variety of actions in the IDE. Using the `Commands`/`Commands2` collection, you can create your own named commands by using the `AddNamedCommand2` method.

To repeat the dissection of the `OnConnection` method, the wizard has created a body of code responsible for creating a new named command, adding it to the Tools menu, and then reacting to the command. The `IDTCommandTarget.Exec` method is the hook used to react to an issued command. Here is its prototype:

```
void Exec (
    [InAttribute] string CmdName,
    [InAttribute] vsCommandExecOption ExecuteOption,
    [InAttribute] ref Object VariantIn,
    [InAttribute] out Object VariantOut,
    [InAttribute] out bool Handled
)
```

To handle a command issued to an add-in, you write code in the `Exec` method that reacts to the passed-in command.

`CmdName` is a string containing the name of the command; this is the token used to uniquely identify a command, and thus is the parameter you will examine in the body of the `Exec` method to determine if and how you will react to the command.

`ExecuteOption` is a `vsCommandExecOption` enumeration that provides information about the options associated with the command (see Table 11.4).

TABLE 11.4   `vsCommandExecOption` Members

Member	Description
vsCommandExecOptionDoDefault	Performs the default behavior
vsCommandExecOptionDoPromptUser	Obtains user input and then executes the command
vsCommandExecOptionPromptUser	Executes the command without user input
vsCommandExecOptionShowHelp	Shows help for the command (does not execute it)

The `VariantIn` parameter is used to pass any arguments needed for the incoming command, and `VariantOut` is used as a way to pass information back out of the add-in to the caller.

Lastly, `Handled` is a Boolean that indicates to the host application whether the add-in handled the command. As a general rule, if your add-in processed the command, it will set this to `true`. Otherwise, it will set it to `false`, which is a signal to Visual Studio that it needs to continue to look for a command invocation target that *will* handle the command.

The code to handle the Tool menu command looks like this:

```
/// <summary>Implements the Exec method of the IDTCommandTarget
///interface. This is called when the command is invoked.</summary>
```

```
/// <param term='commandName'>The name of the command to execute.</param>
/// <param term='executeOption'>Describes how the command should
///be run.</param>
/// <param term='varIn'>Parameters passed from the caller to the command
/// handler.</param>
/// <param term='varOut'>Parameters passed from the command handler to
/// the caller.</param>
/// <param term='handled'>Informs the caller if the command was handled
/// or not.</param>
/// <seealso class='Exec' />
public void Exec(string commandName, vsCommandExecOption executeOption,
    ref object varIn, ref object varOut, ref bool handled)
{
    handled = false;
    if(executeOption == vsCommandExecOption.vsCommandExecOptionDoDefault)
    {
        if(commandName == "MyFirstAddin.Connect.MyFirstAddin")
        {
            handled = true;
            return;
        }
    }
}
```

A Sample Add-in: Color Palette

To cap this discussion of add-ins, let's look at the process of developing a functioning add-in from start to finish. The add-in will be a color picker. It will allow users to click on an area of a color palette, and the add-in will then emit code to create an instance of a Color structure that matches the selected color from the palette. Here is a summary list of requirements for the add-in:

- In a tool window, it will display a visual color palette representing all of the possible colors.

- As the mouse pointer is moved over the palette, the control will display the Red, Green, and Blue values for the point directly underneath the mouse pointer.

- If a user clicks on the palette, it will take the current RGB values and emit C# or VB code into the currently active document window to create a new color structure that encapsulates the given color.

- The selection of language (for example, C# or VB) will be a configurable property of the control.

Getting Started

To start the development process, you will create a new solution and a Visual Studio Add-in Project called `PaletteControlAddIn`. The Add-in Wizard will create a code base for you inside a `Connect` class just as you saw earlier in this chapter. The `Connect` class is the place where all of the IDE and automation object model–specific code will go.

In addition to the core add-in plumbing, you will also need to create a `User Control` class that encapsulates the user interface and the processing logic for the add-in.

Creating the User Control

First, you can work on getting a user control in place that has the functionality you are looking for. After you have a workable control, you can worry about wiring that control into Visual Studio using the `Connect` class created by the Add-in Wizard.

Add a user control (called `PaletteControl`) to the add-in project by selecting Project, Add User Control. After the control is added, you'll immediately add a picture box to the design surface. The picture box will display the palette of colors, stored as a simple bitmap in a resource file. With the palette in place, you now need a few label controls to display RGB values per your requirements. And finally, in the finest tradition of gold-plating, you'll also add an additional picture box that repeats the current color selection and a label that shows the code that you would generate to implement that color in a Color structure.

Figure 11.22 provides a glimpse of the user control after situating these controls on the designer.

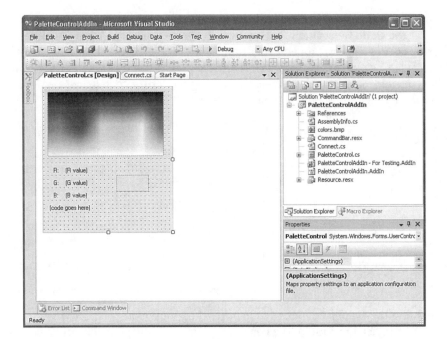

FIGURE 11.22   The `PaletteControl` user control.

Handling Movement over the Palette   With the UI in place, you can now concentrate on the code. First, you can add an event handler to deal with mouse movements over the top of the palette picture box. With the MouseMove event handler, you can update your label controls and the secondary picture box instantly as the pointer roves over the palette bitmap:

```
public PaletteControl()
{
    InitializeComponent();
    this.pictureBox1.MouseMove += new MouseEventHandler(pictureBox1_MouseMove);
    this.pictureBox1.Cursor = System.Windows.Forms.Cursors.Cross;
}


void pictureBox1_MouseMove(object sender, MouseEventArgs e)
{
    // Get the color under the current pointer position
    Color color = GetPointColor(e.X, e.Y);

    // Update the RGB labels and the 2nd pic box
    // using the retrieved color
    DisplayColor(color);

    // Generate our VB or C# code for the Color
    // structure
    SetCode(color);
}
```

Looking at the Code Generation Properties   The PaletteControl class will expose two properties: Code is a string property that holds the Color structure code generated by clicking on the palette, and GenerateVB is a Boolean that specifies whether the control should generate Visual Basic code (GenerateVB = true) or C# code (GenerateVB = false). Here are the field and property declarations for these two properties:

```
string _code = "";
public string Code
{
    get { return _code; }
}


bool _generateVB = false;
public string GenerateVB
{
    get { return _generateVB; }
}
```

Implementing the Helper Routines   Whenever the mouse pointer moves over the picture box region, you need to capture the color components of the point directly below the cursor (GetPointColor), update the label controls and the secondary picture box control to reflect that color (DisplayColor), and then generate the code to implement a matching color structure (SetCode). Here are the implementations of these routines:

```csharp
/// <summary>
/// Returns a Color structure representing the color of
/// the pixel at the indicated x and y coordinates.
/// </summary>
/// <param name="x"></param>
/// <param name="y"></param>
/// <returns>A Color structure</returns>
private Color GetPointColor(int x, int y)
{
    // Get the bitmap from the palette picture box
    Bitmap bmp = (Bitmap)pictureBox1.Image;
    // Use GetPixel to retrieve a color
    // structure for the current pointer position
    Color color = bmp.GetPixel(x, y);

    // Return the color structure
    return color;
}


/// <summary>
/// Displays the RGB values for the given color. Also sets
/// the background color of the secondary picture box.
/// </summary>
/// <param name="color">The Color to display</param>
private void DisplayColor(Color color)
{
    // pull out the RGB values from the
    // color structure
    string R = color.R.ToString();
    string G = color.G.ToString();
    string B = color.B.ToString();
    // set our secondary picture box
    // to display the current color
    this.pictureBox2.BackColor = color;
    // display RGB values in the label
    // controls
    this.labelR.Text = R;
    this.labelG.Text = G;
    this.labelB.Text = B;
}


/// <summary>
/// Generates a string representing the C# or VB code necessary to
```

```csharp
/// create a Color structure instance that matches the passed in
/// Color structure. This string is then assigned to this
/// user control's _code field.
/// </summary>
/// <param name="color">The color to represent in code.</param>
/// <param name="isVB">Boolean flag indicating the language
/// to use: false indicates C#, true indicates VB</param>
private void SetCode(Color color, bool isVB)
{
    // Read in add-in settings from registry
    SetPropFromReg();

    string code = "";

    if (isVB)
    {
        code = "Dim color As Color = ";
    }
    else
    {
        code = "Color color = ";
    }

    code = code + "Color.FromArgb(" + color.R.ToString() + ", " +
        color.G.ToString() + ", " +
        color.B.ToString() + ");";

    _code = code;
    this.labelCode.Text = _code;

}
/// <summary>
/// Reads a registry entry and sets the language output fields
/// appropriately.
/// </summary>
private void SetPropFromReg()
{
    RegistryKey regKey =
      Registry.CurrentUser.OpenSubKey(@"Software\Contoso\Addins\ColorPalette");
    string codeVal = (string)regKey.GetValue("Language", "CSharp");

    if (codeVal == "CSharp")
    {
```

```
        _generateVB = false;
    }
    else
    {
        _generateVB = true;
    }
}
```

Signaling a Color Selection   Because you will need some way for the control to indicate that a user has selected a color (for example, has clicked on the palette), you will also define an event on the user control class that will be raised whenever a click is registered in the palette picture box:

```
public event EventHandler ColorSelected;

protected virtual void OnColorSelected(EventArgs e)
{
    if (ColorSelected != null)
        ColorSelected(this, e);
}

private void pictureBox1_Click(object sender, EventArgs e)
{
    OnColorSelected(new EventArgs());
}
```

> **TIP**
>
> To isolate and test the user control, you may want to add a Windows forms project to the solution and host the control on a Windows form for testing. Just drop the control onto the form and run the forms project.

With the user control in place, you are ready to proceed to the second stage of the add-in's development: wiring the user control into the IDE.

Finishing the Connect Class

The Connect class already has the basic add-in code; now it's time to revisit that code and add the custom code to drive the user control. You'll want the add-in to integrate seamlessly into the development environment, so you can use a tool window to display the user control that you previously created.

Harking back to the discussions of the automation object model, you know that the Windows2 collection has a CreateToolWindow2 method, which allows you to create your own custom tool windows.

> **NOTE**
>
> Prior versions of Visual Studio required you to create a shim control (using C++) that would host a control for display in a tool window. The tool window, in turn, would then host the shim. With Visual Studio 2005 (and its improved `Windows2.CreateToolWindow2` method), this is no longer necessary. Now you can directly host a managed user control in a tool window.

Here is the method prototype:

```
Window CreateToolWindow2 (
    AddIn Addin,
    string Assembly,
    string Class,
    string Caption,
    string GuidPosition,
    [InAttribute] out Object ControlObject
)
```

Displaying the Tool Window and User Control   Because you want the tool window to be created and displayed after the add-in has loaded, this `CreateToolWindow2` method call will be placed in the `Connect.OnConnection` method. First, you set up a local object to point to the `DTE.ToolWindows` collection:

```
// The DTE.ToolWindows collection
Windows2 toolWindows= (Windows2)_applicationObject.Windows;
```

Then you need an object to hold the reference to the tool window that you will create:

```
// Object to refer to the newly created tool window
Window2 toolWindow;
```

And finally, you need to create the parameters to feed to the `CreateToolWindow2` method:

```
// Placeholder object; will eventually refer to the user control
// hosted by the user control
object paletteObject = null;


// This section specifies the path and class name for the palette
// control to be hosted in the new tool window; we also need to
// specify its caption and a unique GUID.
Assembly asm = System.Reflection.Assembly.GetExecutingAssembly();
string assemblyPath = asm.Location;
string className = "PaletteControlAddIn.PaletteControl";
string guid = new Guid().ToString();
string caption = "Palette Color Picker";
```

With that in place, you are only a few lines of code away from creating and displaying the tool window:

```
// Create the new tool window with the hosted user control
toolWindow = (Window2)toolWindows.CreateToolWindow2(_addInInstance, assemblyPath,
    className, caption, guid, ref paletteObject);

// If tool window was created successfully, make it visible
if (toolWindow != null)
{
    toolWindow.Visible = true;
}
```

Capturing User Control Events   The add-in is missing one last piece: You need to react whenever the user clicks on the palette by grabbing the generated code (available from the PaletteControl.Code property) and inserting it into the currently active document. There are two tasks at hand. First, you need to write an event handler to deal with the click event raised by the PaletteControl object. But to do that, you need a reference to the user control. This is the purpose of the paletteObject object that you pass in as the last parameter to the CreateToolWindow2 method. Because this is passed in by reference, it will hold a valid instance of the PaletteControl after the method call completes and returns. You can then cast this object to the specific PaletteControl type, assign it to a field within the Connect class, and attach an event handler to the PaletteControl.ColorSelected event:

```
// retrieve a reference back to our user control object
_paletteControl = (PaletteControl)paletteObject;

// wire up event handler for the PaletteControl.ColorSelected event
_paletteControl.ColorSelected +=
    new System.EventHandler(paletteControl1_ColorSelected);
```

> **TIP**
>
> Getting a reference to the user control can be a bit tricky. If the user control is not a part of the same project as your add-in class, CreateToolWindow2 will return only a null value instead of a valid reference to the user control. If you want to develop your user control outside the add-in project, you have to make sure that the user control is fully attributed to be visible to calling COM components. See the topic "Exposing .NET Framework Components to COM" in MSDN for details on how this is accomplished.

Inserting the Generated Code   You react to the ColorSelected event by grabbing the content of the PaletteControl.Code property and writing it into the currently active document. Again, you will use your automation object model knowledge gained from the preceding chapter to make this happen. The DTE.ActiveDocument class will hold a reference to the currently active document. By using an edit point, you can easily write text directly into the text document:

```
TextDocument currDoc = _applicationObject.ActiveDocument.Object;
EditPoint2 ep = currDoc.Selection.ActivePoint.CreateEditPoint();
```

```
ep.Insert(_paletteControl.Code);
ep.InsertNewLine();
```

Exposing Add-in Settings

The final step is to make the add-in's language choice a configurable option. Users should be able to indicate whether they want the add-in to emit C# or Visual Basic code. To do this, you need to have a user interface in the form of an Options page (that will display in the Options dialog box), and you need a place to persist the option selections.

Creating the Option Page UI   Add-ins can reference an Options page that will appear in the Tools Options dialog box. Again, as you did with the custom tool window, you will build a user control to implement the logic and the user interface for the Options page.

You start by creating a new user control to the existing add-in project. For this example, call this class PaletteControlOptionPage. Adding a label control and two radio button controls will enable you to indicate the language preference for the palette add-in. Figure 11.23 shows the design surface of the Options page.

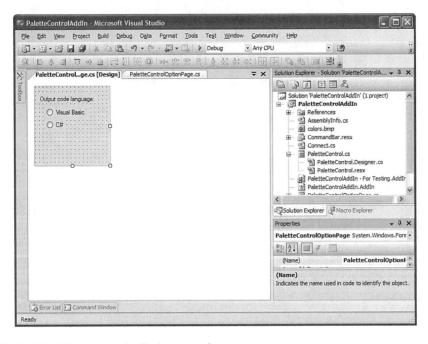

FIGURE 11.23   The user control's design surface.

The user control for the Options page needs to inherit from IDTToolsOptionsPage:

```
public partial class PaletteControlOptionPage : UserControl, IDTToolsOptionsPage
{
    public PaletteControlOptionPage()
    {
```

```
        InitializeComponent();
    }
}
```

The `IDTToolsOptionsPage` interface defines five methods, outlined in Table 11.5.

TABLE 11.5 `IDTToolsOptionsPage` Members

Member	Description
GetProperties	Returns a properties object in response to calling DTE.Properties for this specific Options page
OnAfterCreated	Fires after the Tools Options page is created for the first time
OnCancel	Fires if the user clicks the Cancel button on the Tools Options dialog box
OnHelp	Fires if the user clicks on the Help button on the Tools Options dialog box
OnOK	Fires if the user clicks on the OK button on the Tools Options dialog box

These methods are called as the Options page progresses through its normal sequence of states, as you can see in Figure 11.24.

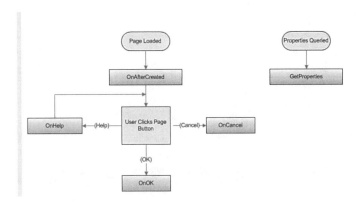

FIGURE 11.24   Tools Options page action sequence.

By placing code within these methods, you can read in and store any configuration changes that a user makes through the Options page. In this case, you can keep things simple: Read in a value from a Registry entry as part of the `OnAfterCreated` method and update that same entry as part of the `OnOK` method:

```
public void OnAfterCreated(DTE DTEObject)
{
    // read our current value from registry
    // TODO: we should really include contingency code here for creating
    // the key if it doesn't already exist, dealing with unexpected values,
    // exceptions, etc.
    RegistryKey regKey =
```

```
        Registry.CurrentUser.OpenSubKey(@"Software\Contoso\Addins\ColorPalette");
    string codeVal = (string)regKey.GetValue("Language", "CSharp");

    if (codeVal == "CSharp")
    {
        this.radioButtonCSharp.Checked = true;
        this.radioButtonVB.Checked = false;
    }
    else
    {
        this.radioButtonCSharp.Checked = true;
        this.radioButtonVB.Checked = false;
    }
}
public void OnOK()
{
    string codeValue = "CSharp";    // our default value

    if (this.radioButtonVB.Checked)
    {
        codeValue = "VB";
    }

    // update the registry with the new setting
    RegistryKey regKey =
        Registry.CurrentUser.OpenSubKey(@"Software\Contoso\Addins\ColorPalette");
    regKey.SetValue("Language", codeVal);
}
```

> **NOTE**
>
> It is up to you to decide where and how you persist your add-in's settings. The Registry is one logical place; you could also elect to store your settings in an XML file that is deployed along with your binaries.

Registering the Options Page   The registration mechanism for an Options page is the same as that for an add-in: The .addin file is used. By adding a few lines of XML, you can indicate to Visual Studio that an Options page exists with the custom add-in. You can do this easily by editing the .addin file right in Visual Studio (because it is automatically created as part of the project).

To include the necessary XML registration information, edit the .addin file and place the following XML before the closing </extensibility> tag:

```
<ToolsOptionsPage>
  <Category Name="Color Palette">
    <SubCategory Name="Code Generation">
```

```
    <Assembly>C:\Documents and Settings\lpowers\My Documents\Visual Studio
➡2005\Projects\PaletteControlAddIn\PaletteControlAddIn\bin\
➡PaletteControlAddIn.dll</Assembly>
        <FullClassName>PaletteControlAddIn.PaletteControlOptionPage </FullClassName>
      </SubCategory>
    </Category>
</ToolsOptionsPage>
```

You use the `Category` tag to specify the name of the option category displayed in the Tools Options dialog box. The `SubCategory` tag specifies the subnode under that category. The `Assembly` tag provides a path to the add-in's DLL file, and the `FullClassName` tag contains the full name for the add-in class.

With this final step complete, the add-in is fully functional. You can compile the project and then immediately load the add-in using the Add-in Manager. Figure 11.25 shows the add-in in action, and a complete code listing for the `Connect`, `PaletteControl`, and `PaletteControlOptionPage` classes (in that order) is provided in Listing 11.6.

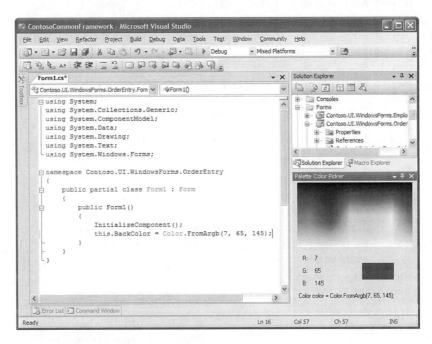

FIGURE 11.25   The color palette add-in.

LISTING 11.6   The `Connect`, `PaletteControl`, and `PaletteControlOptionPage` Classes

```
using Extensibility;
using EnvDTE;
using EnvDTE80;
```

LISTING 11.6   Continued

```csharp
using Microsoft.VisualStudio.CommandBars;
using System.Resources;
using System.Reflection;
using System.Globalization;
using System.Windows.Forms;

namespace PaletteControlAddIn
{
    /// <summary>The object for implementing an Add-in.</summary>
    /// <seealso class='IDTExtensibility2' />
    public class Connect : IDTExtensibility2, IDTCommandTarget
    {
        #region Fields

        private DTE2 _applicationObject;
        private AddIn _addInInstance;
        private PaletteControl _paletteControl;

        #endregion

        #region Events and Event Handlers

        private void paletteControl1_ColorSelected(object sender, EventArgs e)
        {
            try
            {
                TextDocument currDoc =
                    (TextDocument)_applicationObject.ActiveDocument.Object("");
                EditPoint2 ep = (EditPoint2)
                    currDoc.Selection.ActivePoint.CreateEditPoint();
                ep.Insert(_paletteControl.Code);
                ep.InsertNewLine(1);
            }

            catch (Exception ex)
            {
                MessageBox.Show("Exception caught: " + ex.ToString());
            }

        }

        #endregion
```

LISTING 11.6 Continued

```
/// <summary>Implements the constructor for the Add-in object.
/// Place your initialization code within this method.</summary>
public Connect()
{
}


/// <summary>Implements the OnConnection method of the
/// IDTExtensibility2 interface. Receives notification that the
/// Add-in is being loaded.</summary>
/// <param term='application'>Root object of the host application.</param>
/// <param term='connectMode'>Describes how the Add-in is being
/// loaded.</param>
/// <param term='addInInst'>Object representing this Add-in.</param>
/// <seealso class='IDTExtensibility2' />
public void OnConnection(object application, ext_ConnectMode connectMode,
  object addInInst, ref Array custom)
{
    _applicationObject = (DTE2)application;
    _addInInstance = (AddIn)addInInst;

    #region Tool menu command and control setup

    if (connectMode == ext_ConnectMode.ext_cm_UISetup)
    {
        object []contextGUIDS = new object[] { };
        Commands2 commands = (Commands2)_applicationObject.Commands;
        string toolsMenuName;

        try
        {
            //If you would like to move the command to a different menu,
            // change the word "Tools" to the English version of the menu.
            // This code will take the culture, append on the name of
            // the menu then add the command to that menu. You can find
            // a list of all the top-level menus in the file
            //  CommandBar.resx.
            ResourceManager resourceManager = new
              ResourceManager("PaletteControlAddIn.CommandBar",
              Assembly.GetExecutingAssembly());
            CultureInfo cultureInfo = new
System.Globalization.CultureInfo(_applicationObject.LocaleID);
            string resourceName =
              String.Concat(cultureInfo.TwoLetterISOLanguageName,
              "Tools");
```

LISTING 11.6   Continued

```csharp
        toolsMenuName = resourceManager.GetString(resourceName);
    }
    catch
    {
        //We tried to find a localized version of the word Tools,
        //but one was not found.
        //Default to the en-US word, which may work for the current
        //culture.
        toolsMenuName = "Tools";
    }

    //Place the command on the tools menu.
    //Find the MenuBar command bar, which is the top-level command
    //bar holding all the main menu items:
    Microsoft.VisualStudio.CommandBars.CommandBar menuBarCommandBar =
      ((Microsoft.VisualStudio.CommandBars.CommandBars)
      _applicationObject.CommandBars)["MenuBar"];

    //Find the Tools command bar on the MenuBar command bar:
    CommandBarControl toolsControl =
      menuBarCommandBar.Controls[toolsMenuName];
    CommandBarPopup toolsPopup = (CommandBarPopup)toolsControl;

    //This try/catch block can be duplicated if you wish to add
    //multiple commands to be handled by your Add-in,
    // just make sure you also update the QueryStatus/Exec
    // method to include the new command names.
    try
    {
        //Add a command to the Commands collection:
        Command command = commands.AddNamedCommand2(_addInInstance,
          "PaletteControlAddIn", "PaletteControlAddIn", "Executes the
➥command for PaletteControlAddIn", true, 59, ref contextGUIDS,
            (int)vsCommandStatus.vsCommandStatusSupported
              +(int)vsCommandStatus.vsCommandStatusEnabled,
            (int)vsCommandStyle.vsCommandStylePictAndText,
            vsCommandControlType.vsCommandControlTypeButton);

        //Add a control for the command to the tools menu:
        if((command != null) && (toolsPopup != null))
        {
```

LISTING 11.6   Continued

```
                command.AddControl(toolsPopup.CommandBar, 1);
        }
    }
    catch(System.ArgumentException)
    {
        //If we are here, then the exception is probably because a
        //command with that name already exists.
        //If so there is no need to recreate the command
        //and we can safely ignore the exception.
    }
}

#endregion

#region Create Tool Window

// The DTE.ToolWindows collection
Windows2 windows = (Windows2)_applicationObject.Windows;

// Object to refer to the newly created tool window
Window2 toolWindow;

// Placeholder object; will eventually refer to the user control
// hosted by the user control
object paletteObject = null;

// This section specifies the path and class name for the palette
// control to be hosted in the new tool window; we also need to
// specify its caption and a unique GUID.
 Assembly asm = System.Reflection.Assembly.GetExecutingAssembly();
 string assemblyPath = asm.Location;
 string className = "PaletteControlAddIn.PaletteControl";
 string guid = Guid.NewGuid().ToString();
 string caption = "Palette Color Picker";

try
{

    // Create the new tool window and insert the user control in it.
    toolWindow = (Window2)windows.CreateToolWindow2(_addInInstance, _
        assemblyPath, className, caption, guid, ref paletteObject);
```

LISTING 11.6   Continued

```
            // If tool window was created successfully, make it visible
            if (toolWindow != null)
            {
                toolWindow.Visible = true;
            }

            // retrieve a reference back to our user control object
            _paletteControl = (PaletteControl)paletteObject;

            // wire up event handler for the PaletteControl.ColorSelected event
            _paletteControl.ColorSelected += new _
                System.EventHandler(paletteControl1_ColorSelected);

        }

        catch (Exception ex)
        {
            MessageBox.Show("Exception caught: " + ex.ToString());
        }

        #endregion

    }

    /// <summary>Implements the OnDisconnection method of the
    ///IDTExtensibility2 interface. Receives notification that the Add-in
    /// is being unloaded.</summary>
    /// <param term='disconnectMode'>Describes how the Add-in is being
    ///unloaded.</param>
    /// <param term='custom'>Array of parameters that are host application
    //specific.</param>
    /// <seealso class='IDTExtensibility2' />
    public void OnDisconnection(ext_DisconnectMode disconnectMode,
        ref Array custom)
    {
    }

    /// <summary>Implements the OnAddInsUpdate method of the IDTExtensibility2
        /// interface. Receives notification when the collection of Add-ins
        /// has changed.</summary>
    /// <param term='custom'>Array of parameters that are host application
        ///specific.</param>
    /// <seealso class='IDTExtensibility2' />
    public void OnAddInsUpdate(ref Array custom)
```

LISTING 11.6   Continued

```
    {
    }

    /// <summary>Implements the OnStartupComplete method of the
        /// IDTExtensibility2 interface. Receives notification that the host
        /// application has completed loading.</summary>
    /// <param term='custom'>Array of parameters that are host application
        /// specific.</param>
    /// <seealso class='IDTExtensibility2' />
    public void OnStartupComplete(ref Array custom)
    {
    }

    /// <summary>Implements the OnBeginShutdown method of the
        ///  IDTExtensibility2 interface. Receives notification that the host
        ///  application is being unloaded.</summary>
    /// <param term='custom'>Array of parameters that are host
        /// application specific.</param>
    /// <seealso class='IDTExtensibility2' />
    public void OnBeginShutdown(ref Array custom)
    {
    }

    /// <summary>Implements the QueryStatus method of the IDTCommandTarget
        /// interface. This is called when the command's availability is
        /// updated</summary>
    /// <param term='commandName'>The name of the command to determine state
        /// for.</param>
    /// <param term='neededText'>Text that is needed for the command.</param>
    /// <param term='status'>The state of the command in the user
        /// interface.</param>
    /// <param term='commandText'>Text requested by the neededText
        /// parameter.</param>
    /// <seealso class='Exec' />
    public void QueryStatus(string commandName, vsCommandStatusTextWanted _
            neededText, ref vsCommandStatus status, ref object commandText)
    {
        if(neededText == _
                    vsCommandStatusTextWanted.vsCommandStatusTextWantedNone)
        {
            if(commandName == _
                            "PaletteControlAddIn.Connect.PaletteControlAddIn")
            {
                status = _
```

LISTING 11.6   Continued

```
                    (vsCommandStatus)vsCommandStatus.vsCommandStatusSupported¦ _
                    vsCommandStatus.vsCommandStatusEnabled;
                        return;
                }
            }
        }


        /// <summary>Implements the Exec method of the IDTCommandTarget
            /// interface.
            /// This is called when the command is invoked.</summary>
        /// <param term='commandName'>The name of the command to execute.</param>
        /// <param term='executeOption'>Describes how the command should be
            /// run.</param>
        /// <param term='varIn'>Parameters passed from the caller to the command
            /// handler.</param>
        /// <param term='varOut'>Parameters passed from the command handler to the
            /// caller.</param>
        /// <param term='handled'>Informs the caller if the command was handled or
            /// not.</param>
        /// <seealso class='Exec' />
        public void Exec(string commandName, vsCommandExecOption executeOption, _
                ref object varIn, ref object varOut, ref bool handled)
        {
            handled = false;
            if(executeOption == _
                    vsCommandExecOption.vsCommandExecOptionDoDefault)
            {
                if(commandName == _
                            "PaletteControlAddIn.Connect.PaletteControlAddIn")
                {
                    handled = true;
                    return;
                }
            }
        }
    }
}

using System;
using System.Collections.Generic;
using System.ComponentModel;
using System.Drawing;
using System.Data;
```

LISTING 11.6   Continued

```csharp
using System.Text;
using System.Windows.Forms;
using Microsoft.Win32;

namespace PaletteControlAddIn
{
    public partial class PaletteControl : UserControl
    {
        #region fields/properties

        string _code = "";

        public string Code
        {
            get { return _code; }
        }

        bool _generateVB = false;

        public bool GenerateVB
        {
            get { return _generateVB; }
        }

        #endregion

        #region Events and Event Handlers

        public event EventHandler ColorSelected;

        protected virtual void OnColorSelected(EventArgs e)
        {
            if (ColorSelected != null)
                ColorSelected(this, e);
        }

        void pictureBox1_MouseMove(object sender, MouseEventArgs e)
        {
            // Get the color under the current pointer position
            Color color = GetPointColor(e.X, e.Y);

            // Update the RGB labels and the 2nd pic box
            // using the retrieved color
            DisplayColor(color);
```

LISTING 11.6   Continued

```csharp
        // Generate our VB or C# code for the Color
        // structure
        SetCode(color);
    }

    private void pictureBox1_Click(object sender, EventArgs e)
    {
        OnColorSelected(new EventArgs());
    }

    #endregion

    #region Ctor(s)

    public PaletteControl()
    {
        InitializeComponent();
        this.pictureBox1.MouseMove +=
            new MouseEventHandler(pictureBox1_MouseMove);
        this.pictureBox1.Click +=
            new System.EventHandler(this.pictureBox1_Click);

        this.pictureBox1.Cursor = System.Windows.Forms.Cursors.Cross;
    }

    #endregion

    #region Internal Routines

    /// <summary>
    /// Returns a Color structure representing the color of
    /// the pixel at the indicated x and y coordinates.
    /// </summary>
    /// <param name="x"></param>
    /// <param name="y"></param>
    /// <returns>A Color structure</returns>
    private Color GetPointColor(int x, int y)
    {
        // Get the bitmap from the palette picture box
        Bitmap bmp = (Bitmap)pictureBox1.Image;

        // Use GetPixel to retrieve a color
        // structure for the current pointer position
        Color color = bmp.GetPixel(x, y);
```

LISTING 11.6 Continued

```csharp
            // Return the color structure
            return color;
        }


        /// <summary>
        /// Displays the RGB values for the given color. Also sets
        /// the background color of the secondary picture box.
        /// </summary>
        /// <param name="color">The Color to display</param>
        private void DisplayColor(Color color)
        {
            // pull out the RGB values from the
            // color structure
            string R = color.R.ToString();
            string G = color.G.ToString();
            string B = color.B.ToString();

            // set our secondary picture box
            // to display the current color
            this.pictureBox2.BackColor = color;

            // display RGB values in the label
            // controls
            this.labelR.Text = R;
            this.labelG.Text = G;
            this.labelB.Text = B;

        }


        /// <summary>
        /// Generates a string representing the C# or VB code necessary to
        /// create a Color structure instance that matches the passed in
        /// Color structure. This string is then assigned to this
        /// user control's _code field.
        /// </summary>
        /// <param name="color">The color to represent in code.</param>
        /// <param name="isVB">Boolean flag indicating the language
        /// to use: false indicates C#, true indicates VB</param>
        private void SetCode(Color color)
        {
            SetPropFromReg();

            string code = "";
```

LISTING 11.6   Continued

```csharp
            if (_generateVB)
            {
                code = "Dim color As Color = ";
            }
            else
            {
                code = "Color color = ";
            }


            code = code + "Color.FromArgb(" + color.R.ToString() + ", " +
                color.G.ToString() + ", " +
                color.B.ToString() + ");";

            _code = code;
            this.labelCode.Text = _code;

        }


        /// <summary>
        /// Reads a registry entry and sets the language output fields
        /// appropriately.
        /// </summary>
        private void SetPropFromReg()
        {
            RegistryKey regKey = _
              Registry.CurrentUser.OpenSubKey(@"Software\Contoso\Addins\
➥ColorPalette");
            string codeVal = (string)regKey.GetValue("Language", "CSharp");

            if (codeVal == "CSharp")
            {
                _generateVB = false;
            }
            else
            {
                _generateVB = true;
            }
        }

        #endregion
    }
}
```

LISTING 11.6 Continued

```csharp
using System;
using System.Collections.Generic;
using System.ComponentModel;
using System.Drawing;
using System.Data;
using System.Text;
using System.Windows.Forms;
using Extensibility;
using EnvDTE;
using EnvDTE80;
using Microsoft.Win32;

namespace PaletteControlAddIn
{
    public partial class PaletteControlOptionPage : UserControl,
        IDTToolsOptionsPage
    {
        public PaletteControlOptionPage()
        {
            InitializeComponent();
        }

        #region IDTToolsOptionsPage Members

        public void GetProperties(ref object PropertiesObject)
        {
            throw new Exception("The method or operation is not implemented.");
        }

        public void OnAfterCreated(DTE DTEObject)
        {
            // read our current value from registry
            // TODO: we should really include contingency code here for creating
            // the key if it doesn't already exist, dealing with unexpected values,
            // exceptions, etc.
            RegistryKey regKey = _
                Registry.CurrentUser.OpenSubKey(@"Software\Contoso\Addins\
➥ColorPalette");
            string codeVal = (string)regKey.GetValue("Language", "CSharp");

            if (codeVal == "CSharp")
            {
                this.radioButtonCSharp.Checked = true;
```

LISTING 11.6   Continued

```
            this.radioButtonVB.Checked = false;
        }
        else
        {
            this.radioButtonCSharp.Checked = true;
            this.radioButtonVB.Checked = false;
        }

    }

    public void OnCancel()
    {

    }

    public void OnHelp()
    {
        throw new Exception("The method or operation is not implemented.");
    }

    public void OnOK()
    {
        string codeVal = "CSharp";     // our default value

        if (this.radioButtonVB.Checked)
        {
            codeVal = "VB";
        }

        // update the registry with the new setting
        RegistryKey regKey = _
            Registry.CurrentUser.OpenSubKey(@"Software\Contoso\Addins\
➥ColorPalette");
        regKey.SetValue("Language", codeVal);
    }
    #endregion
}
}
```

Creating a Visual Studio Wizard

Visual Studio makes heavy use of wizards to help guide developers through various tasks. The Add-in Wizard that we discussed in the previous sections is one such example of a

New Project Wizard (it is launched when you try to create a new add-in project). There are also wizards for adding new items to projects. You can modify the existing Project/Add New Item Wizards or create your own wizard complete with its own user interface.

In the following sections, we will focus on understanding the wizard landscape and creating a custom Add New Item Wizard.

Examining the Wizard Structure

Each wizard consists of two major components: a class that contains the code (and user interface) for the wizard and a `.vsz` file that provides information about the wizard to Visual Studio.

The `IDTWizard` Interface

To hook into Visual Studio's wizard engine, your `Wizard` class must implement the `EnvDTE.IDTWizard` interface. The `IDTWizard` defines a single method, `Execute`, that is called by Visual Studio whenever the wizard is launched. Here is the prototype for the `IDTWizard.Execute` method (in C#):

```
void Execute (
    [InAttribute] Object Application,
    [InAttribute] int hwndOwner,
    [InAttribute] ref Object[] ContextParams,
    [InAttribute] ref Object[] CustomParams,
    [InAttribute] out wizardResult retval
)
```

The arguments passed to the `Execute` method are used to link the wizard to the Visual Studio environment and to pass relevant data to the wizard:

- `Application`—A DTE instance for the Visual Studio IDE.

- `hwndOwner`—A handle to the parent window; this window will "parent" any user interface elements created by the wizard.

- `ContextParams`—For New Project/Add New Item Wizards, this is an array of objects used to pass information about the type of wizard that was launched and various data necessary for the wizard to function, such as project name, install directory, and so on.

- `CustomParams`—An array of objects used to carry any custom parameters you define for your wizard.

- `wizardResult`—A `wizardResult` enumeration value that indicates the results of the wizard.

The `ContextParams` parameter's content will vary depending on the type of wizard. For instance, for a New Project Wizard, the third value in the `ContextParams` array represents the location where the project file is stored (called the `LocalDirectory`). But for an Add Item Wizard, the third value in the array is a pointer to a `ProjectItems` collection. Table 11.6 maps the various array elements to the three different wizard types.

TABLE 11.6 `ContextParams` Values

Index	NewProject Wizard	AddSubProject Wizard	AddItem Wizard
0	`WizardType` enum	`WizardType` enum	`WizardType` enum
1	Project name	Project name	Project name
2	Local directory	`ProjectItems` object	`ProjectItems` object
3	VS install directory	Local directory	Local directory
4	`FExclusive` flag (create new solution or use current)	Name of added item	Name of added item
5	Solution name	VS install directory	VS install directory
6	`Silent` flag (run with or without UI)	`Silent` flag	`Silent` flag

To determine the results of the wizard, you look at the value placed in the `wizardResult` parameter. Table 11.7 lists the `wizardResult` enum values.

TABLE 11.7 `wizardResult` Enumeration Values

Member	Description
`wizardResultBackOut`	The user exited the wizard by clicking on the Back button.
`wizardResultCancel`	The wizard was canceled.
`wizardResultFailure`	The wizard failed.
`wizardResultSuccess`	The wizard succeeded.

The core content of the `Execute` method is entirely up to you. Within the body of the `Execute` method, you will need to implement all of the code necessary to do the work of the wizard and display its UI to the user.

> **NOTE**
>
> Although you probably think of wizards as a series of pages accessed by Next and Back navigation, a wizard in Visual Studio's terms is nothing more than a COM object that implements IDTWizard. In fact, a wizard doesn't need to display a user interface at all. It could, for instance, merely use the parameters passed to it to do some work and then quit.

The `.vsz` and `.vsdir` Files

If you recall from our discussion of add-ins, every add-in uses an `.addin` file to register the add-in with Visual Studio. The `.vsz` files are the equivalent for wizards; they make Visual Studio aware of the wizard and its implementing class.

Here is a complete, sample .vsz file:

```
VSWizard 8.0
Wizard=ContosoWizard.AddNewClassWizard
Param=
```

The VSWizard line in this file identifies the version information for the wizard. The number 8.0 equates to Visual Studio 2005, while prior version numbers map to prior Visual Studio releases. Next, a class ID is provided for the wizard. And finally, there are one or more (optional) Param lines. These lines define any custom parameters that you want sent to the wizard. Any parameters defined here will come across in the CustomParams parameter in the Execute method.

Visual Studio has a specific folder hierarchy that it uses for storing wizard .vsz files; the folder where you place the .vsz file will dictate exactly where the option to launch the wizard will appear. As an example, if you wanted to create an Add Item Wizard for both Visual Basic and Visual C#, you would need to place a copy of the .vsz file into both the Visual Basic and the C# folders. If Visual Studio 2005 was installed in its default location, that would mean placing the wizard files here:

```
C:\Program Files\Microsoft Visual Studio 8\VC#\CSharpProjectItems

C:\Program Files\Microsoft Visual Studio8\VB\VBProjectItems
```

If you were creating a New Project Wizard, the files would be placed in the VC#\CSharpProjects and the VB\VBProjects folders.

Wizard folders may also contain a .vsdir file. This file is used to provide Visual Studio with icon and other resource information about a particular wizard. The .vsdir file is also a plain-text file. Each line in the file represents a specific .vsz file/wizard and provides multiple fields (separated by the pipe character, |) with optional information about the wizard. Table 11.8 documents the valid fields for each .vsdir line, in order of their appearance. The optional fields are noted.

TABLE 11.8   .vsdir Record Fields

Field	Description
Relative Path	The relative path to the wizard's .vsz file.
Class ID	The Class ID of the wizard component in GUID format. Optional.
Localized Name	The localized name of the wizard that will appear in the Add Item dialog box. Optional.
Sort Priority	A number used to provide a relative grouping number for the wizard in the display dialog boxes. A wizard with a value of 1 will be displayed next to other 1 wizards, and so on.
Description	The description of the wizard. This will appear whenever the wizard is selected in the Add Item dialog box.
DLL Path	A full path to the assembly containing the wizard's icon.
Icon Resource ID	A resource identifier that points within the DLL to the icon to be displayed.

TABLE 11.8   Continued

Field	Description
Flags	One or more bitwise values used to control certain wizard behaviors. See the MSDN documentation for a complete list. Optional.
Name	The name of the wizard to be displayed in the Name field of the dialog box (unlike the Localized Name, this field is required).

Here is a simple .vsdir file example with one wizard record:

```
CSharpContosoDataClass.vsz ¦ ¦ ¦1¦Create a new Contoso storage
➥class¦c:\ContosoFramework\Wizards\DataClassWizard.dll¦ ¦ ¦Contoso Data Class
```

> **NOTE**
>
> The .vsdir record provides a way to associate an icon resource to the wizard by allowing you to specify a DLL path and an icon resource ID. There is also a simpler way to accomplish this: Just create an .ico file, give it the same name as the wizard's .vsz file, and place it in the same directory.

Creating an Add New Item Wizard

Here are the basic steps for creating a wizard:

1. Create a new class library project; in this project, create a new class that implements the IDTWizard interface.

2. In the wizard class, write the code in the Execute method to perform the wizard's tasks and display its UI.

3. Create a .vsz file for the wizard.

4. Create or edit a .vsdir file to reference the new wizard and the .vsz file.

To solidify these concepts, let's look at them in action. We'll follow the development of a wizard from start to finish. In this case, the wizard will be a C# Add Item Wizard. Its purpose will be to collect some basic data from the user and then create a Tools Options page class (much like you manually did earlier in the chapter) that has been customized in accordance with the user's input into the wizard dialog box.

Implementing the Execute Method

The Execute method needs to do two things: It will display a Windows Forms dialog box to capture preferences such as class name; and it will process those preferences, generate a class that implements a Tools Options page, and add that class to the current project.

Creating the Dialog Box   First, the dialog box: It should look roughly like the dialog box in Figure 11.26 (there is nothing special about the implementation of this form, so we won't bother to detail all of its code here).

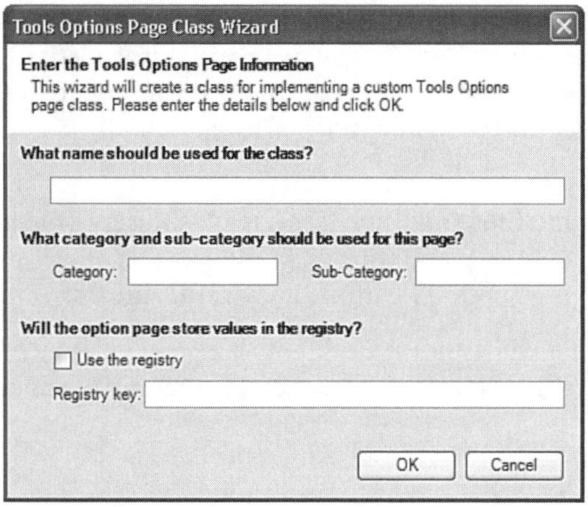

FIGURE 11.26   The wizard form.

When the user clicks on the OK button, you should set several properties on the form that mirror the selections made on the dialog box. For instance, if you implement this form as a class called `WizardDialog`, you will want a `WizardDialog.ClassName` property, a `WizardDialog.Category` property, and so on. The last thing to do when the OK button is clicked is to set the form's `DialogResult` property. The `Execute` method on the wizard (which we will examine in a moment) will query the `DialogResult` property to determine if the user has committed the wizard or canceled it. Here is a look at the OK and Cancel button click event handlers:

```
private void buttonOK_Click(object sender, EventArgs e)
{
    // assign screen control values to our public
    // fields
    this.ClassName = this.textBoxClassName.Text;
    this.Category = this.textBoxCategory.Text;
    this.SubCategory = this.textBoxSubCategory.Text;
    this.UseRegistry = this.checkBoxUseRegistry.Checked;
    this.RegKey = this.textBoxRegKey.Text;

    // indicate dialog was accepted
    this.DialogResult = DialogResult.OK;
}


private void buttonCancel_Click(object sender, EventArgs e)
{
    // indicate dialog was cancelled
    this.DialogResult = DialogResult.Cancel;
}
```

Using a Template File There are two approaches here to creating the Tools Options page class: You could generate every line of code using either the Code DOM API or by brute-force string creation/concatenation, or you could use a template file. The template file approach is a bit simpler and probably more efficient as well, so that is the approach we describe here.

The class template is a file that looks just like any other user control. Using the standard code created for a user control class, you substitute key areas with string placeholders. For instance, the class name is specified within the wizard, and thus something you will want to replace in the template class:

```
public class %TemplateClassName% : UserControl, IDTToolsOptionsPage
{
    ...
}
```

You will also want the `IDTToolsOptionsPage` members—such as `OnAfterCreated`, `OnOK`, and so on—represented in the class. For most of these methods, you will leave a simple `System.NotImplementedException` call to remind the user to fill in code as necessary. For `OnAfterCreated` and `OnOK`, however, you want the option of including a line of code to open the indicated Registry key:

```
public void OnAfterCreated(DTE DTEObject)
{
    // read our current value from registry
    // TODO: Include code to read from registry here
    %StartRegistryCode%
    RegistryKey regKey = Registry.CurrentUser.OpenSubKey(@"%TemplateRegKey%");
    %EndRegistryCode%
}
public void OnOK()
{
    //TODO: include code to save options
    // update the registry with the new setting
    %StartRegistryCode%
    RegistryKey regKey = Registry.CurrentUser.OpenSubKey(@"%TemplateRegKey%");
    %EndRegistryCode%
}
```

Again, you use placeholders here: The `%StartRegistryCode%` and `%EndRegistryCode%` delimits the `OpenSubKey` line of code. If the user unchecks the User Registry check box in the wizard, you will eliminate everything between these two placeholders (including the placeholders themselves). The `%TemplateRegKey%` is used as a token for the Registry key value; this is something else that you collect from the user in the wizard's dialog box.

Executing the Wizard The `Execute` method will open the wizard form and, if the user has not canceled the dialog box, will use the form's properties to call into a few internal routines responsible for generating the output class:

```
public void Execute(object Application, int hwndOwner, ref object[] ContextParams,
    ref object[] CustomParams, ref wizardResult retval)
{
    // instance the dialog for the wizard
    WizardDialog dlg = new WizardDialog();

    // show the dialog
    dlg.Show();

    // process the wizard results
    if (dlg.DialogResult == DialogResult.OK)
    {
        // Load template file, replace tokens, return content
        // as string
        string classContent = ReplaceTokens(dlg.ClassName, dlg.Category,
            dlg.SubCategory, dlg.UseRegistry, dlg.RegKey);

        // Put the returned string content into a file and
        // add the file to the current project
        // (3rd element of ContextParams is the current project's
        // items collection)
        ProjectItems projItems = (ProjectItems)ContextParams[2];
        AddFile(classContent, projItems);

        retval = wizardResult.wizardResultSuccess;

    }
    // wizard was canceled; no action required
    else
    {
        retval = wizardResult.wizardResultCancel;
    }
}
```

To react to the user clicking OK, you call three separate internal routines. The first, ReplaceTokens, opens the template class file and replaces the tokens (because this is a simple string substitution process, we won't reproduce the code here).

The second routine, AddFile, writes the new class content into a new file and adds it to the current project. Because this code may not be entirely obvious, here is one approach:

```
private void AddFile(string className, string classContent,
    ProjectItems projItems)
{
    // determine path to project files
```

```csharp
    string fileName =
        Path.GetDirectoryName(projItems.ContainingProject.FileName);

    // use path and class name to build file name for class
    fileName = fileName + className + ".cs";

    // save class file into project folder
    using (TextWriter writer = new StreamWriter(fileName, false))
    {
        writer.Write(classContent);
        writer.Close();
    }

    // add the newly created file to the current project
    projItems.AddFromFile(fileName);

}
```

Last, you call `UpdateXML`; this routine opens the `.addin` file and adds the appropriate
`<ToolsOptionsPage>` node to the XML content:

```csharp
private void UpdateXml(ProjectItems projItems, string category,
    string subCategory)
{
    // create string XML snippet
    string xml = "";
    xml += "<ToolsOptionsPage>\r\n";
    xml += "    <Category Name=\"" + category + "\">\r\n";
    xml += "        <SubCategory Name=\"" + subCategory + "\">\r\n";
    xml += "            <Assembly></Assembly>\r\n";
    xml += "            <FullClassName></FullClassName>\r\n";
    xml += "        </SubCategory>\r\n";
    xml += "    </Category>\r\n";
    xml += "</ToolsOptionsPage>\r\n";
    xml += "</Extensibility>";

    // iterate items in the project, looking for the
    // .addin file
    string projName = projItems.ContainingProject.FullName;
    foreach (ProjectItem itm in projItems)
    {
        if (itm.Name == projName + ".addin")
        {
            // open the .addin file's document object
            itm.Document.Activate();
            TextDocument txtDoc = (TextDocument)itm.Document.Object("");
```

```
        TextRanges nullObj = null;
        // add in the cat/sub-cat XML snippet
        txtDoc.ReplacePattern("</Extensibility>", xml,
            (int)vsFindOptions.vsFindOptionsFromStart,
            ref nullObj);


    }
  }
}
```

At this point, the wizard code is complete.

Creating the `.vsz` and `.vsdir` Files

All that is left is to create the `.vsz` file and add an entry to the `.vsdir` file. The `.vsz` file is straightforward:

```
VSWizard 8.0
Wizard=ContosoWizards.ToolsOptionsPageWizard
Param=
```

The record you add to the `.vsdir` file looks like this:

```
ToolsOptionsPageWizard.vsz ¦ ¦ ¦1¦Create a new Tools Options Page
➥class¦c:\ContosoFramework\Wizards\ToolsOptionsPageWizard.dll¦
➥¦ ¦Contoso Options Page Class
```

With that, the wizard is fully functional and can be selected from the Add Item dialog box.

Summary

In this chapter, we described how to leverage the power of Visual Studio's automation APIs to create macros, add-ins, and wizards.

You saw that the macro recorder gives you a quick entry point into driving various components of the IDE and that the Macro Explorer itself rounds out that equation by providing a fully featured development environment for building on top of these recorded macros or creating macros from scratch.

You also investigated the nearly unlimited potential for extending Visual Studio by using add-ins that call into the automation API and expose their interfaces in a variety of ways, including custom tool windows and dialog boxes.

And last, you saw how to once again leverage the ubiquitous automation object model and the built-in wizard engine to create your own custom wizards for adding new projects, adding new project items, or executing nearly any other type of algorithm within Visual Studio.

CHAPTER **12**

The .NET Community: Consuming and Creating Shared Code

IN THIS CHAPTER

- The Community Features of Visual Studio

- Discovering and Consuming Shared Content

- Giving Back to the Community

The .NET community is a large and diverse group. A quick look across the Internet and you will find countless bits of content and help for building applications. Microsoft has added new community features to Visual Studio 2005 that help to streamline and manage this content.

This chapter covers how developers can take advantage of the community capabilities of Visual Studio 2005. You will learn how to customize your community content to provide the right mix, how to get community support, and how to find and consume code from the greater developer community. Finally, you will also learn how to bundle your own code for sharing with the community.

The Community Features of Visual Studio

Visual Studio 2005 tries to expand the breadth and reach of the .NET community by making every developer's experience connected beyond his or her local hard drive and network. Its goal is to provide you with important (and targeted) product, development, and learning information where you will find it: in the IDE. It uses Web services, RSS feeds, and community-specific features built into the IDE to ensure you connect with and cull the benefits from the larger .NET world.

The Visual Studio team built these connections and features into the IDE so as to be intuitive and unobtrusive yet readily available. You do not have to go searching to find and connect to your community. Rather, these communities are delivered to you through your development tool. If you are looking to find specific information, just explore, or publish community content, you can do so directly from within Visual Studio 2005. The following sections illustrate what is available from the IDE in terms of the Visual Studio Start Page and the Community menu.

The Visual Studio Start Page

Developers new to Visual Studio 2005 will first encounter the IDE through the Start Page. The Start Page acts as a simple portal to your development experience and includes links to your favorite community. The four principal parts to the Start Page are Recent Projects, Getting Started, Visual Studio Headlines, and the Start Page news channel. Figure 12.1 shows a sample Start Page in the IDE.

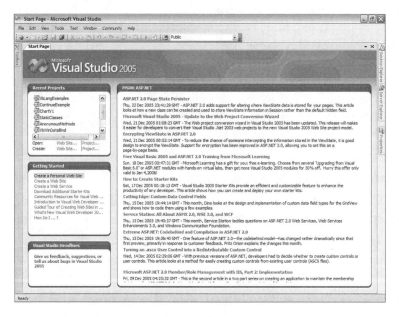

FIGURE 12.1   The Visual Studio Start Page.

Notice that the sample Start Page (or portal) shown in Figure 12.1 is for a developer who has set default settings in the IDE to Web Development Settings. The Start Page (and other items in the IDE such as toolbars and layout) will change to reflect the setup of your default profile in the IDE. For example, if you indicate you are a C# developer, your news channel will be set to the C# news, and the Getting Started information will be targeted to a C# developer. Now let's look at each section on the home page.

TIP

You can change your default IDE settings in terms of your primary usage (VB, C#, C++, Web, and so on). This will change the IDE and the configuration of your Start Page. To do so, open the Tools menu and choose the Import and Export Settings option. From the Import and Export Settings Wizard, you can not only import or export your IDE settings, but you can also reset all of your settings to a default profile. Selecting a new profile will automatically customize your Start Page relative to the new profile.

Recent Projects

The Recent Projects section of the Start Page provides a list of projects you have been working on. This allows you to easily access one or more projects on which you are currently engaged. Of course, clicking on a project in this list will open that project for editing. Figure 12.2 shows an example of a Recent Projects list.

FIGURE 12.2   The Recent Projects list from the Start Page.

Note that the Recent Projects list also contains links to open and create other projects not in the list. Using these links, you can quickly start a new project, create a new website, or browse to another project not listed here. Having quick access to these features makes the Start Page more useful as a launch point for your daily development work.

Getting Started

The Getting Started section of the Start Page provides developers who are new to Visual Studio 2005 (or those looking to learn something new) a common place to start. The links in this list typically revolve around creating a new project, using a template or starter kit, answering a question, or learning something new. This feature can be a great launch point for doing your own exploration. Figure 12.3 shows an example of the Getting Started section from the C# Start Page. Of course, this section changes based on your developer profile (VB, C#, C++, Web, and so on).

From Figure 12.3, you can see that the Getting Started block provides links directly to MSDN in terms of what's new and similar learning opportunities. You can also connect directly to community-related websites or download add-ins and starter kits.

FIGURE 12.3   The Getting Started list from the Start Page.

Visual Studio Headlines

The Visual Studio Headlines section of the Start Page promises to bring announcements and headlines relative to Visual Studio. Figure 12.4 shows an example. You can see here that the content is less a headline and more a link to MSDN and the feedback center. We expect this feature to evolve into more headline-like content as Microsoft begins to make new announcements.

FIGURE 12.4   Visual Studio Headlines from the Start Page.

Start Page News Channel

The news channel information is located inside the main section on the Start Page. In Figure 12.1, this section was titled MSDN: ASP.NET. Figure 12.5 provides a closer look at some of the content that is included in this news channel. It bears repeating that the news channel shown in this graphic is that of a web developer. Therefore, content for the news channel is targeted to the concerns of a web developer. Of course, you can choose from a number of additional news channels. Again, these choices are typically set through your developer profile (VB, C#, C++, Web, and so on).

Customizing the News Channel   The news channel is set based on your default developer settings or profile. For instance, if your principal development language is set to Visual Basic, then your start page will include information from the MSDN Visual Basic site. This information comes to the IDE via RSS feeds.

If you are unfamiliar with RSS, you should be aware that RSS stands for either Rich Site Summary, Really Simple Syndication, or RDF Site Summary, depending on which definition you use. The gist is that RSS is meant to provide an XML-structured list that contains summaries and links to key information found within a particular site. With this technology, Visual Studio users can get the published summary of key news items for a particular development center on MSDN.

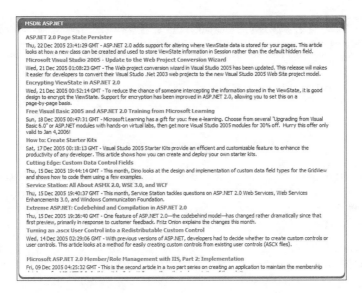

FIGURE 12.5   The Start Page news channel.

To customize the Start Page news channel, you use the Options dialog box (which you access by choosing Tools, Options). You select the Environment item from the tree view on the left side of the dialog box. Under Environment, you select the Startup leaf. This will present you with a couple of options, as shown in Figure 12.6.

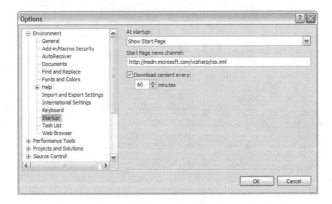

FIGURE 12.6   Customizing the Start Page news channel.

The dialog box's first option allows you to choose what happens when Visual Studio starts. Of course, we suggest you continue showing the Start Page by default. However, you can also open the last project on which you were working or show one of the open project dialog boxes.

> **TIP**
>
> If you choose not to see the Start Page when your IDE starts up, you can still navigate there. You do so by using either the Start Page toolbar icon, shown in Figure 12.7, or choosing View, Other Windows, Start Page.

FIGURE 12.7   Accessing the Start Page using the Toolbar Icon.

The second option, Start Page News Channel, is the focus of our attention. Here, you can set a URL to an RSS feed. This allows for easy customization and connection to any RSS channel. Changing this setting will change the data that is displayed in the news channel section of the Start Page.

Some common news channels and their URLs are listed in Table 12.1. They correspond to the MSDN developer centers Microsoft has created. There are many more developer centers (and RSS feeds) than those listed in the table. For more, look at http://msdn.microsoft.com/developercenters/.

TABLE 12.1   Common RSS Feeds for the VS Start Page

Description	URL
Architecture and the .NET Framework	
.NET Framework	http://msdn.microsoft.com/netframework/rss.xml
Architecture	http://msdn.microsoft.com/architecture/rss.xml
Patterns & Practices	http://msdn.microsoft.com/practices/rss.xml
Mobile	http://msdn.microsoft.com/mobility/rss.xml
Security	http://msdn.microsoft.com/security/rss.xml
Web Development	
ASP .NET	http://msdn.microsoft.com/asp.net/rss.xml
Web Services	http://msdn.microsoft.com/webservices/rss.xml
Visual Studio and Languages	
Visual Studio	http://msdn.microsoft.com/vstudio/rss.xml
Team System	http://msdn.microsoft.com/vstudio/teamsystem/rss.xml
C# News	http://msdn.microsoft.com/vcsharp/rss.xml
VB News	http://msdn.microsoft.com/vbasic/rss.xml
C++ News	http://msdn.microsoft.com/visualc/rss.xml
Development with MS Products & Platforms	
Microsoft Office	http://msdn.microsoft.com/office/rss.xml
SQL Server	http://msdn.microsoft.com/sql/rss.xml
BizTalk	http://msdn.microsoft.com/biztalk/rss.xml
Windows Vista	http://msdn.microsoft.com/windowsvista/rss.xml

> **TIP**
>
> Each URL listed in Table 12.1 not only points to an RSS feed that can be put into Visual Studio, but also provides a link to the related developer center on Microsoft's website. Simply remove the `rss.xml` from the link and you have the URL to the related developer center.

The Community Menu

Visual Studio 2005 now includes a handy Community menu, which provides quick access to various community-related information. The menu exposes a wide range of community-related features, including your ability to get help with a question, send feedback to Microsoft on Visual Studio and .NET, and access .NET-related development sites. Figure 12.8 shows the Community menu. We will cover each item in this menu in the following sections.

FIGURE 12.8   The Visual Studio 2005 Community menu.

Ask a Question

The Ask a Question button on the Community menu allows you to search for answers to questions you might have about Visual Studio or the .NET Framework and languages. When you click this button, Visual Studio launches the MSDN documentation explorer and navigates to a general search page for the MSDN Community Forums. Figure 12.9 shows an example of this search page.

The MSDN Community Forums allow developers to find information relevant to a common problem or post specific issues and receive feedback from the community. The intent of these moderated forums is to provide a community of developers to aid other developers.

When you reach the forum through the Ask a Question button, inside the IDE you start the process of getting an answer by first searching to find out whether your question was already asked (and possibly answered). As an example, Figure 12.9 shows a question pertaining to changing the default language for Visual Studio. When you click the Go button, MSDN searches the community forum for relevant matches. Figure 12.10 shows the matches returned by the sample question.

FIGURE 12.9   Search for an answer to your question.

FIGURE 12.10   Community Forum search results.

In this example, the results show that someone has already asked a similar question. The green icon with a check mark next to the post indicates that this item was an answer to a question. When you ask a question and receive a reply that answers your question, you are able to mark that reply as an "Answer." This makes it much easier to find real answers to your questions and not have to filter through a large number of replies that did not really answer the question.

Of course, if you do want to see the complete thread (and all related replies), you can do so by selecting the item in the list. Figure 12.11 shows an example of the thread. Notice how the answer is clearly highlighted.

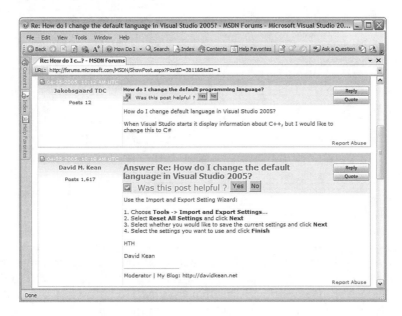

FIGURE 12.11   Community Forum answers.

Starting a New Thread   Sometimes when you ask a question, you cannot find an answer. In these cases, you can post the question to the appropriate community forum. If, for example, you cannot find your answer in the search results, you can use the links on the right side of the page (see Figure 12.10) to navigate to the appropriate forum.

You would navigate to the Visual Studio General Forum if you were unable to find the answer to the question on changing the default language in the IDE. Clicking this link will take you to the main page for this forum. From here, you can click the New Thread button to post the question to the community. This question/thread will be added to the appropriate forum and marked unanswered. Typically, each forum has a group of people who peruse these unanswered questions and try to provide assistance.

Navigating Forums and Topics   The MSDN Community Forums are organized into a wide variety of high-level forum categories. These categories include web development, .NET, XML, Smart Devices, and, of course, Visual Studio. Figure 12.12 shows the Community Forums home page.

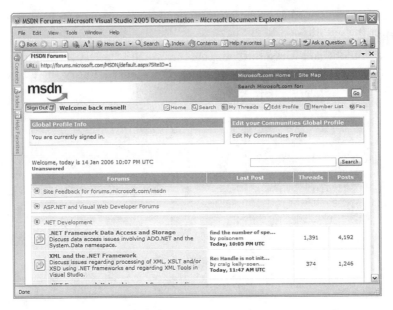

FIGURE 12.12   Community Forums home page.

Each forum category is further refined by the actual forums in the given category. You click on a forum category to navigate to the forums list for the given category. You can find forums that may be of particular interest to you in the Visual Studio category. Figure 12.13 shows the main page for the Visual Studio forums. From here, you can find forums on setup, MSBuild, the Class Designer, and many other IDE topics.

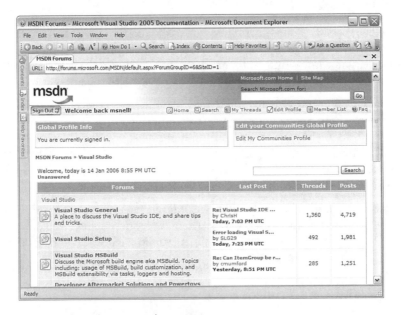

FIGURE 12.13   Visual Studio Forums home page.

Selecting a given forum will take you to the main page for that forum. From here, you can find information such as announcements, FAQs, top five most-viewed answers, and, of course, actual topics that have been posted to the forum. As an example, Figure 12.14 shows some of the topics found on the Visual Studio General Forum.

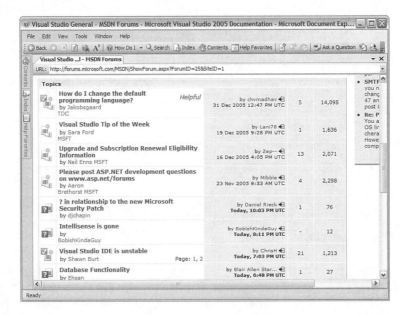

FIGURE 12.14   Forum Topics.

You may have noticed the many icons next to each topic in Figure 12.14. These icons help you to navigate through topics. When doing so, you quickly learn that not all topics are questions and not all questions are answered.

The icons next to each topic help to guide you to the content that is held within a given topic. For instance, a check mark over a document icon indicates that the topic is an answer to a question. Popular items will also have a sun attached to their icon. There are many icons with which you will want to become familiar. Figure 12.15 shows the icons and what they mean next to a given topic.

Managing Your Thread/Topic Alerts   Typically, when you start a new thread or post a new question, you will ask to receive alerts when someone makes a reply to your post or answers your question. In addition, if you find a topic that is of particular interest, you can request to be alerted when new posts are made to the thread. The MSDN Community Forums enable you to receive these alerts via email, instant messenger, or sent to a mobile device. This capability allows the community to stay in touch with its participating members without forcing them to constantly log in and check for activity.

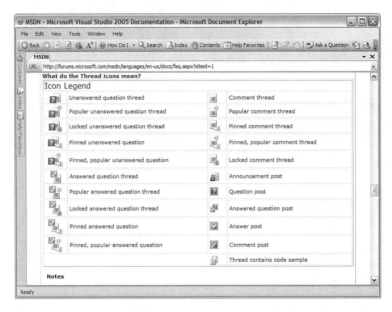

FIGURE 12.15   Topic icon legend.

Figure 12.16 shows some of the options you have for managing forum alerts. Notice that there are basic options and custom delivery. The latter allows for alerts to be sent based on your MSN Messenger status. If you are logged in, you can get an IM; if not, the alert can be forwarded to your email or phone.

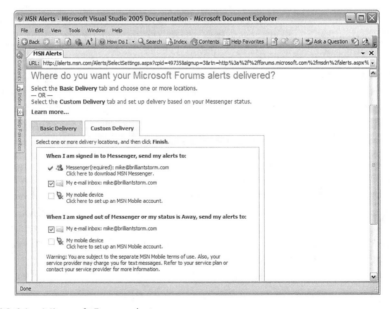

FIGURE 12.16   Microsoft Forum alerts.

Check Question Status

The Check Question Status button on the Community menu provides quick and easy navigation to the My Threads section of the MSDN Forums. From here, you have quick access to the threads you've started, participated in, or to which you've subscribed via alerts. Clicking this menu item is equivalent to selecting My Threads from the MSDN Forums menu.

Send Feedback

Most developers we've met love to work with cool software and are always looking for ways it might be improved. This holds especially true for their tools, the biggest of which is Visual Studio. Often you'll think of something that would make for a great addition or perhaps you'll find a flaw (or bug) in the software. Using the Send Feedback button on the Community menu, you can now post your suggestions and log any bugs you find. These items will go directly to the Visual Studio development team.

Clicking the Send Feedback button will take you to the MSDN Product Feedback Center home page. Figure 12.17 shows an example of this page. From here, you have access to any suggestions and bugs you have submitted; you can also keep tabs on items that you haven't submitted but are still of interest to you.

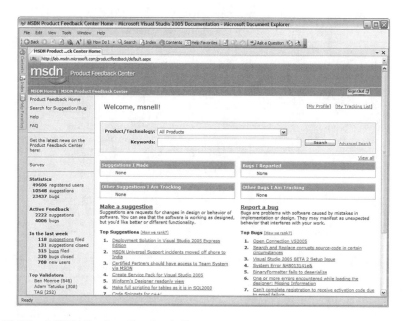

FIGURE 12.17   MSDN Product Feedback Center.

In addition to tracking bugs and suggestions, the site provides some interesting community-related statistics. Down the left side of the page, as shown in Figure 12.17, MSDN publishes the number of registered users, the total number of suggestions and bugs, and the numbers for the prior week. You can see by these numbers that the .NET community is large and very active.

Report a Bug or Make a Suggestion   The process for reporting bugs and making suggestions is similar to that of starting a new thread in the community forums. That is, the process starts by first searching for a similar suggestion or bug. This helps to reduce the creation of duplicate submissions.

If you do find a similar item to the one you had planned to report, you can vote or annotate (comment) the item. Voting allows Microsoft to prioritize an item in terms of its importance. Both the number of voters and the rating help to influence how the item is prioritized. Adding your comments to an item allows you to provide similar evidence or clarification to a reported bug or suggestion.

Microsoft actively monitors these lists. In fact, most items are marked with Microsoft comments and closed or resolved in new builds and service packs. In addition, if you find a bug for which you know a workaround, you can attach your workaround to the item. This is another way the .NET community can help itself.

Finally, you can help the Visual Studio team by trying to validate a specific bug. Typically, this involves following the "steps to reproduce" as posted by the person who logged the issue. You mark an item as either Can or Can't Validate. This allows the Visual Studio team to know more than one person is experiencing the issue.

Figure 12.18 shows the Bug Details toolbar across the top of the page. This toolbar contains links to the features we've discussed in this section.

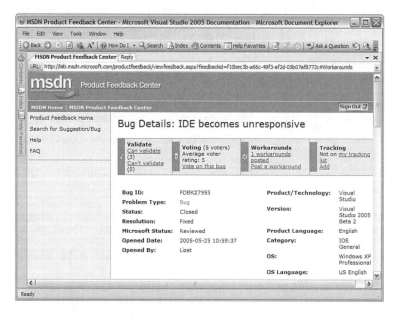

FIGURE 12.18   The Bug Details toolbar.

Developer Center

Clicking the Developer Center option from the Community menu will load one of the many MSDN developer center sites. Which center is loaded depends on how you've configured the IDE in terms of your primary usage. This is the same setting we discussed in the Start Page section. This setting not only controls your news channel but also sets your primary developer center. Refer to Table 12.1 for a list of common MSDN developer centers.

Codezone Community

The Codezone Community menu option is a link to Microsoft's list of independent .NET resources. These resources include sites dedicated to the .NET community, individual experts, user groups, and the like. This feature helps to broaden your access to communities outside just the Microsoft resources. These communities typically publish articles, blogs, code snippets, independent forums, and so on.

Codezone (http://msdn.microsoft.com/community/codezone/) membership is granted by the Visual Studio and .NET teams. This membership policy helps to ensure the quality of the sites. Each member is listed on Codezone, along with a description of what he or she adds to the .NET community. In addition, one member is highlighted each month for community effort. Finally, Codezone community members' content is indexed and made searchable through the Community Search feature (see the related section later in this chapter).

> **NOTE**
>
> If you know a site that should be included in the Codezone community, you can submit it for membership. You do so by sending an email to the Codezone team at codezone@microsoft.com. The email should include the site name, its URL, the primary contact details, and a brief history of the site. The Codezone team reviews each submission and selects its members based on terms they define.

Partner Products Catalog

As the name suggests, the Partner Products Catalog link in the Community menu provides access to Microsoft's partners and their products. The products listed on this site are developer tools and extensions to Visual Studio. Each product is from a Microsoft Visual Studio Industry Partner (or VSIP). The site enables you to browse products by a specific category or do a detailed search to find the exact third-party tool, add-in, or component you're looking for.

Community Search

The Community Search menu option on the Community menu links you to the search feature inside the MSDN help system. Of course, this search tool covers your local help files. However, it also reaches out to MSDN Online and the Codezone community sites to give you a wider coverage for your search results.

Selecting this menu option from the Visual Studio IDE opens a submenu from which to choose (see Figure 12.19). Notice that it allows you to quantify your search by content type. Content types include templates, code snippets, samples, controls, and add-ins. The search tool's content type parameter is set according to your selected option.

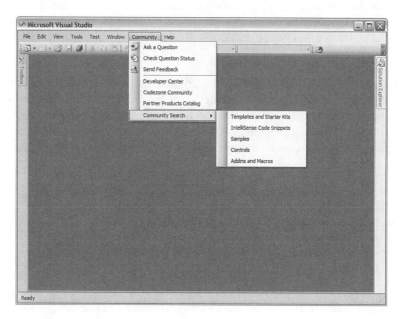

FIGURE 12.19   The Community Search submenu.

A number of parameters control your search. Content type, as we've discussed, is a big one. However, you can also set the development language you are referring to in your search and the technology. Development language indicates that you are looking for community content that is targeted at a particular language (C#, VB, C++, and so on). Of course, as with all of the options, you can select more than one. The technology parameter allows you to narrow your search to a particular set of technologies such as ASP .NET and .NET development. There are a large number of technologies on which you can search.

When you execute a search, the results are grouped by where they came from. This includes your local help, MSDN online, the Codezone community, and the forums (questions). Figure 12.20 shows the results for a particular search. We will look at using these community results in the coming sections.

Managing Search Options   You have some degree of control over Community Search through the Options dialog box. From inside the MSDN documentation, you can access these settings by choosing Tools, Options. You then select the Online item under the Help node. Figure 12.21 provides an example. You can navigate to this same set of options from within Visual Studio (choose Tools, Options and then select the Help node under Environment).

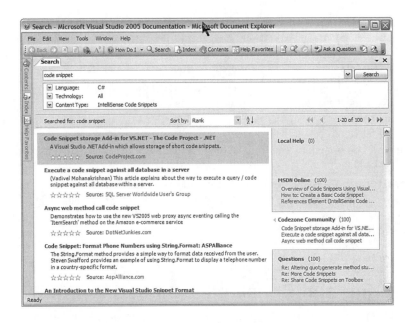

FIGURE 12.20   A Community Search in action.

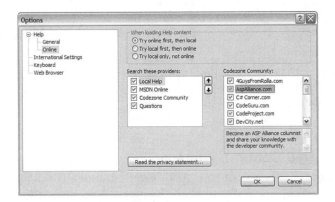

FIGURE 12.21   Community Search options.

These help options allow you to set your order of preference in terms of local versus online help. In addition, you can choose the help provider(s) you want to search. This includes turning on and off individual Codezone communities.

TIP

If you use a proxy server on your network, you might notice that the search does not work properly in the current release. It seems that authentication to the proxy is not being passed by the help system. Fortunately, a quick search of the community forums provided an answer to this issue.

To fix the problem, you need to change the help system's application configuration file located at `Program Files\Common Files\Microsoft Shared\Help 8\dexplore.exe.config`. You can modify this file in one of two ways. If your computer is a stationary desktop, you would add the following element to the `<system.net>` node:

```
<defaultProxy enabled="true" useDefaultCredentials="true">
  <proxy bypassonlocal="True" proxyaddress="http://yourproxy"/>
</defaultProxy>
```

If you use a laptop and have a proxy script that controls when and when not to use the proxy, you would add the following element:

```
<defaultProxy enabled="true" useDefaultCredentials="true">
  <proxy autoDetect="true" usesystemdefault="true" scriptLocation=
➥"file://c:/yourfile"/>
</defaultProxy>
```

Discovering and Consuming Shared Content

We have all been given programming tasks in which we *just know* someone must have already tackled the problem, and we've all faced tight deadlines. In these cases, it is often wise to hit the Internet to find out whether there is community content you can use to your advantage. At a minimum, you may find a partial solution that can speed your development effort and increase your understanding of how you might solve your particular problem.

Visual Studio 2005 provides a formal mechanism for publishing, finding, and consuming community content. In the following sections, we will look at discovering and leveraging this content. We will then demonstrate how you can be an active participant in this community.

Examining Shared Content Types

Visual Studio provides a number of code-sharing opportunities. For example, you might download a project template that defines an observer or singleton pattern, perhaps you'll find a code snippet that inserts a common method for accessing a database, or maybe you'll write a time-saving add-in or macro to share with the community. Visual Studio allows developers to write these types of extensions and more. Table 12.2 describes the many content types that provide opportunities for community sharing and consumption in Visual Studio 2005.

TABLE 12.2   Shared Content Types

Content	Description
Project Template	Project templates are the sets of files that define a new project. When you create a new project using Visual Studio, you are asked to select a project template. Visual Studio allows for the creation of your own project templates and the consumption of the same.

TABLE 12.2   Continued

Content	Description
Starter Kit	Starter kits are just like project templates but typically include additional documentation and step-by-step instruction.
Item Template	Item templates are files that you want to be able to reuse across projects. When you use Visual Studio to add a new item to your project, you are selecting and adding an item template. Item templates define the contents and structure of new items when added to a project. Visual Studio allows you to create and consume custom item templates.
Code Snippet	Code snippets are bits of code that you can add to the Visual Studio IntelliSense feature. You can create your own code snippets and share them with your community. A number of useful snippets are also available for download. We cover creating a custom code snippet in Chapter 7, "Working with Visual Studio's Productivity Aids."
Sample	A number of MSDN sample applications are available for download and installation. These files are typically `.zip` files and come in multiple languages (C# and VB being the most common).
Control	Controls can be both user and custom controls written for .NET. They may be free to the community and include source code, or they may be made for commercial purposes. You can write and share your own controls using Visual Studio.
Add-Ins & Macros	Add-ins and macros are typically extensions and enhancements to the development environment. Visual Studio supports the creation and sharing of these items. We cover add-ins and macros in-depth in Chapter 11, "Writing Macros, Add-ins, and Wizards."

Finding the Right Content

The first trick to leveraging the knowledge that exists out there is finding it. You have already seen the search feature that is built into the Visual Studio help system. However, it is worth noting that one of the search options is Content Type. This allows you to filter your search based on what you are looking for. For example, if you are looking only for a control or a code snippet, you can limit the search to content that has been tagged as such. Figure 12.22 shows the Content Type drop-down options.

Installing and Storing Shared Content

Visual Studio 2005 provides a tool called the Visual Studio Content Installer. Its role is to both allow content consumers to easily install content as well as help content creators package their content (more on this later). The Content Installer is invoked when you run a `.vsi` (Visual Studio Installer) file. The Content Installer is a wizard that walks you through installing shared content. The dialog boxes in the wizard are slightly different depending on what type of content you are installing. For example, Figure 12.23 shows the tool installing a Visual Basic code snippet. Notice that it prompts you as to which branch the snippet should be installed under (and thereby accessed from).

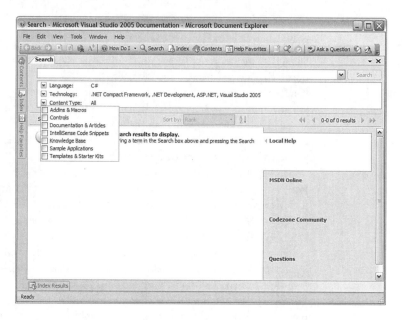

FIGURE 12.22   Content Type search.

FIGURE 12.23   The Visual Studio Content Installer.

Content that is not a macro, add-in, or snippet gets installed in one of the appropriate Visual Studio locations. There are paths for projects, project templates, and item templates. Figure 12.24 shows the Options dialog box that can be used to manage these paths. Note that if you have a lot of varied project and item templates, you may choose to set these paths to a network share.

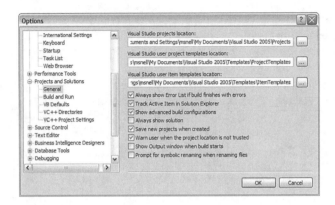

FIGURE 12.24   Setting project and item template storage locations.

We will examine this tool more closely in the upcoming section where we discuss how you can create and package your own content.

Giving Back to the Community

No matter how good Visual Studio gets, most developers often think of great additions or extensions to the existing functionality. These extensions may simply be project specific, or they may apply to all Visual Studio users. Of course, developers also like to write code. Therefore, it is not surprising that some go so far as to write their own custom extensions (add-ins, snippets, macros, and the like). This feat is often successful for single, personal use. The trouble comes when you want to share your time-saving creation with the rest of the team. Often, you end up writing a page of installation instructions and doing one-on-one troubleshooting with each developer as he or she installs your "timesaver."

Visual Studio 2005 offers a solution in the form of a packaging mechanism that allows developers to publish, exchange, and install Visual Studio content. Previously, we looked at consuming community content. Now we will demonstrate how you can package your own creations and exchange them with team members, friends, or through community websites.

Creating Shared Items (Project and Item Templates)

In previous chapters, we demonstrated how to create snippets, macros, and add-ins. What we have not covered is creating project and item templates. These items are very useful for large teams that want to disseminate standards and provide guidance. Rather than dedicating an entire chapter to these two items, we will cover them here as creating shared content.

Creating Project Templates

Project templates are what appear in Visual Studio's New Project dialog box. Projects are grouped by project type (C#, VB, Windows, Office, and so on). In addition, the templates themselves are split between Visual Studio installed templates and My Templates. The latter refers to the custom templates you install. Figure 12.25 shows the New Project dialog box in action. You choose between a project type or group and then between actual templates themselves.

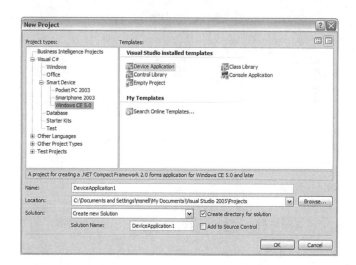

FIGURE 12.25   The New Project dialog box.

You can create a project template manually or use the Visual Studio Export Template Wizard. It simply makes the task of putting together the right XML files and zipping your project slightly easier. To create a project template, you follow these basic steps:

1. Create a project in Visual Studio (or start with an existing project).

2. Determine where (if any) parameters should exist in your template.

3. Choose the Export Template option from the File menu.

4. (Optional) Edit the .vstemplate XML.

Next, let's look at each of these steps.

Step 1: Create Your Project

Most templates you create will start with an existing Visual Studio template (or an empty project). Typically, developers look to templates to enforce standards and practices and provide guidance to teams. Therefore, the hardest part of creating a project template is defining the template itself in terms of what content should go into it. As an example, perhaps your team uses a common set of libraries, resources, or controls. You can define a project template that has these items either built in or referenced.

Step 2: Determine Project Parameters

Project parameters define the items that are set by default when Visual Studio sets up a new project based on the given template. For example, when you create a new project, the namespace of the code files is set to the namespace of the project. This is a project parameter. Visual Studio uses a number of *reserved template parameters* for this purpose. Table 12.3 provides an overview of these parameters.

TABLE 12.3   Reserved Template Parameters

Content	Description
clrversion	The version of the Common Language Runtime (CLR).
GUID[1=10]	A unique project ID. You can set up to 10 using GUID1, GUID2, and so on.
itemname	The name of the given item that the user types into the Add New Item dialog box—for example, MyNewClass.cs.
machinename	The user's computer name.
projectname	The name of the given project that the user types into the Add New Project dialog box—for example, MySmartClient.
registeredorganization	The Registry key value for the organization set during Windows installation.
rootnamespace	The namespace that will be set as the root for the current project.
safeitemname	Similar to the itemname but with all unsafe characters and spaces removed.
safeprojectname	Similar to the projectname but with all unsafe characters and spaces removed.
time	The current time on the user's computer.
userdomain	The domain the user has logged in to.
username	The name of the active user.
year	The current year as represented by the user's computer.

The Export Template Wizard helps you with these parameters. After you define them manually in your code, the Export Template Wizard will pick up the settings.

As an example, suppose you have a project template titled SmartClient. When a user chooses to create a project based on this template, you want the template to behave as another template in the dialog box. For instance, you want the project's namespace to be defined as the project name the user has chosen.

To implement parameters in the template, you define the parameter's position within the code. In the namespace example, you must use the reserved template parameter safeprojectname in place of the actual namespace defined throughout the code files in the project. This indicates to Visual Studio that when a new project is created, the namespace should be set to the safe project name as defined by the user. The following code example shows how to define the code:

```
namespace $safeprojectname$ {
    class Framework {
```

NOTE

Your code will not build with these parameters in place. Therefore, it is best to debug your code prior to setting up parameters.

Now that you've defined your parameters, the Export Template Wizard will pick them up and place them in the .vstemplate XML file. We will look at this in step 3.

Defining Custom Parameters   In addition to the aforementioned Visual Studio parameters, you can define your own custom parameters to be passed to your templates. The process is similar to using the reserved template parameters. You first define the parameters using the $parameter$ syntax in your code as follows:

```
string myCustomValue = "$CustomParameter1$";
```

You then edit the .vstemplate XML to include a <CustomParameters> node in which you define your replacements. We will look at this XML in more detail in the next major section; however, the following defines a custom parameter in the .vstemplate file:

```
<TemplateContent>

    ...

    <CustomParameters>

        <CustomParameter Name="$CustomParameter1$" Value="Some Custom Value"/>

    </CustomParameters>

</TemplateContent>
```

Visual Studio will replace the content of the custom parameter when a user creates a new instance of the project template. In the preceding example, the value of the variable myCustomValue will be set to Some Custom Value.

NOTE

The Export Template Wizard does not recognize custom parameters. You will have to edit the .vstemplate XML manually to include the CustomParameters node.

Step 3: Export Your Template

Now that you have defined your template and decided on template parameters, the next step is to run the Export Template Wizard. This wizard is used for both project and item templates. You access it from the File menu.

Figure 12.26 shows the first step in the wizard. Here, you are asked to choose the template type (project or item). You then must select a project from within the current, open Visual Studio solution. This project will serve as the basis for your template.

The next step in the Export Template Wizard allows you to define a few additional parameters for your template. You can set an icon for the template, you can indicate a name and description that show up in the New Project dialog box, and you can also choose the location where your template will be placed. Figure 12.27 shows an example of this dialog box.

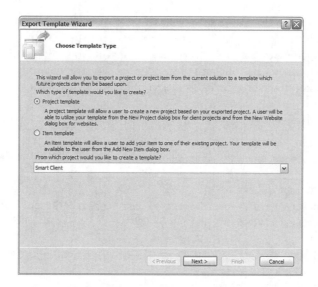

FIGURE 12.26   Export Template Wizard.

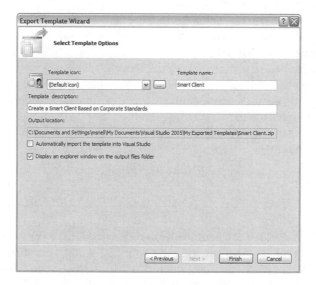

FIGURE 12.27   Export template options.

Notice that in the dialog box shown in Figure 12.27 the option Automatically Import the Template into Visual Studio is not checked. This is for two reasons. First, you want to edit the `.vstemplate` file the wizard generates, and second, you want to package the template for installation (we will look at this topic in the next major section). By default, the template is created in the My Exported Templates directory inside `\My Document\Visual Studio 2005`. The file is created as a `.zip` file (as are all Visual Studio templates).

Step 4: (Optional) Edit the .vstemplate XML

A fourth, optional, step in the process is to edit the .vstemplate XML. The Export
Template Wizard generates a default .vstemplate for you. You can open the .zip file, edit
the XML, rezip (compress) the file, and place it either directly into the template folder or
package for installation. Listing 12.1 shows a sample .vstemplate file.

LISTING 12.1   A Sample .vstemplate File

```
<VSTemplate Version="2.0.0"
  xmlns="http://schemas.microsoft.com/developer/vstemplate/2005" Type="Project">
  <TemplateData>
    <Name>Smart Client</Name>
    <Description>Corporate standard smart client template</Description>
    <ProjectType>CSharp</ProjectType>
    <ProjectSubType>
    </ProjectSubType>
    <SortOrder>1000</SortOrder>
    <CreateNewFolder>true</CreateNewFolder>
    <DefaultName>Smart Client</DefaultName>
    <ProvideDefaultName>true</ProvideDefaultName>
    <LocationField>Enabled</LocationField>
    <EnableLocationBrowseButton>true</EnableLocationBrowseButton>
    <Icon>__TemplateIcon.ico</Icon>
  </TemplateData>
  <TemplateContent>
    <Project TargetFileName="Smart Client.csproj" File="Smart Client.csproj"
      ReplaceParameters="true">
      <ProjectItem ReplaceParameters="true"
        TargetFileName="Framework.cs">Framework.cs</ProjectItem>
    </Project>
  </TemplateContent>
</VSTemplate>
```

Notice that the wizard added the `ReplaceParameters` attribute to the `ProjectItem` node
and set its value to `true`. This setting indicates to Visual Studio that it should swap any
parameters in the target file during project creation. In the example, `Framework.cs` is the
target file containing the parameters (`$safeprojectname$`).

> **TIP**
>
> You can actually create templates that contain multiple projects. To do so, you still create a
> .vstemplate file for each project in the solution. You then create a .vstemplate root file that
> describes the multiproject template. The data inside this XML is used by the New Project dialog
> box. The file also contains pointers to each individual project's .vstemplate file.

Installing the Template

Finally, all that is left to do is to package the template into a `.vsi` file (see the next section) for sharing. You can then install it. Figure 12.28 shows an example of a newly installed template under the My Templates subsection. Also, notice that the item should be installed for C#, Windows applications. This is done through the `.vsi` file. Again, we will cover this topic in the following section.

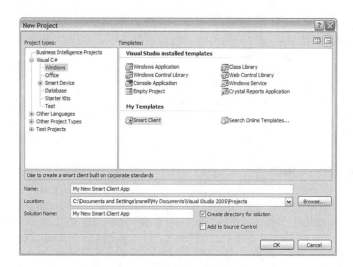

FIGURE 12.28   The installed template in the New Project dialog box.

Finally, when the project is generated, Visual Studio inserts the safe filename for the project namespace. Recall this was the reserved parameter you had set. The following code is inserted into `Framework.cs`:

```
namespace My_New_Smart_Client_App {
    class Framework {
```

Creating Item Templates

Item templates represent the various items or files you can add to Visual Studio projects. Selecting Add New Item opens a dialog box that allows you to select from the various Visual Studio items. You can also create your own items. Custom items could be time-saving devices that stub out the shell of a class or a specific type of class, for instance. Figure 12.29 shows the Add New Item dialog box. Notice the My Templates section, which is where custom templates appear in the list.

The good news is that you create item templates the same way you create project templates. You start with an existing item, edit it, and then use the Export Template Wizard to create a template from the item. You can also define the same set of parameters for items that you can for projects.

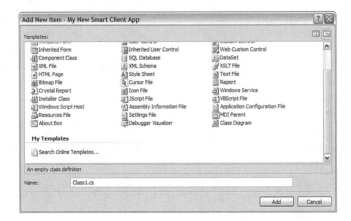

FIGURE 12.29   The My Templates section of the Add New Item dialog box.

Packaging Your Creation

As mentioned previously, Visual Studio 2005 provides a tool called the Visual Studio Content Installer. The role of this tool is to help developers install content that is targeted at the Visual Studio IDE. This content takes the form of Visual Studio content files (with the .vsi extension). After you've bundled your creation inside one of these files, the tool can easily install the content into the IDE. The good news is that creating these files is a relatively straightforward process.

Of course, the first step is to define and debug your creation (see Chapter 10, "The Visual Studio Automation Object Model," and Chapter 11, "Writing Macros, Add-ins, and Wizards," for more information on extending Visual Studio). Creations such as project and item templates, add-ins, macros, and code snippets can all be bundled as .vsi files. When you are ready to share your creation, you need to follow these steps (we will elaborate on them later):

1. Create a .VSContent file that contains XML describing your content.

2. Gather the file or files that define your creation.

3. Compress your files into a .zip file.

4. Rename the .zip file using the .vsi extension.

5. Optional: Sign your .vsi file.

This process is the same no matter the content type. You follow the same steps for macros, add-ins, and snippets. The install tool gets its information regarding your contents through the settings of your .VSContent XML file. Now let's explore this file in detail.

The Elements of a `VSContent` File

The `VSContent` file is an XML structure that contains elements for all pertinent items needed by the Visual Studio Content Installer. Your content is defined by a `Content` node (or element). This element is meant to define a single item of content you want to share (such as a macro file or control defined in a `.dll` file). Listing 12.2 presents the high-level structure of the `VSContent` file. This is neither a real example nor the official XSD. Rather, it serves to present the elements and their relations to one other.

LISTING 12.2   The Structure of a `.VSContent` File

```
<VSContent xmlns="http://schemas.microsoft.com/developer/vscontent/2005">
  <Content>
    <FileName></FileName>
    <DisplayName></DisplayName>
    <Description></Description>
    <FileContentType></FileContentType>
    <ContentVersion></ContentVersion>
    <Attributes>
      <Attribute name="" value=""/>
    </Attributes>
  </Content>
</VSContent>
```

> **TIP**
>
> The actual XSD that defines the structure of a `VSContent` file is a bit lengthy to reprint here. However, if you would like to examine the XSD file that defines the structure for valid `VSContent` XML, you can do so. The file is stored at `C:\Program Files\Microsoft Visual Studio 8\Xml\Schemas\1033\` and is named `vscontent.xsd`.

You can point to multiple content types and their associated files using a single `.vsi` file. You do so by creating multiple instances of the `Content` element, one for each item you want to share. For example, a single `.vsi` file could contain a `Content` node that installs a code snippet and another `Content` node that points to a `.vsmacro` file containing macros.

Each element inside Listing 12.2 is covered in depth in Table 12.4. We will walk through an actual example of creating and using a `VSContent` file in the following section.

TABLE 12.4   Elements of a `VSContent` File

Element	Description
FileName	This element represents the name of the file that contains the item to be installed as the content. A single `Content` element can contain multiple `FileName` elements, depending on the situation. For example, you may define a `VSContent` file to install an add-in. The add-in might contain both an `.Addin` file and a `.dll` file.

TABLE 12.4   Continued

Element	Description
DisplayName	This is the name of your content. The Visual Studio Content Installer displays this name when users install your creation.
Description	This element is used as the ToolTip text for your content inside the Visual Studio Content Installer.
FileContentType	This represents the type of content defined by the given Content node. This value is enumerated and therefore must be one of the following settings: Addin, Macro Project, Code Snippet, VSTemplate, Toolbox Control.
ContentVersion	This element represents a version number for your content. The only valid setting at this time is 1.0. All other settings will result in an error.
Attributes	This element is used to group Attribute elements.
Attribute	You can use attributes to further define code snippet and VSTemplate content. These settings are discussed further in the next section.

Using Attributes to Define VSTemplates and Code Snippets   The Attribute element inside the VSContent file provides the Visual Studio Content Installer additional information for content types that include project templates, item templates, and code snippets. The Attributes node is not used for the content types Addin, Macro Project, and Toolbox Control.

The Attribute element consists of a name/value pair. You set the name and value of the element using XML attributes in the following format:

```
<Attribute name="" value=""/>
```

Both the name and the value attributes are defined with enumerated values. These enumerated values define the possible setting combinations you can define for code snippets and templates.

For code snippets, only the value lang is applicable for the name attribute. Setting the lang attribute on code snippets allows you to indicate the development language to which the snippet applies. Possible entries for the value attribute when defined with lang include csharp, jsharp, vb, and xml. For example, if your code snippet is meant to work with Visual Basic, you would define your attribute as follows:

```
<Attribute name="lang" value="vb"/>
```

When defining content of type VSTemplate, you can use the following enumerated items for the name attribute:

- TemplateType—Defines the type of template your content represents. Values are either Project for project templates or Item for item templates.

- ProjectType—Defines the type of project contained in your template. Possible enumerated items for the value attribute are Visual Basic, Visual C#, Visual J#, and Visual Web Developer.

- ProjectSubType—Defines the subcategory in which your template is placed in the New Project dialog box. Possible entries include Windows, Office, Smart Device, Database, Starter Kits, and Test.

Recall the Smart Client project template you created in the previous section. Listing 12.3 represents the VSContent file used to define the installation for the Smart Client. Notice the three attribute definitions. This combination allows for the configuration shown in Figure 12.28 (the New Project dialog box).

LISTING 12.3   The VSContent File for the Smart Client Example

```xml
<VSContent xmlns="http://schemas.microsoft.com/developer/vscontent/2005">
  <Content>
    <FileName>Smart Client.zip</FileName>
    <DisplayName>Smart Client</DisplayName>
    <Description>Install a smart client project template</Description>
    <FileContentType>VSTemplate</FileContentType>
    <ContentVersion>1.0</ContentVersion>
    <Attributes>
      <Attribute name="TemplateType" value="Project"/>
      <Attribute name="ProjectType" value="Visual C#"/>
      <Attribute name="ProjectSubType" value="Windows"/>
    </Attributes>
  </Content>
</VSContent>
```

An Example: Packaging a Macro

As with most things, the best way to understand the Visual Studio content packaging process is to work through a real example. In this case, we will take a few of the macros defined in Chapter 10 and bundle them for sharing with the community.

Step 1: Create the VSContent **File**   After you've debugged and tested your creation, the first step in packaging it is to define the VSContent file. For this example, we've created a macro file that contains a few macros from previous chapters, including the InsertTemplateFlowerbox macro that places common comment structure above the Visual Basic Subs and Functions, the ResizeIDE macro, and others. The name of the macro file is VS2005_Unleashed.vsmacros.

Any easy way to define the VSContent file is to open the Visual Studio IDE, select File, New, and then select New File. In the resulting dialog box, select XML File. Remember, the VSContent file is nothing more than an XML file with a special extension in the filename (VSContent). In this way, you can create and edit your VSContent file directly in Visual Studio. You will have to edit the filename from .xml to VSContent. However, using Visual Studio allows you to take advantage of the built-in XML editor that includes IntelliSense.

The first step in defining the content of this file is to set the XML namespace (`xmlns`) to the proper schema. You do this by adding the following root node to the file:

```
<VSContent xmlns="http://schemas.microsoft.com/developer/vscontent/2005">
```

After you've done this, Visual Studio will recognize the intended structure for the XML and guide you through defining additional elements. Figure 12.30 shows an example of creating the `VSContent` file inside the IDE. Note that for the example, you define the `FileName` element to point to the macro file. You also must set the `FileContentType` to the enumerated value `Macro Project`. This ensures that the example is installed in the proper location for macros.

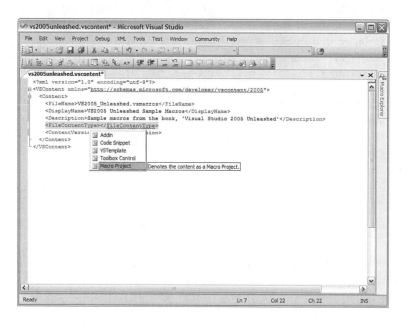

FIGURE 12.30   Defining the `VSContent` file inside the IDE.

Step 2: Gather Files That Define Your Creation   The next step is to place all your files into a single directory where they can easily find each other. You need to include in your bundle any files that are called out in the `VSContent` file (`.vsmacros`, `.dll`, `.addin`) and the `VSContent` file itself. For some files and projects, you may have to dig a little. For this macro project, the `.vsmacros` file created as a new macro project is stored in the `VSMacros80` folder. This folder exists inside the path `\My Documents\Visual Studio 2005\Projects\`.

In this example, you create a folder named `VS2005 Unleashed Macros`. In it, you place the macro file named `VS2005_Unleashed.vsmacros` and the `VSContent` file named `VS2005_Unleashed.vsmacros`.

TIP

If you are creating a macro project and want to include it in a .vsi file, you will first need to find it! By default, Visual Studio stores custom macro projects in the folder \My Documents\Visual Studio 2005\Projects\VSMacros80.

Step 3: Compress (Zip) Files   The process of compressing the files should be familiar to all developers. You can use Window's built-in capability to compress files, or you can use a compression tool. In this example use the Windows compression tool. You select the .vsmacros and VSContent files, right-click, and then choose Send To, Compressed (Zipped) Folder.

Step 4: Rename the .zip **File to** .vsi   The result of step 3 was the creation of a file named vs2005unleashed.zip. Now you're ready for the easiest step. Right-click the .zip file and choose Rename from the context menu. Remove the .zip extension and replace it with .vsi. That's it. If you are on a machine with Visual Studio installed, the new file will take on the .vsi icon (used for both .vsi and VSContent files). Figure 12.31 shows an example of these files and their icons.

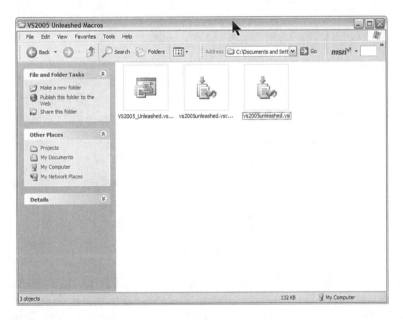

FIGURE 12.31   The packaged files.

Installing the Sample Content   All that remains is to distribute the .vsi file to the intended audience. Of course, it would be prudent to do a couple of test installations first. Let's look at the Visual Studio Content Installer tool in action.

First, in Figure 12.31, notice that both the .vsi and the VSContent files are Visual Studio Content Installer (VSContentInstaller.exe) files. They have the same icon. The reason is that both can be used to install the content.

There are some differences between the two, however. The .vsi file is fully self-contained. It does not require additional files for installation, whereas the VSContent file must exist in a directory that also contains the related content files. In addition, when you run the VSContent file, you are not warned about the lack of a signature (if one is lacking). Therefore, you might think that there is a bug or that these files are more appropriate for internal installations. The .vsi file, on the other hand, prompts you with a security warning dialog box if the content is not signed by a publisher. This, along with the single file and compression factor, seems to make the .vsi file ideal in larger, distributed scenarios.

Let's examine the installation process for the .vsi file. First, you double-click the file to invoke the Visual Studio Content Installer. Figure 12.32 shows the example loaded in the tool.

FIGURE 12.32   The Visual Studio Content Installer.

From this screen, you can select View Files in Windows Explorer to examine the files that will be installed by the .vsi. Also, notice that the Publisher Information section is blank. The reason is that the bundle is not signed. When you click the Next button, the tool prompts you with a warning regarding the lack of signature. Figure 12.33 shows this warning. Again, this warning is not shown if you are installing from the VSContent file directly. For now, click Yes and move on. In the sidebar, we will discuss signing your work.

FIGURE 12.33 No Signature Found warning.

Signing Your Work

To sign your .vsi files with Authenticode, you must get a valid software publisher certificate (.spc) from a certificate authority (CA). Of course, this requires that you have a company set up and that you fill out an application as such. Visual Studio does have a few test tools to help developers understand the process prior to working with a CA. These tools include the following:

- Zip to Exe Conversion Tool (MakeZipExe.exe)
- Certificate Creation Tool (MakeCert.exe)
- Software Publisher Certificate Test Tool (Cert2spc.exe)
- Sign Tool (SignTool.exe)

The vision for these tools is as follows: You use the MakeZipExe.exe tool to convert your .zip file to an .exe file (because code signing requires an .exe or .dll). You then use the SignTool.exe to sign the resulting .exe. You then convert this file into a .vsi file for publication.

If you do not have a valid certificate from a CA, you can create a test certificate (not to be used for publishing) with the MakeCert.exe tool. You then must convert this certificate into a software publisher certificate (.spc) using the Cert2spc.exe.

Be aware that the shipping version of MakeZipExe.exe contains a bug! Therefore, none of this currently works. Look for Microsoft to post a fix soon. There are also some good blog entries out there with possible workarounds.

Next, the installer prepares you to finish the installation. Figure 12.34 shows an example. When you click the Finish button, the installer writes the files to the appropriate folders based on content type. If the given file already exists, the installer prompts you to find out whether you want it left as is or overwritten.

FIGURE 12.34   Finishing the installation.

When you click Finish, the installer finishes its job and reports back. Figure 12.35 shows a successful installation.

FIGURE 12.35   A successful installation.

> **TIP**
>
> To help streamline the creation of .vsi files, a GotDotNet workspace (http://www.gotdotnet.com/workspaces/) was created. If you navigate to the site and search for "Visual Studio Content Installer Power Toys," you will be able to find the workspace. This wizard tool has some related files that aid in the creation of the .vsi files.

Publishing Your Creation

You can publish your `.vsi` files to your coworkers, friends, team, or to other developers. You also can post them on a network share, email them, or drop them on a content-sharing website such as www.gotdotnet.com or similar community sites.

Summary

This chapter presented the many community options inside Visual Studio 2005. Developers can expect to feel part of a larger community that surrounds .NET. Microsoft has tried to build in a community to .NET. You see it with the Start Page inside Visual Studio, the options on the Community menu, and within the capability to search the community from the help file.

Don't forget that being part of the developer community means giving back to it once in a while. Visual Studio provides the tools to make that happen. You can create and share project and item templates, code snippets, macros, add-ins, and controls. After you've created these items, Visual Studio provides the Visual Studio Content Installer framework in which to package your shared content for distribution. Now, the next time you write a great time-saving macro or snippet, you will have the know-how to package it up and share it with others.

12

PART III

Visual Studio 2005 at Work

CHAPTER 13   Creating ASP.NET User Interfaces   465

CHAPTER 14   Building Windows Forms   517

CHAPTER 15   Working with Databases   553

CHAPTER 16   Web Services and Visual Studio   595

Creating ASP.NET User Interfaces

IN THIS CHAPTER

- The Basics of an ASP.NET Website

- Designing Your User Interface

- Working with the ASP.NET Controls

Visual Studio 2005 and the .NET Framework 2.0 represent a major overhaul of all .NET web development. Every place you turn—controls, security, data binding, configuration— you name it, there is something new for web developers. These additions and changes provide additional productivity and confidence in building web applications with .NET.

This chapter is focused on creating user interfaces with ASP.NET. We first cover the basics around defining web projects and web forms. We then move on to designing a cohesive UI with master pages, themes, and web parts. Finally, we focus on the controls inside ASP.NET.

> **NOTE**
>
> ASP.NET is a huge topic. We are not able to dig in on its every aspect. Instead, we will concentrate on areas where you can leverage Visual Studio to increase your productivity in building web-based user interfaces. This is a key topic for all web developers.
>
> We expect that as you build your ASP.NET interface you will discover places that require further exploration. To that end, we will try to point out some of them as we move through the chapter. Some examples include membership, user profiles, advances in caching, website administration, and cross-page posting.

The Basics of an ASP.NET Website

Websites in .NET start with a website project. The website project represents a connection between Visual Studio and the development version of your website (see Chapter 4, "Solutions and Projects," for more information). What is meant by *website*, however, continues to evolve and expand.

Simple HTML sites with hyperlinks and images are rarely created anymore or even discussed seriously as websites. In fact, .NET has pushed the definition well beyond the original ASP model of HTML and script. Today, a website means web forms, compiled code that links those web forms to a middle tier, master pages, themes, configuration, databases and data binding, DLLs, and so on. Visual Studio 2005 brings these concepts together to define the current view of a .NET website. In the following sections, we will examine the makeup of these sites and how to create and configure them.

Creating a New Web Application Project

A web application project represents a template for a site. This template defines default directories, configuration, pages, and other files and settings. Visual Studio ships with a number of website templates. These templates allow you to define a few different versions of a website. You can also use these templates as a basis to define your own, custom templates (see project templates in Chapter 12, "The .NET Community: Consuming and Creating Shared Code," for more information).

Websites are no longer considered just another Visual Studio project (like Windows forms or a library application). Instead, websites have been elevated and given their own status in Visual Studio. To create one, you choose the New Web Site option from the File menu. This launches the New Web Site dialog box, which is very different from your standard new project dialog box. Figure 13.1 shows an example. We'll look at the many items that make defining a website a unique process.

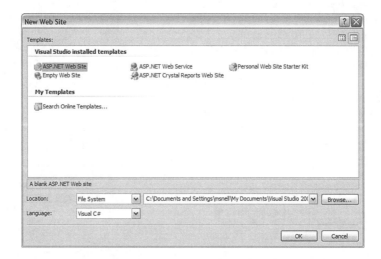

FIGURE 13.1   Creating a new website.

Selecting a Visual Studio Website Template

Visual Studio installs five ASP.NET templates by default. You pick a template based on your needs. However, the majority of sites will be built with the standard template, ASP.NET Web Site. The five default ASP.NET templates are as follows:

- **ASP.NET Web Site**—Represents a basic ASP.NET website with an `App_Data` directory and a `Default.aspx` web form. This is the template most commonly used to start sites.

- **ASP.NET Web Service**—Represents a site focused on creating a web service (see Chapter 16, "Web Services and Visual Studio," for more details).

- **Personal Web Site Starter Kit**—Generates a site meant for individuals to publish their own personal information such as their resume and links. We provide an overview of this template in the following section.

- **Empty Web Site**—Represents a website project devoid of all folders and files. You use this project container as a starting point. It does not presume folders and files. Instead, you explicitly add these items yourself as required.

- **ASP.NET Crystal Reports Web Site**—Creates a site that leverages Crystal reports for the .NET Framework. Creating this site will not only drop a report in your project and set appropriate references, but will also launch a wizard to walk you through configuring a report.

The Personal Web Site Starter Kit   The most ambitious ASP.NET template is the Personal Web Site Starter Kit. This template generates a full working site that you can customize and use to publish a site about yourself. However, more importantly, this site serves as a nice sample showing how to leverage some of the new features of ASP.NET, such as themes, master pages, and object data binding. Figure 13.2 shows the many files and folders inside this template.

Again, using this sample application can be a good way to explore these concepts further. We will cover most of these concepts throughout the chapter. However, we want to make sure you are aware of this template should you want to walk through a sample in the IDE. Figure 13.3 shows the default version of this site running in a browser.

Choosing a Website Location

In prior versions of .NET, you were essentially stuck (or boxed in) when creating a location for your development website. You had to be running IIS locally, and you had to store your web application inside the wwwroot folder structure. This severely limited your options.

This model caused a number of problems. The first was that typically your application was spread all over your machine. You would have your solution file and .dll projects inside one directory and your web application buried on your C drive in a special directory.

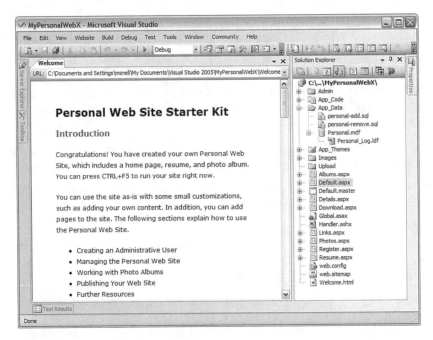

FIGURE 13.2   The Personal Web Site Starter Kit.

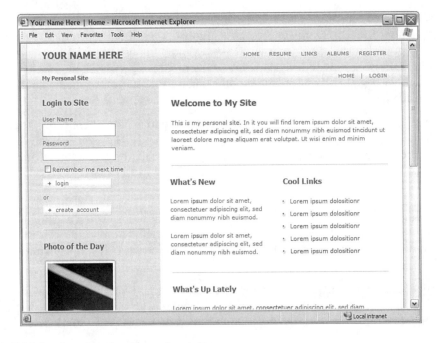

FIGURE 13.3   Running the personal website.

The second was that this model forced IT managers to allow IIS servers on every developer desktop (or not get work done). This typically broke standard policy. In addition, developers were often running a version of IIS that did not match the version of their servers (Windows Server 2003, for example).

Finally, other developers might have a hosted version of their application or might work off a shared development server. Typically, these developers would have access to the server through FTP or HTTP. However, they had no good way to access these files with these protocols and Visual Studio. Therefore, they were forced to work locally and then worry about deployment onto these servers.

Visual Studio 2005 solves every one of these issues. Your options for connecting to the development version of your application are vastly expanded. You can now work with your application using a local IIS server or not. Instead, you might work with the file system and a runtime development web server. Or you may work on a remote server and connect to it with FTP or HTTP. Let's look at configuring these many location options.

You define the location for your website when creating it or connecting to it. Recall that in Figure 13.1 there was a drop-down list for location. This list contains the values, file system, HTTP, and FTP. Each of these locations requires you to navigate to the appropriate location and provide the appropriate credentials to create your site. Alternatively, you can click the Browse button and navigate to each location individually. Clicking this button launches the Choose Location dialog box. In the following sections, we'll look at the many options of this dialog box.

File System You can choose any directory on your machine to store the contents of your website. The Choose Location dialog box allows you to navigate the file system and select or create a new folder. Figure 13.4 shows this dialog box for selecting a folder. The Create New Folder button is in the upper-right corner.

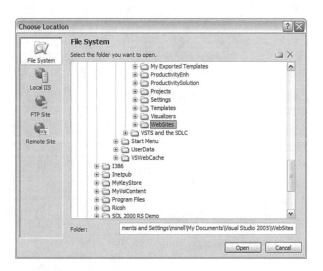

FIGURE 13.4 Selecting a file system location.

If you choose File System for your local website development, then you don't need to have IIS on your machine. Instead, Visual Studio recognizes the content in the directory as a website and runs a local instance of ASP.NET Development Server. This server mimics IIS and can be run and killed on an as-needed basis. You end up with an instance for each website you are currently running, debugging, or even building with Visual Studio.

Each development server instance is listed in your system tray. You can right-click an instance and navigate to it, stop it, or view its details. An example of the development server details window is shown in Figure 13.5.

FIGURE 13.5   The ASP.NET Development Server details window.

TIP

By default, the development server runs on a random port. However, you can force a specific port for the server. To do so, you select the website and view its properties. Figure 13.6 shows an example. You can set the Use dynamic ports property to False and then force a port number using the Port number property.

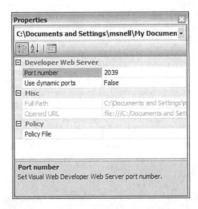

FIGURE 13.6   Forcing a port number for the development server.

Local IIS   Visual Studio still allows you to configure a web application using a local instance of IIS. This capability gives you the benefit of being able to run the server even when you're not developing. It also lets you have more control over the configuration of your site using the IIS administration tool.

Select the Local IIS option to define a website on your local server. Figure 13.7 shows the dialog box with this option selected. There are three buttons in the upper-right corner. In order, these buttons allow you to create a new web application, create a new virtual directory, and delete a selected item. If you choose to create a new virtual directory, you are asked to define a directory name and a folder location where you want to store the site. You are not bound to wwwroot. Instead, you can create your site using any folder. You can also choose to connect to this site via Secure Sockets Layer (SSL). This capability is useful if you need to encrypt sensitive information between the development machine and the server.

FIGURE 13.7   Creating a website on your local version of IIS.

FTP Site   You can define your website to exist on an FTP server. To do so, you must enter the address of the server and the port and provide appropriate credentials. All FTP rules apply (passwords are not secure). Figure 13.8 shows the FTP website settings. Note that sites created using FTP are run using the local ASP.NET Development Server. FTP is simply used to retrieve and store the files.

Remote HTTP Site   Finally, you can choose a remote web server to define your website. This is similar to running on IIS locally. However, here you actually can use a shared development server. The development server must have FrontPage Server Extensions applied to allow this type of connectivity. Figure 13.9 shows an example of configuring a site's location to be a remote IIS server.

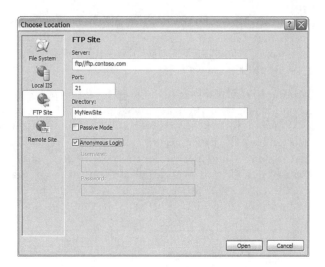

FIGURE 13.8 Defining a website with FTP.

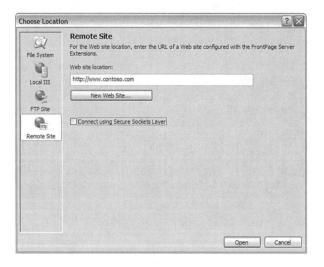

FIGURE 13.9 Creating a website on a remote server.

Choosing a Default Programming Language

Visual Studio 2005 allows you to mix the languages you use to develop the items in your site. When you create a web form or a class file, you determine the language in which each individual item is written. However, when you create a new site, you set a default language for the site. This default language is set in the New Web Site dialog box (recall Figure 13.1). Setting this value tells Visual Studio how to generate your template. In addition, it sets the initial value for the setting that controls the default language of new items being added to your site.

Figure 13.10 shows a website with mixed code. There are two web files: one with a code-behind written in VB and one with a C# code-behind. Also, you can mix C# and VB class files. To do this, you have to put the class files into separate directories.

FIGURE 13.10   A website with mixed VB and C# files.

Understanding the File Makeup of Your Website

A number of files go into the definition of an ASP.NET website. In addition, Visual Studio 2005 adds a number of additional, "special" directories. The following sections provide a reference for the many directories and files that define a .NET website.

Directories   ASP.NET defines a number of folders that it uses to organize and recognize various files that make up your application. These folders have reserved names that mean something special to ASP.NET; therefore, you should use them appropriately. Table 13.1 lists each directory along with a basic explanation of each.

TABLE 13.1   ASP.NET Directories

Directory	Description
Bin	This folder contains the compiled code (.dll files) that your application references.
App_Code	This folder houses the class files that help to define your application. For example, you could choose to put your business object classes in this directory.
	The code in this directory is compiled together. This includes subdirectories. Therefore, all code in the directory must be of the same language.
App_Data	This directory contains data files used by your applications. This can be an .mdf file (SQL Express) or XML data and so on.
App_GlobalResources	This folder contains the resource files (.resx and .resources) that make up your application.
App_LocalResources	This folder also contains resource files. However, these files are specific to a page or control. They are not global to the application.
App_WebReferences	This folder is used for references to web services. It will contain the web service contract (.wsdl), the schemas (.xsd), the discovery files (disco), and other related files.

13

TABLE 13.1 Continued

Directory	Description
App_Browsers	This folder contains browser definition files (.browser). These files are most often used for mobile applications. They define the various capabilities of a given browser.
App_Themes	This folder contains subfolders for each theme in an application. The theme folders contain skins (.skin), styles (.css), and images. See "Creating a Common Look and Feel" later in this chapter.

You can add an ASP.NET directory to your application via the context menu for the site. Figure 13.11 shows this operation and lists many of the ASP.NET-specific content directories.

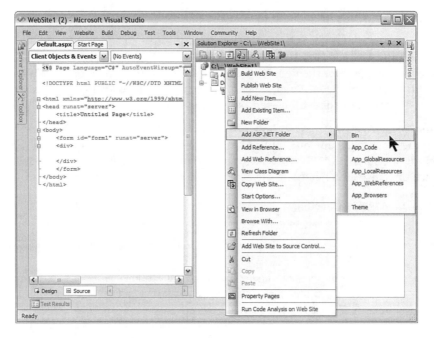

FIGURE 13.11 Adding an ASP.NET directory to your website.

Files   Numerous files and file types define a typical ASP.NET website. Of course, there are files that you use often, such as web form, user control, class, and configuration; and then there are those that are rarer, such as skin, resource, and site map—and there are many in between. Table 13.2 lists some of the more common files in an ASP.NET web application.

TABLE 13.2   ASP.NET Files

File Extension	Description
.aspx	Defines an ASP.NET web form. This is the most common ASP.NET file. See "Creating Web Pages" later in this chapter.
.asmx	Defines an ASP.NET web service. See Chapter 16.
.ascx	Represents an ASP.NET user control.
.asax	Creates a global application class. This class defines application and session-level events.
.cs/.vb	Define a class file. The extension .cs is a C# class file. The .vb extension is a class written in Visual Basic.
.master	Represents a master page. A master page is used to define a common look and feel for an application. See "Master Pages" later in this chapter.
.config	Represents a configuration file for your web application. You use the configuration file to manage settings such as debugging and to store application-specific data (such as an encrypted connection string to a database).
.css	Represents a cascading style sheet. It stores the styles of your application or theme. See "Style Sheets" later in this chapter.
.skin	Represents a skin for one or more controls in your application. A skin is defined for an application theme. See "Themes and Skins" later in this chapter.

You add a new ASP.NET file to your application via the context menu for the site (by right-clicking and selecting Add New Item). Figure 13.12 shows the Add New Item dialog box. The many files that are available to your site are also listed as item templates. Visual Studio will take care to place each file in a special directory if applicable.

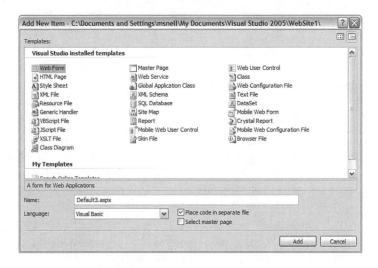

FIGURE 13.12   Adding an ASP.NET file to your website.

Controlling Project Properties and Options

ASP.NET applications have their own set of properties and configuration options. These properties control how an application works, is built, works with the debugger, and so on. You access the properties for your website through the Property Pages dialog box. You can open this dialog box through the context menu for your website. The following sections cover the many options of this dialog box.

References

The references in your application define the code that your application uses by reference. That is, this code is not written as part of this application but exists in another. Figure 13.13 shows the References portion of the Property Pages dialog box.

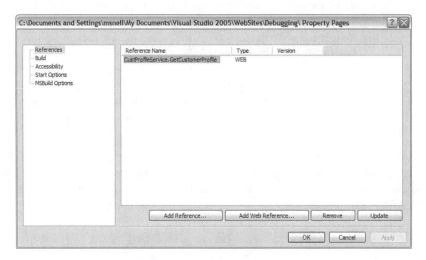

FIGURE 13.13   Managing web application references.

Each current reference for the website is listed along with its associated reference type. In the figure, there is a web reference (web service) listed. From this dialog box, you can add a new reference, remove an existing reference, or refresh (update) the reference.

Adding a New Reference   You can add two types of references to your ASP.NET applications: a standard reference or a web reference (we cover web references in Chapter 16). A standard reference can be made to a `.dll` file that exists as part of another application or project. Establishing this reference will place a copy of the compiled `.dll` file into your `bin` directory. The namespaces, classes, and methods will then be available for you to code against.

Figure 13.14 shows the Add Reference dialog box. You can use the tabs across the top of the dialog box to find the specific item you want to reference. If, for example, you are looking to reference a namespace from the .NET Framework, you would select the .NET tab. You can also set references to COM components, browse for `.dll` files, and view recent references.

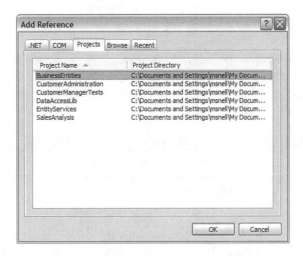

FIGURE 13.14   Adding a new reference to your web application.

Finally, the figure shows project-specific references. These items are projects that exist in the current solution. If you set a project reference, then your references are automatically refreshed when those projects are recompiled.

Build

The Build page of the Property Pages dialog box also allows you to control how your application is built using Visual Studio. Figure 13.15 shows the options that are available.

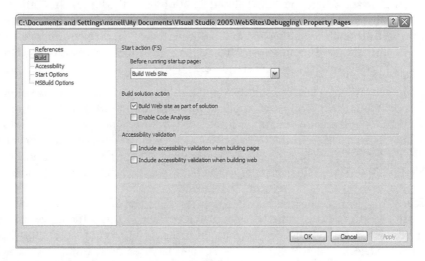

FIGURE 13.15   Controlling the build options for your site.

Start Action   The Start Action section of the Build page allows you to define how your application is compiled when you run it from the IDE. There are three options in this drop-down: No Build, Build Page, and Build Web Site (the default). Let's look at each of these options.

The No Build option tells the IDE to just launch the site in a browser without doing any compilation. In this instance, as pages and items are accessed, they are built. Instead of the errors showing in the IDE before you run the application, the errors are displayed in the browser as you find them.

TIP

The No Build capability can be great when you have a large application that contains pages that you are not working on or that have errors (and you intend to avoid). It also speeds the startup time because no pages are precompiled.

The Build Page option tells the IDE to compile only the current startup page or the page you're working on. This capability is very useful if you work on only one page at a time. If the IDE finds errors, they are shown in the IDE before the page launches.

Last, the Build Web Site option, the default setting, tells the IDE to build the entire website and all dependent projects prior to launching into the browser. This capability can be helpful if you are working on a small site by yourself. However, it can also cause longer build times on larger projects.

Build Solution Action   There are two options under Build Solution Action in the Build page. The first, Build Web Site as Part of Solution, indicates whether Visual Studio should include the website as part of the solution's build. The default for this setting is true (or checked). In this case, when you choose Build Solution from the Build menu, the website will also be built. The second option, Enable Code Analysis, indicates whether you want to have the website analyzed by Visual Studio (formerly FxCop) for performance, unused variables, naming standards, and so on. This can be a great tool for ensuring developers are adhering to common .NET coding standards.

Accessibility Validation   The Accessibility Validation options in the Build page allow you to have Visual Studio check your web application for conformance with accessibility standards. These standards ensure your application will work for people with disabilities. The actual standards are covered in the next section. Here, you have two options: enable validation for the entire site or just the current startup page. If these options are enabled, Visual Studio displays accessibility issues in the IDE when you run the application.

Accessibility

The Accessibility page of the Property Pages dialog box allows you to define what checks should be done relative to your site's conformance. Figure 13.16 shows the options for configuring the checks. There are three levels of checks based on two standards: the W3C's Web Content Accessibility Guidelines (WCAG) 1 and 2, and the U.S. government's standards for accessibility (Access board section 508).

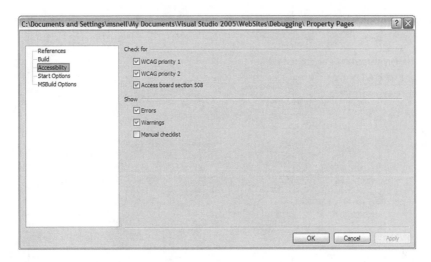

FIGURE 13.16   Managing accessibility options.

13

> **TIP**
>
> Visual Studio checks only your HTML pages for accessibility standards compliance. It does not check ASP controls because those controls emit their own HTML. Therefore, if you need to check an entire page that combines HTML and ASP, you must copy the HTML from the page and embed it as a separate HTML file in your solution. For more information, see "Walkthrough: Creating an Accessible Web Application" at the MSDN website.

Start Options

The Start Options page in the Property Pages dialog box allows you to define what happens when you start (or run) your application. Figure 13.17 shows the many options available. We'll look at each in the following sections.

Start Action   The Start Action section of the Start Options page is useful for defining what happens when a page is loaded when you start your application through the IDE. The first option, User Current Page, tells the IDE to start the application using the current, active page in the IDE. This capability can be great for developers who work on one standalone page at a time. The next option, Specific Page, allows you to set a startup page. This is akin to right-clicking a page and choosing Set as Start Page. The third option, Start External Program, allows you to specify an .exe file to run (instead of the browser) when you start the application. The Start URL option allows you to send the browser to a different URL when running your application. This capability can be useful when debugging a web service. You might launch a client that uses your web service, for example. Finally, you can use the last option to tell Visual Studio to wait for a request (don't start anything). This, too, can be useful for a web service scenario.

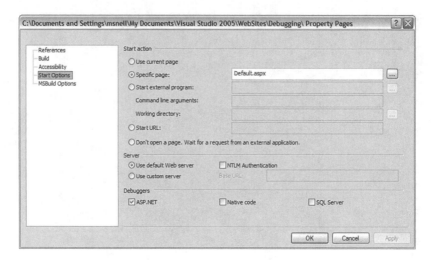

FIGURE 13.17   Configuring the startup options for your application.

Server   The Server section of the Start Options page allows you to specify a server to be launched for your application. Most applications will leave this set to Use Default Web Server. This represents the file system websites. For scenarios that use IIS or FTP, you will specify a URL to the actual server.

Debuggers   The Debuggers group of options on the Start Options page allows you to set the enabled debuggers used when running your application. By default, only ASP.NET is enabled. You can choose to turn off this setting. You can also add both Native code and SQL Server debuggers to the mix.

MSBuild Options

The final page in the Property Pages dialog box, MsBuild Options, allows you to control precompiling of your application. These options are specific to using the MSBuild compilation tool from the command line. Figure 13.18 shows an example. From here, you can set your precompilation output folder and manage related settings.

> **NOTE**
>
> You can get the same results from the Publish Web Site option in the IDE as you would with the MSBuild command-line application.

Creating Web Pages

ASP.NET web pages (also called web forms) make up the bulk of your web application. You create web pages to define your user interface. Web pages in ASP.NET have both a designer component and an event model. The designer allows you to define the controls and look of a given web page. The event model is used on the server to respond to user interaction (or events). This section looks at the basics of both the web page's designer and its event model.

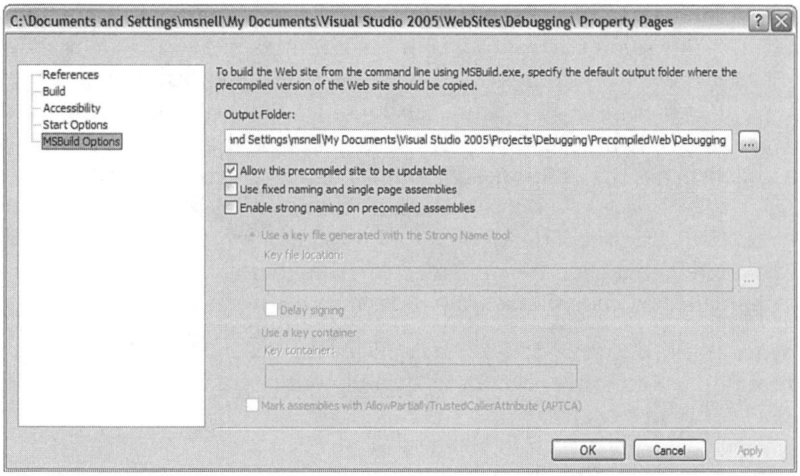

FIGURE 13.18   Managing the options related to MSBuild and ASP.NET.

Adding a Web Page to Your Website

The first step to working with web pages is adding one or more to your website. To do so, you use the Add New Item dialog box and select Web Form from the item templates. Figure 13.19 shows an example of adding a CustomerEdit.aspx page to a website.

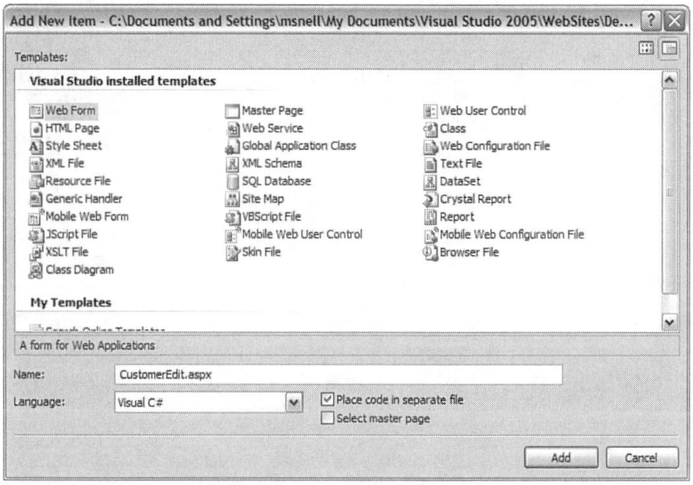

FIGURE 13.19   Adding a new web page to your website.

You have a few options when adding a new web page. First, you can set its name. It is best to use a standard naming scheme and to make sure the name also references the page's primary function. Web page names must be unique in a given directory. The second option is the language on which the form is based. Your website can be made up of C#, VB, and J# web pages. When you define a new page, you can choose its language.

Next, you can indicate whether you want the code for the web page to be in a separate file. ASP.NET 2.0 allows you to create a web form as a single file (code and markup). In fact, you now get IntelliSense in the editor for these types of forms. However, the dominant setting (and default) is code-behind (separate file). Putting code in a new file allows you to manage that code independently of the UI markup. This can be a much cleaner development experience. In addition, ASP.NET 2.0 has a new code-behind model that puts your code into what is called a *partial class*. This partial class contains only the code that you write. Code that is emitted by the tool or framework is not part of this file. Your code and the tool-emitted code are combined together during compilation. In this way, you are not burdened by code that is really not yours.

The final setting on this form is Select Master Page. This setting tells the IDE that you want your form to use a master page for its default content and layout. We will look at master pages later in this chapter.

Adding Controls to Your Web Page

You add controls to a web page by dragging them from the Toolbox to the form. There are two views of your form: design and source view. The design view allows you to build your form using a visual editor (or designer). This is similar to building a Windows form. You drag items on the page and see how they lay out. The source view allows you to see (and edit) the markup related to the web page. You toggle between these views using the options at the bottom of the form window. Figure 13.20 shows the designer view of a web page. The Toolbox items are on the left of the figure. You can see how to toggle the form's two views at the bottom of the figure.

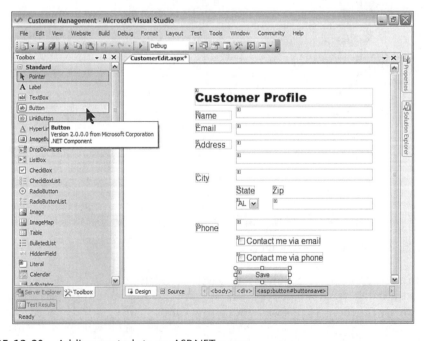

FIGURE 13.20   Adding controls to an ASP.NET page.

> **TIP**
>
> You can change how Visual Studio brings up your web forms. You can choose between viewing in source view or design view by default. To do so, choose Options from the Tools menu. You then select the HTML Designer node from the tree. Figure 13.21 shows an example of this window. The Start Pages In group box allows you to modify this setting.

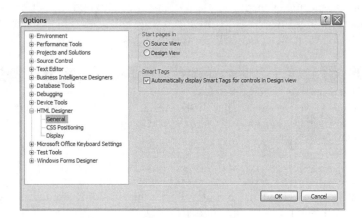

FIGURE 13.21   Choosing between default source or design view.

Responding to Events

When you write ASP.NET web pages, it is important to understand how the event model works. The event model represents how events are fired on the server when users make requests (or trigger actions). The ASP.NET event model is different from the standard Windows form event model because it combines events that process on a server with the nature of a web application delivered inside a web browser. The basics of the web page event model are as follows:

1. `Page Init`—This event is called to create the controls used by the web page. It also initializes the properties of these controls. This event is typically created automatically by the IDE.

2. `Page Load`—This event is called when the page is loaded and after the controls are initialized. This is a common event for web developers to use. You can use this event to determine whether a user is requesting a page or executing a postback (submitting data). You then call the appropriate code based on this information.

3. `Control Specific Event(s)`—Next, the page framework executes the event or events that are associated with the control the user used to submit the form (if any). For example, if a user clicked a button on your form, the button's click event is called (after page load).

4. `Page Pre Render`—This event is called just before the final rendering of the page is sent back to the browser. You can use this event to make changes to the page after all events are called.

5. Page Unload—This is the last event that is called for the page (after the page is rendered). You use this event to do cleanup. For example, you might close page-level connections or do some form of logging.

These steps represent the basic event model for a page. However, there are additional events for the page. In addition, user controls have their own events that are called during the control-specific event stage. Master pages can also add default processing for all pages. Understanding the events in any given page will always help when you're debugging or trying to achieve a specific result.

> **NOTE**
>
> For more information on what happens inside the ASP processing framework. see "ASP.NET Application Life Cycle Overview" on the MSDN website. This article provides a detailed view of how ASP works with user requests and renders a page. It also covers application- and session-specific events (inside global.asax).

Adding Page Event Handlers   There are a couple ways to ensure that your event handlers are called by ASP.NET when a page executes. First, you can call them automatically. If you set the AutoEventWireup page-level attribute to True, then ASP.NET will find events that follow the Page_ naming convention and automatically call them at their appropriate time. This approach can be convenient but requires you to recall each event's name so that you can define it appropriately.

You can also explicitly bind page events to methods in your code. In this way, you can use your own event names. You can also let Visual Studio generate the event names (so you don't have to remember them). You do so in the same way you bind events to controls: from the Properties window. However, to access the page's events, you must view the Component Designer for the page. You get there by right-clicking the given page and choosing View Component Designer. Selecting this option opens that page's Properties window including the events. Figure 13.22 shows an example.

The right side of the figure shows the properties for the CustomerEdit.aspx page. Notice that the lightning bolt icon is selected from the Properties toolbar. This shows the events (and not the properties). You can double-click an event in this list to generate a method stub for the given event. You can also choose a method from your code and explicitly bind that to an event.

Adding Control Event Handlers   You add server events to controls in a similar manner. You select the control and view its properties. From the Properties window, you can select the lightning bolt icon to show all the events for the given control. You then double-click an event to add it to your code-behind.

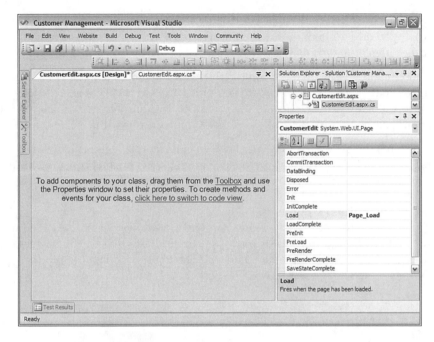

FIGURE 13.22   Adding page events.

Designing Your User Interface

The first step in creating a good web user interface is to create a design plan. In the design plan, you should

- Determine how users will navigate your site

- Decide which links will constitute top-level menu items

- Figure out how to create a unique, consistent look across the pages of the site

- Decide whether you will support multiple themes or user-configurable options

These and many more decisions go into the planning of a good, web-based UI.

When you have your plan, Visual Studio 2005 is there to help. It allows you to create master pages for determining a common look and feel. There are controls for managing links and menus. You can support themes through skin files. You can even allow users to participate in the customization of their layout using web parts. The following sections demonstrate the many features of ASP.NET that go into creating web UIs.

Determining Page Layout and Control Positioning

If you use the Visual Studio web page designer, then you will want to manage how controls are placed on a web page. For example, if you are used to building Windows forms, you may be more comfortable controlling the positioning of each individual item. In this case, you drag an item on the form and move it around relative to other items. This is called *absolute positioning* in web terms.

On the other hand, if you are more comfortable with the dynamic nature of a page in a browser, you may prefer to control your positioning through *flow layout*. This refers to your controls moving with the flow of the page. This capability is great if you intend to lay out your page with multiple tables and place your controls within table cells.

You can also mix both flow and absolute layouts. For example, you could define a page that flows based on tables. Inside a given cell, you might set a panel control. This panel control might be set to allow absolute positioning for items within the panel.

Setting Control Position Options

Visual Studio 2005 gives you a few options for managing how controls are added to pages by default. Within the Options dialog box, you can set these choices. You navigate to the HTML Designer/CSS Positioning node to do so. Selecting this node brings up the Options dialog box, as shown in Figure 13.23.

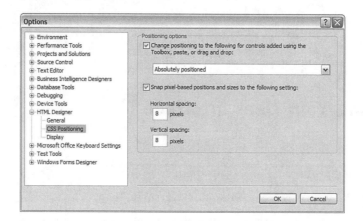

FIGURE 13.23   Selecting a form layout position.

You set your positioning options from the drop-down list. From here, you have four options that determine how controls are added to a page. Table 13.3 lists those options along with a description of each.

TABLE 13.3   Control Positioning Options

Option	Description
Absolutely Positioned	This option indicates that controls added to the web page have a defined position in terms of their left and top. They also have a layer or z-order. This option is useful if your controls overlap one another.
Relatively Positioned	This option is similar to Absolutely Positioned. The difference is that items are added to the page in a flow layout mode with top and left set to zero. You can then modify this information as and when necessary.

TABLE 13.3   Continued

Option	Description
Statically Positioned	This option indicates that controls should be placed on the form using flow layout. That is, if a text box is placed as the first item on the form and then you add a button, the button is added to the right of the text box. In this way, the UI "flows."
No Positioning Attribute	With this option, controls are added to the form with flow layout. However, their layout can be changed or affected by a style.

Visual Studio also lets you control the positioning of individual items on a given form. To do so, you select the item and then choose the Position item from the Layout menu. See Figure 13.24 for an example. This foldout menu gives you easy access to the Options dialog box discussed in the preceding paragraphs. It also lets you override the positioning for individual controls.

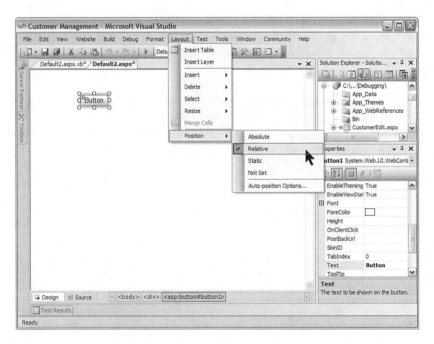

FIGURE 13.24   Setting the positioning of individual items.

Creating a Common Look and Feel

When you create a website, you want the pages to look as if they all belong to one application. The navigation should be standard, the colors and fonts should match for like items, and sizing should be consistent. In addition, you don't want to have to manage this consistency across every single page in the site. This would be extremely tedious. In addition, if you decide to make a change, you would have to do so in every file.

Thankfully, you have the tools to support a consistent look across pages and make the management of it all much easier. Visual Studio provides styles, master pages, and themes to do so.

Style Sheets

Style sheets allow you to define a common look and behavior. You can then apply that common group to multiple items within your page and application. In this way, if you decide to change something, you can change it in one place and all the places that use the style will be updated.

As an example, suppose you want to manage how hyperlinks on your site look when a user hovers the mouse pointer over them. To do so, you can define a style inside a style sheet for the anchor tag's hover (A:hover) behavior. Inside the style, you might set the color, name, and size of the font. You might also toggle underlining. After you've defined your style, you then apply the style sheet to the page. All anchor tags on the page will then use the given style definition.

Creating a Style Sheet   You can add one or more style sheets to an application through the Add New Item dialog box. Style sheets have the extension .css. You can open a style sheet in the editor. When you do, Visual Studio presents a Style Sheet toolbar, CSS outline window, and the actual contents of style sheet. Figure 13.25 shows these items.

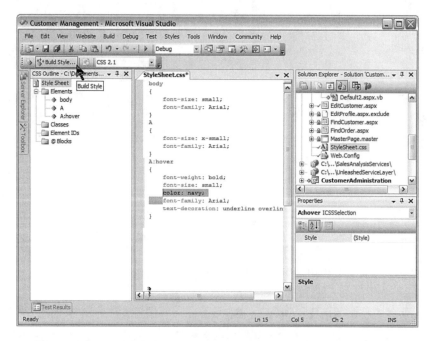

FIGURE 13.25   Working with a style sheet in the IDE.

The middle pane of Figure 13.25 shows the contents of the style sheet. You can manually edit the style sheet from here. Of course, being able to edit it requires you to have a good working understanding of CSS. Like anything, the more you work with it, the more familiar you will become. You can also use the context menu inside this pane to gain access to adding a new style rule and building a style with the style builder tool.

The Style Sheet toolbar has just a few options. The first one on the left launches the Add Style Rule dialog box. The second option opens the Style Builder window. The next button allows you to view the results in a browser window. Finally, the drop-down allows you to set a CSS standard with which to work.

The CSS Outline pane on the left of Figure 13.25 shows an outline view of the style sheet. If you don't intend to work with the raw `.css` file, this view and the related dialog boxes provide a nice set of tools. Items in this view are organized in two primary groups: Elements and Classes. The Elements group shows styles that define the look HTML elements. When a style sheet is applied to a page, the page's elements pick up these styles.

The Classes folder groups your custom styles. These styles are not related to elements. Rather, you define a custom style, give it a unique name in the sheet, and then explicitly apply it to individual items on your page.

Adding a Style Rule   A style rule defines a style for an element or class. You can create a new style rule by typing it directly into the editor (using the correct syntax, of course). For example, to create a new style class, you would type `.myClass {}` in the editor.

You can also define a style rule by using the Add Style Rule dialog box. You access this dialog box from either a right-click in the CSS outline pane, a right-click in the editor pane, a button on the Style Sheet toolbar, or the Add Style Rule option on the Style menu. This dialog box is useful in that it lists the many HTML elements for which you can define styles. It also allows you to define a style hierarchy. Figure 13.26 shows an example.

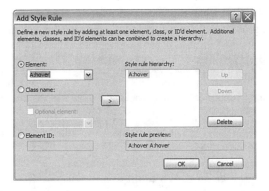

FIGURE 13.26   Adding a style rule.

Building a Style   You edit the contents of a given style either through the editor pane or the Style Builder dialog box. The latter provides a tool for setting the many options that can define a given style. This tool emits the correct markup for your style. You access the dialog box by right-clicking inside an existing style, selecting an option from the Style menu, or using a tool on the Style Sheet toolbar. Figure 13.27 shows an example of the dialog box. This figure represents the many options for controlling the font on a style. The Style Builder dialog box has many more options such as backgrounds, positioning, and borders.

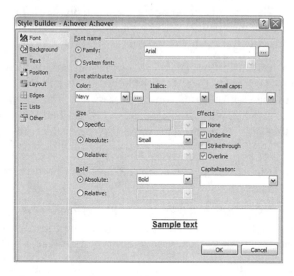

FIGURE 13.27   Building your style markup.

Applying a Style Sheet to a Page   Your next step after creating a style sheet is to have it applied to your page. This is easy enough to do. You can drag and drop the style sheet from the Solution Explorer to any web page in the same Solution Explorer. You can also manually add the link tag to your page and point it to your style sheet. Next, we will look at master pages. It is worth noting that you can apply a style sheet to your master page. All pages that use the master will then have this style sheet applied.

> **NOTE**
>
> You can also define style for a single page. This is not a style sheet. In addition, you can use the inline style attribute to define styles on individual controls. This capability can be useful for overriding style sheet–defined styles.

Master Pages

Master pages are one of the greatest new additions to ASP.NET 2.0. They allow you to visually design a common look for your application in one file and then use that look across other files. This result was previously achieved through include files and user controls. However, these items were difficult to use in that they did not visually represent the final page in the designer. Instead, you had to run your browser to see the results of your combined HTML. In addition, you were often opening a table in one file that you had to remember to close in another. Master pages eliminate these issues. When you derive a page from a master file, Visual Studio displays the contents of both pages at once inside the designer.

Creating a Master Page   You add a master page to your project through the Add New Item dialog box. You can have multiple master pages in your application. This capability can be especially useful if your application has more than one default layout (or look) for certain areas of the site. It is most common to have a master page that includes common navigation, common graphics, and a common footer.

A master page defines the main HTML for the page. This includes the opening and closing HTML tags, head, body, and form. Inside the master page are one or more ContentPlaceHolder controls. These controls indicate areas on the page where content pages (pages that derive from the master) may place their content (such as a form definition).

Master pages also have their own code-behind file. This file should contain all code that relates to the workings of the master page itself. If there are working controls on the page, for example, their code would go inside this code-behind file. In addition, the master page has its own set of page events (just like an .aspx page).

Figure 13.28 shows an example of a master page. Notice that the page is laid out as a table. The cell in the center row contains a ContentPlaceHolder control. This is the only place where content pages that use the master page can add their content.

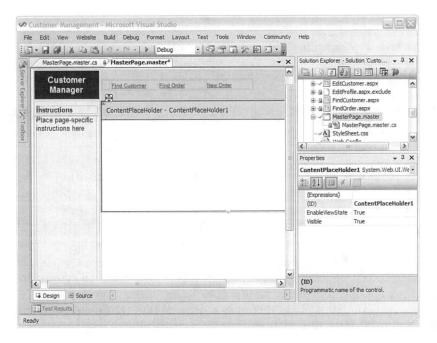

FIGURE 13.28   Creating a master page.

Creating a Content Page   Users do not access master pages directly. Instead, they call the content pages that derive from the master. When they do, .NET combines the contents of both pages and returns a single response as if there were only one page.

You create a content page by selecting a master when adding a web page to your site. When you do, there is an option titled Select Master Page at the bottom of the dialog box (recall Figure 13.12). Selecting this option will present you with available master pages in your application.

When your content page opens, you will see the content of the master page in the background. In the foreground will be the `ContentPlaceHolder` controls. It is here that you will add controls specific to your page. This provides a discrete separation of functionality between what is your page and what belongs to the master. You work with the page as you would any other ASP.NET web page. You add controls to the form and write event code in the code-behind file.

NOTE

Control layout and positioning can be important when you work with content areas. If, for example, you have turned on absolute positioning, then the content placeholder acts more as a guide. Due to the nature of this layout option, the content placeholder cannot restrict you from placing your controls anywhere on the page. The flow layout option, however, has the opposite effect. If you are working with static positioning, controls will be allowed only inside the content areas.

Figure 13.29 shows an example. This web page was created to edit a customer's profile; it is based on the application's master page. Notice that the content page has the same extension as any web form (`.aspx`).

TIP

You can use the `Master` object to reference the master page from the code within your content page's code-behind file. For example, suppose you want to set the instruction text on the master page from within each content page. Figure 13.29 shows an example. You would need to find the control used by the master page for the instruction text. This code would look like the following:

```
Label lb = (Label)this.Master.FindControl("LabelInstructions");
```

Themes and Skins

Visual Studio 2005 introduces the concept of themes for web pages and entire sites. This feature allows you to define one or more specific looks for the controls that make up your application. After you do, you can then switch between them based on user preference, their company affiliation, or similar.

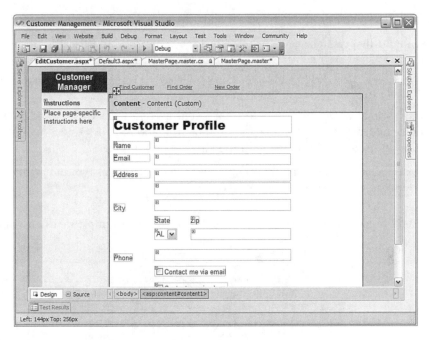

FIGURE 13.29   Creating a content page.

At first glance, it seems themes provide nearly the same experience as style sheets. However, themes go a few steps further. First, they leverage style sheets. Each theme can have an associated style sheet. Themes can also be applied in such a way as to work with an existing style sheet or to override it (see "Applying a Theme to a Site or Page"). The next difference is that themes allow you to embed graphic files as part of the themes. In this way, you can switch between one set of graphics to another based on a theme's name. Style sheets cannot do this. Last, themes allow you to define skin files for your ASP.NET controls. These skin files enable you to set property values of a control that fall outside mere styles (these property values must be nonbehavioral, however).

> **NOTE**
>
> Only one theme can apply to a site at any given time (unlike style sheets).

Creating a Theme   Themes are created inside the App_Themes folder. Each theme gets its own theme folder. The name of the theme is the name of the folder (which must be unique). This ensures there is no confusion when applying a theme. You apply it based on the folder's name.

As an example, suppose you are building an application to manage customer details and orders. Assume this application is accessed from multiple company sites. Therefore, company A would manage its customers, and company B would manage its customers. In this scenario, the site owner might define a different theme for each company. Perhaps the theme is based on each company's colors, fonts, and graphics.

To create a theme, you typically follow a standard set of steps:

1. You must first create the App_Theme directory. You can do so through the context menu. You choose Add ASP.NET Folder and then Theme. You can also choose to add a skin file to your application, and then Visual Studio will create the App_Theme directory for you.

2. When you have the App_Theme directory, you can right-click on it to add a new theme folder. This can again be found under the Add ASP.NET Folder menu. You will want to name this folder with the name of your theme.

3. Next, you add the files that make up your theme. These files typically include a style sheet, any images or resources, and a skin file.

Figure 13.30 shows the folder and file structure based on the example we discussed here.

FIGURE 13.30   Application themes.

Creating a Skin File   We have already discussed style sheets. What we need to look at now is defining a skin file. You can have one or more skin files in your theme. You might want to create a new skin file for each control you intend to skin. Alternatively, you may want to define a single skin file for your entire theme. The choice is yours.

Inside the skin file are control skin definitions called *skins*. You declare each skin just as you would write the markup for a given control on a web page. The syntax is similar. However, you omit the property assignments for the control that do not pertain to the skin.

There are two types of skin definitions: named skins and unnamed skins. A named skin is created by using the attribute SkinId. This allows you to define a unique name for the skin declaration. In this case, only controls in your site with this same SkinId will be affected by the skin declaration. On the other hand, unnamed skins apply to all controls of a similar type. For example, if you want all your button controls to look a similar way, you create an unnamed skin for the button control. When you apply the skin to a page, then all buttons will pick up this look. Let's look at an example.

For this example, say you want to define a few skins to define your theme. You will define named skins for the customer logo on the master page and the title labels on each screen. You will then create unnamed skins for label, text box, button, and grid view controls.

Listing 13.1 shows the sample skin file. At the top are the named skins. Notice the use of the SkinId attribute. Again, this attribute will be used when applying this skin to specific instances of these types of controls (image and label in this case). Below this are the skins that apply to standard controls. There is one for all buttons, labels, text boxes, and grid views. Notice that the GridView definition includes definitions for the many parts of the control. You nest these definitions within the GridView definition as you would on any ASP.NET page.

You also need a similar file for company B. To create it, you copy and paste this file to that company's directory. You then make minor edits to the image skin and the fonts and colors of the other skin definitions. We will next look at applying these skins to the pages in the site.

LISTING 13.1   Company A Skin File

```
<%-- named skins --%>
<asp:Image runat="server" SkinID="CustomerLogo"
 Height="60px" Width="128px"
 ImageUrl="~/App_Themes/CompanyA/compaAlogo.jpg" />


<asp:Label runat="server" SkinID="TitleLabel"
 Font-Names="Arial Black"
 Font-Size="X-Large" />


<%-- default, control skins --%>
<asp:Button runat="server" Width="100px" Height="25px"
 BackColor="Silver" ForeColor="MidnightBlue"
 Font-Name="Arial" Font-Size="10px"
 BorderColor="MidnightBlue" BorderStyle="Ridge" />


<asp:Label runat="server" ForeColor="MidnightBlue"
 Font-Names="Arial" Font-Size="Small" />


<asp:TextBox runat="server" Width="265px" BackColor="White"
 BorderColor="MidnightBlue" BorderStyle="Solid" BorderWidth="1px"
 Font-Names="Arial" Font-Size="Small" />


<asp:GridView runat="server" CellPadding="4" ForeColor="#333333" GridLines="None">
  <FooterStyle BackColor="#5D7B9D" Font-Bold="True" ForeColor="White" />
  <RowStyle BackColor="#F7F6F3" ForeColor="#333333" />
  <EditRowStyle BackColor="#999999" />
  <SelectedRowStyle BackColor="#E2DED6" Font-Bold="True" ForeColor="#333333" />
  <PagerStyle BackColor="#284775" ForeColor="White" HorizontalAlign="Center" />
  <HeaderStyle BackColor="#5D7B9D" Font-Bold="True" ForeColor="White" />
  <AlternatingRowStyle BackColor="White" ForeColor="#284775" />
</asp:GridView>
```

> **TIP**
>
> There is not much tool support for defining skin declarations. You are forced to manually enter this markup. However, a common shortcut can be to create a page that includes each control in the theme. You then use the designer to edit the controls on the page. Finally, you copy this markup from the page to the skin declaration and then delete any unwanted declaration code (including the ID tag).

Applying a Theme to a Site or Page   There are a few ways in which you can apply a theme. Each is meant to provide a different level of control. For example, you can set a global theme for an entire server. You can configure a theme for just one website. You can also choose to configure a theme at the individual page level. Finally, you can apply a single skin to a single control. You can see that these levels go from the very macro (server) to the granular (control). Most websites will fall somewhere in the middle, like applying a theme at the page or site level.

You apply a theme at the page level by using the @ Page directive inside the page's markup. You have a couple of options here. You can decide that your theme should always trump all control settings. That is, if a developer explicitly sets a control value and that value is overridden by the theme, then the theme takes precedence. This type of declaration would look like the following:

```
<%@ Page Theme="MyPageTheme" %>
```

Alternatively, you can set what is called a StyleSheetTheme at the page level. This indicates that the theme applies only where controls do not have explicit overriding values. In the previous declaration, the theme would override local control settings. Using the StyleSheetTheme, you can set the theme to apply only to control settings that are not explicitly set. That is, if the control has a value for a given attribute, then that value is used. If it does not, then the theme's value is used. You set this type of theme for the page as follows:

```
<%@ Page StyleSheetTheme="MyPageTheme" %>
```

You can define the theme for an entire website through the configuration file. This allows you to set a theme and then change it without recompiling your code. To do so, you add the Theme or StyleSheetTheme (see the preceding example) attributes to the pages element inside the system.web node. The following is an example:

```
<system.web>
  <pages theme="MySiteTheme" />
</system.web>
```

To define just the style sheet theme, you would use the following:

```
<system.web>
  <pages StyleSheetTheme=" MySiteTheme" />
</system.web>
```

You can also set a theme inside your code. This capability can be useful if you are allowing users to choose their theme or you are dynamically setting a theme based on some user information. Recall the example with two companies: company A and company B. Remember, a theme file was defined for each. If you determine within your code that a member of company A , for example, has logged in, then you would set the theme as follows:

```
Page.Theme = "CompanyA"
```

Figure 13.31 shows an example of the theme defined in Listing 13.1. This theme was set programmatically.

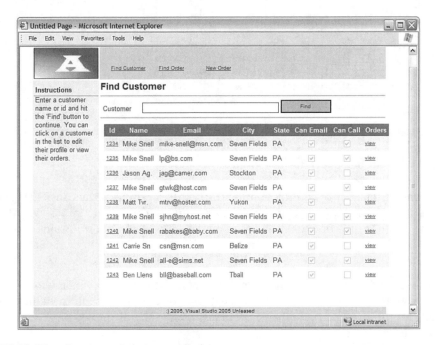

FIGURE 13.31   Company A theme applied.

Figure 13.32 shows the same theme for company B. Here, the theme has been modified and applied programmatically to the entire site.

TIP

You can make changes to a theme file or skin without recompiling your site. These changes will simply be applied on the next browser refresh.

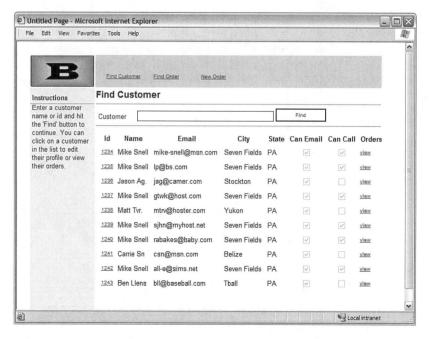

FIGURE 13.32   Company B theme applied.

To set a theme for a single control, you use the `SkinID` attribute of the control. This ID can be set to reference a particular skin inside a skin file. The skin definition would have the same skin ID as the one used inside the markup. The markup for this looks as follows:

```
<asp:SomeControl runat="server" ID="ControlID" SkinID="MySkinId" />
```

You can set the skin ID from the markup or by using the Properties window for a given control open in the designer. This window will provide a drop-down list of skins that are available for the given control type. You can also set the skin ID programmatically. The following is an example:

```
SomeControl.SkinId = "MySkinId"
```

Creating a User-Configurable UI

ASP.NET 2.0 provides support for creating a user interface that can be configured and personalized by each individual user of a site. As an example, if you have ever worked with SharePoint Portal Server or visited MSN.com, you will notice that blocks of functionality define a given page. These blocks can be removed, added, moved around, and configured by users. To enable this functionality, the blocks all must work together as part of a portal framework. .NET now has just such a framework built into the product.

The following sections provide an overview of creating a configurable user interface using the new Web Part controls. We will walk through the basics of building a Web Part page that allows users to monitor customers in a customer management application. In doing so, we will cover the many basics of Web Parts. Note that this is another large topic. When you become familiar with the basics, you will want to do additional exploring to find out more.

Working with the Web Part Controls

There are many Web Part controls and classes; the Visual Studio Toolbox alone defines 13 Web Part controls (see Figure 13.33). In addition, the System.Web.UI.WebControls. WebParts namespace contains nearly 100 classes. These controls and objects work together to manage the structure of a Web Part page, its personalization and configuration, and the presentation itself.

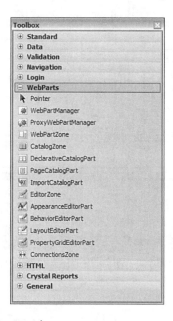

FIGURE 13.33   The Web Part controls.

When you create a basic Web Part page, you typically work with three types of controls: the WebPartManager, WebPartZone, and presentation controls themselves. The first control, WebPartManager, is actually required of all Web Part pages. It is the control responsible for managing the Web Parts on the page. You must define this control on each Web Part page and can define only one per page. The WebPartManager is responsible for tracking the controls and their zones throughout the page. It also manages the state that a page might be in, such as view or edit mode.

The second control, WebPartZone, enables you to manage the layout or "zones" of your page. A zone represents an area of the page where controls or features can be placed. To understand zones, you can think of your page in terms of horizontal and vertical content zones. For example, you may have a zone at the top of your page that presents the header for the application. Beneath this, you may have two vertical zones. The leftmost zone may be used for links and navigational controls. The middle zone may contain content Web Parts. Finally, you may have another zone at the bottom of the page to manage footer-type content.

Figure 13.34 shows an example of a Web Part page broken into zones. Of course, you can define any number of zones and lay them out as you like. This is simply one example.

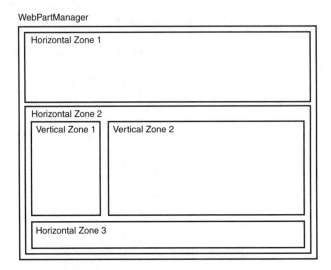

FIGURE 13.34   Web Part zones.

> **NOTE**
>
> Zones also have an associated style. That is, they define a header, title, border, buttons, and so on. This is known as the "chrome" of the controls.

Last, you put controls into each zone of the Web Part page. These controls can be any .NET control that you want to be managed by the zone. You can also create your own Web Parts and user controls that can be placed in these zones. The advantage of the latter is that you can provide configuration capabilities for these Web Parts. This allows users to edit a given Web Part's properties from within the web browser (similar to SharePoint).

Table 13.4 provides a brief reference to the primary controls that you use to manage a Web Part page. Each of these controls can be found on the Visual Studio Toolbox. These controls are all zone controls (except the manager control). As such, they constrain what type of control should be added to the given zone.

TABLE 13.4   The Web Part Zone Controls

Control	Description
WebPartManager	This control tracks the zones on the page and the WebPart controls that are in those zones. Each Web Part page requires one (and only one) instance of this control.
CatalogZone	This control defines a zone that contains one or more CatalogPart controls. The CatalogPart control provides a list of Web Parts that are available for the page. When a user is editing the page, this zone is enabled. Users then use the CatalogPart control to select one or more Web Part objects and drag them into WebPartZones.
WebPartZone	You use this control for defining the primary zones of your user interface. You can add ASP.NET controls and Web Part controls into these zones. Most Web Part pages define two or more WebPartZones.
EditorZone	You use this zone for providing an area for users to edit and configure a given Web Part. The editor for a Web Part is defined as an EditorPart control. This zone contains these types of controls.

Creating a Web Part Page

You create a Web Part page using any standard web form (.aspx). For the following example, you will create a form titled MonitorCustomer.aspx. The first step is to drag a WebPartManager control onto this form. This control has no visual appearance on the form. Instead, it is simply necessary to create a Web Part page.

TIP

Inside the form designer, you can decide to show or hide controls that have no visual appearance. To do so, you use the View menu and check or uncheck the option Non-Visual Controls. Non-visual controls show up as gray boxes inside the designer. A box typically contains a control's name and ID.

Defining Zones   Next, you add the zones to the page. Recall that the zones define where your Web Parts can exist and how they look and are sized. You can lay out your zones inside a table, use absolute positioning to place zones in specific areas, or use relative positioning. If you allow users to hide or close the controls in a zone, you might consider a table or relative positioning. If, on the other hand, your zones are static, you would use absolute positioning. In the example, you will do the latter. You can follow these steps to create the example:

1. Place two WebPartZone controls on a web page.

2. Name the first control Customer Links; it will take up the left side of the page.

3. Set the first control's ID property to WebPartZoneCustomerLinks.

4. Set the `HeaderText` property of the first control to `Customer Links`. This allows people editing the page to see a zone name (and, you hope, your intentions for the zone).

5. Next, you define the chrome for the Web Parts that are placed in this zone. You can configure this through numerous properties of the zone or use the smart tag associated with the control to autoformat the zone. Figure 13.35 shows an example of the Auto Format dialog box. On the left are possible formats. On the right is a preview showing how the Web Parts in the zone will look. This preview is based on actual content for the zone.

FIGURE 13.35   Setting the chrome for a zone.

Repeat these steps for the other zone control. Place this one in the middle of the page and set its `HeaderText` property to `Customer Statistics`. This zone will be used to display statistics relative to customers shopping in the site.

Adding Web Parts to Zones   Now you're ready to add Web Parts to the zones you have defined. There are few ways to go about this. You can create actual controls that implement the `WebPart` class. This allows the most flexibility for creating Web Parts. It also allows you to create user configuration for your Web Parts. This configuration is shown when a user edits a given Web Part. This also happens to be the most involved method. Of course, it is recommended for portal developers. Alternatively, you can add ASP.NET controls or user controls to the zones. When you do so, ASP will define a Web Part around the given control. This makes for an easy way to create Web Parts.

For the example, you will implement the latter method. You will first create a Customer Links Web Part. This Web Part will provide a series of links around managing a customer. The following outlines the process for creating this Web Part:

1. Drag an ASP `Label` control inside the `WebPartZone` control.

2. This label will be automatically turned into a `WebPart` control. You can see this in the markup. The `<ZoneTemplate>` element is added inside the `<asp:WebPartZone>` node. Inside this goes the `Label` control you added to the form.

3. Set a title for the Web Part. To do so, add the `title` attribute to the `Label` control. This attribute is picked up by ASP and applied to the Web Part.

4. Add some links within the confines of the `<asp:Label>` declaration. The final markup looks something like Listing 13.2.

LISTING 13.2   The Customer Links Web Part

```
<asp:WebPartZone ID="WebPartZoneCustomerLinks" runat="server">
  <ZoneTemplate>
    <asp:Label title="Customer Links" runat="server" ID="LabelCustActions">
      <a href="FindCustomer.aspx">Find Customer</a><br />
      <a href="FindOrder.aspx">Find Order</a><br />
      <a href="FindCustomer.aspx">Offer Discount</a><br />
    </asp:Label>
  </ZoneTemplate>
</asp:WebPartZone>
```

Repeat this method for a Help Web Part. Then create some user controls. Create one for showing active shoppers, one for searching for an order, and one that shows the top products sold in a given day. You add the user controls to a zone in a similar way you added the ASP.NET controls. ASP turns each into its own Web Part and applies the zone's chrome to each control. Figure 13.36 shows what the page now looks like inside the designer.

Enabling Users to Configure the Page   There are many options available for allowing users to customize the look and behavior of Web Parts. You can create editors for your controls that allow for full configuration. You might have Web Parts that can connect (or talk to) other Web Parts. They require configuration. You might allow users to pick from a catalog of controls in order to determine which controls they would like to see on the page. It is also common to allow users to minimize, close, and move your controls from zone to zone. The first two features come by default with Web Parts. We will look at enabling this last feature.

There are a few steps you need to take to enable users to change the layout of the page. These steps are as follows:

1. Add an `EditorZone` control onto the page. Adding this control creates a zone where you can put `EditorParts`. It is typical for you to show this zone when your page is in edit mode. In the example, assume you are using the zone but do not intend to display to users.

2. Add the `LayoutEditorPart` control to the `EditorZone` you just created. This Web Part allows for the page's layout to be edit-enabled.

3. Create a user control for managing the edit mode. This user control will contain a single `LinkButton` control. This control should look like every other Web Part when added to the page.

4. Write some code for the user control. First, add an event to pick up the `WebPartManager` instance that is managing the control. Next, respond to the button's `Click` event and then toggle the state of the `WebPartManager` between either edit or browse mode. Listing 13.3 shows this code.

5. Add the control to a zone on the Web Part page. Figure 13.37 shows both this control and the editor Web Parts in the designer.

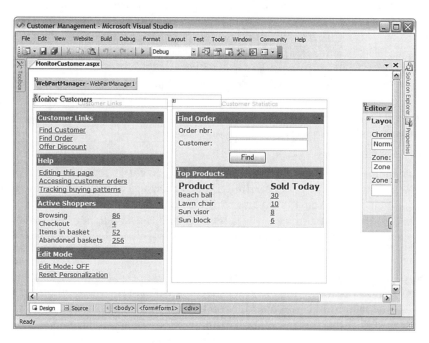

FIGURE 13.36   The Web Parts inside the designer.

LISTING 13.3   Controlling Edit Mode for the Page

```
public partial class EditMode : System.Web.UI.UserControl {
  WebPartManager _wpManager;
  void Page_Init(object sender, EventArgs e) {
    Page.InitComplete += new EventHandler(InitComplete);
  }
  void InitComplete(object sender, System.EventArgs e) {
```

LISTING 13.3   Continued

```
  wpManager = WebPartManager.GetCurrentWebPartManager(Page);
}
protected void LinkButton1_Click(object sender, EventArgs e) {
  if (LinkButton1.Text == "Edit Mode: OFF") {
      wpManager.DisplayMode = _wpManager.SupportedDisplayModes["Edit"];
      LinkButton1.Text = "Edit Mode: ON";
  }
  else {
    wpManager.DisplayMode = _wpManager.SupportedDisplayModes["Browse"];
    LinkButton1.Text = "Edit Mode: OFF";
  }
}
}
```

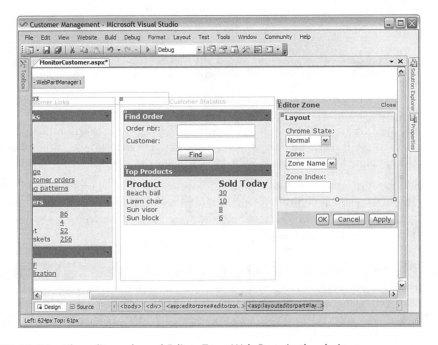

FIGURE 13.37   The edit mode and Editor Zone Web Parts in the designer.

Viewing the Results   The final step is to view and debug the results. Figure 13.38 shows the Monitor Customers page in a standard browse view. Notice that the Customer Links Web Part has been minimized. In addition, the menu off the Web Part toolbar has been highlighted. In browse mode, this menu contains links for closing the Web Part and minimizing it. Of course, these actions are configurable.

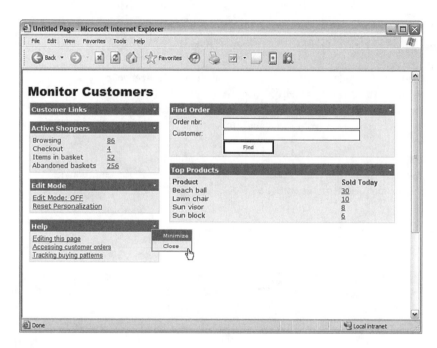

FIGURE 13.38   Choosing to minimize or close a Web Part.

If you click the Edit Mode link button, you can toggle the page into edit mode. When in edit mode, users see the available zones and their titles. They are now allowed to move Web Parts from zone to zone. Figure 13.39 show this movement in action.

When the page is in edit mode, users get the edit action inside the toolbar's menu by default. This action enables editing for the given Web Part. In this example, this means displaying the Editor Zone, which contains the LayoutEditorPart control. Figure 13.40 shows an example of this zone enabled.

TIP

Web part personalization is persisted from session to session. If users (or developers) close controls, you need to give them a way to get them back. For this example, a link was added in the edit mode control to do just this. Inside the Click event is the following, which is used to reset the personalization for the page:

_wpManager.Personalization.ResetPersonalizationState().

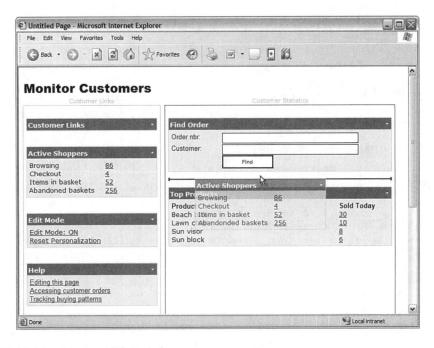

FIGURE 13.39   Moving Web Parts between zones.

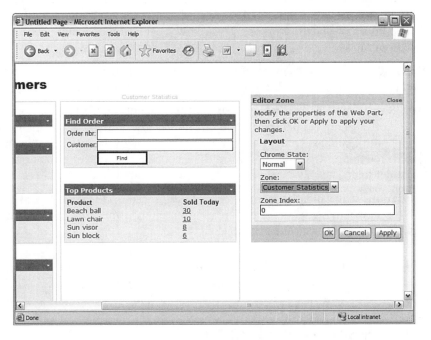

FIGURE 13.40   Invoking the layout editor for a Web Part.

Working with the ASP.NET Controls

Visual Studio 2005 and the new version of ASP.NET introduce a large number of control enhancements and a similar number of new controls. Wherever you turn in the product, there is something new, designed to make you more productive. We have already covered a few of these new items in this chapter. Our intent for the following sections is to call out some of the major enhancements as well as walk you through the new controls.

ASP.NET Control Enhancements

Most control enhancements apply to the entire group of ASP.NET controls. This is due to the fact that they are all built on the same control framework. Control enhancements include

- **XHTML Compliance**—The ASP.NET controls are sent back to the user's browser as standard HTML. In this release, all controls generate XHTML 1.1–compliant markup. This ensures there are fewer surprises when viewing your pages in different browsers.

- **Data Binding**—There is a new data-binding model for ASP.NET 2.0. This model allows you to bind to many data sources such as a database, a business object, XML, and so on. In most scenarios, the binding requires no coding on your part. In addition, the controls still support the old binding model.

- **Adaptive Rendering**—The ASP.NET 2.0 controls can now adapt their markup output based on the requesting browser. Therefore, they are browser-compatible by default for most modern browsers. This can save a lot of time when you're testing your application.

- **Skins**—We have already described how themes and skins can be used to change the look of a site. Each ASP.NET 2.0 control has support for skins built in.

- **Data Entry**—ASP.NET controls now support, by default, some of the data entry features of Windows applications. You can now define a tab order, set the focus to a given control, and assign a hotkey (or access key) to a given control. All of this is done through properties on the control. The controls themselves generate script on the client to enable this feature.

- **Validation**—The validation controls are also improved in this release. For example, you can now group a set of validation controls and control validation for groups of controls (or sections of your page).

This list represents some of the big enhancements. However, each control has its own set of new features and enhancements. If you are familiar with prior versions of .NET, you should be sure to look for any feature you previously felt was missing.

The New Controls Inside ASP.NET

The Visual Studio Toolbox continues to grow. In fact, there are whole new sets of controls. For example, we have already looked at the new Web Part family of controls.

Another set of controls exist for managing user logins and security. In addition, Visual Studio now has controls that help you better define site navigation. There are also new data source controls and a new grid in which to display data. There is a new wizard control for defining multistep processes in the UI, a new control for uploading files, an image map control, and so on. The list of new (and improved) controls is a large one. The following sections examine a number of these new controls.

> **NOTE**
>
> If you still can't find the perfect control, Visual Studio provides you with the framework to create your own controls. You can take the simple approach and define a *user control*. This is a file that you can design like a page and then use across other pages. User controls are made up of one or more existing ASP.NET controls. They also have their own code-behind file for processing their own events. In this latest version of Visual Studio, user controls are also shown inside the designer (previously, they were just gray boxes).
>
> If a user control is still not right and you want to provide design-time support for the Toolbox, configuration, and the Properties window, then you can create a *custom control*. Custom controls follow the same framework as the existing ASP.NET controls. You can even subclass and extend an existing control and turn it into your own custom version.

Login Controls

ASP.NET has a built-in set of login controls. These controls are meant to provide a complete low-code (sometimes no-code) solution for managing and authenticating users inside web applications.

By default, the login controls use what is called *ASP.NET Membership*. This feature allows these controls to work with an authentication database and related features without your writing code. Membership allows for the creation of users and groups and the management of user data (including passwords). The membership services inside ASP.NET can work with a SQL Express database or Active Directory. You can also write your own custom provider that can be plugged into the model.

We will look at configuring membership in a moment. First, let's examine the many login controls. Figure 13.41 shows a list of all these controls in the Toolbox. Each control has a purpose and is aptly named. Table 13.5 provides a brief overview of these many controls.

FIGURE 13.41   The login controls for ASP.NET.

TABLE 13.5   The Login Controls

Control	Description
Login	This control provides the primary interface for challenging users for their credentials (usernames and passwords). You can format the look of the control as well as display other links and messages such as authentication errors. The control is set up to work with ASP.NET Membership by default. If you configure it, you do not need to write code. However, if you want to write your own code, you can use the Authenticate event to write your custom scheme.
LoginView	This control allows you to define two views: a view for users who are logged in and a view for anonymous users. You add controls to each view to define what users see based on their current status.
PasswordRecovery	This control is used for users to recover their passwords. Typically, you configure this control to email users their passwords. However, there are a number of other options.
LoginStatus	This control shows the authentication status of the current user. Users are either logged in or not. If they are, the control enables them to log out. If they are not logged in, the control gives them the opportunity to do so.
LoginName	This control displays the username of the currently logged-in user.
CreateUserWizard	This control allows users to create their own accounts or helps in password recovery. Users can request an account (and fill in their details) with this control.
ChangePassword	This control allows users to enter their current passwords and new passwords. The control can then validate the passwords and make the change if successful.

Configuring User Authentication   You can create a login page (or control) by dropping the Login control directly on a form. After you place it, you can begin to set the properties that define your application's security. Figure 13.42 shows an example. Notice that the login control provides access to the Administer Website link. This link takes you to the Web Site Administration Tool (WSAT) for your site where you can begin to define your authentication.

> **NOTE**
>
> By default, user data is sent to the server from the client as plain text. Therefore, you should enable SSL and HTTPS for securing your site.

The WSAT is a web-based tool that allows you to configure your site, including security. Figure 13.43 shows the home page of the tool. From here, you can access the Security tab, define application configuration (turn on tracing, for example), and select an administration provider. The default administration provider is configured for SQL Server or SQL Express. This is the place where the configuration data (such as users) for your site is stored.

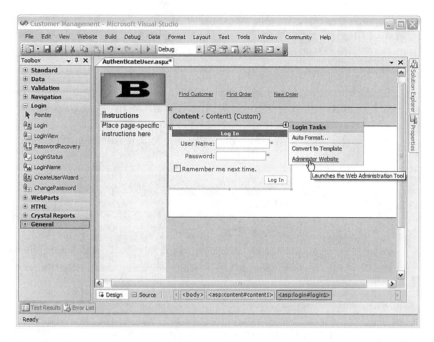

FIGURE 13.42   The Login control.

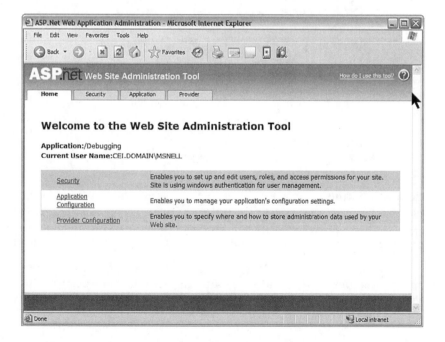

FIGURE 13.43   The ASP.NET Web Site Administration Tool (WSAT).

You can use the WSAT to change from Windows security to Internet security. The former is best when working on a LAN environment. The latter is required for most public-facing, secure sites. After you configure this model, ASP switches you over to using membership. As a result, you get a membership database.

You can use the Security tab, shown in Figure 13.44, inside WSAT to configure the users, roles, and access for this database. Notice the three groups at the bottom of the screen: Users, Roles, and Access Rules. These groups provide links for managing the accounts in your system. Your login control will automatically respect the information configured here.

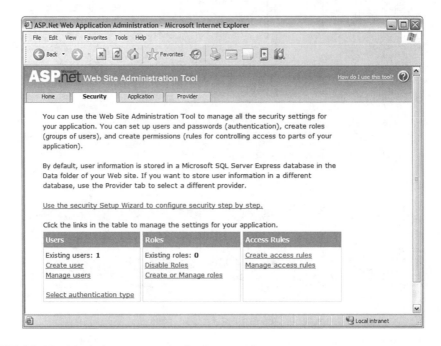

FIGURE 13.44   Managing users and roles for your site.

Site Navigation Controls

It can be easy to become lost on a lot of websites out there. If you don't provide good user navigation, then chances are users will complain (or stop visiting). ASP provides a few controls to help deal with defining and controlling navigation. The controls include the following:

- Menu—You can now create menus for your web page out-of-the-box with Visual Studio. The menus support submenus and flyout menus. You can even bind your menus to an XML data source.

- `SiteMapPath`—This control allows you to leave *cookie crumbs* as users navigate your site. That is, you can tell them where they came from and where they are. When you do so, users can use this list to jump backward to a place they just were.

- `TreeView`—This control could always show hierarchical data. However, it can now be bound to an XML representation of your site called a *site map*. In this way, you can quickly define a navigation structure for your site that is updated in a single place.

Using the SiteMapPath Control   Recall that the `SiteMapPath` control is used to orient users in your site. You control this orientation definition through the use of a `.sitemap` file. You add this file to your site through the Add New Item dialog box. Inside it, you define the logical hierarchy of your site by nesting pages inside `siteMapNode` elements.

For example, if users start at a home page, this would be your outer node. As they navigate into your site, you create nested nodes. Listing 13.4 shows a simple example that includes a three-tier definition: Home, Find Customer, Edit Customer. This makes a logical progression through the sample site.

LISTING 13.4   A `.sitemap` File

```
<siteMap xmlns="http://schemas.microsoft.com/AspNet/SiteMap-File-1.0" >
  <siteMapNode url="Default.aspx" title="Home" description="">
    <siteMapNode url="FindCustomer.aspx" title="Find Customer" description="">
      <siteMapNode url="EditCustomer.aspx" title="Edit Customer" description="" />
    </siteMapNode>
  </siteMapNode>
</siteMap>
```

Figure 13.45 shows the results users see in their browser. In this case, the `SiteMapPath` control was added to the master page so that it appears throughout the site.

Data Controls

ASP.NET has a full set of controls that you can use for working with, displaying, and binding to data. These controls are meant to work with little to no additional code. Instead of writing code, you should be able to configure the controls to behave as you want. Figure 13.46 shows a list of all the data controls in the Toolbox. Table 13.6 provides a brief overview of each of these controls.

> **NOTE**
>
> We will cover ways to work with data and databases in Chapter 15, "Working with Databases."

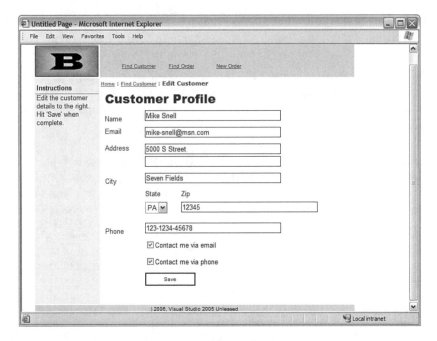

FIGURE 13.45   The SiteMapPath control in action.

FIGURE 13.46   The data controls in ASP.NET.

TABLE 13.6   The Data Controls

Control	Description
GridView	This is the new control in ASP.NET for binding to and working with tabular data. The control works with multiple data sources. It also allows sorting, paging, edit, add, and delete features.
DataList	You use this control when you want to control how your data is displayed and formatted. You can use this control with templates to gain control over when and how your data is displayed.

TABLE 13.6   Continued

Control	Description
DetailsView	This is another new control in ASP.NET. It lets you display a single row of data (or row detail). You can display this row as an editable set of fields inside a table. The DetailsView control can be used in conjunction with the GridView control to obtain a master-detail editing structure.
FormView	This control is also new to ASP.NET. It offers the same features as the DetailsView control with the added benefit of being able to define the templates that make up the display of a given row.
Repeater	This control is a container for repeating data. You use the Repeater control with a template to show the contents.
Data Source Controls	Several data source controls are new to ASP.NET. These sources can be configured to work with the source data and execute select, update, new, and delete methods. You use a data source control to bind to other controls (such as a GridView). The ASP.NET data source controls allow access to SQL Server data, Microsoft Access data, data contained in an object, XML data, and data defined as a .sitemap file.

Summary

In this chapter, we described how to create a web application and build web forms. In addition, we looked at how to leverage the new features of ASP.NET to create a consistent (sometimes configurable) user interface. We also looked at some of the new controls. Some key points in this chapter include the following:

- You can create a website using a local built-in server. You can also create your site on a remote server using HTTP (and IIS) or FTP.

- The website project property pages allow you to set what happens when you start your application from Visual Studio (among other things).

- You can create themes to switch the look and feel of your site without writing code or recompiling. The themes contain style sheets, images, and skin files.

- Web parts allow you to define a user-configurable user interface. You lay out this interface with zones and place Web Parts inside these zones.

- ASP.NET ships with Login controls, Membership provider, and WSAT to help you manage the authentication of users on your site.

- New data controls inside ASP.NET make data binding, editing, and updating easier (often requiring no code).

CHAPTER 14

Building Windows Forms

IN THIS CHAPTER

• The Basics of Form Design

• Creating a Form

• Adding Controls and Components

• Creating Your Own Controls

One of the core goals for Visual Studio is enabling rapid Windows Forms construction. Using the Windows Forms Designer, the Controls Toolbox, and the various common controls provided by the .NET Framework, this chapter will serve as your guide to the drag-and-drop creation of rich form-based applications. Specifically, we'll look at how best to leverage the built-in capabilities of the Forms Designer and the Visual Studio project system to quickly build a baseline form from scratch.

We won't worry about the code behind the form at this point; instead, the focus will be on the user interface and Visual Studio's inherent Rapid Application Development (or RAD) capabilities with the Windows Forms Designer. In other words, we will focus on the design-time capabilities of the IDE as opposed to the runtime capabilities of the form and control classes.

The Basics of Form Design

Designing the appropriate user interface for a Windows application is still part art and part science. In the Windows Forms world, a user interface is a collection of images, controls, and window elements that all work in synergy. Users absorb information through the UI and also use it as the primary vehicle for interacting with the application.

The task in front of any developer when creating a user interface is primarily one of balance: balancing simplicity of design with the features that the application is required to implement. Also thrown in the mix is the concept of standards, both formal and experiential.

NOTE

Although we use the term developer in this chapter, much of the UI design and layout process is actually squarely in the camp of the designer. Although many development teams don't have the luxury of employing a full-time UI designer (developers handle this area on many teams), this is rapidly becoming a key competitive differentiator as software development firms look to distinguish their applications and rise above their competitors at the "look and feel" level.

Considering the End User

You simply can't start the design process unless you understand how the application will be used and who its intended audience is. Even applications that contain similar feature sets might need to provide significantly different user experiences. An application designed to store medical information might have the same data points and functions but would likely have a different persona if it was designed for the average consumer as opposed to a physician or registered nurse.

Use cases and actual usability labs are both great tools for understanding user expectations, and they provide great data points for preserving that function versus simplicity of design balance.

Location and Culture

Location and culture figure into the equation as well. The typical form application used in the United States would cater to this culture's expectations by anticipating left-to-right, top-to-bottom reading habits. In this environment, the most important elements of the UI are typically placed in the most prominent position: top and left in the form. Other cultures would require this strategy to change based on right-to-left and even bottom-to-top reading traits.

Most controls in Visual Studio 2005 directly support right-to-left languages through a `RightToLeft` property. By setting this property to an appropriate `RightToLeft` enum value, you can indicate whether the control's text should appear left to right, right to left, or should be based on the setting carried on the parent control. Even the Form class supports this property.

In addition to the `RightToLeft` property, certain controls also expose a `RightToLeftLayout` property. Setting this Boolean property will actually affect overall layout within the control. As an example, setting `RightToLeftLayout` to `True` for a Form instance will cause the form to mirror its content.

TIP

Search for "Best Practices for Developing World-Ready Applications" in MSDN for more detailed information on how to design an application for an international audience.

In addition, simple things such as the space allocated for a given control are impacted by language targets. A string presented in U.S. English might require drastically more space when translated into Farsi. Again, many controls support properties designed to overcome this design issue; setting the `AutoSize` property on a control to `True` will automatically extend the client area of the control based on its contained text.

Understanding the Role of UI Standards

Applications must also strive to adhere to any relevant standards associated with their look and feel. Some standards are documented for you by the platform "owner." Microsoft, for example, has a set of UI design guidelines documented within MSDN. The book *Microsoft Windows User Experience*, published by MSPress, is included in its entirety within MSDN. By tackling topics such as Data-Centered Design, Input Basics, and Design of Graphic Images, this book provides a structured baseline of UI design collateral for Windows application developers.

Design guidelines and UI standards are often specific to a given platform. The current look and feel expected from a Windows application trace primarily back to the "new" design that debuted with Windows 95. Windows XP further refined those expectations. Now, Windows Vista—the next generation operating system from Microsoft—will feature an entirely new set of user experience guidelines.

> **TIP**
>
> For a peek at the future of UI, take a look at the Windows Vista Developer Center: http://msdn.microsoft.com/windowsvista/experience/. This page includes a summary of the Windows Vista experience and also includes a link to the revised UX guidelines.

Visual Studio 2005 surfaces some of these design guidelines and standards to make it easy to develop conforming interfaces. For instance, default button heights match the recommended standard, and Visual Studio assists developers with standard control positioning relative to neighboring controls by displaying snaplines as you move controls on the form surface. We cover this topic more fully later in this chapter.

De Facto Standards

Sometimes the influence of a particular application or suite of applications is felt heavily in the UI design realm. One example here is Microsoft Outlook. There are various applications now in the wild that mimic, for instance, the structure and layout of Microsoft Outlook even though they are not, per se, email applications. The Microsoft Outlook designers struck a vein of usability when they designed its primary form, and now other companies and developers have leveraged those themes in their own applications. A similar comment can be made about the visual appearance of toolbars made popular with Microsoft Office 2003.

Although there are limits, Visual Studio enables developers to achieve the same high-fidelity UIs used in Microsoft Office and other popular applications. In fact, if you look at the official Windows Forms website, you'll see demo applications written with VS2005, showcasing how you can develop replicas of the Microsoft Outlook, Quicken, or even Microsoft Money facades (visit the "Samples" page at http://www.windowsforms.net).

Planning the User Interface

Before you embark on the design process in Visual Studio, it is probably a decent idea to first draft a mockup of the form's general landscape. This can be a simple pen and paper sketch; what we are looking for is a simple, rough blueprint for the application.

As a sample scenario, consider a Windows Forms application written for Contoso customer service representatives. The application needs to expose a hierarchical list of orders placed with Contoso, and it should allow the reps to search on orders and edit data.

Preliminary Design

A few basic components have been established as de facto standards for a Windows form: Menus, toolbars, and status bars are all standard fare and can certainly be leveraged within this fictional order application.

Beyond those staples, you know that you need to list orders on the screen and also provide for a region that will show order details. By borrowing liberally from an existing layout theme a la Microsoft Outlook, you might arrive at a tentative form layout plan like the one shown in Figure 14.1.

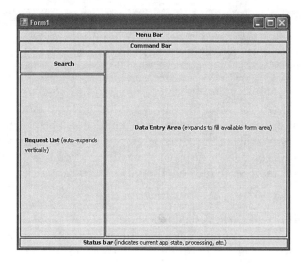

FIGURE 14.1   Initial layout plan.

It is important to pay some attention to the concept of resizing: How will the form's constituent controls respond relative to one another when a user resizes the form? What if a control element is resized because of a language change or a change in the underlying data? By fleshing out some of the resizing design intent now, you can save a mountain of work later. The prototype sketch in Figure 14.1 includes some simple text to remind you how to accommodate the different form regions during resizing.

Creating a Form

Although there are many different ways of approaching form design, the starting point for all of them within Visual Studio is the Windows Application project template. From the New Project dialog box, select this template, give the project an appropriate name, and click OK (see Figure 14.2).

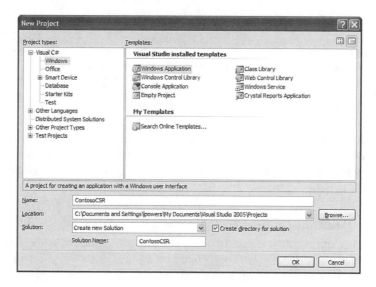

FIGURE 14.2   Creating a new Windows forms project.

The Windows Application Project Type

Windows Application projects consist of a default form class and, in the case of C#, a default static Program class. After creating the project, you are immediately presented with a blank, default form opened in the Windows Forms Designer. For a refresher on the basic capabilities and components of the Windows Forms Designer, reference Chapter 6, "Introducing the Editors and Designers."

Setting the Startup Form

Although the default project creates only a single form, you can, of course, add multiple forms at any time. This then raises the question of how to indicate at design time which form you initially want displayed at runtime (if any). There are two methods:

- For Visual Basic projects, the startup form is set using the Project Properties dialog box. The Startup Object drop-down in this dialog box contains a list of all valid form objects. You simply select the form you want launched on startup, and you're all set.

- For Visual C# projects, a slightly more complex approach is needed. The notion of a C# startup object is simply any class that implements a Main() method. Within the body of the Main method, you need to place a line of code that passes in a form instance to the Application.Run method, like this: Application.Run(new OrderForm()). Assuming that you have a class that implements Main and code that calls Application.Run in that Main method, you can then select the specific startup object via the Project Properties dialog box.

Inheriting Another Form's Appearance

If your form will look similar to another form that you have already developed, you have the option of visually inheriting that other form's appearance. Visual Studio provides an Inherited Form project item template to help you along this path.

To create a form that visually inherits another, select Project, Add New Item. In the Add New Item dialog box, select the Inherited Form item type. The Inheritance Picker dialog box then lists the available forms within the current project that you can inherit from. Note that you also have the option of manually browsing to an existing assembly if you want to inherit from a form that doesn't appear in the list. After you select the base form, Visual Studio will create the new form class; its code will already reflect the base class derivation.

Form Properties and Events

A form is like any other control: You can use the Properties window in the IDE to control its various properties. Although we won't touch on all of them here, you will want to consider a few key properties as you begin your form design process.

Startup Location

You use the form's StartPosition property to place the form's window on the screen when it is first displayed. This property accepts a FormStartPosition enumeration value; the possible settings are documented in Table 14.1.

TABLE 14.1   FormStartPosition Enumeration Values

Value	Description
CenterParent	Centers the form within its parent form.
CenterScreen	Centers the form within the current display screen.
Manual	The form will position itself according to the Form.Location property value.
WindowsDefaultBounds	Positions the form at the Windows default location; the form's bounds are determined by the Windows default as well.
WindowsDefaultLocation	Positions the form at the Windows default location; the form's size is determined by the Form.Size property (this is the default setting).

Appearance

Given our discussion on the priority of UI design, it should come as no surprise that the appearance of the form is an important part of the overall application's user experience.

For the most part, the default appearance property values are sufficient for the typical application. You should set the ForeColor and BackColor properties according to the color scheme identified for your application. Note that when you add controls to the form, most of them have their own individual ForeColor values set to mimic that of the form.

Some properties allow you to implement a more extravagant user interface. The Opacity property allows you to implement transparent or semitransparent forms. This capability might be useful for situations in which users want to see a portion of the screen that actually sits behind the form's window. In addition to the Opacity property, you use the Form.BackgroundImage property to set an image as the form's background. This property is best used to display subtle color gradients or graphics not possible with just the BackColor property.

Keeping in mind our goal of rapidly crafting the form, most of the activities within the designer described in this chapter consist of tweaking the form's properties and adding controls from the Toolbox to the form.

Form Events

Forms inherit the same event-driven architecture as other controls do. Certain public events defined on the Form class are useful as injection points across the continuum of a form's life.

Figure 14.3 shows the various stages (and corresponding events) from form inception to close. To react to a form event, you first need to create an event handler.

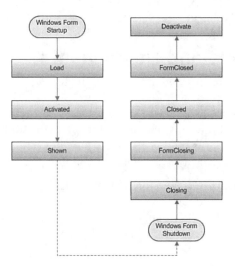

FIGURE 14.3   The events in the life of a Windows form.

Creating an Event Handler   Visual Studio's Properties window provides a speedy mechanism for defining an event handler. First, select the form of interest. Then click on the Events button in the Properties window's toolbar. The window will now show a list of every event defined on the form. Double-clicking on the event will create a blank event handler routine and open it in the code editor for you. The event handler will have the correct arguments list and will follow established standards for event handler naming (typically, *object_eventname*).

Figure 14.4 depicts the form events within the Properties window.

FIGURE 14.4   Form events in the Properties window.

With the form in place, you can start placing controls onto its surface.

Adding Controls and Components

When you are building a form-based application, the user interface design really involves three separate tools within Visual Studio: the Forms Designer tool, which provides the canvas for the form; the Toolbox, which contains the controls to be placed onto the canvas; and the property browser, which is used to affect the form and its child controls, appearance, and behavior. This triad of IDE tools provides the key to rapid form construction with Visual Studio, especially as it relates to building a form's content.

The term *control* technically refers to any .NET object that implements the Control class. In practice, we use the term to refer to the visual controls hosted by a form. This is in contrast to a *component*, which has many of the same characteristics of a control but doesn't expose a visual interface. A Button is an example of a control; a Timer is an example of a component.

Controls and components alike live in the Toolbox window (see additional coverage of the Toolbox in Chapter 6). Adding either a control or component to a form is as easy as dragging its likeness from the Toolbox and dropping it onto the form's surface.

After you place a control on a form, the Windows Forms Designer will paint the control onto the form to give you a WYSIWYG view of how the form will look at runtime. As we noted in Chapter 6, components are handled in a slightly different fashion. The Forms Designer has a special region called the *component tray*; any components placed onto the form are represented here. This allows you to interact in a point-and-click fashion with the component as you would with a control but doesn't place a representation onto the form itself because a component has no visual aspect to it.

Figure 14.5 highlights the component tray area of the Windows Forms Designer.

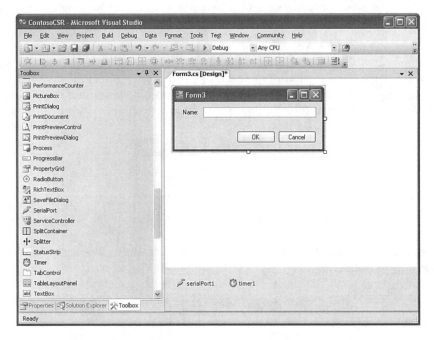

FIGURE 14.5   The component tray.

TIP

The Toolbox is customizable: You can add or remove controls from the Toolbox within any of the Toolbox tabs. Right-click anywhere in the interior of the Toolbox window and select Choose Items. This launches the Choose Toolbox Items dialog box; from here, you can select or deselect the Toolbox control population. If a control doesn't show up in the .NET Framework Components tab or the COM Components tab of the dialog box, you can browse to the control's assembly and add it directly.

Control Layout and Positioning

When a few controls are on a form, the Windows Forms Designer has a few functions designed to automate common layout tasks, such as aligning a group of controls vertically to one another. We again refer you to Chapter 6 to see how you can leverage these productivity tools. But these layout functions, although nice from a design perspective, do nothing for you at runtime.

As previously noted, controlling runtime behavior within its parent form is an important area that needs attention if you are to implement your form according to your design intent. That is, you not only want controls to look a certain way, but you also want them to act a certain way when the form is resized.

The simplest way to underscore the issue presented during a form resize is to look at a few figures. Figure 14.6 shows the simplest of forms: a label, a text box, and OK and Cancel buttons. The controls on the form have been carefully placed to maintain equal spacing, the controls are nicely aligned in the vertical and horizontal planes, and in short, this form looks just like the developer intended it to look.

FIGURE 14.6   Controls aligned on a form.

But then a user becomes involved. Figure 14.7 shows the results of resizing the form horizontally and vertically.

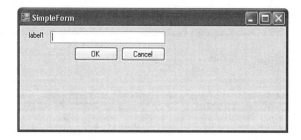

FIGURE 14.7   Form resize effects on design.

This appearance is clearly not what was intended; the nice clean design of the form has failed to keep up with the form's size. Perhaps the user resized the form in an attempt to get more room to type in the text box. Or perhaps the user tiled this application's window with other applications, causing its size to change. Whatever the reason, it is clear that further intervention by the developer is needed to keep the design "valid," regardless of the size of the form.

Just by viewing the before and after figures, you can decide on a strategy and answer the question "What should happen when a user resizes the form?" Figure 14.8 is a snapshot of the ideal; the text box has "kept pace" with the resize by horizontally extending or shrinking its width. The command buttons have kept their alignment with one another and with the text box, but they have not altered their overall dimensions. Plus, the label has stayed in its original location.

FIGURE 14.8   Reacting to a form resize.

Every form object has a resize event that fires whenever the form boundary size changes (most commonly as the result of a user dragging the form's border to increase or decrease the size of the form). Because every control has positioning properties such as Top, Left, Height, and Width, you could implement a brute-force approach to achieving the form in Figure 14.8. By writing several lines of code for each control, you can manually move or redimension the controls in response to the form size and the position of the other controls. But this approach is tedious at best and results in brittle code that has to be touched every time the layout and placement of controls are tweaked.

Thankfully, the Visual Studio Windows Forms Designer, in conjunction with some standard control properties, allows you to take all of the common resize optimizations into account during the layout of the form. By *anchoring* and *docking* your controls, you can dictate their position relative to one another and to their position within the borders of the form.

Anchoring
Anchoring, as its name implies, is the concept of forcing a control's left, top, right, or bottom border to maintain a static, anchored position within the borders of the form. For instance, anchoring a label control to the top and left of a form (this is the default) will cause the label to maintain its exact position regardless of how the form is resized. Each control's Anchor property can be set to any combination of Top, Left, Bottom, and Right. The control's property browser provides a convenient property editor widget, shown in Figure 14.9, which graphically indicates the sides of the control that are anchored.

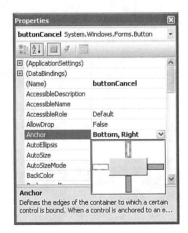

FIGURE 14.9   Setting the `Anchor` property.

Anchoring opposite sides of a control has an interesting effect. Because each side must maintain its position relative to the sides of the form, the control itself will stretch either vertically or horizontally depending on whether the `Top` and `Bottom` or `Right` and `Left` anchors have been set. In fact, this is the exact behavior you want with the text box: You want its width and height to adjust whenever the form is resized. By anchoring all sides of the control, you get the behavior shown in Figure 14.8; the control has automatically adjusted its dimensions with no code required from the developer.

> **NOTE**
>
> By default, controls are typically anchored on their top and left sides. You may be wondering what happens if no anchors are specified at all. In that case, the control will maintain its exact position regardless of form resize actions. This is, in effect, the same behavior as top and left anchors would have because forms have their top, leftmost points as their "origin."

Anchoring also solves the positioning problem with the command buttons. If you change their `Anchor` property to `Bottom, Right`, they will anchor themselves to the bottom right of the form, which is consistent with their recommended placement on a form. Because you aren't anchoring opposing sides of the control, you aren't forcing the buttons to resize; they are merely repositioned to keep station with the right and bottom edge of the form. Contrast this with the anchoring performed for the text box: Because you anchored all sides, you are not only keeping a uniform border between the edge of the text box and the form, but you are also causing the text box to stretch itself in both dimensions.

Docking

For the simple form in Figure 14.8, you can implement the majority of your layout logic using the `Anchor` property. But if you refer to the overall plan for the CSR screen (see Figure 14.1), you can see that you have some positioning needs that would be cumbersome to solve using anchors. For instance, the data entry region of the form should automatically expand vertically and horizontally to fill any space left between the list of requests, the status bar, and the command bar. This is where the concept of *docking* comes to the rescue. Docking is used to either stick a control to a neighbor control's edge or the form's edge, or it is used to force a control to fill all of the available space not taken by other controls.

As with the Anchor property, the property browser provides a graphical tool to set a control's Dock property (shown in Figure 14.10).

FIGURE 14.10   Setting the Dock property.

Control Auto Scaling

The Windows Forms engine supports the capability to dynamically adjust a control's dimensions in order to preserve its original design proportions. This capability is useful if the form or control is displayed at runtime on a system with different display characteristics (resolution, DPI, and so on) than the system the form or control was designed on.

A simple example of this occurs when an application that uses a reasonable 9-point font during design becomes almost unusable when displayed on a system whose default font size is larger. Because many UI elements auto-adjust based on the font of their displayed text (such as window title bars and menus), this can impact nearly every visual aspect of a form application.

Controls in .NET 2.0 support two properties that enable them to counter these issues automatically without a lot of developer intervention: AutoScaleMode and AutoScaleDimensions. AutoScaleMode specifies an enumeration value indicating what the scaling process should use as its base reference (DPI or resolution). Table 14.2 shows the possible AutoScaleMode values.

TABLE 14.2   AutoScaleMode Enumeration Values

Value	Description
Dpi	Scale relative to the resolution
Font	Scale relative to the dimensions of the font being used
Inherit	Scale according to the base class AutoScaleMode value
None	No automatic scaling is performed

AutoScaleDimensions sets the dimensions (via a SizeF structure) that the control was originally designed to. This could refer to a font size or the DPI.

Using Containers

Containers are .NET controls designed to hold other controls. You can use containers in conjunction with the Anchor and Dock control properties to create intricate design scenarios. Although there are various container controls, the ones most applicable to control layout are the FlowLayoutPanel, TableLayoutPanel, and SplitContainer classes.

Both the TableLayoutPanel and FlowLayoutPanel classes derive from the more generic Panel class. The Panel class provides very high level capabilities for grouping controls. This is beneficial from a placement perspective because you can aggregate a bunch of controls into one group by positioning them within a panel. This way, you can act on them as a group; for instance, disabling a panel control will disable all of its child controls. The TableLayoutPanel and FlowLayoutPanel build on that functionality by also providing the capability to dynamically affect the positioning of their child controls.

The TableLayoutPanel

Consider a series of labels and text boxes for entering address information. They are typically arrayed in a column-and-row fashion. The TableLayoutPanel is ideal for implementing this behavior because it automatically forces the column and row assignment that you make for each of the controls. Figure 14.11 shows a series of label and text box controls embedded within a TableLayoutPanel. Notice that resizing the form (and thus the panel, which is docked to fill the form interior) causes the panel's controls to auto-adjust their alignment.

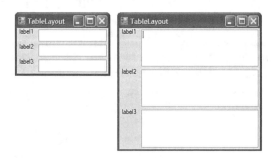

FIGURE 14.11   The TableLayoutPanel.

If an item within one of the cells extends beyond the cell's boundaries, it will automatically overflow within the cell. This provides you with the same layout capabilities that HTML provides for web browser–based interfaces.

> **NOTE**
>
> When a control is added to a `TableLayoutPanel`, it is decorated with five additional properties: `Cell`, `Column`, `Row`, `ColumnSpan`, and `RowSpan`. These properties can be used to change the control's row/column position within the layout panel at runtime. The `ColumnSpan` and `RowSpan` properties are used the same way as their namesakes in the HTML world. In .NET, controls that imbue other controls with additional properties are called *extender providers*.

The `FlowLayoutPanel`

The `FlowLayoutPanel` has a simpler layout algorithm: Items are ordered either vertically or horizontally by wrapping control sets across rows or columns as needed. The two screens shown in Figure 14.12 illustrate the effect of resizing a flow layout panel containing a series of radio buttons.

FIGURE 14.12   The `FlowLayoutPanel`.

The `SplitContainer`

The `SplitContainer` control is a much enhanced alternative to the original `Splitter` control included with .NET 1.0/1.1/Visual Studio 2003. This control represents the marriage of two panels and a splitter; the splitter separates the two panels either horizontally or vertically and allows a user to manually adjust the space (in the horizontal or vertical) that each panel consumes within the overall container.

Figure 14.13 shows the versatility of this control; two split containers, one embedded within a panel hosted by the other, are used to provide both vertical and horizontal resizing capabilities for the panels on a form (panel 2 isn't visible because it is the panel functioning as the container for the split container with panels 3 and 4). By dragging the split line to the right of panel 1, you can increase or decrease the horizontal real estate it occupies on the form. The same is true for the split line between panel 3 and panel 4: Dragging this will adjust the ratio of space that both panels vertically occupy in relation to one another.

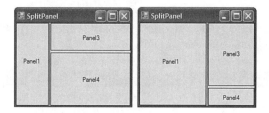

FIGURE 14.13 Resizing with the `SplitContainer`: a horizontal `SplitContainer` embedded in a vertical `SplitContainer`.

The `ToolStripContainer`

Many applications support the ability to drag and dock a toolbar, menu, and the like to any side of a form: top, bottom, left, or right. Visual Studio itself is an example of just such an application. By grabbing and dragging a Visual Studio toolbar, you can reposition it, for example, to the left side of the form. The `ToolStripContainer` control enables this functionality in your applications as well; it is a combination of four panels, each positioned on the four different edges of the containing form. These panels are used to host `ToolStrip` controls (more on these in a bit) and—at runtime—allow users to move tool strips within and between the four panels.

> **NOTE**
>
> Although the `ToolStripContainer` provides a convenient vehicle for snapping tool strips to the sides of a form, there is unfortunately no built-in support for "floating" tool strips.

The design experience is simple: You can shuffle controls around to the four different panels depending on where you want them positioned within the parent form. Figure 14.14 shows a `ToolStripContainer` in design mode. The smart tag offers up control over the visibility of the top, left, right, and bottom panels. Each panel is hidden by default. You can click on any of the arrows on the sides of the container to expand the corresponding panel and give you room to place tool strips within the panel.

Although it is convenient to be able to place items in a `ToolStripContainer` within the designer, the real benefit that you get from the control is the automatic support for dragging and dropping between panels at runtime. This means that, without writing a single line of layout or positioning code, you have enabled functionality that allows users to place their menus or toolbars wherever they want within the form. Figure 14.15 shows a toolbar, hosted in a `ToolStripContainer`, which has been redocked from the top panel to the left panel at runtime.

Multiple `ToolStrip` controls can also be stacked within any of the given panels in the `ToolStripContainer`. Figure 14.16 shows multiple command bars stacked within the rightmost panel. As noted later in the chapter, a control's z-order dictates its place within the stack.

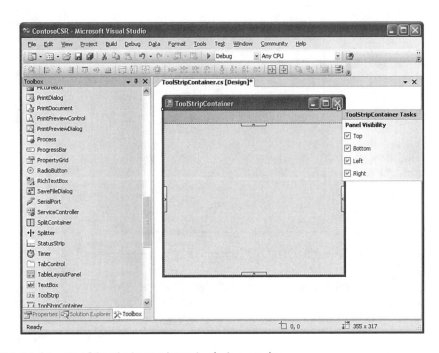

FIGURE 14.14   ToolStripContainer in design mode.

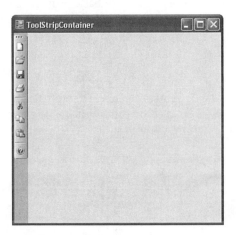

FIGURE 14.15   A toolbar repositioned within a ToolStripContainer.

NOTE

The sharing of space—vertically or horizontally—within a tool strip container is sometimes referred to as rafting: The tool strip controls are free to float anywhere within the panel.

FIGURE 14.16   Multiple toolbars stacked within the same panel.

There are a few other intricacies involved with form/control layout and positioning, but we have now covered the basics. With these concepts in hand and a general design for your form, you can start using the Windows Forms Designer.

Control Appearance and Behavior

A control's appearance is set via the same set of basic properties used to control form appearance: items such as ForeColor, BackColor, and Font all make an appearance on most controls.

Visual Styles

One item of interest, however, is the capability for a control to automatically alter its appearance to conform to the currently selected "Desktop Theme" if running on Windows XP. This capability is enabled by calling the Application.EnableVisualStyles method. Figure 14.17 shows a form without visual styles enabled (left) alongside one with visual styles enabled (right).

FIGURE 14.17   The effects of Application.EnableVisualStyles.

Tab Order

By default, the order in which the controls on a form receive focus (tab order) is the same as the order in which they were placed on the form. To explicitly set the tab order for all of the controls on a form, the IDE has a tab order selection mode.

To enter tab order selection mode, select View, Tab Order from the menu. The Windows Forms Designer will annotate every control on the form with a number. This number represents that control's position within the overall tab order for the form. To set the tab order that you want, just click sequentially on the controls; their tab order number will automatically change as you click.

ToolTips

ToolTips are small "balloons" that display text as a user moves his or her cursor over a control. Typically, they are used to provide helpful hints or descriptions of a control's purpose, action, and so on. ToolTips are implemented with the `ToolTip` class and can be assigned to controls at design time.

The `ToolTip` class is an example of an *extender provider* (see the previous note on extender providers in our discussion on the `TableLayoutPanel` control). When you add a ToolTip component to a form, every control on the form will now implement a `ToolTip` property that is used to assign a ToolTip to that specific control.

For illustration, if you wanted to add a ToolTip to a ToolStrip button, you would first drag the ToolTip component over to the form from the Toolbox. You would then select the ToolStrip button that you want to add the ToolTip to, and you would set its `ToolTip` property to reference the ToolTip instance on your form.

Working with `ToolStrip` Controls

Many of the standard, core visual elements of a form will be realized with `ToolStrip` controls. A `ToolStrip` control functions as a container for other controls that derive from `ToolStripItem`; it can host various types of controls: buttons, combo boxes, labels, separators, text boxes, and even progress bars. The `ToolStrip` class itself is used to directly implement toolbars on a form and also functions as a base class for the `StatusStrip` control and the `MenuStrip` control.

`ToolStrip` controls come with an impressive list of built-in capabilities. They intrinsically support, for example, dragging an item from one tool strip to another, dynamically reordering and truncating items in the tool strip as users resize the strip or its parent form, and fully supporting different OS themes and rendering schemes.

All of the different flavors of the `ToolStrip` control have some common traits:

- A design-time smart tag provides quick and easy access to common commands.

- In-place editing of child controls is supported (for example, a point-and-click interface is offered for adding, removing, and altering items within the `ToolStrip`, `StatusStrip`, or `MenuStrip`).

- An Items Collection Editor dialog box allows you to gain finer control over child control properties and also allows for add/reorder/remove actions against the child controls.

- Tool strips support a pluggable rendering model; you can change the visual renderer of a tool strip to a canned rendering object or to a custom object to obtain absolute control over the appearance of the tool strip.

From the initial form design, you know that you will need menus, toolbars, and status bars, so the ToolStrip control and its descendants will play a crucial role.

Creating a Menu

MenuStrip controls enable you to visually construct a form's main menu system. Dragging and dropping this control from the Toolbox onto the blank form will automatically dock the menu strip to the top of the form (see Figure 14.18).

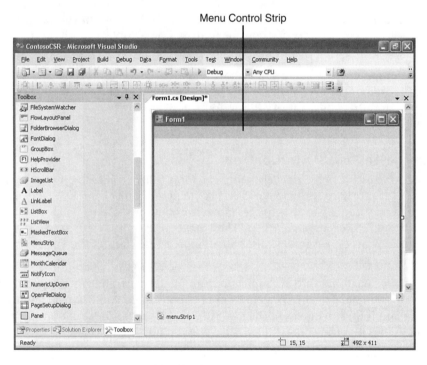

FIGURE 14.18   A menu positioned on the form.

After you place this control on the form, selecting the MenuStrip control will activate the smart tag glyph (smart tags are covered in Chapter 7, "Working with Visual Studio's Productivity Aids"). Clicking on the smart tag allows you to quickly do three things:

- Automatically insert standard items onto the menu

- Change the menu's RenderMode, Dock, and GripStyle properties

- Edit the menu items

Leveraging the ability to automatically equip a menu strip with a standard set of menus shaves a few minutes of design time off the manual approach. Figure 14.19 shows the result.

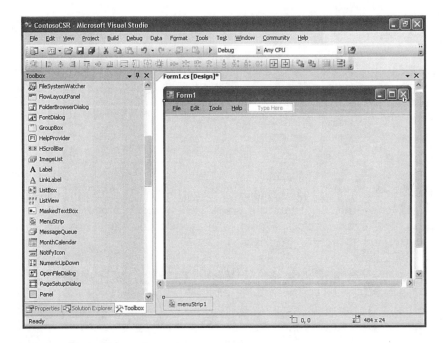

FIGURE 14.19   Menu with standard items.

Not only has the designer inserted the standard File, Edit, Tools, and Help top-level menu items, but it has also inserted subitems below each menu. Table 14.3 indicates the exact menu structure that results from using the menu's Insert Standard Items feature.

TABLE 14.3   Standard Menu Items

Main Menu	Menu Items
File	
	New
	Open
	Save
	Save As
	Print
	Print Preview
	Exit
Edit	
	Undo
	Redo
	Cut

TABLE 14.3   Continued

Main Menu	Menu Items
	Copy
	Paste
	Select All
Tools	
	Customize
	Options
Help	
	Contents
	Index
	Search
	About

If you want to manually add additional menu items into the menu strip, you can use the placeholder block within the menu strip labeled with the text "Type Here." Every time you type in the placeholder block, additional placeholders become visible, and a menu item is added to the menu strip (see Figure 14.20).

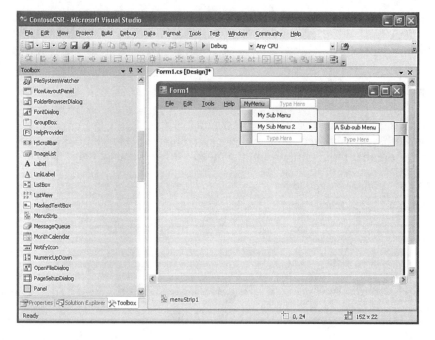

FIGURE 14.20   Manually adding menu items.

Creating a Toolbar

The next item up for inclusion on the form is a toolbar. Toolbars in .NET 2.0 are implemented directly with ToolStrip controls. As mentioned before, ToolStrip controls can host a variety of child controls; each inherits from the `ToolStripItem` base class. Figure 14.21 shows the controls that can be implemented inside a tool strip.

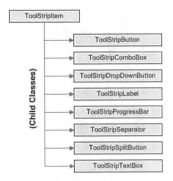

FIGURE 14.21   Classes inheriting from `ToolStripItem`.

In fact, the interactive layout features of the tool strip work the same way as the menu strip: Dragging the control onto the form will result in a blank `ToolStrip` control docked to the top of the form just under the existing menu control, and you can quickly add a roster of standard items to the tool strip by using its smart tag and selecting Insert Standard Items.

> **NOTE**
>
> Controls use the concept of *z-order* to determine their "depth" on the form. If two controls occupy the same space on a form, the control's individual z-order determines which of the two controls is on top and which is on the bottom. You control this layering in the IDE by right-clicking a control and using the Send To Back and Bring To Front menu commands.
>
> Z-order plays an important role in the placement of docked controls. Docked controls are arrayed in increasing order of their z index on the form. For instance, if you select the `ToolStrip` and issue the Send To Back command, the order of the `MenuStrip` and `ToolStrip` containers will be altered to place the `ToolStrip` first (at the top of the form) and the `MenuStrip` second (just below the `ToolStrip` instance).

Figure 14.22 shows the in-progress form with the added `ToolStrip` control.

If you wanted to enable users to drag and drop the toolbar or menu onto one of the form's four sides, you would use the `ToolStripContainer`. In fact, there is a shortcut option here: You can take any of the `ToolStrip` controls currently on the form and add them to a `ToolStripContainer` with just a couple of clicks of the mouse. One of the items available via a tool strip's smart tag is the command Embed in a ToolStripContainer. If you issue this command against the toolbar that you just added to the sample form, Visual Studio will do two things for you: It will add a `ToolStripContainer` to the form, and it will place the selected `ToolStrip` into the container, specifically, in the top panel of the `ToolStripContainer`.

14

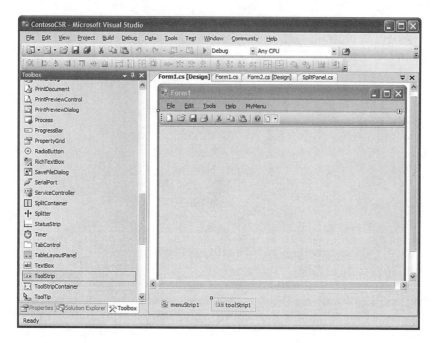

FIGURE 14.22   Main form with complete menu and toolbar.

Creating a Status Bar

Status bars provide the user feedback on an application's current status, progress within an action, details in context with an object selected on a form, and so on. The StatusStrip control provides this functionality in .NET 2.0/Visual Studio 2005, and it supplants the StatusBar control found in previous versions.

As with the other ToolStrip descendants, the StatusStrip control functions as a container; its ability to host labels in addition to progress bars, drop-downs, and split buttons makes it a much more powerful control than the StatusBar.

Figure 14.23 shows the fictional Contoso CSR form with a StatusStrip docked at the bottom of the form. In design mode, you see a drop-down button that holds a selection for each of the four supported child controls. For the purposes of this demonstration prototype, add a label control to report general application status and an additional label and progress bar to be used if you run into any long-running retrieval or edit operations.

By default, child controls will be added in a left-to-right flow layout pattern within the StatusStrip pattern. With just six clicks (two per item), you can add these controls to the strip. The in-place editing capabilities are great for quickly building out the look and feel of the strip; for greater control of the strip's child controls, you can use the Items Collection Editor dialog box.

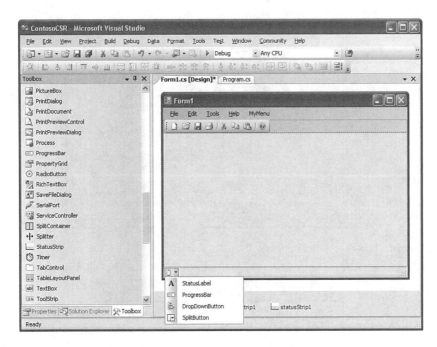

FIGURE 14.23   StatusStrip in design mode.

14

NOTE

By right-clicking on any of the StatusStrip child controls and selecting Convert To, you can quickly change the type of the control. For instance, if you have a label control currently on the strip but you really want a drop-down button, you right-click the label and select Convert To, DropDownButton. This saves you the hassle of deleting the control and adding a new one.

Editing the StatusStrip Items   You use the StatusStrip's smart tag and select Edit Items to launch the Items Collection Editor dialog box. The editor provides direct access to all of the hosted control's properties and also allows you to edit, delete, and reorder items within the status strip (see Figure 14.24).

By tweaking some properties here, you can improve the layout and appearance of your items. Figure 14.25 shows the default layout of the controls you added; ideally, you want the progress bar and its label control to sit at the far right of the status strip and the status label to sit at the far left to consume any remaining space.

To make this happen, you need to set the Spring property to True for the leftmost label. This will cause the label to expand and contract to fill the available space on the status strip. Next, set its TextAlignment property to situate the text to the left of the label region and change the Text property to something more appropriate.

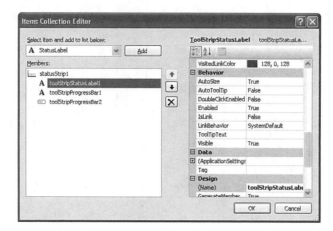

FIGURE 14.24   The Items Collection Editor.

FIGURE 14.25   Default `StatusStrip` items.

Figure 14.26 shows the fruits of our labor.

FIGURE 14.26   Final `StatusStrip` look and feel.

Displaying Data

So far, we have only touched on form elements that provide the basic framework user navigation, status, commands, and so on. However, the capability to access, display, and edit data from an underlying data store (relational or otherwise) is the real value of an application like the fictional Contoso CSR application. We'll touch on the details of working with databases in the next chapter; here, we will describe some of the basic controls used to display data in a form.

Hierarchical Data

The `TreeView` control is ideal for presenting data with hierarchical relationships and is thus a good candidate for housing the list of order records (which can be grouped by different criteria). First, add a `SplitContainer` control. This will partition the leftover interior space in the form into two discrete panels. Yet another panel will house the search function for orders; this will be docked to the top of the left split panel. A `TreeView` will dock-fill the remainder of this leftmost panel, and the right panel will house the data fields (text boxes, labels, radio buttons, and so on) for an individual CSR record.

`TreeView` controls present data as a list of nodes; each node can serve as a parent for additional nodes. Typically, with applications that front a database, you would build the contents of the `TreeView` by binding to a resultset from the database, or by programmatically looping through the resultset and adding to the `TreeView`'s node list through its API. But you also have control over the `TreeView` content in the designer by launching the TreeNode Editor.

The TreeNode Editor   The TreeNode Editor (see Figure 14.27) is a dialog box that acts much the same as the Items Collection Editor examined previously. It enables you to add, edit, and remove items from the `TreeView` control. You launch the editor dialog box by selecting Edit Nodes from the `TreeView`'s smart tag.

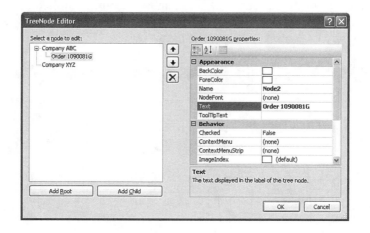

FIGURE 14.27   Using the designer to edit notes in the tree view.

Using the Add Root and Add Child buttons, you can insert new nodes into the tree's data structure at any given nesting level. Figure 14.27 shows manually inserted nodes with test data so that you can get an idea of what the order list would look like using the company as a parent node and order instances as child nodes under the corresponding company. Each item, or node, in the `TreeView` consists of two parts: an image and text. The image is optional; if you want the ability to attach an icon to a node, you start by first assigning an `ImageList` control to the `TreeView` control.

Using an `ImageList`   `ImageList` controls function as an image provider for other controls. They maintain a collection of Image objects that are referenced by their ordinal position or key within the collection. Any control that provides an `ImageList` property can reference an `ImageList` component and use its images. `ListView`, `ToolStrip`, and `TreeView` are some examples of controls that can leverage the `ImageList` component.

NOTE

Visual Studio 2005 ships with a large library of images that you can use with the `TreeView` or any other control that requires these types of standard graphics such as toolbars and menus. By default, the image files are placed in `C:\Program Files\Microsoft Visual Studio 8\Common7\VS2005ImageLibrary`.

An `ImageList` doesn't have a visual presence on a form; in other words, you can't see the `ImageList` itself. Its sole use is as a behind-the-scenes component that feeds images to other controls. Dropping an `ImageList` onto the designer will put an instance of the component in the component tray (see Figure 14.28). You can then use the Images Collection Editor dialog box to add, edit, and remove the images hosted by the component. Changing the images associated with the image list will automatically change the images used by any controls referencing the `ImageList`.

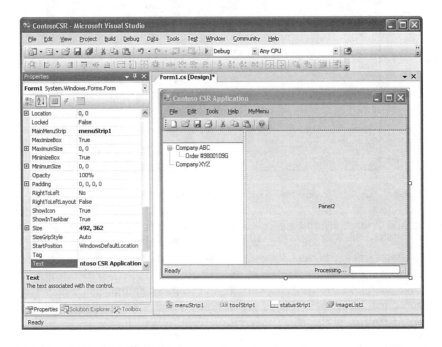

FIGURE 14.28   An `ImageList` added to the Forms Designer.

Figure 14.29 shows a few images added for use in the `TreeView` control. To enable the `TreeView` to use these images, you have to do two things:

1. Assign the `TreeView.ImageList` property to point to the instance of the `ImageList` component (in this case, `imageList1`).

2. Set the image associated with a node either programmatically or via the TreeNode Editor dialog box.

FIGURE 14.29 An ImageList added to the Forms Designer.

With the ImageList component in place and the TreeView dropped in the SplitContainer's left panel, the form is almost there from a design perspective. The remaining piece is the series of fields that will display the data for a record selected in the TreeView control.

You could add this piece by just dragging a bunch of text boxes and labels over into a TableLayoutPanel and then docking the whole mess in the open SplitContainer panel. But because you really want to treat this as one cohesive unit to simplify positioning, eventual data binding, and so on, you will instead create a user control for displaying a CSR record.

Tabular Data

The DataGridView control is the premium Visual Studio 2005 control for displaying data in a tabular format. It provides a row/column format for displaying data from a wide variety of data sources. Figure 14.30 shows a DataGridView with its smart tag menu opened; the smart tag menu provides fast access to the column properties of the grid control and also allows you to directly bind the DataGridView to a data source.

Data Sources   The DataGridView control supports a variety of possible data sources. For instance, scenarios like displaying name/value pairs from a collection are supported, in addition to mainstream support for datasets returned from a relational data store. If you select a data source for the grid, a column will be added to the grid for every column that appears in the data source, and the row data will automatically be provided inside the DataGridView control.

Data can be displayed in the grid control in an "unbound" mode as well; using the grid's row/column API, you can programmatically define the structure of the grid and add data to it at runtime.

14

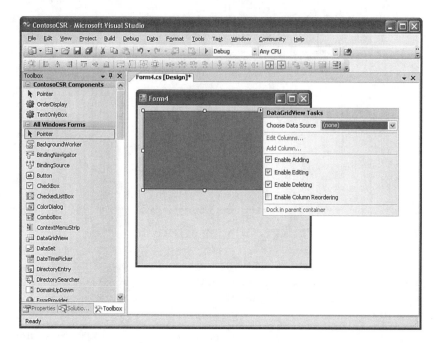

FIGURE 14.30   The DataGridView control.

Cell Types   Each individual cell in a DataGridView functions as if it is an embedded control. Each cell can express the underlying data that it contains in various ways; check boxes, drop-downs, links, buttons, and text boxes are all supported cell types. In addition to the data visualization possibilities, each cell also has its own set of events that can be hooked within your code. For example, you can hook the mouse enter and leave events for a specific cell.

We cover this control in depth in Chapter 15, "Working with Databases."

Creating Your Own Controls

If none of the stock .NET controls will meet your specific needs, you can create your own controls for use on a Windows Form in three ways:

- You can subclass an existing control and modify or extend its behavior and appearance.

- You can create a user control by compositing together two or more existing controls.

- You can create a custom control from scratch, implementing your own visuals and behavior.

Subclassing an Existing Control

Subclassing an existing control is the best approach if your needs are only slightly different from one of the standard .NET Framework controls. By inheriting from an existing control class, you are riding on top of its behavior and appearance; it's up to you to then add the specialized code to your new control class.

For example, suppose that you wanted a text box that would turn red any time a numeric (that is, nonalphabetic) character was entered. This is easy to do with just a few lines of code sitting in the TextBox control's TextChanged event, but consolidating this behavior into its own class will provide a reuse factor.

You start by adding a new user control to the project. User controls actually inherit from the UserControl class; because you want to inherit from the TextBox class, you will need to change the class definition by using the code editor. After you do that, you can place the new component on a form and use its functionality.

Working with an Inherited Control

Because TextBox already has a UI, you don't need to do anything with regards to the appearance of the control. In fact, it will work just like any other text box control within the Windows Forms Designer (see Figure 14.31).

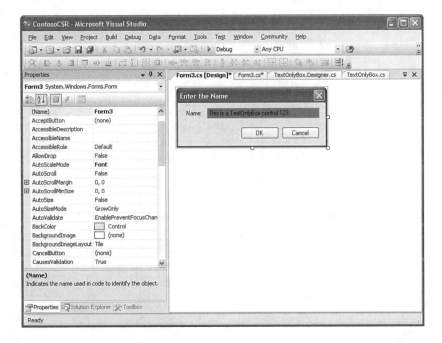

FIGURE 14.31 A derived control on a form.

The Properties window for the control behaves as expected, and double-clicking on the control will immediately take you to an open code editor window. In short, the design-time experience remains fully functional and requires no effort on the part of the developer.

Designing a User Control

A user control is technically the same as any other class that you would author as a developer; because a user control has a visual aspect to it, Visual Studio provides a designer, just as with Windows forms, to help in the drag-and-drop creation of the control.

User controls are composite controls; that is, they are constructed from one or more existing .NET controls. As with a derived control, their user interfaces inherit from the native controls they are composed of, making them simple to build and use in the designer.

There are two approaches to the user control creation process: You can create a separate Windows Control Library project, or you could simply add a user control class to an existing Windows Forms project.

Creating a separate project would allow the user control to live in its own assembly. If it is a separate assembly, you can treat the user control as the quintessential black box, giving you greater flexibility from a source control perspective and allowing you to share the control among multiple projects. For production scenarios, this is clearly the best route. However, for simple prototyping work, as you are doing here with the CSR form application, the ease and simplicity of just adding a new class to the existing project make this approach preferable to using the separate project approach. The class would live inside the same namespace as the form class.

If you were ever in a position to transition from prototyping to actual production development, nothing would preclude you from refactoring the control by simply copying the user control class file and embedding it in a separate control library project.

As soon as you add the user control class to the project, you are presented with the User Control Designer (see Figure 14.32). The designer works in exactly the same way as the Windows Forms Designer; to build the user control, you drag components or controls from the Toolbox onto its surface.

Adding Controls

Obviously, the controls that you use to build your composite control will entirely depend on its envisioned functionality. As an example, to create an order display control, you need to think about the underlying data structure of an order. An order record might contain the following:

- An order number
- A series of dates that capture the date the order was placed, date the order was shipped, and so on
- A list of items included on the order
- Billing information and shipping address
- Miscellaneous comments

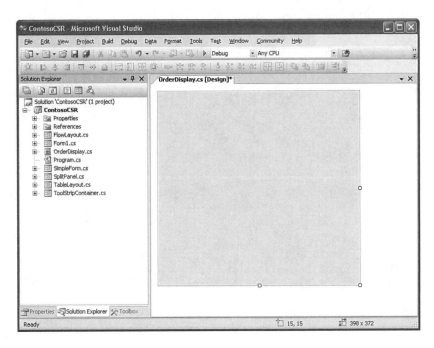

FIGURE 14.32   The User Control Designer.

Because this is a lot of information to try to cram onto one screen, you can turn to the `TabControl`. A tab control is another general-purpose container control that allows you to organize content across several pages that are accessed via tabs. Within each tab, you can leverage the `TableLayoutPanel` and implement most of the order fields with simple label and text box pairs.

The whole process of getting these controls into the user control works identically to the Windows Forms Designer: You drag and drop the controls from the Toolbox onto the user control design surface. Figure 14.33 shows the `OrderDisplay` user control with its user interface completed.

Embedding the User Control

Now that you have a completed design for your user control, the only remaining step is to embed the control into your primary form. If you compile the project, Visual Studio will automatically recognize the user control class and include an entry for the control in the Toolbox. From there, you are just a drag and drop away from implementing the `OrderDisplay` control.

In Figure 14.34, you can see the `OrderDisplay` item in the Toolbox and the results of dragging it onto the form surface.

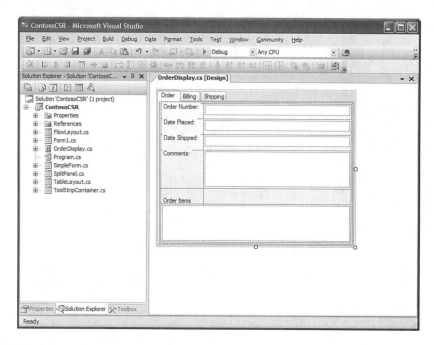

FIGURE 14.33   Designing a user control.

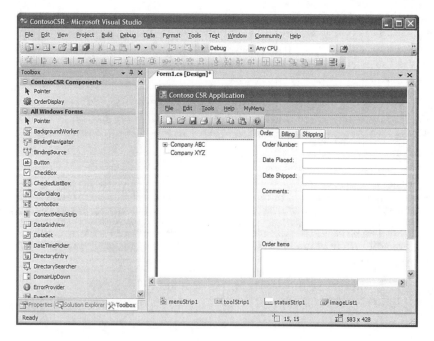

FIGURE 14.34   The user control in the Toolbox and on the form.

Creating a Custom Control

Custom controls represent the ultimate in extensibility because they are built from scratch. As a result, they are relatively hard to develop because they require you to worry not only about functionality but also about every single aspect of the control's visual appearance. Because the physical user interface of the custom control needs to be drawn 100% by custom code, a steep learning curve is associated with authoring a custom control.

Because much of the work that goes into creating a custom control is at the code level, we won't try to tackle this subject with any useful degree of detail in this book. You should note, however, that the process starts the same way as with other control options: Visual Studio has a custom control project item template; adding this to your project will give you a baseline of code to start with. From there, it's up to you.

> **NOTE**
>
> The OnPaint event is where you place the code to draw your control's user interface. Although so-called "owner draw" controls can involve complex drawing code, the good news is that the Windows Forms Designer will leverage whatever code that you place in the OnPaint event in order to render the control at design time. This means that you can still rely on the Windows Forms Designer to provide you with a WYSIWYG experience even with custom controls.

Summary

In this chapter, we described the various design-time capabilities of the Windows Forms Designer tool. Windows forms are a powerful presentation layer technology, and Visual Studio 2005 provides an array of tools for quickly building impressive, rich user interfaces based on this technology.

The role of the Windows Forms Designer, the Toolbox, and the Properties window were introduced in the context of delivering a modern, well-thought-out, standards-based user interface for a .NET Windows application. Using the tools documented here, you can wring the most out of your forms development experience.

CHAPTER 15

Working with Databases

This chapter is all about how you can manage databases and build data-aware applications using Visual Studio 2005 and SQL Server.

Five different Visual Studio tools allow you to interact with a database and assist with building applications that leverage data from a database:

- Solution Explorer

- Server Explorer

- Database Diagram Designer

- Table Designer

- Query and View Designer

Collectively, they are referred to as the *Visual Database tools*. We introduced a few of these tools earlier in Chapter 5, "Browsers and Explorers." Now we have the opportunity to explore how developers can use these tools together to create database solutions.

We'll start by examining how to build databases and database objects with the visual database tools. From there, we can cover the specifics of creating data-aware applications with data-bound controls.

Creating Tables and Relationships

The primary entities in any database are its tables. Tables are composed of a structure and data. Server Explorer is the Visual Studio instrument used to define or edit the structure or data of any table within a connected database. In fact, using Server Explorer, it is possible to create a new SQL Server database instance from scratch.

IN THIS CHAPTER

- Creating Tables and Relationships

- Working with SQL Statements

- Using Database Projects

- Creating Database Objects in Managed Code

- Binding Controls to Data

NOTE

As we noted in Chapter 5, the Express and Standard editions of Visual Studio refer to the Server Explorer as the Database Explorer. For simplicity, we will always refer to this window as the Server Explorer in this chapter.

Creating a New SQL Server Database

Data connections are physical connections to a database. In Server Explorer, the Data Connections node has a list of every established database connection. To start the database creation process, right-click on the Data Connections node and select the Create New SQL Server Database option. In the resulting dialog box (see Figure 15.1), you will need to provide a server name, login credentials, and a name for the new database.

FIGURE 15.1   Creating a new SQL Server database.

This will immediately create the indicated database and add a connection to the new database under the Data Connections node. Figure 15.2 shows the newly created Contoso database added to the list of connections.

Adding an Existing Database

Of course, you can also establish a connection to an existing database. Again, you right-click the Data Connections node; this time, though, you select the Add Connection option. The Add Connection dialog box (see Figure 15.3) is similar to the new database dialog box: You specify a data source, server name, login credentials, and a database name/database filename to connect to the database.

FIGURE 15.2   The new database added to the data connections.

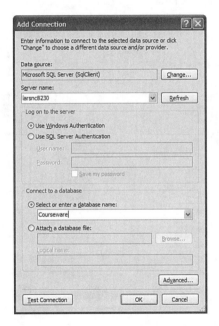

FIGURE 15.3   Connecting to an existing database.

Under each connection are folders for the following classes of database objects:

- Database Diagrams

- Tables

- Views

- Stored Procedures

- Functions

- Synonyms

- Types

- Assemblies

These folders are the launching point for creating corresponding objects within the database.

Defining Tables

The Table Designer is the Visual Studio tool you use to define or edit the definition for a table. Using the Server Explorer window, right-click the Tables folder under an existing connection and select Add New Table. The Table Designer will open in the main document pane of the IDE.

The designer is implemented in a tabular format; you add a row in the designer for every column you want to define in the table. For each table column, you specify a name, data type, and nullability. In addition to the tabular designer interface, a Properties window is also present that provides complete access to all of the different properties for any given column in a table (see Figure 15.4).

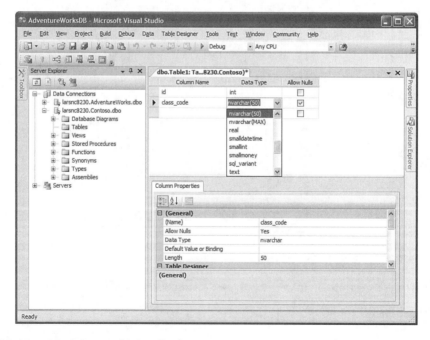

FIGURE 15.4   Defining a table's columns.

In addition to the basics, the Table Designer also allows you to define a column, or group of columns, as part of the primary key for the table, or as part of an index.

Setting a Primary Key

With the Table Designer active in the IDE, a new Table Designer top-level menu item is available. You can use this menu, or the shortcut menu displayed whenever you right-click within the Table Designer, to access a list of useful actions. For instance, to create a primary key for the table, you would select the column or columns that constitute the key and then select Set Primary Key from the designer's menu. A key icon will indicate any primary keys defined in the table.

Creating Indexes, Foreign Keys, and Check Constraints

Indexes, foreign keys, and check constraints are all created using the same interface and process: Select the appropriate action from the Table Designer menu; use the settings dialog box to first add the index, key, or constraint; and then set its properties in the property grid. As an example, to create an index across one or more columns in the table, select the Indexes/Keys item from the Table Designer menu. In the Indexes/Keys dialog box (see Figure 15.5), you can add a new index and then set its properties in the property grid.

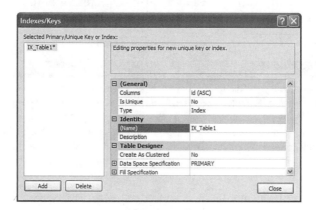

FIGURE 15.5   Creating an index.

Column population for the index is controlled with the index's Columns property; a separate Index Columns dialog box (see Figure 15.6) enables you to change the column membership and specify the sort order for each column.

Using the Database Diagram Designer

The aforementioned Table Designer and dialog boxes allow you to define tables and table-related constructs on a table-by-table basis. The Database Diagram Designer provides the same functionality in a more visual format. It allows you to build a diagram of the whole database showing tables, table columns, keys, and table relationships, and also allows you to create each of these items from within the Diagram Designer tool.

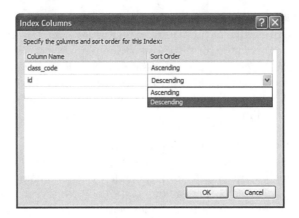

FIGURE 15.6   Column membership in an index.

Like the Table Designer, the Database Diagram Designer is implemented within the IDE's document pane. It has its own menu and toolbar associated with it; many of the commands on the menu/toolbar can be accessed through the designer's shortcut menu by right-clicking anywhere within the designer.

> **TIP**
>
> Within a diagram, you can change the view style on a per-table basis. Right-click the table and select one of the available Table views: Standard (shows column name, data type, and allow nulls), Column Names, Keys, Name Only, and Custom (you select the data you want to display). The Name Only view is particularly useful if you want to see an entire database diagram to get a sense of the relationships without necessarily caring about the table details themselves.

Creating a Database Diagram

To create a database diagram, right-click on the Database Diagrams node in the Server Explorer window and select Add New Diagram. A blank diagram will open, and the designer will immediately display a dialog box for adding tables to the diagram (see Figure 15.7).

After you've added a few tables, the diagram shows a graphical representation of the tables' columns and any relationships that the tables participate in. The diagram is fully interactive; you can directly edit column definitions, keys, relationships, and so on.

> **TIP**
>
> Here is a quick shortcut for adding groups of related tables: Add a table to the diagram, select it, and click on the Add Related Tables button in the designer's toolbar. This will automatically add to the diagram any table in the database that has a current relationship with the selected table.

FIGURE 15.7   Adding tables to a diagram.

Modifying Table Definitions

Tables can be edited "in-line" within the diagram. To change column details, you click within the table and then enter column name information or change the data type and nullability rules. To add a column, just fill out a new row within the table representation in the diagram.

Building Table Relationships

Table relationships are easy to define within a diagram: Just drag and drop the primary key column from one table to the foreign key column on another table. This will automatically kick off two dialog boxes: Foreign Key Relationships and Tables and Columns (these are the same dialog boxes used to create foreign keys in the Table Designer). Figure 15.8 captures the foreign key and primary key assignments for the creation of a common one-to-many relationship between a category table and an order table. The order table has a category ID column (category_id) that will be foreign-keyed to the primary key on the category table (id).

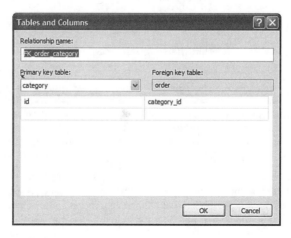

FIGURE 15.8   Creating a foreign key.

After committing the column assignments, you complete the relationship by changing any properties (if needed) on the relationship itself in the Foreign Key Relationships dialog box (see Figure 15.9).

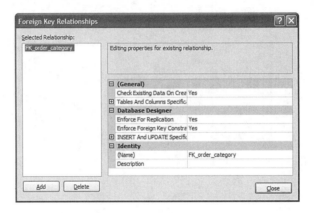

FIGURE 15.9   Creating a foreign key.

Relationships are depicted within the diagram as a line between the two tables. The line indicates the direction of the relationship by showing a key on the primary key side and an infinity symbol on the foreign key side (or the "many" side) of the relationship. Figure 15.10 illustrates the order category table to order table association as it would appear within the Database Diagram Designer.

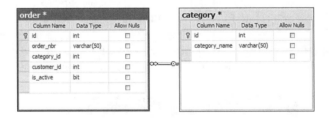

FIGURE 15.10   Two tables related in the Database Diagram Designer.

NOTE

By default, relationships will enforce referential integrity. That is, they will prevent any action (insert, update, delete) that would result in a mismatch of keys between the two related tables. This would include inserting a foreign key (FK) value when it doesn't exist as a primary key (PK) in the related table, changing a PK value that is referenced as a FK value, and so on.

You can control whether a relationship enforces referential integrity through the Enforce Foreign Key Constraint setting in the Foreign Key Relationship dialog box. Relationships that do not enforce referential integrity are depicted as banded lines instead of solid lines within the Diagram Designer. You should also note that the Diagram Designer will show only relationships that have been explicitly defined through the process we cover in the preceding paragraphs. Just having similarly named foreign keys and primary keys will not automatically create a relationship for you.

In addition to one-to-many relationships, you can also model one-to-one, many-to-many, and reflexive relationships using the Database Diagram Designer.

One-to-One Relationships   You build a one-to-one relationship in the same way you create a one-to-many relationship. The difference is this: One-to-one relationships are between two primary keys instead of a primary and a foreign key. If you drag a primary key column from one table to a primary key column on another table, this will automatically create a one-to-one association. These relationships are depicted with a key icon on both ends of the relationship line.

Many-to-Many Relationships   You create a many-to-many relationship with the help of a junction table. If you had to model a many-to-many association between an order table and an item table (an order can have many items, and an item can belong to many orders), you would first add a third table to the database to hold the foreign keys of this relationship.

After adding the junction table, you would then establish a one-to-many relationship between the order and orderitem table and the item and orderitem table. The last step is to define the multicolumn primary key on the junction table. Figure 15.11 shows the results in the diagram.

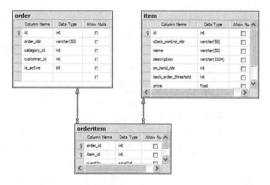

FIGURE 15.11   A many-to-many relationship.

Reflexive Relationships   A reflexive relationship is a relationship between a table and itself. A typical example used to illustrate reflexive relationship is that of a *part* table that relates back to itself to represent the fact that a part could be made up of other parts. In this case, the part table might carry a parent_part_id field that is meant to be a foreign key related to the employee table's primary key.

To create a reflexive relationship, select the primary key column and drag it back onto the same table. The configuration of the key associations and the relationship values is the same as with any other relationship. Figure 15.12 shows a diagram of a reflexive relationship.

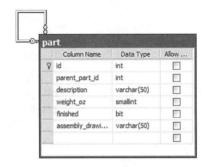

FIGURE 15.12   A reflexive relationship.

Working with SQL Statements

There is full support within the Visual Database Tools set for crafting and executing SQL statements against a connected database. This includes support for compiling SQL statements as stored procedures, creating views and triggers, and writing user-defined functions.

Writing a Query

The primary tool that facilitates the development of SQL statements is the Query/View Designer, which is a graphical tool that allows you to build queries with a point-and-click interface. After a query is constructed, this tool also allows you to view and interact with any results returned as a result of executing the query.

Now you're ready to put this tool through its paces.

Creating a new select query against a table is as simple as selecting the database in Server Explorer and then selecting Data, New Query. An initial prompt gathers a list of the tables, views, functions, and/or synonyms to use as the target of the query (see Figure 15.13).

After you have selected the objects you want the query to target, the Query Designer will open. As Figure 15.14 illustrates, there are four separate panes to the designer:

- **Criteria Pane**—This pane allows you to select, via a point-and-click diagram, the data columns to include in the select statement, sorting, and alias names.

- **Diagram Pane**—This pane is similar to the diagram in the Database Diagram Designer; it graphically depicts the database object relationships. This makes creating joins a simple action of using existing relationships or creating new ones right within this tool.

- **Results Pane**—After the query is executed, this pane holds any data returned as a result. Note that this pane is equipped with navigation controls to allow you to page through large resultsets.

- **SQL Pane**—The SQL pane holds the actual SQL syntax used to implement the query. You can alter the statement manually by typing directly into this pane, or you can leverage the designer and let it write the SQL for you based on what you have entered in the diagram and criteria panes.

FIGURE 15.13   Adding tables to the query.

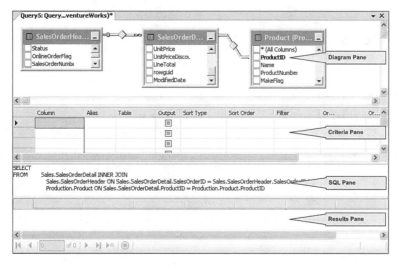

FIGURE 15.14   The Query/View Designer.

Each of these panes can be shown or hidden at will. Right-click anywhere in the designer and select the Pane fly-out menu to select or deselect the visible panes.

Fine-Tuning the SQL Statement

To flesh out the select statement, you can indicate which columns from which tables you want returned by placing a check next to the column in the diagram pane. You use the criteria pane to specify a sort order, provide alias names for the return columns, and establish a filter for the resultset. As you select these different options, the designer turns them into SQL, visible in the SQL pane.

> **NOTE**
>
> We are using the AdventureWorks sample database in a SQL Server 2005 instance for most of this chapter. If you want to follow along, you can download a copy of this database by visiting the main Microsoft website (www.microsoft.com) and searching for "AdventureWorks." This is also the sample database used by the SQL Server 2005 Books Online help collection.

Figure 15.15 shows the completed "Order" query, with results visible in the bottom pane.

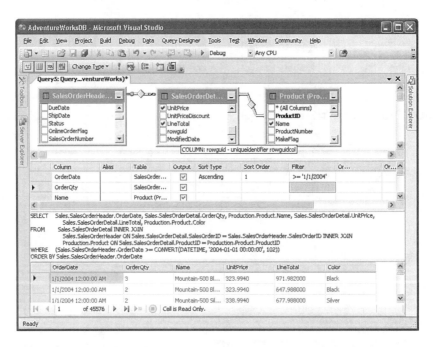

FIGURE 15.15   Querying for order information in the AdventureWorks database.

Specifying Joins and Join Types

When you add multiple, related tables to the Query Designer, the designer uses their key relationships to automatically build a JOIN clause for the query. You also have the option to create joins on table columns that don't have an existing relationship. You do this the same way that you specify relationships in the Database Diagram Designer: You select and drag the column from one table to another within the diagram pane. The columns to be joined must be of compatible data types; you can't join, for instance, a varchar column with an integer column.

Joins are created using a comparison operator. By default, this is the equals operator; in other words, return rows where the column values are equal across the join. But you have control over the actual comparison operation used in the join. As an example, perhaps you want the resultset to include rows based on a join where the values in Table A are greater than the values in Table B on the joined columns. You can right-click the join relationship line in the diagram pane and select Properties to see the properties for the join; clicking the ellipsis button in the Join Condition and Type property will reveal the Join dialog box, depicted in Figure 15.16.

FIGURE 15.16   Setting join type and operator.

Other Query Types

By default, creating queries from the Server Explorer will result in a *select* query. But the Query Designer is equally adept at building other query types. If you want, for instance, an insert query, you can change the type of the query loaded in the designer by selecting Query Design, Change Type.

Table 15.1 shows the different query types supported by the designer.

TABLE 15.1   Supported Query Types

Query Type	Comments
Select	Returns data from one or more tables or views; a SQL SELECT statement
Insert Results	Inserts new rows into a table by copying them from another table; a SQL INSERT INTO...SELECT statement
Insert Values	Inserts a new row into a table using the values and column targets specified; a SQL INSERT INTO...VALUES statement
Update	Updates the value of existing rows or columns in a table; a SQL UPDATE...SET statement
Delete	Deletes one or more rows from a table; a SQL DELETE statement
Make Table	Creates a new table and inserts rows into the new table by using the results of a select query; a SQL SELECT...INTO statement

---

TIP

If you just want to quickly see the data contents of any given table, you can right-click the table within the Server Explorer and then select Show Table Data. This will initiate a new Query/View Designer with a SELECT * statement for the given table. By default, only the results pane is visible. This functionality is ideal for testing scenarios in which you need to quickly edit data in the database or observe the effects of SQL statements on a table.

Creating Views

Views are virtual tables. They look and act just like tables in the database but are, in reality, select statements that are stored in the database. When you look at the content of a view, you are actually looking at the resultset for a select statement.

Because views are implemented as select statements, you create them using the Query/View Designer tool. In Server Explorer, right-click the Views folder under the database where you want to create the view. From there, you build the select statement just as you would for any other SQL statement.

Saving the view will refresh the database's copy of the view's select statement.

Developing Stored Procedures

A stored procedure is a SQL statement (or series of statements) stored in a database and compiled. With SQL Server, stored procedures consist of Transact-SQL (T-SQL) code and have the capability to involve many coding constructs not typically found in ad hoc queries. For instance, you can implement error-handling routines within a stored procedure and even call into operating system functions with so-called extended stored procedures.

For a given database, right-click the stored procedures folder in Server Explorer and select Add New Stored Procedure. A template for a stored procedure will open in the SQL Editor. The SQL Editor is a close sibling to Visual Studio's Code Editor; although it doesn't have IntelliSense, it does support syntax coloring, breakpoints, and the more general text-editing features (cut-copy-paste, word wrapping, and so on).

Figure 15.17 shows the beginnings of a stored procedure in the SQL Editor window.

With the template loaded into the SQL Editor, writing a stored procedure involves typing in the lines of code and SQL that will perform the required actions. But stored procedure developers haven't been left out in the cold with regards to productivity in Visual Studio. You can leverage the power of the Query/View Designer to write portions of your stored procedure for you.

Using the SQL Editor with the Query/View Designer

As you build the body of the procedure, the editor window will highlight and box in certain parts of the procedure. These boxed-in areas represent SQL statements that can be edited using the Query Designer. Consider the stored procedure featured in Figure 15.18.

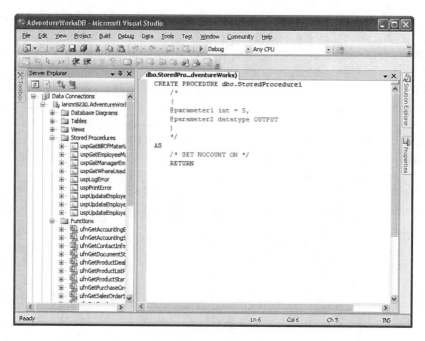

FIGURE 15.17   The start of a new stored procedure.

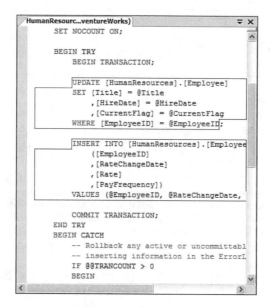

FIGURE 15.18   SQL statements in a stored procedure.

This procedure, from the AdventureWorks database, essentially consists of two update queries. Both of them are contained within a blue-bordered box in the SQL Editor window. This is the editor's way of indicating that it has recognized a SQL statement within the procedure that can be designed using the Query/View Designer. If you right-click within the boxed-in area, the shortcut menu will include an option titled Design SQL Block. If you select this option, the Query/View Designer will open in a separate dialog box.

Figure 15.19 shows the first of the two update statements as they appear in the Query/View Designer. Using the same process outlined before for writing queries, you can construct the SQL within the relative luxury of the Query Designer's drag-and-drop interface. Clicking OK on the designer dialog box will save the query back into the stored procedure, updating the code in the editor window.

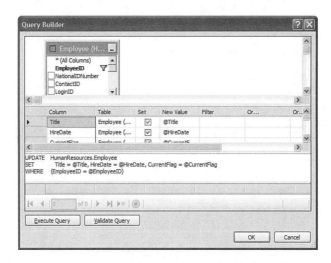

FIGURE 15.19   Designing a query for a stored procedure.

Notice that the Query Designer fully supports the use of parameters. When you fill in the parameter names in the New Value column (see the criteria pane in Figure 15.19), the designer is able to construct the appropriate SQL.

> **NOTE**
>
> The capability to create and edit stored procedures is supported only in Microsoft SQL Server. You cannot use the Visual Studio tools to create a procedure in, say, an Oracle database.

The Query Designer can also be pressed into play for inserting new blocks of SQL into a stored procedure (as opposed to editing existing SQL statements). First, in the SQL Editor window, right-click on the line within the procedure where you want to place the new query. From the pop-up menu, select Insert SQL. The Query/View Designer can now be used to craft the appropriate SQL. After you close out the dialog box by clicking OK, the new SQL will be inserted into the procedure and can be saved into the database.

Debugging Stored Procedures

In addition to coding stored procedures, you can leverage the Server Explorer tool to help you debug them. With the stored procedure open in the SQL Editor window, set a breakpoint in the procedure by clicking in the Indicator Margin (for more details on the Indicator Margin and general editor properties, see Chapter 6, "Introducing the Editors and Designers"). With a breakpoint in place, right-click on the stored procedure's name in the Server Explorer tree and select Step Into Stored Procedure (see Figure 15.20).

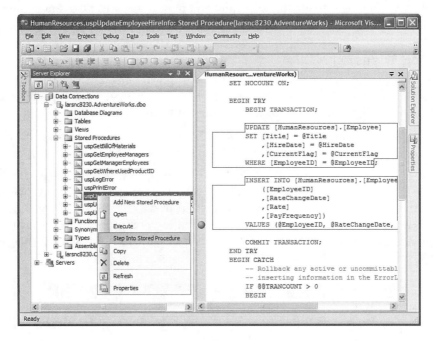

FIGURE 15.20   Debugging a stored procedure.

The SQL Debugger is also parameter-friendly. If the stored procedure uses any parameters, the debugger will show a dialog box to capture values for the parameters (see Figure 15.21).

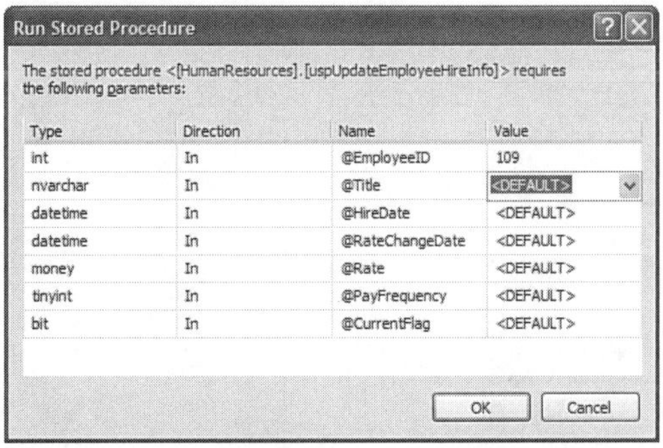

FIGURE 15.21   Entering parameter values in the SQL Debugger.

You can quickly cycle through the list of parameters, supplying appropriate values. After you click OK, the stored procedure will be executed. If you have set a breakpoint, execution will pause on the breakpoint (a yellow arrow is used to indicate the current line of execution within the editor, just the same as with the code editor window). With execution stopped, you can use the Locals and Watch windows to debug the procedure's code. See Chapter 9, "Debugging with Visual Studio 2005," for a more thorough treatment of the Locals and Watch windows as debugging tools in Visual Studio.

The Debug menu is used to control execution and flow. If you select Continue, the procedure will continue running up to the next breakpoint (if present).

Creating Triggers

Triggers are a type of stored procedure designed to run when the data in a table or view is modified. Triggers are attached to an individual table; when a query—an update, insert, or delete query—affects data in the table, the trigger will execute.

Because a trigger is really a stored procedure with a controlled execution time (hence, the name *trigger*), it can have quite complex SQL statements and flow execution logic.

To create a trigger, use Server Explorer and locate the table to which the trigger is to be attached. Right-click the table name, select Add New Trigger, and then use the SQL Editor to write the SQL for the trigger. When the trigger is saved to the database, it will show up under its related table in Server Explorer (alongside the columns in the table). Figure 15.22 shows a simple trigger designed to raise an error if an update statement changes the Availability column in the Location table.

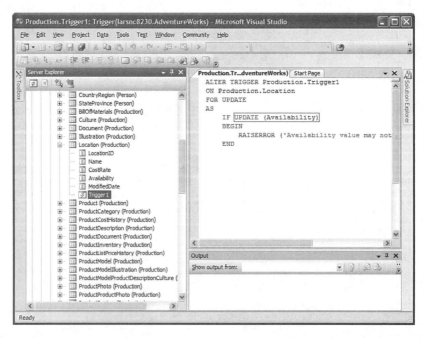

FIGURE 15.22 Creating a trigger.

Creating User-Defined Functions

User-defined functions are bodies of code/SQL designed to be reusable across a variety of possible consumers: stored procedures, applications, or even other functions. In that respect, they are no different from functions written in C# or Visual Basic. They are routines that can accept parameters and return a value. User-defined functions return scalar values (for example, a single value) or a resultset containing rows and columns of data.

One example of a user-defined function might be one that accepts a date and then determines whether the day is a weekday or weekend. Stored procedures or other functions in the database can then use the function as part of their processing.

Because user-defined functions are T-SQL statements with a format similar to stored procedures, the SQL Editor again is the primary tool for writing them. For each data connection visible in Server Explorer, a Functions folder will contain any existing functions. To create a new function, you can right-click on this folder, select Add New, and then select the type of function to create. There are three options:

- **Inline Function**—Returns values as a resultset; the resultset is built from the results of a `SELECT` query

- **Table-valued Function**—Returns values as a resultset; the resultset is built by programmatically creating a table within the function and then populating the table using `INSERT INTO` queries

- **Scalar-valued Function**—Returns a single value

After selecting the appropriate function type, template code for the function will be delivered inside a new SQL Editor window. Feel free to use the Query/View Designer to construct any required lines of SQL within the function.

For the specifics on how to write a function and put it to best use within the database, consult your database's documentation.

Using Database Projects

Up to this point, we have discussed the use of the Visual Database Tools outside the context of a Visual Studio solution/project. Now let's investigate the role of the Database project type. Database projects hold a database connection (referred to as a *database reference*) and SQL scripts or queries that relate to that database. One benefit of housing scripts in a project like this is that they are available for storage in a source control system.

> **NOTE**
>
> Scripts are nothing more than SQL statements stored in a file. They are useful because they can be executed in batch to do such things as create tables in a brand-new database or add a canned set of stored procedures to a database. Because they are merely files, they can be transferred from computer to computer, enabling you to duplicate database structures across machines with ease.

The SQL scripts in the database project can create many of the database objects that we have already discussed: tables, views, triggers, stored procedures, and so on. Queries developed using the Query/View Designer can also be directly saved into a database project. In short, you use the Visual Database Tools in conjunction with a Database project to create and save SQL scripts and queries.

Creating a Database Project

To generate a database project, pick New Project from the File menu and then look under the Other Project Types category in the New Project dialog box (see Figure 15.23).

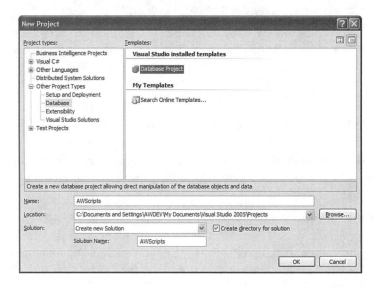

FIGURE 15.23 The database project type.

The project wizard will first prompt you for a database reference to add to the project; you do this by using the same set of dialog boxes used to add data connections in the Server Explorer (refer to Figure 15.3).

Once created, the default project will have the structure that you see in Figure 15.24.

As you can tell from this project structure, it has predefined folders for holding scripts, queries, and database references.

Scripts are added to the project in two ways. You can use the traditional "add new item" process just as you would with any other project. Select the item type (see Figure 15.25), and a script (or query) will be added to the project with the standard template skeleton code added to the file for you. An easier way to create scripts, however, is to let the database tools do the work for you.

FIGURE 15.24   Database project structure.

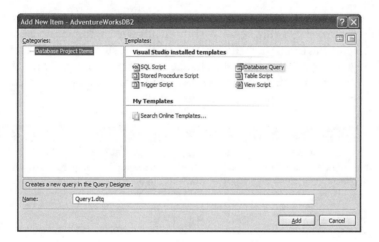

FIGURE 15.25   Database project items.

Auto-Generating Scripts

There are two major types of auto-generated scripts: create scripts and change scripts. As their names imply, create scripts are used to create a new database object of some sort: a table, a stored procedure, and the like. Change scripts are used to update an existing database object.

Create Scripts

Using Server Explorer, you can generate a create script for any object in the database. For example, to capture the create script for the BillOfMaterials table in the AdventureWorks database, you would right-click the table and select Generate Create Script to Project. All of the SQL necessary to create the table (and its associated objects such as keys, indexes, and so on) will be written to a file under the Create Scripts folder in the current database project.

You even can script an entire database with one click: Instead of selecting an individual table, select the database node in Server Explorer and then select the Generate Create Script to Project command.

When the script is created, double-clicking on its file in the project will launch the SQL Editor with the script's content.

> **NOTE**
>
> As an indication of the manual work that script generation saves, consider this: The create script for the BillOfMaterials table weighs in at more than 120 lines of SQL.

Change Scripts

The concept with change scripts is the same with two differences: Change scripts can be automatically generated only for tables, and the script will capture only changes made to the table instead of the creation of the table. The Table Designer provides easy access to change script generation. After making a change to the table within the designer, select Table Designer, Generate Change Script. The script will be constructed and placed within the Change Scripts folder in the current project.

> **NOTE**
>
> Because Visual Studio generates the change script by looking at your current edits and comparing them to the table structure as it exists in the database, you can only generate a change script before you have saved your changes down to the database.

Executing a Script

After a script is created, you have the option to run the script against a database. You kick off script execution in the Solution Explorer by right-clicking on the script file. There are two options in the pop-up menu for running the script: a Run command and a Run On command. The Run command will run the script against the database specified in the default database reference. The Run On command allows you to manually specify which database, from the list of database references, should be the target of the script.

Database References

If you recall from the Database Project Wizard, you are prompted for a database reference to include in the project. But database projects support the ability to have more than one reference. If you have more than one reference, you can specify which of the available references is the default reference by right-clicking on it in Solution Explorer and selecting Set As Project Default.

Creating Database Objects in Managed Code

Database objects are commonly implemented using some dialect of the SQL language. This is true with SQL Server as well. SQL Server 2005, however, introduces the capability of authoring SQL objects in managed code. So, instead of using Transact SQL, you can actually write your stored procedures, queries, views, and so on using your favorite .NET language.

The key enabler in Visual Studio that makes this happen is the SQL Server Project. Not to be confused with the formerly discussed Database Project, the SQL Server Project is a language-specific project type that provides class templates for implementing managed code versions of database routines.

Starting a SQL Server Project

In the Add New Project dialog box, SQL Server projects are located under the Database category within each language. Creating a new SQL Server project kicks off the same Add Database Reference dialog box that you have already seen with the Server Explorer and with the Database Project; the new project structure laid down by the project wizard is shown in Figure 15.26.

FIGURE 15.26   SQL Server Project.

The SQL Server Project directly supports the creation of the following database objects:

- Stored procedures
- Triggers
- Aggregates
- User-defined functions
- User-defined types

The following sections look at how to go about creating a straightforward stored procedure.

Creating a Stored Procedure in C#

First, you add a stored procedure item to your project by using the Project menu and selecting Add Stored Procedure. A new class will be added to the project. Listing 15.1 shows the base code that shows up within the new class file. You can add your custom code to the static void routine `UpdateEmployeeLogin`.

LISTING 15.1   The Start of a Managed Code Stored Procedure

```
using System;
using System.Data;
using System.Data.SqlClient;
using System.Data.SqlTypes;
using Microsoft.SqlServer.Server;


public partial class StoredProcedures
{
    [Microsoft.SqlServer.Server.SqlProcedure]
    public static void UpdateEmployeeLogin()
    {
        // Put your code here
    }
};
```

Managed code objects in SQL Server all leverage the .NET Framework data classes (that is, ADO .NET) to do their work. This means that stored procedures that you write will end up instantiating and using classes like `SqlConnection` and `SqlCommand`. The code that you write is identical to data access code that you would write from within any other .NET project type: class libraries, web projects, and Windows forms projects. Because the common denominator is the use of ADO .NET classes, developers don't need to learn another language (like T-SQL) to perform work in the database.

> **NOTE**
>
> It's outside the scope of this chapter to cover the relative merits or disadvantages of writing your database objects in managed code as opposed to T-SQL. Check out the whitepaper available on MSDN titled "Using CLR Integration in SQL Server 2005" by Microsoft. Although fairly old (it was written in November 2004), it is a great treatment of this subject and is highly recommended reading.

Listing 15.2 shows a fleshed out C# routine that will update the AdventureWorks Employee table with login information. None of this code is complicated and can be easily understood (and written) by anyone with C# data access experience.

LISTING 15.2   Managed Code for Updating Employee Login Values

```
using System;
using System.Data;
using System.Data.SqlClient;
using System.Data.SqlTypes;
using Microsoft.SqlServer.Server;


public partial class StoredProcedures
{
    [Microsoft.SqlServer.Server.SqlProcedure]
    public static void UpdateEmployeeLogin(SqlInt32 employeeId,
SqlInt32 managerId, SqlString loginId, SqlString title,
SqlDateTime hireDate, SqlBoolean currentFlag)
    {
        using (SqlConnection conn =
            new SqlConnection("context connection=true"))
        {
            SqlCommand UpdateEmployeeLoginCommand =
              new SqlCommand();

            UpdateEmployeeLoginCommand.CommandText =
                "update HumanResources.Employee SET ManagerId = " +
              managerId.ToString() +
                ", LoginId = '" + loginId.ToString() + "'" +
                ", Title = '" + title.ToString() + "'" +
                ", HireDate = '" + hireDate.ToString() + "'" +
                ", CurrentFlag = " + currentFlag.ToString() +
                " WHERE EmployeeId = " + employeeId.ToString();

            UpdateEmployeeLoginCommand.Connection = conn;

            conn.Open();
            UpdateEmployeeLoginCommand.ExecuteNonQuery();
            conn.Close();


        }
    }
};
```

One line of code, however, deserves a more detailed explanation. The SqlConnection object is created like this:

```
SqlConnection conn = new SqlConnection("context connection=true")
```

The connection string "context connection=true" tells the data provider engine that the connection should be created in the same context as the calling application. Because this routine will be running inside a database, that means you will be connecting to the host database and will run using the context (transactional and otherwise) of the calling application. Because you are piggy-backing on the context of the database that the routine is running in, you don't need to hard-code a full SQL connection string here.

For comparison purposes, Listing 15.3 shows the same update query implemented in T-SQL.

LISTING 15.3   T-SQL for Updating Employee Login Values

```
ALTER PROCEDURE [HumanResources].[uspUpdateEmployeeLogin]
    @EmployeeID [int],
    @ManagerID [int],
    @LoginID [nvarchar](256),
    @Title [nvarchar](50),
    @HireDate [datetime],
    @CurrentFlag [dbo].[Flag]
WITH EXECUTE AS CALLER
AS
BEGIN
    SET NOCOUNT ON;

    BEGIN TRY
        UPDATE [HumanResources].[Employee]
        SET [ManagerID] = @ManagerID
            ,[LoginID] = @LoginID
            ,[Title] = @Title
            ,[HireDate] = @HireDate
            ,[CurrentFlag] = @CurrentFlag
        WHERE [EmployeeID] = @EmployeeID;
    END TRY
    BEGIN CATCH
        EXECUTE [dbo].[uspLogError];
    END CATCH;
END;
```

Building and Deploying the Stored Procedure

When you build your SQL Server project, the typical compilation process takes place. Assuming that your code will build, you can now deploy the resulting assembly to the database. Use the Build menu to access the Deploy command.

After the assembly has been deployed, you can test it by calling it from an application or from a query window. For detailed information on how to call managed assemblies and write them, consult the SQL Server 2005 Books Online.

Binding Controls to Data

You have now seen all of the various ways that you can use Visual Studio to create and manage databases. The following sections look at the tools available for consuming data within Windows forms or web applications.

An Introduction to Data Binding

There is a common problem and solution pattern at hand with applications that front databases. Typically, data has to be fetched from the database into the application, and the applications user interface has to be updated to display the data in an appropriate manner. For large datasets, the concept of paging comes into play. Because it is inefficient to load in, say, a 100MB dataset, a paging mechanism needs to be pressed into action to allow the user to move forward and back through the data "stream." After the data has safely made it into the application's UI, the application-to-database flow needs to be handled. For any pieces of data that have been changed, those changes have to be reconciled and committed back into the database.

Data binding is the term given to the implementation of a design pattern that handles all facets of this roundtrip of data from a data structure, into an application's controls, and back again (see Figure 15.27). Although the data structure will most commonly be a database, it could be any sort of container object that holds data, such as an array or a collection. With .NET, .NET further stratifies the concepts of data binding into *simple data binding* and *complex data binding*. Both of these terms refer to a control's intrinsic capabilities in the larger context of the data-binding process.

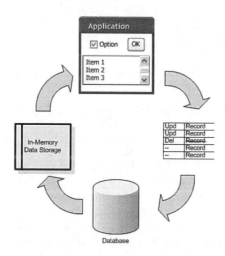

FIGURE 15.27   The data-binding process.

Simple Data Binding

Simple data binding is the capability for a control to bind to and display a single data element within a larger dataset. A TextBox control is a great example of a control commonly used in simple data-binding scenarios. You might use a TextBox, for example, to display the last name of an employee as it is stored within the employee table of a database.

Support for simple data binding is widespread throughout both the Windows and web forms controls. When you use the built-in capabilities of the Windows and Web Forms Designer, it is trivial to add a group of controls to a form and simple-bind them to a dataset (more on this in a bit).

Complex Data Binding

The term *complex data binding* refers to the capability of a control to display multiple data elements at one time. You can think of this as a "multirow" capability: If a control can be leveraged to view multiple rows of data at one time, then it supports complex data binding.

The DataGridView control (for Windows forms) and DataGrid control (for web forms) are premier examples of controls that were purpose-built to handle tabular (multirow and multicolumn) data.

Although the internals necessary to implement data binding are messy, complex, and hard to understand, for the most part the Visual Studio tools have abstracted the cost of implementing data binding out to a nice, easy, drag-and-drop model. Now let's look at how to rapidly build out support for roundtrip data binding.

Auto-Generating Bound Windows Forms Controls

Although there are various ways to approach and implement data-bound controls with Visual Studio, they all involve the same basic two steps. You need to

1. Establish a data source.

2. Map the data source members to controls or control properties.

From there, the Visual Studio Form Designers are capable of generating the correct controls and placing them on the form. All of the data-binding code is handled for you; all you need to worry about is the layout, positioning, and UI aspects of the controls.

As you might imagine, your form might have controls that use simple data binding or complex data binding or a mix of both. Now you're ready to look at the steps involved with creating a series of controls that will leverage both simple and complex data binding to display information from the AdventureWorks Employee table. In this scenario, you will work with the Windows Forms Designer. The ASP .NET Web Forms Designer works in a similar fashion, and you'll have a chance to investigate drag-and-drop approaches for data binding in the web environment in just a bit. As we have already established, the first step is selecting a data source.

Selecting a Data Source

In Visual Studio, make sure you are working inside a Windows Application project and use the Data Sources window to select a data source. If this window isn't already visible, select Show Data Sources from the Data menu in the IDE. If your current project doesn't have any defined data sources, you will need to create one. Select the Add New Data Source button in the toolbar of the window to start the Data Source Configuration Wizard. On the first page of this wizard (see Figure 15.28), you select the type of the data source. There are three options here:

- **Database**—The data source resides as a table within a relational database.

- **Web Service**—The data source is a web service that will return the data to be bound to the form controls.

- **Object**—The data source is an object that will provide the data (this is useful in scenarios in which a business object from another layer of the application will be responsible for delivering the data to the form).

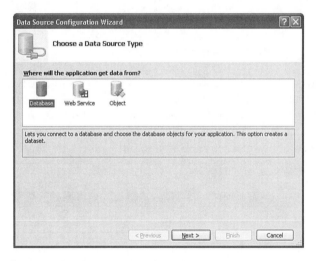

FIGURE 15.28   Choosing the data source type.

Because the concepts of data binding are most easily understood within the context of a database, we will use the database data source type as the underpinning for our walk-throughs in this chapter.

If you have selected the database data source type, the second page of the wizard focuses on selecting a connection for the database. Any connections previously established for other data sources or for use in the Server Explorer will show up here by default in the drop-down (see Figure 15.29). You also have the option of specifying a new connection. If the connection string to the database has private information such as a user password, you have the option at this point to exclude that information from the string.

The next step in the wizard allows you to save the connection string information to your application's local configuration file. Saving the information is usually a good idea because it allows you to tweak the string when needed (such as when changing database environments), but caution should be used if you have elected to store sensitive information in the string (refer to the previous wizard page).

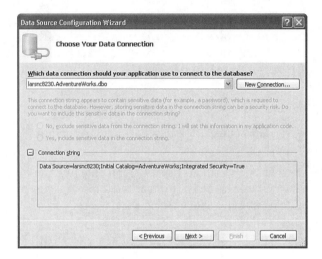

FIGURE 15.29   Selecting the connection.

On the final page of the wizard, shown in Figure 15.30, you indicate which of the objects in the database should be used for the source data. You can select from any of the data elements present in any of the various tables, views, stored procedures, or user-defined functions in the database. For purposes of this example, select a few employee table data columns that are of interest: Employee ID, Title, Birth Date, Gender, Hire Date, and Modified Date.

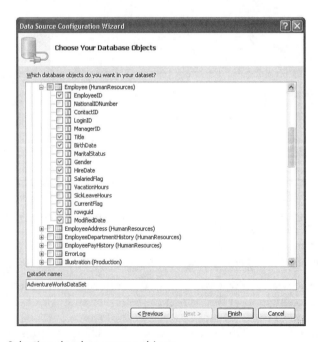

FIGURE 15.30   Selecting the data source objects.

At the conclusion of the wizard, your selected data source will be visible in the Data Sources window (see Figure 15.31).

NOTE

Behind the scenes, Visual Studio is really just using the data source information collected in the Data Source Configuration Wizard to create a typed dataset. This dataset is then stored as a project item in the current project.

FIGURE 15.31   The Data Sources window.

With the data source in place, you're ready to move on to the next step: mapping the data source elements to controls on your form.

Mapping Data Sources to Controls

The really quick and easy way to create your data-bound controls is to let Visual Studio do it for you. From the Data Sources window, click on the drop-down button on the data source name to reveal a menu (see Figure 15.32).

FIGURE 15.32   Changing the data table mapping.

This menu enables you to set the control generation parameters and really answers the question of what controls you want generated based on the table in the data source. By setting this to `DataGridView`, you can generate a `DataGridView` control for viewing and editing your data source. The Details setting allows you to generate a series of simple data-bound controls for viewing or editing data in the data source. For this example, select Details and then drag and drop the data source itself from the Data Sources window and onto a blank form.

Figure 15.33 shows the results. In just two short steps, Visual Studio has done all of the following for you:

- Auto-generated a set of `Label`, `TextBox`, and `DateTimePicker` controls

- Auto-generated a tool strip with controls for navigating between records in the data source, saving changes made to a record, deleting a record, and inserting a new record

- Created all of the necessary code behind the scenes to establish a connection to the data source, read from the data source, and commit changes to the data source

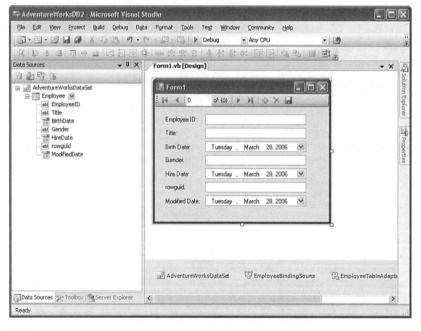

FIGURE 15.33   Auto-generated controls: viewing employee data.

You have essentially created an entire data-enabled application from scratch with absolutely no coding on your part.

The approach of using simple data binding may not fit in to the user interface design, so you always have the option of working in the complex data binding world and using the

`DataGridView` as an alternative. Figure 15.34 shows the results of auto-generating a `DataGridView` instance using this same process.

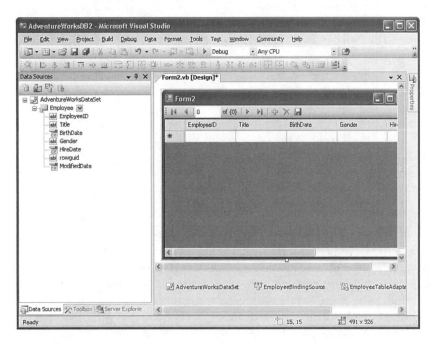

FIGURE 15.34   An auto-generated `DataGridView`.

Customizing Data Source Mappings   Refer again to Figure 15.31 and look at the individual data elements that show up under the Employee data source. Each of these is displayed with a name and an icon. The name is, of course, the name of the data element as defined in the database. The icon represents the default mapping of that data type to a .NET control. For example, the Title field maps to a `TextBox` control, while the BirthDate field maps to a `DateTimePicker` control. Visual Studio actually attempts to provide the best control for any given data type. But feel free to manually indicate the specific control you want used. If you wanted to display the value of the Employee ID column in a label instead of a text box (in recognition of the fact that you cannot edit this value), it would be easy enough to change this before generating the controls by selecting the `EmployeeID` column in the Data Sources window and then clicking on the drop-down arrow to select `Label` instead of `TextBox`.

In addition to changing the control to data type mapping on an individual level, you can affect the general default mappings that are in place by selecting the Customize option from that same drop-down menu. This will pop up the Visual Studio Options dialog box with the Windows Forms Designer page selected. Using the settings there (see Figure 15.35), you can specify the default control type that you want applied for each recognized data type.

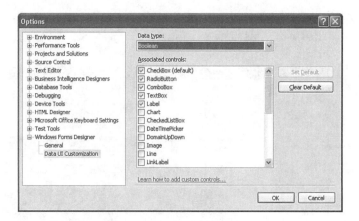

FIGURE 15.35   Customizing the data to control type mappings.

Manually Binding Windows Forms Controls

In many situations, you don't want Visual Studio to create your data-bound controls for you, or you may need to bind existing controls to a data source. Data binding in these cases is just as simple and starts with the same step: creating or selecting a data source. Some controls, such as the `DataGridView`, have smart tag options for selecting a data source. Others don't have intrinsic data dialog boxes associated with them but can be bound to data just as easily by working, again, with the Data Sources window.

Binding the `DataGridView`

Grab a `DataGridView` from the Toolbox and drag it onto the form's surface. After you've created the control, select its smart tag glyph and use the drop-down at the top of the task list to select the data source to bind to (see Figure 15.36).

With a data source selected, you have again managed to develop a fully functional application with two-way database access. All of the code to handle the population of the grid and to handle committing changes back to the database has been written for you.

Customizing Cell Edits   The power of the `DataGridView` lies in its capability to both quickly bind to and display data in a tabular format and also to provide a highly customized editing experience. As one small example of what is possible in terms of cell editing, follow through with the Employee table example. When you auto-generated form controls to handle Employee table edits, you ended up with `DateTimePicker` controls to accommodate the date- and time-based data in the table. With the `DataGridView`, the cell editing experience is a simple text box experience: Each cell contains text, and you can edit the text and save it to the database. But you can provide a more tailored editing experience. You can use a variety of stock controls (such as the `DataGridViewButtonColumn`, `DataGridViewComboBoxColumn`, and others that inherit from `DataGridViewColumn`; see Chapter 14, "Building Windows Forms") to display data within the columns of the grid.

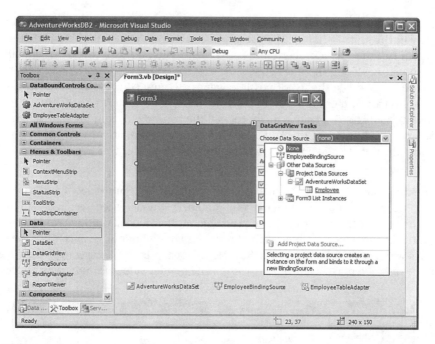

FIGURE 15.36   Selecting the `DataGridView`'s data source.

For instance, you can use the `DataGridViewComboBoxColumn` class to provide a drop-down edit for the `Gender` column in the grid. To do this, you first need to change the default column type. Select the grid control, open the smart tag glyph, and select the Edit Columns action. In the Edit Columns dialog box, find the column for the employee gender data and change its column type to `DataGridViewComboBoxColumn`. (see Figure 15.37).

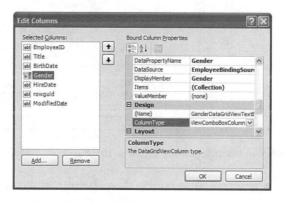

FIGURE 15.37   Changing the column type.

With the column type changed, you now need to specify how the grid should retrieve the list of possible values to display in the drop-down; the grid is smart enough to already know to use the underlying gender values from the table to select the one value to display in the grid. To handle the list of possible values, you could hard-code them in the column (see the Items property in Figure 15.37), or you could wire up a separate query—something along the lines of SELECT DISTINCT(Gender) FROM Employees—and have that query provide the list of possible values. Because constructing another query or data source is easy and doesn't lead to a brittle hard-coded solution, that's the approach we'll investigate here. To create a query to feed the combo-box column, you can visit the Data Sources window, select the Add New Data Source action, and follow the same steps you followed before to add the original Employee data source. This time, though, select only the Gender column.

After the data source is created, right-click on the data source and select Edit DataSet with Designer. Visual Studio's XSD Designer will launch. In the designer (see Figure 15.38), you can see the Fill query used to populate the dataset. If you click on the query (that is, click on the last row in the table graphic in the designer window), you can use the Properties window to directly edit the SQL for the query. By modifying this to reflect SELECT DISTINCT syntax, you can return the valid gender values for inclusion in the grid.

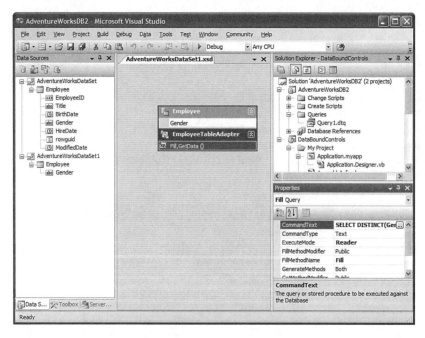

FIGURE 15.38 Changing the query for a data source.

Figure 15.39 shows the results of these efforts. If you need to implement a cell edit control that doesn't currently exist, you need to roll your own by inheriting from the DataGridViewColumn base control. This employee grid could benefit from a DateTimePicker control for the date- and time-based data such as birth date and hire date.

15

> **NOTE**
>
> If you look in the MSDN documentation, there is a specific example of creating a
> DataGridViewDateTimePickerColumn control and then wiring it up within the grid. Search for
> the phrase "How to: Host Controls in Windows Forms DataGridView Cells."

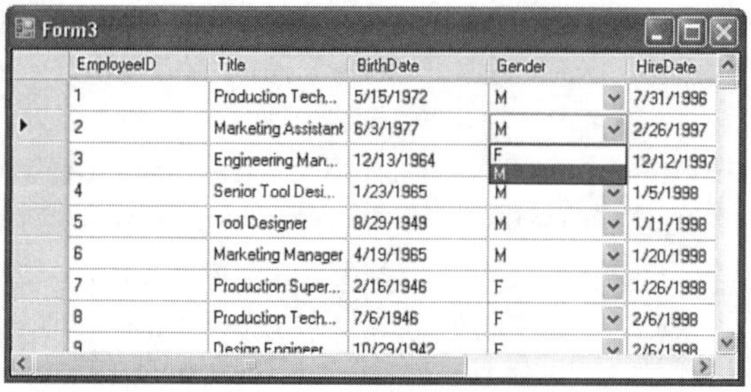

FIGURE 15.39   A drop-down within a `DataGridView`.

Binding Other Controls

For other controls that don't have convenient access to binding via their smart tag, you can leverage the Data Sources window. Drag a data source from the Data Sources window and drop it onto an existing control. The designer will create a new binding source, set it appropriately, and then make an entry in the control's DataBinding collection. If you try to drag a data element onto a control that doesn't match up (for instance, dragging a character field onto a check box), the drop operation won't be allowed.

Data Binding with Web Controls

Although the general concepts remain the same, data binding web-based controls is a slightly different game than in the Windows forms world. The first obvious difference is that data sources for web forms are implemented by data source controls in the `System.Web.UI.WebControls` namespace; there is no concept of the Data Sources window with web applications. Because of this, instead of starting with a data source, you instead need to start with a data control and then work to attach that control to a data source.

Selecting a Data Control

There are five primary controls that you will work with in a web application to deliver data-bound functionality:

- **`GridView` Control**—Provides a tabular presentation similar to the `DataGridView` control.

- **`DetailsView` Control**—Displays a single record from a data source; with a DetailsView control, every column in the data source will show up as a row in the control.

- **`FormView` Control**—Functions in the same way as the DetailsView control with the following exception: It doesn't have a built-in "default" for the way that the data is displayed. Instead, you need to provide a template to tell the control how exactly you want the data rendered onto the web page.

- **Repeater** Control—Simply renders a list of individual items fetched from the attached data source. The specifics of how this rendering looks are all controlled via templates.

- **DataList** Control—Displays rows of information from a data source. The display aspects are fully customizable and include header and footer elements.

For demonstration purposes, continue working with the AdventureWorks employee table and see how you can implement a data-bound web page for viewing employee records.

Using the GridView   First, with a web project open, drag a GridView control from the Toolbox onto an empty web page. The first thing you will notice is that the GridView's smart tag menu is just as efficient as the DataGridView's menu. You are directly prompted to select (or create and then select) a data source as soon as you drop the control onto the web page surface (see Figure 15.40).

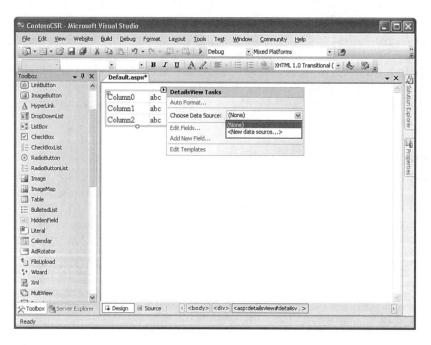

FIGURE 15.40   Selecting the GridView's data source.

Selecting the <New Data Source...> option will use the same data source wizard (refer to Figure 15.28) to collect information about your data source and add it to the project.

Once again, because of the data binding support in the designer, you now have a fully functional application without writing a line of code. Figure 15.41 shows this admittedly ugly web page with live employee data.

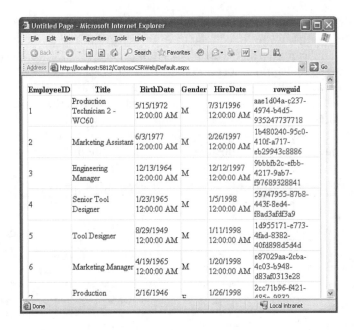

FIGURE 15.41 Employee records in the `GridView`.

Thankfully, you can just as easily put some window dressing on the table and make it look nice as well. By using the `GridView`'s smart tag menu again, you can select the Auto Format option to apply several different flavors of window dressing to the table (see Figure 15.42). And, of course, by applying a style sheet, you can really impact the look and feel of the page.

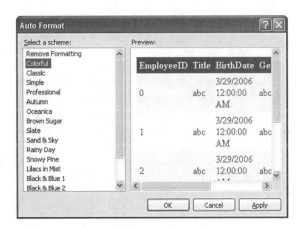

FIGURE 15.42   Autoformatting options for the `GridView` control.

Updating Data with the GridView   Creating the web grid was easy, and no data access coding was required on your part, but there is one thing missing here: How can you update data back to the database? The GridView you currently have is great for static reporting, but what if you want to edit data within the grid just like you did earlier in the Windows forms application? The key here is a set of properties on the GridView: AutoGenerateEditButton and AutoGenerateDeleteButton. When you set these properties to True, the GridView will automatically include an Edit and a Delete link. The Edit link comes fully baked with rendering code so that when it is clicked, that particular row in the grid will become editable. In Figure 15.43, notice that by setting the AutoGenerateEditButton to True and then clicking on one of the edit links, you now have a fully interactive set of columns that you can use to modify the record's data.

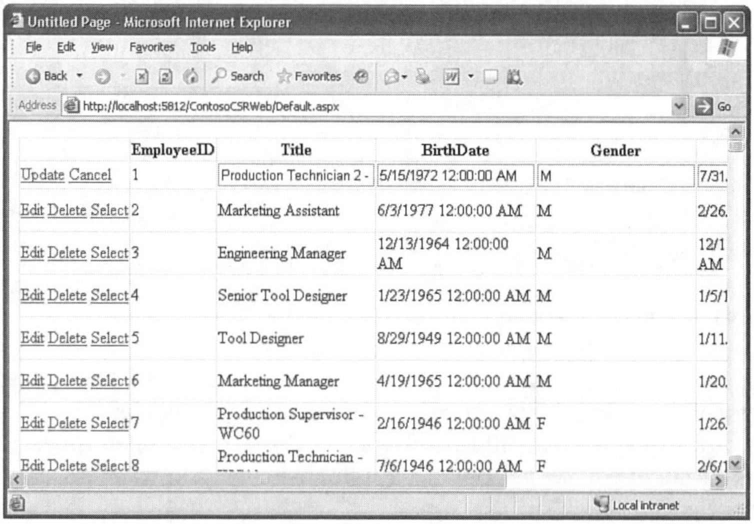

FIGURE 15.43   Editing a record in the GridView.

After changing the data in one or more of the columns, you can click on the Update link to send the data back to the database. For the update to work, however, you need to explicitly tell the data source control (in this case, a SqlDataSource control) what query to use for processing updates. This is done with the SqlDataSource.UpdateQuery property. By specifying a parameterized UPDATE query in this property, you have fully informed the data source on how to deal with updates. You can take advantage once more of the Query Builder window to write this query for you: Select the data source control on the web form, and in the Properties window, select the UpdateCommand property. This will launch the Query Builder window and allow you to construct the parameterized update command (see Figure 15.44).

With that last piece of the puzzle in place, you now have a fully implemented and bound grid control that pages data in from the database and commits changes back to the database.

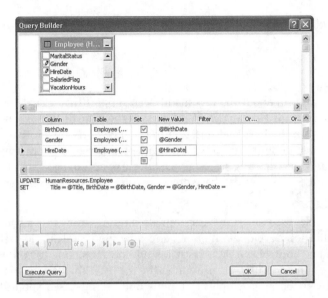

FIGURE 15.44   Specifying an `UpdateCommand` query.

NOTE

To implement delete capabilities for a record, you perform the same steps using the DeleteQuery property and setting the AutoGenerateDeleteButton to True.

Data Source Controls

As mentioned, data sources are surfaced through one or more data source controls placed onto the web form. In the `GridView` example, the designer actually adds a `SqlDataSource` control to the form for you (based on your creation of a new db-based data source). But there is nothing preventing you from adding one or more data source controls to a web page directly. Just drag the control from the Toolbox onto the form surface. Table 15.2 itemizes the available data source controls.

TABLE 15.2   Data Source Controls

Data Source Control	Description
ObjectDataSource	Exposes other classes as data sources.
SqlDataSource	Exposes a relational database as a data source. Microsoft SQL Server and Oracle databases can be accessed natively; ODBC and OLE DB access is also supported.
AccessDataSource	Exposes a Microsoft Access database as a data source.
XmlDataSource	Exposes an XML file as a data source.
SiteMapDataSource	A special case data source that exposes an ASP .NET site map as a data source.

After configuring the data source, you can then visit any data-aware control and bind it to the source.

Summary

In this chapter, you read about the broad and deep support that Visual Studio 2005 has for building and managing databases. We discussed the suite of Visual Database tools, available right within the IDE, that function in synergy with one another and with the various Visual Studio designers to provide a seamless experience for writing queries, creating table structures, and crafting stored procedures. We also investigated the newfound support for writing SQL Server database procedures and functions using entirely managed code.

We spent some time discussing the basics of data binding—how it is a core problem space with many application development efforts and how the Visual Studio Web and Windows Form Designers and controls provide first-class support for simple to complex data binding scenarios. In particular, we examined the role that the designers play in the data binding world by enabling developers to rapidly build forms-based applications with sophisticated data needs without writing a single line of code.

Hopefully, by exposing you to all of these great built-in tools, we have started you on the road to becoming even more efficient in leveraging Visual Studio across a range of database interactions.

CHAPTER 16

Web Services and Visual Studio

IN THIS CHAPTER

- Web Services Defined
- The Components of a Web Service Project
- Developing a Web Service
- Consuming a Web Service
- Managing Web Service Exceptions

Web services are currently transforming the way we think of the Web and how we leverage it to build software. Prior to web services, the Web was mostly considered a delivery mechanism for user interfaces. Of course, that was a huge deal given that these user interfaces did not require deployment but instead worked inside a browser. Web services have a similar potential. At their core, they represent a method (or service) that executes on a server and then leverages the ubiquitous communication mechanism that is the Web. In addition, web services are not bound to any one environment or operating system, and they are built on open standards such as XML. As a result, web services provide new potential in terms of connecting disparate systems, enabling rich clients that work across the web, and rethinking architectures to focus on the set of services they might provide.

Visual Studio 2005 provides the tools to make web services easier for developers. Just like a good user interface designer that abstracts the need to work directly with HTML, Visual Studio enables developers to create web services without working directly with the XML, SOAP, and so on. The tool embraces web services and the standards on which they operate. It then simplifies the web services world and allows developers to write web methods the way they write other Visual Basic or C# methods.

In this chapter, we first cover the basics of a web service and discuss the standards on which they are based. We then walk through creating and consuming web services using Visual Studio. Finally, we look at some finer points on working with web services such as handling exceptions.

NOTE

The web service topic is a big and growing one. After you complete this chapter, you should have a solid understanding of how to create and work with web services in Visual Studio. From there, you can use this foundation to begin exploring WSE 3.0, Service-Oriented Architecture (SOA), BizTalk, and other web service–related topics.

Web Services Defined

A web service defines a contract between a client and the service itself. In English, this contract states something like, "If you send me data in this format, I will process it and return you the results in this other format." The format of this data and the communication parameters of these calls are all based on open standards such as XML and SOAP. Similar standards allow a client to often "discover" a web service and its contract and then work to program against it. These web service standards apply across technology boundaries and therefore make web services very attractive for exchanging data between heterogeneous environments.

Visual Studio 2005 does a lot to abstract the intricacies of these standards away from everyday programming tasks. This is no different from the manner in which the .NET Framework abstracts "plumbing" code for developers. The intent (and result) is a more productive development experience. You spend less time worrying about how to create a proper SOAP message and more time building business value.

Web Service Terms

It is important that developers understand the key concepts and standards around web services. This knowledge ensures you know what is happening in your application. It also helps when you are reading the .NET documentation and articles related to web services. Therefore, we have put together the following glossary of key terms related to web services:

- **Web Service**—A web service represents a cohesive set of application logic that performs actions and provides data. A web service groups web methods. It can therefore be helpful to think of a web service as a component or class.

- **Web Service Method (or Web Method)**—A web service method represents a method exposed by a web service. A web method can take parameters and return a response.

- **XML (Extensible Markup Language)**—XML is used to both represent and describe data in a platform-neutral manner. XML can be used to represent both simple and complex data elements and relationships. It is the XML standard that makes web services possible.

- **WSDL (Web Service Description Language)**—WSDL is used to describe the contents of a web service and its web methods. The WSDL provides the message data contracts that allow clients to work with a given service.

- **XSD (XML Schema Document)**—XSD contains a set of predefined types (string, decimal, and so on) and a standard language for describing your own complex types. An XML Schema Document (also referred to as an XSD) uses these types to describe (and restrict) the contents of an XML message.

- **SOAP (Simple Object Access Protocol)**—SOAP is an XML-based protocol for communicating between client and web service. It is helpful to think of SOAP as representing the format of the messages as they pass over the wire. SOAP wraps XML messages (in envelopes) for communication across the Web. Most SOAP messages are sent over HTTP. However, they can also be sent with transport protocols such as SMTP and FTP.

- **HTTP (Hypertext Transfer Protocol)**—HTTP represents the communication protocol used by web services to transfer SOAP-formatted (or encoded) messages. HTTP is also the way standard web page requests (GET and POST) communicate.

- **UDDI (Universal Description, Discovery, and Integration)**—UDDI is used to define a registry of web services. This capability is useful for the publication of services for developers to find and consume.

- **URI (Uniform Resource Identifier)**—URIs provide a means for locating items on the web. In most cases URIs are URLs (uniform resource locators) that point to a given service.

- **DISCO (Discovery Document)**—A DISCO file provides information that links to other key elements of a web service. This includes links to XSDs, SOAP bindings, and namespaces. A program can use a DISCO file to determine how to work with a given web service.

- **WS-***—This term represents the overall standards for web services.

- **WSE (Web Service Enhancements)**—Microsoft's implementation of WS-* standards. Currently, WSE 3.0 is the latest version. It enables web service transactions and enhanced security. WSE is a plug-in to Visual Studio.

The Components of a Web Service Project

Visual Studio and the .NET Framework abstract the complexities involved with defining web services in terms of SOAP, WSDL, XSD schemas, and the like. You still have access and control over these low-level items if you need them. However, for the most part, you define a web service the same way you create a class. You then define web methods similar to the way you would define methods on a class. Visual Studio takes on the job of creating the appropriate schema contract for your method signatures and describing your web services in terms of WSDL. The .NET Framework then worries about properly packaging your data into a SOAP message and transmitting it across HTTP.

.NET Web Services

Web services in .NET are built and delivered on the same ASP .NET framework that delivers ASP .NET websites. This means that web services share the same server technology (Internet Information Server or IIS) as well as the same objects such as `Application`, `Session`, and `Context`. In this way, developers who are familiar with delivering ASP .NET applications can leverage this experience for web services. You can take advantage of the built-in state management, authentication services, and performance of ASP .NET, for instance.

A web service in .NET is simply a web address to a web service file that contains the extension `.asmx`. The service has a standard `http:\\...` address. This file is used as the URI for the web service (just like a form). You write your code "behind" this file, and Visual Studio and .NET do the rest by attaching the appropriate WSDL and enabling the SOAP calls over HTTP. Let's take a closer look at how to leverage Visual Studio and ASP .NET to deliver web services.

ASP.NET Web Service Project

A web service can be added to any ASP .NET web project. Visual Studio also provides a web service–specific project template. This template is useful if you intend to create an entire service layer or want to separate your services from any user interface elements. You create a project from this template the same way you define other web projects: Selecting File, New, Website will launch the New Web Site dialog box, as shown in Figure 16.1. Here, you can select the template, ASP.NET Web Service, to define a web service–specific project.

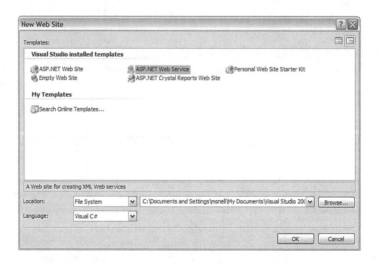

FIGURE 16.1   Create a web service project.

As with defining a new website, you can indicate the location of the web service. You can choose a location by using the file system or by browsing to a web server using HTTP, or by leveraging FTP to indicate where to store the web service. In addition, you can define the default language in which the web service should be programmed.

The Web Service Files

The actual web service project that is created through the web service template contains exactly one service. The service is referenced by an .asmx file. Again, this file is used as the URI (and URL) for the web service. The actual contents of this file are depicted in Figure 16.2.

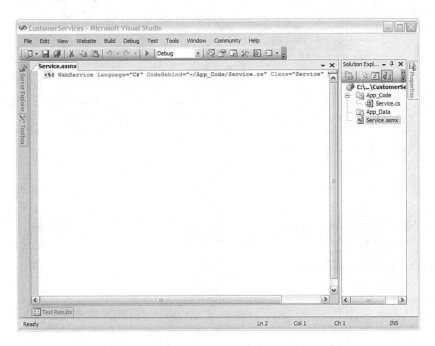

FIGURE 16.2   The web service project.

The .asmx file in the figure contains a single WebService directive. This directive indicates that the web service file is a pointer to the code for the service. The CodeBehind attribute indicates this information. Here, it points to the code file called Service.cs inside the App_Code directory. This is the place where the application logic for the service resides. Finally, this directive uses the Class attribute to indicate a class contained inside Service.cs;. this class is the web service. The methods in this class are the web methods.

NOTE

You can actually choose to define a web service as a single file. In this case, both the directive and the code are stored together (instead of the code-behind model).

Figure 16.3 shows the contents of Service.cs. First, note that this class is just a standard C# class (it could also be VB). It has a constructor, using statements, a method, and so on. The web service programming model should be very familiar to .NET developers.

FIGURE 16.3   The web service code.

Of course, you still have to let .NET know that this code is a web service. There are two ways the code does this. First, it uses attributes. The Service class in Figure 16.3 is decorated with the WebService attribute. This defines the class as a web service. Notice also that the HelloWorld method has the WebMethod attribute applied. This attribute indicates this method is a web method that can be called for the web service.

Another way this class indicates itself as a web service is through inheritance. The class inherits System.Web.Services.WebService. This is actually optional. You could define a class as a web service without inheriting from WebService. However, through this inheritance, the class will actually have full access to the ASP.NET features such as Session and Context objects. Having access to these objects provides many of the familiar ASP.NET features to web service developers.

Developing a Web Service

Thus far, you've looked at the standard web service files created by the Visual Studio web service template. Now you're ready to explore developing an actual web service with Visual Studio 2005. For this example, you will develop a CustomerProfile web service. This web service will provide methods for retrieving customer information from a data store and saving changes to that information. Along the way, you will look at the finer points of developing a .NET web service.

Creating the Web Service

To create the web service, you add a new web service item to an ASP .NET application. For this example, you start with a web service project and create the `CustomerProfile.asmx` service. Next, you remove the `HelloWorld` sample method and in its place develop your web methods. These sample methods include `GetCustomerProfile` and `SaveCustomer`.

The `GetCustomerProfile` method takes a customer ID as a parameter and returns a customer object. The `SaveCustomer` method takes an instance of this same customer object but does not return a value. Listing 16.1 shows the sample code for the service.

LISTING 16.1   Customer Profile Web Service

```
using System;
using System.Web;
using System.Web.Services;
using System.Web.Services.Protocols;
using System.Data;

[WebService(Namespace = "http://www.brilliantstorm.com/")]
[WebServiceBinding(ConformsTo = WsiProfiles.BasicProfile1_1)]
public class CustomerProfile: WebService {
    public CustomerProfile() {
    }
    [WebMethod(Description = "Used to return a customer's profile.")]
    public BusinessEntities.Customer GetCustomerProfile(int customerId) {
        EntityServices.CustomerProfile custProfile =
          new EntityServices.CustomerProfile();
        return custProfile.GetCustomer(customerId);
    }
    [WebMethod(Description = "Saves a customer")]
    public void SaveCustomer(BusinessEntities.Customer customer) {
        EntityServices.CustomerProfile custProfile =
          new EntityServices.CustomerProfile();
        custProfile.SaveCustomer(customer);
    }
}
```

16

It is important to note that Listing 16.1 references a couple of projects that are outside the web service project. The first is the `BusinessEntities` project. This project (and namespace) contains the actual definition for the `Customer` object. You reference this project the same way you add a reference to any other project.

The second project referenced is `EntityServices`. This namespace provides the actual implementation of the code that executes on behalf of the service. In fact, the `SaveCustomer` web method is actually a proxy for the `EntityServices.CustomerProfile.SaveCustomer` method. This latter method does the work to actually save the customer.

This proxy implementation pattern is optional. You could define all your execution logic right inside the web service. However, we are showing this example for two reasons. The first is that most applications built today leverage some existing code. It can be useful to build a proxy to expose this existing code through web services. The second point is that this is just good design. Having the implementation code inside a separate object can lead to reuse, can enable easier unit testing, and can enable client scenarios that are more traditional (and do not rely on web services).

> **TIP**
>
> When you're building a web service, it is best to group functionality into course-grained interfaces. You don't want web methods that do a number of fine-grained operations such as setting properties prior to calling a method. This chatty nature can be expensive when communicating across the Internet.
>
> Of course, this approach is also contrary to most object-oriented application designs. Therefore, the use of a proxy object to bundle operations around a business object is ideal. The business object can be serialized and passed across the wire. On the other side, it can be deserialized and then worked with in an in-process manner (where chatty calls are not expensive).

Now that you have built the sample service, you're ready to look at what makes this class a web service. In addition, the following sections elaborate on the definition of web methods.

The `WebService` Attribute Class

The `WebService` attribute class (also called `WebServiceAttribute`) can be used to provide additional details about a given web service. You may apply this attribute when declaring a class as a web service. However, the attribute is not required. It merely gives context about a web service. For example, we used the `WebService` attribute on the `CustomerProfile` class declaration to provide details about the web service's namespace.

The following are the descriptive elements you can define with the `WebService` attribute class:

- `Description`—Used to define a description of the web service. This description will be provided to consumers of your web service and in related documentation. You should always supply this web service description.

- `Namespace`—Used to declare the namespace for your web service (`tempuri.org` by default). This is similar to namespaces as you know them inside .NET. However, these namespaces are meant to be unique across the web on which they operate. Therefore, you should always define a namespace using a URL that you own and control. This can be a company Internet address, for example.

- Name—Used to define a different name for your web service. The name of your web service need not be restricted to the naming confines of .NET. Therefore, you can use this parameter to create a new name for your web service.

The WebService Class

The WebService class represents the base class for .NET web services. This is not to be confused with the WebService attribute class (see the preceding section). You derive from this class in order to use the common ASP.NET objects (Session, Application, Context, and so on). However, it is not mandatory that you do so. Visual Studio enforces this inheritance when you define a new web service, but you can remove this code if you have no intention of leveraging the ASP objects within your web service. If you choose to derive from WebService, then you access these ASP.NET objects the same way you would inside any web application.

The WebMethod Attribute Class

The WebMethod attribute class is used to indicate that a method in your service should be exposed via the web service. This declaration is mandatory for all methods that you intend to make available through the web service.

There are a number of parameters you can set when defining a web method. These parameters control how the web method operates. For the example, you will simply set the Description parameter to document a description of the method. However, the following provides a more comprehensive list of parameters on the WebMethod attribute:

- Description—Used to provide a description of the web method. This description will appear to calling clients and on help documentation related to the web method.

- EnableSession—Used to indicate whether session states should be enabled for the given web method. Setting this value to True allows you to store and retrieve items in the session. If you set this parameter to True and inherit from WebService, you access the session from the Session object (WebService.Session). If you are not inheriting from WebService, you can still set this parameter to true. However, to get to the session object, you will have to traverse the HttpContext.Current.Session path.

- CacheDuration—Used to indicate that the results of the web service should be cached for a specific duration. You set the duration (in seconds) for this parameter. Enabling this cache will result in the caching of the response for every unique set of parameters passed to the web service (similar to ASP.NET output caching).

- MessageName—Used to define an alias or separate name for a given web method. This capability is useful if you intend to have overloaded methods that .NET supports but web services do not. In this way, you can keep your overloaded methods and then apply a unique name to each one using this parameter.

- BufferResponse—Used to indicate whether the entire response should be buffered in the server's memory before passing it back across the wire to the calling client.

16

The default setting for this parameter is True. If you set it to False, the response will be buffered in chunks of 16KB, with each chunk being sent to the client one at a time.

- TransactionOption—Used to indicate whether the web service should be the root of a transaction. By default, web services cannot be enlisted in other transactions. They can, however, invoke objects that participate in a transaction along with the single web service.

Accessing and Invoking the Web Service

Visual Studio and the .NET Framework enable you to view a given web service inside the web browser. This capability can be useful for both testing a web service and discovering how one works (the messages they require and return). To access a web service, you first build (compile) it in Visual Studio and then access the .asmx file in a browser.

Figure 16.4 shows the CustomerProfile web service example in a browser window. Notice that both methods of the service are listed. Each method's description is also provided. This is the same description entered in the web method definition (WebMethodAttribute).

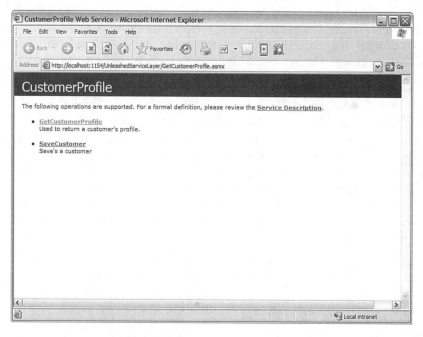

FIGURE 16.4 Navigating to the web service.

Viewing the Formal Web Service Description

To see the actual formal description of the web service as it is defined in WSDL, you can select the link Service Description from the page shown in Figure 16.4. When you click this link, the WSDL parameter is passed to the .asmx file on the QueryString. This tells .NET to return the WSDL of the service.

This WSDL is generated for you by .NET. It conforms to the WSDL standards and can therefore be used by clients that want to access your service. These clients use this WSDL to understand how your web service operates.

> **NOTE**
>
> .NET ships with a tool named Disco.exe. Visual Studio uses this tool to generate files related to the understanding and discovery of web services. You, too, can leverage this tool from the command line to generate these documents and store them for examination and use.
>
> The documents created by Disco.exe serve as the input for client applications that consume the web service. These client applications are created using a related tool called WSDL.exe.

You can find the complete listing of the WSDL for the CustomerProfile service in Listing 16.2. This listing is easier to view in a browser (where you get color-coding and a tree-like structure to navigate the XML). However, the listing is provided here for your reference. As you scan it, notice how each service is defined. Also notice how the Customer complex type is embedded inside the WSDL. This complex type was generated based on the sample Customer object (BusinessEntities.Customer). Recall that this type is a return value to one method and a parameter to another. You can see that .NET is converting this to an XML type for use by web services.

LISTING 16.2   The Web Service WSDL

```xml
<?xml version="1.0" encoding="utf-8"?>
<wsdl:definitions xmlns:soap="http://schemas.xmlsoap.org/wsdl/soap/"
➥xmlns:tm="http://microsoft.com/wsdl/mime/textMatching/"
➥xmlns:soapenc="http://schemas.xmlsoap.org/soap/encoding/"
➥xmlns:mime="http://schemas.xmlsoap.org/wsdl/mime/"
➥xmlns:tns="http://www.brilliantstorm.com/"
➥xmlns:s="http://www.w3.org/2001/XMLSchema"
➥xmlns:soap12="http://schemas.xmlsoap.org/wsdl/soap12/"
➥xmlns:http="http://schemas.xmlsoap.org/wsdl/http/"
➥targetNamespace="http://www.brilliantstorm.com/"
➥xmlns:wsdl="http://schemas.xmlsoap.org/wsdl/">
  <wsdl:types>
    <s:schema elementFormDefault="qualified"
➥targetNamespace="http://www.brilliantstorm.com/">
      <s:element name="GetCustomerProfile">
        <s:complexType>
          <s:sequence>
            <s:element minOccurs="1" maxOccurs="1" name="customerId"
➥type="s:int" />
          </s:sequence>
```

16

LISTING 16.2   Continued

```
          </s:complexType>
        </s:element>
        <s:element name="GetCustomerProfileResponse">
          <s:complexType>
            <s:sequence>
              <s:element minOccurs="0" maxOccurs="1"
➡name="GetCustomerProfileResult" type="tns:Customer" />
            </s:sequence>
          </s:complexType>
        </s:element>
        <s:complexType name="Customer">
          <s:sequence>
            <s:element minOccurs="0" maxOccurs="1" name="Email" type="s:string" />
            <s:element minOccurs="0" maxOccurs="1" name="Address1"
➡type="s:string" />
            <s:element minOccurs="0" maxOccurs="1" name="Address2"
➡type="s:string" />
            <s:element minOccurs="0" maxOccurs="1" name="City" type="s:string" />
            <s:element minOccurs="0" maxOccurs="1" name="State" type="s:string" />
            <s:element minOccurs="0" maxOccurs="1" name="Zip" type="s:string" />
            <s:element minOccurs="0" maxOccurs="1" name="Phone" type="s:string" />
            <s:element minOccurs="1" maxOccurs="1" name="ContactViaEmail"
➡type="s:boolean" />
            <s:element minOccurs="1" maxOccurs="1" name="ContactViaPhone"
➡type="s:boolean" />
            <s:element minOccurs="0" maxOccurs="1" name="Name" type="s:string" />
            <s:element minOccurs="0" maxOccurs="1" name="Description"
➡type="s:string" />
            <s:element minOccurs="1" maxOccurs="1" name="Id" type="s:int" />
          </s:sequence>
        </s:complexType>
        <s:element name="SaveCustomer">
          <s:complexType>
            <s:sequence>
              <s:element minOccurs="0" maxOccurs="1" name="customer"
➡type="tns:Customer" />
            </s:sequence>
          </s:complexType>
        </s:element>
        <s:element name="SaveCustomerResponse">
          <s:complexType />
        </s:element>
      </s:schema>
    </wsdl:types>
```

LISTING 16.2   Continued

```
<wsdl:message name="GetCustomerProfileSoapIn">
  <wsdl:part name="parameters" element="tns:GetCustomerProfile" />
</wsdl:message>
<wsdl:message name="GetCustomerProfileSoapOut">
  <wsdl:part name="parameters" element="tns:GetCustomerProfileResponse" />
</wsdl:message>
<wsdl:message name="SaveCustomerSoapIn">
  <wsdl:part name="parameters" element="tns:SaveCustomer" />
</wsdl:message>
<wsdl:message name="SaveCustomerSoapOut">
  <wsdl:part name="parameters" element="tns:SaveCustomerResponse" />
</wsdl:message>
<wsdl:portType name="CustomerProfileSoap">
  <wsdl:operation name="GetCustomerProfile">
    <wsdl:documentation xmlns:wsdl="http://schemas.xmlsoap.org/wsdl/">
➥Used to return a customer's profile.</wsdl:documentation>
    <wsdl:input message="tns:GetCustomerProfileSoapIn" />
    <wsdl:output message="tns:GetCustomerProfileSoapOut" />
  </wsdl:operation>
  <wsdl:operation name="SaveCustomer">
    <wsdl:documentation xmlns:wsdl="http://schemas.xmlsoap.org/wsdl/">
➥Saves a customer</wsdl:documentation>
    <wsdl:input message="tns:SaveCustomerSoapIn" />
    <wsdl:output message="tns:SaveCustomerSoapOut" />
  </wsdl:operation>
</wsdl:portType>
<wsdl:binding name="CustomerProfileSoap" type="tns:CustomerProfileSoap">
  <soap:binding transport="http://schemas.xmlsoap.org/soap/http" />
  <wsdl:operation name="GetCustomerProfile">
    <soap:operation soapAction="http://www.brilliantstorm.com/GetCustomerProfile"
➥style="document" />
    <wsdl:input>
      <soap:body use="literal" />
    </wsdl:input>
    <wsdl:output>
      <soap:body use="literal" />
    </wsdl:output>
  </wsdl:operation>
  <wsdl:operation name="SaveCustomer">
    <soap:operation soapAction="http://www.brilliantstorm.com/SaveCustomer"
➥style="document" />
    <wsdl:input>
      <soap:body use="literal" />
    </wsdl:input>
```

16

LISTING 16.2   Continued

```
      <wsdl:output>
        <soap:body use="literal" />
      </wsdl:output>
    </wsdl:operation>
  </wsdl:binding>
  <wsdl:binding name="CustomerProfileSoap12" type="tns:CustomerProfileSoap">
    <soap12:binding transport="http://schemas.xmlsoap.org/soap/http" />
    <wsdl:operation name="GetCustomerProfile">
      <soap12:operation soapAction=
➥"http://www.brilliantstorm.com/GetCustomerProfile" style="document" />
      <wsdl:input>
        <soap12:body use="literal" />
      </wsdl:input>
      <wsdl:output>
        <soap12:body use="literal" />
      </wsdl:output>
    </wsdl:operation>
    <wsdl:operation name="SaveCustomer">
      <soap12:operation soapAction="http://www.brilliantstorm.com/SaveCustomer"
➥style="document" />
      <wsdl:input>
        <soap12:body use="literal" />
      </wsdl:input>
      <wsdl:output>
        <soap12:body use="literal" />
      </wsdl:output>
    </wsdl:operation>
  </wsdl:binding>
  <wsdl:service name="CustomerProfile">
    <wsdl:port name="CustomerProfileSoap" binding="tns:CustomerProfileSoap">
      <soap:address
➥location="http://localhost:1154/UnleashedServiceLayer/GetCustomerProfile.asmx" />
    </wsdl:port>
    <wsdl:port name="CustomerProfileSoap12" binding="tns:CustomerProfileSoap12">
      <soap12:address
➥location="http://localhost:1154/UnleashedServiceLayer/GetCustomerProfile.asmx" />
    </wsdl:port>
  </wsdl:service>
</wsdl:definitions>
```

Viewing the Web Method

When you click on the web method name, .NET generates a web form for you to use to test the given web service. This form is accessed from the .asmx file (URI) with the

QueryString parameter op (operation). You pass the name of the web method to this parameter. For the example, look at the web method named GetCustomerProfile. Figure 16.5 shows this web form.

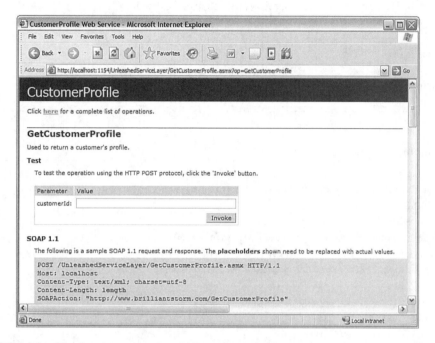

FIGURE 16.5   The GetCustomerProfile web method.

The top part of the form allows you to enter parameters for the web method and then invoke the actual web method using the HTTP POST protocol. This protocol is just one way to invoke the web method. Recall that you also use SOAP over HTTP and so on. This page shows actual examples of a SOAP request and response as well as HTTP. These examples can be useful if you want to see how messages should be constructed for these protocols.

As an example, Listing 16.3 shows a SOAP message request for this web method. Notice that it indicates the <customerId> element must be passed to the method. This is of the primitive type int. Listing 16.4 shows the correlated SOAP response from the call. Notice here the SOAP result is contained in the element <GetCustomerProfileResult>. This page also contains examples of SOAP 1.1 and HTTP POST requests and responses.

LISTING 16.3   SOAP 1.2 Request

```
POST /UnleashedServiceLayer/GetCustomerProfile.asmx HTTP/1.1
Host: localhost
Content-Type: application/soap+xml; charset=utf-8
Content-Length: length
<?xml version="1.0" encoding="utf-8"?>
```

LISTING 16.3   Continued

```
<soap12:Envelope xmlns:xsi="http://www.w3.org/2001/XMLSchema-instance"
➥xmlns:xsd="http://www.w3.org/2001/XMLSchema"
➥xmlns:soap12="http://www.w3.org/2003/05/soap-envelope">
  <soap12:Body>
    <GetCustomerProfile xmlns="http://www.brilliantstorm.com/">
      <customerId>int</customerId>
    </GetCustomerProfile>
  </soap12:Body>
</soap12:Envelope>
```

LISTING 16.4   SOAP 1.2 Response

```
HTTP/1.1 200 OK
Content-Type: application/soap+xml; charset=utf-8
Content-Length: length
<?xml version="1.0" encoding="utf-8"?>
<soap12:Envelope xmlns:xsi="http://www.w3.org/2001/XMLSchema-instance"
➥xmlns:xsd="http://www.w3.org/2001/XMLSchema"
➥xmlns:soap12="http://www.w3.org/2003/05/soap-envelope">
  <soap12:Body>
    <GetCustomerProfileResponse xmlns="http://www.brilliantstorm.com/">
      <GetCustomerProfileResult>
        <Email>string</Email>
        <Address1>string</Address1>
        <Address2>string</Address2>
        <City>string</City>
        <State>string</State>
        <Zip>string</Zip>
        <Phone>string</Phone>
        <ContactViaEmail>boolean</ContactViaEmail>
        <ContactViaPhone>boolean</ContactViaPhone>
        <Name>string</Name>
        <Description>string</Description>
        <Id>int</Id>
      </GetCustomerProfileResult>
    </GetCustomerProfileResponse>
  </soap12:Body>
</soap12:Envelope>
```

Invoking the Web Method

To invoke the web method, you enter a value for the parameters and click the Invoke button (as shown in Figure 16.5). Doing so executes the web service and returns the results. The results are sent back as XML (as defined by the message). Remember, this invocation is HTTP POST. Figure 16.6 shows the results from the example.

> **NOTE**
>
> You can use this method only to invoke web methods that take simple (primitive) data types as parameters. If your web method takes a complex type (`SaveCustomer`, for example), then you can still see the request/response examples but cannot invoke the web method in this manner.

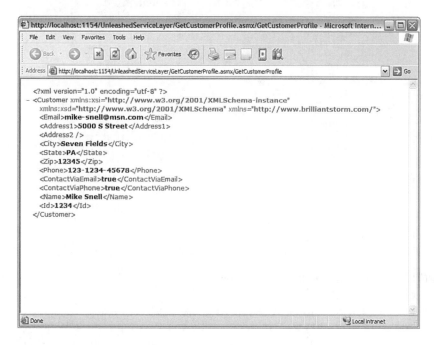

FIGURE 16.6 `GetCustomerProfile` results.

Consuming a Web Service

A web service can be consumed by any client capable of calling the service and managing its results. Visual Studio makes this task easy. It allows you to set a *web reference* to a web service. This process is similar to setting a reference to another .NET library or COM component. After you define this web reference, Visual Studio generates a proxy class for consuming the web service. This allows you to program against the proxy class and not worry about writing web service–specific code. Web references can be set inside web applications, windows applications, even console applications. Let's look at this process.

Defining a Web Reference

You define a web reference for your project by selecting the Add Web Reference option from the context menu for a given project. This will launch the Add Web Reference dialog box. You use this dialog box to browse to a web service and add that service as a reference.

Figure 16.7 shows the first screen of this dialog box. From here, you can search for a web service. You have a couple of options to find a service. You can navigate directly to it through the URL field. You can also browse services defined in the current solution, on the local machine, or those exposed through a local UDDI server.

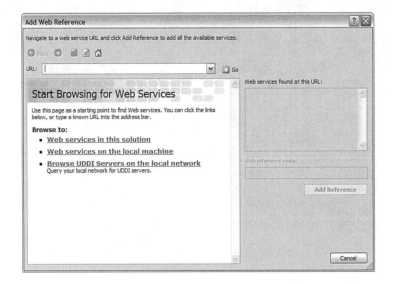

FIGURE 16.7   The Add Web Reference dialog box.

For the example, you will bind a Windows form application called CustomerAdministration to the CustomerProfile web service. Both the Windows form application and the service happen to be in the same solution. Therefore, you can select the link Web services in this solution to bring up as list of services in the solution. This list is shown in Figure 16.8.

In this example, the solution list contains a couple of web services. You can use the browser window (middle left) to navigate to these services, test them, and select the one you want to add as a reference. Of course, you are looking for the GetCustomerProfile service. Selecting this service brings up the service shown in Figure 16.9.

A web service is now selected; it has an associated URL. You are also on the same web page you saw back in Figure 16.4. You can use this window to view details about the service and even test its invocation.

When you are comfortable with the service, you need only define the reference name and add it to your project. You set the reference name using the Web Reference Name field on the right side of the dialog box. Typically, you set this to the name of the web service. In this case, use CustomerProfile. Next, click the Add Reference button to add the web reference to the project.

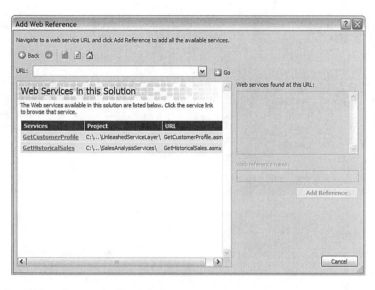

FIGURE 16.8   Web reference in the solution.

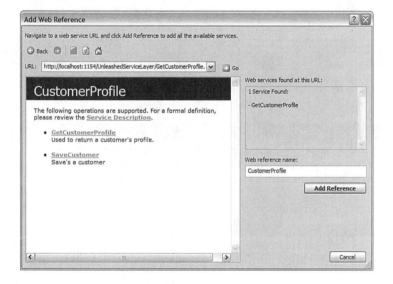

FIGURE 16.9   Set the web reference name.

Viewing the Web Reference

In Figure 16.10, the proxy class is open in the editor. This proxy class is a C# class that represents the web service. The intent of the class is to encapsulate and abstract the intricacies of calling this service. This allows developers to work with the service the same way they might work with any other .NET component or class. The contents of the proxy class include methods that mimic the web methods and objects that are used for the parameters (such as the `Customer` object in the example).

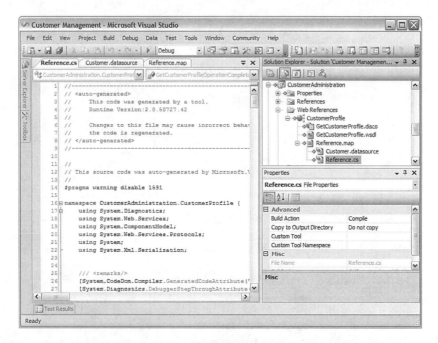

FIGURE 16.10   The web reference.

> **TIP**
>
> If you update or modify your web service, you will need to update the web reference. To do so, you right-click the web reference and choose Update Web Reference. This will instruct Visual Studio to refresh the reference and regenerate files as necessary.

Calling the Web Service

You call the web service the same way you would call any other .NET class. This capability is courtesy of the proxy class that was generated for you. For example, to get a `Customer` instance, you need only to create an instance of the `CustomerProfile` proxy and then call its `GetCustomerProfile` method. Figure 16.11 shows a working example.

The code for the `Find` click event simply translates the customer ID text box into an integer and passes that value to a private routine that loads the form. This private routine creates an instance of the proxy class and then calls the appropriate method. Listing 16.5 shows this private routine for your review.

FIGURE 16.11   The customer profile service in action.

LISTING 16.5   Calling the `GetCustomerProfile` Web Method

```
private void LoadCustomer(int custId) {
  CustomerProfile.CustomerProfile custProfileServ =
    new CustomerProfile.CustomerProfile();
  CustomerProfile.Customer cust = custProfileServ.GetCustomerProfile(custId);
  //bind customer information to form
  textBoxName.Text = cust.Name;
  textBoxEmail.Text = cust.Email;
  textBoxAddress1.Text = cust.Address1;
  textBoxAddress2.Text = cust.Address2;
  textBoxCity.Text = cust.City;
  textBoxZip.Text = cust.Zip;
  textBoxPhone.Text = cust.Phone;
  checkBoxEmail.Checked = cust.ContactViaEmail;
  checkBoxPhone.Checked = cust.ContactViaPhone;
  comboBoxState.SelectedText = cust.State;
}
```

All web services in .NET are called this same way. A proxy is generated, and you then
work with the proxy to call the service. This is true of web applications that call web
services, console applications, and so on.

> **NOTE**
>
> To debug your web service from a client application, you must attach to the ASP worker process
> responsible for hosting the service. Refer to Chapter 9, "Debugging with Visual Studio 2005,"
> for details on doing just that.

16

Managing Web Service Exceptions

.NET can make it easy to forget that you are calling a web service. When you deal with proxy classes, you often get used to working with a web service as if it were no different than any other method. However, this can be dangerous. Web methods are different. One big difference is the way in which you throw exceptions from a web service. The following sections explore how to throw exceptions.

Creating a Web Service Exception

Fortunately, the SOAP specification describes how an exception is thrown over the Web through this protocol. These exceptions can be business logic exceptions or those generated by .NET when processing a call. The important point is that if you wrap these exceptions appropriately, the client should be able to understand how to manage them.

.NET provides the `SoapException` object for wrapping an exception for SOAP transmission. This class has a number of parameters that you may not be used to working with when throwing exceptions. The parameters and properties include the following:

- `Message`—Used to define a descriptive message of the exception. If you are passing a standard .NET exception through SOAP, you can set the `Message` property to the `Message` property of the standard exception.

- `Code`—Used to indicate whether the error was server or client related. You set the property to `ServerFaultCode` if the client passed the message correctly but the server failed to process the request (was down or broken). You set this value to `ClientFaultCode` is the client passed a bad message or bad parameter values.

- `Actor`—Used to set the value to the URI of the web service. The actor is the code that caused the exception.

- `Detail` (Optional)—Used to pass more information about a given error. The `Detail` property can include nothing or as much detail as you want to include about the exception.

Listing 16.6 shows a new version of the `GetCustomerProfile` web method. This version checks to see whether the customer exists. If not, it throws a `SoapException` with the `Code` property set to `ClientFaultCode`.

LISTING 16.6   Creating a SOAP Exception

```
[WebMethod(Description = "Used to return a customer's profile.")]
public BusinessEntities.Customer GetCustomerProfile(int customerId) {
  EntityServices.CustomerProfile custProfile =
➥new EntityServices.CustomerProfile();
  BusinessEntities.Customer customer = custProfile.GetCustomer(customerId);
  if (customer == null) {
    SoapException soapEx = new SoapException("Could not find Customer",
      SoapException.ClientFaultCode, Context.Request.Url.AbsoluteUri.ToString());
```

LISTING 16.6   Continued

```
    throw soapEx;
  }
  return customer;
}
```

Handling a Web Service Exception

You handle the SOAP exception by catching it the same way you might catch any other
.NET exception. You can use the .NET SoapException class for this purpose. .NET will
automatically translate the SOAP exception into this object for your use. The following
simple example shows how to catch the exception and display it in a message box. We
added this code to our Windows form example.

```
} catch (System.Web.Services.Protocols.SoapException ex) {
  string msg = "Message: " + ex.Message + ", Actor: " + ex.Actor
    + ", Fault Code: " + ex.Code.ToString();
  MessageBox.Show(msg);
}
```

Summary

In this chapter, you saw how .NET abstracts the programming of web services. With this
abstraction, you can concentrate on building business functionality and exposing this as
web services in a similar manner as you might expose other .NET libraries. Some key
points in this chapter include the following:

- Web services are based on open standards. .NET adheres to these standards to ensure
  that heterogeneous applications can all work together with web services.

- A .NET web service consists of an .asmx file that points to the code behind the
  service. This .asmx file represents the URI to the service.

- You use the WebMethod attribute class to indicate a given method should be defined
  as a method of a web service.

- To consume a web service, you set a web reference to that service. Doing so results
  in a proxy class that you work with to call the web service.

- You can throw exceptions from a web service using the SoapException class. This
  same class can be used to catch and handle web service exceptions.

PART IV

Visual Studio 2005 Team System

IN THIS PART

CHAPTER 17	Team Collaboration and Visual Studio Team System	621
CHAPTER 18	Managing and Working with Team Projects	633
CHAPTER 19	Source Control	659
CHAPTER 20	Work Item Tracking	687
CHAPTER 21	Modeling	731
CHAPTER 22	Testing	769
CHAPTER 23	Team Foundation Build	811

Team Collaboration and Visual Studio Team System

We have spent the majority of this book specifically describing how to best press Visual Studio into action for writing a variety of different application types: Windows forms applications, web applications, database-connected applications, class libraries, and so on. And in our discussion of the various Visual Studio tools that enable those development scenarios, we have focused squarely on the role of the developer in writing quality code quickly using the Visual Studio IDE. But to talk solely about coding is to miss the larger picture. Software development projects involve other equally important roles and skill sets. Software projects are also a whole lot more complicated than simply producing code; they have a life all their own that involves variables across a variety of work activities.

Visual Studio Team System is the graduation of Visual Studio from a developer-focused Integrated Development Environment to a collaborative suite of tools that targets all of the different roles involved on a software project, and enables productive work across all phases of the Software Development Life Cycle (SDLC). In this chapter, we will look at this suite of collaborative tools collectively referred to as *Visual Studio Team System (VSTS)*. We will first establish some baseline knowledge of SDLCs to provide context for the problems faced by development teams. Then we will discuss exactly what we mean when we refer to the Visual Studio Team System and take a brief tour through the Team System toolset. The balance of the chapters in this book will look in detail at the various scenarios enabled through VSTS.

A View of Software Development Projects

Software development projects are complex projects that involve a variety of different moving parts: Yes, developers are an important component of the software development machinery, but they are far from the only component. With any sufficiently sized project, architects are also involved. They act as the keepers of the technical blueprint for a solution and work closely with developers to ensure that the blueprint is achievable in code and that it matches the requirements and expectations of the project. Testers are also involved. They test the validity of the code produced by the developers against a gamut of quality benchmarks. And finally, one or more individuals are usually needed to manage the logistics of the project: who is working on what, schedule achievement, and general process management.

In addition to the different roles and skill sets involved, any given project progresses through a series of phases from inception to completion. Over time, the software industry has evolved various models that are useful in describing the software development life cycle and the interactions between the various roles and parties.

Microsoft has developed its own series of models and guidance around the SDLC and the involved roles called the *Microsoft Solutions Framework*. The Microsoft Solutions Framework, or MSF, is in its fourth major incarnation. It documents a process model for describing the phases and activities within the SDLC and a team model for describing the roles that participate on the software development project team. It is also a collection of best practices, project-specific guidance, and templates.

The MSF is available in two flavors: MSF for Agile Software Development (MSF Agile) and MSF for CMMI Process Improvement (MSFCMMI). A basic understanding of MSF is important to this discussion of Visual Studio Team System for two reasons:

- To understand the value of VSTS, you first have to understand the problem space presented with software development projects; by using a common set of terms and semantics to describe this problem space, you'll have a much easier time understanding the benefits that the Visual Studio Team System brings to the table.

- In addition, VSTS is capable of using template models that actually impact tool behavior within Visual Studio. MSF Agile and MSF for CMMI are two templates delivered by Microsoft for direct use with Visual Studio Team System.

MSF Agile

MSF Agile maps the concepts of a solutions framework into the values favored by an agile development methodology. Although it is hard to come up with a universal definition of what makes a development process agile, in general these methodologies can be said to adhere to and prize the following characteristics:

- Individuals and interactions trump processes and tools.

- Valid, quality software is valued over comprehensive documentation.

- Collaboration with the customer and between team members is advocated over contract negotiation.

- The project team is empowered to react to change as opposed to following a prescriptive project plan.

The MSF Agile Process Model

The MSF v4 Agile process model deals with the development process in terms of tracks, checkpoints, and work products. *Tracks* are a set of activities (some sequential, known as *workstreams;* others not). *Checkpoints* are consensus points where the team collaboratively examines progress and determines whether to continue on the current path, change paths, or stop altogether. *Work products* is the term given to the tangible outputs from one or more activities; these are the source code, documents, spreadsheets, and so on, that are generated throughout the course of a project.

The MSF Agile model also incorporates the concept of cycles. *Cycles* represent the frequency with which activities are performed. For instance, a daily build is an example of a cycle that involves a discrete set of activities that, in turn, result in a discrete set of work products.

The MSF Agile Team Model

Beyond the activities you expect to see within an SDLC, it is also useful to understand the interaction between the various roles you encounter on a software project. The MSF Agile team model represents the project team as a set of different constituencies. The needs of each constituency are represented by its team members, and all members are considered to be peers on the project team. No one role is more important than another. Figure 17.1 documents the Agile team model.

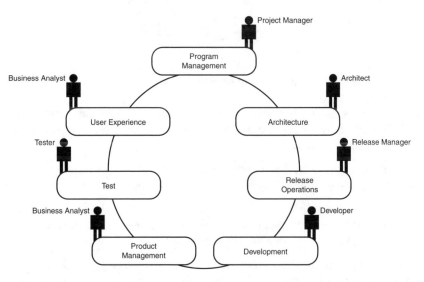

FIGURE 17.1   Constituencies and roles in the MSF Agile team model.

MSF for CMMI

The Software Engineering Institutes Capability Maturity Model (CMM) is "a reference model of mature practices in a specified discipline, used to improve and appraise a group's capability to perform that discipline" (see http://www.sei.cmu.edu). The Capability Maturity Model for Integration (CMMI) is a collection of four CMMs focused on the disciplines of software engineering, systems engineering, integrated product and process development, and supplier sourcing. MSF v4 for CMMI (MSFCMMI) is a framework tied directly to this four-discipline CMMI.

The MSF for CMMI Process Model

Just like MSF Agile, the MSF for CMMI process is described in terms of tracks and checkpoints. The tracks within MSFCMMI are more formally defined, and the checkpoints are also all well defined with expected deliverables.

Figure 17.2 shows the tracks and checkpoints espoused by the MSF for CMMI process model.

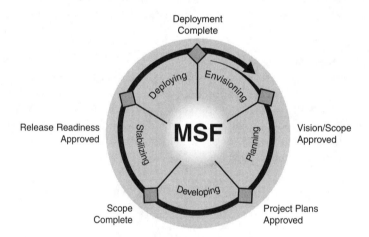

FIGURE 17.2   Tracks and checkpoints in MSF for CMMI.

These tracks are a recognition of the fact that although there are many competing models for the SDLC, they really all distill down to project activities spread across the natural rhythm of the project process:

- First, all the parties involved need to agree on the vision for the project. What are they setting out to achieve? How will they know whether they are successful?

- After a common vision has been agreed upon, boundaries have been set, and goals have been documented, the project team needs to agree on both what they are going to build and how they are going to build it.

- Then the plans are put into action, and the software application is actually architected, designed, and written.

- As various components of the system are written, they need to be tested to ensure that they are actually realizing the requirements of the project and that they meet the project team's commitments with respect to quality.

- And finally, after all of the parts have been written, tested, and approved, the software application has to actually be deployed so that it can be used.

These phases are termed, respectively, *Envisioning, Planning, Developing, Stabilizing,* and *Deploying.* Each of these phases has a different set of anticipated work activities, work outputs, and culminating checkpoints.

The MSF for CMMI Team Model

The MSFCMMI team model is identical in principle and structure to the MSF Agile team model, but it defines and maps many more roles. Compare Figure 17.1 with Figure 17.3.

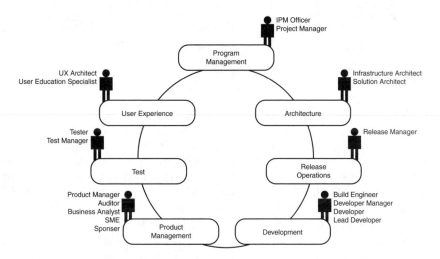

FIGURE 17.3 Constituencies and roles in the MSF for CMMI team model.

Introducing the Visual Studio Team System

Only three variables in play at any given time affect the impact and success of a software project: speed, quality, and money. Put another way, you can "improve" the success of any given application by delivering the application faster, by delivering a better application, or by spending less money to develop the application. If you truly want to optimize against this "faster, better, cheaper" troika, you need to look beyond the role of the developer and the singular process of writing code and start to contemplate how you can enable the other roles and skill sets that are prevalent in the software development life cycle. You also have to pay attention to more than just the development phase of any project. You need to pay attention to project planning, initial architecture analysis, test suites, and work item management.

Visual Studio Team System recognizes this basic premise and elevates the role of Visual Studio in the software development process by providing a suite of interconnected tools that focus on all roles and all phases of the SDLC.

Visual Studio Team System is the name applied to a set of Visual Studio versions, each of which targets a different role in the software development process. From a product capabilities perspective, you can think of Visual Studio Team System as a team-focused superset of the other available Visual Studio versions such as Visual Studio Professional or Visual Studio Standard (see Figure 17.4).

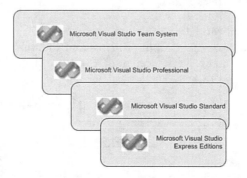

FIGURE 17.4   The Visual Studio versions.

We discussed earlier the MSF team models: Visual Studio Team System provides tools useful for the architect, developer, tester, and project manager roles. This means that separate products are tailored to the architect, developer, and tester work sets: Visual Studio Team Architect, Visual Studio Team Developer, and Visual Studio Team Test. Project managers are enabled via a set of add-ins, utilities, and reporting functions delivered with the Visual Studio Team Foundation Server. Team Foundation Server also functions as the keystone collaboration and storage component within the team system. Each of these different products surfaces role- and track/activity-specific tools within the familiar IDE.

> **NOTE**
>
> Keep in mind the superset relationship between the Visual Studio Team System products (such as Team Architect) and the other Visual Studio versions: The VSTS versions add capabilities (specific to a role) over and above the features and functions found in Visual Studio Professional. Another way to think about it is like this: Anything you can do in Visual Studio Professional, you can also do in Visual Studio Team Architect (or Team Developer or Team Test).

Let's look at the different VSTS products and how they map into the software development process/team model space.

Visual Studio Team Architect

Visual Studio Team Architect is, obviously, focused on the architect role. Part of an architect's job is to help the development team and the project management team crisply communicate the design of a system. The design and architecture of a system are typically visualized through the use of models; models are a superb way to construct and think about all the different aspects and variables involved in a large system and from that perspective are great documentation vehicles. Their historical problem is that they are difficult to translate into code and must then be updated to match the code any time the code base changes.

Visual Studio Team Architect provides the architect with tools that overcome those problems. Specifically, four designers—the Distributed Application Designer, Logical Infrastructure Designer, Deployment Designer, and Class Designer—work together to deliver dynamic models of a software system. Besides working together in an integrated fashion, these designers are also capable of synchronizing with the system's code.

This is the key benefit realized within Visual Studio Team Architect:

- You can visually author code using the Class Designer.

- You can describe the network infrastructure using the Logical Infrastructure Designer.

- The Distributed Application Designer enables you to construct services-based architectures around the code described in the Class Designer.

- The Deployment Designer enables you to deploy a specific system or subsystem into the specified environment that was described using the Logical Infrastructure Designer.

- Changes made to any of the models in these designers are immediately recognized and synchronized with the code base.

We cover these four designers in depth in Chapter 21, "Modeling."

Visual Studio Team Developer

Visual Studio Professional already does a terrific job as an integrated development environment; its code authoring editors and designers are both powerful and easy to use. The Visual Studio Team Developer extends the embrace of the developer role by delivering tools to validate code. Using VS Team Developer, you can verify the performance and quality of your code. This edition provides static and dynamic code analysis tools, code profiling, code coverage, and unit testing facilities.

Static Code Analysis

Static code analysis is a design-time check of source code that goes beyond the syntax-checking capabilities of the compiler. In fact, if we extend that analogy, if compiler checks are analogous to spelling checks in a word processor, then static code analysis is similar in concept to grammar checking in a word processor: It attempts to determine the meaning of your code and then highlight areas of concern.

Code analysis happens at build/compile time; the various analysis checks are controlled on the Code Analysis tab on the project properties dialog box (as shown in Figure 17.5).

17

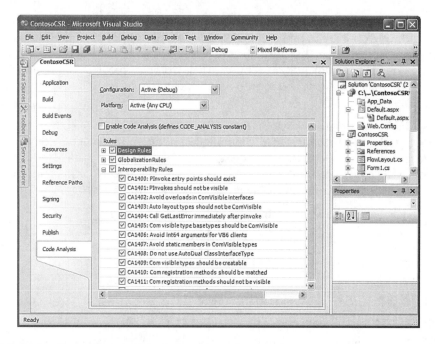

FIGURE 17.5   Controlling code analysis options.

Dynamic Code Analysis and Code Profiling

Just like static code analysis works against your code at design time, dynamic code analysis works against your code at runtime. Code profiling analyzes your code to give you information on how your application is running. There are two code profilers. A sampling profiler polls your application and retrieves information about it. An instrumented profiler injects probes into your code at compile time; these probes emit data, which is collected by the profiler.

Application profiling is set up using the Performance Explorer. We discussed the Performance Explorer in Chapter 5, "Browsers and Explorers."

Code Coverage and Unit Testing

Code coverage and unit testing work together. Unit testing is accomplished via an attribute-based framework (similar to that employed by JUnit and NUnit if you are familiar with those tools). When you place an attribute on a block of code, it will show up in the Test Manager tool (see Figure 17.6).

After creating a test, you can then use the test facilities to determine which lines of code were actually covered by the test. This is done interactively in the code editor window (tested lines of code are shaded green, missed lines of code shaded red) and via a Code Coverage Results window.

We cover unit testing and code coverage with VSTS in Chapter 22, "Testing."

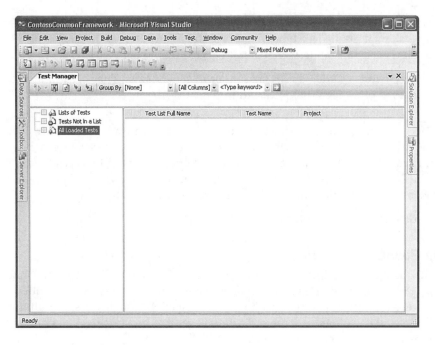

FIGURE 17.6   The Test Manager.

Visual Studio Team Test

Visual Studio Team Test picks up the testing activities where Team Developer leaves off. In addition to the same profiling, unit testing, and code coverage tools, this edition has tools for load testing web applications, running and analyzing unit tests, and managing test cases.

Creating Tests

You can create tests of the following types within Team Test:

- **Unit Tests**—These are the same unit tests supported by Team Developer

- **Web Tests**—These are a series of HTTP requests designed to web application functionality; they could be used in performance or stress testing cycles.

- **Load Tests**—Load tests are used to simulate traffic against a website (see the following section).

- **Manual Tests**—Certain tests may be impossible to automate or script (such as user interaction with the applications UI). In these cases, a manual test can be generated. Manual tests in VSTS are nothing more than Word documents that outline the discrete tasks that constitute a test. Even though the tests are manual, by capturing the task sequence and results in a document, you can manage and view it along with the other tests in the system.

- **Generic Tests**—Generic tests are simply wrappers around any other tests that return a pass or fail result. This type of test is useful as an extensibility mechanism because it allows you to wrap tests that aren't covered by the native test types in VSTS.

- **Ordered Tests**—Ordered tests are similar to generic tests. They are wrappers around a series of other tests that must run in sequence.

Load Tests   Load tests are somewhat unique: VSTS can create a logical testing unit called a *rig*. Rigs are client computers (known as *agents*) and a controller used to generated load demand against a system. There are full management capabilities in Visual Studio Team Test to create agents, assign them to a controller, encapsulate a group of agents and a controller as a rig, and run and monitor tests from the rig.

We cover load tests in Chapter 22, "Testing."

Team Foundation Server

The individual team products can all function individually, but adding Team Foundation Server (TFS) allows the entire team to collaborate seamlessly across work activities and tracks. It even has its own set of enabling technologies. Although TFS serves all the individual roles and constituencies, the project manager role in particular is shored up by the tools provided with Team Foundation Server.

> **NOTE**
>
> Team Foundation Server requires Microsoft SQL Server 2005.

Source Control

Team Foundation Server includes a brand-new source control engine that far exceeds Visual Source Safe's capabilities when used with large development teams. The TFS source control engine uses SQL Server 2005 as its backing store instead of the file system and is very scalable up to the largest development teams. In addition to native support for access over HTTP/HTTPS, the TFS source control system also supports check-in policies and *shelving*:

- Check-in policies allow you to add rules that are run on check-in to ensure that procedures and best practices are enforced. A common example of this is a check-in policy that requires a clean bill of health from the static code analyzer before the check-in is allowed.

- Shelving is a technique whereby you can check in a file to a "shelveset" instead of checking in to the live source code tree. This allows you to check in a work in progress without overwriting the work in progress that is maintained on the main source code branch for your project.

NOTE

Although most users will leverage the TFS source system within Visual Studio, it also ships with a standalone user interface that can provide administrator and contributor level functionality to individuals who don't own Visual Studio Team System.

Source control is covered in Chapter 19, "Source Control."

Work Item Tracking

A work item is the atomic unit within VSTS for tracking and managing activities and work products within the context of a project. Work items can be assigned to any role within the project team and can be assigned to a specific workflow. Work items are powerful in that they can be related to a multitude of items to create a web of connected work products. For example, you may create a work item for a bug report and then link that bug report to a checked-in source code file, a developer, a tester, and the test case that revealed the bug.

A set of Microsoft Office add-ins ship with Team Foundation Server to allow project managers to tie into work items from within Office. For instance, a project manager can use the Microsoft Word add-in to generate a status report directly linked to work items in the TFS database. Or the project manager may use the Microsoft Project add-in to automatically generate and sync work items with the action items in the Microsoft Project plan file.

Although simple in concept, work items are the single most important collaboration element in VSTS. Consider an end-to-end scenario: You are assigned a work item to fix a bug in your code. You would first review the work item, check out the section of offending code, make the fix, and then use the VSTS development/test tools to automatically run the tests that cover that code section. From there, you would check the changed code back into the source repository. Test would then pick up the ball. When the fix makes it into a build, that build is also linked to the work item. All the while, notifications are sent to interested parties so that others can track the progress of the work item through its workflow.

We cover work items in depth in Chapter 20, "Work Item Tracking."

Build Automation

Team Foundation Build is a part of the Team Foundation Server. It enables release management roles to run tests against a code base, build the code base, release the code base to a file server, and generate reports about the build and distribute them to the team.

Team Foundation Build is a tool and graphical user interface that sits over the top of the MSBuild tool. Chapter 23, "Team Foundation Build," has all the details on using the TFS build automation features.

Reports

Because all the work items and other work products in VSTS are stored in a SQL Server 2005 database, TFS is able to leverage the SQL Server 2005 Reporting Services and the SQL

Server 2005 Analysis Services to deliver reports about build quality, work item progress, test results, build results, and so on.

The Project Portal

Team Foundation Server uses the project template to generate a Windows Sharepoint site containing the correct document libraries and document templates that map to the chosen project type. For instance, creating a project based on the MSF Agile template will produce a SharePoint site with artifact document templates specifically generated for the agile process.

By using the SharePoint site as a universal portal, even non–Visual Studio project stakeholders can interact with the VSTS work items and participate in project collaboration.

Summary

Visual Studio Team System focuses on enabling all tracks of the SDLC, not just the development track. A holistic approach toward managing progress through the SDLC is key. VSTS extends the reach of Visual Studio from the developer to include other pivotal roles in the SDLC such as architects, business analysts, QA, and project management, and by doing so aims to

- Avoid unplanned scope increases

- Improve communication

- Minimize duplication of effort

- Optimize resources

- Streamline the development process

- Manage and mitigate risks

- Facilitate postmortem analysis and capture of best practices

In this chapter, you learned that VSTS is a set of different Visual Studio versions, each targeted at a different role within the SDL landscape. These VS versions are available separately or in a package known as the Visual Studio Team Suite. There is also a server-side component known as the Team Foundation Server that sits in the middle of a VSTS deployment. Because these tools all work together in an integrated fashion, Visual Studio Team System enables consistent support of work activities ranging from architecture to development to test, and management of the work items associated with each.

In the following chapters, we will look at the individual tools associated with Visual Studio Team System and see how they can be utilized within the fabric of a development team.

CHAPTER 18

Managing and Working with Team Projects

IN THIS CHAPTER

- Anatomy of Team Foundation Server

- Managing a Team Project

- Contributing to a Project Team

The preceding chapter described the cohesive tools ecosystem delivered with Visual Studio Team System. Now, it's time to look at the specifics involved with the Team Foundation Server.

You can think of Team Foundation Server as the central collaborative hub in a Visual Studio Team System environment: Visual Studio provides role-specific tools for architects, developers, testers, and managers, whereas Team Foundation Server provides the central repository and information-sharing services necessary to bind a project team together into one cohesive unit. In this chapter, we will focus on implementing a Team Foundation Server setup and leveraging its team-enabling capabilities.

Anatomy of Team Foundation Server

As discussed in Chapter 17, "Team Collaboration and Visual Studio Team System," Team Foundation Server (TFS) serves as the core collaboration hub for the Visual Studio Team System. It is TFS that enables source control, work item tracking, project alerts, reporting, and a host of other collaboration features.

You can best think of TFS as a suite of web services running over the top of a data store. Physically, this means that TFS functionality is surfaced through Windows IIS web services, with data storage, warehousing, analysis, and reporting services provided by SQL Server 2005. These two parts of TFS are referred to as the *application tier* and the *data tier*. These tiers are logical and physically may map onto one or more servers. Some organizations may deploy both of these tiers onto a single server, whereas others might deploy the application tier into a web farm and the data tier onto several SQL Server installations.

> **NOTE**
>
> The decision on how to deploy TFS is largely driven by the infrastructure and needs specific to your organization. Team Foundation Server ships with a lengthy set of installation instructions that you should consult closely before determining the best infrastructure arrangement.

The Application Tier

The application tier is composed of a set of web services (running under ASP .NET/Microsoft Internet Information Server) that provide source code control, work item tracking, reporting, and core TFS functionality. Figure 18.1 shows the general structure of a TFS application server.

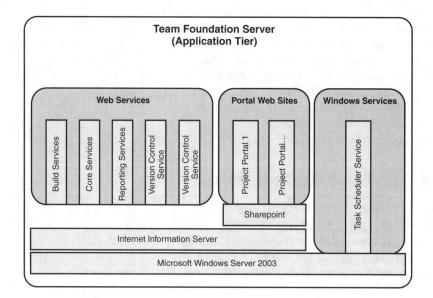

FIGURE 18.1   Team Foundation Server: application tier.

The web services on the application tier act as wrappers over the top of the TFS API, which provides the actual functionality delivered by TFS. These services are hosted in virtual directories under the root Team Foundation Server website. Figure 18.2 shows these web service directories within IIS Manager.

Within each service directory, there are one or more web service endpoints. The list is provided in Table 18.1.

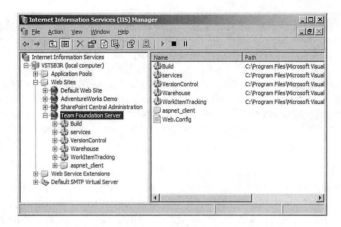

FIGURE 18.2   Team Foundation Server web services.

TABLE 18.1   Application Tier Web Services

Service Directory	Web Service(s)
Build Services	BuildController
	BuildStore
	Integration
	PublishTestResultsBuildService
Core Services	EventService
	AuthorizationService
	CommonStructureService
	GroupSecurityService
	ProcessTemplate
	ProjectMaintenance
	Registration
	ServerStatus
Warehouse	WarehouseController
Version Control	Administration
	Integration
	ProxyStatistics
	Repository
Work Item Tracking	ClientService
	ConfigurationSettingsService
	ExternalServices
	Integration
	SyncEventsListener

18

> **TIP**
>
> In general, you don't need to worry about the TFS web services. They function as the server's API, which is used by various TFS tools such as the Team Explorer. However, if you want to extend TFS functionality, the web services are a great place to start. Documentation on the TFS web services is spotty, but you can find some information on extending and integrating with TFS in the Visual Studio 2005 SDK (see http://msdn.microsoft.com/vstudio/extend/default.aspx). You can also get a small glimpse of web service functionality by simply calling the web service from your browser. This will give you a brief description of the service and a list of its supported methods.

In addition to these web services, a Windows service is also deployed and run on TFS application tier servers: the task scheduler service. The task scheduler service—which runs under the name `TfsServerScheduler`—is a generic service for scheduling a variety of TFS tasks. For example, the VSTS build system leverages this service to schedule builds.

> **NOTE**
>
> Team Foundation Build is the server application designed to run and manage automated software builds. It relies on its own service, the Team Build Service, which runs independently from the task scheduler. The Team Build Service can be deployed onto the application tier server but doesn't have to be. It also can be deployed on a client or on a standalone server.

The Data Tier

The data tier is essentially a SQL Server 2005 machine. It acts as the data repository for TFS and provides analysis and reporting services that are directly leveraged by Team Foundation Server (see Figure 18.3).

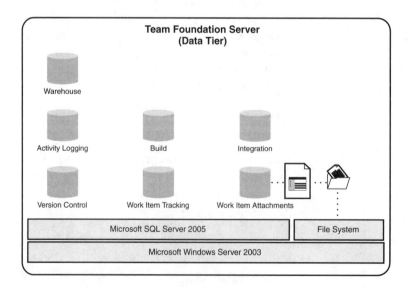

FIGURE 18.3   Team Foundation Server: data tier.

Physically, TFS stores its data across seven different databases:

- An activity log database (`TfsActivityLogging`)

- A build database (`TfsBuild`) that holds data related to system builds such as build steps and build quality indicators

- An "integration" database (`TfsIntegration`) that stores core team project information, security settings, and event registrations

- A version control database (`TfsVersionControl`)

- A data warehouse database (`TfsWarehouse`) that serves as the analysis and reporting store

- A work item database (`TfsWorkItemTracking`) that stores work items

- A work item attachment database (`TfsWorkItemTrackingAttachments`) that has a single table, `Attachments`, that serves as a collection of pointers to the work item attachment files

Work item attachments are actually stored in the file system.

It is important to note that the relationship between TFS and SQL Server is a close one: TFS relies on and requires SQL Server Analysis Services and SQL Server Reporting Services to complete its various reporting requirements.

Security

Team Foundation Server uses the traditional and well-understood model of users and groups to implement security. Two broad categories of users need to be accommodated: server administrators and project members. Server administrators are responsible for the administration of all the TFS components from the web service configurations within IIS to the database setup under SQL Server. Project members are those users who comprise a project team. Although these broad categories may overlap, and certainly there is nothing preventing someone from sharing server administration responsibilities with project management responsibilities, they are served by different groups within a default Team Foundation Server install.

Global Security Groups

Global security groups are the high-level, universal groups that broadly organize users into administrator or user-level permission sets: The Team Foundation Administrators group has full rights to all pieces of the TFS deployment, and the Team Foundation Valid Users group contains the user population that is allowed to access the resources of a Team Foundation Server.

Team Foundation Valid Users are further broken down at the project level by the project security groups.

Project Security Groups

For each individual project, TFS defines permissions and access levels by classifying users into three different groups: project administrators, contributors, and readers. Each of these groups has a decreasing level of privileges with respect to one another (see Figure 18.4).

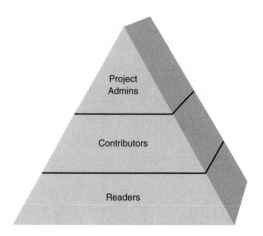

FIGURE 18.4   Team Foundation Server security roles.

Project Administrators   Project administrators have permission to manage individual projects en masse. They control content in the project portal sites, determine team membership, set security parameters, and have full control over a project's work items.

Contributors   Contributors represent the bulk of the team members; they are the individuals responsible for executing the project and therefore are imbued with permissions to add, edit, and delete work items in a given project, and can view information published on the project portal site.

Readers   Readers are individuals who have a vested interest in looking at project artifacts but don't contribute principally to the project. As the group name implies, they have only view permissions and will primarily interact with project data through the project portal site.

Mapping Roles to Groups

In Chapter 17, we covered two of the project process models that are supported. TFS uses *process templates* to describe how to physically implement a particular process using the components of TFS and Visual Studio Team System. We cover process templates in more depth in the following section; they are important to mention here because security is one area covered by a process template. It effectively takes the roles defined by the process and maps them into the security groups that TFS cares about. Table 18.2 shows how the MSF Agile and MSF CMMI roles map into the three project-level groups used by the Foundation Server security subsystem.

TABLE 18.2   MSF Roles and TFS Security Groups

MSF Agile Roles	
Role	Group
Architect	Contributor
Business Analyst	Contributor
Developer	Contributor
Project Manager	Project Administrator
Release Manager	Project Administrator
Tester	Contributor

MSF for CMMI Roles	
Role	Group
Auditor	Contributor
Build Engineer	Project Administrator
Business Analyst	Contributor
Developer	Contributor
Development Manager	Project Administrator
Infrastructure Architect	Contributor
IPM Officer	Contributor
Lead Developer	Project Administrator
Product Manager	Contributor
Project Manager	Project Administrator
Release Manager	Project Administrator
Solution Architect	Contributor
Sponsor	Reader
Subject Matter Expert	Reader
Test Manager	Project Administrator
Tester	Contributor
User Education Architect	Contributor
User Experience Specialist	Contributor

18

Managing a Team Project

Now that you have a decent understanding of what Team Foundation Server looks like from an architectural perspective, you're ready to see how you can create and host a *team project* within TFS. The term *team project* is used to distinguish a TFS-based collaboration project from a Visual Studio project.

The first step is installing the Team Foundation Server client software; this is available on the Team Foundation Server install media. After this software has been installed on your machine, several additions are made to Visual Studio to allow it to interact with a Team Foundation Server: A new option under the Tools menu will allow you to connect to a Team Foundation Server, a new Team menu is added to the Visual Studio menu bar, and new options are available under the File menu. We'll get to the Team menu in just a bit. In addition to these Visual Studio enhancements, a variety of Microsoft Office add-ins are also installed; they allow you to surface certain TFS capabilities, such as work item tracking, within applications like Microsoft Word, Microsoft Excel, or even Microsoft Project.

Creating a New Team Project

Creating a new team project works much the same as creating a new Visual Studio project: From the File menu, choose New, Team Project. The New Team Project Wizard will start.

> **NOTE**
>
> If you don't see the Team Project option available under the Visual Studio File menu, you may not have the Team Foundation Server client software installed. Another possibility is your choice of VS environment settings. Your Visual Studio environment settings will alter the way your File menu is structured. For instance, if you have the Visual Basic Development settings profile loaded, you will see the New Team Project option located directly under the File menu instead of under the New submenu. You can change environment settings by using the Import and Export Settings Wizard (which you access by choosing Tools, Import and Export Settings).

The wizard will collect all the information needed to create the various TFS structures used by a team project, including the databases and websites.

Selecting a Team Project Name

On the first page of the wizard (see Figure 18.5), you are prompted to select a name for the team project. Keep in mind that the name you choose here will, in one form or another, be embedded in many of the TFS structures from database names to SharePoint websites. Therefore, you need to select a name that doesn't conflict with any of the current projects hosted in the target TFS server.

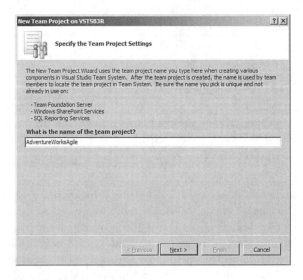

FIGURE 18.5   Selecting a project name.

Selecting a Process Template

The second page of the wizard (see Figure 18.6) asks you to identify a process template. As we have mentioned, the default selections here are the MSF Agile template and the MSF for CMMI template.

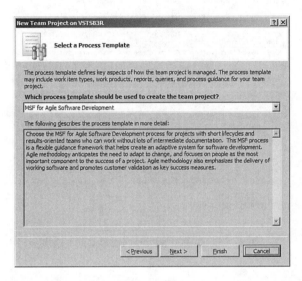

FIGURE 18.6   Choosing a process template.

Your template selection will drive many of the behaviors in the Team System environment. For instance, the default work items, documents, and team roles that are populated when you start a new team project are all based on the information contained within the process template.

Naming the Project Portal

The next page is used to name the project portal website (see Figure 18.7). The project portal is a Windows SharePoint Services website designed to be the one-stop shop for all of a team project's collateral from the standard work items and documents to team announcements, links, and process guidance information.

The portal name will default to the team project name that you specified on the initial wizard page; you can change it to something else, keeping in mind that the project portal has a potentially larger and more diverse audience than the other team project entry points.

Specifying Source Control Settings

The source control settings page (see Figure 18.8) enables you to control how this new project should be configured with regards to its source control repository. You have the option to create a new folder under the root source control tree, create a new branch under an existing source control folder, or leave the source control creation for a later date.

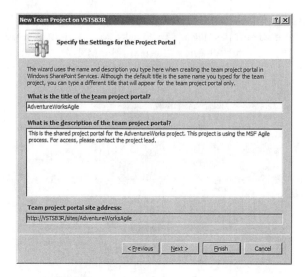

FIGURE 18.7   Naming the project portal.

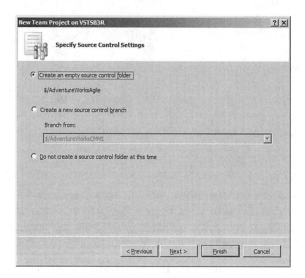

FIGURE 18.8   Source control settings.

Confirming Your Settings

At this point, the wizard will display a confirmation page of the settings you have chosen. Clicking Finish will start the project generate process on the server. A progress page will show you what process is currently running. After everything has been created, a final notice page (see Figure 18.9) will confirm the team project has been created and offer you the option of viewing the project process guidance (more on the guidance page later in this chapter).

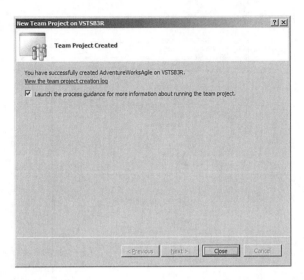

FIGURE 18.9   Final confirmation.

You have now successfully created a new team project within TFS. The next step is to add team members to the project.

Adding Users to a Project Team

As a project administrator, you have access to the security groups that control access to your projects. In Visual Studio, you can access the group membership settings through the Team Explorer tool or through the Team menu. Take a moment to briefly examine the Team Explorer window. As a project administrator or contributor, you will want to thoroughly understand the various Team Explorer features. And indeed, in later sections of this chapter and later chapters in this book, we will provide even more focus on this tool and its use scenarios. For now, though, a high-level acquaintance is sufficient.

Working with the Team Explorer Window

When you are connected, display the Team Explorer window by selecting View, Team Explorer within Visual Studio. The Team Explorer window is a full-fledged tool window that operates just like other tool windows such as the Solution Explorer.

With a connection established to a running TFS application tier server, you will see a variety of different nodes within the Team Explorer window (see Figure 18.10). The top-level node represents the Team Foundation Server itself. Below this node are the various projects available on that server. And within each project are folders for Work Items, Documents, Reports, Team Builds, and Source Control. Also, below the server node is a Favorites folder.

18

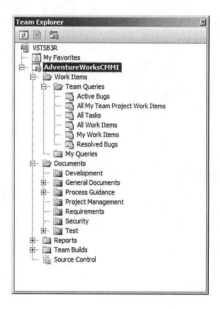

FIGURE 18.10   The Team Explorer window.

Team Project Folders   Just as with the Solution Explorer, the folders within team project nodes serve to organize the artifacts generated within the team project. Each of the folders provides a context menu: Just right-click on the folder to access the valid actions for that particular node. Figure 18.11 shows the context menu for the Work Items node.

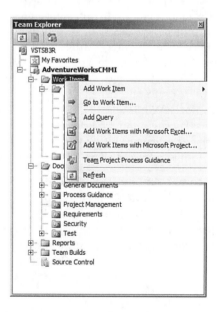

FIGURE 18.11   Team Explorer context menu for Work Items.

Double-clicking on any of the items within the project will load that item into its appropriate window within Visual Studio. We'll cover how to view and create items within a project in the section titled "Contributing to a Project Team."

Team Explorer Favorites   The Favorites folder holds shortcuts to other nodes within the explorer window. Typically, you would place links to frequently used project nodes here because they may be buried within the tree structure or at the end of a long list of explorer items.

The quickest way to add a shortcut is simply to drag the target node into the Favorites folder.

Controlling Project Groups

As we explained earlier in the discussion on the TFS security model, access to TFS functionality is controlled by privilege levels and permissions that are doled out based on group membership. Put another way, what you can do and see within a team project is based on what group your user ID belongs to. The Project Group Membership dialog box can be accessed by project administrators and is used to control group membership.

There are two ways to access this dialog box: through the Team menu or through the Team Explorer window. On the Team menu (shown in Figure 18.12), select Team Project Settings, Group Membership. Using Team Explorer, you perform the identical action by right-clicking on the project node to access the Team Project Settings menu items.

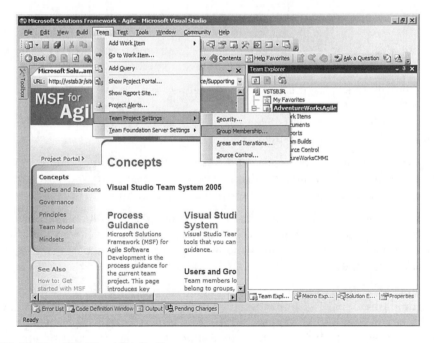

FIGURE 18.12   The Visual Studio Team menu.

Adding Users to a Group   The Project Group Membership dialog box is the principal mechanism for adding or removing users from a project group (see Figure 18.13).

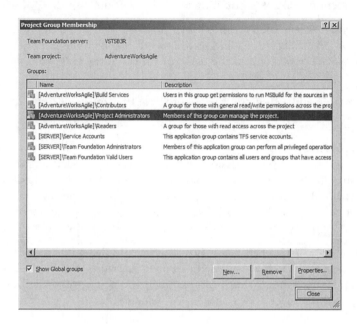

FIGURE 18.13   Project Group Membership dialog box.

To add a new user to an existing group, select the group and then click on the Properties button. This will launch a properties window for that group (see Figure 18.14).

From the properties window, make sure you have the Members tab selected, select the Windows User or Group radio button, and then click the Add button. This will yield the standard Windows user selection dialog box (see Figure 18.15). Selecting a user here and clicking OK will add that user to the group.

Adding Custom Groups   Some organizations may want to implement their own group scheme within TFS. There is nothing that prevents you from adding your own groups or, in fact, deleting the default groups that are part of the TFS setup.

To add a new group, you start at the same Project Group Membership dialog box shown in Figure 18.13. Instead of clicking on the Properties button, however, you will instead click the New button. In the resulting window (see Figure 18.16), you can enter a name for the new group and a description.

Fine-tuning Permissions   Each group has a default set of permissions applied to it. As a project administrator or TFS administrator, you can change the permissions associated with each group. From the Team menu, select Team Project Settings, Security. The security dialog box (see Figure 18.17) will enable you to fine-tune the exact permissions associated with any of the project-level or global security groups on the Team Foundation Server machine.

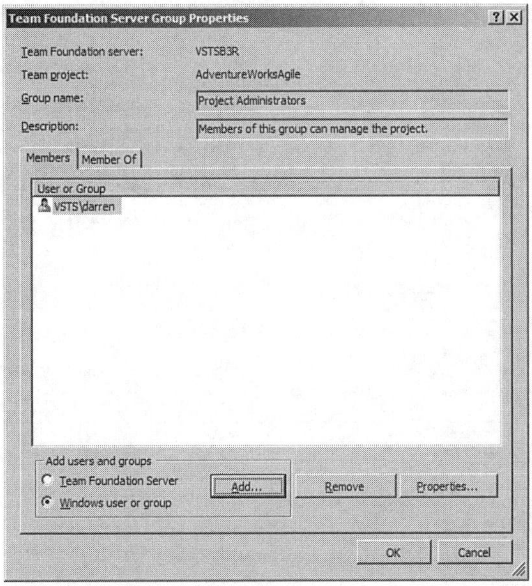

FIGURE 18.14   Project group properties.

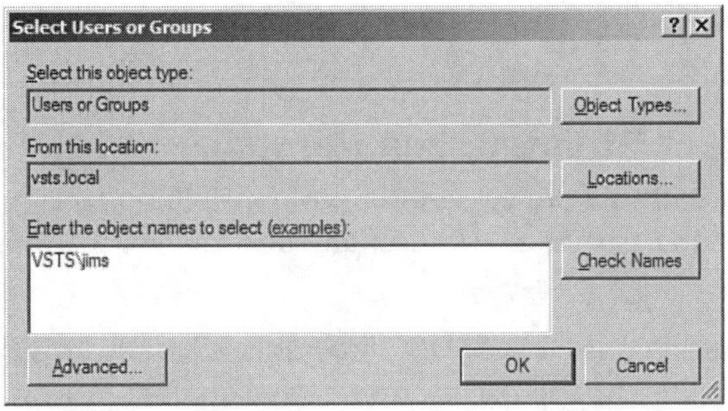

FIGURE 18.15   Selecting users and groups.

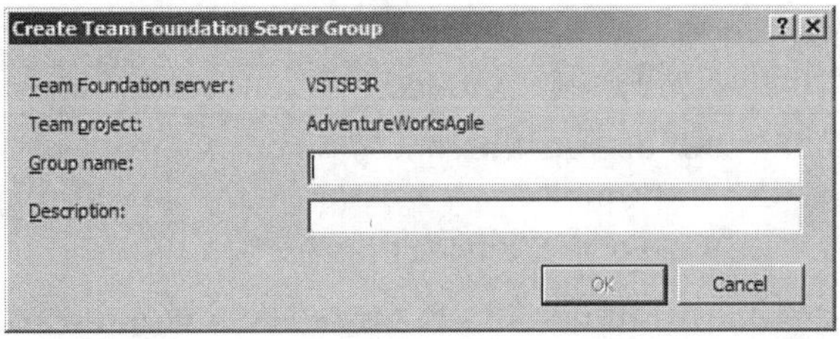

FIGURE 18.16   Creating a new project group.

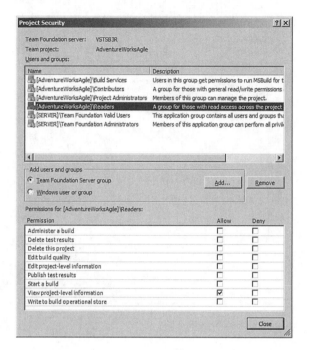

FIGURE 18.17   Setting group permissions.

Controlling Project Structure and Iterations

Besides controlling access to a project, another responsibility of the project administrator is to define the structural aspects of a project and also control the number of *iterations* planned for a project.

From the previous discussions on the SDLC process in Chapter 17, you know different methodologies have different approaches to the development process. But in general, an iteration is a complete work cycle that results in a working release of the software. Subsequent iterations build on the previously generated artifacts and lessons learned until, finally, enough iterations have been processed to achieve a releasable product. Using the team settings in Visual Studio, project administrators can control how many iterations any given project will progress through.

In addition to iterations, TFS supports the concept of *areas*. Areas are simply logical ways to group work efforts within the project. For software development projects, an area may define the boundary of a functional group or feature set.

Both areas and iterations are controlled using the same Areas and Iterations dialog box (reached through Team Project Settings, Areas and Iterations).

Adding or Changing Project Areas

Figure 18.18 shows the Areas and Iterations dialog box, with the Area tab active. This is the work surface used for creating and structuring areas within a project. For instance, you may want to flesh out some project structure by creating `OrderTracking`, `OrderProcessing`, and `OrderIntake` areas. You could then further subdivide these functional areas into specific breakouts for each major component.

FIGURE 18.18   Adding areas to a project.

Areas are depicted within a tree control in the dialog box. To add a new area, first select the parent area and then click on the Add New Node button (on the toolbar within the Area tab). You can then edit the area's name inline within the tree. Removing a node is as simple as selecting it and then clicking on the Delete Node button in the toolbar. Nodes can also be moved within the tree hierarchy. First, select the node you want to move and then use the four buttons on the right of the dialog box's toolbar to move them up within their siblings list or move the node up or down within the parent/child relationship.

Any areas created are then used to help structure the work items for the project. In that way, they can function as a mechanism for organizing work against these functional area breakouts.

> **NOTE**
>
> Because areas will likely be very specific to a given project, no areas are created by default when you instantiate a new team project.

Adding or Changing Iterations

Iterations are handled in exactly the same fashion as areas. First, click on the Iteration tab and then add or move nodes as necessary. Unlike areas, the process template that you have selected for the current project will initially default to a number of iterations. As an example, the MSF Agile project already has three iterations defined (see Figure 18.19).

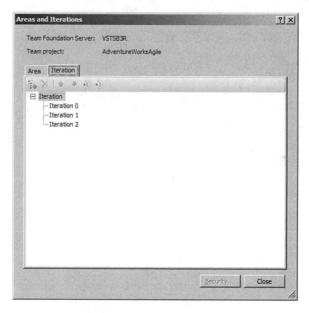

FIGURE 18.19   Managing project iterations.

Contributing to a Project Team

Team members interact with a team project in a variety of ways that will differ depending on the unique role of that user. The following sections cover how team contributors can use the Visual Studio Team Explorer to interface with a Team Foundation Server.

Connecting to a Team Foundation Server

Before using the Team Explorer tool, you will first need to connect to a Team Foundation Server—specifically, an application tier server.

From the Tools menu in Visual Studio, select Connect to Team Foundation Server. This will launch a dialog box that shows any "known" TFS instances (see Figure 18.20). You can either select from this list or, if your intended server isn't shown, you can add it to the list by clicking on the Servers button.

To add a new TFS server to the dialog box, click on the Add button and fill out the HTTP connection properties: server name, port, and protocol.

Select one of the listed servers, select one or more of the projects hosted on that server, and then click OK.

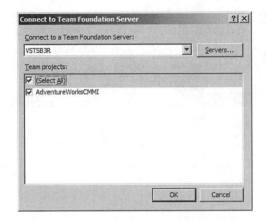

FIGURE 18.20   Connecting to a Team Foundation Server.

Assuming that the project administrator has added your credentials to that project's groups, you are now wired into the selected TFS team projects and can use Team Explorer to access the items within those projects.

Using Team Explorer

You have already had a decent look at the Team Explorer tool; it provides an interactive, organized view of items within a particular project. As a project contributor, you can edit or view those items or create new items within the various categories (for example, work items, reports, documents).

Using Team Explorer isn't complicated: By right-clicking on a node, you get a context-sensitive menu with the various actions that correspond to the folder's content. For instance, you can upload a document in this fashion by right-clicking on one of the document folders. Or you can create a new work item.

Dedicated chapters following this one discuss work item, build, and source control management.

Using the Project Portal

As we stated previously, the project portal is the nexus of all the various components of a project. Because it is a SharePoint Services–based site, it follows the standard composition theme for a SharePoint site: It is composed of a mix of standard web parts—such as links, announcements, and so on—and TFS-specific web parts to provide users a holistic view of the current state of the project (see Figure 18.21).

You can visit the project portal from a web browser by manually navigating to the site; by default, it is located at http://<*tfs app server*>/sites/<*project name*>/default.aspx. You can automatically navigate there by right-clicking on a project in Team Explorer or selecting the Team menu. Both have a Show Project Portal option, which will launch a new browser window pointed at the portal site.

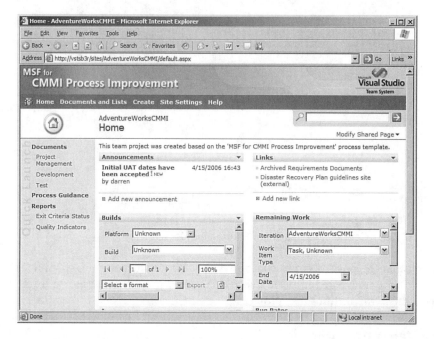

FIGURE 18.21   Connecting to projects on a Team Foundation Server.

Contributors will typically use the portal site to gain access to team project documents from outside Visual Studio and check on announcements, general progress reports, and the like. The portal site will also be heavily used by users in the "reader" role because it represents the only way to access team project information without using Team Explorer.

Default web parts are available for viewing build information, checking on remaining work, seeing bug rates, and looking at the open issues list. You can also gain access to the entire roster of reports (served up from SQL Server Reporting Services) or look at process guidance.

Process Guidance
Process guidance refers to a collection of HTML-based material that describes and documents the SDLC process. For each team project, guidance specific to the process used by that project is made available within the project portal site: Just click on the Process Guidance link in the left navigation bar.

Figure 18.22 shows the process guidance material for an MSF Agile-based project.

Using Microsoft Office
Microsoft Office is the third tool that you can use to work with items stored in a Team Foundation Server. Through various add-ins and templates, you can use Office applications such as Word, Excel, and Project to talk directly to a TFS server and update items stored there.

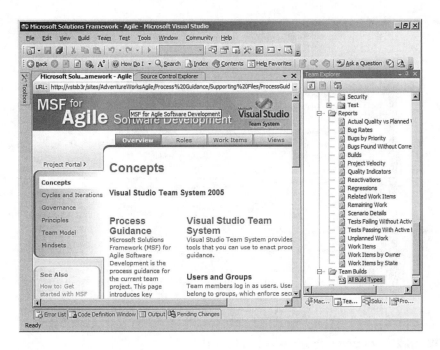

FIGURE 18.22   Project process guidance.

The use of Microsoft Word is limited to working with the various document templates (.dot files) that are included with the MSF Agile and MSF for CMMI process templates. Microsoft Project and Microsoft Excel offer actual integration with TFS and allow you to manage work items directly from these Office applications.

Managing Work Items with Project and Excel

After the Team Foundation Server client software is installed, a new toolbar and Team menu will appear in the Office application. Figure 18.23 shows Microsoft Project with the TFS add-in installed. Using the toolbar or the Team menu, you can connect to a Team Foundation Server (using the same process you saw in Figure 18.19) and then import work items from TFS into project. After editing the project plan in Microsoft Project, you can then push those work item changes back into TFS by using the Publish button.

You also can access several custom project views via the MS Project View menu.

Similar capabilities are present with Microsoft Excel. You can use the Team menu to retrieve a list of work items, import them into Excel, and even make round-trip changes back to the TFS database (see Figure 18.24). We will cover both Excel and Project integration in more depth in Chapter 20, "Work Item Tracking."

18

> **NOTE**
>
> Microsoft also provides a centralized project collaboration server called Project Server. Currently, Team Foundation Server does not integrate at all with Project Server.

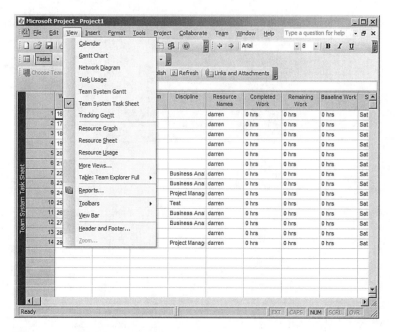

FIGURE 18.23   Microsoft Project working with TFS.

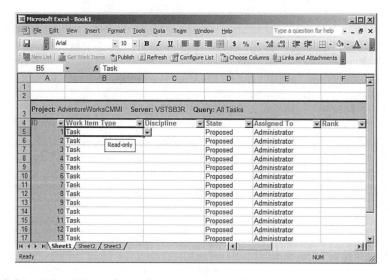

FIGURE 18.24   Using Microsoft Excel to manage work items.

Using Project Alerts

Alerts are email notifications that are sent from the TFS server whenever a specific event occurs. Project team members can subscribe to the alerts that they need to react to by using the Project Alerts dialog box. From the Team menu, select Project Alerts. The dialog box that is displayed shows all the possible alert categories; from there, you can type in your email address (or someone else's) to receive a notification when that event transpires (see Figure 18.25).

FIGURE 18.25   Managing project alerts.

You can elect to receive alerts in HTML or plain-text format. When an alert arrives in your Inbox, you can view the basics of the alert and then follow the embedded links to get more detail. As an example, if you receive an alert because someone has changed one of your work items, you can actually retrieve information about exactly who changed the work item and what items were changed.

Working with Project Reports

For the most part, you handle project reports in the same way as any of the other project artifacts such as documents or work items: You can double-click on a report within Team Explorer (or select a report from the project portal) to view its content. Figure 18.26 shows a report on work items opened within Visual Studio.

Remember that the reporting feature of TFS relies on SQL Server Reporting Services. We cover some of the basics in the following sections.

Using the Data Warehouse

Reports are generated directly from an OLAP cube that is derived from the TfsWarehouse relational database (see Figure 18.27). This allows reports to deliver information across several different sources and aggregate information on builds, tests (including test cases, code coverage, and load testing), source control, and work items.

Designing Reports

Team members can take an existing canned report and alter it to suit their needs. You can also build custom reports from scratch. Again, owing to the SQL Server Reporting Services dependency, the best way to do this is to actually use the Report Designer inside Visual Studio. Create a new Report Server project (under the Business Intelligence Reports category) in Visual Studio (see Figure 18.28). If the Business Intelligence Reports category isn't visible to you, you will need to install the SQL Server Business Intelligence Server Studio from the SQL Server install media.

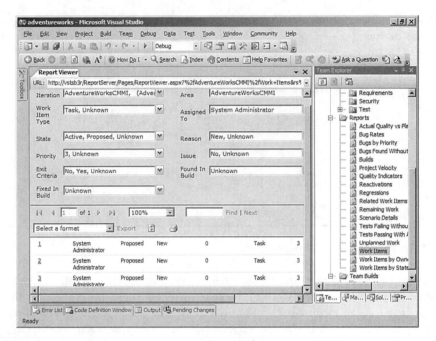

FIGURE 18.26   Viewing a TFS report in Visual Studio.

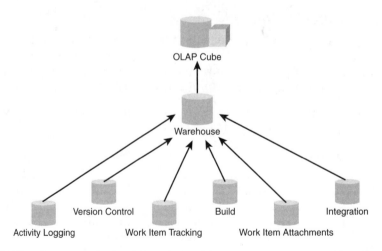

FIGURE 18.27   The reporting database relationship.

After creating the project, you can then add a new Report project item and use the Report Wizard to graphically build your report. Figure 18.29 shows a report being built to disseminate build information for the project.

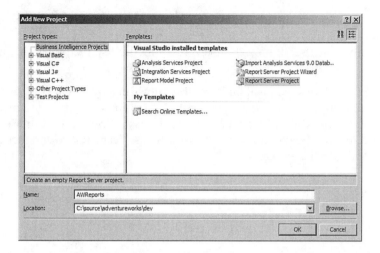

FIGURE 18.28   Creating a new report project.

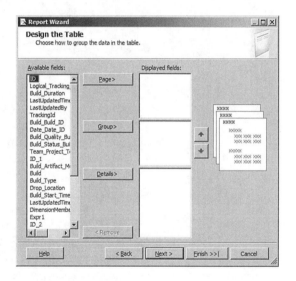

FIGURE 18.29   Building a custom report.

Summary

Team Foundation Server is the core set of application and data tier components that enable collaboration within team projects. In this chapter, we reviewed the system architecture of the data tier and application tier of the Team Foundation Server. We also discussed how security is handled within a TFS deployment.

We covered how project managers interact with a Team Foundation Server and tools such as Team Explorer to create new team projects, manage process templates, assign team members to a project, and maintain the project portal site. For project contributors, you learned how to effectively work as part of a team and use the various TFS features to participate within the overall project process by using the Team Explorer, the project portal, and even Microsoft Office.

In the following chapters, you will build on this knowledge by digging deeper into the process for managing work items, working with the TFS source control system, and managing builds. You will also examine how architects and developers can use the VSTS modeling features and how testers can use Visual Studio Team Test to conduct unit and load testing and manage test cases.

CHAPTER 19

Source Control

This chapter covers source control with Visual Studio Team System: specifically, the source control system and repository provided by Team Foundation Server and its integration with Visual Studio.

The premise of source control is relatively simple: On a software project, there is a need to centrally store and control access to the files that constitute the core artifacts. In other words, a source control system centrally manages access not just to source code files, but also to any other file-based artifact produced during the execution of the project. These artifacts could include items such as requirements documents, network diagrams, and test plans.

IN THIS CHAPTER

- The Basics of Team Foundation Source Control
- Getting Started with Team Foundation Source Control
- Editing Files Under Source Control
- Branching and Merging

> **NOTE**
>
> The terms source control and version control are synonymous, at least as far as this book is concerned. Although the term version control is in some ways preferable because it alludes to the fact that there is more than just source code being controlled, we use the term source control in this chapter so that we conform to the majority of the MSDN documentation on team systems—even though the source control database in the Team Foundation Server data tier is, ironically, named `TfsVersionControl`.

The job of a source control system can be broken down into the following responsibilities:

- It centrally stores files in a secure and reliable fashion.

- It provides a way to bundle sets of file versions together to constitute a "release."

- It allows multiple users to interact with the same file at the same time through the concepts of check-in, check-out, and merging.

- It keeps track of which changes were made to a file, who made them, when they were made, and why.

The source control system that ships as part of Team Foundation Server and Visual Studio handles all those requirements and more. It is a robust client/server-based solution specifically targeted at the source control needs of large, enterprise-level development teams.

The Basics of Team Foundation Source Control

The source control system that ships as a part of VSTS and Team Foundation Server is a brand-new system from Microsoft; it is not an enhanced version of Microsoft's previous source control system, Visual Source Safe. Team Foundation Source Control (TFSC) was built from the ground up to be an enterprise-class system capable of handling hundreds or even thousands of concurrent users.

NOTE

Visual Source Safe (VSS) has not, in fact, gone away. A new version, VSS 2005, was produced in conjunction with Visual Studio 2005, and it remains the preferred source control mechanism for individual developers or small teams (those with five or fewer members).

TFSC was built around some fundamental design goals:

- To provide a scalable solution for enterprise-class development teams

- To provide a reliable solution

- To allow the system to be accessed remotely using the HTTP/HTTPS web protocols

- To allow more than one developer at a time to work on a source file

- To provide a completely integrated user experience from within Visual Studio

From a high level, the following sections cover the basics of the Team Foundation source control system before moving on to more in-depth topics around actually interacting with the system.

Basic Architecture

Because the Team Foundation source control system is merely another service provided by TFS, it rides on top of the same three-tier architecture. It relies on SQL Server as the database to house the source control repository, exposes access to the repository through a set of services hosted on a TFS application tier server, and leverages Visual Studio as the client. Figure 19.1 shows a diagram depicting this system architecture.

FIGURE 19.1   The Team Foundation source control system.

In support of its design goals, this architecture allows the TFS source control system to scale up by adding additional servers on the application tier. In addition, storage space can be increased by adding additional storage devices to the database server or adding additional database servers.

TIP

For geographically dispersed teams, Team Foundation supports the ability to use proxy servers to cache source control data on servers that are local to a particular team segment. Proxy server settings are controlled via the Team Foundation Settings dialog box and are handled by the Team Foundation administrators. For more details on how to configure proxy servers to increase performance, see the MSDN documentation and search for the phrase "How to: Configure Team Foundation Source Control to Use Proxy Server."

Security Rights and Permissions

TFSC uses the same Windows integrated security system as the application tier Team Foundation Server that it is hosted on. This means that the same user/group model is used to determine permission levels specific to source control operations and that the same process for adding and removing users is used. In other words, TFSC does not maintain its own specific user base or security system; it participates in the larger Team Foundation Server infrastructure. In general, a user will play either a *contributor* or an *administrator* role in the source control system.

The contributor group is usually filled by team members in the developer, tester, sponsor, or other role. These individuals will interact with the source control system to perform a basic set of common tasks: checking out files for modification, checking in changes made to a file, viewing a file in the repository, and adding or deleting files to the repository.

Administrators, as the name implies, are more focused on maintaining the source control server as a whole. Administrators manage access to the source repository and are tasked with maintaining the integrity and security of any items in the repository. Administrators may also have project-specific tasks such as determining when a new branch should be created in the project tree and handling merges between branches. Membership in this group is typically limited to the global TFS administrators and team roles such as project manager or project lead.

At the permission level, TFSC supports a variety of granular rights that can be assigned or denied to an individual user or a group of users. The specific permissions/rights supported by TFSC are documented in Table 19.1.

19

TABLE 19.1   Team Foundation Source Control Permissions

File/Folder Permissions

Permission	Description
AdminProjectRights	User can set permission levels for users/groups.
Checkin	User can check in a file to the source control repository.
CheckinOther	User can check in another user's file to the source control repository.
Label	User can label an item.
LabelOther	User can label another user's item.
Lock	User can lock an item.
PendChange	User is able to check out, add, delete, branch, merge, or undelete.
Read	User can read the contents of a file or folder.
ReviseOther	User can change another user's changeset comments or check-in notes.
UndoOther	User can undo another user's pending changes.
UnlockOther	User can remove a lock that another user has placed on an item.
Global Permissions	
AdminConfiguration	User can function as an administrator and change the basic source control settings.
AdminConnections	User can stop any in-progress source control action.
AdminShelvesets	User can delete another user's shelveset.
AdminWorkspaces	User can edit another user's workspace.
CreateWorkspace	User can create a workspace.
UseSystem	User can access the source control system (this is the base-level permission required to use any portion of the TFSC system).

Armed with this basic understanding of the Team Foundation source control system, you're ready to look at the tooling integrated into Visual Studio that allows VS users to perform basic and advanced source control tasks.

Getting Started with Team Foundation Source Control

You will use two primary tools within Visual Studio to perform both basic and advanced source control tasks: Solution Explorer (a tool that we have discussed in many of the chapters in this book) and the Source Control Explorer tool. Solution Explorer can be used to directly manage solution and project items under source control. Source Control Explorer provides many of the same functions and also allows you to browse the Team Foundation Source Control items that are stored in the TFS data tier.

Before you can use either of these tools, however, or use any of the Visual Studio source control–specific features, you have to ensure that Visual Studio is configured for use with Team Foundation Server.

Configuring Visual Studio

Visual Studio source control settings are configured from the Options dialog box. Select Tools, then Options, and then navigate to the Source Control page. From there, you use the drop-down to select the source control system that you want to use; Visual Studio Team Foundation Server is one option in this list (see Figure 19.2) and, in this case, is the option to select.

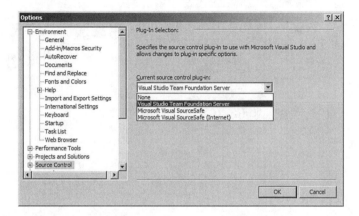

FIGURE 19.2 Selecting the source control system in Visual Studio.

With TFS selected as the source control provider, you automatically can use VS as a source control client whenever you connect to a Team Foundation Server. From within Visual Studio, you can

- Browse Team Projects and workspaces

- Examine the individual files within the source repository

- Retrieve and check out files from the source repository

- Check in changes made to a file or reverse changes made to a file

- View the change history associated with a file

We'll cover all these actions and more a bit later in this chapter. For now, it's time to get comfortable with the Source Control Explorer user interface.

Using the Source Control Explorer Window

Figure 19.3 shows the Source Control Explorer (SCE) window open in Visual Studio. You can see that the SCE is hosted as a document window (as opposed to a tool window), that it has several different panes in which source control information is visible, and that these panes are arranged so that the window looks similar to the Windows File Explorer window.

19

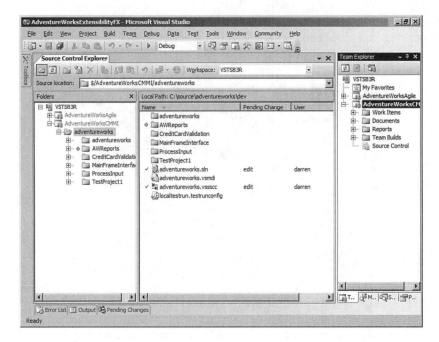

FIGURE 19.3   The Source Control Explorer window.

The Toolbar

The toolbar on the SCE window provides easy access to common activities; moving left to right, these buttons allow you to

- Hide or show the folders pane

- Refresh the contents of all of the panes (for example, requery the server)

- Create a new folder within the source control tree structure

- Add files to the source control repository

- Remove files from the source control repository

- Retrieve the latest version of the file from the server (this command functions recursively; by selecting the root of the source control tree, you can retrieve the latest version of *all* the files)

- Check out a file for editing

- Check in changes made to a file

- Undo changes made to a file

- Compare the server copy of a file with the local copy

The toolbar also has two drop-downs that you can use to change the workspace that you are working in (more on workspaces in a bit) or change your location within the source control tree.

The Folders Pane
The folders pane contains a hierarchical view of the server source control "folders" in the selected *workspace*. If you are familiar with Visual Source Safe terminology, a workspace is analogous to a working folder; it is a local working area on your hard drive that is mapped to a specific source control project on the server. When you retrieve files from the server, they are placed in the local folder that you have associated with the workspace. Because workspaces map onto your local file system, and because projects are naturally organized in a hierarchical fashion in terms of the artifacts they generate, it is natural that the view you use to look into a workspace is a folder/file view *even though the files are actually stored in a set of tables in a SQL Server database.*

The Files Pane
Each time you select a folder in the folders pane, the files pane will refresh to show you any files (or subfolders) that exist in that workspace/folder. Notice that the files pane uses specific icon overlays to indicate the status of a particular file. For instance, a red checkmark is used to indicate a file that you have already checked out, whereas a yellow plus indicates a file or folder that is waiting to be added to the source repository on the server. These same icons are used by the Solution Explorer window.

So that you can readily identify a given file's status, the overlay graphics for the more common statuses have been reproduced for you in Table 19.2. For the complete list, consult the MSDN documentation (search for "Identify Source Control Item Status in Source Control Explorer").

TABLE 19.2   Source Control Explorer File/Folder Status Indicators

Icon	Description
✔	The file is checked out by you; other users, however, may check out the file as well and make their own changes.
✔!	The file is checked out exclusively to you; no other users can check out the file.
🔒	The file is checked out by another user (or by you in another workspace); you can still check out the file and make changes.
⊘	The file is checked out exclusively by another user (or by you in another workspace); you cannot make any changes to the file.
⊖	The file is not under source control.
✕	The file is to be deleted during the next check-in.

Managing Workspaces

As we have mentioned, workspaces are areas in your local file system. Any local copies of files under source control are stored in a workspace. Local copies of files are created the first time you connect to a source repository. From then on, your local files become your working set; whenever you modify one of the local files, the changes that you have made are marked as pending within the workspace, and not committed to the TFSC server until you explicitly elect to do so during a check-in. Put another way, a workspace is like a sandbox. You can do anything you want to the files in your workspace without worrying about affecting other team members or damaging the viability of the project.

> **NOTE**
>
> Workspaces can be owned by only one user on the local machine. This means that if there are multiple user accounts on one machine, and each of those accounts participates in a TFS Team Project, each would have its own workspaces.

Creating a Workspace

Besides having Visual Studio configured for source control, the other requisite step for interacting with the source control server is to create a workspace on your computer. Without one, you won't be able to retrieve any files from the source repository, and therefore you won't be able to view those files or make changes to them—which is the whole point of being a team member in the first place.

To create a new workspace, select File, Source Control, Workspaces. This will start the Manage Workspaces dialog box (see Figure 19.4).

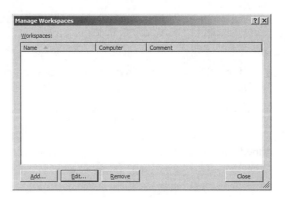

FIGURE 19.4 Managing workspaces.

From here, click on the Add button to open the Add Workspace dialog box (see Figure 19.5). In this dialog box, you provide the required information about the workspace and map the server-side source to a client-side folder.

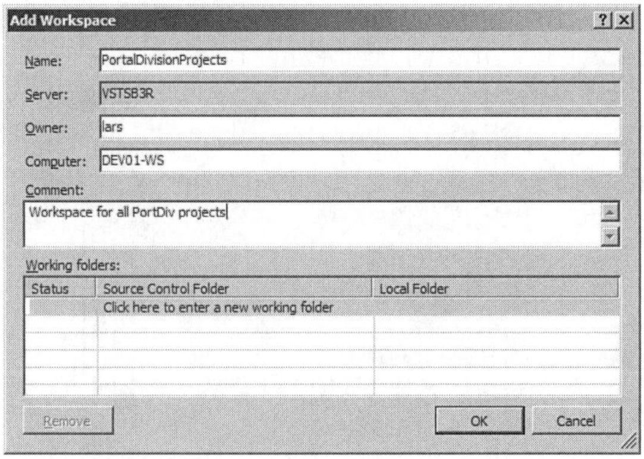

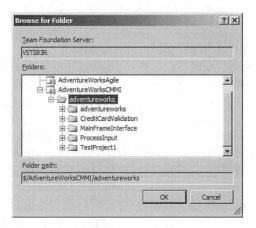

FIGURE 19.5   Creating a workspace.

After giving the workspace a name and indicating the owner and local machine name for it, you need to map a local folder to the source tree on the server. In the Working Folders table at the bottom of the dialog box, click in the Source Control Folder column on the line "Click here to enter a new working folder." This will create a new line in the table; you will now need to click on the ellipses button in the Source Control Folder column and select the source control project folder from the server that you want to mirror within your workspace (see Figure 19.6).

FIGURE 19.6   Selecting the server source project.

NOTE

Don't get confused about the concept of project folders on the source control server. Although source control is implemented with a relational database, and not the file system, you still interact with the TFSC's repository as if it were a hierarchical folder-like store of the various projects and items stored in the source control system.

19

The last step is to select a folder from your file system that will function as the root level for your new workspace. Click in the Local Folder column, click on the ellipses button, and then select the local folder to link to the server source repository (see Figure 19.7). Clicking OK will bring you back to the Add Workspace dialog box.

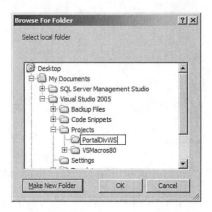

FIGURE 19.7   Selecting the local folder.

Click OK on the Add Workspace dialog box to actually create the workspace.

With the workspace established, you can now view the workspace using the Source Control Explorer. To open it, on the View menu, select Other Windows and then select Source Control Explorer.

Every workspace will initially be empty. If a file exists on the server but not locally, its filename will be grayed out. Figure 19.8 shows the workspace immediately after creation; all the files are grayed out, indicating that these are server-only copies at this point.

To actually populate the local workspace with the files from the Team Foundation source repository, you need to execute a Get Latest command. To do this, make sure you have the right workspace selected in the SCE's workspace drop-down (refer to Figure 19.3), select the server project folder in the folders pane, and then click on the Get Latest (Recursive) button in the SCE's toolbar (again, see Figure 19.3).

Adding Files to Source Control

Of course, you might be the one tasked with initially placing the source code files under source control. Suppose, for instance, that you have an existing Visual Studio solution that you need to place under source control. The same steps apply in terms of creating a workspace, but there won't be any files on the server yet—they will all be local. The source control system won't know anything about them, even though you may have mapped your local workspace folder onto the folder containing your solution files. In this case, you need to take the local files and add them to the server.

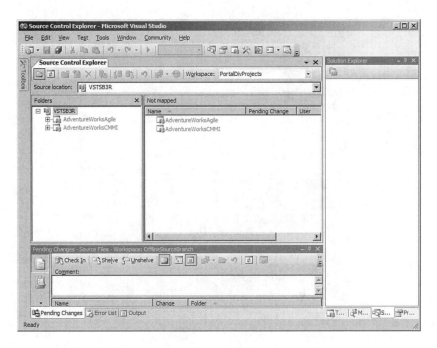

FIGURE 19.8   Server-side files in the Source Control Explorer.

The Solution Explorer is the tool used to do this: Right-click on the solution node in the Solution Explorer window and select Add Solution to Source Control. The resulting dialog box (see Figure 19.9) allows you to select a Team Project folder in the source repository or create a new one. Visual Studio will attempt a default mapping of the solution projects into folders based on the project name. If you want to manually control this, you can click on the Advanced button and specify different folder names.

At this point, the files will be placed into the pending changes list as *adds*. This means that the next time you perform a check-in, you will have the option of completing the operation and physically adding the files to the server. After the adds have been committed, the files will be available for check-out.

Using the Solution Explorer is the easiest way to add solutions and projects en masse to the source control system, but you can also use the Source Control Explorer to place files under source control. This is the preferred way to handle nonproject-related items. To add a file with the Source Control Explorer, follow these steps:

1. Open the Source Control Explorer window.

2. Using the folders pane, browse to the Team Project source folder where you want to place the file.

3. Select the File, choose Source Control, and then Add to Source Control.

4. In the dialog box, click OK.

19

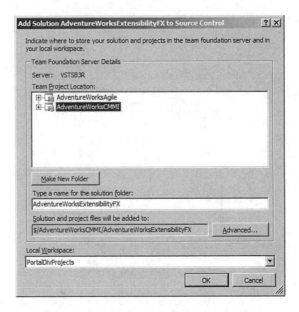

FIGURE 19.9   Adding solution projects to source control.

Figure 19.10 shows the Add to Source Control dialog box.

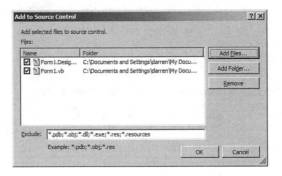

FIGURE 19.10   Adding files using the Source Control Explorer.

Again, as with the Solution Explorer, this procedure really only flags the file or files as pending adds. You must complete the operation by checking in the files. In the next section, we'll examine the check-in process and tool support from beginning to end.

Editing Files Under Source Control

So far, we have examined the fundamentals of getting the client workspace set up and using both the Solution Explorer and the Source Control Explorer to retrieve files from the Team Foundation source server or add files to the server. Now let's get to the heart of the source control mechanism: change management.

Retrieving a File from the Source Repository

There are two ways to pull a file from the server source repository and place it into the local workspace: by using a Get Latest command or using the Check Out command. Get Latest, as you saw in the previous examples around workspace management, simply retrieves the current version of the file as it exists on the server and copies it down into your workspace. You use the Check Out command to tell the system that you not only want the latest version of the file, but that you also intend to make changes to the file. This can mean one of two things depending on whether the TFSC system has been configured for exclusive or shared access: If exclusive, a lock will be placed on the file and no one else will be able to make changes as long as it is checked out by you. If shared, then others are permitted to make changes to the file; these changes will later be merged with any changes that you make to generate a new version that will ultimately be the one stored in the source repository.

> **NOTE**
>
> The exclusive versus shared access setting is actually dictated by the process template being used within your Team Project. For more information on process templates, consult Chapter 18, "Managing and Working with Team Projects," or the MSDN documentation for Team Foundation Server.

Checking in Your Changes

When you are done with your changes, it is time to check those changes back into the source server. There are three ways to do this: You can right-click on the file in the Solution Explorer, you can right-click on the file in the Source Control Explorer, or you can use the Pending Changes window.

Using the Solution Explorer window, you right-click on the file that you want to check in and select the Check In command from the context menu. The Check In dialog box, shown in Figure 19.11, is the place where the action happens. This dialog box contains a list of all the files currently available for check-in. Each file can be selected or deselected using a check box (the file that you previously selected will already have its selection check box checked for you). You simply select any of the files that you want included in the check-in process and then click on the Check In button. Notice that you can provide a comment as well (which is always a best practice to provide the check-in with some historical context on the reason for the change/check-in).

Buttons in the top toolbar allow you to control how the files are viewed, hide or show the comment area, or even filter the list of files based on the solution.

You can access this same window from the Source Control Explorer window: Select your file or files, right-click, and select the Check In command to view the Check In dialog box.

19

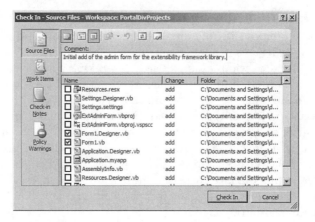

FIGURE 19.11   The Check In dialog box.

To the left side of the Check In dialog box are buttons—referred to as *channels*—used to place the dialog box into different modes. Besides the Source Files channel (which is shown in Figure 19.11), you can select channels for working with Work Items, Check In Notes, and Policy Warnings. Before we get into these topics, let's examine the third way to check changes back into the source repository: through the Pending Changes window.

Checking Changes with the Pending Changes Window

The Pending Changes window is implemented as a tool window in Visual Studio. You open it by selecting View, Other Windows, Pending Changes. You can also launch the window by right-clicking on any item within the Solution Explorer and selecting View Pending Changes.

As its name implies, this window, shown in Figure 19.12, contains a list of all pending changes within your current workspace. Every file that you have checked out is visible in the window.

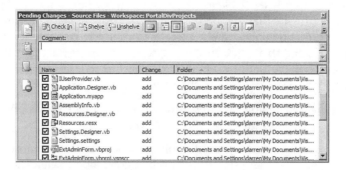

FIGURE 19.12   Viewing pending changes.

The Pending Changes window is structured identically to the Check In window and supports the same channels; there are just a few minor differences with the toolbar, which supports two new buttons: Shelve and Unshelve. We cover shelving later in this chapter.

Understanding Check-In Policies

Project teams will have different rules that users will need to follow in determining whether a check-in is appropriate. For instance, checking in a class file that doesn't compile probably isn't a good idea. Anyone else performing a Get Latest operation or Check Out on the file would have his or her project "broken" because of your changes. Team Foundation Source Control recognizes the importance of vetting check-ins and provides a way to enforce certain rules on check-in through the use of check-in policies.

Three check-in policies are available out of the box with TFS:

- **Code Analysis Policy**—Ensures that certain code analysis tests have been run against the code before a check-in is allowed

- **Testing Policy**—Ensures that certain tests (selected from a list of all known tests) have been run against the code before check-in

- **Work Items Policy**—Requires that one or more work items be associated with a check-in

Check-in policies are typically set up and configured on a per-project basis by project administrators; a default set of selected policies is usually turned on by the TFS process template currently in use. To configure which policies are in effect for your current project, you would access the Team Foundation Server source control settings available by selecting Team, Team Project Settings, Source Control Settings. The Source Control Settings window (see Figure 19.13) has a Check-In Policy tab, which allows you to select the specific policies to be enforced for the current project.

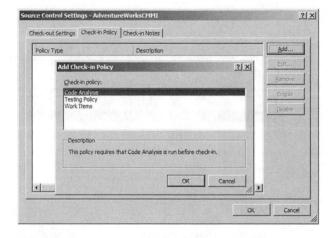

FIGURE 19.13   Adding a check-in policy to the current project.

Each policy may require additional settings. For instance, adding the Code Analysis policy will spawn yet another dialog box used to specify the exact code analysis tests that should be required (see Figure 19.14).

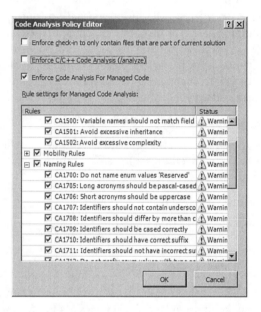

FIGURE 19.14   Configuring the code analysis check-in policy.

If check-in policies are in effect, select the Policy Warnings channel (in either the Check-In or Pending Changes window), and you will see any policy violations. As an example, Figure 19.15 shows the policy warnings that result from enabling the Code Analysis policy and then attempting to check in a VB class file without running the Code Analyzer.

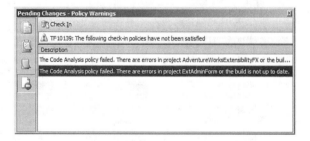

FIGURE 19.15   Policy warnings.

If you were to try to check in these files, a Policy Failure dialog box would launch (see Figure 19.16). You can either choose to abort the check-in and satisfy the policy, or you can override and provide a comment that explains your decision to circumvent the policy.

FIGURE 19.16   Overriding a policy failure.

Adding a Check-In Note

Check-in notes are short pieces of text that you can attach to the check-in items during the check-in process. Check-in notes become a part of the file's historical metadata, are stored in the source repository, and can be viewed at a later date so that you can get a sense for an item's change history.

A check-in note consists of a category name or prompt and the actual note text. By default, there three note categories: security reviewer, code reviewer, and performance reviewer. When performing a check-in, you can click on the Notes channel button to enter notes. Each note prompt/category will appear with a corresponding text box that holds the text of the note (see Figure 19.17).

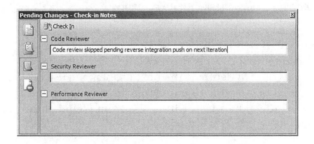

FIGURE 19.17   Adding notes to a check-in.

Check-in notes can be required for a project, and you can also add your own check-in note categories. These settings are managed from the Source Control Settings dialog box, which we covered during our discussion of check-in policy management. The Check-In Notes tab (see Figure 19.18) allows you to add or remove note categories.

For example, you could add a new note prompt for a knowledgebase article number. Just click on the Add button, fill in the category/prompt text, and then select whether the note should be required (see Figure 19.19).

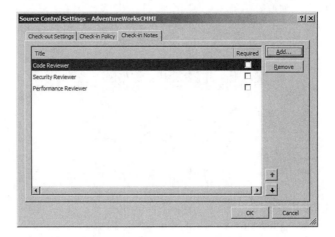

FIGURE 19.18   Managing check-in notes for a project.

FIGURE 19.19   Adding a new check-in note category.

Using Work Items

The last check-in feature we'll cover is the concept of relating check-ins to work items. *Work items*, which we cover in depth in the next chapter, are used to represent tasks within the project from bug reports to traditional "to do" items. Work items can be linked to a variety of different artifacts within the Team Foundation system; check-ins are merely one of those items.

To associate a check-in with a work item, select the Work Items channel and then select from the list of available work items. By associating work items with a check-in, you help to integrate the various work sets from across the project into one cohesive representation of the project's progress. Consider, for example, a developer who has created a class library as part of her project tasks. After testing, she determines that one of her classes isn't responding as expected to one of the test cases. Instead of reporting an exception, the class is swallowing the exception. To fix this problem, the developer checks out the class file, fixes the bug, and then checks the file back in. During the check-in process, she would ensure that the bug work item that initially prompted the work was associated with the check-in, as shown in Figure 19.20.

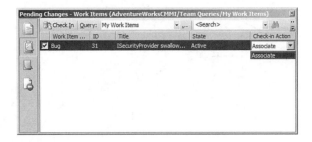

FIGURE 19.20 Associating a work item.

The work items that appear in the list are actually returned from a query that is run against the work item database. You can change the query by using the drop-down at the top of the Work Items channel window, or you can even perform a search across all work items. As mentioned, work items, queries, and many more work item topics are covered in Chapter 20, "Work Item Tracking."

Understanding the Concept of Changesets

Until now, our discussion of the check-out/check-in process has been fairly simplistic, focusing on checking out a file, making changes, and then checking that file back in. In reality, what we have been talking about is the concept of *changesets*. A changeset is a compilation of *all* the information associated with a check-in operation.

To extend the prior bug fix example, you may check out three different files to fix a bug. When you perform a check-in, you will check in all three of these files at the same time and associate their check-in with the bug work item. This is where the changeset concept comes into play: The changeset bundles these three files into a single entity. In other words, the bug is, rightly, associated with the three files as a whole. It is associated with the changeset. Any related work items, notes, and metadata about the code change (date, time, user) are all associated to the changeset as a whole, and not to the individual files.

> **NOTE**
>
> It is worth noting that check-ins and, by extension, changesets are atomic in nature. That is, Team Foundation Server guarantees that the entire changeset was committed in its entirety; you would never, for instance, attempt a check-in of three files and have only two of those files succeed in the transaction. All three of them go, or (in the case of an error) none of them go.

The diagram in Figure 19.21 shows how changesets figure into the overall source control process.

19

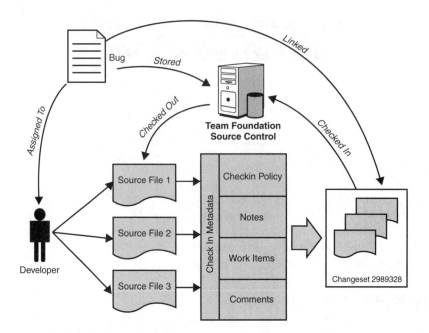

FIGURE 19.21   Changesets.

Each changeset is assigned an incremental, numeric ID.

Shelving Your Code

Sometimes, developers may need to set aside their current work or move on to other tasks before the files are ready for check-in. For instance, you may be in the middle of working on some code files when an urgent bug is logged that requires your attention. Or perhaps you haven't quite completed a required code change before leaving on vacation. In these scenarios, you don't want to check in your work because it is incomplete. You also don't want to leave the work checked out locally onto your box for what may be a lengthy time period. Shelving allows you to take some or all of your pending changes and store them back into the TFS source repository database without checking them in.

Shelving works in a similar way to the check-in process, and is handled by the Shelve window. To open the Shelve window, you can click on the Shelve button in the Pending Changes window, or you can click on the Shelve Pending Changes button in the Source Control Explorer. Alternatively, you can use the Solution Explorer: Right-click on a file and select Shelve Pending Changes.

When you shelve your code, you are creating a *shelveset,* which is identical to a changeset but applies to shelved code only. You will be prompted to name your shelveset so that it can be retrieved later. Figure 19.22 shows code files being shelved from the Shelve window.

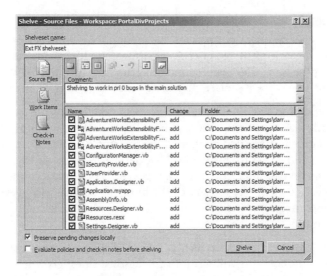

FIGURE 19.22   Shelving code changes.

Unshelving Files

After a shelveset has been created, you have the option to unshelve that shelveset at any point in time. This will return all the shelved files into your workspace. Click on the Unshelve button in the Pending Changes window to launch the Unshelve window.

All your previously created shelvesets will be visible; you simply select the one you want and click the Unshelve button (see Figure 19.23). Note that you can change the owner name field and initiate a new search for any shelvesets that belong to that user.

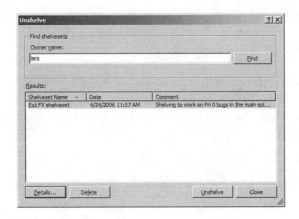

FIGURE 19.23   Unshelving code changes.

19

Merging Changes

When we introduced the check-out process, we mentioned that check-outs can be exclusive or shared. In the case of shared check-outs, in which more than one person is actively changing the same file, Team Foundation provides a way to merge those changes into a new changeset that will replace the current file version on the server.

Let's examine a common scenario: Developer A checks out a class file and works on a method within the class. While the file is checked out, Developer B is assigned a bug and has to work on a different method contained in the same code file. Developer B then checks out the file and works on his method. Developer A checks in her changes and then a day later Developer B checks in his changes. At this point, a conflict exists: Because Developer B never had a copy of the source file in his workspace with Developer A's changes, something needs to be done to merge the two files. This situation is handled with the merge tool.

When Developer B starts to check in his file, Team Foundation source control will automatically detect a conflict. This will result in the Resolve Conflicts window being displayed (see Figure 19.24).

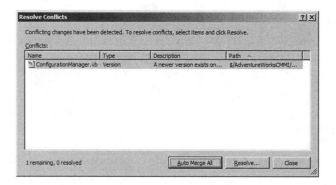

FIGURE 19.24 The Resolve Conflicts window.

To resolve the conflicts in the identified file, you click on the Resolve button, which launches yet another screen—the Resolve Version Conflict window, shown in Figure 19.25—that provides some more details on the file conflict and offers some options for rectifying the conflict.

There are four options available for proceeding:

- Allow Visual Studio to automatically merge the changes.
- Merge the changes in the two files using the merge tool.
- Undo the changes that were made to the local copy of the file.
- Undo the changes that were made to the server copy of the file.

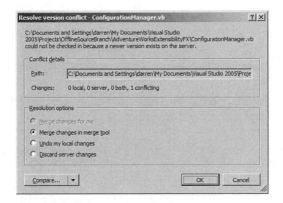

FIGURE 19.25   The Resolve Version Conflict window.

In all but the simplest cases, you will need to use the merge tool to explicitly tell Visual Studio how to handle the conflict. To assist with understanding the nature of the conflict, you can also launch the File Comparison tool from this window.

Comparing File Differences

The File Comparison tool, shown in Figure 19.26, provides a simple side-by-side view of the two files, the server file and the local file, and visually highlights the textual differences between the two through a highlighting scheme. Blue represents changed text, green represents inserted text, and red represents deleted text.

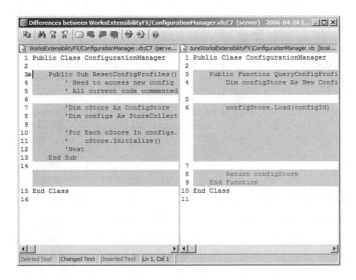

FIGURE 19.26   Using the File Comparison tool.

You can't actually edit the files using this tool; that needs to take place with the merge tool.

Using the Merge Tool

The merge tool provides a similar view to the file comparison window: It highlights the textual differences between the two windows. But this tool shows a third view as well: the results of a merged file. See Figure 19.27 for a look at the merge tool window.

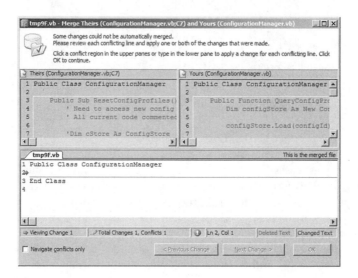

FIGURE 19.27   Merging changes.

By moving the cursor in the merged file pane, you can move your current position and then insert changes from either of the two conflicting files. In this specific example, we wanted to add two methods to the merged file. One method exists in the server copy, and the other method exists in the local copy. To create the merged file, you would first select the change highlighted in the server copy (top-left pane). This will insert that block of changed text into the blank merged copy (bottom pane). You can then reposition the cursor location to some point after the newly added method text and then click on the highlighted, changed text in the local copy (top-right pane). The merge tool will add this text into the merged file as well, resulting in the desired outcome: a new version of the source file that combines the content of the server copy and the local copy.

Branching and Merging

Branching and *merging* refer to two different but related processes for managing the source code tree within the Team Foundation Server repository. These operations are often performed by development teams that need to execute on different versions of the code in parallel and then, at some point, bring those changes back together for a release path through the source tree.

Owing to both the nature of iterative development and the circumstances of the modern software market, development teams often have complex needs in terms of maintaining their source code tree. The source code tree is essentially a hierarchical look at the various code files that constitute a solution by version. To solidify the idea behind branching, let's discuss the problem space in the context of a work scenario.

Assume that a development team is hard at work on a market-revolutionizing piece of software. Part of the team's product plan involves a rapid version 1.0 release to really nail the fundamentals, with a very quick follow-up that contemplates some of the more difficult design problems. The product management team decides to tackle this effort with two different development teams. One will start the initial architecture and development work for version 1.0. When enough architecture, design, and code base exists, the second team will start working on version 2.0. Because their development phases overlap, in a sense, their source code will as well.

Consider the diagram in Figure 19.28; it depicts a versioned view of the source tree and highlights the need for the version 2.0 efforts to work from, or branch from, the initial 1.0 efforts. Then, at some point in time, the fully complete 1.0 bits will be merged into the 2.0 tree. Notice as well that the product team anticipates a patch release to address the inevitable issues in the 2.0 code base. These changes will also need to branch and merge in the source tree.

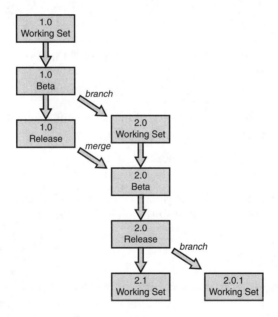

FIGURE 19.28   Branching and merging a source tree.

Branching

Branching, just as it sounds, is the act of copying code from the current source tree and putting that code into a new branch of the tree. An easy way to understand this concept is to think of this space in terms of folders: To branch is to take a current folder of code (called the source) and create a new folder with a copy of the source's code (called the target). In other words, you can think of branching as a file system copy operation: You take the files in one location and make a copy of them in another location. Development is then free to continue within both folders in a parallel fashion.

Branching in Team Foundation is performed using the Source Control Explorer. You first need to navigate to the source folder on the server; then you right-click on the folder and select Branch. In the Branch dialog box (see Figure 19.29), you provide a name for the new branch (or target folder) and select a version of code from the source folder. If you select the Lock New Branch option, this will prevent anyone else on the team from creating a branch with the same name. Click OK to create the branch; it will be immediately visible in the Source Control Explorer.

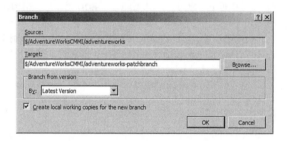

FIGURE 19.29   Branching source using the Source Control Explorer.

Merging

Merging is the opposite of branching: Instead of forking one element of the source tree, it combines two elements of the source tree into one.

As with branching, you kick off the process from the Source Control Explorer. Right-click one of the source folders that will participate in the merge and then select Merge.

The Source Control Merge Wizard (see Figure 19.30) will collect all the needed information about the merge operation. Specifically, you will be asked to provide

- The source branch

- The target branch

- The changes you want to merge (all within the source branch or only specific changesets)

- The source versions that you want to merge

Clicking Finish at the end of the wizard will complete the merge.

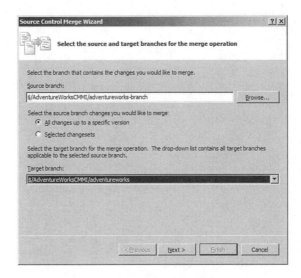

FIGURE 19.30   Using the Source Control Merge Wizard.

Summary

In this chapter, we took an end-to-end look at the tools and capabilities of the Team Foundation source control system. We presented the architecture of the server-side aspects and discussed how Team Foundation leverages Windows and SQL Server to provide an eminently reliable and scalable infrastructure for source control services.

We described the basic concepts behind source control and investigated how Team Foundation delivers on those essentials.

In addition, we painted a picture of the powerful suite of tools that Visual Studio Team System users have at their disposal for handling policy compliance, branching and merging, and source management. We also examined how to use the source control tools for a variety of tasks:

- Setting up new workspaces

- Checking out files from the source repository

- Checking in changesets

- Shelving file changes

- Resolving check-in conflicts

- Branching and merging the source tree

Because all these tools are integrated into the Visual Studio IDE, and because the source control system itself is integrated into the larger concepts of process management, Team Foundation source control truly provides a seamless experience with the rest of the project development tasks and activities.

CHAPTER 20

Work Item Tracking

IN THIS CHAPTER

- Understanding Work Items
- Using Team Explorer to Manage Work Items
- Understanding Team Role Perspectives
- Customizing Work Items

The process of developing software on a team can be as difficult as writing the actual code. Developers want to be free to focus on writing great code. Clients, project sponsors, project managers, testers, architects, even other developers, on the other hand, are all interested in tracking the progress of that code and determining the overall state of the project. Keeping everyone in the loop requires time-consuming meetings. These meetings generate reports that are often out of sync with what is really happening before the target audience has a chance to review them.

A similar challenge is getting actual, meaningful metrics. This can be problematic at best. Project managers are often left to interpret the ramblings of team members as they take turns reporting their progress in weekly meetings. This data, by its very nature, represents only a small view of reality on the project. Therefore, in the absence of real statistical measures, a divide begins to open between what is happening on a project and what is being reported.

Many software development shops have become good at managing this divide. They become better and better at estimating, reporting, and tracking progress. To do so, they have implemented methodologies such as RUP, MSF, CMMI, eXtreme programming, and so on. These methodologies have been an important part of maturing the software development process. However, the tools to support these methodologies within a development platform have been lacking, too expensive, not cohesive, or all the above.

With Team Foundation Server and work items, Microsoft is addressing the desire for developers to get back to writing great code while still giving other team members the information they need. This chapter covers work items in depth. It presents work items from the perspective of various team members in the Software Development Life Cycle (SDLC).

We then explore the tools built into Visual Studio 2005 for working with and customizing work items.

NOTE

Review Chapter 17, "Team Collaboration and Visual Studio Team System," for a better under-standing of the methodologies that ship with TFS. This chapter focuses specifically on work items and how they relate to the development process and Visual Studio 2005. Where appropri-ate, we discuss work items in context with MSF Agile and CMMI. However, work items are only part of the overall methodology picture.

When you define a project website, Team System creates pages that define process guidance around the selected methodology. These pages are required reading and can provide a quick reference if you ever lose your context within the methodology.

Understanding Work Items

A *work item* in Visual Studio Team System is just what it sounds like: a definition of work for a development project. A work item is responsible for recording that work, allowing the work to be assigned, tracked, related to other work, and reported on. Like a project task, a work item may have a title and description of the work to be done, a current owner, a history, related information, an associated life cycle, and a current state. The difference, however, is that unlike a simple project task, all the work item information is maintained in a central server and is at once accessible to all team members as work happens. It is for this reason that work items are the fundamental driver behind the power of communication and collaboration in Team System.

Understanding the Role of Work Items and the SDLC

The actual work items themselves can be defined to represent the wide variety of work that is executed on any given project. Work items can be created for project requirements, tasks, change requests, code reviews, bugs, and so on. Work items provide enough customization to cover the entire SDLC and its associated roles. They can be created by, assigned to, and worked on by developers, architects, business analysts, testers, and project managers. For these reasons, work items are the core nugget for driving a software project. All work can be done through and tracked by a work item.

Picking the Work Item Set for Your Project

Most projects that leverage Team Systems will use a set of predefined work items. Each work item set covers the SDLC for a given development methodology. You can create custom work items and even custom methodologies for Team Systems (more on these later). However, the most common scenario is to define a project based on one of the methodologies that ship with Team Systems: MSF for Agile Software Development and MSF for CMMI Process Improvement (both discussed in Chapter 17).

Team system generates a set of work item definitions for your project when you choose the methodology you want to employ on your new project. The actual work items associated with a methodology are based on the driving principles behind the given methodology. These work items define the fields, states, and transitions of the work that will be done on the project. In addition, they generate the metrics for reports that let team members know the state of the project at any given time. Let's explore these core work items across both methodologies that ship with TFS.

MSF for Agile Work Items

The MSF Agile methodology is driven by scenarios and the tasks that are derived from them. It also defines various service-level requirements for performance and security, for example. It is meant to get the team working together with customers on a common vision while staying flexible with respect to change. For these reasons, the MSF Agile methodology defines the following work items: scenario, quality of service requirement, task, bug, and risk. Let's look at each of these items in more depth.

Scenario Work Item   A scenario defines a user's interaction with the system to complete a specific goal or task. If you have ever created or worked with use cases, then scenarios will seem very familiar. Typically, a scenario will define a common, successful path to achieve a user's goal. In addition, it may relate to alternate scenarios that define alternative (sometimes unsuccessful) paths through the system.

MSF process guidance suggests that the team initially brainstorm the list of possible scenarios for the system. Of course, these scenarios should relate to the overall vision of the project. Each scenario is then assigned to a business analyst (or customer/subject matter expert) to define and describe. Ultimately, the scenarios will be broken down into tasks that the team members can complete to realize the given scenario (and thus the project's vision).

Some of the key fields defined for a scenario include its description, history, rank, integration build, and rough order of magnitude. The description field provides a high-level overview of the given scenario. However, MSF Agile recommends the actual scenario be created as a Word document (a template is provided for this inside the project portal). The history field tracks the scenario as changes are made. Rank is used to indicate priority relative to other scenarios in the system. Integration build indicates the actual build where the scenario is implemented. Finally, the rough order of magnitude is used to indicate the relative complexity of the scenario.

Quality of Service (QoS) Requirement Work Item   A QoS requirement defines how a given system should operate after it is complete. These work items come in the form of load, performance, platform, stress, security requirements, and the ubiquitous "other" category. Their purpose is to get the team on the same page with respect to what is expected overall for the system. For instance, a QoS requirement might define that all user interaction in the user interface can be performed in less than a second. This requirement may dictate that the team creates a SmartClient application rather than a browser-based client.

The fields used to define a QoS requirement are nearly identical to that of a scenario. The MSF Agile process guidance suggests that the QoS requirement is fully defined inside the work item (there is no need to create a separate document like a scenario).

Task Work Item   A task work item is just what it sounds like as well: a project task that signals a team member to execute some work on the project. Like other work items, tasks are assigned to team members. However, task items are typically the work items that make the project schedule. For example, there may be a task to create a new scenario. This task might be assigned to a business analyst on the team.

When you define a task, you select the discipline to which the task belongs. Disciplines are similar to the roles on the project; they include architecture, development, project management, release management, requirements, and testing. These disciplines help to imply meaning behind the state (closed), which describes the current progress of a task (more on this in a moment).

Bug Work Item   A bug work item is used to report a problem with the system. These work items allow for defect management and tracking in Team Systems.

A few key fields related to a bug include priority, found in build, resolved in build, test name, test path, and triage. Priority indicates whether the bug is a show-stopper or something minor. The build fields allow you to indicate which version of the code the bug was originally found in and where it was fixed. The test fields allow you to indicate which actual tests were used to produce the bug. This information can help a developer reproduce the bug. Finally, the triage field is used to indicate whether the bug has been approved to work on or requires further investigation.

Risk Work Item   A risk work item allows the team to proactively track and manage project risk. Risks to a project represent anything that might have a negative impact on the project in terms of quality, cost, schedule, and so on.

You define a risk by indicating its description (and related fields). Some additional key fields include severity and rank. Severity indicates the likelihood of the risk to occur along with the impact of that risk. Severity is defined as critical, high, medium, or low.

MSF for CMMI Work Items

The MSF for CMMI methodology is not unlike that of MSF Agile. In fact, they share some of the same core principles and ideas around quality, customers, and adaptation to change. The CMMI methodology, however, allows development teams to be assessed by a third party in terms of their commitment to process and continuous improvement. It is not meant to be a larger or more complex process. It, too, should be lightweight and right-sized to the project.

The work items that drive MSF for CMMI are also similar to those found in the MSF for Agile method. For example, MSF for CMMI also drives a project through requirements and tasks. The full set of work items for MSF for CMMI includes requirement, task, change request, risk, review, bug, and issue. Let's examine each of these items in turn.

Requirement Work Item   We've discussed how MSF for Agile defines two work items for defining requirements (scenario and QoS). MSF for CMMI, on the other hand, defines a single requirement work item. When you create a new requirement work item under MSF for CMMI, you define the requirement's type. You can then delineate between a scenario or QoS requirement. In fact, the requirement work item for CMMI has seven types by default: functional, interface, operational, quality of service, safety, scenario, and security.

Some additional fields of note for the requirement work item include subject matter experts, impact assessment, and user acceptance test. The subject matter experts section allows you to choose up to three people who can provide additional expert-level information with respect to the given requirement. The impact assessment allows you to indicate the overall impact of the given requirement if it is not realized or implemented. Finally, the user acceptance test (UAT) field allows you to track whether the requirement is ready for UAT or has passed/failed UAT.

Task Work Item   The task work item is meant to trigger a team member to execute work and to track that work. For example, an architect may break down a scenario into a number of developer implementation tasks. These tasks are assigned and tracked by the project manager. Tasks can be assigned to all roles on the project.

Change Request Work Item   The change request work item allows you to track and manage the inevitable on all software projects: change. Some projects might simply roll with the changes. Other, more formal projects will require documentation of the change and an assessment of its impact. This change will then be presented to a change control board for a decision. When the decision is made to accept the change, a new set of task work items will result, altering the baseline schedule and costs.

Typically, a business analyst (or similar) creates the change request work items and obtains impact and analysis relative to the request. This information is stored in a few key areas on the work item: description, justification, and analysis. The description field is used to describe the request. Justification tells readers why the request is being logged and the value it brings to the overall project. The analysis section of the work item lets you address the impact of the request across five key project elements: architecture, user experience, test, development, and technical documentation.

Risk Work Item   The risk work item allows team members to log items that have a potential to impact the project in a negative way. The MSF for CMMI risk work item allows users to enter a mitigation plan along with events that might trigger that plan. In addition, users document a contingency plan that describes what to do in the event the risk actually presents itself on the project.

Review Work Item   The review work item allows you to document the outcome of a given code or document review. A best practice on most development projects is to do a review of scenarios, requirements, design, and code. These reviews may be offline or done as a meeting. In addition, these reviews may be iterative in that they continue to occur until the item passes the review. All of this can be tracked by the review work item.

The review work item has a type field to indicate whether the review was a meeting or done offline. In addition, there are fields to indicate who did the review (or attended the meeting). These fields allow for up to eight iterations through a given review. The results of the review are tracked via the minutes field. This is where a reviewer might document requested action items relative to the review.

Bug Work Item   A bug work item allows team members to indicate perceived problems with the system. These bugs are documented, triaged, prioritized, and categorized by severity.

Issue Work Item   The issue work item allows team members to log issues that are blocking progress on the project. These are not risks. Rather, issues are real things that require actions (not potential risks). After an issue is identified, a set of tasks should be created to resolve the issue.

The issue work item allows for the definition of priority, impact to project, escalation, and corrective action. Priority indicates the order in which issues should be dealt with. The impact of the issue is defined in terms of critical, medium, high, or low. The escalate field indicates whether the issue should be escalated because it is blocking the project in some manner. Finally, corrective action allows you to define the agreed-to plan for solving the issue.

Identifying Work Item Commonalities

You should now have a basic understanding of the many work items defined by both MSF methodologies. Again, you choose a single methodology for your project and inherit the work item set associated with your choice. By examining all work items across both methodologies, you've seen that there are many similarities between the two. In fact, work items in general have a lot in common with one another.

Work item commonalities are not an accident. The term *work item* itself is a generic abstraction, the concrete implementation of which are the various work items we've been discussing (bug, task, risk, and so on). Work items are created and managed by a work item framework. Therefore, when you understand how a work item works in that framework, you will essentially understand how they all work. The following sections define and discuss those commonalities.

> **NOTE**
>
> For the remainder of this chapter, we will discuss and present sample work items from the MSF for CMMI methodology. Everything we discuss is still applicable to MSF for Agile. However, focusing on a single methodology will simplify discussion. In addition, you should find it easy to move from the MSF for CMMI to MSF for Agile if required.

Work Item Areas and Iterations

Work item areas and iterations allow you to categorize and group work and define when that work will be executed. This information is defined for your entire project (typically by the project manager). Areas and iterations are typically project-specific and are therefore not predefined by the methodology. Each work item is then classified in terms of its area and iteration.

Although we covered the basics of areas and iterations in Chapter 18, "Managing and Working with Team Projects," let's dig deeper and see how they directly relate to work items and project management.

You define areas and iterations through the Areas and Iterations dialog box, which you can access from Team Explorer. To open it, you right-click the team project you want to define and then choose Team Project Settings, Areas and Iterations. Figure 20.1 provides an example of accessing this dialog box.

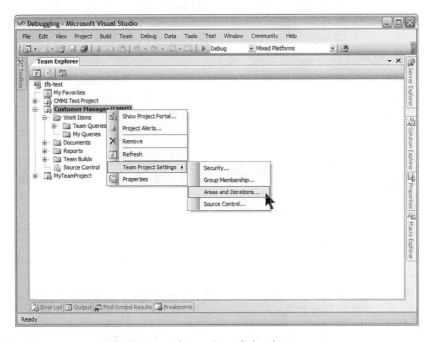

FIGURE 20.1   Accessing the Areas and Iterations dialog box.

Areas   An area represents a category used to group work. Many times this is referred to as a module or feature set. For example, a project may break down work by defining a user account profile module, an order entry module, an order history module, or an inventory module. These modules or areas are used to group tasks and other work items in the system. This capability is useful for reporting and tracking. Areas can also be defined in a hierarchical structure. This allows for the definition of subareas and the like.

You create areas using Visual Studio Team Explorer and the Areas and Iterations dialog box. You've already seen how to access this dialog box. Figure 20.2 shows the dialog box along with a definition of a few areas (modules) for a sample project.

Notice that you can define areas in a hierarchy. This allows for the creation of areas and subareas (modules and submodules). The toolbar in this dialog box allows you to position each item in the correct order and hierarchy.

Notice the Security button at the bottom of the dialog box. It allows you to configure the security associated with this area. For example, you can indicate who on the team is allowed to create, edit, and view work items associated with a given area.

20

FIGURE 20.2 Defining the areas for a project.

Clicking the Security button brings up the User Profile Node Security dialog box. It is important to note that this dialog box is specific to the actual node (area) you have selected. For example, if you select the User Profile node and click this button, you will be defining security for the area, User Profile. Figure 20.3 shows this dialog box and the permissions that can be set.

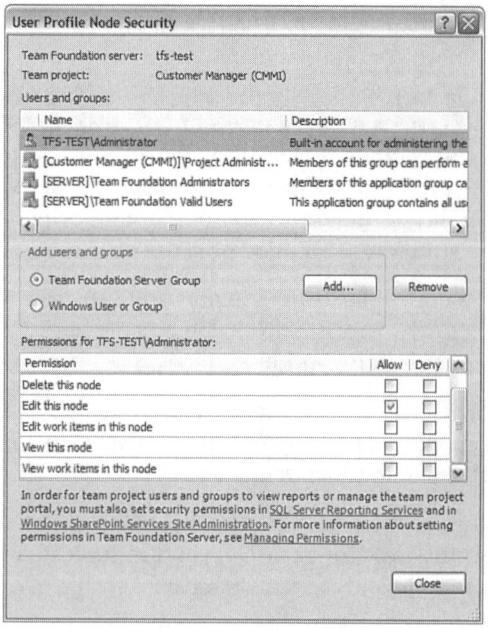

FIGURE 20.3 The User Profile Node Security dialog box.

Iterations   An iteration represents a time period on the project in which you will execute some portion of the work. The intent of an iteration is to time-box some set of work items that will be delivered in a specific window of time. You may define 30-day sprints, for example. In addition, iterations may overlap one another for various reasons. Typically, this is the result of a hand-off between team members or groups on the project.

For example, suppose you define four iterations for your project. Each iteration may be defined as a 30-day time-box. You would go through the full life cycle of development for a subset of functionality during each of these iterations. You might define two to four areas or modules to be developed during each iteration.

Suppose you start the first iteration by doing architecture and design for the first two modules. After those modules are designed, the iteration might continue with the designers passing the specification off to the development team. The designers might then begin working on the next iteration. When the first iteration is developed and unit-tested, it might be passed to a quality assurance team. At this time, the developers might begin working on coding the design for the second iteration. This process would continue through the iterations. Notice how each iteration overlaps the others.

Clearly, this process requires a mature team and toolset to work smoothly. In addition, there can be many variations on these cycles. Team Systems allows you to define the iterations for your project and then classify work items in terms of their iteration. Figure 20.4 shows the Iteration tab on the Areas and Iterations dialog box.

FIGURE 20.4   Defining the iterations for a project.

Notice that you can define subiterations under a given iteration. This capability can be helpful for certain reporting purposes. However, we've discovered that most teams find it sufficient to have four to six top-level iterations for the project. Each might be time-boxed into eight-week increments: two weeks for design, four weeks for development, and two more weeks for integration and user acceptance testing.

TIP

If you modify areas or iterations, you will have to execute a refresh in Team Explorer before these changes are reflected in the work item definitions.

Work Item States and Transitions

Work items are tracked through the State and Reason fields. Together, these fields define the state in which a work item exists at any given time, the state to which it can transition (move), and the reason the work item might move from one state to another. This seemingly simple process is used to track all work items in Team Systems. Let's look at an example of how this works.

For this example, we will look at the states of a bug work item. Figure 20.5 shows the state diagram for a bug (from the process guidance).

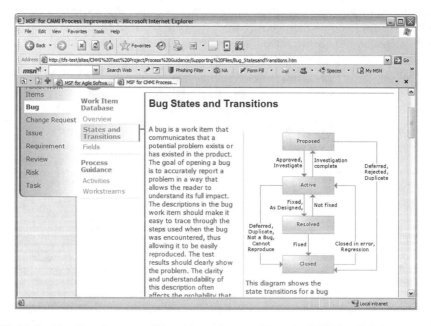

FIGURE 20.5 The Bug States and Transitions diagram from the MSF for CMMI process guidance.

The boxes on the state diagram indicate the states in which a bug can exist. The arrows represent the transitions between the states. An arrow from one state to another indicates a possible transition. The verbiage associated with the transition represents the reason behind the transition.

As an example, suppose you have a bug in the Active state. This bug could be transitioned back to the Proposed state or on to Resolved or Closed. Moving the bug back to Proposed would be valid only when the bug was moved to Active for the purpose of doing more investigation. When that investigation is complete, it would move back to Proposed so that it could be triaged. If the bug is moved to Resolved, it was either fixed or determined not to be a bug (as designed). If the bug is moved to Closed from Active, the possible reasons include that it was deferred, was a duplicate item, was not really a bug, or cannot be reproduced.

All work items in Team Systems work in this manner. Again, the work item State and Reason fields make this workflow easy to manage. In fact, the work item editor inside Team Explorer enforces these transitions and reasons. It will allow a work item to move only to a valid state and the transition reasons are also enforced. Figure 20.6 demonstrates this through a bug work item moving from the Active state to Closed.

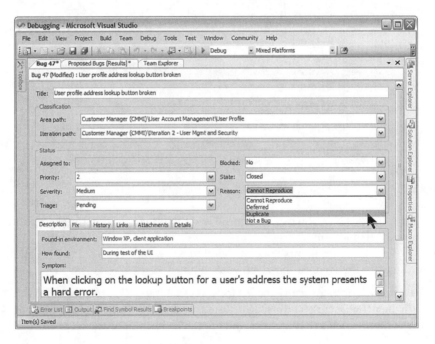

FIGURE 20.6   Moving a bug from Active to Closed.

Tracking Work Item History

As a work item is changed, Team System automatically logs the history of that change. You can review an item's history through the History tab on the given work item. Each change is stored in an entry. The entries are categorized by date and time of change, along with the name of the person who executed the change. Figure 20.7 shows a bug work item's history.

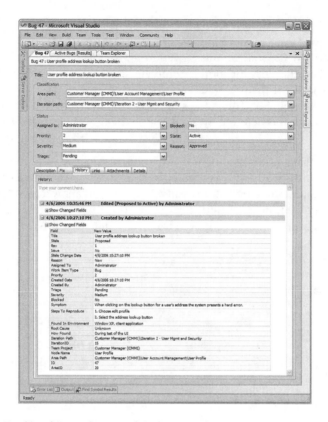

FIGURE 20.7   Tracking history for a work item.

Notice that in Figure 20.7 you can determine what fields changed between work item history records. In addition, users can enter their comments in this tab (Type your comment here). These comments are embedded in the work item history. This allows for a recorded discussion relative to the given work item.

Figure 20.8 shows another history record for the same item. This record was the result of moving the bug from Active to Resolved. Note the comment in the history record. Also notice that only the fields that are changed are tracked in the history.

Linking Work Items

Often you will need to link work items together. Linking these items helps provide a better understanding of the system and the work that is being created. It keeps people on the same page and facilitates better reporting. As an example, suppose you write a user scenario. It would be good to know which requirements were created as a result of the scenario. You might also like to know which tasks were generated from each requirement. If you take this example even further, you might want to link issues and change requests to tasks and/or requirements.

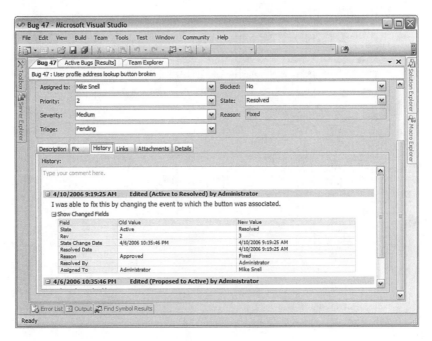

FIGURE 20.8   User comments stored as history.

Ultimately, you can then use metrics to determine the success of a given requirement or scenario. A scenario that resulted in no change requests and fewer issues means that the scenario was well written, understood, and agreed to by the team. Whereas a scenario that ended up spawning many issues and change requests could mean the scenario was either not understood, agreed to, or poorly written.

As another example, if you have a task that is blocked because of an issue or risk, you might want to link that task to the work items that were created to unblock the task.

You define a work item link using the Links tab for the given work item. This tab presents the various links already established for the work item. You can view, edit, and delete an existing link. You can also establish a new link from here. Figure 20.9 shows the Add Link dialog box.

Notice that when adding a link to a work item, you are asked to browse to that work item. Clicking the Browse button will bring up the Choose Related Work Item dialog box, which is shown in Figure 20.10. From here, you can search the work item database and find those items you want to link. In the example used for these dialog boxes, a bug is being linked to a related development task.

After you've selected the link and clicked OK, you are returned to the Add Link dialog box (see Figure 20.11). The work item ID and description are populated for you. You can add a comment to the link and then click OK to establish your link.

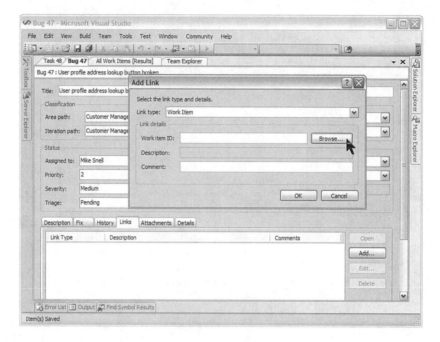

FIGURE 20.9   Adding a link to a work item.

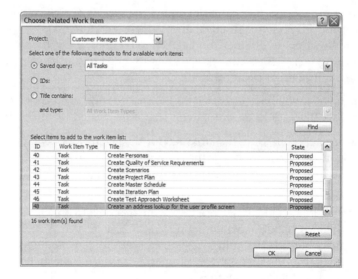

FIGURE 20.10   Finding the work item to link.

Not all links are between two work items. You can establish a link from a work item to other things, too. This includes linking a work item to a web page (hyperlink), a changeset, a versioned item, or a test result. You use a similar set of dialog boxes for each of these additional items.

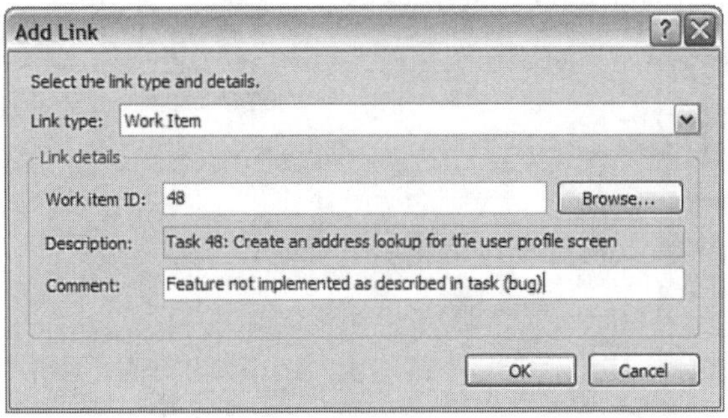

FIGURE 20.11   Adding a work item link.

Attaching Files

You can also attach files directly to work items. This capability is useful if, for example, you want to attach a screenshot to a bug or perhaps a portion of a design document to a task.

The interface for attaching files is similar to that of establishing links. An Attachments tab lists all attachments. From here, you can add, delete, view, and update file attachments to work items.

Using Team Explorer to Manage Work Items

If you install one of the Team editions of Visual Studio, you have the right license to connect to Team Foundation Server. However, you may not have the tools. You need to install the Team Explorer client tools. You can find this install on the Team Foundation Server media. These tools are the principal means for interacting with work items using Visual Studio. The following sections cover the basic functionality of these tools. Following this discussion, we will illustrate how various project roles work using these same tools.

Creating a New Work Item

You can create a new work item through Team Explorer or the Team menu. When you do so, you must choose the work item type. Again, the types available for your project are dependent on methodology and customizations that might have been made. Figure 20.12 shows how to create a new task work item using the Team menu.

When you select the work item type, you are presented with a screen to define the work item. From here, you can define the work item's title, assign the work item, enter a description, add attachments, and so on. Figure 20.13 shows the definition of a new task work item. Notice the task work item's Discipline field. Here, you can indicate if this is a development task, business analysis, test, and so on.

20

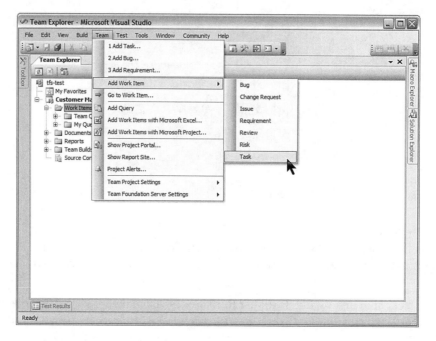

FIGURE 20.12   Creating a new work item.

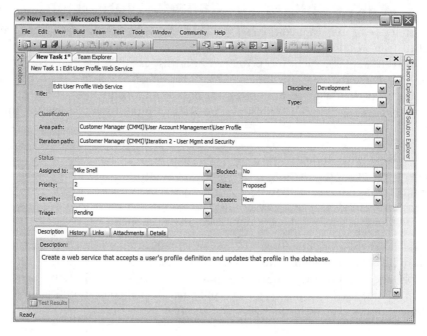

FIGURE 20.13   New work item dialog box.

Note the Details tab on the work item. It contains some key functionality that we have not yet discussed. Most of these features apply to all work items. Features include scheduling the task, identifying its related build, indicating it requires review, and associating it to a test. Figure 20.14 shows the Details tab.

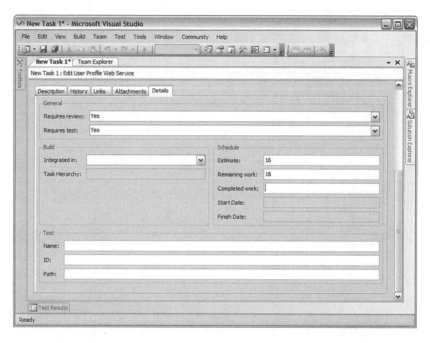

FIGURE 20.14   Work item details.

A work item task is scheduled through estimation. You indicate the number of hours estimated and the number of hours completed; then you estimate the number of hours remaining. This information is used by Project and other applications to show scheduling. The start and finish dates are entered as tasks are started and finished.

Finding and Filtering Work Items

You often need to find the work item or work item set with which you want to work. For doing so, Team Explorer provides a query engine. Each query is run against the work item database and returns a subset of information. In this way, you can quickly zero in on your next task.

A number of default queries ship out of the box (dependent on chosen methodology). You can find them under the folder heading Team Queries. Figure 20.15 illustrates a set of queries for an MSF for CMMI project.

Team queries are shared across project team members. That is, each team member sees the list of team queries. If you have proper credentials, you can define a new team query. In this way, you can write queries of which everyone can take advantage.

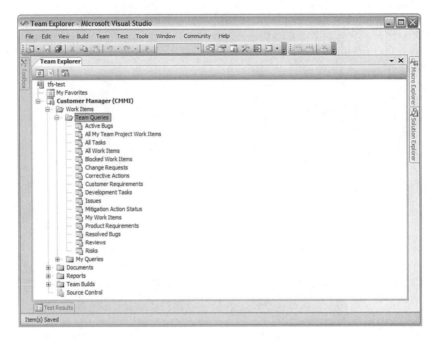

FIGURE 20.15   Work item team queries.

You also have a folder to store your personnel set of queries. This folder is aptly named My Queries. It is useful for storing queries that are pertinent to you. For instance, you may create queries that are associated with your user ID, or you might simply write a few queries that are specific to your job function.

Running a Query and Viewing Results   To run a query, you select it in the Team Explorer tree and choose Run Query from the Team menu (or press F5). You can also right-click the query and choose View Results or Open. There is also a toolbar for work item queries. You can run a query from here by clicking the Run Query button.

The results of your query are displayed in a list that includes the work item's ID, its type, state, and title. As you scroll through items in this list, the selected work item's details are displayed at the bottom of the screen. You have full interaction with a work item from this screen. Figure 20.16 shows a sample result set.

You can customize the list that is returned as a result of the query. To do so, you click the Column Options toolbar item (far right) or select this option from the context menu to bring up the Column Options dialog box. With it, you can determine which fields you want in the list and each field's width using the Fields tab. You can even define a multi-column sort from here by using the Sorting tab. Figure 20.17 shows this dialog box.

TIP

The changes you make in the Column Options dialog box can be saved back to the query definition.

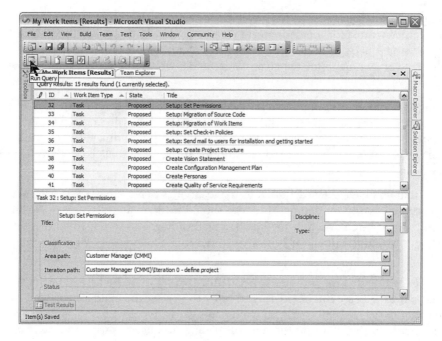

FIGURE 20.16   View query results.

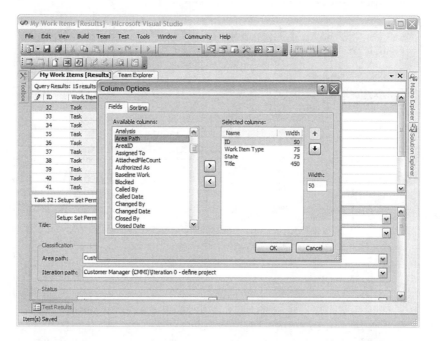

FIGURE 20.17   Customizing query results.

20

Creating a Custom Query   You can create custom queries for Team Explorer. These queries can be created for the entire team (Team Queries) or just yourself (My Queries). To create a custom query, you select the Add Query menu option from either the Team menu or from the context menu for the given folder under which you want to store the new query.

Selecting this option brings up the query view. From here, you define filter clauses that allow you to narrow your query to just those items for which you are searching. Each clause in your query defines a field, an operator, and a value (think WHERE clause in SQL). In addition, you can relate clauses to one another using AND and OR conditions. Let's look at an example.

Suppose that you have been identified to triage all bugs that are proposed. This makes you the central person for determining who should work on a bug, whether the bug requires more research, whether the bug is actually a bug, and so on. To do this work, you might want to define a query in your My Queries that allows you to view all proposed bugs.

When setting the filter for this query, you define two clauses. The first is for the Work Item Type field. You are interested only in bugs, so you set the operator to = and the Value field to Bug. This will return all work items whose type is a bug. You then add another clause to your filter for the state of the bug. You need to see only bugs that are in the state of Proposed. This clause is inclusive, so you set the And/Or field to And. Figure 20.18 shows this filter example using the tool.

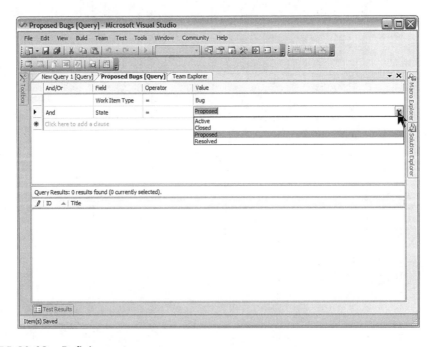

FIGURE 20.18   Defining a new query.

Next, to select the fields that are shown as a result of your query, you use the Column Options dialog box, which also allows you to indicate a sort order. This is the same dialog box we discussed previously (refer to Figure 20.17). You can then run your query and test the results. When you're happy, you can name it and save it for future use.

> **NOTE**
>
> You edit queries using the save interface. To open a query for edit, select the View Query option from the context menu for the given query.

Understanding Team Role Perspectives

As we've discussed, work items are the key collaborative element that connect all team members on the project. They are used to communicate tasks, status, issues, risks, and so on. They also emit status information and define metrics for reporting. Work items touch the entire team. Therefore, in the following sections, we will cover how some of the key roles across the SDLC interact with work items. We will present a few common activities per role and then demonstrate how those activities are realized through work items.

The roles we will discuss include project manager, business analyst, developer, and tester. There are many more roles defined for most processes (including MSF). However, in general, these roles tend to interact the most with work items on any given software project.

> **NOTE**
>
> Only the roles of architect, developer, and tester are assumed to have an installed version of a Visual Studio team client. Other team members (such as business analysts, project managers, and customers) will connect to the project using tools such as Excel and Project. They can also view reports and information via the project team site (portal). Of course, each of these team members should have a client access license (CAL) for Team Foundation Server.
>
> One question we are always asked is "Can a customer (or someone who does not have access to Visual Studio) update or view a work item through a browser?" The answer is no; the feature does not come out of the box. You can allow these people to integrate using Excel or Project. You can also write custom code to extend Team Systems for this purpose.

Project Vision

It is helpful to discuss each role's interaction with work items in the context of an actual project. So for this section, we will assume the following as the parameters and vision that define the sample project:

- There is an existing e-commerce application.

- A project has been envisioned to develop an application that allows both sales and customer service representatives (CSRs) to proactively manage the user accounts in this e-commerce system.

20

- Sales will interact with customer accounts to offer special direct marketing. They would also like to do data mining to prioritize top accounts.

- CSRs will manage user accounts and handle customer requests. They need to be able to look up information, change orders, determine tracking information, and so on.

We will use this as the basis for describing how various roles work on this project through work items. Let's first look at the project manager's role.

> **NOTE**
>
> MSF defines actual workstreams to group activities by role. It is recommended you become familiar with these workstreams, their activities, and their associated roles. In addition, MSF illustrates how a work item is used inside each workstream. Our approach is simpler: We want to show common activities by role and illustrate how work items come into play and how those work items are reflected in Visual Studio and Team Explorer.

Project Manager

For this example, assume you are the project manager (PM) who is the leader in charge of the project. It is therefore your responsibility to set up the project in Team Systems, select a methodology, control security, and so on. Given that many PMs have little experience with Visual Studio, you may want to assign a technical lead to aid with these tasks.

We will not cover these project setup tasks here. Instead, assume a project has been defined with the MSF for CMMI methodology, security is in place for each role, and the iterations and areas have been defined similar to those found in Figures 20.3 and 20.4. We will now focus on a few common tasks the PM will execute involving work items.

Identifying the PM's Work Items

In general, project managers focus on tasks, risks, and issues on a day-to-day basis. Many are also occasionally concerned with requirements, reviews, and bugs. For this example, we will discuss the former set and cover the latter with other, more pertinent roles.

Using Excel

As the PM, you may have a copy of Team Explorer (this is recommended). From here, you can query and update work items as we have discussed. Many project managers, however, also like to work with lists of information in both Excel and Project. Team Explorer has support for two-way integration with these products, as we introduced in Chapter 18. You therefore can view, create, and update work items using these common Office tools. Of course, this feature is not limited to project managers; we simply will walk through a few of scenarios pertinent to their role.

Viewing Open Issues   For this example, assume that you, as the project manager, want to view the list of active issues on the project, update them, and then publish this list back to server.

To start, you launch Excel. Provided you have installed the Team Explorer tools, you will have a Team toolbar inside Excel. This toolbar provides interaction with a team server. From this toolbar, you click New List to launch the Connect to Team Foundation Server dialog box. This allows you to select a TFS server and a project on that server.

TIP

Work item lists can also be opened in Excel directly from Team Explorer. To do so, run a query. Then, in the results window, select the Open Selection in Excel toolbar item.

Next, you are presented with the New List dialog box. From here, you can indicate whether you want to query for work items or create an input list. Query allows you to get back a list, work with the list items, and then update the server. We will look at the Input list in a moment. Recall that you want to work with the current issues on this project. For this reason, you will select Query List and choose the Issues List from the Query drop-down (which includes the list of both team and private queries). Figure 20.19 shows this interaction.

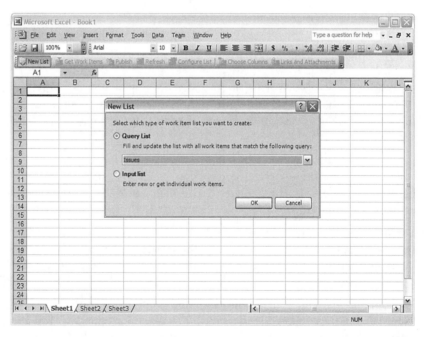

FIGURE 20.19   Opening a list in Excel.

When the query runs, you are then presented with all open issues on the project. Using the features of Excel, you can filter and sort this list. Figure 20.20 shows the results of the query.

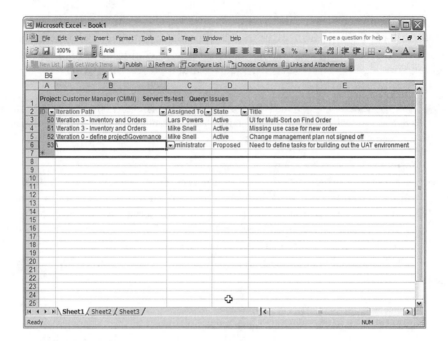

FIGURE 20.20   The list of issue work items in Excel.

Notice the Team toolbar now has many more active buttons. From here, you can publish changes you make to the list, refresh the list from the server, configure the list, determine which columns you want to view, and manage links and attachments to the various work items in the list.

Let's suppose you, as the project manager, need to update the Escalation field and the Target resolution date for these items. To do so, you click the Choose Columns item from the toolbar to bring up the related dialog box. This dialog box allows you to determine which fields are displayed in the Excel sheet. Figure 20.21 shows this task in action.

The next step is to update the data for the work items. The good news is that Excel provides drop-downs for data entry that match the work item drop-downs in Team Explorer. This ensures the data conforms to the right business rules and eases the data entry.

For changes, assume that you updated the escalation fields and target resolution dates and changed the status of the Proposed work item to Active (and assigned it). You also have to enter a new issue. You can do so at the bottom of the list.

When entering a new issue to the list, you will go to the Choose Columns dialog box, select the work item type, and then click the Add Required button. This will push all the required fields to the form.

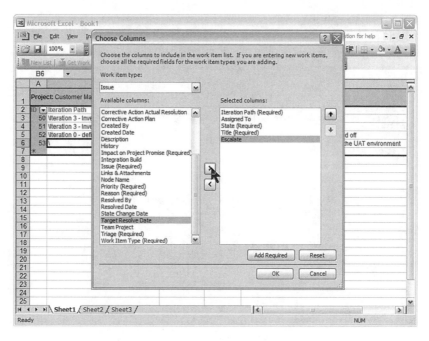

FIGURE 20.21 Selecting work item fields to display in Excel.

TIP

Because you work with multiple types of work items in Excel, one of the required fields is Work Item Type. It is important to set this field first when entering a new work item. This way, all other fields in the row will be updated as to allowed values. You will then get the correct data entry experience.

Now that you are finished doing updates and have even added a new issue to the list, the next step is to publish these items to the server. To do so, you click the Publish button on the toolbar. This will start the synchronization process.

Note that you may run into errors when publishing. If problems are detected, you will be presented with the Work Item Publishing Errors dialog box. This dialog box lists the results of the operation and shows the work items that have errors. Figure 20.22 shows the work items that did not successfully publish.

You can click the Edit Work Item button to resolve the errors for each item. Clicking this button brings up the work item in the standard view (not Excel). The errors are listed at the top of the form, and the fields in error are also highlighted. From here, you can make your fixes and then click the Close button. Figure 20.23 shows an error with the State field being fixed. A new work item must start in the state Proposed, and not Active. You will click the Publish button on the Work Item Publishing Errors dialog box after each error is fixed.

20

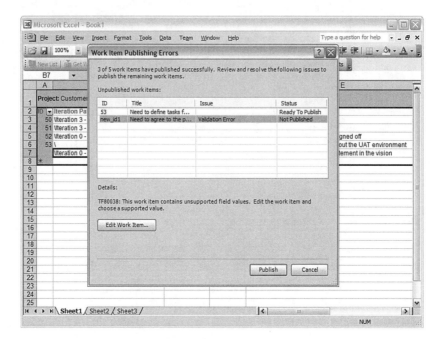

FIGURE 20.22   Publishing errors.

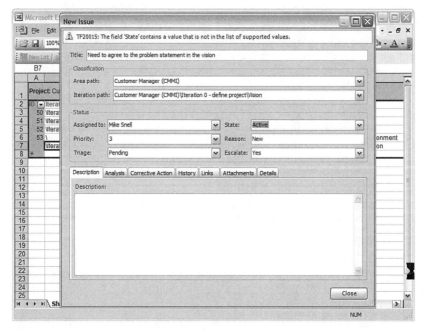

FIGURE 20.23   Resolving a publishing error.

> **NOTE**
>
> You can add links and attachments to work items from Excel. The interface is similar to that of Team Explorer's. However, you can only do so after a work item is published. Therefore, if you create a new work item in Excel, you will need to publish before adding attachments and links. After the item is published, you can make your additions. You will then have to republish to post those additions.

Creating a Risk List   For the next example, suppose you, as the PM, want to create a project risk list in Excel. Each risk will be entered in a blank worksheet and then published to the Team Foundation Server. The steps involved in this task are not unlike what we discussed previously. To create a risk list in Excel, follow these steps:

1. Open Excel and select the New List menu option.

2. Connect to a TFS and project.

3. On the New List dialog box (see Figure 20.19), select Input List to indicate you do not want to start with a query or set of work items. Rather, you simply want to have the correct schema for entering items.

4. You will be presented with an Excel sheet that allows you to enter work items. One of the fields is Work Item Type. Selecting this field will define the data entry for the remaining fields on the sheet.

5. In the example, you want to enter Risk work items. Therefore, you need to click the Choose Columns button from the toolbar. This will invoke the Choose Columns dialog box (see Figure 20.21). From here, choose the Risk work item type and click the Add Required button. Then click OK to be taken back to the Excel sheet.

6. Enter the risks associated with the project.

7. When the risk list is complete, click the Publish button to update the server.

These steps allow any team member to create work items in Excel and then publish them to the server.

> **TIP**
>
> You may want to save your Excel workbooks after they're created. Doing this can be a great way to get team members to use work items in Excel. You define a workbook for risks, for instance, and then publish that workbook to the project portal. Team members can now simply open the workbook, add or edit the given item, and then publish to the server. The MSF for Agile project portal has a couple examples of this.

20

Using Project

Work items can also be viewed, edited, created, and scheduled using Microsoft Project. The integration of work items and Project is nearly identical to that of Excel. As an example, suppose you, as the PM, need to schedule the tasks on the project.

First, you may run a query inside Team Explorer. Next, you select the Open Selection in Project item from the toolbar. Selecting this item will open a new project file and feed it the selected tasks from the query. Within Project, you are free to do project-related tasks. This includes rolling up tasks under a group name, defining the hours for a task and its predecessors, and so on. Figure 20.24 shows an example of the sample project's task work items being scheduled in Project.

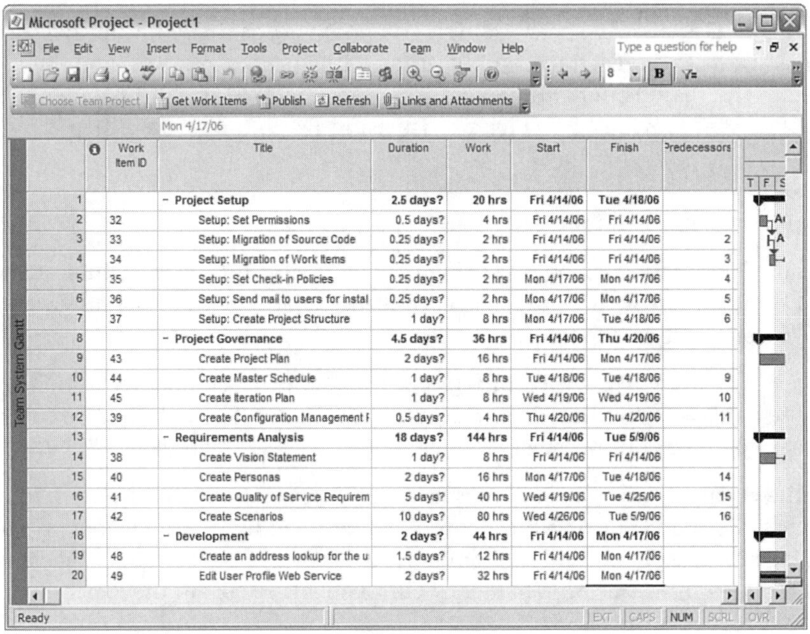

FIGURE 20.24   Working with task work items in Project.

You then click the Publish button after scheduling is complete. This will update the team server. The synchronization will attempt to push all lines in the project into new work items. For categories and the like in Project, you can simply choose to ignore these errors.

The schedule information for each task is now available inside each work item. For example, if developers open a development task work item, they can click on the Details tab to see the remaining work and scheduled start and end dates. Figure 20.25 shows an example.

Project managers can save their schedules and use them as a basis to receive updates to tasks. This way, they can handle work items with the tool they're most comfortable using.

Business Analyst

A business analyst's (BA's) primary interaction with work items will be to define requirements and user scenarios. These items will represent the interaction with the system that a user must have to consider the project a success. Therefore, these scenarios are typically defined at the beginning of an iteration. The scenarios drive other work items such as development tasks. Let's look at a standard method that a BA might follow with respect to work items and a project.

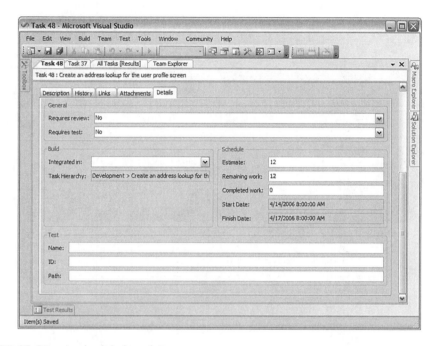

FIGURE 20.25   A scheduled work item.

For this example, imagine you are now the business analyst. Your first step is to meet with stakeholders and brainstorm possible user scenarios. Suppose this meeting defined 25 possible scenarios. The first step would be to create Requirement work items of type Scenario for each of these 25 possible scenarios. This will allow for the work items to be named, assigned, and tracked. In addition, the PM can now track these work items on the schedule as you estimate the time required to complete each scenario.

Next, you begin to write the various scenarios. You may query the set of scenarios to determine which are of the highest priority and do those first. When writing a simple scenario, you may use the Description tab on the work item. You may write longer, more complex scenarios using a Word document. Let's look at an example of the latter.

Suppose that you have a work item for the scenario titled Login Scenario. When you write this scenario, you use a scenario Word template for the project. You then upload this scenario to the project. You can do so using the project portal or through Team Explorer. Suppose that you used Team Explorer. From here, you expand the Documents folder and then right-click the Requirements folder. You then choose Upload Document to navigate to the document and upload it to the server.

This document is uploaded to the same library used by the project portal. There are simply two views: one from Team Explorer and one from the portal. Figure 20.26 shows the scenario document in both views.

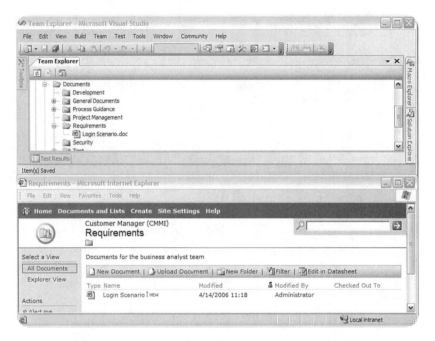

FIGURE 20.26   A requirements document viewed from Team Explorer and the portal.

Finally, you will want to link the scenario document to the work item. It may seem intuitive for you, as the BA, to use the Link tab for this work. However, this is not the case. Instead, this link is made through the Attachment tab. You add an attachment and navigate to the document stored on the portal (see Figure 20.27). Adding this attachment actually defines a link between the work item and the file. This way, if the file is updated from the portal, the updates are reflected when the file is opened from the work item.

Developer

Developers get their task lists from the work items database. In addition, they use work items to get clarification on requirements, user scenarios, bugs, and so on. Developers are probably the prime consumers of work items in Team Systems. We have already discussed the majority of these scenarios. Therefore, we will focus on one primary activity of the developer: associating code to work items.

Associating work items and code provides vital statistics to Team Foundation Server. It allows for reporting on code churn, task progress, and bug status. In addition, it provides a vital link when going back over code and doing maintenance. The capability to look at a piece of code and then read the associated requirements, tasks, and scenarios is extremely helpful.

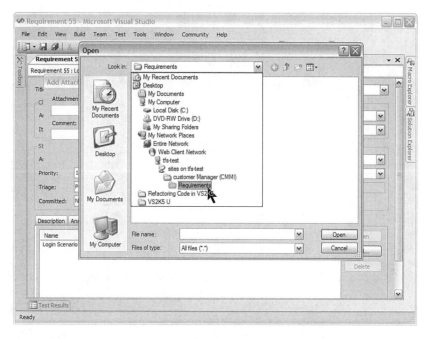

FIGURE 20.27   Linking to a scenario document on the project portal.

> **TIP**
>
> It is often a best practice to create a check-in policy that forces developers to associate all check-ins with one or more work items. This ensures that development work is properly tracked (and therefore can be reported on).

Associating Code and Work Items Through Check-In

The principal means for a developer to associate code with a work item is to do so during the source control check-in procedure. We cover source control in Chapter 19. However, it is important to illustrate this process here from the perspective of work items.

As an example, suppose you are the project's technical lead and have been assigned the task for generating the skeletal structure of the application. Of course, this task would be a work item. Your activity as the tech lead might include creating the solution and the projects and scripting out code stubs for many of the items in the project.

When the code is complete, you would check in the entire code structure. During the check-in process, you would associate the check-in to the task for generating the code structure. You would do so by selecting the Work Items icon on the Check In dialog box. Selecting this option will open a window that allows you to query and search for work items to associate to code. Figure 20.28 shows this example in progress.

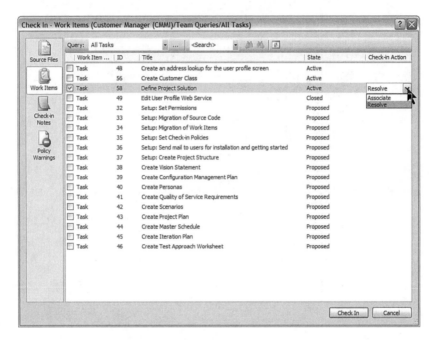

FIGURE 20.28   Linking a changeset to a work item.

After you find the task, you click the check box to make the association. In addition you can indicate whether the check-in resolves the given task. You do this by setting the Check-In Action (far right of figure). This indication automatically marks the task's status as Resolved.

Finally, this process also creates a link back to the work item. When you open the work item and click the Links tab, you will see the changeset that was checked in as part of the previous process. This linked changeset represents the history of what code was resolved or checked in relative to this work item. Figure 20.29 shows this link and the open changeset.

TIP

You will most often link check-ins to multiple work items. This capability is fully supported and a best practice. For instance, if your check-in resolves a bug, is related to a requirement, and resolves a task that was created to fix the bug, you will want to relate to all three work items.

Linking Code to Work Items

You can also associate code to a work item through the Link tab on the work item. This capability can be useful if you want to make the association outside a check-in (or you forget).

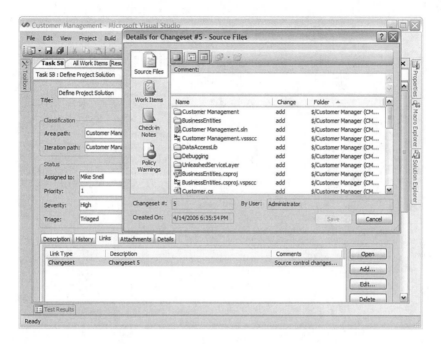

FIGURE 20.29 The changeset link on the work item.

To link the code this way, navigate to the work item and select the Links tab. Click the Add button to bring up the Add Link dialog box. In this dialog box, select Versioned Item from the Link type field. Then, next to the Item field, click the Browse button. Figure 20.30 shows an example.

For this example, your task is to create a `Customer` class. The class is created and checked in. It now needs to be manually associated with the work item. After clicking the Browse button, you can now navigate the source tree to find the correct code files with which to associate the item. Figure 20.31 shows this process in action. After making a selection, you can then indicate whether the link should always point to the latest version or a changeset.

Tester

A tester interacts with work items by writing and tracking bugs and issues for the project. You have seen examples of these tasks. What we want to discuss here is how a tester might associate a test to work items.

As a simple example, let's look at the requirement work item. Each requirement in the system should be verified by someone representing the user. This is referred to as a user acceptance test (UAT). The Details tab of the Requirement work item has a space to track the UAT status. Figure 20.32 shows an example. In this way, the team knows which requirements have made it all the way through UAT (and are thus ready to ship).

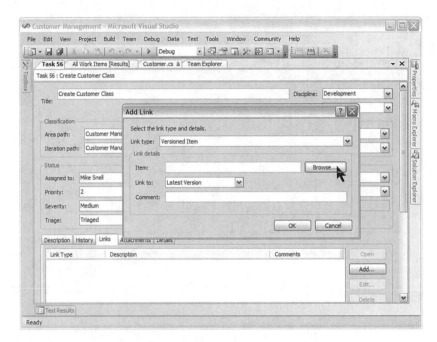

FIGURE 20.30   Adding a versioned item link to a work item.

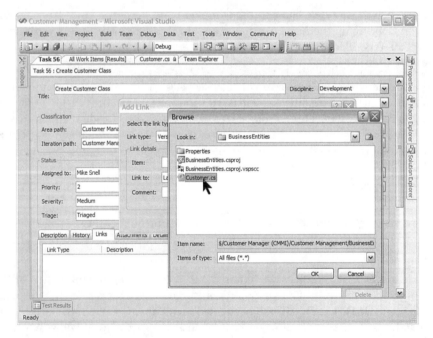

FIGURE 20.31   Selecting the versioned item to link to a work item.

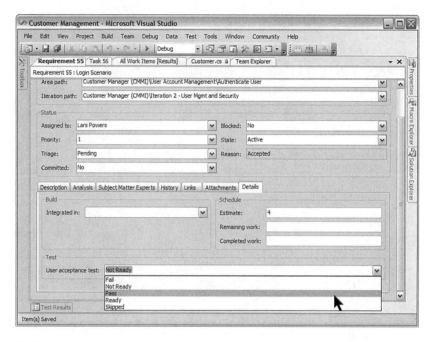

FIGURE 20.32   Setting the UAT results for a requirement.

Testers may also be asked to indicate what test satisfies a given requirement or task. For example, suppose you, as the tester, have a development task to create the Customer class. This work item might indicate on the Details tab that a test is required before the item can be resolved. In this case, the item's test details must be filled out.

You add test details to a task work item in the Test group on the Details tab. Unfortunately, there is no way to associate tests and work items from within the IDE. Instead, this is currently a manual process. The test information you need to enter includes the name of the test, its ID, and a path to the test. This information is available from the Test Manager screen. Figure 20.33 shows a horizontal split between the Test Manager and the details of a given work item.

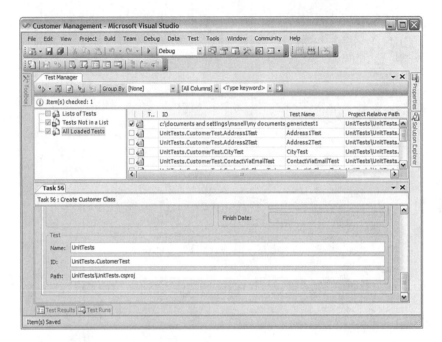

FIGURE 20.33   Filling in the Test Details for a Task.

Customizing Work Items

You can customize and extend the features of Team Systems in a number of places. Customizing is the process of taking the existing functionality and tweaking it to fit your needs. This is the typical scenario for most development shops. Extending involves using the Team System API and report engine to write new functionality into Team Systems. The following are all possible customization and extension points:

- **Process Methodology**   You can customize the existing methodologies or write your own.

- **Work Items**   You can edit the existing work items or create your own new work items.

- **Reporting**   You can create new reports and customize existing ones.

- **Project Portal**   You can modify the project portal to contain your own templates and default project documents.

We cannot cover all these extension points here. Instead, we will look at three common scenarios related to work items: seeding your process with standard work items for a project, customizing an existing work item, and creating a new, custom work item.

Seeding the Process with Work Items

When you create a new project based on one of the MSF methodologies, the team server is seeded with an initial set of work items. These items represent common tasks that are required for the execution of the project. A number of these tasks involve starting the project moving (such as creating a project plan and master schedule).

This initial set of work items is part of the overall methodology. A common request is to seed your own tasks (work items) into an existing methodology. Let's look at how this is done.

> **NOTE**
>
> You can apply this process of adding work items to a methodology to extend the methodology in a number of other directions as well. You can even use it as a basis for writing your own methodology.

Downloading (Exporting) a Methodology

Methodologies in Team Systems are defined as process templates. A process template is a set of files that Team Systems can use to define a given process or methodology. As we have discussed, Team Systems ships with two process templates: MSF for Agile and MSF for CMMI. As you tweak your process, you will want to tweak these templates to stay in tune.

You use the Process Template Manager to modify a process template. This tool lets you export a process, tweak it, and then re-import it. You can access this tool from Team Explorer. Figure 20.34 shows the menu structure for accessing the tool.

The Process Template Manager presents the process templates installed on your TFS. From here, you can export (download), import (upload), set one process as the default, and even delete a process if needed. Figure 20.35 shows this dialog box.

For this example, you will export the MSF for CMMI process template. You will then add a few custom work items to this template and re-import.

The Process Template Manager saves all the files that define the process to a folder upon download. This folder contains XML files that define a lot of the process. It also contains the default documents, queries, and process guidance associated with the methodology. Figure 20.36 shows the folder structure that defines the CMMI process.

Notice that the file you will be working with in this example, WorkItems.xml, has been highlighted. You will edit this file in Visual Studio. Figure 20.37 shows the file open in the IDE.

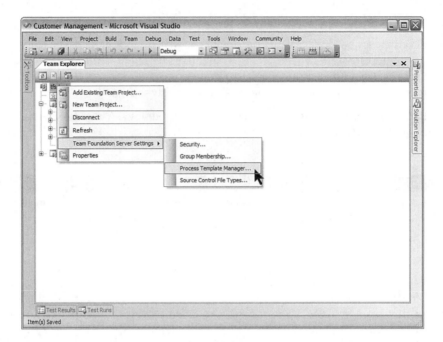

FIGURE 20.34   Accessing the Process Template Manager.

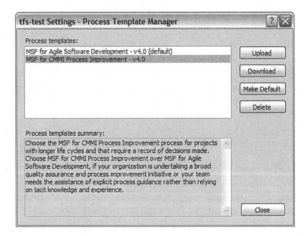

FIGURE 20.35   The Process Template Manager.

There are three sections to this file: work item type definitions, work items, and queries. The type definitions section indicates the location of the XML files used to describe each work item. The work items section identifies the set of seed work items to be loaded at project creation (this is the focus). The query section lists the location of each query file to be loaded as part of the methodology.

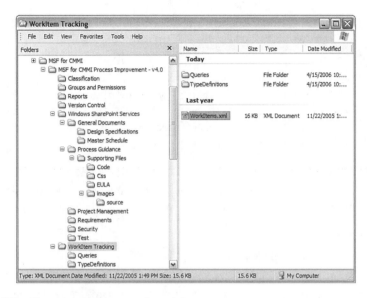

FIGURE 20.36   The exported process template.

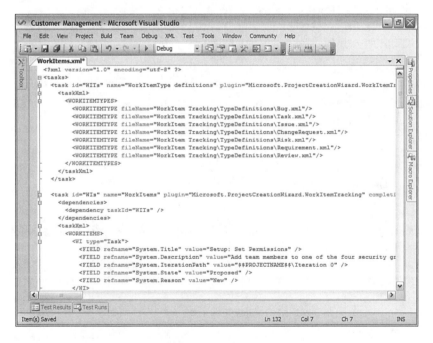

FIGURE 20.37   The WorkItems.xml file.

Adding Work Items to the Methodology

Again, the focus in this example is the set of work items to be seeded for the project. If you look at an existing work item, you can understand its structure. This will help you create a few new tasks and tweak existing ones. The following represents the task titled Setup: Set Permissions (we've truncated the description):

```
<WI type="Task">
  <FIELD refname="System.Title" value="Setup: Set Permissions" />
  <FIELD refname="System.Description" value="Add team members to … " />
  <FIELD refname="System.IterationPath" value="$$PROJECTNAME$$\Iteration 0" />
  <FIELD refname="System.State" value="Proposed" />
  <FIELD refname="System.Reason" value="New" />
</WI>
```

You can see that to seed the methodology with additional work items you need to define a type, title, description, state, and so on. Now you can add the work items as defined in Listing 20.1.

LISTING 20.1   New Tasks to Be Seeded

```
<WI type="Task">
  <FIELD refname="System.Title" value="Setup: Execute project setup checklist" />
  <FIELD refname="System.Description" value="Fill out the Excel file,
    'ProjectStartupChecklist.xls' from the portal." />
  <FIELD refname="System.IterationPath" value="$$PROJECTNAME$$\Iteration 0" />
  <FIELD refname="System.State" value="Proposed" />
  <FIELD refname="System.Reason" value="New" />
</WI>
<WI type="Task">
  <FIELD refname="System.Title" value="Create billing report" />
  <FIELD refname="System.Description" value="Fill out the Excel file,
    'ProjectBillingReport.xls' from the portal." />
  <FIELD refname="System.IterationPath" value="$$PROJECTNAME$$\Iteration 0" />
  <FIELD refname="System.State" value="Proposed" />
  <FIELD refname="System.Reason" value="New" />
</WI>
<WI type="Task">
  <FIELD refname="System.Title" value="Enter project in Time Tracking System" />
  <FIELD refname="System.Description"
➥value="Go to TimeTrack2006 and enter new project information." />
  <FIELD refname="System.IterationPath" value="$$PROJECTNAME$$\Iteration 0" />
  <FIELD refname="System.State" value="Proposed" />
  <FIELD refname="System.Reason" value="New" />
</WI>
```

Uploading (Importing) the Methodology

The next step is to import the refined methodology. To do so, you return to the Process Template Manager and choose Upload. You are then presented with a folder selection screen. You use this screen to navigate to the folder that contains the updated methodology.

The process template name is very important. If the name matches the name of an existing process template, then the Template Manager will ask to overwrite the existing template. This is great if it is your intention. However, if you want to keep the Visual Studio core templates, then you should rename your process template before uploading.

You rename the process template at the top of the `ProcessTemplate.xml` file found in the root folder for the template. You can also use this file to change the process template description that shows up in the Template Manager. Figure 20.38 shows the uploaded process template.

> **NOTE**
>
> If you choose to overwrite an existing process, this will not affect projects that are already defined by this process. Instead, these projects use a copy of this core methodology. What you will overwrite is the core that drives new projects.

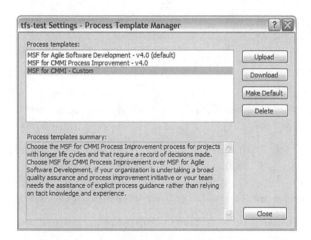

FIGURE 20.38   The newly uploaded process template.

You can now use your newly customized process to create new projects. You can use this same process of export, tweak, and import to make all kinds of modifications to team systems. You can also use the import to load third-party processes. Figure 20.39 shows the results of this work: a new project with a new set of seed work items.

Customizing an Existing Work Item

You can customize the definition for an existing work item by using the same steps we outlined in the preceding section: export, tweak, and import. Customizing existing work items is probably the most common Team System customization. Let's look at an example.

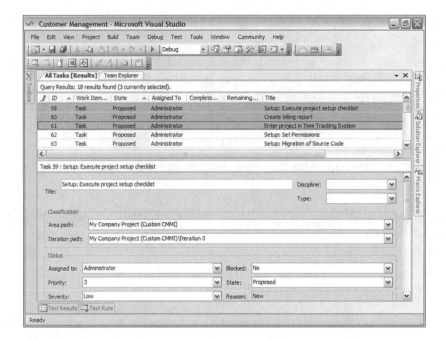

FIGURE 20.39   The new tasks in a new project.

Suppose you want to customize the Bug work item. You want to add a field to indicate bug type. This will allow the person triaging bugs to categorize them. You can then report and prioritize bugs that are of type error versus cosmetic and the like.

To make your edits, you again would export a methodology. For this example, use the one you exported previously (CMMI). You then navigate to the work item type definitions (\WorkItem Tracking\TypeDefinitions). This folder contains definitions for each work item defined by the process. Of course, you are interested in the Bug.xml file.

This definition file contains the core fields defined for bugs as well as common fields that apply to most work items. The definition is long and does not bear repeating here. You will add your new field to the core fields area in this XML. Listing 20.2 represents the new field.

LISTING 20.2   A New Field Inside Bug.xml

```
<FIELD name="Bug Type" refname="Unleashed.BugType" type="String"
  reportable="dimension">
  <HELPTEXT>Represents the type of bug</HELPTEXT>
  <REQUIRED/>
  <ALLOWEDVALUES>
    <LISTITEM value="Error"/>
    <LISTITEM value="Requirement"/>
    <LISTITEM value="Change"/>
    <LISTITEM value="Navigation"/>
```

LISTING 20.2 Continued

```
   <LISTITEM value="Text"/>
   <LISTITEM value="Cosmetic"/>
 </ALLOWEDVALUES>
 <DEFAULT from="value" value="Error"/>
</FIELD>
```

This field is added to the Fields section of the XML. Notice that you restrict the values that can be entered in this field by using the AllowedValues node. This will tell Team Systems to display this field as a drop-down list for users. This field is also marked as required (<REQUIRED/>) and has a default value set using the Default element. Finally, the field definition indicates that the field is reportable. This tells Team System to include this field when doing analysis for reports.

You must also define how the field should appear on the form. You do this inside the Form section of the XML. You want the field to appear at the top of the form to the right of the Title field. To accomplish this, you add a column to the Group element that contains the Title field. Listing 20.3 illustrates adding the Bug Type field to this group.

LISTING 20.3 Adding the Field to the Form

```
<Group>
  <Column PercentWidth="70">
    <Control Type="FieldControl" FieldName="System.Title" Label="&amp;Title:"
      LabelPosition="Left"/>
  </Column>
  <Column PercentWidth="30">
    <Control Type="FieldControl" FieldName="Unleashed.BugType"
➥Label="&amp;Bug Type:" LabelPosition="Left"/>
  </Column>
</Group>
```

Finally, you upload the new process template. Figure 20.40 shows the results of this work.

> **NOTE**
>
> You can also make changes to existing work items (without exporting and importing) on a project that is in progress. Microsoft has created the Visual Studio Team System Extensibility Kit to allow for greater customizations of VSTS. This tool ships separately from the product. It does require you to become an affiliate member of the Microsoft Visual Studio Integrator Program (VSIP). You can start the download process at http://msdn.microsoft.com/vstudio/extend/default.aspx.
>
> This SDK ships with examples of work item customizations. It also provides detailed documentation of the work item type definitions. This is a must-read for creating your own work items.

20

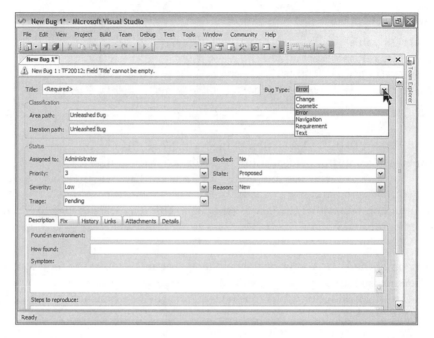

FIGURE 20.40   The new bug type field in action.

Summary

Work items are the driving force behind team collaboration using Team Systems. If used correctly, they can define all work and then track the progress and related metrics associated to that work. In this chapter, we discussed the many work items defined by both MSF for Agile and MSF for CMMI. We covered the basics behind these items, including workflow, work item history, linking, file attachments, and more.

Work items are also integrated into the IDE. You can query them and work on them directly inside Visual Studio. This capability provides a great experience for developers and testers. For example, you saw how developers can associate work items to their code during the check-in process.

Team Systems provides integration with Excel and Microsoft Project for nondevelopers (such as project managers). Work items can be pulled into these tools, updated (even new ones can be added), and then published back to the server. This chapter presented both these scenarios.

Finally, in this chapter, we showed a few of the ways you might customize work items and Team Systems to meet the needs of your team. We demonstrated the process of downloading, tweaking the XML, and then uploading the results as a new process inside TFS.

CHAPTER **21**

Modeling

Software modeling is moving out of the documentation phase and becoming a core development task. All too often software is modeled during initial design when expectations are high and intentions are great. However, as the project progresses, it can become difficult to keep the models updated. When the code base starts diverging from the models, this documentation can be quickly rendered useless.

Visual Studio 2005 is Microsoft's first step at moving software modeling out of this documentation mode and into the IDE. Having the models in the IDE means they are closer to the code and systems you write. This helps ensure these models are useful to the development process and the team. It also provides a better chance that they stay in sync with the project.

In this chapter, we focus on the models and related tools used to develop software with Visual Studio 2005. These models include the following diagrams:

- **Application**—The application diagram is used to define the components that make up your application.

- **System**—The system diagram is used to group applications into systems for deployment purposes.

- **Class**—The class diagram is used to visualize code and make changes to its structure.

- **Logical Datacenter**—The logical datacenter diagram is used to define the infrastructure that will house your application.

- **Deployment**—The deployment diagram represents the logical deployment of your systems into the datacenter.

IN THIS CHAPTER

- Team Architect Artifacts
- Designing Your Application
- Defining a System
- Defining Your Infrastructure
- Deploying Your Application
- Implementing Your Application
- Visually Developing Code

Each of these diagrams has an associated set of tools or a designer that can be used to create and edit the diagrams. We cover each of these diagrams and their related tools through the rest of this chapter.

NOTE

The majority of what we discuss in this chapter is related to the Visual Studio 2005 Team Architect product. The only exception is the Class Designer. This tool is available to all team members with Visual Studio Professional or a Team Edition.

Team Architect Artifacts

Visual Studio Team Architect installs a couple of additional project templates and a few new item templates. These templates are focused on a single role called *architect*. However, in most organizations there is a split between infrastructure and application architects. These are typically two distinct roles played by people with different skill sets. For example, the infrastructure architect is often concerned with server software, networks, firewalls, and VPNs. The application architect, on the other hand, is more involved in determining whether an application's interface will be web or Windows, whether it will leverage web services, what external interfaces it will connect to, and so on. Visual Studio Team Architect tries to unite these roles and increase the communication between them.

Project Templates

Team Architect defines a project template for both the application and infrastructure architects. These templates can be found in the New Project dialog box under Distributed System Solutions. Figure 21.1 shows an example of this dialog box.

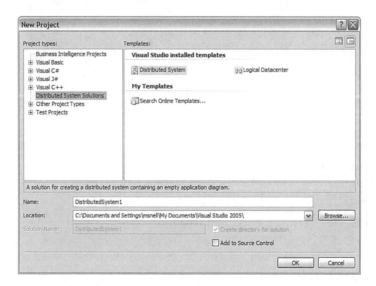

FIGURE 21.1   The Distributed System Solutions.

21

The Distributed System template is meant for the application architect. Visual Studio creates a new solution with a blank Application Diagram file when you choose this project type. This project type cannot be added to existing solutions. Instead, you would simply add a new application diagram to that solution.

> **NOTE**
>
> You can have only one application diagram per solution. The reason is that the contents of this file should represent the entirety of your solution.

The Logical Datacenter template is for the infrastructure architect. Visual Studio creates a new solution with a blank Logical Datacenter Diagram file upon selecting this project type. It, too, cannot be added to existing solutions. Instead, you can add the diagram itself to the solution (and not the project).

Item Templates

Visual Studio Team Architect provides three items templates: Application Diagram (`.ad`), Logical Datacenter Diagram (`.ldd`), and System Diagram (`.sd`). These templates can be added to existing solutions from the Add New Item dialog box. Figure 21.2 shows an example of this dialog box in action.

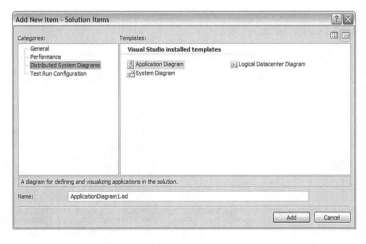

FIGURE 21.2   The team architect diagrams.

All distributed system diagrams are added to the Solution Items folder in the Solution Explorer. The reason is that they refer to the entire solution and are not project specific.

A couple of diagrams that may seem to be missing from the item templates list are the class diagram (`.cd`) and the deployment diagram (`.dd`). The class diagram, as we have stated, is not solely tied to Team Architect. It can be added to a project from the New Item Template dialog box.

The deployment diagram does not have an item template. It can be created only through the logical datacenter diagram (see "Deploying Your Application" later in this chapter).

Designing Your Application

Typically, the first step in designing an application is for the application architect to define the components that make up the application, the communication between those components, and their settings and constraints. The application diagram directly supports this activity. Doing this step first in the process allows the application architect to lay out the components of the system and have those elements verified for deployment by a logical datacenter diagram. Once verified, these components can then generate stub projects and code for the solution. This will give the development team a head start.

The following lists the logical order of using the diagrams in Visual Studio 2005 to build a new application:

1. Create an application diagram to define the clients, services, components, and communication paths of the application.

2. Group applications together to form systems with the System Designer.

3. Create a logical datacenter diagram that represents the infrastructure in which the application will be deployed.

4. Use the Deployment Designer to verify your application definition (diagram) will deploy in the logical infrastructure.

5. Use your application diagram to generate the project stubs for your solution.

6. Finally, use the Class Designer to visually define classes and their relationships to one another.

We will walk through each of these steps throughout the rest of this chapter. Our examples will follow the design of the application begun in Chapter 20, "Work Item Tracking." Recall that this application represents a customer management system for an existing e-commerce application.

TIP

Visual Studio will generate the model of your application if you add an application diagram to the existing application. This can be a great way to understand the relationship between components of an application. It is also a great place to start when you're working with an existing application to extend its functionality.

In fact, all application models are synchronized with the solution that contains them. This ensures the models stay in step with the code base.

Working with the Application Diagram

You've seen how to add an application diagram to a solution. Now you're ready to look at the application diagram in greater detail. Figure 21.3 shows an open application diagram in the IDE using the Application Designer toolset.

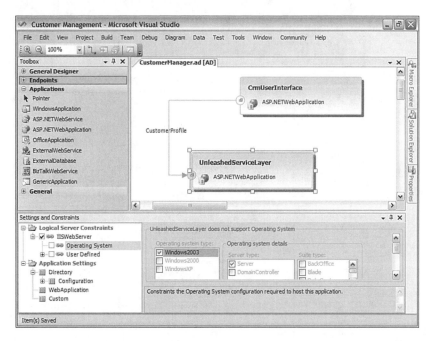

FIGURE 21.3   The Application Designer.

The four main parts of the Application Designer are the diagram itself, the Toolbox items, the Settings and Constraints window, and the Diagram menu. These four items allow you to design the details of your application. Now let's look at each of these items in more detail.

The Diagram Menu

The Diagram menu is active only when you have an architectural diagram loaded in the active window. The contents of the menu change depending on what type of diagram you have loaded. In fact, even the application Diagram menu changes depending on what is selected in the actual diagram. Figure 21.4 shows an example of this menu for an application diagram with a web service application selected.

Some key features worth discussing are that the menu provides access to include Define Deployment, Design Application System, and Add to Toolbox. The Define Deployment menu item enables you to select the deployment details of the application. We will cover this item later when we discuss the deployment diagram. The Design Application System menu item allows you to create a system from components of your application. We'll cover this item in the next section. Finally, the Add to Toolbox menu item allows you to take an existing application, endpoint, or group of applications and create a reusable Toolbox item from it. This capability can be useful if you are consistently reusing an element across diagrams.

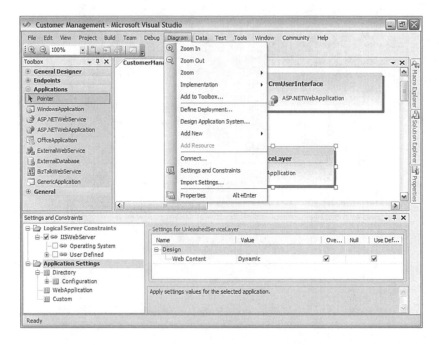

FIGURE 21.4   The Diagram menu.

Application Designer Toolbox

The Application Designer Toolbox provides access to the items that can be added to the application diagram. These items are grouped into three sections: General Designer, Endpoints, and Applications. The General Designer section contains elements that are common to many of the architect designers. The Endpoints section groups the endpoint connections that define the communication between applications. Finally, the Applications section groups the various applications that can be defined on the diagram. Figure 21.5 shows a visual representation of this Toolbox.

For the most part, these Toolbox items are aptly named, and you should have no problem using them. We will cover adding applications and using the endpoints in the coming section.

> **NOTE**
>
> The applications in the Toolbox are either clients, web services, or databases. There is no support for adding frameworks or class libraries to the Application Designer. These items are not part of the Application Designer by design.

FIGURE 21.5   The Application Designer Toolbox.

The Application Diagram

The application diagram represents the canvas for the application architect. It is here that you drag applications from the Toolbox and connect them together to form a solution. Figure 21.6 shows an application diagram in progress.

There are two ASP.NET web application items on the diagram. The top one, CrmUserInterface, represents the web-based user interface screens for the customer management sample application. The one below that, CrmServiceLayer, is a web service for the CustomerProfile service. Notice that once they are placed on the diagram it is difficult to distinguish between a web application and web service; this is by design because either application could contain both .aspx and .asmx files.

There is also an arrow that connects the two applications. This arrow is a Connection item; it is used to connect endpoints of an application. Notice that each application has an associated endpoint. Each endpoint is a web service endpoint. The CrmUserInterface endpoint has a hollow or white background, indicating it is the client endpoint. The CrmServiceLayer endpoint is solid to indicate it represents the server. The arrow also indicates the direction of caller (client) to server. Finally, the arrow contains a decorator or label. This label indicates the web service that connects the two applications (CustomerProfile). This relationship will become a web reference upon implementation.

Now let's look at adding a couple of new applications to the diagram and connecting them.

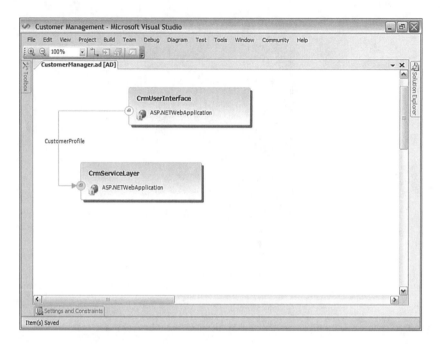

FIGURE 21.6   The application diagram.

Adding Applications   You add applications to the diagram through drag-and-drop. For the example, you will add an external database to which the service layer can connect. This external database belongs to the existing e-commerce application that the CRM application extends. You will also add a Windows user interface to allow the sales and marketing team to do their data analysis work. Figure 21.7 shows the results of this work.

Connecting Applications   Now you're ready to add endpoints to the applications and connect them. The Toolbox shows three endpoints, but there is actually a fourth one: `DatabaseServerEndpoint`. This endpoint exists on database applications by default. It can also be dragged to connecting applications. The following list describes the possible endpoints for connecting applications in the diagram:

- `WebServiceEndpoint`—Used to connect to SOAP-based web services. Each web service endpoint represents an actual web service. You can create a one-to-one relationship between web service application and web service endpoint. Or you can create as many endpoints as you need for your web service application.

- `WebContentEndpoint`—Used to connect to web-based content through HTTP (such as files).

- `GenericEndpoint`—Used to set an endpoint without specifying an exact communication protocol. It defines a connection but not the mechanics of the connection.

- `DatabaseServerEndpoint`—Used to connect to a database server.

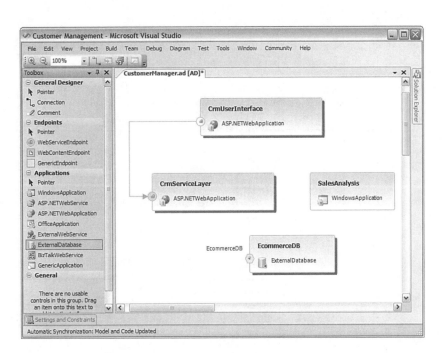

FIGURE 21.7   Additional applications added to the model.

You will use these endpoints to connect applications. First, the `SalesAnalysis` Windows client application will need to connect to the `CrmServiceLayer` through a web service endpoint. Next, the `CrmServiceLayer` will require a connection to the `EcommerceDB` database.

First, you add all the endpoints to the various applications. Next, to connect the endpoints, you can use the Connection item from the Toolbox. Alternatively, you can hold down the Alt key and select and drag the endpoint from one application to another.

When you connect an application to a database application, Visual Studio presents you with the Connection Properties dialog box for establishing a connection to an actual database. You can cancel this step or define the actual connection details if they are set up.

Figure 21.8 shows the applications connected. Notice the addition of a new web service layer: `SalesAnalysisServices`. The `SalesAnalysis` client application will connect to both the CRM layer and this newly defined layer. Also, notice the endpoint names. You can turn these labels off for each endpoint, show for each, or show for only one endpoint. The labels connecting to a web service represent the actual web service's name that is defined by the endpoint.

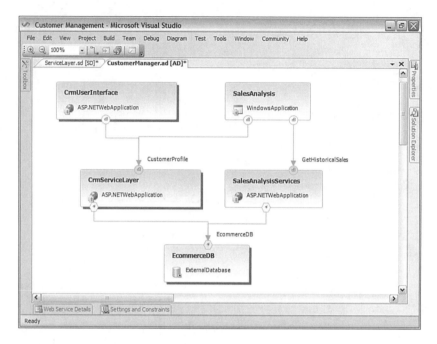

FIGURE 21.8   The connected applications.

Application Settings and Constraints

Each application on the diagram has a set of properties, settings, and constraints. This metadata helps further define how this application will be built and deployed. For example, suppose the web user interface must be deployed on a Windows 2003 Enterprise server that is running the .NET Framework version 2.0.

To indicate this setting, you would select the CrmUserInterface application from the diagram, right-click, and choose Settings and Constraints. Visual Studio will present the related window in the IDE. Figure 21.9 shows this window and related setting.

Notice that the Settings and Constraints window is split between Logical Server Constraints and Application Settings. The former represents the server on which the application will be deployed. Constraints entered here will be enforced when you try to deploy against a logical datacenter diagram. The Application Settings section is essentially the configuration file for the application. You can set all related settings here. These settings will be emitted when you implement the application diagram.

On the right side of the screen, you modify the settings. Notice in the example the operating system, server type, suite type, and .NET Framework version have been selected.

Application Properties   You can define additional implementation details about the application using the Properties window. Again, select an application from the diagram, right-click, and choose Properties. This will open the Properties window for the given application. Of course, the settings in this window are dependent on the type of application selected.

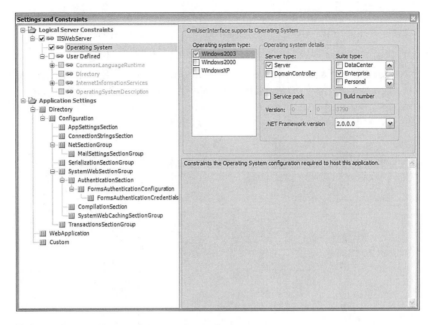

FIGURE 21.9 The Settings and Constraints window.

As an example, assume that the development team for the SalesAnalysis Windows client application intends to work in Visual Basic. You can add this implementation detail in the Properties window. This setting will affect how Visual Studio emits the project when implementing the diagram. Figure 21.10 shows this process in action.

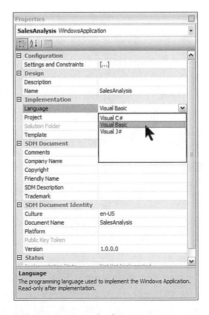

FIGURE 21.10 The Application Properties window.

Web Service Settings   Recall that each endpoint on a web service application represents an actual web service that will be implemented. The Application Designer allows you to indicate the implementation details of each of these web services.

To add these details, you select a web service endpoint, right-click, and choose Define Operations from the context menu. Selecting this menu item will open the Web Service Details window. Figure 21.11 shows an example of this window along with the web service's Properties window.

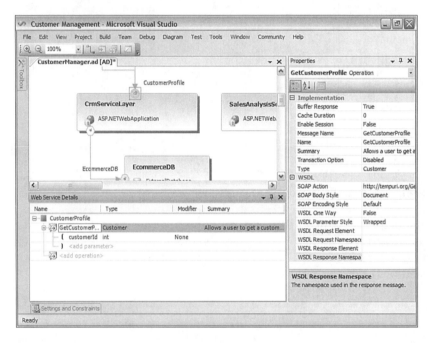

FIGURE 21.11   The Web Service Details window.

When defining web service details, you can add operations, set their return types, and indicate parameters. You can also define summary information that will be used for the XML documentation of the web service.

Defining a System

We have now described the basic application architecture. The next step is to compose actual systems using the System Designer. The concept and use of system diagrams can be difficult to grasp. They are also somewhat optional, which adds to their being obtuse. Simply put, a system is an actual configuration of one or more applications you intend to deploy.

This definition may already seem confusing given that an application diagram already represents the configuration (settings and constraints) of the applications you intend to deploy. This is what makes system diagrams optional. You can simply use the application diagram and move it into your infrastructure. However, there is a real use for system diagrams.

System diagrams can group applications into a system. The only reason to do so is for actual deployment. Also, a system is based on the original application architecture. However, the system diagram can be reconfigured for the actual deployment.

It helps to think of an example. Suppose you intend to deploy your service layer twice: once in your intranet zone and again in your Internet zone. The base application architecture does not change. What changes are the settings for a specific deployment. Therefore, you can create two systems, one for each deployment. Each system draws on the base application architecture. In addition to allowing configuration overrides, the system diagram also enables you to control which portions of the application actually are deployed in any system.

System Diagram

There are a couple of ways to add a system diagram to your solution. You can use the item template, as we described earlier; or you can select one or more applications, right-click, and choose Design Application System. In either case, you will be working with the applications defined in your application diagram. Recall that a given solution may contain only one application diagram. All system diagrams will use the applications defined in this diagram. Figure 21.12 shows an example of selecting three applications and starting the System Designer.

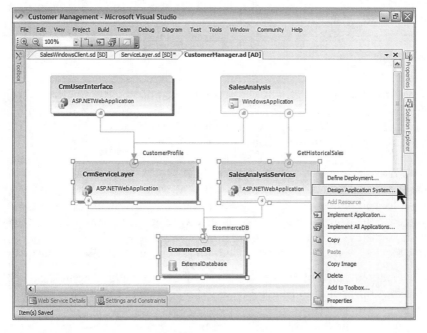

FIGURE 21.12 Defining an application system.

The System Designer contains a System View window and the System Designer (SD) window. The system view is like a Toolbox of items that can be added to the SD window. Its contents are directly linked to your application architecture diagram. Each application you defined there is available to be added to the system from the System View window. Figure 21.13 shows an example of a system in the designer.

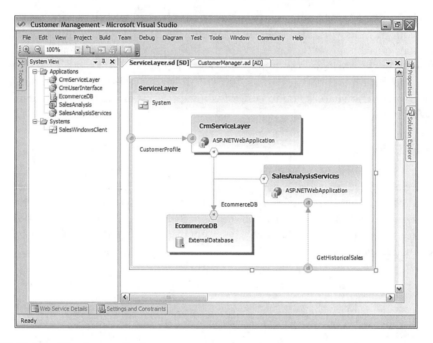

FIGURE 21.13   The System Designer.

Notice that this system view is not unlike the view you had on the application diagram. The difference here is that this view is constrained to this single system. You also have access to the Settings and Constraints from this designer. This will allow you to do the setting overrides for the system, as we discussed.

Creating Proxy Endpoints
The outer box of the System Designer represents the way in which you intend to expose the system for communication from other applications and systems. Notice that in Figure 21.13 there are two endpoints on this outer box: One points to the CrmServiceLayer and one points to the SalesAnalysisServices application. These endpoints are called *proxy endpoints;* they allow you to define the communication that is allowed to the system.

The proxy endpoints are not on the outer system box by default. You must explicitly select and drag the application endpoints to the other box to create these proxy endpoints.

Connecting Applications to Systems

You can use the System Designer to connect an application inside a system to another, previously defined system. This way, you can reuse the configuration of the system for defining new systems.

As an example, suppose you want to define a system for the sales client application. Recall this is a Windows-based client that connects to the service layer. It would be useful to create one or more systems for the actual deployment of this client. However, each system will talk to a deployed version of the service layer system.

Therefore, you add a new system diagram to the solution. On this diagram you will drag the SalesAnalysis application. The System View tool window also gives you access to the other systems you have created. Under the Systems folder, you will see the ServiceLayer system created in the prior example. You will drag this onto the designer as well.

The ServiceLayer shape is represented as a system (and not an application). You have access only to the proxy endpoints exposed by the system. You will use the SalesAnalysis endpoints to connect to the two proxy endpoints of the ServiceLayer system. The diagram will enforce that you connect the proper endpoints (based on the WSDL).

Figure 21.14 shows the completed system diagram. We will come back to these diagrams when we deploy the application into the logical datacenter.

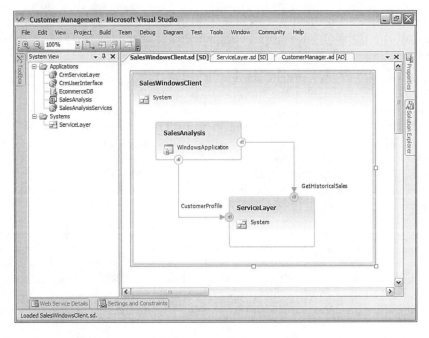

FIGURE 21.14 Creating a system that uses another system.

> **TIP**
>
> It is helpful to remember that the systems defined here do not physically exist. Rather, they define application configurations at the time of deployment.

Defining Your Infrastructure

An important, and often overlooked, step in any software project is ensuring what the development team plans to build will deploy in the production infrastructure. This includes hardware, software versions, configuration of that software, and communication between the various servers involved. The sooner you can get a comfort level (or identify the risks), the more likely your project will succeed.

It is the job of the application architect and the infrastructure architect to make sure they get on the same page, while the design is simply that, a page. When that design moves from paper to code, the wrong infrastructure assumptions can cause costly delays (or worse) in deployment. The new logical datacenter diagram in Team Architect can help.

Logical Datacenter Diagram

The logical datacenter diagram (.ldd) allows you to represent an infrastructure environment in a model. In fact, for most projects you may want to represent more than one infrastructure model. Perhaps a development, staging, and production infrastructure will exist. Knowing the anomalies between these infrastructures can be very helpful. Having this logical representation allows you to test whether your application, as modeled, will deploy.

The current version of the Logical Datacenter Designer is not a networking diagram or even a similar tool. Those tools are still important for the infrastructure team. This diagram is less for the infrastructure team and more for the application architect's benefit. The infrastructure team may be concerned about switches, routers, firewalls, trusts, virus protection, VLANs, and so on (as well they should be). The logical datacenter diagram does not represent this information. It is meant solely to logically represent servers and their related software configuration and their allowed connection points. This gives the application architect and the infrastructure team confidence that a new application project will be deployable in the environment.

The logical nature of this designer is evident from the first use. For example, a logical server in the datacenter diagram would be an IIS web server, a database server, a generic server, and so on. These logical servers do not have physical mappings. Instead, one IIS server might represent an entire farm of web servers, or a database and web server may be deployed on the same box. This information is important to the infrastructure team but is not as relevant to the application architect's need to ensure the new project will deploy correctly.

Instead, the focus is on software, configuration of that software, and communication channels between servers. For example, as an application architect, you may need to ensure that your production environment supports the 2.0 version of the .NET Framework, or that the IIS server that hosts your web services is capable of communicating to your database. These are the types of details that can be embedded in a logical datacenter diagram.

Logical Datacenter Diagram Toolbox

The Logical Datacenter Designer Toolbox provides the access to the items that can be added to the logical datacenter diagram. These items are grouped into three sections: General Designer, Endpoints, and Logical Servers. The General Designer section contains elements that are common to many of the architect designers. The Endpoints section groups the endpoint connections that define the communication between servers in the datacenter. Finally, the Logical Servers section groups the various logical servers and zones that can be defined on the diagram. Figure 21.15 shows a visual representation of this Toolbox.

FIGURE 21.15   The Logical Datacenter Designer Toolbox.

Defining Zones

A zone in a logical datacenter is used to group servers and provide an abstraction of the same. Zones do not, by default, represent any one thing or group of things. You are free to define zones to group servers as you see fit. You can even nest zones within other zones to represent complex relationships.

The principal benefit of using a zone is to indicate what type of communication (traffic) is allowed in and out of the zone. The servers within the zone may talk to one another, but connecting to the zone can be a different story. As an example, a zone can be used to represent any number of things, including an intranet, an extranet, the Internet, a firewall, and a VPN.

As an example, say you want to define zones that will host servers to support the application and systems you have defined previously. You will want a client zone to represent the Windows client application for the sales analysis tool. You will also create an Internet or public access zone for the CRM user interface, as well as to expose a set of proxies for the service layer. Next, you will define a zone for the intranet; you will call this zone ServiceLayer. Finally, you will create a zone for the database. Figure 21.16 shows an example of these zones.

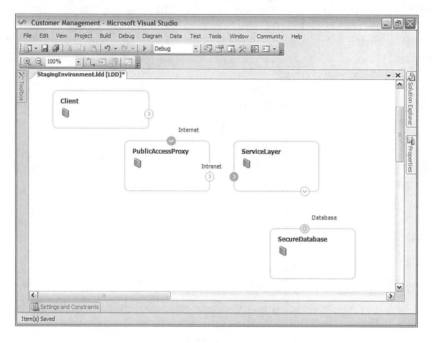

FIGURE 21.16   Logical datacenter zones.

The next step is to add servers to these zones. After you do this, you'll define the connections between the zones and servers within the zones. You will then work to set the constraints on both servers and zones.

Adding Servers

Servers do not have to be added to a zone. They can be added directly to the diagram. However, it helps to think of servers inside communication zones or boundaries. Therefore, the example will use the zones you defined earlier when adding servers.

The Logical Datacenter Designer allows you to use a few different server types on your diagram. These server types and their descriptions are as follows:

- WindowsClient—Represents a user's machine or desktop running Windows

- IISWebServer—Represents a Windows web server running IIS

- DatabaseServer—Represents a server in the datacenter that is running a relational database

- GenericServer—Represents custom or other types of servers in the datacenter

For the example, you will end up with one logical server per zone. Many times you will have more than one server in a zone. For example, if you have both an application server and a front-end web server in your intranet, you might define them in the same zone. The servers would talk to one another, but the zone boundary would dictate the incoming and outgoing traffic. Figure 21.17 focuses back on the example.

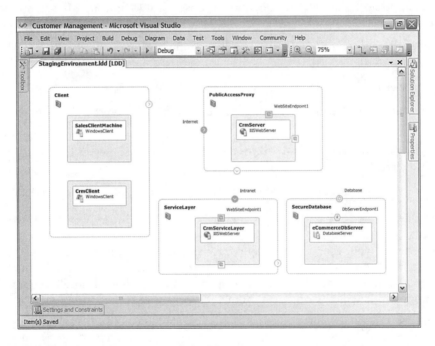

FIGURE 21.17   Logical datacenter zones and servers.

This diagram shows the five added servers. The Client zone contains two servers: one to represent each type of client that will connect to the solution. These are not really servers. Rather, they represent an application host that also has configuration implications. Next, the logical database server was added to the SecureDatabase zone. Then two web servers were added. The web server in the PublicAccessProxy zone is meant to host the CrmUserInterface application. In addition, this server has proxy web services that call into the server in the ServiceLayer zone. These are used for the SalesClient application. The next step is to connect the communication channels between these servers and zones.

Connecting Servers and Zones

Servers and zones are connected via endpoints. Endpoints define the type of traffic (and related constraints) that is allowed for a zone or server. If a zone endpoint, for instance, allows only inbound web traffic, there is no other open communication method allowed into that zone. The servers in the zone may have their own endpoints and communicate with one another using different traffic patterns.

The Logical Datacenter Designer allows you to define a few different endpoints. These endpoints and their descriptions are as follows:

- `ZoneEndPoint`—Represents the traffic flow into and out of zones. These endpoints also indicate direction of that traffic using arrows. An arrow pointing into a zone or server represents inbound traffic, whereas an arrow pointing out of a zone or server represents outbound traffic. An arrow pointing in both directions represents bidirectional traffic. `ZoneEndPoints` can also be constrained to indicate what type of traffic is allowed.

- `HTTPClientEndpoint`—Used to constrain communication to a web server from a client.

- `WebSiteEndpoint`—Used to manage server traffic for a web server.

- `DatabaseClientEndpoint`—Used to manage communication to a database server from a client.

- `DatabaseServerEndpoint`—Used for defining the allowable server traffic for a database server.

- `GenericClientEndpoint`—Used to manage client communication to a generic server.

- `GenericServerEndpoint`—Used to manage traffic allowed on a generic server.

For the example, your goal is to wire up the zones and servers within the zones. When there is traffic coming into a zone, typically that traffic is destined for a server (and not simply routed through the zone). The same is true on the outbound side. The outbound traffic from a zone typically originates from a server.

Figure 21.18 shows the endpoints added to the diagram and connected accordingly.

The following provides a step-by-step walkthrough illustrating how to connect the items in the diagram:

1. First, in each of the client servers (or hosts), add an `HTTPClientEndpoint`. This allows these machines to talk using the HTTP protocol. You then connect these endpoints to the outbound traffic for the Client zone.

2. Next, connect the inbound traffic endpoint for the `PublicAccessProxy` zone to a `WebSiteEndpoint` on the logical web server (`CrmServer`). This allows you to then connect the outbound traffic from the Client zone to the Internet endpoint of the `PublicAccessProxy` zone. The HTTP client traffic is now routed to a web server.

3. The next step is to follow a similar pattern for the server in the ServiceLayer zone. You connect the inbound zone endpoint to the WebSiteEndpoint of the CrmServiceLayer server. You then connect the HTTPClientEndpoint on the CrmServer to the outbound endpoint for the PublicAccessProxy zone. You could then connect the two zones (outbound PublicAccessProxy to inbound ServiceLayer).

4. Finally, remove the HTTPClientEndpoint from the CrmServiceLayer server. You replace it with a DatabaseClientEndpoint. You then connect the inbound zone endpoint for the SecureDatabase zone to the database server. The last step is to connect the ServiceLayer zone outbound endpoint to the inbound endpoint of the SecureDatabase zone.

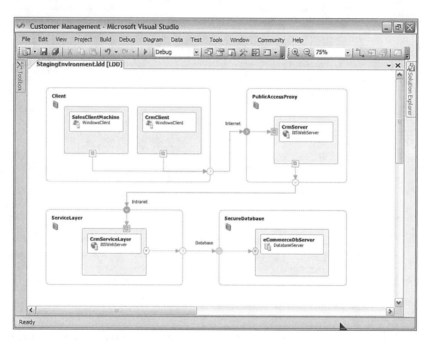

FIGURE 21.18   Logical datacenter connected zones and servers.

Defining Settings and Constraints

Configuring the zones and the servers is the final step. The logical datacenter diagram will then represent your infrastructure—at least for the purpose of the application architect. This architect can then use this zone to determine whether the proposed architecture will fit with the real infrastructure environment. Of course, the logical datacenter diagram works only if it truly matches your physical system configurations.

Configuring a Zone   There are a number of settings you can control with respects to zones. These settings include the capability to constrain the types of logical servers that can be added to the zone, the communication allowed in and out of the zone, whether zones can be nested within the zone, and the capability to define custom settings. The Datacenter Designer respects these constraints. It will not allow you, for instance, to add a web server to a zone that is configured for database servers only.

As an example, each zone defined previously should be constrained as to what servers are allowed in the zone. The client zone should allow only clients, the two zones that participate in web traffic should allow only web servers, and the database zone should be constrained to database servers. You set these types of constraints in the Settings and Constraints window (just like the application diagram). Figure 21.19 shows an example.

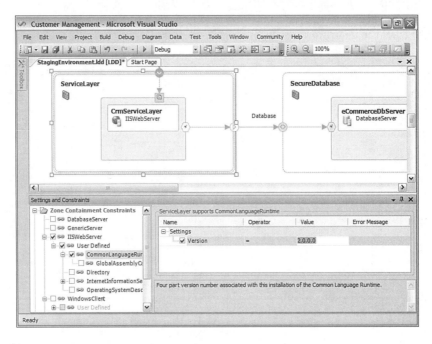

FIGURE 21.19   Zone settings and constraints.

In the example, the ServiceLayer zone has been selected. Notice on the left side of the Settings and Constraints window that servers other than an IISWebServer have been disabled (and thus disallowed) to be in this zone. Next, for this type of server, another constraint has been added: Web servers in this zone must be running version 2.0 of the .NET Framework.

For each constraint you set, you can craft a custom error message that is displayed when this constraint is broken. To do so, you click the ellipsis button in the Error Message field for the constraint. This brings up the dialog box shown in Figure 21.20. Here, you can set the error message. Notice you can use the macro text to show special fields for the given message.

FIGURE 21.20   A custom constraint error message.

Configuring a Server   You configure servers in the same manner. You select each and then control their settings through the Settings and Constraints window. From here, you can indicate the types of applications that are allowed to run on the server, the constraints for each, and the various server settings.

Figure 21.21 shows an example. The `CrmServer` has been selected. To restrict this server to running ASP.NET and web service applications, you can use the check boxes on the left side of the window.

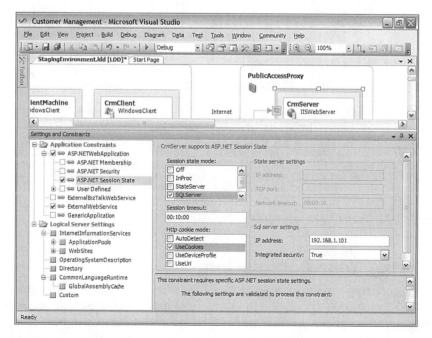

FIGURE 21.21   Setting a server constraint.

Next, you can define various settings for the server. Notice that the ASP.NET Session State parameter has been selected (left side, settings tree). You can now use the configuration area on the right side of the dialog box to control these constraints. Figure 21.21 indicates that session state is managed via SQL Server.

Again, your settings should closely match the servers in your environment. These settings will be used to restrict what the application architect can deploy.

Importing Server Settings   The datacenter diagram is a logical representation of your servers. However, you can use an import feature to point a server at a real, physical machine and import its settings. This capability can be helpful if you have access to servers that already represent the correct environment.

You access this feature from the Diagram menu with the Import Settings item. Selecting this menu item launches the Import IIS Settings Wizard. The imported settings apply to the server you have selected in the diagram. The wizard will walk you through the import.

Figure 21.22 shows the key step in the wizard. Here, you provide login credentials to the server. You also indicate what settings you want to import. If you import website settings, the diagram tool can add a new endpoint for each website on your server. You can also pick and choose which sites to import on another screen in the wizard.

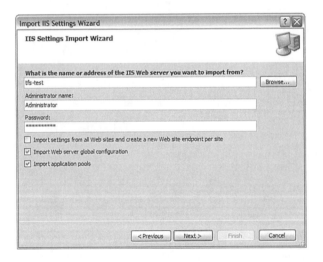

FIGURE 21.22   The IIS Settings Wizard.

Deploying Your Application

The intent of modeling the logical infrastructure is to avoid problems that might arise during deployment of an application. It can be extremely frustrating to get your application built and tested in one environment only to see it fail to deploy in the production environment. Often these issues are not found until late in the project and end up causing great delays and other headaches. If you've been doing development for a while, you've undoubtedly come across the statement "Deploy early, deploy often." This adage is in direct response to those who have experienced these headaches. You can be thankful that the Deployment Designer was built to try to avoid these types of issues. It allows you to deploy as often as you like.

Deployment Diagram

Team Architect ships with the Deployment Designer. This tool ties together the application and the logical datacenter diagrams. With it, you can use an application diagram to do a test deployment against your logical infrastructure. This test deployment will show where the application should run smoothly when you deploy it and where errors exist.

To start, you need to create a deployment diagram (.dd). You can do so from an existing application diagram. With it open, you can use the Diagram menu or the context menu and choose the Define Deployment option. Selecting this menu item brings up the Define Deployment dialog box (see Figure 21.23). From here, you select a logical datacenter diagram that represents the environment to which you want to test deploy.

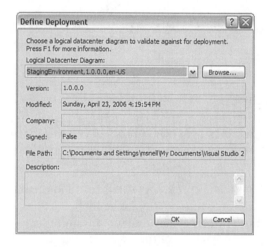

FIGURE 21.23   Define Deployment dialog box.

Visual Studio then brings up the deployment diagram. Remember, it is meant to be a marriage between your logical datacenter and application diagrams. Figure 21.24 shows an example. Notice that the diagram itself looks mostly like your infrastructure. The reason is that you are deploying your application into this diagram. Each server in the infrastructure has a box below it to which you can add an application. The applications from the application diagram are listed in the tree (System View) on the left side of the figure. Finally, notice that each application is added to its respective server.

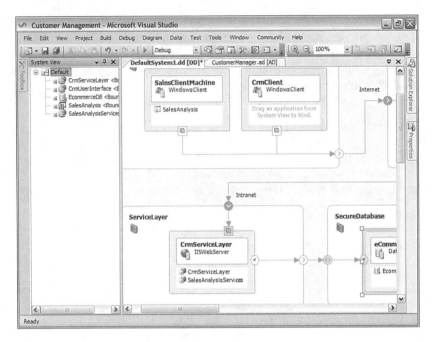

FIGURE 21.24   The deployment diagram.

Validate Deployment

The next step is to test the deployment. Some testing occurs when adding applications to the servers. The Deployment Designer will not allow you to add applications if you are breaking a hard rule in the deployment. For example, you cannot add a web application to the database server.

To validate the deployment, you choose the Validate Diagram option from the diagram or context menu. This checks the configuration of your applications against all the pieces of the infrastructure diagram. It then generates a set of warnings and errors for you to review. Figure 21.25 shows the results of the example. You can see there were no errors but plenty of warnings to work on.

Deployment Report

You can also generate a report that details your deployment. This lengthy document indicates every aspect of the application, datacenter, and deployment.

You can set a few options for generating the report. For example, you can indicate whether you want to see copies of the diagrams in the report. You set these options from the Properties window of the deployment diagram itself.

To access the report generation tool, you use the Diagram or context menu and choose the Generate Deployment Report option. Selecting this menu item creates the detailed report. Figure 21.26 shows a sample portion of the report. The contents of this report are all inclusive. You may prefer to pull a few sections out and paste them into a smaller report for archiving.

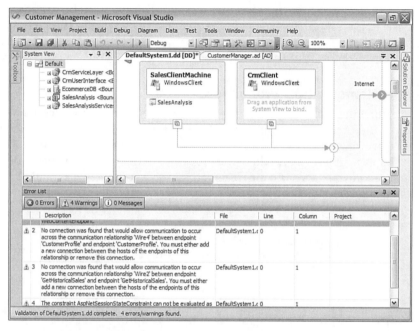

FIGURE 21.25 Warnings generated from the validate diagram.

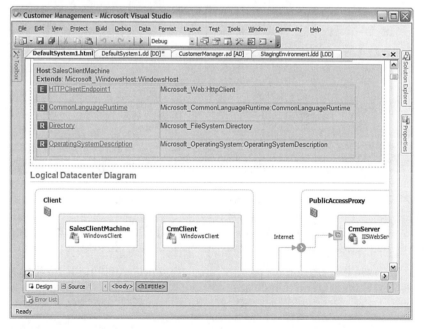

FIGURE 21.26 The deployment report.

Implementing Your Application

After you have the application designed and tested through deployment, the next step is to set up the actual project for the development team. The application architect performs this task. The Application Designer allows the architect to implement the applications defined in the diagram. This implementation is used to generate projects with the appropriate settings, references, and template files.

Setting Implementation Properties

Before generating the actual projects, you will want to define the implementation details of each application on the diagram. You can do this through the Properties window. When you're viewing properties for a given application, the Properties window will present an Implementation subsection. The properties in this section are based on the type of application you are configuring. Figure 21.27 shows the implementation properties for a web application.

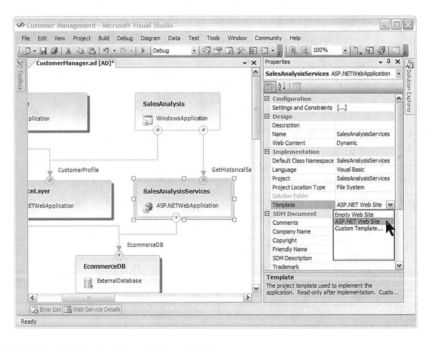

FIGURE 21.27   Setting implementation details.

Notice that you can set the language with which the application will be built. You can also define the project template, the default namespace, and so on.

You select each application and set its implementation properties in turn. When you're happy with these implementation details, it's time to generate the actual implemented templates.

Generating Projects

You do the actual implementation through the Implementation menu option on the Diagram menu. With it, you can choose to implement all applications on the diagram or only a single application.

Note that if you're working in a solution that already contains some of the applications used for the application diagram, then those applications will not be available for implementation (because they are already implemented). This happens to be the case with the example here. If you choose Implement All Applications, a confirmation dialog box is presented. Figure 21.28 shows the example. Notice that only two additional applications will be added to the existing solution.

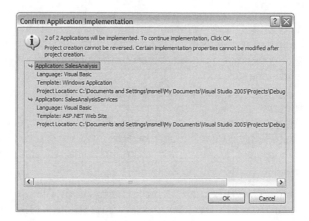

FIGURE 21.28   Confirm Application Implementation.

When complete, the new projects are generated with their properties and references set. You can now begin coding against your application architecture.

Visually Developing Code

As an architect, you get used to seeing things as diagrams. It is useful to think of your application as objects with specific semantics and relationships between one another. Most application architects and developers have been creating these types of diagrams for some time using the Unified Modeling Language (UML) or similar. These tools and modeling languages offer a great, abstract view of systems. However, they are difficult to keep in sync as your objects change. They also do not offer much assistance in terms of productivity or refactoring.

Visual Studio 2005 provides the Class Designer as a new aid in this area. You can think of it as a modeling tool. However, its greatest strength lies in what it can do over and above representing your objects visually. It provides a real-time view of your code, along with the capability to edit this view. With the Class Designer, you can both model your application and visually develop code at the same time.

TIP

The class designer is a great way to come up to speed on existing code. With it, you can open an existing set of objects and quickly find out how they work with one another.

Class Diagram

The class diagram is a modeling tool that is very important to the architect. However, unlike the models we have discussed previously, the class diagram is not specific to just the Team Architect version of Visual Studio. Instead, it is available to all roles in Team Systems. In fact, it is included in the Professional Edition. This is due to its nature as both a modeling tool and a development aid.

With the class diagram, you can get actual, real-time synchronization with your code. Developers should think of it more like a visual code editor (and less like a diagram). If you make a change to code, that change is reflected in the diagram. When you change the diagram, your code changes, too.

Creating a Class Diagram

There are a couple of ways to create a class diagram. The first is to add a class diagram to your project from the Add New Item dialog box. Here, you select a class diagram template (.cd) and add it to the project. You can then add items to this diagram from the Toolbox or from existing classes in the Solution Explorer.

The second way to add a class diagram to a project is to choose View Class Diagram from the context menu for a given project. In this way, Visual Studio will generate a class diagram from an existing project. You still end up with a .cd file in your project, but you save yourself the time of dragging everything onto the diagram. Figure 21.29 shows an example of the Class Designer. We will cover each window shown in this designer.

Displaying Members

You use the arrow icon in the upper-right corner of each object to toggle whether to show or hide its members. This capability is helpful if you need to fit a lot of classes on a screen or if you are interested only in members of a particular class.

You can also use the Class Designer toolbar to indicate how members are grouped for display and what additional information is shown. For example, you can sort members alphabetically, group them by their kind (property, method, and so on), or group by access (public, private, and so on). You can then indicate if you want to display just member names, their name and type, or the full signature.

Adding Items

You add items to the Class Designer by using either the Toolbox or the Solution Explorer. The Toolbox is for new items. You use the Solution Explorer to add existing classes to the diagram. In both scenarios, you simply drag and drop the item to the Class Designer window. If the item already exists, then Visual Studio will build out the class details for you. In fact, if the class file contains more than one class, each class will be placed as an object on the diagram.

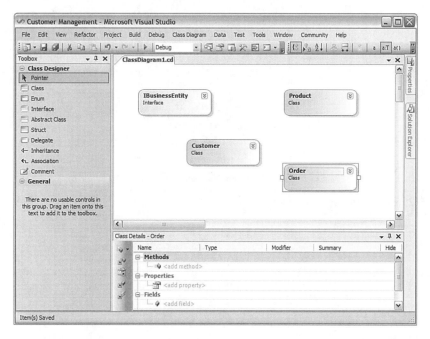

FIGURE 21.29   The Class Designer.

To add new items to the diagram, you use the Class Designer Toolbox. Figure 21.30 shows an example of these tools. Notice that you can define all object-oriented concepts here, including classes, interfaces, inheritance, and so on.

When you add a new item such as a class or struct to the designer, it will prompt you for its name and location. You can choose to generate a new file to house the item or place it in an existing file. Figure 21.31 shows the New Class dialog box. Here, you can give the class a name, set its access modifier, and indicate a filename.

TIP

The Class Designer can automatically add related classes to the diagram. For example, suppose you add a class from the Solution Explorer. If you want to show classes that inherit from this class, you can right-click the class and choose Show Derived Classes. This will add to the model all classes that derive from the selected class.

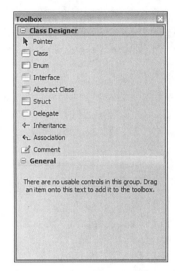

FIGURE 21.30   The Class Designer Toolbox.

FIGURE 21.31   Adding a new class to the designer.

Defining Relationships Between Classes

One of the biggest benefits of the class diagram is that it visually represents the relationships between classes. These relationships are much easier to see in a diagram than through code. The following relationships can be represented:

- **Inheritance**—Indicates if a class inherits from another class

- **Interface**—Indicates if a class implements one or more interfaces

- **Association**—Indicates an association between classes

Let's look at implementing each of these relationships through an example.

Inheritance

First, let's look at inheritance with the class designer. Suppose you have a base class called `Product`. This class represents a generic product in your system. You then want to create a concrete `Book` class that inherits from `Product`. To do this with the Class Designer, you make sure both classes are on the screen. You then select the Inheritance tool from the Class Designer Toolbox. This tool has its own special icon that shows an arrow pointing upward. This visual cue indicates you want to draw the inheritance from the implementation class to the base class. Figure 21.32 shows this drawing in action.

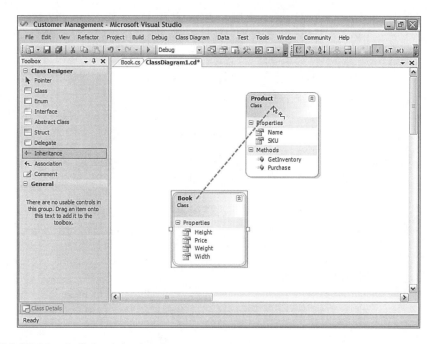

FIGURE 21.32 Defining inheritance.

When the drawing is complete, the inheritance arrow should point toward the base class. Figure 21.33 shows an example. Also, notice the `Book` class now contains an icon indicating that it inherits `Product`.

Interface

The next visual relationship we'll look at is an interface. For this example, suppose that all the business entities in your system implement a similar contract. This contract may define properties for ID and name. It may also define methods such as `Get`, `Delete`, and `Save`.

To implement this interface, you again use the Inheritance tool from the Class Designer Toolbox. You drag it from the class doing the implementation toward the interface. Figure 21.34 shows the result of an implemented interface. Notice the lollipop icon above the Customer class; it denotes the interface implementation.

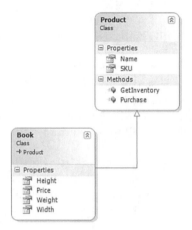

FIGURE 21.33   Inheritance defined.

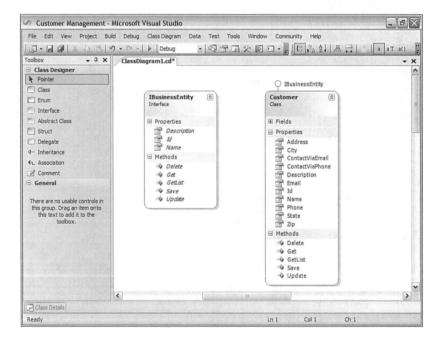

FIGURE 21.34   Implementing an interface.

Association

The final relationship to look at is association. This relationship is typically a very loose one in the UML world. However, in the Class Designer, an association is very real. Typically, this means that two classes have an association through the use of one of the classes. This relationship is also optional in terms of viewing. It can exist, but you do not have to show it in the diagram.

For example, suppose you have an `Order` object. This object might expose an `OrderStatus` property. Suppose it also has a property for accessing the Customer record associated with the order. These two properties are associations. You can leave them as properties, or you can choose to show them as associations.

You can also draw these property associations on the diagram. To do so, you select the Association tool from the Toolbox. This tool has the same icon as Inheritance. You then draw the association from the class that contains the association to the class that is the object of the association. Figure 21.35 shows an example. Notice that the association property is displayed on the association arrow. This indicates that the class from where the association originates contains this property (it is shown only on this line, however).

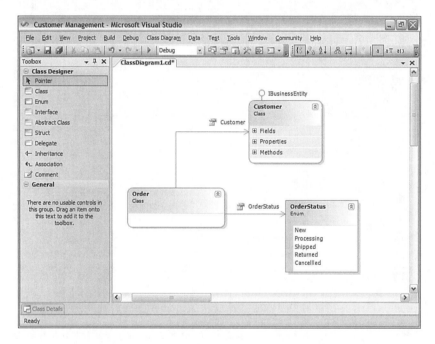

FIGURE 21.35   Creating an association.

Defining Methods, Properties, Fields, and Events

The most exciting part of the Class Designer is that it allows you to do more than define classes and relationships. You can actually stub out code and do refactoring (see Chapter 8, "Refactoring Code," for details).

There are two ways to add code to your classes, structs, interfaces, and the like. The first is to type directly into the designer. For example, if you are in the Properties section of a class, you can right-click and choose to add a new property. This will place the property in your class and allow you to edit it in the diagram. This method works for other class members as well. It does have a couple of drawbacks, however. You can't, for instance, define a full method signature or indicate access levels. For that, you need the Class Details window.

The Class Details window allows you to fully define methods, fields, properties, and events for a class. It also works with other constructs such as interfaces, delegates, and enums. To use this window, you right-click a class and choose Class Details from the context menu. Selecting this menu item brings up the Class Details editor for the selected class. Figure 21.36 shows an example.

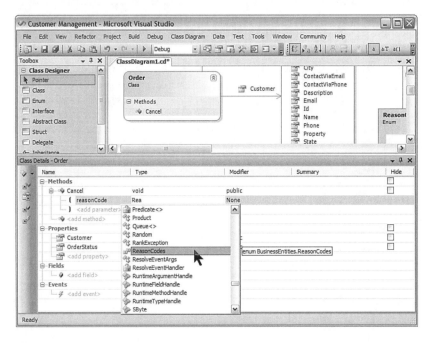

FIGURE 21.36   The Class Details window.

Notice that when working in the Class Details window, you still get IntelliSense. In this example, the Cancel method is being added to the Order class. You can indicate a return type for the method with the Type column. You can define the access modifier with the Modifier column. You can also set the parameters of the method. In this case, the method takes the parameter reasonCode.

Finally, there are the Summary and Hide columns. The Hide column indicates whether you want to show an item on the diagram. This capability allows you to hide various members when printing or exporting as an image. The Summary column allows you to add your XML documentation to the class. Clicking the ellipsis button in this field will bring up the Description dialog box. Here, you can enter your XML summary information for the given member. Figure 21.37 shows an example.

FIGURE 21.37   The Method Description dialog box.

Summary

You have seen how Visual Studio Team Architect can be used to move software modeling beyond just raw documentation. The models you create with it are much more: They are real tools that help increase productivity and reduce errors.

In this chapter, you looked at the standard approach for modeling applications. You first created an application diagram to represent the interfaces, services, and database that existed in the example. You then created a system diagram to group key application elements. Next, you learned how the logical datacenter diagram can be used to represent a physical infrastructure environment. This diagram became the basis of a test deployment for the application. Finally, you saw how the Class Designer can be leveraged to build diagrams and code at the same time.

These tools form the basis for modeling with Visual Studio 2005. They also represent a milestone step in what is sure to be a great future for visually modeling applications and code.

CHAPTER 22

Testing

IN THIS CHAPTER

- Creating, Configuring, and Managing Tests
- Developer Testing
- Web Testing
- Load Testing
- Manual Tests
- Generic Tests
- Ordered Tests

Testing is one of the most important parts of the Software Development Life Cycle (SDLC). All too often, however, testing is pushed to the back of the project as a last-minute exercise. Or, just as bad, developers are put in charge of testing their own code. In either case, you can expect poor results. If you have ever released software like this, you know that the release is just a point in time on a calendar. When users get a hold of the application, the real testing begins. In fact, this is where we get alpha and beta releases. Developers and testers do not have the tools to be confident in a release of software. Therefore, they throw it over the wall with a name like *alpha release* to get a read on everything that is actually wrong with the code. The tags *alpha* and *beta* mean that the users can't get too mad when things break. This typical cycle is changing, however.

Visual Studio 2005 provides developers and testers with tools that allow for repeatable, automated tests. These tools bring testing into all phases of the SDLC (including development). The tools allow you to test early and test often. The result is an increased confidence in the software. This confidence can turn the tables on the alpha and beta releases. Instead of users fettering out the errors, they can focus on usability and requirements mapping. The result is an application delivered with predictability and fewer bugs.

In this chapter we focus on the testing tools built into Visual Studio 2005. They include unit testing in Team Developer and the many tools inside Team Test, such as test case management, web testing, and load testing. This chapter will get you well on your way to creating software of a higher quality.

NOTE

You can create unit tests with Visual Studio Professional or Team Developer. However, you cannot create the many other tests we will discuss in this chapter without Team System's Team Test Edition. Therefore, if your edition does not have a specific feature, you may need to install Team Test or Team Suite.

Creating, Configuring, and Managing Tests

Testing is no longer a manual process tracked inside an Excel spreadsheet. Instead, testing is now built into the Visual Studio IDE. Here, you can create test projects and tests. You can control, configure, and manage these tests in a central area. You can also execute tests and publish the results to Team Foundation Server. In the following sections, we'll look at the basics of test projects, test items, and test management.

Test Projects

You define tests inside test projects. This is a familiar paradigm for all Visual Studio users: create a project, add items to that project. In this way, you can group test items under one or more projects. You can also check that project (and associated items) into source control as you would any other project.

In most cases you create a single test project for an application. That is, if your application is contained within a single solution, you would add a test project to that solution. Of course, there are exceptions. For larger projects, you may want to break out the test project by component, module, or even iteration.

Creating a Test Project

You create a test project like any other. You can choose New Project from the File menu, or you can right-click a solution and indicate the same. In either case, you are presented with the New Project dialog box. Figure 22.1 shows an example.

From the New Project dialog box, you navigate to Test Projects and then Test Documents. This will allow you to use the Test Project template. Notice that when adding a new test project, you can indicate whether Visual Studio should create a new solution or add your new project to the existing solution.

Configuring the Creation of Test Projects

By default, when you create a new test project, a new manual test and unit test are added to the project. Your project template also gets an automatic reference to the UnitTestFramework namespace. Figure 22.2 shows the Solution Explorer with a new test project highlighted, CustomerManagerTests.

The Test Project template is actually configurable. To configure it, you can bring up the Options dialog box (by selecting Tools, Options) and select the Test Project node under Test Tools. Figure 22.3 shows an example.

FIGURE 22.1   Creating a new test project.

FIGURE 22.2   A new test project.

From this Options dialog box, you can indicate the default test project type (C#, VB, and so on). You can also indicate the default items that are added to the test project upon creation. Notice the default settings include a unit test, a manual test, and an introductory file. You can override these settings by selecting the check boxes.

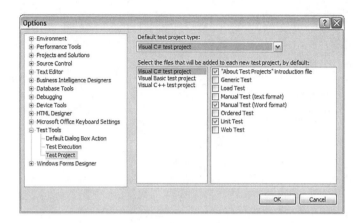

FIGURE 22.3   New test project options.

Test Items

A number of test item templates are defined for Visual Studio. Each represents a different test or a version of a test. These items are added to a test project. Each is a file that can be versioned inside source control. Figure 22.4 shows the Add New Test dialog box.

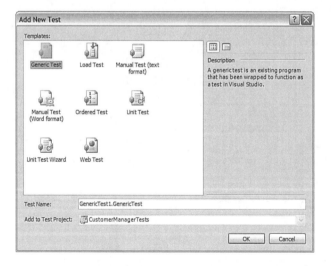

FIGURE 22.4   The Add New Test dialog box.

The figure shows the full list of the test items available. We will cover each one throughout this chapter. However, Table 22.1 provides a brief overview of each test item.

TABLE 22.1   Visual Studio Test Items

Test	Description
Generic Test	A generic test is an application or third-party tool that should be treated like a test. The generic test wraps this application.
Load Test	A load test is used to test your application's behavior when many concurrent users are accessing it.
Manual Test (text format)	A manual test is a set of steps that must be performed by a tester. This test is described as text. When the test is run, a tester has to indicate the results of the manual test.
Manual Test (Word format)	A manual test (see above) is written using Microsoft Word.
Ordered Test	An ordered test allows you to execute existing tests in a set order.
Unit Test	A unit test is a bit of code that executes a portion of your application and asserts the results.
Unit Test Wizard	The Unit Test Wizard allows you to automatically generate unit tests for existing code.
Web Test	A web test is used to test your web application. These tests can be recorded and then seeded with data to exercise an entire web user interface.

Test Manager

The larger the project, the more tests you will have. It is not uncommon for a project to have hundreds of tests. Each unit test, web test, load test, or manual test needs to be managed. Thankfully, Visual Studio provides the Test Manager tool to solve this issue. With it, you can organize tests into lists, group tests together, filter which test details you want to view, search for tests, run a group of tests, and more. It is the principal tool for the tester to bring order to his or her work. You access this tool from the Test menu (by selecting Test, Windows, Test Manager) or from the Test Tools toolbar. Figure 22.5 shows the Test Manager window in the IDE.

Notice the selection to view tests that are not in a list (by default this is all tests) in the tree view on the left. The tests themselves are shown in the list to the right. You can group the test list by namespace, project, test type, and so on using the Group By option on the Test Manager toolbar. This toolbar also allows you to indicate which columns, search for tests, run tests, and so on.

Test Lists

Test lists allow you to choose the grouping of tests in the test case manager. You can define your own custom lists and then add tests to those lists. Perhaps the biggest benefit to test lists is that you can run a list as a single unit. This gives you control over what tests to group together to form, for instance, a module test.

To define a test list, you can right-click the Lists of Tests node on the Test Manager navigation tree view. You can also select Create New Test List from the Test menu. Selecting this menu option brings up the Create New Test List dialog box. Figure 22.6 shows this dialog box in action.

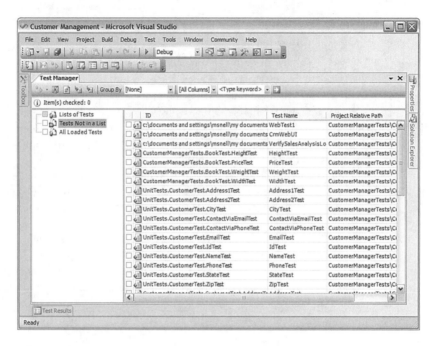

FIGURE 22.5   The Test Manager.

FIGURE 22.6   The Create New Test List dialog box.

In the Create New Test List dialog box, you define the list name, provide a description, and indicate where the list should exist in the test list hierarchy. Finally, you add tests to the list through drag-and-drop in the IDE.

> **TIP**
>
> A test may exist in one or more lists. This capability can be very helpful. You can reuse tests across lists and then execute that list as a group. For example, you may put a specific unit test in a regression test list you create and then reuse it again in a specific module test.

Testing Configuration

When you create a test project, Visual Studio adds a test configuration file to the solution. This file, with the extension .testrunconfig, can be found under the Solution Items folder. You use this configuration file to set a number of settings related to code coverage, web tests, test setup and cleanup, and so on. An example of the dialog box is shown in Figure 22.7. We will refer back to this configuration as we move through the chapter.

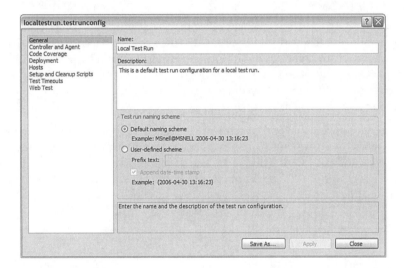

FIGURE 22.7   Test run configuration.

Developer Testing

Developers have always been responsible for testing their code prior to its release to the testers. In the past, this meant walking through every line of code in the debugger (including all conditions and errors). Going through all the code made for a fine goal but was not always realized (and very difficult to verify). In fact, the entire exercise was often skipped when doing code changes and updates. The result was lower-quality builds sent to the testers.

Clearly, this system highlights a need to automate unit testing. As a result, unit test frameworks were developed. The first such framework for .NET was nUnit, which is an open source project that allows you to write code that tests other code. A similar framework is now built into Visual Studio 2005. With it, developers can write unit tests that call their code and test possible conditions and outcomes.

The unit test framework in Visual Studio allows you to build tests as you build your application. Alternatively, if you subscribe to test-driven development, you can write your tests before you write your code. In either case, a disciplined approach to unit testing can lead toward building a full set of tests in unison with your application.

This full set of tests can often represent a regression test for most components or even the entire system. The result is increased confidence in activities that were previously very high risk, such as last-minute fixes, refactoring, and late additions. When these activities occur, you can leverage your full set of unit tests to find out what, if anything, was broken as a result of the change.

A Sample Unit Test

Before we go too much further, it makes sense to look at unit tests to better understand them. Remember, a unit test is simply test code you write to call your application code. This test code asserts that various conditions are either true or false as a result of the call to your application code. The test either passes or fails based on the results of these assertions. If, for example, you expect an outcome to be true and it turns out false, then a test fails. Let's look more closely at a real example.

Suppose you have a web service that returns a customer's profile from the database. This web service takes the customer's ID as a parameter. You might write a simple test to call this web service and pass a known ID from the database. This test might then confirm that what is returned not only works but is also correct. Listing 22.1 shows an example of such a test.

LISTING 22.1   A Sample Unit Test

```
[TestMethod()]
public void GetCustomerProfileTest() {
  CustomerProfile cutProfileService = new CustomerProfile();
  int customerId = 1234;
  Customer customer = cutProfileService.GetCustomerProfile(customerId);
  Assert.AreEqual(customer.Id, 1234);
}
```

Notice that this code is similar to other C# code. You simply make the call to the object. If this call fails (or any exception is thrown), then the test fails. You then do an assertion in the test to make sure the object returned matches the expected results. If this assertion is false (the values are not equal), then the test fails. If it is true, the test succeeds. You might add a few more assertions to round out this test. In addition, you might create some additional tests for this method. However, you should now have an understanding of the basics of a unit test. We will dig a little deeper in a moment.

Writing Effective Unit Tests

The more unit tests you write, the better you get at writing them. There are a few tenants (or best practices) to keep in mind to write effective unit tests. They include the following:

- Each unit should be tested independently. If your method has a number of possible, expected outcomes, then you need a unit test for each.

- Unit tests should exist independently from other tests. A unit test should not require other tests (or a sequence of tests) to be run prior to its executing.

- Unit tests should cover all cases. An effective set of unit tests covers every possible condition for a given method, including bounds checks, null values, exceptions, conditional logic, and so on.

- Unit tests should run (and rerun) without additional configuration. You should be able to run your unit tests easily. If you create an environment that requires configuration every time you run unit tests, you decrease the likelihood they will be run (or written) by the team.

- Test a standard application state. If your unit tests work with application data, for example, you should reset this data to common state prior to each unit test executing. This way, you ensure that tests are not causing errors in other tests. You also give developers a common platform on which to test.

These best practices represent a few guidelines for writing effective tests. As you write more and more tests, you may come up with your own effective unit test tenets.

Using Unit Test Classes and Methods

Visual Studio 2005 provides the `Microsoft.VisualStudio.TestTools.UnitTesting` namespace, which contains the attribute classes used to define tests. Attributes are used to decorate classes and methods for execution by the unit test framework. Table 22.2 presents a list of common attribute classes used for unit testing.

TABLE 22.2   Visual Studio Test Attribute Classes

Test	Description
TestClass	Used to indicate that a class is a test class containing unit tests.
TestMethod	Used to decorate a method as a unit test. Test methods must have no return value (void) and cannot expect parameters (because there is nothing to pass parameters to the method).
TestInitialize	Used to indicate a given method should be run before each test. This capability is useful if you need to reset the system state prior to each test.
TestCleanup	Used to indicate that the method should be run after each test. You can use this method to do any cleanup after each test.

TABLE 22.2   Continued

Test	Description
ClassInitialize	Used to indicate that the method should be run once before running any tests in the class.
ClassCleanup	Used to indicate the method should run once after all tests in the class are executed.
ExpectedException	Used to indicate that a given test is expected to throw a certain exception. This capability is useful for testing expected error conditions.

The UnitTesting namespace also includes the Assert static type. This object contains a number of methods for evaluating whether the results of a test were as expected. Table 22.3 lists some key assertion methods.

TABLE 22.3   Test Assertions

Test	Description
AreSame / AreNotSame	Used to test whether two objects are the same object (or not)
AreEqual / AreNotEqual	Used to test whether two values are equal to one another (or not)
IsNull / IsNotNull	Used to test whether an object contains a null reference (or not)
IsInstanceOfType / IsNotInstanceOfType	Used to determine whether an object is of a specified type (or not)
IsTrue / IsFalse	Used to test whether a condition is true (or false)

The UnitTesting namespace contains a couple of additional assertion classes. The CollectionAssert class is used to verify the contents of collections. As an example, you can call the Contains method to assert whether a given collection contains a specific element. The StringAssert class contains methods for matching strings and portions of strings. You can use the StartsWith method, for example, to assert whether a string begins with a certain set of characters.

Creating Unit Tests

There are a few ways you can initiate the creation of unit tests. You can do so manually by creating a class file, adding the appropriate references, attributes, and the like. You can also add a unit test item to a test project via the Test menu or the context menu associated with a test project. These methods create blank unit tests to which you can add your code.

Visual Studio also provides two means of automating the creation of unit tests. You can right-click an existing class and choose CreateUnitTests. You can also run the Unit Test Wizard from the Test Items dialog box (alternatively, you can launch this wizard from the context menu of a test project by selecting Add, Unit Test). In all cases Visual Studio will actually generate a set of unit tests based on the code in your class. What gets generated is more than just stub code. Visual Studio actually examines the methods and properties in your class and writes out real, possible tests. Of course, you have to finish adding the appropriate values and assertions, but what is generated is a nice start.

Let's look at an example. Suppose you have a `Customer` object that contains standard properties such as `Name`, `Address`, `Phone`, `Email`, and so on, It also may contain methods such as `Save`, `Update`, and `Delete`. Also, suppose you choose to add a new unit test to your test project. Visual Studio will present the Create Unit Tests dialog box. Figure 22.8 shows an example.

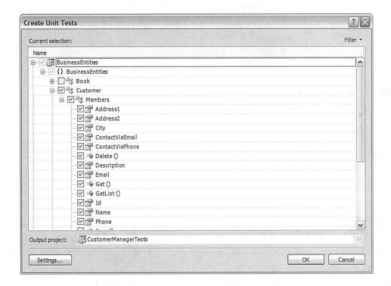

FIGURE 22.8   Unit Test Creation Wizard.

In this dialog box, you can select the members that need to have tests generated. For this example, the members of the `Customer` object have been selected. The Settings button opens a dialog box that allows you to indicate various settings for generating your unit tests. Figure 22.9 shows an example of this dialog box. Notice you can use the macro text `[File]`, `[Class]`, and `[Method]` to indicate that Visual Studio should use key portions of the class to name portions of the test.

Visual Studio generates a test for every method and every property in the object. As an example, consider the `Name` property. Listing 22.2 shows what Visual Studio generated as a unit test for this property. Notice this test creates a new instance of the `Customer` object. It then attempts to set the value of the `Name` property. Finally, it confirms that this property set was successful via the assertion. This is a valid property test. All that is left for a developer is to put a valid value into the variable `val` (note the `TODO`) and remove the `Inconclusive` assertion.

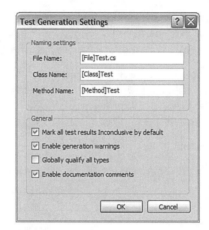

FIGURE 22.9   The Test Generation Settings dialog box.

LISTING 22.2   A Sample of an Autogenerated Unit Test

```
/// <summary>
///A test for Name
///</summary>
[TestMethod()]
public void NameTest() {
  Customer target = new Customer();
  string val = null; // TODO: Assign to an appropriate value for the property
  target.Name = val;
  Assert.AreEqual(val, target.Name,
    "BusinessEntities.Customer.Name was not set correctly.");
  Assert.Inconclusive("Verify the correctness of this test method.");
}
```

Running Unit Tests

You can run your tests from the Test Tools toolbar or the Test menu. You have a couple of options: Run with the debugger or run without. The former allows you to break into the debugger if a test fails. This capability can be useful if you are troubleshooting code through tests. The latter is a more likely scenario. You simply want to run your set of unit tests and determine their results.

The Test Tools toolbar runs all tests in a given project. You will want to use the Test Manager to run a group, list, or subset of tests. For example, if you simply want to run the Customer unit tests, you can open the Test Manager. You then would apply a filter to the All Loaded Tests list. This filter would be by Class Name. You then check which tests you want to run. Finally, from the toolbar on the test manager, you can choose a Run option. Figure 22.10 shows an example. Notice the Test Manager window on top, the Run menu item, and the Test Results window below.

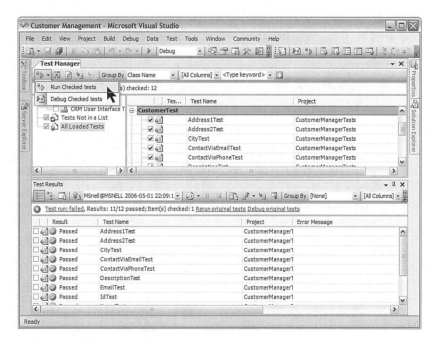

FIGURE 22.10   Running tests from the Test Manager.

NOTE

When you run a test project, only the test project is recompiled. If you make changes to a project you are testing, you must recompile that project. This approach is different from "running" applications with the debugger and can therefore take some time to get used to.

Viewing Test Results

The Test Results window provides an overview of which tests passed and which failed. Figure 22.11 shows this window in action. Notice that the given test run is considered failed if one or more tests fail. In this case, 10 of 11 tests passed. However, the overall test failed due to the one test failure.

You can navigate through the results in the Test Results window. If you double-click a test, you are presented with statistics relative to the test. The top of Figure 22.11 shows the failure information for the CityTest; this includes the error message and stack trace.

You can also publish the results of your testing to Team Foundation Server. Doing so provides vital statistics on the quality of a given build, including which tests were run and what the results were. In addition, you can right-click a test and generate a Team Systems work item. This capability is useful if you have a failure. You can right-click it and log it as a bug or task for someone to fix.

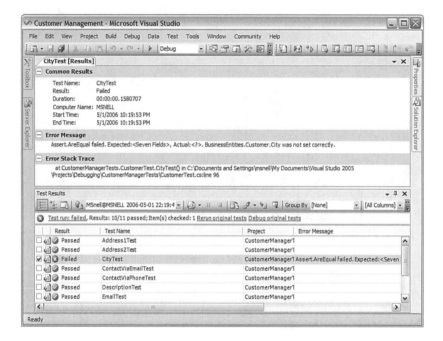

FIGURE 22.11   Test results.

Code Coverage Analysis

Automated unit tests are wonderful. However, you also need some assurance that the unit tests cover all the code in the system. This is true especially for project managers and other stakeholders. To date, they have had no real measure of how much code was being tested. Instead, they had to rely on the word of the developers (who are often also unsure).

To help solve this problem, Visual Studio provides code coverage analysis. This analysis matches unit tests to code and indicates what code is being covered and what code is not. The result is a shared view into the state of testing. For example, all your tests may pass; however, it makes for a different report if only 30% of your code is being called by those tests.

Configuring Code Coverage

Looking at code coverage can help developers write effective unit tests. It can also help to measure those tests. You configure (or turn on) code coverage for a given assembly from the .testrunconfig file. Figure 22.12 shows this file. In this example, code coverage is turned on for the BusinessEntities.dll project.

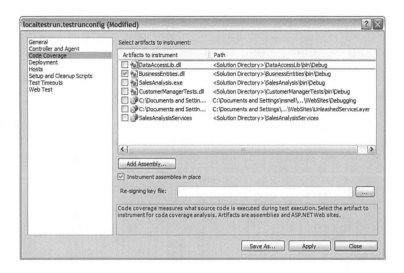

FIGURE 22.12   Configuring code coverage.

Evaluating Code Coverage

The next step is to rerun your tests. Visual Studio then captures the coverage data. This data is then presented to you in the Code Coverage Results window. You can access this window from the toolbar on the Test Results window. Figure 22.13 shows an example of these test results.

Hierarchy	Covered (% Blocks)	Not Covered (Blocks)	Not Covered...	Covered (Blocks)
Customer	71.74 %	13	28.26 %	33
Delete()	0.00 %	2	100.00 %	0
Get()	0.00 %	2	100.00 %	0
GetList()	0.00 %	2	100.00 %	0
Save()	0.00 %	2	100.00 %	0
Update()	0.00 %	2	100.00 %	0
get_Address1()	100.00 %	0	0.00 %	2
get_Address2()	100.00 %	0	0.00 %	2
get_City()	100.00 %	0	0.00 %	2
get_ContactViaEmail()	100.00 %	0	0.00 %	2
get_ContactViaPhone()	100.00 %	0	0.00 %	2
get_Description()	100.00 %	0	0.00 %	2
get_Email()	100.00 %	0	0.00 %	2
get_Id()	100.00 %	0	0.00 %	2
get_Name()	100.00 %	0	0.00 %	2
get_Phone()	100.00 %	0	0.00 %	2
get_State()	0.00 %	2	100.00 %	0
get_Zip()	100.00 %	0	0.00 %	2
set_Address1(string)	100.00 %	0	0.00 %	1
set_Address2(string)	100.00 %	0	0.00 %	1
set_City(string)	100.00 %	0	0.00 %	1

FIGURE 22.13   Code coverage results.

Notice that only approximately 72% of the code is covered inside the `Customer` class. You can navigate through this list to find gaps. Plus, you can quickly see that a number of methods do not have unit tests (0% coverage).

You can navigate to this code directly from the coverage window. In fact, you can turn on code-coloring from the Coverage toolbar. Code-coloring highlights in blue the code that is being called by the test. It turns red the code that is not called. These colors give you an easy way to find dead spots in your testing. Figure 22.14 shows an example of this coloring (although the distinction is difficult to see in this black-and-white book). The `Id` property is covered by the executing tests, but the methods below it are not.

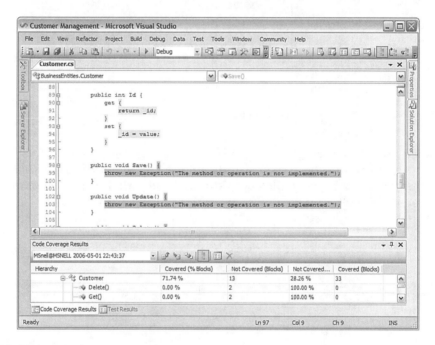

FIGURE 22.14   Code coverage coloring.

Web Testing

Testing a web user interface does not have to be a manual process. In fact, if it is, testers cannot be expected to test every permutation of a data-driven user interface. Instead, they often test a common path through the system and rely on (and hope) the other combinations produce similar results.

Visual Studio 2005 automates web testing. It provides the web test tools for this purpose. These tools enable you to record navigation paths through your site, manage these requests, bind these requests to data in a database, and then run the tests over and again. You can also review and save the test results to TFS.

Recording a Web Test

You create a new web test by adding a web test item template to a test project. When you do this, Visual Studio automatically launches the web test recording tool in the browser. The intent of this tool is to allow a tester to record a set of web requests in the system. This recording will serve as the basis for defining the web test.

As an example, suppose you want to define a web test for a Customer Manager CRM application. Assume the current release being tested contains web forms that allow a user to find customers, edit their profiles, and view their orders. The tester would then navigate to each of these features in turn using the recorder. Figure 22.15 shows an example.

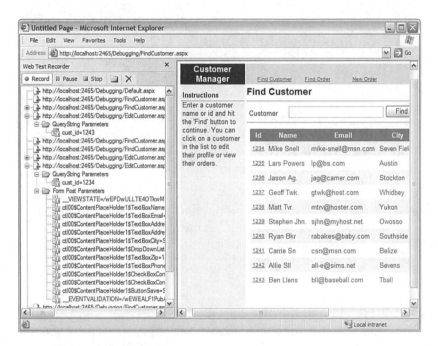

FIGURE 22.15   The Web Test Recorder.

Notice the recording being captured on the left. The Web Test Recorder provides a toolbar for pausing your recording, stopping it, deleting a request from the list, and adding comments (or notes) in between requests. Finally, notice that the details of requests containing QueryStrings and form posts are captured. We will cover more on this in a moment.

Visual Studio writes the requests to the web test upon stopping the recording. The complete set of requests is captured and contained within the test. Figure 22.16 shows the details of the sample web test inside the web test viewer.

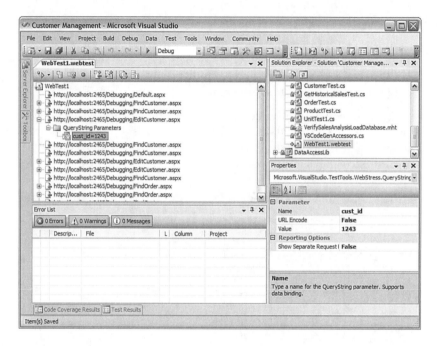

FIGURE 22.16   The recorded web test.

Notice the web test toolbar. The buttons on this toolbar allow you to (from left to right) rerun the test, bind the test to a data source, set user credentials for test execution, do more recording, set a web test plug-in, set a request plug-in, generate code from the web test, and parameterize web servers. We will cover most of these items in the following sections.

Managing Web Test Requests

The requests in the web test can be manipulated. You can move them up and down in the list (they are run in order), delete them, and add new requests between them. When you define an effective web test, you should be sure to cover all requests and possible request conditions. However, you often end up with a lot of redundancy in your recorded requests. Therefore, it makes sense to go through each request and pare down your test to the essentials.

In the example, you want the following list of requests:

- Request for the home page (`Default.aspx`)

- Request to `FindCustomers.aspx`

- A form post on `FindCustomers.aspx` that searches for customers by clicking the Find button

- Request to `EditCustomer.aspx` that passes the customer ID on the `QueryString`

- A form post on `EditCustomer.aspx` that saves the details of the customer using the Save button

- Request to `FindOrder.aspx` that passes the customer name on the `QueryString` (from the `FindCustomer` page)

- A form post on `FindOrder.aspx` that searches for a customer's order based on the user's entering a portion of the customer name and clicking the Find button

You can see that this list covers all the bases for the pages you are testing. Figure 22.17 shows the list cleaned up inside the IDE.

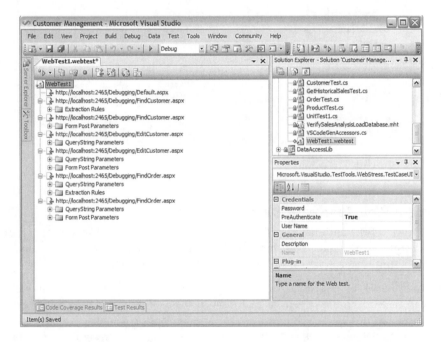

FIGURE 22.17   Cleaned-up web tests.

Running the Web Test and Viewing Results

You can run your web test from the web test toolbar. When you do so, Visual Studio executes each request and captures all statistics relative to the same. This includes the outcome of the request, its size, response time, and actual details of what happened. Figure 22.18 shows the results of the web test created earlier.

Notice that you can navigate each request and view its details. These details can be stored for later review. This provides proof of what exactly happened when the test ran. You have access to the actual HTML that was returned, the request details, the response details, the context of the request, and other details such as exceptions and extraction rules (we will look at these rules in a moment).

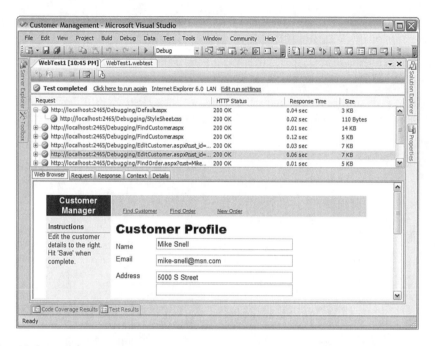

FIGURE 22.18   Web test results.

Seeding a Web Test with Data

The real power of the automated web test is the capability to seed it with data from a database. In this way, you can test many more possible permutations of your web application. This is simply not practical when you're doing manual testing.

Using the example, you have a few options for database seeding. First, say you want to be able to call the edit profile screen for each user in the database. You then might also want to save those profiles back to the database. As another option you might also seed the find pages with data elements and filter the lists accordingly. Running this small number of tests with a lot of data rows should give the web interface a good workout.

Defining the Web Test Data Source

The first step is to define a source for the data that will seed your web test. You can do this from the web test toolbar (database icon). Selecting this toolbar button brings up the Connection Properties dialog box, which is the standard database connection dialog box.

After you define the connection information, Visual Studio asks which tables you want to use for the web test. You select them in the Choose Tables dialog box. For the example, use the customer and order tables.

Figure 22.19 shows the data source added to the test. You can add multiple data sources to a given test. These data sources are specific to each test. That is, they do not have an effect on any other portion of your code. Finally, notice that in the figure the customer table is selected and its properties are shown. Here, you can set how data is accessed or loaded for each web test. You can have that data pulled in one of the following ways:

- **Random**—Access rows in the table randomly.

- **Sequential**—Access each row in the table in order. After the entire table has been executed, the process will start over (loop) for the duration of a load test.

- **Unique**—The same as sequential without the looping.

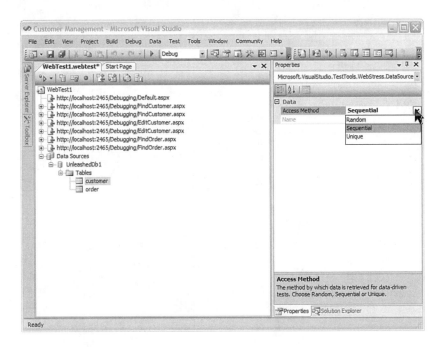

FIGURE 22.19   Web test data source.

As you can see, this setting is more important in a load test where the test is executed over a duration of time. In a web test, you will indicate how many (or all) rows you want to execute as part of the test.

Binding Tests to Data

The next step is to bind the tests to the data. Typically, binding is done to the QueryString parameters and the form post values. To bind the parameters and values, you select the QueryString parameter from beneath the given request in the web test. You then view the properties of the parameter. Here, you can set the value property to a field in the database. Figure 22.20 shows an example.

Before you run the test, you must tell the tool to run your web test once per row in the database. You can also determine a fixed count for your web test. You modify this setting through the .testrunconfig file. Figure 22.21 shows an example. Here, you select the option button One Run Per Data Source Row.

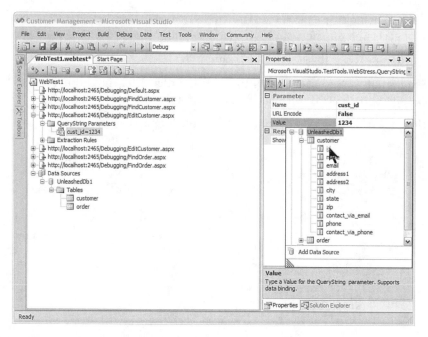

FIGURE 22.20   Binding the test to the data.

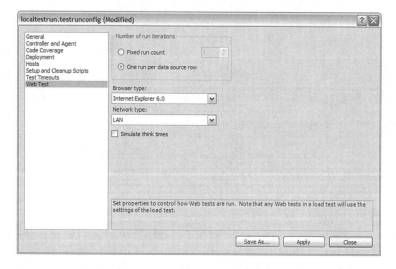

FIGURE 22.21   Configuring the web test to run once per data row.

Finally, you run the web tests. The tool will take care of pulling the data from the table and executing each test once per row in the database. Each execution is considered a run. All runs are saved and presented in a list for your review.

Figure 22.22 shows the results of the sample runs. Notice that run 2 executed fine but run 3 had errors. This is what you hope to find with a web test: errors that only present themselves based on certain data conditions. In this case the value stored in the state field in the database cannot be found in the drop-down list control on the user interface. You can take this test and generate the appropriate work item bug to get the problem fixed.

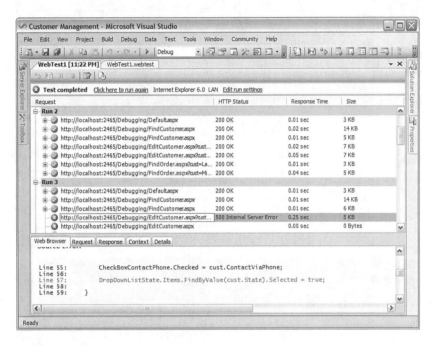

FIGURE 22.22   Web test results.

Binding to Form Posts

Thus far, we've looked at binding a simple request to a data source. Next, we want to examine how to bind a form post to the database. The good news is that the process works the same way. The form post parameters are listed in the web test request. Each parameter can then be bound to a database field from the Properties window.

The web test example has a few form posts: each time the user clicks the Find button to search for a customer, again when he or she searches for an order, and then when the user clicks Save to write customer details to the database. The first two posts you simply bind to the name field on the customer table. This will ensure each customer name is searched for in the list. Searching for all customer names in the database will provide a nice test that is easy to configure. However, if you prefer to seed this test with your own values (not from the database), you can take a couple of steps: Create an object or XML data source with your own values or simply copy the test and manually enter a series of search values (one for each copy).

To bind the save parameters, you need to ensure the `QueryString` parameter is bound to the `customer.id` field and then bind each form element to a field on the customer table.

In this case, you have text boxes, a drop-down, and some check boxes. Figure 22.23 shows the results of the binding.

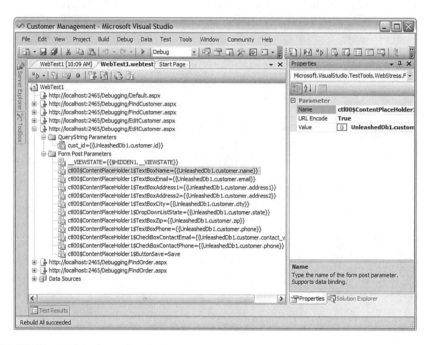

FIGURE 22.23   A data-bound web test.

The final step is to run the tests and view the results. Figure 22.24 shows the results of the web test created earlier. Notice that we have navigated to the EditCustomer.aspx test. Clicking the Context tab in the results window will show you the context in which the test was run. In this case, you can see which values were used to seed the test (and thereby posted to the form and saved).

> **TIP**
>
> Visual Studio provides complete control over the web tests for those testers who can write code. On the web test toolbar, there is an option to generate code. Selecting this option will create a class file that represents the web test. The web test uses the Microsoft.VisualStudio. TestTools.WebTesting namespace and can be coded manually or edited from this generated code. Listing 22.3 shows a portion of the generated code. This test is for the FindOrder.aspx page. The QueryString and the post parameters are bound to the database.

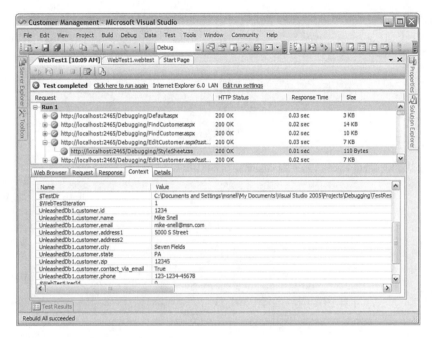

FIGURE 22.24   Data-bound web test results.

LISTING 22.3   Web Test Autogenerated Code

```
WebTestRequest request7 = new
  WebTestRequest("http://localhost:2465/Debugging/FindOrder.aspx");
request7.Method = "POST";
request7.QueryStringParameters.Add("cust",
  this.Context["UnleashedDb1.customer.name"].ToString(), false, false);
FormPostHttpBody request7Body = new FormPostHttpBody();
request7Body.FormPostParameters.Add("__VIEWSTATE",
  this.Context["$HIDDEN1.__VIEWSTATE"].ToString());
request7Body.FormPostParameters.Add("ctl00$ContentPlaceHolder1$TextBoxCustomer",
  this.Context["UnleashedDb1.customer.name"].ToString());
request7Body.FormPostParameters.Add(
➥"ctl00$ContentPlaceHolder1$Button1", "Find Order");
request7.Body = request7Body;
yield return request7;
```

Extracting Values from Web Tests

You can further refine your web tests by creating your own extraction rules. These rules allow you to extract key information from the request and save it as part of the test results. As an example, you might want to extract the values inside an HTML attribute such as an anchor tag's URL or button's name. Other examples might include extracting text from the page, form field values, values of hidden fields, and so on. Figure 22.25 shows an example.

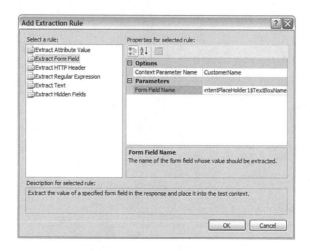

FIGURE 22.25   Defining the extraction rule.

You access this dialog box by right-clicking a web test request and choosing Add Extraction Rule. From here, you can define various rule types. For this example, say you are creating a rule to extract the value from a form field, TextBoxName. Notice that this rule's Context Parameter Name is CustomerName. This name will allow you to identify the parameter in your test results. Figure 22.26 shows these results. On the Context tab, you can find the extracted values. Also, on the Details tab (not shown), you can review the results of your extraction tests.

Linking Pages with Extracted Values

In addition to viewing these extracted values, you can also use this information to link requests together. You can pull a value from one page and then pass it to another. For example, when defining the extraction rule, you gave the parameter a name, CustomerName. This name becomes a variable name that you can use inside the Properties window when binding test items to values. Figure 22.27 shows an example of binding the CustomerName extracted value to the FindOrder.aspx search request.

Requesting Validation Rules

You can also add validation rules to each of the requests in your web test. Validation rules allow you to check a page (or request) for certain expected values. These additional tests are run against the request. Validation rules include the capability to check for expected form field values, verify HTML tags, check expected request times, and more.

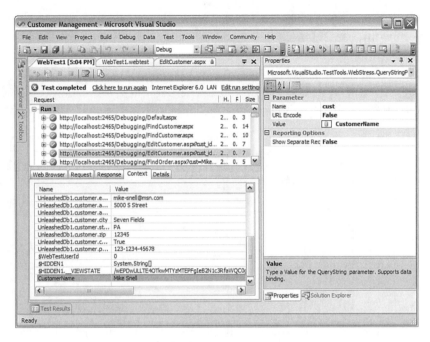

FIGURE 22.26   Viewing the extracted value.

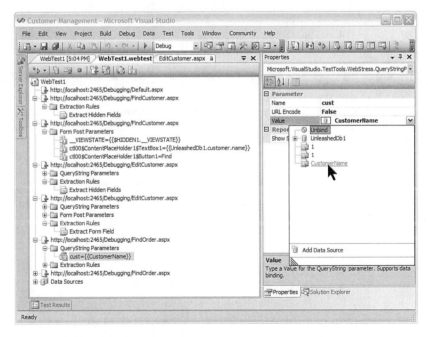

FIGURE 22.27   Binding to the extraction.

You add a validation rule by right-clicking a web test request and choosing Add Validation Rule. Selecting this option brings up the Add Validation Rule dialog box. Here, you can define the rule type and its parameters.

As an example, on the FindCustomer.aspx page, a set of instructions is loaded on the master page. You can create a validation rule to check for these instructions. To do so, you create a FindText validation rule and enter the appropriate parameters. Figure 22.28 shows an example.

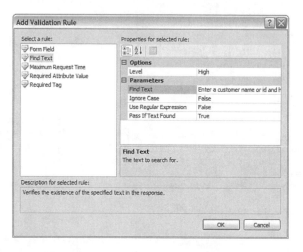

FIGURE 22.28   Defining a validation rule.

> **NOTE**
>
> Validation rules can sometimes have an effect on performance. Therefore, you can use the Level property to indicate when a given validation rule should run. Typically, you set your validation rules to High and then on a load test you indicate that you want to run tests on a Low level to get a more accurate view of performance.

The results of the validation rule are shown on the Details tab for the request. Figure 22.29 shows the results of the sample validation rule.

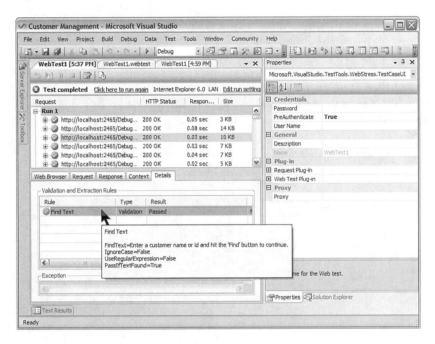

FIGURE 22.29   Validation rule results.

Load Testing

It is important to know how your application handles user load. Typically, you will define a performance benchmark for the application. This benchmark is best represented in terms of the number of users that an application can support at a given time (concurrent users). Without load testing, it is very difficult to know whether you have reached your goal. Clearly, you do not want to wait until after deployment to find out whether you've fallen short of your benchmark.

Visual Studio Team Test provides a load testing tool to do just that. With it, you can create a load test. The load test can be configured to simulate multiple users accessing a site concurrently. While the load test runs, you capture instrumentation output from the environment. This data lets you know how the environment and your application held up under stress.

Creating a Load Test

Visual Studio provides a load test wizard to walk you through the process of creating a load test. The good news is that load tests leverage the web and unit tests you've already defined for the initial stages of application testing. By walking through the wizard steps, you can select the existing tests you will use to simulate load and then configure the actual load. The load test is then added to a testing project where it, too, can be saved, edited, versioned, and run over and again.

Let's walk through an example with the New Load Test Wizard. You will simulate load on the customer management application and will leverage the web test created previously. Recall that this test hits most of the pages in the site and is fed from the database.

Starting the New Load Test Wizard

You launch the New Load Test Wizard by simply adding a load test to a test project. The first screen of the wizard is introductory in nature. Figure 22.30 shows an example.

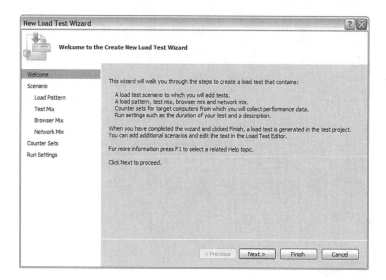

FIGURE 22.30   The New Load Test Wizard welcome screen.

Defining Your Load Scenario

You define a name for your scenario on the second screen of the New Load Test Wizard. This name is simply a label for the test to help others understand exactly what you want to test. For this example, load test the FindCustomer.aspx, EditCustomer.aspx, and FindOrder.aspx pages. Therefore, call this scenario Find and edit customer, find order.

The second screen also allows you to define a *think time* profile. Think times represent the time a user might spend thinking between requests. This time is used to read the page, fill it out, and so on. Think times are important in that you want to simulate actual users with your load test. You have a few options here. You can use recorded think times. These times were recorded when you created the web test. Therefore, this is a great option. You can smooth out these recorded think times by indicating a standard distribution based on the recorded think times. Last, you can turn think times off altogether. This setting is useful only if you are trying to spike load on the server (and not simulate users).

Finally, the second screen allows you to indicate the time between test iterations. This value is in seconds. It is useful if you know something about your users. For example, if you know that approximately every 5 seconds a user initiates a find-and-edit customer process, you could indicate that number here. Figure 22.31 shows the sample setup for the scenario.

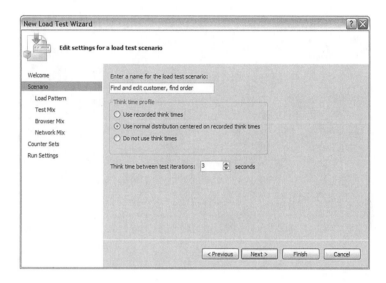

FIGURE 22.31   Defining the scenario using the New Load Test Wizard.

Defining a Load Pattern for Your Test

The next wizard screen is used to indicate a pattern for the load test. You have a couple of options here: constant load and stepped load. The first allows you to execute the test with a steady, constant load of users. For standard load testing scenarios, this is sufficient. You already have think times for the users. If you want to test how the system performs with a constant, target load, you would use this setting.

Stepping the load represents a different twist on the load test. For example, you might be trying to determine how the system behaves as more and more users are added to the load. This capability is great if you are testing for a breaking point or bottleneck relative to server and application stress. To define your stepped load, you indicate a starting number of users and a maximum number of users to be stepped up to. You then indicate the time period (duration) between each jump (or step) and the size of each step. Figure 22.32 shows an example of a stepped load.

Choosing Tests to Simulate Load

On the next screen of the wizard, you choose the tests to run to simulate the user load. You can add multiple web tests and unit tests based on your scenario. You can then choose the percentage distribution of each test relative to the overall load test.

For example, suppose you have a web test to simulate editing customers and another for looking up their orders. You might also know that for every five customer edits, users do an order lookup. In this case, you can distribute these two tests across your load test. The customer web test would represent 80% of the load, and the order web test would be the other 20%.

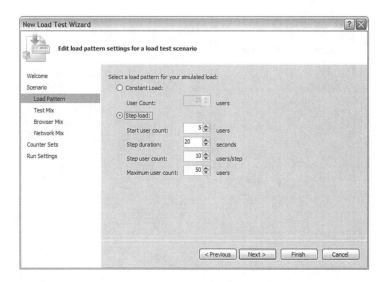

FIGURE 22.32   Defining the load pattern using the New Load Test Wizard.

The example shows one web test created for simulating load. Figure 22.33 shows an example of the Test Mix screen.

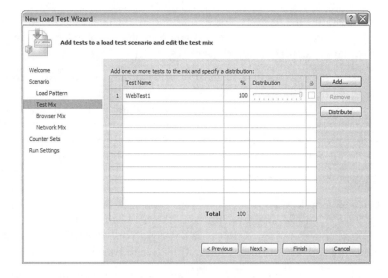

FIGURE 22.33   Defining tests using the New Load Test Wizard.

NOTE

Remember to set your web test data source to pull data randomly or sequentially. If you use the Unique setting, then each row will be pulled from the database and the load test will report an error, indicating there was insufficient data to finish the test.

Indicating a Browser Mix

The fifth screen of the load test allows you to simulate the browsers that users might use to visit your application. Again, you can distribute these browsers across a percentage. Figure 22.34 shows an example.

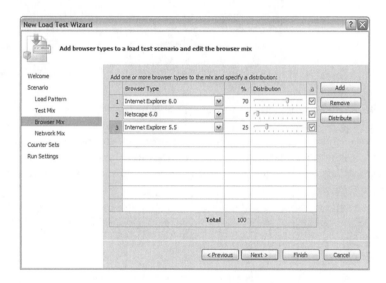

FIGURE 22.34   Defining the browser mix using the New Load Test Wizard.

Indicating a Network Mix

Next, you indicate the user's network mix. If you know that 100% of the users are on the LAN, then you can indicate that information here. If, however, a portion of the user base comes from outside the LAN, you can set up that distribution on this page. Of course, setting up the distribution this way requires you to have some data about your user base (or do projections). Figure 22.35 shows an example of this screen.

Choosing Computers to Monitor

The next screen in the wizard is used to determine which servers the load test should monitor. If your application is distributed on multiple servers, you would indicate the details of these computers here. You also want to indicate the controller computer. This is the computer running the tests. Of course, for best results you will want the controller computer and the server computers to be physically different machines.

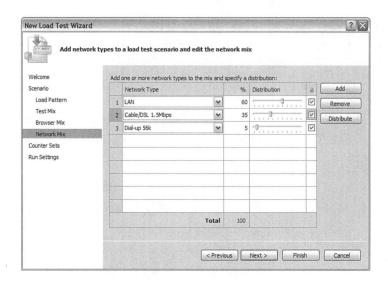

FIGURE 22.35   Defining the network mix using the New Load Test Wizard.

In addition, for each computer you intend to monitor, you can define a counter set. A counter set represents a standard set of performance indicators you want to monitor. There are counter sets for IIS, SQL, and so on. Figure 22.36 shows an example of the Counter Sets screen.

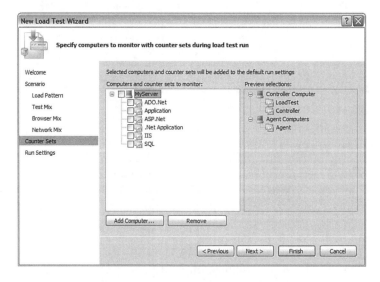

FIGURE 22.36   Defining counters using the New Load Test Wizard.

Indicating Execution Timings and Run Settings

The final screen of the wizard is used to define configuration settings for the load test. These settings include the timings, the number of errors to trap, and the validation level. Recall the validation level from the web tests; this is the level of validations to run to simulate load. If, for example, you define a number of validations for your web test, these validations take away from performance and have nothing to do with simulating actual users. Therefore, you can indicate a level here that excludes these validations. Figure 22.37 shows an example of this final screen in the wizard.

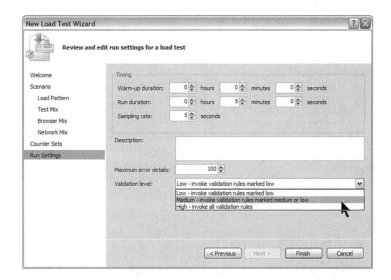

FIGURE 22.37   Configuring run settings using the New Load Test Wizard.

Reviewing and Editing a Load Test

When the wizard finishes, it creates a `.loadtest` file. This file can be opened and edited within the IDE. Figure 22.38 shows an example of the file open in the IDE. Notice that each section defined in the wizard is represented here.

If you need to edit an item, you can select it and modify its settings through the Properties window. You can also right-click a section and bring up an editor. For example, if you want to change the Network mix, you can right-click this section and choose Edit Network Mix to bring up a dialog box that looks just like the wizard page for this setting.

Running Load Tests and Reviewing Results

You are finally ready to run the load test. When you click the Run button on the load test page (refer to Figure 22.38), Visual Studio opens the load test monitor window. This window is shown in Figure 22.39.

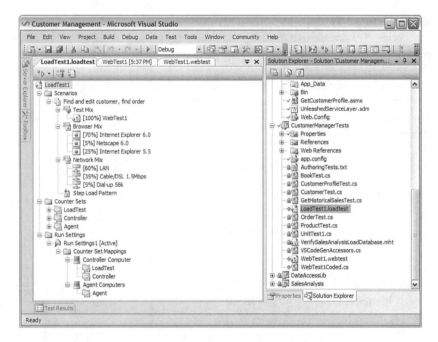

FIGURE 22.38   The load test viewer.

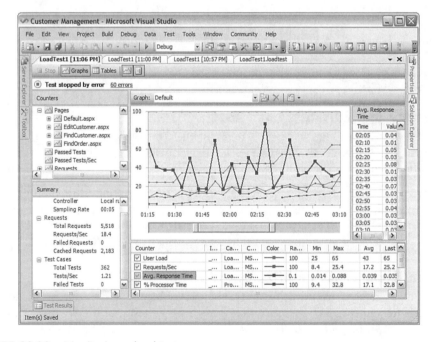

FIGURE 22.39   Monitoring a load test.

If you have used the Performance Monitor in Windows, you will find similarities with this screen. At the center of the monitor is a graph that tracks the counters over time. The counters being tracked are listed at the bottom of the screen, along with their general statistics. It is helpful to select one of these counters to see the line of the graph highlighted. Notice that the figure focuses on the Average Response Time for the duration of 1:45 to 2:30. You can also see in the counter window the average response time and the minimum and maximum times. Everything here responds in less than a second (0.088 max).

There are a couple of other windows here. The Counters window to the left allows you to navigate counters and add them to the monitor. The Summary window shows a summary view of the tests. You can locate some key statistics in this window, such as the total requests, requests per second, use of the cache, and so on.

Last, when the load test stops running, the data is stored. You can work with this data and review it in detail. In addition, you can look for trends and breaking points. You can also review errors that occurred during execution. In the example, there were 60 errors. However, these errors were all the result of a bad counter that could not be found.

Manual Tests

Even with all the automated testing inside Team Test, a user will still need to perform some tests manually. The good news is that these tests can be defined for the project and tracked just like other tests.

Creating a Manual Test

You create a manual test by adding the manual test item to a test project. A manual test can be defined as a text file or a Word document. Manual tests have the extension .mht and are stored inside the test project.

As an example, suppose that you want a tester to view a page in your application to confirm its layout across browsers. You can define a manual test to do just that. Figure 22.40 shows an example. You give the test a title and indicate the steps to execute the test.

Executing a Manual Test

You run a manual test the same way you run all other tests. In fact, if you execute a manual test as part of a group (using the Test Manager), that manual test will be presented to the tester for completion. In addition, the details of the manual test's execution will be saved as part of the test results. This ensures that all test results make it back to the team.

Figure 22.41 shows the sample manual test inside the IDE. Notice that the tester must indicate the test results (pass/fail). The tester can also add comments here. In addition, the actual test that the tester must perform is shown in the space at the bottom of the window.

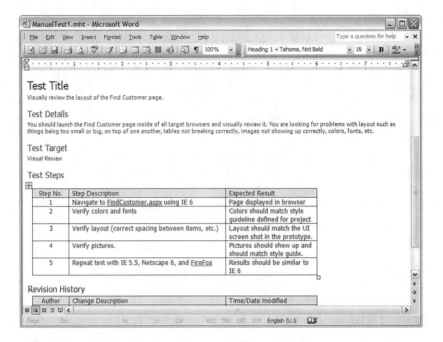

FIGURE 22.40   A manual test in Word.

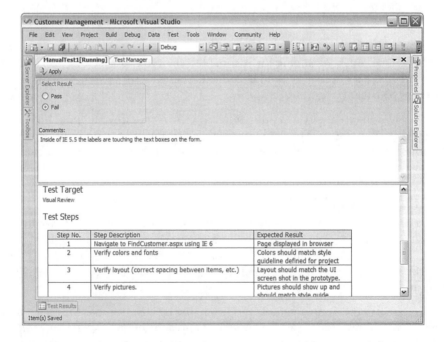

FIGURE 22.41   Executing the manual test.

Generic Tests

A generic test is used to wrap existing test code and have that code executed as part of the testing system. Performing a generic test ensures that the result of these test scripts will be published along with the other application test results.

You create a generic test by adding it to a test project. Figure 22.42 shows some of the fields used to define generic tests.

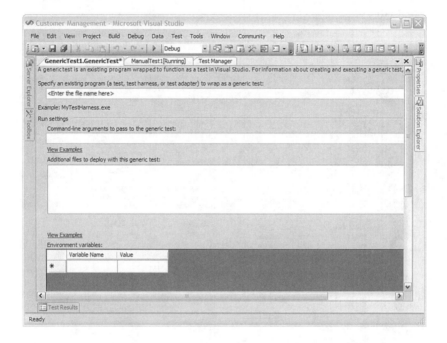

FIGURE 22.42   A generic test.

Generic tests are outside the bounds of a typical testing scenario for most applications. It is good to know, however, that they exist in case you ever need them. For more information, including a detailed walkthrough of generic tests, you can search MSDN for "Generic Tests."

Ordered Tests

The last test we need to look at is the ordered test. An ordered test is simply a test you create that groups and orders other tests. This type of test can be useful if you want to define an overall module test, for instance. The ordered test is treated as a single test even though it groups many tests. This is also true for the results of an ordered test. The ordered test either fails or succeeds.

Creating an Ordered Test

You add an ordered test to a test project just like any other test. You can then use the ordered test definition window to add any type of test to the ordered test, with the exception of a load test. Load tests are outside the bounds of an ordered test.

Figure 22.43 shows an example of an ordered test. You can select tests from the left and add them to the ordered test on the right. You can then choose the order in which these items get executed. Finally, you can indicate whether the ordered test should continue upon the first failure.

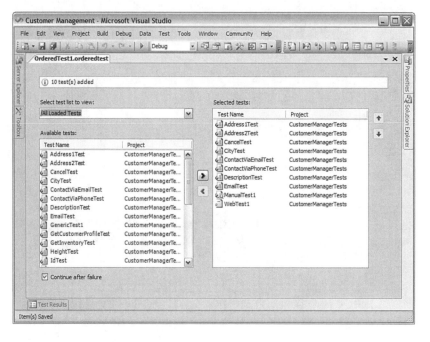

FIGURE 22.43 An ordered test.

Summary

You have seen how developers can build unit tests to increase the quality of their code and the code they deliver to production. You have also seen the power of Visual Studio Team Test to create web tests, load tests, manual tests, generic tests, and ordered tests. Some key points in this chapter include the following:

- You can define a test project to group test items.

- A Test Manager tool enables you to review and group tests inside the IDE.

- You configure test settings through the .testrunconfig file.

- Developers create code called unit tests that run their application code and assert the expected results.

- You can record a navigation path through a web application and save these requests as a web test.

- The parameters of a web test can be seeded from a data source.

- You can leverage your web and unit tests to define load tests.

- Load tests can be configured to simulate actual users visiting your site.

- You can define a manual test for execution by a tester. The results of this test can be maintained along with the other tests.

- You can create an ordered test to treat a group of tests as a single, atomic test.

22

CHAPTER 23

Team Foundation Build

IN THIS CHAPTER

- An Overview of Team Foundation Build

- Creating a New Build

- Starting a Build

- Monitoring and Analyzing Builds

The last Visual Studio Team System tool we will cover in this book is Team Foundation Build (TFB). It is distributed as part of the Team Foundation Server and, like the other tools we have discussed, is an integrated part of the overall project experience offered by VSTS.

As projects march through their lifecycle, you reach a point at which it is time to pull together all the various components, compile them, distribute them, and test them. This overall process is known as a *build*. And as you will see, building software is much more than simply compiling source code into executable binaries. In fact, builds can be amazingly complex and can involve a huge amount of manual work by various members of the project team. This process presents some unique issues:

- The lack of a comprehensive, universal set of build tools that integrate with the project environment leads to unpredictable and unrepeatable ad hoc build processes.

- Monitoring the build process and gaining an understanding of the health of any given build can be difficult.

- Typically, no mechanisms are available to troubleshoot problems when they occur within a build.

Team Foundation Build is intended to automate many aspects of the build process and address the problems listed here by providing the entire project team with a holistic set of tools for creating and analyzing builds.

This chapter covers the capabilities of the Team Foundation Build tool. It overviews the basics of build systems, discusses how a typical build process is accommodated within Visual Studio Team System, and details the ways you can interact with the build tools from within Visual Studio.

An Overview of Team Foundation Build

Many development organizations leverage a build lab to create both public and private builds of their software releases. Distilled to its basics, a build lab is a set of hardware and software resources that take all the source code files from the team project, centralize them on a Build server, and then compile the system with all the latest changes. Ideally, this build is then packed up and copied over to a central, accessible location that everyone on the team can access. Quality Assurance (QA) resources are then free to run their test suites against the software and determine what sorts of changes need to be fed back to the development team.

Team Foundation Build's stated goal is to provide a build lab in a box. In essence, it strives to eliminate much of the manual work from the build process while at the same time enabling team members to gain information about the health of a particular build. The Team Foundation Build platform provides a variety of benefits to the project team:

- It enables a build process to be constructed and initiated quickly and easily from within Visual Studio.

- It provides the project team with the tools necessary to determine the overall health of the build.

- It allows for build-to-build comparison for a historical look at overall project progress as each build is created and tested.

Team Foundation Build Architecture

Team Foundation Build services are provided by four subsystems within the Visual Studio Team System ecosystem. Each plays a specific role in the high-level build process:

- The Team Build client (Visual Studio) will define a build (which can be stored in the Team Foundation Source Control system) and then initiate the build.

- The Team Foundation Server application tier will listen for any build requests that come through from the Team Build client; it then passes off the build request to the Build server.

- The Build server is the workhorse here: It runs the Team Build Service, which will examine the specifics of the build, grab the necessary files from the source control system, compile the source files, run tests, and publish results. Notifications of the build completion can then be sent to the team. In addition, the Build server will publish the build out to a specified location.

- The Team Foundation Server data tier fills its typical role as data repository: The build details and log events are all stored here, allowing the Build client to view and analyze the build.

Figure 23.1 identifies how these components work with one another.

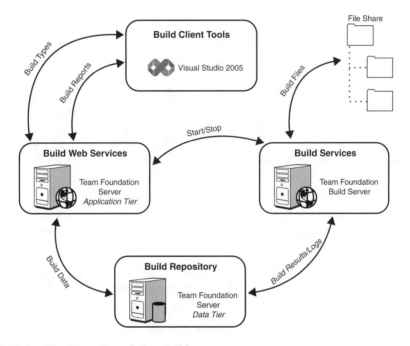

FIGURE 23.1   The Team Foundation Build system.

NOTE

The diagram presented in Figure 23.1 is a logical architecture. The Team Foundation system can be physically structured in a variety of ways. For example, although it makes sense to have a dedicated Build server for larger projects, you could host the Build server on the same machine that is hosting the Team Foundation Server application tier or, for that matter, the data tier.

In fact, for very large projects, it may make sense to have an entire farm of Build machines running the Build server components.

The Team Build Client

Team Explorer, hosted inside Visual Studio, functions as the primary client for the Team Foundation Build system. Within Team Explorer, builds are managed and configured through the Builds node. Under the Builds node, every defined build within the scope of the current team project is visible. Each of these entities represents a variety of settings, including which files should be incorporated in the build, what tests should be run as part of the build, where the build should be published, and so on.

Figure 23.2 shows a list of build definitions (known as a *build types*) within the Team Explorer window.

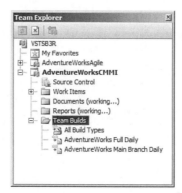

FIGURE 23.2   Builds within the Team Explorer window.

The Application Tier

The Team Foundation Server application tier exposes Team Foundation Build as a set of four web services (see Chapter 18, "Managing and Working with Team Projects," for a look at all the web services implemented by the TFS application tier machine):

- The Build Controller web service exposes the API for managing and controlling builds. It is capable, for instance, of issuing start and stop commands for a build and signaling build completion, among other things.

- The Build Store web service provides methods for saving and retrieving build information to the TFS data tier.

- The Build Integration web service allows the Build server and other clients to interface with other team project entities.

- The Publish Test Results web service is the API used to distribute test results run against the build to the project team as a whole.

The Build Server

As mentioned previously, the Build server is the core engine that really implements the build process. It consists of a windows service (named Team Build Service) that processes commands issued from the application tier. This service is responsible for invoking the underlying build engine (MSBuild) based on the build information retrieved from the build database. We'll discuss the MSBuild technology later in this chapter.

The Build Repository

The build repository is implemented by the Team Foundation Server data tier within its own SQL Server database called `TfsBuild`. This database contains more than 20 tables that store information related to build definitions, test results, and related work items.

As an example of the information stored here, Figure 23.3 shows the data model for a few of the core tables used to define a build.

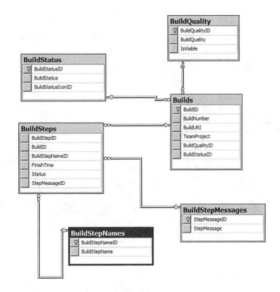

FIGURE 23.3   Partial data model for the Build database.

Now that you have the fundamentals in hand, it's time to see how to manage the build process within the Visual Studio Team System.

Creating a New Build

Team Foundation Build uses the concept of build types. A build type is simply the container for all the configuration information related to a build. In essence, it defines all the different parts of a particular build.

You create a new build type by using the Team Explorer window. Right-click the Team Builds node and then select New Team Build Type. This will launch the New Build Type Creation Wizard.

Specifying New Build Information

The wizard will ask a series of questions about the desired build process. After you've provided the answers, the wizard will write them out into a specific file format used by the build engine.

Naming the Build

The first step is to provide a name for the build. This is the same name that is reflected within the Team Explorer Builds node and in the build reports. Figure 23.4 shows the first page in the build type wizard.

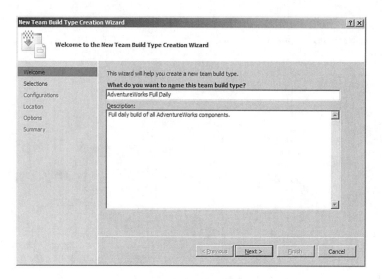

FIGURE 23.4   Specifying the build type name.

Selecting the Solutions to Build

The second step involves selecting the projects that you want to be included as a part of the build (see Figure 23.5). The drop-down at the top of the wizard page is used to essentially filter the list of available projects based on a given workspace (refer to Chapter 19, "Source Control," for a discussion of workspaces). Every solution that exists in the workspace selected in the drop-down will be displayed in the list box. Checking or unchecking the individual solutions will include or exclude them from the build.

Note that this page of the wizard also allows you to specify the order of the build. The order is important in cases in which there may be an order dependency between the different binaries generated between solutions. You change the build order of the solutions by using the up and down arrows next to the list of solutions.

Selecting the Build Configurations

Build configurations dictate parameters for the build such as whether this is a release or debug build, and what the target CPU platform is. You can specify multiple configurations on the third page of the wizard (see Figure 23.6); they will be built in the order shown.

Providing a Build Location

Team Foundation Build will need to know which server to use as the Build server. Remember, you must have already prepared this server as a Build server by running the appropriate setup files from the Team Foundation Server install media; this will deploy the build service onto the server (which must, of course, be running before you can start a build).

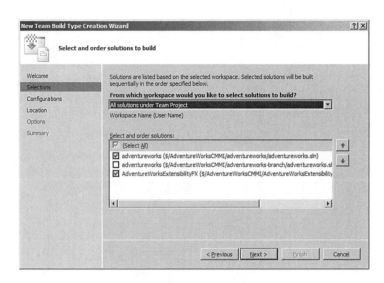

FIGURE 23.5   Selecting the projects to build.

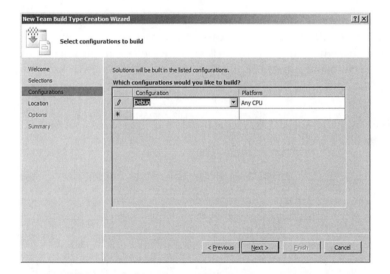

FIGURE 23.6   Selecting the build configuration.

The build engine will need to know where to place the build files locally on the Build server and where the build output should be published so that the team can access it. All of these parameters are captured on the Location page of the wizard, shown in Figure 23.7.

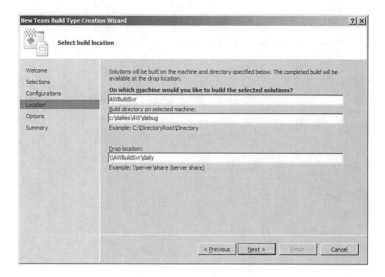

FIGURE 23.7   Supplying location information for the build.

Selecting Build Tests

Tests can be run as part of the build process. This next page of the build type wizard (see Figure 23.8) gathers information on which tests should be run during or after the build process. By selecting a test metadata file, you can pick and choose from among any of the tests defined within the Team Project (team project tests were covered in the preceding chapter).

By using the bottom check box, you can elect to run static code analysis against the source files included in the build.

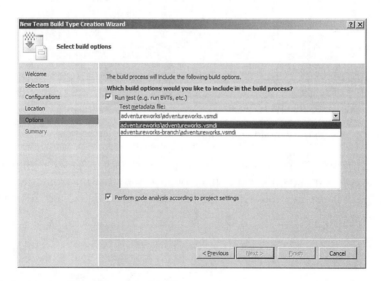

FIGURE 23.8   Options for testing the build.

Confirming Your Selections

The sixth and final page of the New Team Build Type Creation Wizard (see Figure 23.9) summarizes all the build definition selections you have made.

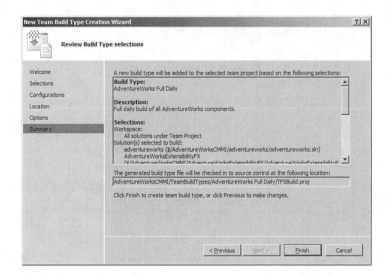

FIGURE 23.9   Validating the build type information.

Clicking Finish will do two things: It will write the various build settings into an XML file called TFSBuild.proj, and it will add that XML file to the source control system within a new project that is named the same as the build.

For instance, Figure 23.10 shows two new build projects as they appear within the Source Control Explorer window. They are located under the team project node and then within a folder labeled TeamBuildTypes.

Editing a Build Type

TFSBuild.proj is an XML file used as input to the MSBuild engine. Visual Studio Team System does not offer a user interface for making changes to a build after it has been initially defined. To do this, you need to directly edit the TFSBuild.proj file.

The TFSBuild.proj Project File

Listing 23.1 shows the results of a complete sample AdventureWorks build type as it is represented within the TFSBuild.proj file. Reading through the XML, you will notice that it has captured all the major build type information categories within its individual nodes: There are nodes for storing general build, solution, configuration, location, and test option information.

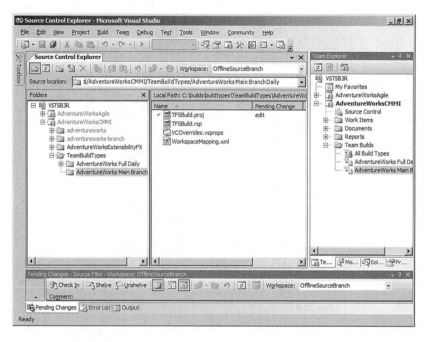

FIGURE 23.10   Build type files in the Source Control Explorer.

TIP

You are not limited to a stock set of build tasks. It is fairly straightforward to extend any given build type with custom tasks that will run during the build process. Because a task is really just a body of code that is executed during the build, creating a new task involves writing code to implement your custom action. For information on how to extend a build using custom tasks, see the MSDN topic "Walkthrough: Extending Team Foundation Build."

The XML in the build project files is extremely well commented, and the files are fairly short. Editing a build project file is straightforward and simple. As an example, if you wanted to change the server used as the Build server, you would edit the following XML node:

```
<BuildMachine>NewBuildServer</BuildMachine>
```

LISTING 23.1   Sample Build File

```
<?xml version="1.0" encoding="utf-8"?>
<Project DefaultTargets="DesktopBuild"
➥xmlns="http://schemas.microsoft.com/developer/msbuild/2003">
  <!-- TO EDIT BUILD TYPE DEFINITION
```

LISTING 23.1   Continued

```
To edit the build type, you will need to edit this file which was generated
➥by the Create New Build Type wizard.  This file is under source control and
➥needs to be checked out before making any changes.

The file is available at - $/{TeamProjectName}/TeamBuildTypes/{BuildTypeName}
➥where you will need to replace TeamProjectName and BuildTypeName with your
➥Team Project and Build Type name that you created

Checkout the file
   1. Open Source Control Explorer by selecting View -> Other Windows ->
➥Source Control Explorer
   2. Ensure that your current workspace has a mapping for the
➥$/{TeamProjectName}/TeamBuildTypes folder and that you have done a
➥ "Get Latest Version" on that folder
   3. Browse through the folders to {TeamProjectName}->TeamBuildTypes->
➥{BuildTypeName} folder
   4. From the list of files available in this folder, right click on
➥TfsBuild.Proj. Select 'Check Out For Edit...'

Make the required changes to the file and save

Checkin the file
   1. Right click on the TfsBuild.Proj file selected in Step 3 above and
➥select 'Checkin Pending Changes'
   2. Use the pending checkin dialog to save your changes to the source control

Once the file is checked in with the modifications, all future builds using
➥this build type will use the modified settings
   -->
   <!-- Do not edit this -->
   <Import Project="$(MSBuildExtensionsPath)\Microsoft\VisualStudio\
➥v8.0\TeamBuild\Microsoft.TeamFoundation.Build.targets" />
   <ProjectExtensions>
     <!-- DESCRIPTION
     The description is associated with a build type. Edit the value for making
➥changes.
     -->
     <Description>Full daily build of all AdventureWorks components.</Description>
     <!-- BUILD MACHINE
     Name of the machine which will be used to build the solutions selected.
     -->
     <BuildMachine>VSTSb3</BuildMachine>
   </ProjectExtensions>
   <PropertyGroup>
```

23

LISTING 23.1   Continued

```
<!--  TEAM PROJECT
The team project which will be built using this build type.
-->
<TeamProject>AdventureWorksCMMI</TeamProject>
<!--  BUILD DIRECTORY
The directory on the build machine that will be used to build the
➥selected solutions. The directory must be a local path on the build
➥machine (e.g. c:\build).
-->
<BuildDirectoryPath>c:\builds\daily</BuildDirectoryPath>
<!--  DROP LOCATION
  The location to drop (copy) the built binaries and the log files after
  the build is complete. This location has to be a valid UNC path of the
  form \\Server\Share. The build machine service account and application
  tier account need to have read write permission on this share.
-->
<DropLocation>\\VSTSb3\dailbuild</DropLocation>
<!--  TESTING
  Set this flag to enable/disable running tests as a post build step.
-->
<RunTest>false</RunTest>
<!--  WorkItemFieldValues
  Add/edit key value pairs to set values for fields in the work item created
  during the build process. Please make sure the field names are valid
  for the work item type being used.
-->
<WorkItemFieldValues>Priority=1;Severity=1</WorkItemFieldValues>
<!--  CODE ANALYSIS
    To change CodeAnalysis behavior edit this value. Valid values for this
    can be Default, Always or Never.

  Default - To perform code analysis as per the individual project settings
  Always  - To always perform code analysis irrespective of project settings
  Never   - To never perform code analysis irrespective of project settings
  -->
<RunCodeAnalysis>Default</RunCodeAnalysis>
<!--  UPDATE ASSOCIATED WORK ITEMS
  Set this flag to enable/disable updating associated workitems on a
➥successful build
  -->
<UpdateAssociatedWorkItems>true</UpdateAssociatedWorkItems>
</PropertyGroup>
<ItemGroup>
  <!--  SOLUTIONS
```

LISTING 23.1 Continued

```
The path of the solutions to build. To add/delete solutions, edit this
value. For example, to add a solution MySolution.sln, add following line -
    <SolutionToBuild Include="$(SolutionRoot)\path\MySolution.sln" />

To change the order in which the solutions are built, modify the order in
which the solutions appear below.
-->
<SolutionToBuild Include="$(SolutionRoot)\adventureworks\adventureworks.sln"
➥/>
    <SolutionToBuild Include="$(SolutionRoot)\AdventureWorksExtensibilityFX\
➥AdventureWorksExtensibilityFX.sln" />
</ItemGroup>
<ItemGroup>
  <!-- CONFIGURATIONS
  The list of configurations to build. To add/delete configurations, edit
  this value. For example, to add a new configuration, add following lines -
      <ConfigurationToBuild Include="Debug¦x86">
          <FlavorToBuild>Debug</FlavorToBuild>
          <PlatformToBuild>x86</PlatformToBuild>
      </ConfigurationToBuild>

  The Include attribute value should be unique for each ConfigurationToBuild
➥node.
  -->
  <ConfigurationToBuild Include="Debug¦Any CPU">
    <FlavorToBuild>Debug</FlavorToBuild>
    <PlatformToBuild>Any CPU</PlatformToBuild>
  </ConfigurationToBuild>
</ItemGroup>
<ItemGroup>
  <!-- TEST ARGUMENTS
  If the RunTest is set to true then the following test arguments will be
  used to run tests.

  To add/delete new testlist or to choose a metadata file (.vsmdi) file, edit
➥this value.
  For e.g. to run BVT1 and BVT2 type tests mentioned in the Helloworld.vsmdi
➥file, add the following -

  <MetaDataFile Include="$(SolutionRoot)\HelloWorld\HelloWorld.vsmdi">
      <TestList>BVT1;BVT2</TestList>
  </MetaDataFile>
```

LISTING 23.1   Continued

```
      Where BVT1 and BVT2 are valid test types defined in the HelloWorld.vsmdi
➥file.
      MetaDataFile - Full path to test metadata file.
      TestList - The test list in the selected metadata file to run.


      Please note that you need to specify the vsmdi file relative to
➥$(SolutionRoot)
      -->
      <MetaDataFile Include="$(SolutionRoot)\adventureworks\adventureworks.vsmdi">
        <TestList> </TestList>
      </MetaDataFile>
    </ItemGroup>
    <ItemGroup>
      <!-- ADDITIONAL REFERENCE PATH
      The list of additional reference paths to use while resolving references.
      For example,
          <AdditionalReferencePath Include="C:\MyFolder\" />
          <AdditionalReferencePath Include="C:\MyFolder2\" />
      -->
    </ItemGroup>
</Project>
```

> **NOTE**
>
> To open the build project file in Visual Studio, you either right-click on the build type in the
> Team Explorer and select View Build Type, or navigate to the specific TFSBuild.proj file in
> Source Control Explorer and double-click on the filename.

The Role of MSBuild

As mentioned earlier, the core of the TFS Build server is a technology called MSBuild. This build engine is implemented in a single executable, msbuild.exe. Although MSBuild ships with Visual Studio, it does not have any dependencies on the IDE, which means you can run the file on machines that don't have the development environment installed. In fact, MSBuild may actually be distributed within future operating systems from Microsoft, such as Microsoft Windows Vista.

MSBuild works by taking in an XML file that describes the sequence of events for the build. It then processes those events in the order specified. MSBuild is a robust engine in that it can handle conditional builds, incremental builds, and dependencies between targets and builds. Because the TFSBuild.proj file conforms to the MSBuild specifications for its input file, Team Foundation Build is able to simply pass this file over for execution when the build is kicked off. In summary, Team Foundation Build overlays the MSBuild engine with a user interface and a series of functions to integrate the build into the overall fabric of the project team (thus allowing for notifications, changeset selections, and so on).

Starting a Build

With one or more builds defined, team members can initiate any of them at any time by manually invoking them from the Team Explorer window or by scheduling them for an automatic start.

Scheduling Builds

Team Foundation Build does not natively support the capability to schedule builds for one-off or recurring execution. However, by using a TFS command from the command line, you can use the standard window scheduler task scheduler.

To schedule a build, you need to have the following pieces of information handy:

- The URL to the Team Foundation application tier server

- The name of the team project that contains the build type

- The name of the build type that you want to schedule

The TFS command for executing and controlling builds is `TFSBuild.exe` (located in `<TeamBuildInstallDir>\Common7\IDE\`). If you pass in a few parameters, this executable will reach out to the indicated build server, locate the team project, and download its build configuration information. It will then execute the build.

Using Notepad or any other text editor, create a batch file (for example, a `.cmd` or `.bat` file) that runs the `tfsbuild start` command with the parameters in the order outlined in the preceding list.

The exact syntax looks like this:

```
tfsbuild start TFSApp01:8080 AdventureWorksCMMI DailyDebug
```

You could also pass in other parameters to override some of the settings contained within the build type such as the Build server to use and the drop location for the published build.

> **NOTE**
>
> Consult the MSDN documentation, under the topic "Team Foundation Build Commands," for a complete reference guide to all the supported command-line commands available for use with Team Foundation Build.

After you have created and saved this batch file, you can schedule its execution by using the Windows Scheduled Task Wizard. Figure 23.11 shows a task to run this build command every night at midnight.

FIGURE 23.11   Scheduling a build.

Invoking a Build

To invoke a build from Visual Studio, right-click on the build type in Team Explorer and select Build Team Project. As you can see from Figure 23.12, the build dialog box will provide the opportunity to select a build type and change some of the settings contained within that build type, such as the machine to use to conduct the build and the build directory on that machine.

After a build has been started, it will proceed through its steps until failure or success.

Figure 23.13 shows the general process that each build will follow.

As the build progresses through its various steps, the build engine constantly writes and logs information about its progress back to the build repository, enabling interested team members to monitor its progress at runtime from within Visual Studio.

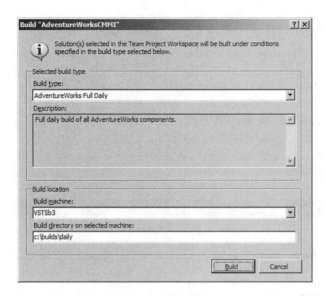

FIGURE 23.12   Running a build.

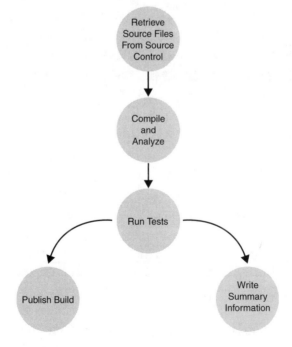

FIGURE 23.13   The general build process.

Monitoring and Analyzing Builds

Build information is provided in Visual Studio through the Team Build Browser. This browser window provides a list of completed or in-flight builds, and it functions as the principal mechanism for viewing build progress or completed summary reports.

Introducing the Team Build Browser

The Team Build Browser, shown in Figure 23.14, provides a snapshot of any build by indicating whether it succeeded, failed, or is in progress; the name of the build; the quality of the build; and the date it was completed.

> **TIP**
>
> If you or other members of the project team want to be notified when a build has been completed, you can use the Team Foundation Server project alerts feature. TFS defines two build-related events that you can subscribe to: Build Completed and Build Quality Changed.

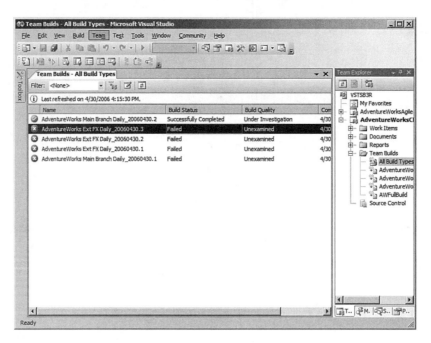

FIGURE 23.14 The Team Build Browser.

The browser enables you to access the report for a specific build and set the build's quality state.

Setting a Build's Quality State

Team Foundation Build comes with a stock set of quality states that the QA group can select from when indicating the quality of a given build:

- Initial Test Passed

- Lab Test Passed

- Ready for Deployment

- Ready for Initial Test

- Rejected

- Released

- UAT Passed

- Under Investigation

- Unexamined

As part of the build process, the QA group would visit the Team Build Browser and change a build's quality state to indicate to the rest of the team what their tests have found. You can do this quite easily by clicking in the column and selecting one of the states, as shown in Figure 23.15.

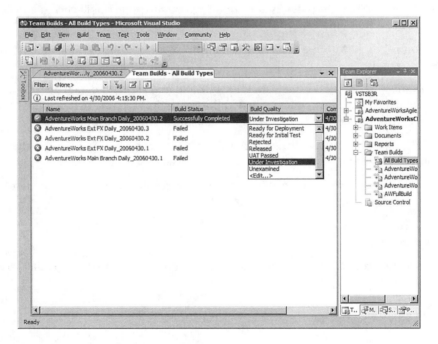

FIGURE 23.15   Setting the build quality state.

In addition to the stock quality states, you can also add your own. Just select the Edit option in the Build Quality drop-down. Using the Edit Build Quality dialog box (see Figure 23.16), you can add new states or remove one of the existing ones.

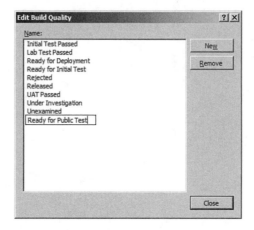

FIGURE 23.16   Adding a new build quality state.

The Build Report

To view reports for both in-progress and completed builds, you double-click the build within the Team Build Browser.

Each report is hosted within a document window opened in Visual Studio and has the following sections:

- **Summary**—Summarizes the details of the build and includes data points such as the build name, the person who requested the build, the machine that executed the build, the current quality state of the build, and a link to the build log.

- **Build steps**—Contains a list (which is dynamic if the build is in progress) that provides date and time stamp information for each stage of the build.

- **Result details**—Contains errors and warnings generated by the build, the results of any tests run with the build, and the code coverage results.

- **Associated changesets**—Contains a hyperlinked list of any changesets that were a part of the build.

- **Associated work items**—Provides a hyperlinked list of any work items that were associated with the build.

Figure 23.17 shows a build report open in Visual Studio.

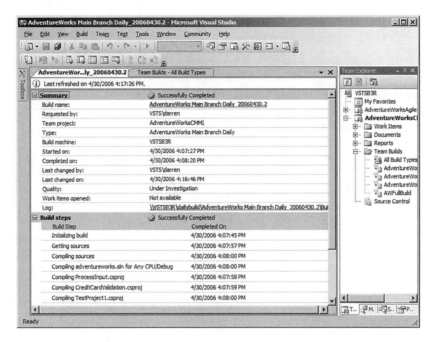

FIGURE 23.17   A build report.

Work items once again provide a correlation mechanism for associating builds and other team project artifacts. For example, consider the following chain of information:

1. A developer fixes a bug and checks in its changes to the source control system.

2. The bug work item with the changeset is created from the check-in.

3. Because the changeset is associated with the work item, and builds work against changesets within the source repository, you can now easily tell which bugs have been fixed in what build.

Summary

In this chapter, we covered the use of Team Foundation Build to automate and manage simple to complex build processes within a team project. Team Foundation Build allows you to treat builds as an integral piece to the team project.

On the server, Team Foundation Build provides a database, build engine, and common web services interface for defining, executing, and analyzing software builds. This chapter presented the logical and physical architecture of the Team Foundation Build components and showed how they coexist within the larger Visual Studio Team System technical framework. By using loosely coupled tiers, Team Foundation Build enables you to scale out build environments by assigning Build server functionality to a shared server, a dedicated server, or even multiple servers in a farm configuration.

On the client, a series of windows integrated into Visual Studio allows team members in all roles to easily participate in the build process. In this chapter, we described how the Team Explorer is used to define new build types and run those builds from within the IDE. And finally, this chapter toured the capabilities of the Team Build Browser to monitor and analyze the results of builds.

Index

Symbols

64-bit support (.NET Framework), 83

:: (double colon) alias qualifier, 74

? (question mark) type modifier, 71

A

About Box dialog box, setting text for add-ins, 377

absolute positioning, 486

    of controls, 193

access modifiers, mixed access modifiers, 73-74

accessibility options for website projects, 479

accessibility standards compliance, HTML designer, 196-197

accessing

    code within projects, 307-309

    windows, 310-311

ACL support (.NET Framework), 83

active hyperlinking (productivity tool), 205

adaptive menus, 330

adaptive rendering, ASP.NET controls, 509

Add Connection dialog box, 554

Add Link dialog box, 699

Add New Item–Solution Items dialog box, 96

Add New Item dialog box, 197, 476, 482, 522

Add New Item wizard example, 418

    creating .vsz and .vsdir files, 423

    implementing Execute method, 419-423

Add New Project dialog box, 575

Add New User Control dialog box, 197

Add Reference dialog box, 477

Add Style Rule dialog box, 184, 490

Add to Source Control dialog box, 670

Add Workspace dialog box, 667

Add-in Manager, 372-373

Add-in Wizard, 374

    About Box dialog box text, 377

    application host selection, 375-376

    code generation, 377-383

    language selection, 374-375

    name and description of add-in, 376

    options, setting, 376-377

add-ins

    Add-in Wizard, 374

        About Box dialog box text, 377

        application host selection, 375-376

        code generation, 377-383

        language selection, 374-375

        name and description of add-in, 376

        options, setting, 376-377

    color palette example, 390-391

        code generation properties, 392

        code listing for, 402-415

        color selection event handler, 395

        creating Options page, 398-402

        creating user control, 391-395

        displaying tool window, 396-397

        helper routines, 393-395

        inserting generated code, 398

        integrating user control, 396-398

        mouse movement event handlers, 392

        user control event handling, 397

    defined, 372

    IDTExtensibility2 interface methods, 383-389

    loading, 373

    managing, 372-373

    purpose of, 351

    reacting to commands, 389-390

    registered add-ins, 373

    shared add-ins, Visual Studio add-ins versus, 376

    structure of, 383

.addin files, 373

adding

    applications to application diagram, 738-739

    items to class diagrams, 761-763

    servers to zones, 749-750

adds (source control), 669

administrator group, source control security, 661

ADO.NET, new features, 84

Advanced Properties property page, performance sessions, 141

agents, defined, 630

agile development, MSF Agile, 622-623

alerts

    managing in MSDN Community Forums, 435-436

    in Team Foundation Server, 654-655

aliases, 216

    :: (double colon) alias qualifier, 74

alignment of form controls, 526-530

Allocation subreport, 150

alpha releases, 769

ambiguous namespaces, 74-75

analyzing builds, 828-831

Anchor property (form controls), 527-528

anchoring controls, 527-528

anonymous methods (C#), 79-80

appearance properties

    controls, 534-535

    forms, 522-523

application architects, 732

application design, steps in, 734

Application Designer, 8-9, 735, 737-740

    application implementation, 758-760

    application settings and constraints, 740-742

    Diagram menu, 735-736

    Toolbox, 736-737

application diagrams, 731-740

    Application Designer Toolbox, 736-737

    application settings and constraints, 740-742

    Diagram menu, 735-736

    generating models, 734

    item templates for, 733

application host, selecting for add-ins, 375-376

application implementation, 758-760

Application property page, 111-112

application settings, defined, 114

application testing tools, 28-29

application tier (Team Foundation Server), 634-636

    role in Team Foundation Build architecture, 812-814

Application.EnableVisual Styles method (form controls), 534

applications

    adding to application diagram, 738-739

    connecting in application diagram, 738-740

    connecting to systems, 745-746

    debugging. See debugging

applying themes, 496-499

architect (project role in Team System), 32

architect role

    application architects, 732

    infrastructure architects, 732

    Visual Studio Team Architect, 626-627

        application design steps, 734

        application diagrams, 735-742

        application implementation, 758-760

        deployment diagrams, 755-758

        item templates, 733-734

        logical datacenter diagrams, 746-755

        project templates, 732-733

        system diagrams, 742-746

architecture of Team Foundation Build, 812-815

architecture modeling tools, 8-12

areas

    team projects, 648-650

    work items, 692-694

Areas and Iterations dialog box, 648-650, 693

arrays, upper/lower bounds (VB), 77

Ask a Question button (Community menu), 431-436

.asmx files (web services), 599-600

ASP.NET

    controls

        custom controls, 510

        data controls, 515

        enhancements, 508-509

        login controls, 510-513

        site navigation controls, 513-515

        user controls, 510

    event model, 481-485

    new features, 84

    user interfaces

        consistency, maintaining, 488-499

        creating user-configurable UIs, 499-508

        master pages, 491-493

        page layout, 486-488

        planning, 485-486

        style sheets, 489-491

        themes, 493-499

    website projects, 466

        accessibility options, 479

        build options, 478-479

        creating, 466-467

        creating web pages, 481-485

        file types for, 475-476

        folders for, 473-475

        MSBuild options, 480-482

        Property Pages dialog box, 476-482

        references, 476-478

        selecting default programming language, 473

        selecting template, 467-469

        selecting website location, 467-473

        start options, 479-480

ASP.NET Crystal Reports Web Site template, 467

ASP.NET Development Server, 470-471

ASP.NET Membership, 510

ASP.NET Web Development Server, 25-26

ASP.NET web service projects, 598-599

ASP.NET Web Service template, 467

ASP.NET Web Site template, 467

assemblies

    friend assemblies (C#), 83

    multiple assembly versions (C#), 81-82

assertion methods, unit tests, 778

associating

    code with work items, 717-720

    icons with wizards, 418

    work items with check-ins, 676-677

association, 765-766

at-rest state (Debug menu), 270

attaching

    files to work items, 701

    to processes, 265-267

attribute classes, unit tests, 777-778

authenticated streams (.NET Framework), 83

Auto Format dialog box, 503

auto scaling controls, 529-530

auto-generating

    bound controls, 580-586

    SQL scripts, 573-574

AutoCorrect feature, 12

automation object model, 299-300

    categories, list of, 302

    Command object, 344-346

        executing commands, 346

        mapping key bindings, 346-347

        properties/methods, 345

    CommandBar object, 327-331

    Debugger object, 347-348

    Document object, 331

        properties/methods, 332-333

        text documents, 333-344

    DTE/DTE2 root object, 302

        properties/methods, 303-304

    EnvDTE/EnvDTE80 assemblies, 300

        types, list of, 300-302

    event handling, 348-349

    Project object

        code access, 307-309

        properties/methods, 306-307

        solution/project hierarchy, 304-305

    Solution object

        properties/methods, 305-306

        solution/project hierarchy, 304-305

    Window object, 310

        command window, 322-323

        linked windows, 325-327

        output window, 323-325

        properties/methods, 311-312

        querying Windows collection, 312-314

        referencing windows, 310-311

        task list window, 317-319

        text windows, 314-316

        tool windows, 316-317

        Toolbox, 319-322

Autos window (debugger), 292

AutoScaleDimensions property (form controls), 530

AutoScaleMode property (form controls), 529

AutoSize property (form design), 519

B

BackColor property (forms), 523

best practices, unit tests, 777

beta releases, 769

Binary Properties property page, performance sessions, 140

binding

    data binding. See data binding

    extracted values to web test requests, 794-795

    form posts to data, 791-793

    key bindings, 346-347

    tests to data, 789-791

bookmarks, 166-168

    indicator margin, 164-165

Bookmarks window, 167-168

brace matching (productivity tool), 224-225

Branch dialog box, 684

branching source code tree, 683-685

Break All command, 278

breaking execution for exceptions, 263-264

Breakpoint Condition dialog box, 285-287

Breakpoint Filter dialog box, 287

Breakpoint Hit Count dialog box, 287-288

breakpoints, 280. See also Run To Cursor command; tracepoints

    Breakpoints window, 283-285

    clearing, 269

    conditions, setting, 285-287

configuring, 177-178

continuing execution after, 267-268

controlling flow of code, 178-179

defined, 176

filters, setting, 287

hit count, setting, 287-288

icons for, 282-283

indicator margin, 164-165

setting, 176-177, 267, 281-282

Breakpoints window, 283-285

Breakpoints window toolbar, 283-284

browsers

selecting for load tests, 801

targeting, 196

bug reports, sending via Community menu, 438

bug work items

MSF for Agile, 690

MSF for CMMI, 692

build automation in Team Foundation Server, 631

Build Configuration property page, 100

build configurations

properties, 100

selecting, 816-817

build events, 112

Build Events property page, 112

build management in Team Foundation Server, 34

Build menu, 47

build options for website projects, 478-479

build order, specifying, 816

Build property page, 112

build reports, 830-831

build repository, 813-815

Build server, 812-814

location information for build, 816-818

build tests, selecting, 818

build types, 815

editing, 819-824

builds, 811. See also Team Foundation Build

creating, 815

editing build type, 819-824

MSBuild, role of, 824-825

specifying build information, 815-820

monitoring/analyzing, 828-831

naming, 815-816

quality states, setting, 829-830

running, 826-827

scheduling, 825-826

selecting solutions for, 816-817

business analysts, role with work items, 714-717

Button Editor, 369

buttons. See toolbar buttons

C

C#

Code Snippet Inserter, 216

creating stored procedures, 576-578

language enhancements

anonymous methods, 79-80

friend assemblies, 83

list of, 78

multiple assembly versions, 81-82

static classes, 80-81

refactoring tools. See refactoring tools

C# code editor, 54-55

"C# Language Specification 2.0" document, 78

caching (.NET Framework), 84

Call Stack (debugger), 265

Call Tree subreport, 150

Caller/Callee subreport, 150

calling web services, 614-615

Capability Maturity Model for Integration (CMMI), 624

capturing outer variables, 80

cascading style sheets, 184

ccessibility Validation dialog box, 197

cells, DataGridView control, 546

change request work items, MSF for CMMI, 691

change scripts, 574

change tracking (productivity tool), 203-204

ChangePassword control, 512

changesets in source control, 677-678

channels, 672

check constraints, creating, 557

Check In dialog box, 671-672

Check Out command (source control), 671

Check Question Status button (Community menu), 437

check-in notes, 675-676

check-in policies, 673-675

   in Team Foundation Server, 630

checking in files to source control, 671-677

checkpoints

   MSF Agile, 623

   MSF for CMMI, 624

Choose Columns dialog box, 710

Choose Location dialog box, 470

Choose Related Work Item dialog box, 699

Choose Toolbox Items dialog box, 525

choosing. See selecting

chords, defined, 239

Class Designer, 9-10, 760

   class diagrams, 760

      adding items, 761-763

      creating, 760, 762

      defining methods/properties/fields/events, 766-767

      displaying members, 761

      relationships between classes, 763-766

   refactoring with, 235-236

class diagrams, 731, 760

   adding items, 761-763

   creating, 733, 760-762

   defining methods/properties/fields/events, 766-767

   displaying members, 761

   relationships between classes, 763-766

class templates, 420

Class View, 124

   members pane, 127-128

   objects pane, 125-127

   search bar, 125-126

   toolbar buttons, 124-125

class view search feature, 15

clearing breakpoints, 269

clickable hyperlinks, 205

client versions (Visual Studio 2005), 34-35

clients, Team Build client, 812-814

CMMI (Capability Maturity Model for Integration), 624. See also MSF for CMMI

code

   accessing within projects, 307-309

   associating with work items, 717-720

   debugging. See debugging

   writing in Windows Forms designer, 189-192

Code Analysis Policy, 673

Code Analysis property page, 113

code coverage in Visual Studio Team Developer, 628

code coverage analysis, 782-784

code definition window, 14-15, 180-181

code editor, 161. See also text editor

   code definition window, 180-181

   customizing, 55-57

   debugging in, 176

      configuring breakpoints, 177-178

      controlling flow of code, 178-179

      setting breakpoints, 176-177

   invoking tools from, 12-14

   navigation tools, 166

      bookmarks, 166-168

      line numbering, 166

   new features for, 16-20

   opening, 161

   printing from, 179-180

   productivity tools

      code outlining, 206-208

      HTML navigation, 208-210

      smart tags, 211-212

   smart tags, refactoring with, 234-235

   toolbar, 166

   windows

      components of, 163-165

      selecting, 161

   writing code in, 162-163

code navigation, 14-16

code outlining (productivity tool), 206-208

code pane (code editor), 164

code profiling in Visual Studio Team Developer, 628

code sharing, shared content

    installing, 443-445

    searching for, 443-444

    types of, 442-443

Code Snipper Inserter, 216-218

code snippets

    productivity tool, 216-224

    as shared content, 443

Code Snippets Manager, 223

code stepping. See stepping through code

code validation with Visual Studio Team Developer, 627-629

code window, search-and-replace modes, 168

    Find In Files mode, 171-173

    Find Symbol mode, 174-175

    Incremental Search mode, 175-176

    Quick Find mode, 168-170

    Quick Replace mode, 170-171

    Replace In Files mode, 173-174

CodeElements collection, 307-309

Codezone Community option (Community menu), 439

coding problem indicators (productivity tool), 204-205

collaboration. See VSTS (Visual Studio Team System)

collections, generic collections, 70

color in code coverage analysis, 784

color palette example (add-ins), 390-391

    code generation properties, 392

    code listing for, 402-415

    color selection event handler, 395

    creating Options page, 398-402

    creating user control, 391-395

    displaying tool window, 396-397

    helper routines, 393-395

    inserting generated code, 398

    integrating user control, 396-398

    mouse movement event handlers, 392

    user control event handling, 397

colors

    printer settings, 180

    syntax coloring (productivity tool), 205-206

column mode, selecting text, 158

Column Options dialog box, 704

columns in performance reports, 143-149

Columns property (indexes), 557

command bars, 327-331

command keys

    Encapsulate Field refactoring tool, 256

    Extract Interface refactoring tool, 248

    Extract Method refactoring tool, 241

    Promote Local Variable to Parameter refactoring tool, 252

    Remove Parameters refactoring tool, 251

    Rename refactoring tool, 239

    Reorder Parameters refactoring tool, 254

    smart tags, 235

Command object, 344-346

    executing commands, 346

    mapping key bindings, 346-347

    properties/methods, 345

command window, 322-323

    running macros from, 371-372

CommandBar object, 327-331

commands, 344-346

    add-ins reacting to, 389-390

    executing, 346

    mapping key bindings, 346-347

CommandWindow object, 322-323

comment tasks, 227-229

comments, inserting into text windows, 340

community code sharing, 20-21

community features (Visual Studio 2005), 425

    Community menu, 431

        Ask a Question button, 431-436

        Check Question Status, 437

        Codezone Community, 439

        Community Search option, 439-442

        Developer Center option, 439

        Partner Products Catalog, 439

        Send Feedback button, 437-438

    Start Page, 426

        Getting Started section, 427-428

        news channel, 428-431

Recent Projects section, 427

Visual Studio Headlines section, 428

community forums. *See* MSDN Community Forums

Community menu, 49, 431

Ask a Question button, 431-436

Check Question Status button, 437

Codezone Community option, 439

Community Search option, 439-442

Developer Center option, 439

Partner Products Catalog option, 439

Send Feedback button, 437-438

Community Search option (Community menu), 439-442

comparison operations, in joins, 565

Compile property page, 113

compiler, productivity tools (coding problem indicators), 204-205

compiler warnings, 204

Complete Word (productivity tool), 213

complex data binding, 580

component designer, 197

creating components, 197-198

Component Designer

viewing, 485

writing code, 199-200

component tray, defined, 187, 525

components

creating, 197-198

defined, 187, 197, 524

writing code for, 199-200

composite controls. *See* user controls

compressing files for macro packaging example, 457

conditions for breakpoints, setting, 285-287

configurable UIs, creating, 499-506, 508

configuration file for testing, 775

configurations, build configurations (selecting), 816-817

configuring

breakpoints, 177-178

code coverage analysis, 782-783

IDE, 39-41

load tests, 803

performance sessions, 138-142

Visual Studio for source control, 663

zones and servers, 752-755

confirmation of build selections, 819-820

confirmation of settings, creating team projects, 642-643

Connect class, color palette example (add-ins), 396-398

connecting

applications in application diagram, 738-740

applications to systems, 745-746

servers to zones, 750-751

connections

database connections, creating, 554-556

to Team Foundation Server, 650-651

consistency for user interfaces, maintaining, 488-499

constant load pattern (load tests), 799

constraints, generic constraints, 68-69

constructors, static constructors (C#), 81

consuming web services, 611

calling web services, 614-615

defining web references, 611-613

updating web references, 614

viewing web references, 613-614

containers, 530-534

Content Installer. *See* Visual Studio Content Installer

content pages, creating from master pages, 492-493

Content Type searches, 443-444

Continue command, 280

Continue statement (VB), 76

continuing executing after breakpoints, 267-268

contributor group, source control security, 661

contributors, Team Foundation Server security, 638

control event handlers, adding, 485

control positioning for user interfaces, 486-488

controls

adding, 193-194

to forms, 186-187

to web pages, 483

appearance properties, 534-535

arranging, 187-188, 193

as shared content, 443

bound controls
    auto-generating, 580-586
    manual binding, 586-589
changing type of, 541
containers, 530-534
creating, 197-198, 546-551
custom controls, 510
    creating, 551
data controls, 515
    selecting, 589-593
data presentation, 542-546
data source controls, 593
defined, 197, 524
enhancements, 508-509
login controls, 510-513
non-visual controls, hiding, 502
positioning, 526-530
resizing, 189
    planning form design, 520
site navigation controls, 513-515
skins, 495
subclassing, 547-548
in Toolbox, customizing, 525
ToolStrip controls, 535-542
user controls, 510
    designing, 548-550
for web applications, 24
web controls, data binding, 589-594
web forms, data binding, 27-28
Web Part controls, 499-508
z-order, defined, 539
cookie crumbs, 513
counter sets (load tests), 802
Counters property page, performance sessions, 141-142
create scripts, 573-574
CreateUserWizard control, 512
CSS editor, 184
culture, form design and, 518-519
custom comment tokens, 228
custom component set (Object Browser), editing, 134-135

custom controls, 198, 510
    creating, 551
custom events (VB), 78
custom parameters, defining, 448
custom reports (TFS), designing, 655-657
Customize dialog box, 346, 368-369
customizing
    data source mappings, 585-586
    form appearance, 185-186
    IntelliSense, 225-226
    Toolbox, 525
    work items, 722, 727-730
cycles (MSF Agile), 623

D

data binding, 26-28, 579-580
    ASP.NET controls, 509
    form controls
        auto-generating bound controls, 580-586
        manually bound controls, 586-589
    web controls, 589-594
Data Connections node, Server Explorer, 130
data controls, 515
    selecting, 589-593
data entry, ASP.NET controls, 509
Data Explorer. See Server Explorer
Data menu, 47
data presentation controls, 542-546
data source controls, 515, 593
data sources
    DataGridView control, 545
    mapping to controls, 583-586
    seeding web tests, 788-793
    selecting, 580-583
data tier (Team Foundation Server), 636-637
    role in Team Foundation Build architecture, 813-815
data view (XML editor), 182-183
data warehouse, TFS reports and, 655

Database Diagram Designer, 557-562

database diagrams

creating, 558-559

table relationships, building, 559-562

Database Explorer. *See* Server Explorer,

database objects, creating in managed code, 574-578

database projects, 571

creating, 572-573

SQL scripts

auto-generating, 573-574

executing, 574

database references, setting default, 574

databases

connections, creating, 554-556

SQL statements

query writing, 562-566

stored procedures, 566-570

triggers, creating, 570

user-defined functions, creating, 571

views, creating, 566

tables

adding to database diagram, 558

defined, 553

defining, 556-558

editing definitions, 559

relationships, building, 559-562

showing contents of, 566

viewing, 558

DataGridView control, 545-546

binding, 586-589

DataList control, 515, 590

DataTips, 19

DataTips window (debugger), 293-294

de facto standards (form design), 519

Debug menu, 47, 270-274

debug mode, starting, 261-263

debug mode (Debug menu), 270

Debug Options dialog box, 275

Debug property page, 113-114

Debug Source Files property page, 99-100

Debug toolbar, 274

debugger, 113-114. *See also* debugging

breakpoints, 280

Breakpoints window, 283-285

clearing, 269

conditions, setting, 285-287

continuing execution after, 267-268

filters, setting, 287

hit count, setting, 287-288

icons for, 282-283

setting, 267, 281-282

Debug menu, 270-274

Debug Options dialog box, 275

Debug toolbar, 274

Edit and Continue feature, 296-297

pointing at source files, 99-100

stepping through code, 268-270, 276

Break All command, 278

Continue command, 280

ending session, 280-281

Run To Cursor command, 277

Start Debugging command, 278

Step Into command, 276-279

Step Out command, 280

Step Over command, 278

tracepoints, 280, 288-290

viewing data, 290

Autos window, 292

DataTips window, 293-294

Locals window, 291

QuickWatch window, 293

visualizers, 294-296

watch windows, 292-293

windows in, 264-265

Debugger object, 347-348

debugging, 260. *See also* debugger; troubleshooting

attaching to web service process, 265-267

breaking execution for exceptions, 263-264

in code editor, 176

configuring breakpoints, 177-178

controlling flow of code, 178-179

setting breakpoints, 176-177

debug mode, starting, 261-263

enabling for websites, 262

macros, 361-362

new features for, 16-20

phases of, 260-261

remote debugging, 297-298

stored procedures, 569-570

windows in debugger, 264-265

declaring

nullable types, 71

partial types, 73

static classes, 80-81

default constructor constraints, 69

default database reference, setting, 574

default IDE settings, changing, 427

default programming language for website projects, selecting, 473

default values, avoiding with nullable types, 70-71

delegates, anonymous methods (C#), 79-80

delimiters, brace matching (productivity tool), 224-225

dependencies (projects), 98-99

Deployment Designer, 10, 12, 755-756

deployment reports, 757-758

validating deployment, 756-758

deployment diagrams, 731, 755-756

creating, 734

deployment reports, 757-758

validating deployment, 756-758

deployment reports, 757-758

derivation constraints, 69

deriving. See inheriting

description pane, Object Browser, 136-137

design view, web pages, 483

designers, 481

defined, 157, 160

designing

applications, steps in, 734

user interface, 517-520

desktop themes, 534

Detach All command, 280

DetailsView control, 515, 589

developer (project role in Team System), 32

Developer Center option (Community menu), 439

developer role, Visual Studio Team Developer, 627-629

developer testing. See unit tests

developers, role with work items, 716, 718-720

development servers, 25-26

Development Tools Environment. See DTE/DTE2 root object

DevExpress, 18

Diagram menu (Application Designer), 735-736

diagrams. See database diagrams

directories. See folders

DISCO (Discovery Document), defined, 597

Disco.exe, 605

Dock property (form controls), 528-529

docked controls, z-order, 539

docking

controls, 528-529

IDE windows, 60-61

Document object, 331

properties/methods, 332-333

text documents, 333-335

editing, 335-344

Document Outline, 152-154

editing in, 154

toolbar buttons, 154

Document Outline window, 209-210

document view (XML editor), 182

document windows, 310

documents, 331-333

text documents, 333-335

distinguishing from nontext documents, 333

editing, 335-344

double colon (::) alias qualifier, 74

downloading process templates, 723-725

DPAPI support (.NET Framework), 84

drag-and-drop operations with Server Explorer, 133-134

DTE.AddIns collection, 373

DTE/DTE2 root object, 302

properties/methods, 303-304

dynamic code analysis in Visual Studio Team Developer, 628

E

Edit and Continue feature (debugger), 296-297

Edit menu, 45

Edit, Outlining menu, 207-208

edit-and-continue feature (debugging), 18

editing

    build types, 819-824

    custom component set (Object Browser), 134-135

    in Document Outline, 154

    files in source control. See source control, files, 671

    load tests, 803-804

    recorded macros, 357-361

    text documents, 335-344

    variables in Locals or Autos windows, 291

    .vstemplate XML file, 450

editors

    code editor. See code editor

    defined, 157

    productivity tools. See productivity tools

    text editor. See text editor

EditPoint object, 335

    adding text, 338-339

    editing text, 339

    properties/methods, 336-338

    repositioning, 339

Empty Web Site template, 467

enabling website debugging, 262

Encapsulate Field dialog box, 256-257

Encapsulate Field refactoring tool, 255-257

    accessing, 256

ending debug sessions, 280-281

endpoints

    connecting

        applications in application diagram, 738-740

        servers to zones, 750-751

    proxy endpoints, 744

enhancements. See Visual Studio 2005, new features

EnvDTE/EnvDTE80 assemblies, 300

    types, list of, 300-302

environment settings

    changing, 640

    configuring IDE, 39-41

EnvironmentEvents module, 362-365

errors. See also exceptions

    productivity tools. See productivity tools

    publishing errors (work items), 711

evaluating code coverage analysis, 783-784

event declarations, adding to macros, 366-367

event definitions in macros, 362-365

event handlers

    color palette example (add-ins), 392, 395-397

    creating, 523-524

event handling, 348-349

    in macros

        adding event declarations, 366-367

        event definitions, 362-365

        initializing event object, 367-368

        writing event handler, 365-366

Event Logs node, Server Explorer, 131

event model, ASP.NET, 481-485

event objects, initializing, 367-368

event trace providers, 142

events

    custom events (VB), 78

    defining in Class Designer, 766-767

    forms, 523-524

Events property page, performance sessions, 142

Excel

    managing work items with, 653-654

    work items, project manager role and, 708-713

Exception Assistant, 265

exceptions

    breaking execution for, 263-264

    web service exceptions

        handling, 617

        throwing, 616-617

exclusive access (source control), 671

Execute method, implementing in Add New Item wizard example, 419-423 executing. See running

    commands, 346

    SQL scripts, 574

execution, continuing after breakpoints, 267-268

explicit naming, 211

Export Report dialog box, 143

Export Template Wizard, 447-449

exporting

    macros, 356-357

    process templates, 723-725

    project templates, 448-449

Express Editions (Visual Studio 2005), 29-30

expression builder, 170

extender providers, defined, 531

Extensible Markup Language. See XML

Extract Interface dialog box, 249

Extract Interface refactoring tool, 248-250

    accessing, 248

Extract Method refactoring tool, 241-246

    Accessing, 241

    method stubs, generating, 247-248

    single line of code, extracting, 246-247

extracting values from web tests, 793-795

extreme programming, 231

F

Favorites folder (Team Explorer), 645

feature sets. See areas

feedback, Send Feedback button (Community menu), 437-438

fields

    defining in Class Designer, 766-767

    Encapsulate Field refactoring tool, 255-257

        accessing, 256

File Comparison tool (source control), 682

File menu, 45

file system as website location, 470-471

file types

    for ASP.NET website projects, 475-476

    project definition files, 103

    for solution items, 96

files

    adding to source control, 669-671

    attaching to work items, 701

    checking into source control, 671-677

    merging changes, 680-683

    retrieving from source control, 671

    shelving in source control, 678-680

    unshelving in source control, 680

files pane (source control), 665

filtering work items, 703-707

filters for breakpoints, setting, 287

Find All References feature, 16

Find and Replace window, 168

    Find In Files mode, 171-173

    Find Symbol mode, 174-175

    Quick Find mode, 168-170

    Quick Replace mode, 170-171

    Replace In Files mode, 173-174

Find In Files mode, 171-173

Find Results window, 171-173

Find Symbol mode, 174-175

finding. See searching

floating IDE windows, 62

flow layout, 486

flow of code, controlling, 178-179

FlowLayoutPanel class, 531

folders

    for ASP.NET website projects, 473-475

    for bookmarks, 167-168

    solution folders, 97

    team project folders, 644

folders pane (source control), 665

fonts, printer settings, 180

Fonts and Colors Options dialog box, 180

ForeColor property (forms), 523

Foreign Key Relationships dialog box, 559

foreign keys
    creating, 557
    referential integrity, 560
form access (VB), 77
form posts, binding to data, 791-793
Form.BackgroundImage property (forms), 523
Format menu, 48
formatting HTML, 195-196
forms. *See also* web forms; web pages; Windows
    Forms designer
    components, defined, 524
    controls
        adding, 186-187
        appearance properties, 534-535
        arranging, 187-188
        auto-generating bound controls, 580-586
        changing type of, 541
        containers, 530-534
        creating, 546-551
        custom controls, 551
        data presentation, 542-546
        defined, 524
        manually bound controls, 586-589
        positioning, 526-530
        resizing, 189
        subclassing, 547-548
        ToolStrip controls, 535-542
        user controls, 548-550
        z-order, 539
    creating, 521-524
    customizing appearance of, 185-186
    Document Outline, 152-154
        editing in, 154
        toolbar buttons, 154
    events, 523-524
    inheriting from, 522
    menus, creating, 536-538
    properties, 522-523
    resizing, 526-530
    startup forms, setting, 521-522
    status bars, creating, 540-542
    toolbars, creating, 538-540
    user interface, designing, 517-520
    web forms, data binding, 27-28
    Windows forms, data binding, 27
Forms Designer, component tray, 525
FormStartPosition enumeration value (forms), 522
FormView control, 515, 589
forums. *See* MSDN Community Forums
friend assemblies (C#), 83
FTP servers as website location, 471-472
FTP support (.NET Framework), 84
function breakpoints, setting, 281
functions, creating user-defined functions, 571
Functions subreport, 150
FxCop, 20

G

General Properties property page, performance ses-
    sions, 138-139
generic collections, 70
generic constraints, 68-69
generic methods, 65
    creating, 67-68
generic tests, 807
    in Visual Studio Team Test, 630
generic type instantiation, 65
generic types, 65
    creating, 65-67
generics, 64-65
    benefits of, 65
    generic type instantiation, 65
    type parameters, 65-68
Get Latest command (source control), 668, 671
get method, mixed access modifiers, 73-74
Getting Started section (Start Page), 427-428
global security groups in Team Foundation Server, 637
globalization (.NET Framework), 84
Go To Line dialog box, 166

GotDotNet workspace, 460

grid positioning (Windows Forms designer), 187-188

GridView control, 515, 589-593

groups (TFS security), mapping to process roles, 638-639

GUI (graphical user interface). *See* user interfaces

H

handling web service exceptions, 617

handling events. *See* event handling

HasValue property (nullable types), 71, 73

Help menu, 49

hiding non-visual controls, 502

hierarchical data, form controls, 542-545

history (work items), tracking, 697-699

hit count for breakpoints, setting, 287-288

Hit Count command, 287-288

HTML designer, 192-193

    controls

        adding, 193-194

        arranging, 193

    HTML source editor and, 193-196

    productivity tools, smart tags, 210

    validation options, 196-197

HTML navigation, 208-210

HTML source editor, HTML designer and, 193-196

HTTP (Hypertext Transfer Protocol), 597

hyperlinks, active hyperlinking, 205

I

icons

    associating with wizards, 418

    for breakpoints, 282-283

    files pane (source control), 665

    members pane (Class View), 128

    objects pane (Class View), 126

    Solution Explorer, 118-121

        signal icons, 121

IDE

    configuring, 39-41

    default settings, changing, 427

    menu bar, 44-49

    projects, creating, 43-44

    Properties window, 58-59

    Solution Explorer, 57-58

    Start Page, 42

    startup options, 43

    text editors, 53

        code editors, 54-56

        customizing, 55-57

    toolbars, 49-51

    Toolbox, 51-52

    Visual Designers, 53

    windows

        docking, 60-61

        floating, 62

        pinning, 59-60

IDTCommandTarget interface, 383

IDTExtensibility2 interface, 383

    methods in, 383-389

IDTToolsOptionsPage interface, methods, 399

IDTWizard interface, 415-416

IIS (Internet Information Server), 25-26

    local IIS version as website location, 471

    remote IIS servers as website location, 472-473

ImageList controls, 543-545

Images Collection Editor dialog box, 544

Immediate window (debugger), 265

implementing applications, 758-760

implicit naming, 211

Import and Export Settings Wizard, 41

importing

    macros, 356-357

    process templates, 726-728

    server settings, 754-755

incremental search, TextPane object, 315

Incremental Search mode, 175-176

Index Columns dialog box, 557

indexes, creating, 557

Indexes/Keys dialog box, 557

indicator margin (code editor), 164-165

infrastructure architects, 732

infrastructure design, logical datacenter diagrams, 746-747

    adding servers to zones, 749-750

    configuring zones and servers, 752-755

    connecting servers to zones, 750-751

    Logical Datacenter Designer Toolbox, 747

    zones, 747-748

inheritance, 763-765

Inheritance Picker dialog box, 522

inheriting

    controls, 547-548

    from forms, 522

initializing event objects, 367-368

inline functions, 571

inner variables of anonymous methods, 80

Insert Table dialog box, 195

inserting comments into text windows, 340

installing

    macro packaging example content, 457-460

    project templates, 451

    shared content, 443-445

    source control, 38-39

    Team Foundation Server (TFS), 639

    Visual Studio 2005, 37-41

Instrumentation Properties property page, performance sessions, 140-141

IntelliSense, 201, 212

    brace matching, 224-225

    code snippets, 216-224

    Complete Word, 213

    customizing, 225-226

    in Watch window, 19

    List Members, 214

    Parameter Info, 215

    Quick Info, 214

interface (visual relationship), 764-765

interfaces, Extract Interface refactoring tool, 248-250

    accessing, 248

Internet Information Server (IIS), 25-26

invoking web methods, 610-611

IsNot operator (VB), 76

issue work items, MSF for CMMI, 692

item templates

    creating, 451-452

    as shared content, 443

    in Visual Studio Team Architect, 733-734

Items Collection Editor dialog box, 541

iterations (team projects), 648-650

iterations (work items), 692-693, 695-696

J

JIT (just-in-time) compiler, generic type instantiation, 65

Join dialog box, 565

joins, creating, 564-565

just-in-time (JIT) compiler, generic type instantiation, 65

K

key bindings, mapping, 346-347

keyboard shortcuts

    Incremental Search mode, 175

    jumping to code lines, 166

    mapping key bindings, 346-347

    running macros from, 370-371

    Toolbox (Windows Forms designer), 186

keyboard shortcuts. See command keys, 239

L

languages

    selecting, 38

    selecting for add-ins, 374-375

    target source language for website projects, 103

Launch Properties property page

    performance sessions, 139

    session targets, 143

launching, 161

layout

    of form controls, 526-530

        containers, 530-534

    of forms, 187-188

layout grid (Windows Forms designer), 187-188

Layout menu, 48

line numbering, 166

line wrapping, 158

linked windows, 325-327

linking

    code to work items, 718-720

    tool windows, 325-327

    work items, 698-701

links, 205

List Members (productivity tool), 214

listings

    adding and removing items in Toolbox window, 320

    adding fields to forms, 729

    autogenerated unit test sample, 780

    bookmarking For loops in documents, 334

    calling the GetCustomerProfile web method, 615

    code generated by the Add-in Wizard, 378

    component designer–generated code, 199

    Connect, PaletteControl, and PaletteControlOptionPage classes, 402-415

    controlling edit mode for page, 505

    controlling incremental search, 315

    creating SOAP exceptions, 616

    Customer Links Web Part, 503

    customer profile web service, 601

    EnvironmentEvents module, 363

    executing commands in command window, 322

    inserting comments into text windows, 340

    linking and unlinking tool windows, 326

    macro to expand/collapse all Solution Explorer nodes, 360

    namespace and class implementation, 307

    new field inside Bug.xml, 728

    new tasks to be seeded, 726

    querying CommandBar object, 328

    recorder-generated macro code, 357

    resizing the IDE, 371

    sample build file, 820

    sample unit test, 776

    .sitemap file, 515

    skin file example, 495

    SOAP 1.2 request, 609

    SOAP 1.2 response, 610

    static class, 81

    toggling task item completion, 318

    VB macro for querying Windows collection, 313

    VSContent file for smart client example, 455

    .VSContent file structure, 453

    .vstemplate file sample, 450

    web service WSDL, 605

    web test autogenerated code, 793

    Windows Forms designer–generated code, 189-192

    writing to output window, 325

lists, test lists, 773-775

load tests, 797

    creating, 797-803

    editing, 803-804

    running, 803-805

    in Visual Studio Team Test, 629-630

loading

    add-ins, 373

    macros with events, security issues, 366

local IIS version as website location, 471

local variables

    Promote Local Variable to Parameter refactoring tool, 252-254

    refactoring and, 252

Locals window (debugger), 265, 291

location, form design and, 518-519

locations for website projects, selecting, 467-473

Logical Datacenter Designer, 10-11, 746-747

    Toolbox, 747

    zones, 747-748

        adding servers to, 749-750

        configuring, 752-755

        connecting servers to, 750-751

logical datacenter diagrams, 731, 746-747

    adding servers to zones, 749-750

    configuring zones and servers, 752-755

    connecting servers to zones, 750-751

    item templates for, 733

    Logical Datacenter Designer Toolbox, 747

    zones, 747-748

login controls, 510-513

LoginName control, 512

LoginStatus control, 512

LoginView control, 510

lower array bounds (VB), 77

M

Macro Explorer, 151, 354-355

    macros, 152

    Macros root node, 151

    modules, 152

    projects, 152

Macro Recorder toolbar, 352-353

macros, 152

    event handling

        adding event declarations, 366-367

        event definitions, 362-365

        initializing event object, 367-368

        writing event handler, 365-366

    limitations of, 372

    Macro Explorer, 354-355

Macros IDE, 355

    adding macro projects, 357

    debugging macros, 361-362

    editing recorded macros, 357-361

    project files, 355-356

    sharing macros, 356-357

    modules, 152

    packaging, 455-460

    with parameters, 371-372

    projects, 152

    purpose of, 351-352

    recording, 352-353

    running, 354, 368

        from command window, 371-372

        from keyboard shortcuts, 370-371

        from toolbars/menus, 368-370

Macros IDE, 355

    adding macro projects, 357

    debugging macros, 361-362

    editing recorded macros, 357-361

    project files, 355-356

        saving, 359

    sharing macros, 356-357

Macros root node, 151

Manage Workspaces dialog box, 667

managed code, creating database objects, 574-578

Management Classes node, Server Explorer, 131-132

management commands, Solution Explorer

    for projects, 123-124

    for solutions, 122-123

Management Events node, Server Explorer, 132

managing

    tests, 773-774

    web test requests, 786-787

manual tests, 805

    creating, 805-806

    running, 805-806

    in Visual Studio Team Test, 629

manually binding controls, 586-589

many-to-many relationships, 561

mapping

data sources to controls, 583-586

key bindings, 346-347

process roles to TFS security groups, 638-639

markup (HTML), 193-196

master pages, 25

for user interfaces, 491-493

members

displaying with Class Designer, 761

explicit naming, 211

implicit naming, 211

List Members productivity tool, 214

members pane

Class View, 127-128

Object Browser, 135

membership (ASP.NET), 510

menu bars, 44-49, 327

determining with CommandBar object, 330

Menu control, 513

menus

creating, 536-538

running macros from, 368-370

MenuStrip controls, 536-538

merge tool (source control), 682-683

merging

changed files (source control), 680-683

source code tree, 683-685

Message Queues node, Server Explorer, 132

method stubs, generating, 247-248

methodologies, seeding with work items, 723-728.
See also **MSF for Agile, MSF for CMMI**

methods

anonymous methods (C#), 79-80

Command object, 345

CommandBar object, 330-331

defining in Class Designer, 766-767

Document object, 332-333

DTE2 root object, 303-304

EditPoint object, 336-338

Extract Method refactoring tool, 241-244, 246

accessing, 241

method stubs, generating, 247-248

single line of code, extracting, 246-247

IDTToolsOptionsPage interface, 399

in IDTExtensibility2 interface, 383-389

OutputWindowPane object, 324

Project object, 306-307

Promote Local Variable to Parameter refactoring
tool, 252-254

Remove Parameters refactoring tool, 251-252

Reorder Parameters refactoring tool, 254-255

Solution object, 305-306

TaskItem object, 317-318

TextDocument object, 333

Window object, 311-312

Microsoft Excel, managing work items with, 653-654

**Microsoft Intermediate Language (MSIL), generic type
instantiation, 65**

**Microsoft Office, Team Foundation Server and,
652-654**

Microsoft Project. *See* **Project**

Microsoft Solutions Framework. *See* **MSF 622**

Microsoft Windows User Experience, 519

mobile applications, 22-24

modeling tools. *See* **architecture modeling tools**

models. *See also* **Class Designer, Visual Studio Team
Architect**

in Visual Studio Team Architect, 627

modules. *See also* **areas, 693**

Marco Explorer, 152

monitoring builds, 828-831

**mouse movement event handlers, color palette exam-
ple (add-ins), 392**

MSBuild, 824-825

MSBuild options, for website projects, 480-482

MSDN, Professional Editions of Visual Studio 2005, 31

MSDN Community Forums, 431-433

alerts, managing, 435-436

navigating, 433-436

new threads, starting, 433

MSF (Microsoft Solutions Framework), 622

    MSF Agile, 622-623

    MSF for CMMI, 624-625

MSF Agile, 622-623

MSF Agile roles, mapping to TFS security groups, 638-639

MSF CMMI roles, mapping to TFS security groups, 638-639

MSF for Agile work items, 689

    bugs, 690

    QoS requirements, 689

    risk, 690

    scenarios, 689

    tasks, 690

MSF for CMMI, 624-625

MSF for CMMI work items, 690

    bugs, 692

    change requests, 691

    issues, 692

    requirements, 690-691

    reviews, 691

    risk, 691

    tasks, 691

MSIL (Microsoft Intermediate Language), generic type instantiation, 65

multiple assembly versions (C#), 81-82

My feature, 13-14

navigation in HTML, 208-210

navigation controls, 513-515

navigation tools in code editor, 166

    bookmarks, 166-168

    line numbering, 166

.NET Framework

    list of enhancements, 83-84

    targeting customer experiences, 21-26

.NET web services, 598

network change discovery (.NET Framework), 84

network types, selecting for load tests, 801-802

New Breakpoint dialog box, 281

new features. See Visual Studio 2005, new features, 7

New File dialog box, 161

New List dialog box, 709

New Load Test Wizard, starting, 798

New Project dialog box, 90-91, 101-102, 184, 521, 572

New Web Site dialog box, 102-103, 466

news channel (Start Page), 428-431

non-visual controls, hiding, 502

nontext documents, distinguishing from text documents, 333

notes, check-in notes, 675-676

nullable types, 70-71

    declaring, 71

    HasValue and Value properties, 71-73

N

named commands, add-ins reacting to, 389-390

named regions, creating, 206

named skins, 495

namespaces, conflicts, 74-75

naming

    builds, 815-816

    project portals, 641-642

    team projects, 640

naming. See renaming

navigating MSDN Community Forums, 433-436

navigating code, 14-16

O

Object Browser, 134-136

    custom component set, editing, 134-135

    description pane, 136-137

    Rename refactoring tool, accessing, 238

    scoping options, 134

Object Property dialog box, 143

Objects Lifetime subreport, 151

objects pane

    Class View, 125-127

    Object Browser, 135

Office, VSTO (Visual Studio Tools for Office), 22

OnAddInsUpdate method, 384-385

OnBeginShutdown method, 385

OnConnection method, 385-386, 388

OnDisconnection method, 388

one-to-one relationships, 561

OnMacrosRuntimeReset event, 367

OnPaint event, 551

OnStartupComplete event, 367

OnStartupComplete method, 388

Opacity property (forms), 523

opening code editor, 161

operations (project role in Team System), 33

operator overloading (VB), 77

Options dialog box. See Visual Studio Options dialog box

Options page (color palette add-in example), creating, 398-402

ordered tests, 807-808

    in Visual Studio Team Test, 630

outer variables of anonymous methods, 80

outlining

    code outlining (productivity tool), 206-208

    Edit, Outlining menu, 207-208

    HTML navigation, 208-210

output window, 323-325

OutputWindow object, 323-325

OutputWindowPane object, 323-324

    properties/methods, 324

overloaded operators (VB), 77

P

packaging

    macros, 455-460

    shared content, 452-460

page event handlers, adding, 484-485

page layout for user interfaces, 486-488

paging, 579

Panel class, 530

Parameter Info (productivity tool), 215

parameters. See also variables, project parameters

    debugging stored procedures, 569

    macros with, 371-372

    Parameter Info productivity tool, 215

    Promote Local Variable to Parameter refactoring tool, 252-254

    Remove Parameters refactoring tool, 251-252

    Reorder Parameters refactoring tool, 254-255

partial classes, 482

partial types, 73

Partner Products Catalog option (Community menu), 439

PasswordRecovery control, 512

patterns (for load tests), defining, 799-800

Pending Changes window, checking in source control files, 672-673

Performance Counters node, Server Explorer, 133

Performance Explorer, 137

    performance reports

        Allocation subreport, 150

        Call Tree subreport, 150

        Caller/Callee subreport, 150

        columns in, 143-149

        functions subreport, 150

        Objects Lifetime subreport, 151

        Summary subreport, 150

    performance sessions

        configuring, 138-142

        creating, 137-139

        targets, 142-143

    Reports node, 143-144

    toolbar buttons, 137-138

performance reports

    Allocation subreport, 150

    Call Tree subreport, 150

    Caller/Callee subreport, 150

    columns in, 143-149

    Functions subreport, 150

    Objects Lifetime subreport, 151

    Summary subreport, 150

performance sessions
  configuring, 138-142
  creating, 137-139
  targets, 142-143
permissions, source control system, 661-662. *See also* security
Personal Web Site Starter Kit template, 467-469
personalized menus, 330
pinning IDE windows, 59-60
placeholder values, code snippets, 218
planning
  form design, 520
  user interfaces, 485-486
policies, check-in policies, 673-675
Policy Failure dialog box, 675
port numbers for ASP.NET Development Server, 471
portals, project portals, 641
positioning controls for user interfaces, 486-488
positioning. *See* layout
post-build events, 112
pre-build events, 112
Preview Changes dialog box, 236-237
previewing refactoring changes, 236-237
primary keys
  creating, 557
  referential integrity, 560
Print dialog box, 179-180
printing from code editor, 179-180
process guidance, 652
process model
  MSF Agile, 623
  MSF for CMMI, 624-625
Process Template Manager, 723
process templates
  exporting, 723-725
  importing, 726-728
  security, 638
  selecting, 641
processes, attaching to, 265-267

productivity tools, 201-203
  in code editor
    code outlining, 206-208
    HTML navigation, 208-210
    smart tags, 211-212
  in HTML designer, smart tags, 210
  IntelliSense, 201, 212
    brace matching, 224-225
    code snippets, 216-224
    Complete Word, 213
    customizing, 225-226
    List Members, 214
    Parameter Info, 215
    Quick Info, 214
  Task List, 227
    comment tasks, 227-229
    shortcut tasks, 228
    user tasks, 229
  in text editor, 203
    active hyperlinking, 205
    change tracking, 203-204
    coding problem indicators, 204-205
    syntax coloring, 205-206
  in Windows Forms designer, smart tags, 211
Professional Editions (Visual Studio 2005), 31
profiling, 137. *See also* performance sessions
programming with Server Explorer, 133-134
programming language for website projects, selecting, 473
Project
  managing work items with, 653-654
  work items, project manager role and, 713-715
project administrators, Team Foundation Server security, 638
project alerts. *See* alerts
project definition files, 103-110
Project Dependencies property page, 98-99
Project Designer, 111
project files in Macros IDE, 355-356
  saving, 359
Project Group Membership dialog box, 645-648

project items, 110

project management in Team Foundation Server, 33

project manager (project role in Team System), 33

project manager role, Team Foundation Server. *See* Team Foundation Server

project managers role with work items, 708

   with Excel, 708-713

   with Project, 713-715

Project menu, 47

Project object

   code access, 307-309

   properties/methods, 306-307

   solution/project hierarchy, 304-305

project parameters, 447-448

project portal, 651-653

   in Team Foundation Server, 632

project portals, naming, 641-642

project properties, 111-114

Project Properties dialog box, 521

project reports. *See* reports, 655

project roles in Team System, 32-33

project security groups in Team Foundation Server, 638, 645-648

project teams. *See* team projects, 643

project templates

   creating, 445-451

   as shared content, 442

   in Visual Studio Team Architect, 732-733

projects. *See also* solutions; team projects

   accessing code within, 307-309

   creating, 43-44, 90-92, 101-102

   database projects, 571

      auto-generating SQL scripts, 573-574

      creating, 572-573

      executing SQL scripts, 574

   defined, 89, 100

   dependencies, 98-99

   Macro Explorer, 152

   management commands in Solution Explorer, 123-124

   project definition files, 103-110

project items, 110

project properties, 111-114

startup projects, 123

   specifying, 98

supported types, 101-102

test projects, creating, 770-772

usage, 110

website projects. *See* website projects

Promote Local Variable to Parameter refactoring tool, 252-254

properties

   Command object, 345

   CommandBar object, 330-331

   defining in Class Designer, 766-767

   Document object, 332-333

   DTE2 root object, 303-304

   EditPoint object, 336-338

   Encapsulate Field refactoring tool, 255-257

      accessing, 256

   forms, 522-523

   mixed access modifiers, 73-74

   OutputWindowPane object, 324

   Project object, 306-307

   project properties, 111-114

   Solution object, 305-306

   solution properties, 97-100

   TaskItem object, 317-318

   TextDocument object, 333

   Window object, 311-312

Properties dialog box, performance sessions, 138

Properties window, 58-59

Property Pages dialog box, 476, 478-480, 482

proxy endpoints, 744

proxy implementation in web services, 602

proxy servers

   Community Search option (Community menu) and, 441

   source control and, 661

Publish property page, 114

publishing

   errors (work items), 711

   shared content, 461

Q

QoS (quality of service) requirement work items, MSF for Agile, 689

quality states (builds), setting, 829-830

queries

types of, 565

on work items, 703-707

writing, 562-566

Query/View Designer, 562-566

SQL Editor and, 566-568

querying Windows collection, 312-314

question mark (?) type modifier, 71

Quick Find mode, 168-170

Quick Info (productivity tool), 214

Quick Replace mode, 170-171

QuickWatch window (debugger), 293

R

rafting, defined, 533

readers, Team Foundation Server security, 638

Recent Projects section (Start Page), 427

recorded macros, editing, 357-361

recording

macros, 352-353

web tests, 785-786

Refactor menu, 46, 233-234

refactoring, 16-18

defined, 231

refactoring tools

Encapsulate Field, 255-257

Extract Interface, 248-250

Extract Method, 241-246

accessing, 241

method stubs, generating, 247-248

single line of code, extracting, 246-247

invoking, 233-236

list of, 232

local variables and, 252

previewing changes, 236-237

Promote Local Variable to Parameter, 252-254

Remove Parameters, 251-252

Rename, 237-238

accessing, 238-239

Rename dialog box, 239-241

Reorder Parameters, 254-255

for Visual Basic, 232

Reference Paths property page, 114

reference/value constraints, 69

references

web references. See web references

in website projects, 476, 478

References property page, 114

referencing windows, 310-311

referential integrity, 560

reflexive relationships, 561

region keyword, 206

registered add-ins, 373

registering Options page (color palette add-in example), 401-402

regular expressions in Find and Replace window, 170

relationships between classes, 763-766

relationships (tables), building, 559-562

relative positioning of controls, 193

remote debugging, 19, 297-298

Remote Debugging Monitor, 297

remote IIS servers as website location, 472-473

Remove Parameters dialog box, 251-252

Remove Parameters refactoring tool, 251-252

Rename dialog box, 239-241

Rename refactoring tool, 237-238

accessing, 238-239

Rename dialog box, 239-241

renaming

process templates, 727

solutions, 92

zipped files, 457

Reorder Parameters dialog box, 255

Reorder Parameters refactoring tools, 254-255

Repeater control, 515, 590

Replace In Files mode, 173-174

replace. *See* search-and-replace modes

reports

build reports, 830-831

deployment reports, 757-758

in Team Foundation Server, 631, 655-657

Reports node, Performance Explorer, 143-144

reports. *See* performance reports

repositioning EditPoint objects, 339

requests, managing web test requests, 786-787

requirement work items, MSF for CMMI, 690-691

reserved template parameters, 447-448

resizing

controls, 189

planning form design, 520

forms, 526-530

Resolve Conflicts window, 681

Resolve Version Conflict window, 681

resources, defined, 114

Resources property page, 114

retrieving files from source control, 671

review work items, MSF for CMMI, 691

rights, source control system, 661-662

RightToLeft property (form design), 518

RightToLeftLayout property (form design), 518

rigs, defined, 630

risk work items

MSF for Agile, 690

MSF for CMMI, 691

RSS feeds, 428

URLs for, 430

Run To Cursor command, 277

running

builds, 826-827

load tests, 803-805

manual tests, 805-806

unit tests, 780-782

web tests, 787-788

S

samples as shared content, 443

Sampling Properties property page, performance sessions, 140

saving

macro project files, 359

temporary macros, 353-354

scalar-valued functions, 571

scaling controls, 529-530

SCE (Source Control Explorer) window, 663-664

files pane, 665

folders pane, 665

toolbar, 664-665

scenario work items, MSF for Agile, 689

scenarios (for load tests), defining, 798-799

scheduling builds, 825-826

schemas, creating, 183

scoping options (Object Browser), 134

scripts, SQL scripts

auto-generating, 573-574

defined, 571

executing, 574

SDLC (Software Development Life Cycle), 621

MSF (Microsoft Solutions Framework), 622

MSF Agile, 622-623

MSF for CMMI, 624-625

team roles, 622

VSTS (Visual Studio Team System), 625-626

Team Foundation Server, 630-633

Visual Studio Team Architect, 626-627

Visual Studio Team Developer, 627-629

Visual Studio Team Test, 629-630

search bar, Class View, 125-126

search features

Community Search option (Community menu), 439-442

for shared content, 443-444

search-and-replace modes, 168

Find In Files mode, 171-173

Find Symbol mode, 174-175

Incremental Search mode, 175-176

Quick Find mode, 168-170

Quick Replace mode, 170-171

Replace In Files mode, 173-174

searching

with class view search feature, 15

for work items, 703-707

security

areas (work items), 694

in Team Foundation Server, 637-639

project security groups, 645-648

macros with events, 366

source control system, 661-662

Security property page, 114

seeding

methodology with work items, 723-728

web tests with data, 788-793

selecting

add-in application host, 375-376

add-in language, 374-375

browsers for load tests, 801

build configurations, 816-817

build tests, 818

default programming language for website projects, 473

languages, 38

locations for website projects, 467-473

network types for load tests, 801-802

process templates, 641

servers for load tests, 801-802

solutions for builds, 816-817

templates for website projects, 467-469

text, 158

web tests and unit tests for load tests, 799-800

windows in code editor, 161

selection margin (code editor), 165

self-checking. See debugging

semantic errors, 204

Send Feedback button (Community menu), 437-438

serial I/O device support (.NET Framework), 84

Server Explorer, 129, 553

Data Connections node, 130

database connections, creating, 554-556

programming with, 133-134

Servers node, 130-131

Event Logs node, 131

Management Classes node, 131-132

Management Events node, 132

Message Queues node, 132

Performance Counters node, 133

Services node, 133

servers

adding to zones, 749-750

Build server, 812-814

location information for build, 816-818

configuring, 752-755

connecting to zones, 750-751

selecting for load tests, 801-802

Servers node, Server Explorer, 130-131

Event Logs node, 131

Management Classes node, 131-132

Management Events node, 132

Message Queues node, 132

Performance Counters node, 133

Services node, 133

Services node, Server Explorer, 133

sessions. See performance sessions

set method, mixed access modifiers, 73-74

Settings property page, 114

shared access (source control), 671

shared add-ins, Visual Studio add-ins versus, 376

shared content

installing, 443-445

item templates, creating, 451-452

packaging, 452-460

project templates, creating, 445-451

publishing, 461

searching for, 443-444

signing, 459

types of, 442-443

shared development servers as website location,
472-473

SharePoint sites in Team Foundation Server, 632

sharing macros, 356-357

sharing code, 20-21

Shelve dialog box, 680

shelvesets, 680

shelving in Team Foundation Server, 630

shelving files (source control), 678, 680

shortcut keys. *See also* command keys

   Code Snippet Inserter, 217

   Complete Word, 213

shortcut tasks, **228**

signal icons

   objects pane (Class View), 127

   Solution Explorer, 121

signing .vsi files, **459**

Signing property page, **114**

simple data binding, 579

Simple Object Access Protocol. *See* SOAP

single line of code, extracting, 246-247

site maps, 513

.sitemap file, 514-515

site navigation controls, 513-515

SiteMapPath control, 513-515

skin definitions, 495

skin files, creating, 495-496

skins, 495, 509

SKUs. *See* Visual Studio 2005, versions of

smart clients, 22, 24

smart devices, 22, 24

smart tags, 210

   in code editor, 211-212

   in HTML designer, 210

   refactoring with, 234-235

   in Windows Forms designer, 211

smart tasks. *See* smart tags, 210

SMTP support (.NET Framework), 84

snap lines (Windows Forms designer), **188**

snippets. *See* code snippets

SOAP (Simple Object Access Protocol)

   defined, 597

   requests, 609

   responses, 610

SOAP exceptions, 616-617

Software Development Life Cycle. *See* SDLC

software models. *See* Class Designer

software models. *See* Visual Studio Team Architect

solution definition file, 92-95

Solution Explorer, 57-58, 95, 117-118

   adding files to source control, 669-670

   checking in source control files, 671

   icons, 118-121

   projects, management commands, 123-124

   Rename refactoring tool, accessing, 239

   signal icons, 121

   solutions, management commands, 122-123

   toolbar buttons, 121-122

solution folders, 97

solution items, 95-97

solution properties, 97-100

Solution Property Pages dialog box, 97-100

solution user options file, 92-93

Solution/Solution2 object

   properties/methods, 305-306

   solution/project hierarchy, 304-305

solutions. *See also* projects

   creating, 90-92

   defined, 89-90

   management commands in Solution Explorer, 122-123

   renaming, 92

   selecting for builds, 816-817

   solution definition file, 92-95

   Solution Explorer, 95

   solution folders, 97

   solution items, 95-97

   solution properties, 97-100

   solution user options file, 92-93

   startup projects, 123

Sort options (Class View), **127**

sorting tasks, 227

source code tree, branching and merging, 683-685

source control, 659-660

   architecture of, 660-661

   associating code with work items, 717-720

   changesets, 677-678

   configuring Visual Studio for, 663

design goals, 660

files

    adding, 669-671

    checking in, 671-677

    merging changes, 680-683

    retrieving, 671

    shelving, 678, 680

    unshelving, 680

installing, 38-39

proxy servers and, 661

security, 661-662

source code tree, branching and merging, 683-685

Source Control Explorer (SCE) window, 663-664

    files pane, 665

    folders pane, 665

    toolbar, 664-665

in Team Foundation Server, 34, 630-631

workspaces, 666

    creating, 666-669

Source Control Explorer

adding files to source control, 669-671

checking in source control files, 672

Source Control Explorer (SCE) window, 663-664

files pane, 665

folders pane, 665

toolbar, 664-665

Source Control Merge Wizard, 685

source control settings, 641-642

Source Control Settings dialog box, 674

source files, pointing debugger at, 99-100

source view, web pages, 483

SplitContainer class, 531-532

SQL Editor, 566

Query/View Designer and, 566-568

SQL scripts

auto-generating, 573-574

defined, 571

executing, 574

SQL Server, data tier (Team Foundation Server) and, 636-637

SQL Server projects, creating, 575

SQL statements

queries, writing, 562-566

stored procedures, 566-570

triggers, creating, 570

user-defined functions, creating, 571

views, creating, 566

squiggles, 204-205

Standard Edition (Visual Studio 2005), 30

Standard toolbar, 50-51

standards, form design, 519

standards compliance, HTML designer, 196-197

Start Debugging command, 278

start options for website projects, 479-480

Start Page, 42

community features, 426

    Getting Started section, 427-428

    news channel, 428-431

    Recent Projects section, 427

    Visual Studio Headlines section, 428

starter kits as shared content, 443

starting

debug mode, 261-263

New Load Test Wizard, 798

threads in MSDN Community Forums, 433

StartPosition property (forms), 522

startup forms, setting, 521-522

startup options, IDE, 43

Startup Project property page, 98

startup projects, 123

specifying, 98

states (work items), 696-697

static classes (C#), 80-81

static code analysis in Visual Studio Team Developer, 627-628

static constructors (C#), 81

status bars, creating, 540-542

StatusStrip controls, 540-542

Step Into command, 276-279

Step Out command, 280

Step Over command, 278

stepped load pattern (load tests), 799

stepping into code, 263

stepping through code, 268-270, 276

Break All command, 278

Continue command, 280

ending session, 280-281

Run To Cursor command, 277

Start Debugging command, 278

Step Into command, 276-279

Step Out command, 280

Step Over command, 278

Stop statement, 178

stored procedures, 566-570

creating in C#, 576-578

Style Builder dialog box, 184, 490

style rules, 490

adding to CSS, 184

style sheets

CSS editor, 184

for user interfaces, 489-491

XSLT style sheets, running against XML, 183

subclassing controls, 547-548

subreports, 149

Allocation subreport, 150

Call Tree subreport, 150

Caller/Callee subreport, 150

Functions subreport, 150

Objects Lifetime subreport, 151

Summary subreport, 150

suggestions, sending via Community menu, 438

Summary subreport, 150

Surround With snippets, 218-219

syntax coloring (productivity tool), 205-206

syntax errors, 204

System Designer, 742-744

connecting applications to systems, 745-746

proxy endpoints, 744

system diagrams, 731, 742-744

connecting applications to systems, 745-746

item templates for, 733

proxy endpoints, 744

System.Collections.Generics namespace, 70

systems, connecting applications to, 745-746

T

tab order, form controls, 534-535

TabControl class, 549

Table Designer, 556-558

table-valued functions, 571

TableLayoutPanel class, 530-531

Tables. *See also* databases

adding to database diagram, 558

defined, 553

defining, 556-558

editing definitions, 559

HTML, 195

joins, creating, 564-565

relationships, building, 559-562

showing contents of, 566

viewing, 558

views, creating, 566

Tables and Columns dialog box, 559

tabular data, form controls, 545-546

tag navigator (productivity tool), 209

target source language for website projects, 103

targets performance sessions, 142-143

Task List, 227

comment tasks, 227-229

shortcut tasks, 228

user tasks, 229

task list window, 317-319

task scheduler service, 636

task work items

MSF for Agile, 690

MSF for CMMI, 691

TaskItem object, 317-319

TaskList object, 317-319

tasks, 227

comment tasks, 227-229

shortcut tasks, 228

sorting, 227

user tasks, 229

Team Build Browser, 828-830

Team Build client, 812-814

Team Build Service, 636, 812, 814

team collaboration. *See* VSTS (Visual Studio Team System)

Team Explorer, 701-707

Team Explorer window, 643-645, 651

    as Team Build client, 813

Team Foundation Administrators group, 637

Team Foundation Build, 631, 811-812

    architecture of, 812-815

    builds

        creating, 815-825

        monitoring/analyzing, 828-831

        running, 826-827

        scheduling, 825-826

    Team Build Service, 636

Team Foundation Server, 32-34

    application tier, role in Team Foundation Build architecture, 812-814

    data tier, role in Team Foundation Build architecture, 813-815

    source control. See source control

Team Foundation Server (TFS), 630-633

    alerts, 654-655

    application tier, 634-636

    connecting to, 650-651

    data tier, 636-637

    installing, 639

    Microsoft Office and, 652-654

    project portal, 651-653

    reports, 655-657

    security, 637-639

        project security groups, 645-648

    Team Explorer window, 651

    team projects

        adding users to, 643-648

        controlling structure and iterations, 648-650

        creating, 640-643

Team Foundation Source Control (TFSC). See source control, 660

Team Foundation Valid Users group, 637

team model

    MSF Agile, 623

    MSF for CMMI, 625

team project folders, 644

team projects, 639. *See also* projects

    adding users to, 643-648

    builds. *See* builds

    controlling structure and iterations, 648-650

    creating, 640-643

    naming, 640

Team System. *See* VSTS

template code. *See* code snippets

templates. *See also* item templates; project templates

    class templates, 420

    for website projects, selecting, 467-469

temporary breakpoints, 277

temporary macros

    running, 353

    saving, 353-354

Terminate All command, 280

test configuration file, 775

test items, creating, 772-773

test lists, 773-775

Test Manager, 773-774

Test menu, 48

test projects, creating, 770-772

test results, viewing, 781-782

tester (project role in Team System), 32

tester role, Visual Studio Team Test, 629-630

testers, role with work items, 719, 721-722

testing, 769

    generic tests, 807

    load tests, 797

        creating, 797-803

        editing, 803-804

        running, 803-805

    manual tests, 805

        creating, 805-806

        running, 805-806

    ordered tests, 807-808

    test configuration file, 775

    test items, creating, 772-773

    Test Manager, 773-774

    test projects, creating, 770-772

unit tests, 775-776

  assertion methods, 778

  attribute classes, 777-778

  best practices, 777

  code coverage analysis, 782-784

  creating, 778-780

  running, 780-782

  sample unit test, 776

web tests, 784

  extracting values from, 793-795

  managing test requests, 786-787

  recording, 785-786

  running, 787-788

  seeding with data, 788-793

  validation rules, 794, 796-797

Testing Policy, 673

testing tools, 28-29

tests, selecting build tests, 818

text

  adding to text documents, 338-339

  selecting, 158

text documents, 333-335

  distinguishing from nontext documents, 333

  editing, 335-344

text editor, 53

  code editors, 54-56

  customizing, 55-57

  defined, 157

  in Macros IDE, saving project files, 359

  productivity tools, 203

    active hyperlinking, 205

    change tracking, 203-204

    coding problem indicators, 204-205

    IntelliSense. See IntelliSense

    syntax coloring, 205-206

  selecting text, 158

  virtual space, 159-160

  word wrapping, 158-160

Text Editor Options dialog box, 159

text view, 182

text windows, 314-316

  inserting comments, 340

TextDocument object, 333-335

  properties/methods, 333

TextPane object, 314-316

TextPoint object, 335

  adding text, 338-339

TextSelection object, 336

TextWindow object, 314-316

TFB. See Team Foundation Build

TFS. See Team Foundation Server

TFSBuild.proj project file, 819, 821-824

TFSC (Team Foundation Source Control). See source control

themes, 24

  for user interfaces, 493-496, 498-499

think times in load tests, 798

threads

  managing alerts in MSDN Community Forums, 435-436

  starting in MSDN Community Forums, 433

throwing web service exceptions, 616-617

tokens, custom comment tokens, 228

tool windows, 310, 316-317

  displaying for color palette example (add-ins), 396-397

  linking/unlinking325-327

toolbar buttons

  Class View, 124-125

  Document Outline, 154

  Performance Explorer, 137-138

  Solution Explorer, 121-122

toolbars, 49-51. See also command bars

  code editor, 166

  creating, 538-540

  determining with CommandBar object, 330

  Object Browser, 135

  running macros from, 368-370

Toolbox, 51-52, 524

  Application Designer, 736-737

  code snippets in, 224

  customizing, 525

Logical Datacenter Designer, 747

Windows Forms designer, 186-187

ToolBox object, 319-322

Tools menu, 48

ToolStrip controls, 535-542

ToolStripContainer class, 532-534, 539

ToolStripItem class, 539

ToolTip class, 535

ToolTip property, 535

ToolTips, defined, 535

tracepoints, 20, 280, 288-290. *See also* breakpoints

tracking work items in Team Foundation Server, 631

tracks

MSF Agile, 623

MSF for CMMI, 624

transactions (.NET Framework), 84

transitions (work items), 696-697

tree view

Class View, 125-127

Macro Explorer, 151

Object Browser, 135

Performance Explorer, 138

Solution Explorer, 118

TreeNode Editor, 543

TreeView control, 513, 542-545

triggers, creating, 570

troubleshooting. *See also* debugging

event object initialization, 368

with productivity tools. See productivity tools

type arguments, 67

type parameters, 65-68

U

UDDI (Universal Description, Discovery, and Integration), 597

UI. *See* user interfaces

Uniform Resource Identifier (URI), 597

unit testing in Visual Studio Team Developer, 628

unit tests, 775-776

assertion methods, 778

attribute classes, 777-778

best practices, 777

code coverage analysis, 782-784

creating, 778-780

running, 780-782

sample unit test, 776

selecting for load tests, 799-800

in Visual Studio Team Test, 629

Universal Description, Discovery, and Integration (UDDI), 597

unlinking tool windows, 325-327

unnamed skins, 495

unshelving files (source control), 680

unsigned types (VB), 76

updating

GridView control data, 591-593

web references, 614

uploading process templates, 726-728

upper array bounds (VB), 77

URI (Uniform Resource Identifier), defined, 597

URLs for RSS feeds, 430

usability, form design and, 518-519

User Control Designer, 548-550

user controls, 198, 510

creating for color palette example (add-ins), 391-395

designing, 548-550

event handling for color palette example (add-ins), 397

integrating for color palette example (add-ins), 396-398

user experience, web applications and, 24-25

user interfaces

consistency, maintaining, 488-499

creating user-configurable UIs, 499-508

designing, 517-520

master pages, 491-493

page layout, 486-488

planning, 485-486

style sheets, 489-491

themes, 493-499

User Profile Node Security dialog box, 694

user tasks, 229

user-configurable UIs, creating, 499-508

user-defined functions, creating, 571

users, adding to team projects, 643-648

Using block (VB), 77

V

validating deployment, 756-758

validating code with Visual Studio Team Developer, 627-629

validation controls, 509

validation options (HTML designer), 196-197

validation rules on web tests, 794-797

Value property (nullable types), 71-73

variables. *See also* parameters

    default values, avoiding with nullable types, 70-71

    inner variables of anonymous methods, 80

    local variables

        Promote Local Variable to Parameter refactoring tool, 252-254

        refactoring and, 252

    outer variables of anonymous methods, 80

    watching

        Autos window, 292

        Locals window, 291

        QuickWatch window, 293

        watch windows, 292-293

VB (Visual Basic)

    language enhancements

        array upper/lower bounds, 77

        Continue statement, 76

        custom events, 78

        form access, 77

        IsNot operator, 76

        list of, 75-76

        operator overloading, 77

        unsigned types, 76

        Using block, 77

    static classes, 80

version control. See source control

versions of Visual Studio 2005. *See* Visual Studio 2005, versions of

View menu, 46

viewing

    Component Designer, 485

    debugging data, 290

        Autos window, 292

        DataTips window, 293-294

        Locals window, 291

        QuickWatch window, 293

        Visualizers, 294-296

        watch windows, 292-293

    test results, 781-782

    web methods, 608-610

    web references, 613-614

    work items, 707

    WSDL, 604-608

views, creating, 566. *See also* subreports

Virtual Point object, 335

virtual space, 159-160

Visual Basic (VB)

    Code Snippet Inserter, 216

    language enhancements

        array upper/lower bounds, 77

        Continue statement, 76

        custom events, 78

        form access, 77

        IsNot operator, 76

        list of, 75-76

        operator overloading, 77

        unsigned types, 76

        Using block, 77

    refactoring in, 18

    refactoring tools, 232

    static classes, 80

Visual Basic code editor, 55-56

Visual C# project definition files, 104-105

Visual C++ project definition files, 106-110

Visual Database tools, defined, 553

Visual Designers, 53

Class Designer, refactoring with, 235-236

Visual Source Safe (VSS) 2005, 660

installing, 39

Visual Studio 2005

community features, 425

Community menu, 431-442

Start Page, 426-431

configuring for source control, 663

environment settings, changing, 640

IDE. *See* IDE

installing, 37-41

new features, 7

architecture modeling, 8-12

code editor, invoking tools from, 12-14

code navigation, 14-16

community code sharing, 20-21

data binding, 26-28

editing and debugging, 16-20

.NET Framework for targeting customer experiences, 21-26

testing tools, 28-29

versions of, 29

Express Editions, 29-30

Professional Editions, 31

Standard Edition, 30

Team System, 31-35

Visual Studio add-ins, shared add-ins versus, 376

Visual Studio automation object model. *See* automation object model

Visual Studio Content Installer, 443-445

macro package example installation, 457-460

packaging shared content, 452-460

Visual Studio debugger. *See* debugger

Visual Studio Headlines section (Start Page), 428

Visual Studio Options dialog box, 225-226

Visual Studio Team Architect, 35, 626-627

application design steps, 734

application diagrams, 735, 737-740

Application Designer Toolbox, 736-737

application settings and constraints, 740-742

Diagram menu, 735-736

application implementation, 758-760

deployment diagrams, 755-756

deployment reports, 757-758

validating deployment, 756-758

item templates, 733-734

logical datacenter diagrams, 746-747

adding servers to zones, 749-750

configuring zones and servers, 752-755

connecting servers to zones, 750-751

Logical Datacenter Designer, 747

zones, 747-748

project templates, 732-733

system diagrams, 742-744

connecting applications to systems, 745-746

proxy endpoints, 744

Visual Studio Team Developer, 34, 627-629

Visual Studio Team Suite, 35

Visual Studio Team System Extensibility Kit, 729

Visual Studio Team System. *See* VSTS

Visual Studio Team Test, 35, 629-630

load tests, 797

creating, 797-803

editing, 803-804

running, 803-805

Visual Studio Tools for Office (VSTO), 22

visual styles, form controls, 534

visualizers, 19

debugger, 294-296

visually developing code with Class Designer, 760

class diagrams, 760-767

vsCMElement enumeration values, 308-309

VSContent files

creating for macro packaging example, 455-456

.vsi files versus, 458

.VSContent XML file, elements of, 453-455

.vsdir files, 417-418

creating, 423

.vsi files

publishing, 461

renaming zipped files to, 457

signing, 459

VSContent files versus, 458

VSInstr command-line tool, 141

.vsmacros file, 356

VSS (Visual Source Safe) 2005, 660

   installing, 39

.vstemplate XML file, editing, 450

VSTO (Visual Studio Tools for Office), 22

VSTS (Visual Studio Team System), 621, 625-626

   source control. See source control, 660

   Team Foundation Build. See Team Foundation
   Build

   Team Foundation Server. See Team Foundation
   Server

   Visual Studio Team Architect, 626-627

   Visual Studio Team Developer, 627-629

   Visual Studio Team Test, 629-630

   work items, 688-689, 692

      areas, 692-694

      associating code with, 717-720

      attaching files, 701

      business analyst role, 714, 716-717

      creating, 701-703

      customizing, 722, 727-730

      developer role, 716-720

      history tracking, 697-699

      iterations, 692-696

      linking, 698-701

      MSF for Agile work items, 689-690

      MSF for CMMI work items, 690-692

      project manager role, 708-715

      queries on, 703-707

      seeding methodology with, 723-728

      states and transitions, 696-697

      Team Explorer tools, 701-707

      tester role, 719-722

      viewing, 707

      workstreams, 708

.vsz files, 417-418

   creating, 423

W

warnings (compiler). See compiler warnings, 204

Watch window, IntelliSense in, 19

watch windows (debugger), 265, 292-293

watching variables

   Autos window, 292

   Locals window, 291

   QuickWatch window, 293

   watch windows, 292-293

web applications, new features for, 22-26

web controls, data binding, 589-594

Web designer. See HTML designer

web forms, 192. See also HTML designer

   controls

      adding, 193-194

      arranging, 193

   data binding, 27-28

   defined, 192

web methods

   defined, 596

   invoking, 610-611

   viewing, 608-610

web pages

   adding controls to, 483

   creating for website projects, 481-485

Web Part controls, 499-508

web references

   defining, 611-613

   updating, 614

   viewing, 613-614

Web Service Description Language. See WSDL

Web Service Enhancements (WSE), 597

web service methods. See web methods

web service process, attaching to, 265-267

web service projects, components of, 597

   ASP.NET web service projects, 598-599

   .NET web services, 598

   web service files, 599-600

web services, 595-596

accessing, 604

invoking web method, 610-611

viewing web method, 608-610

viewing WSDL, 604-608

in application tier (Team Foundation Server), 634-636

calling, 614-615

consuming, 611

calling web services, 614-615

defining web references, 611-613

updating web references, 614

viewing web references, 613-614

creating, 601-602

WebMethod attribute class, 603-604

WebService attribute class, 602-603

WebService class, 603

defined, 596

exceptions

handling, 617

throwing, 616-617

settings, 742

terminology, 596-597

Web Site Administration Tool (WSAT), 512-513

web tests, 784

extracting values from, 793-795

managing test requests, 786-787

recording, 785-786

running, 787-788

seeding with data, 788-793

selecting for load tests, 799-800

validation rules, 794-797

in Visual Studio Team Test, 629

web user interfaces. *See* **user interfaces**

WebMethod attribute class, 603-604

WebPartManager control, 500

WebPartZone control, 500

WebService attribute class, 602-603

WebService class, 603

Website menu, 46

website projects, 466

accessibility options, 479

build options, 478-479

creating, 102-103, 466-467

creating web pages, 481-485

file types for, 475-476

folders for, 473-475

MSBuild options, 480, 482

Property Pages dialog box, 476-482

references, 476-478

selecting default programming language, 473

selecting template, 467-469

selecting website location, 467-473

start options, 479-480

websites, enabling debugging, 262

When Breakpoint Is Hit dialog box, 289

wildcards in Find and Replace window, 170

Window menu, 49

Window object, 310

command window, 322-323

linked windows, 325-327

output window, 323-325

properties/methods, 311-312

querying Windows collection, 312-314

referencing windows, 310-311

task list window, 317-319

text windows, 314-316

tool windows, 316-317

Toolbox, 319-322

window panes, 314-316

windows

document windows, 310

in code editor, components of, 163-165

in debugger, 264-265

linked windows, 325-327

referencing, 310-311

selecting in code editor, 161

task list window, 317-319

text windows, 314-316

inserting comments, 340

tool windows, 310, 316-317

linking/unlinking, 325-327

windows (IDE)

   docking, 60-61

   floating, 62

   pinning, 59-60

Windows Application project template, creating forms, 521-524

Windows collection, querying, 312-314

Windows forms, data binding, 27

Windows Forms designer, 184-185

   controls

      adding, 186-187

      arranging, 187-188

      resizing, 189

   customizing form appearance, 185-186

   productivity tools, smart tags, 211

   writing code in, 189-192

Windows Forms Designer, 525

Windows Management Instrumentation (WMI) classes, 131-132

WinForms. *See also* **forms**

   new features, 84

wizards

   Add New Item wizard example, 418

      creating .vsz and .vsdir files, 423

      implementing Execute method, 419-423

   associating icons with, 418

   IDTWizard interface, 415-416

   purpose of, 352

   structure of, 415-418

   .vsdir files, 417-418

   .vsz files, 417-418

WMI (Windows Management Instrumentation) classes, 131-132

word wrapping, 158-160

Work Item Publishing Errors dialog box, 711

work items, 688-689, 692

   areas, 692-694

   associating code with, 717-720

   associating with check-ins, 676-677

   attaching files, 701

   business analyst role, 714-717

   creating, 701-703

   customizing, 722, 727-730

   developer role, 716-720

   history tracking, 697-699

   iterations, 692-693, 695-696

   linking, 698-701

   managing with Project and Excel, 653-654

   MSF for Agile work items, 689

      bugs, 690

      QoS requirements, 689

      risk, 690

      scenarios, 689

      tasks, 690

   MSF for CMMI work items, 690

      bugs, 692

      change requests, 691

      issues, 692

      requirements, 690-691

      reviews, 691

      risk, 691

      tasks, 691

   project manager role, 708

      with Excel, 708-713

      with Project, 713-715

   queries on, 703-707

   seeding methodology with, 723-728

   states and transitions, 696-697

   Team Explorer tools, 701-707

   tester role, 719-722

   tracking in Team Foundation Server, 631

   viewing, 707

   workstreams, 708

work items (Team Foundation Server), 34

Work Items Policy, 673

work products (MSF Agile), 623

workspaces, 665-666

   creating, 666-669

workstreams, 708

How can we make this index more useful? Email us at indexes@samspublishing.com

writing

code

in code editor, 162-163

in Windows Forms designer, 189-192

component code, 199-200

WS-*, defined, 597

WSAT (Web Site Administration Tool), 512-513

WSDL (Web Service Description Language)

defined, 596

viewing, 604-608

WSE (Web Service Enhancements), 597

zipping files for macro packaging example, 457

zones, 500-501

adding servers to, 749-750

adding Web Parts to, 503-505

configuring, 752-755

connecting servers to, 750-751

defining, 502-503, 747-748

X-Y

XHTML compliance, ASP.NET controls, 508

XML (Extensible Markup Language)

defined, 596

code snippets, creating, 219-224

XML editor, 182-183

schemas, creating, 183

XSLT style sheets, running, 183

XSD (XML Schema Document)

creating, 183

defined, 597

XSLT style sheets, running against XML, 183

Z

z-order, defined, 539

zero-code data binding, 26-28

.zip files, renaming, 457

zipped files, renaming, 457